• "It started with a boot and a promise—L. L. Bean's soon-to-be-famous Maine Hunting Shoe and a money-back guarantee—that became the underpinnings of a hunting, fishing, and outdoor apparel business that would be known and admired throughout the world. Jim Witherell's thorough and engaging account of the ups (many) and downs (a few) of Maine's most famous merchandizer and his company leaves the reader thinking Horatio Alger's real name was Leon L. Bean."

    —David R. Getchell, Sr.
        Former editor of *National Fisherman*
        Co-founder of Maine Island Trail

• "This is the story of an enterprise and of two ambitious men born sixty-two years apart. One extolled the joys of the great Maine woods, the other the gifts of capitalism bestowed upon a community. One spent fifty years building a business from scratch, the other fifty years building an institution of global significance. Each one owes the other everything for the company's astounding success. This book chronicles in detail the successes and failures, conflicting levels of ambition, the significance of place, and the opportunities gained through vision, focus, and being in the right place at the right time."

    —Thomas F. Moser
        Founder, Thos. Moser Cabinetmakers
        Auburn, Maine

Leon Leonwood Bean, 1941
FROM *HUNTING IN MAINE* BY HENRY MILLIKEN,
COURTESY OF PROFESSOR ROBERT MILLIKEN

L. L. BEAN

The Man and His Company

The Complete Story

James L. Witherell

TILBURY HOUSE PUBLISHERS
GARDINER, MAINE

TILBURY HOUSE, PUBLISHERS
103 Brunswick Avenue
Gardiner, Maine 04345
800-582-1899
www.tilburyhouse.com

First paperback edition: June 2011
10 9 8 7 6 5 4 3 2 1

Library of Congress Cataloging-in-Publication Data
Witherell, James L.
  L.L. Bean : the man and his company : the complete story / James L. Witherell.
     p. cm.
  Includes bibliographical references and index.
  ISBN 978-0-88448-329-8 (pbk. : alk. paper)
  1. Bean, L. L. (Leon Leonwood), 1872-1967. 2. L.L. Bean, Inc.--History.
3. Camping equipment industry--United States--History. 4. Mail-order business--United States--History. 5. Businesspeople--United States--Biography. I. Title.
  HD9993.C354L189 2011
  338.7′685530973--dc22
                              2010053997

Front cover image by Tom Stewart, Penobscot, Maine
Back cover image courtesy of Maine Historic Preservation Commission
Copyedited by Genie Dailey, Fine Points Editorial Services, Jefferson, Maine
Printed and bound by Versa Press, East Peoria, Illinois

For Sue

Contents

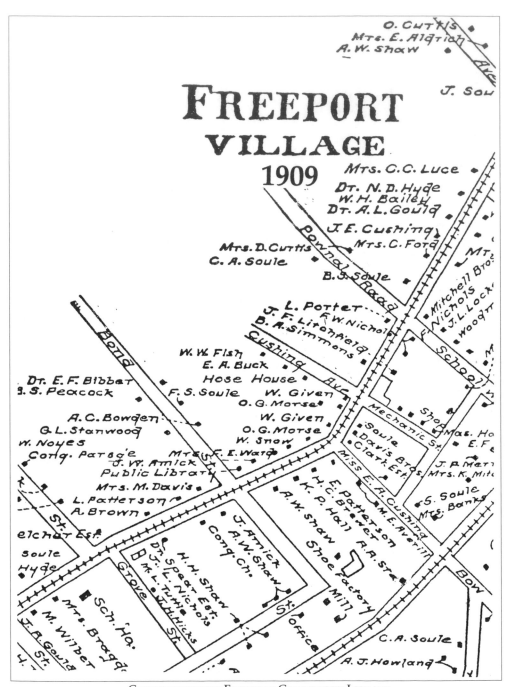

FREEPORT VILLAGE 1909

COURTESY OF THE FREEPORT COMMUNITY LIBRARY

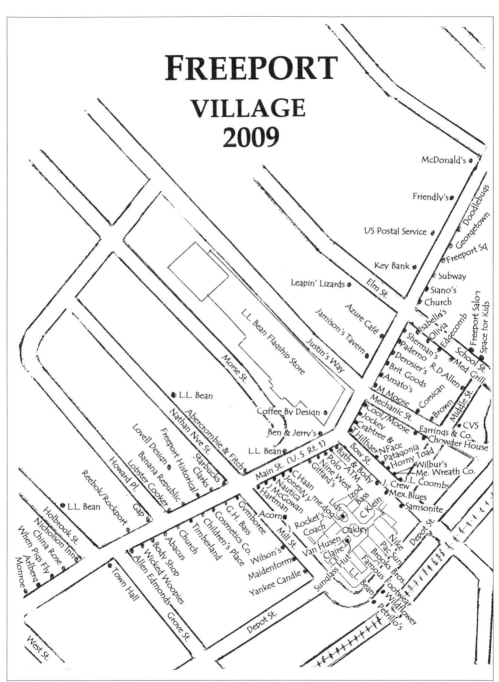

FREEPORT
VILLAGE
2009

McDonald's

Friendly's

US Postal Service

Key Bank

Leapin' Lizards

Elm St.

Subway

Siano's

Church

Doodlebugs

Georgetown

Freeport Sq.

Azure Café

Jamison's Tavern

Justin's Way

L.L. Bean Flagship Store

Morse St.

L.L. Bean

Coffee By Design

Ben & Jerry's

L.L. Bean

Main St. (U.S. Rt. 1)

Isabella's

Olivia

Sherman's

Paderno

Derosier's

Brit. Goods

Amato's

M Moose

Mechanic St.

Cool/Moose

Jockey

Crabtree &

T.Hilfiger

Bow St.

Bath & Body

Nine West

Polo ATM

Giffani's

Freeport Salon

Space for Kids

School St.

Med Grill

Edgecomb

R.D. Allen

Corsican

Brown

Middle St.

Earrings & Co.

NFace

Patagonia

Horny Toad

Wilbur's

Me. Wreath Co.

J.L. Coombs

J. Crew

Mex. Blues

CVS

Chowder House

Abercrombie & Fitch

Nathan Nye St.

Lovell Design

Freeport Historical

Banana Republic

Starbucks

Clarks

C.Haan

JonesNY

Nautica

J. McGowan

Hartman

Izod

Bass

C.Klein

Samsonite

Howard Pl.

Lobster Cooker

Reebok/Rockport

Gap

L.L. Bean

Holbrook St.

Nicholson Inn

China Rose

When Pigs Fly

Arlberg

Monroe

Gymboree

G.H. Bass

Cosmetics Co.

Children's Place

Timberland

Church

Abacus

Body Shop

Wicked Woopies

Allen Edmonds

Town Hall

Grove St.

West St.

Acorn

Wilson's

Maidenform

Yankee Candle

Mill St.

Rocket's

Coach

Van Husen

Claire's

Sunglass Hut

L.L. Bean

Oakley

Me.dog

Lids

Nike

Pac.Sun

Brooks Bros.

Famous Footwear

Depot St.

Wildflower

Petrillo's

Depot St.

MAP BY JAMES L. WITHERELL

Introduction

L. L. BEAN, HAD HE A CHOICE, probably wouldn't have chosen any other time or place to be born than in Greenwood, Maine, on October 13, 1872. Growing up in western Maine during the latter part of the nineteenth century would provide young Leon Leonwood Bean with ample opportunities to hunt and trap in the region's deep, dark forests of pine and maple and to fish in its cold, clear ponds and mountain streams. These hobbies would bind him to the sporting lifestyle and eventually bring him worldwide fame—not to mention a fairly sizable fortune—at least for the time in which he lived.

For the first forty years of his long life, L. L. Bean would, by his own admission, accomplish very little other than clerking in one or another of several small clothing stores to support his growing family. What he really wanted to be doing was enjoying the Maine outdoors, preferably while hunting or fishing. These were the activities that brought him the most happiness—except for the toll they took on his poor flat feet. His solution to this problem was to come up with a pair of lightweight, water-resistant boots that would allow him to walk all day in relative comfort.

Not long after a local farmer said he liked Mr. Bean's leather and rubber creation, which was called the Maine Hunting Shoe, L. L. would scrape together enough money to have durable bottoms made for his footwear, which he featured in a crude circular. Soon Bean would be offering socks and other articles of sturdy wool clothing to go with his increasingly popular boot, all of it guaranteed or your money back, and a great American business was off and running, so to speak.

Leon L. Bean was a man with little formal education, but instead of holding him back, it may actually have helped him sell his merchandise. L. L.'s catalog, filled with his own spare, to-the-point copy, would soon become required reading for nearly every sportsman in the region, thanks to his tenacious style of marketing and his creation of an ingenious method of tracking his orders.

L. L. would never have guessed where his first foray into business would eventually take him and, later, the huge company he'd started. Sports stars, politicians, and other famous people would come to Freeport to search out L. L. Bean—often literally—after getting lost in his rambling manufacturing facility. L. L. would even become the "author," as he'd put it, of a couple of books. (Eventually, L. L.'s company would become so successful it would be the subject of articles in *Life* and the *Saturday Evening Post*, and several case studies by the Harvard Business School.)

As L. L. aged, his company continued to grow, but this later growth seemed to come more out of necessity (staying open twenty-four hours a day, for example) or at the urging of others (his store's first ladies' department), than out of any real desire on his part to expand. By now his sales had leveled off and L. L. seemed content to put a map in his catalog directing customers to his store from the new highway that bypassed downtown Freeport. At this point he was happy let to his son Carl run the company while he spent his winters deep-sea fishing in Florida with his second wife.

It wouldn't be until L. L.'s passing in 1967 that his grandson, who'd just happened to get hired because he needed a job after getting out of the navy, would set his grandfather's mail-order company on its course toward phenomenal growth. The success of Bean's new leader wouldn't come easily, though. The story of the Freeport firm's growing pains is replete with Preppies, MBAs, infighting, and even parodies of a company that would eventually get its own ZIP Code. The fortunes of his company would cause L. L. Bean's adopted hometown of Freeport to change dramatically from a sleepy little coastal town to Maine's largest outdoor mall, complete with a parking garage. All because his feet got sore while he was hunting.

Chapter 1

. . . even prominent Maine writers and publications
aren't altogether clear on the exact location of the
future merchant's birth

How L. L. Bean had come about his love of the sporting life in northern New England can probably be best understood by taking a quick look at the history of Beans in the region from the beginning—the *very* beginning.

The Beans of western Maine were about as close as they could have come to being native New Englanders without having been a member of one of the area's Wabanaki tribes (Penobscot, Passamaquoddy, Maliseet, Micmac, or Abenaki). The first Bean to arrive in North America was John, who emigrated from Scotland[1] to New Hampshire, where he and his wife had eleven children, two of whom died in infancy.

On January 21, 1661 . . . the town of Exeter made a grant of land to JOHN BEAN, who not long previously had gone to that town to settle. Of his previous history nothing is known; but he was a Presbyterian and very certainly of Scottish descent. He was married before he came to this country and had at least one child; but according to tradition, his wife died on the voyage and he married again; nothing is known of his first wife, and but little of his second save that her given name was Margaret. . . . John Bean [born c. 1643] died in 1718, having survived his wife.[2]

During or shortly after the American Revolution, Jonathan Bean, the great-grandson of Scottish immigrant John Bean, settled in Sudbury Canada (now Bethel, Maine). Jonathan was born in

1720 (in his autobiography, *My Story: The Autobiography of a Down-East Merchant*,[3] L. L. Bean says Jonathan was born on September 10, 1736) in Kingston, New Hampshire, on territory that was once part of Exeter. On September 14, 1744, he married Abigail Gordon, with whom he had eight children. The family lived near his brother Benjamin in Chester for a number of years before moving to Standish, Maine, around 1760. Jonathan sold his Standish homestead on March 29, 1780, and moved with his wife and three sons—Josiah, Jonathan Jr., and Daniel—to Sudbury Canada Plantation in the fall of 1781. There they settled on "the farm which David Marshall left when he fled to New Gloucester, and afterward known as the Sanborn Farm."[4] A conflicting account has Jonathan living in Standish at the outbreak of the Revolutionary War and notes that "he came to Bethel before it was over. He is said to have served at Kittery and Portsmouth."[5]

In his later years, Jonathan Bean started acting strangely:

> He became insane and did many queer and ridiculous things. On one occasion, he fancied he could cross the Androscoggin River in summertime on snowshoes. So binding the shoes to his feet, he stepped off the bank into deep water. Of course, he immediately sank, and had not assistance been near, he would have been drowned. He left a large posterity scattered through Bethel, Mason, about the Umbagog Lake region, and on the Androscoggin, while very many of his descendants went west.[6]

Jonathan Bean died in 1809. It is said he committed suicide. "[H]is widow [died] in eighteen hundred and twenty-one at a great age."[7]

Josiah Bean (1752–1826), born in Chester, New Hampshire, was the second child of Jonathan and Abigail and their first son. In 1772 he married Molly Crocker of Standish, where the couple's first three children were born before the family moved to what is now Bethel. "He settled in the lower parish where his sons afterwards lived. On November 3rd, 1780, he bought of Aaron Richardson, intervale lot number 10, south of river, in Sudbury Canada."[8] There the couple added six more children to their brood.

Timothy Bean, born on June 8, 1775, was the second child and first son of Josiah and Molly Bean. He married Hannah, the daughter of Asa and Huldah (Tapley) Kimball, of Bethel. The couple lived near Swan's Hill, where they raised six children. Timothy Bean, who would die in 1830, was L. L. Bean's great-great-grandfather.

Kimball Bean, the first child of Timothy and Hannah, was born on April 26, 1796. At the age of eighteen, he served as a private during the War of 1812, being assigned to Captain Joseph Holt's company in Lieutenant Colonel William Ryerson's regiment, which protected the Maine coast in Portland from September 25 to November 9, 1814. The men of Captain Holt's company, who'd come from Bethel and the neighboring towns, were paid for their service and also for three days' travel. About 1818 Kimball Bean married Lavinia Powers, daughter of Arnold and Betsey (Lane) Powers, and the pair had seven children. After Lavinia's death, Kimball married Maria H. Russell around 1837 and fathered two more children.

At the turn of the nineteenth century, growth was coming fast to the region. In 1796 the Commonwealth of Massachusetts approved the request of the citizens of Sudbury Canada Plantation on the "Amerescoggin River" (the Androscoggin) to incorporate and form the town of Bethel. At first the name Ai was suggested for the town but "Rev. Eliphaz Chapman suggested the name of Bethel and it was adopted by the petitioners. The town was named for that Bethel so called by the patriarch Jacob, formerly known as Luz, and mentioned in the book of Genesis."9

George Warren Bean, L. L.'s grandfather, was born on November 28, 1818, the first child of Kimball and Lavinia Bean. On November 25, 1839, he married Mary Ann, daughter of Isaac and Rebecca (Moody?) Estes. The couple had five children between 1839 and 1857. One account of his later life says that during the Civil War, George enlisted in the 56th Massachusetts Regiment in 1862 and was captured and taken to the Andersonville (Georgia) Confederate Military Prison, where he died in June 1864 at the age of sixty-one. (While the date of his death corresponds with the period that the squalid, 27-acre prison was operational—between

February 1864 and April 1865—George W. Bean would have been only forty-five in June of 1864.[10]) Another account of George Bean's family tree states simply: "He died in the army and his widow married Daniel Cummings of Albany [Township]."[11]

BOTH OF L. L. BEAN'S PARENTS were born in Bethel. Benjamin Warren Bean, L. L.'s father, arrived in this world on November 8, 1841, the second of five children born to George and Mary Ann. Their first child, Fanny M., was born in 1839 and was followed by four boys: Benjamin, Sylvanus M. (1843), Emery I. (1850), and Charles W. (1857). At least two of the Bean brothers served their country during the Civil War. An "Abstract of Town Records" from 1861 states: "The enrolled militia was returned this year by the selectmen as follows . . ." with "Benjamin W. Bean" the first name appearing on the list. Also, "Sylvanus M. Bean was mustered in Company A, Twelfth Maine Volunteers, June 24, 1861, and was discharged for disability, July 17, 1862." (This is the same Uncle Sylvane on whose West Minot farm a fifteen-year-old L. L. Bean would work for $12 a month in 1887 and 1888 following the deaths of his parents.)

Moses and Fanny (Cummings) Sweat (most subsequent accounts—including those of L. L. Bean himself—spell the surname "Swett") lived at the east side of town on the road between Rumford and Paris. They had nine children, the fourth of whom was Sarah, the future Mrs. Benjamin W. Bean, who was born on March 9, 1846.

Sarah Sweat and Benjamin Bean married in Milton Plantation on May 9, 1864, and moved to the town of Greenwood, where they began farming the rock-strewn land of Howe Hill. Howe Hill lies at the base of Mount Abram, just off what is now Route 26 and about a mile south of the northern Greenwood village of Locke Mills. The Beans' first child, Henry Warren, was born on February 17, 1865. This same year, Bertha Porter, who would become L. L.'s first wife, was born in Freeport to Charles U. and Charity Ann (Davis) Porter. Young Henry Bean was soon followed by a brother, Otho Ralph, on January 7, 1867, and a sister, Inez Alice, on August 23, 1868.

Leon Leonwood Bean was born at Howe Hill in Greenwood, Maine, on October 13, 1872. And almost every fact in the preceding sentence seems to have been called into question at one time or another—sometimes by L. L. himself. First there's the matter of L. L. Bean's actual birth name: while there's no doubt that his first name was Leon (even though he went by "Lennie" well into adulthood), it's his middle name that remains the subject of some debate.

Was it really Leonwood or was L. L. Bean originally Leon Linwood Bean? His grandson Tom Gorman suggests it was Linwood, and points to L. L.'s full name on a page of the 1900 baby book for his first son, Carl. On the line for the father's signature, "Leon Linwood Bean" is clearly written. But the signature doesn't match the merchant's later autograph. Also, the entire page appears to have been filled out by the same person—probably a woman—possibly L. L.'s mother-in-law, Charity Porter, whose name appears on the line reserved for the nurse's signature. Maybe the writer was told that the father's middle name was "Leonwood" but heard it as "Linwood." This is certainly a possibility; well-known Maine writer John Gould (1908–2003) noted that "Leonwood was pronounced 'Linwood,' and in Freeport, Leon Leonwood was generally called Lin." Even L. L.'s grandson Tom Gorman says that "the Maine pronunciation of 'Leon' is closer to 'lin' than 'le-on.'"

Though the truth will probably never be known, the second L definitely stood for Leonwood by 1918, when L. L. Bean filled out his draft registration form. Even so, some confusion continues to this day, thanks to the *Reader's Guide to Periodical Literature*'s incorrect listing of Arthur Bartlett's 1946 *Saturday Evening Post* story about the Freeport merchant:

[T]he number of people who stopped with the index is considerable. There is, for example, a black Labrador retriever in Cincinnati, Ohio, named Linwood, on the owner's assumption that he had figured out the mystery of L. L. Bean. That is what happens when you ask your secretary . . . to check something for you at the library. I will bet you a year's supply of dog food that there is no dog in North America named after either Mr. Sears or Mr. Roebuck, let alone by one of their middle names.[12]

There's no disputing the fact that L. L. Bean was born on Howe Hill in Greenwood, Maine. But does Greenwood, Maine, still exist? According to the first line of L. L. Bean's slender 1960 autobiography, *My Story*, it doesn't, with L. L. clearly stating that Greenwood, Maine, the first place his name ever appeared (on his birth certificate) "no longer exists." This "fact" of Greenwood's demise is one that has been repeated many times since. Despite reports to the contrary, the town of Greenwood—which encompasses the perhaps better-known village of Locke Mills and the lesser-known Greenwood ice caves on Long Mountain—is still alive and well in the twenty-first century.

All this confusion about Greenwood probably isn't surprising, considering the fact that even prominent Maine writers and publications aren't altogether clear on the exact location of the future merchant's birth. Writer John Gould, who grew up in Freeport and knew L. L. Bean about as well as anybody, once wrote, "The five Bean brothers were born in Wild River Township, on the western edge of the Great North Maine Woods."[13] The Wild River actually runs between western Maine and New Hampshire, and is where L. L. went on his first deer-hunting trips as a teenager with a borrowed rifle and in the company of his cousin Louvie Swett of South Paris. The area of New Hampshire through which the river runs is now part of the White Mountain National Forest. (Gould also persisted in spelling the name of L. L.'s brother Otho as "Ortho.")

Even Maine's venerable *Down East* magazine got it wrong in a March 1970 article which put Greenwood somewhere in northern Maine: "Leon Leonwood Bean was born on a farm near Greenwood, an Aroostook County town that no longer exists." While there is no Greenwood up in "The County," as Mainers call it, there is a *Glen*wood Plantation, which may have confused someone at the magazine. Coincidentally, Glenwood Plantation is right next to Haynesville, the location of what would become L. L.'s favorite camp. So, while L. L. Bean wasn't born in Glenwood, he would probably do a lot of hunting and fishing there.

To further confuse the matter of where L. L. was born, his 1953 hunting and fishing license—which used to be on display in a case at the retail store's former Dew Drop Inn Café—says his birthplace was Milton Plantation. (By the way, the cost of a combination hunting and fishing license in 1953 was $4.50.)

And finally there's the matter of the dates of L. L. Bean's birth and death. Many sources, especially computerized library card catalogs, list his dates as 1873–1966. In fact, he was born in Greenwood, Maine, on October 13, 1872, and he died in Pompano Beach, Florida, on February 5, 1967. Even L. L.'s grandson, Leon Gorman, who served as president of L.L. Bean, Inc., for well over three decades, has been mistaken about the precise year of his grandfather's birth, once telling the *Maine Times* newspaper that "L. L. was brought up here from the time he was born in 1869."

Even before L. L. Bean had taken his first steps, others were already laying the groundwork for mail-order sales from Maine. Despite the country's being in the throes of the 1872 depression, the three-year-old E. C. Allen Company of Augusta was thriving by selling everything from recipes for washing powder to engravings by mail. Three years earlier, Allen had realized that he could sell a whole line of varied products, which he promoted in his paper, the *People's Literary Companion*, through the mail. His business quickly took off and his fifty-cent publication soon had a circulation of 500,000. During the 1870s, Augusta, Maine, became "the direct-mail capital of the United States."[14]

Merchants in Augusta weren't alone in their mail-order ambitions. During the latter part of the nineteenth century, Edward A. Buck of Bangor sold an all-leather hunting boot described as a "calf-high, laced moccasin" through the mail. The footwear, which had a riveted seam to prevent tearing, was shipped to customers throughout the U.S., especially out west, and in Canada. Ironically, the boots sold by E. A. Buck were probably very similar to the ones that would cause L. L. Bean great discomfort years later, prompting him to invent the Maine Hunting Shoe.

But it was a local event that would have a more immediate impact on young L. L.'s life.

IN THE LAGGING POSTWAR ECONOMY, L. L.'s father decided that there must be a better way to make a living than by farming the rocky fields around Howe Hill. As luck would have it—for Benjamin Bean, at least—1872 was the year that the Locke's Mills House, then owned by D. A. Coffin, burned to the ground. The following year, Benjamin Bean partnered with Coffin and Eben E. Rand to rebuild the hotel, which had originally been constructed by Luther Briggs in 1846 as the Alder River House.

By Thanksgiving of 1873, Bean, who was now supporting his still-growing family as a carpenter, had completed construction of the new hotel at the riverside site of the original structure. The new building, now called the Mount Abram Hotel, had an ell added to it, known locally as Bean's Hall, as well as an outside bandstand. The new hall was reportedly built with a "spring floor" that added much excitement to the contradances held there.

In 1874 the elder Bean bought out his partners and continued to make improvements to the building, including the addition of a partial cellar, which required the removal of some ledge beneath the hotel. During the project, it became the responsibility of his daughter Inez, then six, to ensure the safety of her two-year-old brother. Every time the crew got ready to blast, Inez carried little Leon outside to make sure he was safe from any flying debris.

Soon after the structure was completed, Benjamin Bean apparently decided that the hotel business wasn't for him and sold it back to D. A. Coffin. The building would survive for another seven decades, its name being changed to the Hotel Greenwood in the early 1920s before it was purchased by Raymond Langway, who would tear it down in 1945.

Around 1877, Benjamin Bean moved his family out of Locke's Mills and returned to farming in nearby Milton Plantation. (In his autobiography, L. L. recalls that the move took place in 1874, when he was two years old.) An old photo shows the farmhouse built by Benjamin Bean in the neighborhood then known as Allenville. It was a very large, two-story affair with an attached barn. One newspaper account of the merchant's boyhood says "his parents moved onto a smaller farm in Milton Plantation which, when Leon had attained the age of eight, only had a population of 270."[15] The town, which then had a valuation of $40,966, had one hotel and one general store, owned respectively by R. T. Allen and M. T. Look, who were better known to young L. L. as "Rat Tail Allen and Mouse Tail Look." A week's stay at the hotel cost $3 at the time.

While the general consensus holds that Benjamin Bean's last homestead was indeed located in Milton Plantation, there is some evidence that shows the farm was actually located just across the town line in Bethel. An illustrated history of Bethel says that L. L. lived from the "mid-1870s to 1884 in a Bethel farmstead on present-day Route 232 near the Milton line," adding that the house was "destroyed by fire in the twentieth century." A line from the *Oxford County Advertiser*'s obituary of his parents also supports this theory, reporting that "Mr. B. Warren Bean, who has been hopelessly sick for some time, died at his residence in Bethel Nov. 13th." L. L. himself stated that he used to trap "on a small stream (where I used to fish) that ran through our farm." This stream could be Barkers Brook, which lies a quarter mile west of the short stretch of Route 232, and runs through the eastern corner of Bethel. About a mile to the west of the brook lies Kimball Hill, which is interesting because the first name of L. L.'s great grandfather was Kimball and he was the son of Timothy and Hannah (Kimball) Bean.

The farm, wherever it was actually located, was where Leon's two younger brothers were born. Ervin Arthur Bean (aka "Irwin") was born on January 15, 1877, and Guy Chester on August 5 of the following year. L. L. would remain close to all his brothers, Henry, Otho, Ervin, and Guy, until they died off during the 1940s and 1950s. L. L.'s sister, Inez, who wed a local man named Eli "Eugene" Cummings, would die in March of 1919. One memory the great merchant would recall in his autobiography was attending Milton Plantation's traditional red, one-room schoolhouse from 1878 until his parents' deaths in 1884. "I am quite sure," he wrote in 1960, "the building is still in use."

Other memories from L. L.'s days in Milton Plantation involve his parents and some of the other local folk and might be among his fondest, since he managed to recall quite vividly things like the Saturday night dances at R. T. Allen's hotel, and his mother bringing home any leftover oyster stew she'd made for the event. L. L. also recalled the excitement of seeing the stagecoach driven by Byron Tuttle that used to stop at his house to feed and rest the horses. But his favorite event of the year was his parents' annual fall trip to Bethel Hill and Seal Rowe's store, where his father would purchase provisions for the winter (including a barrel of molasses), and shoes and candy for the three youngest children.

At this point, it's worth noting that L. L. Bean's father, who had made his living as a farmer and a carpenter, probably considered himself to be neither. By his son's recollection, Benjamin Bean was more of a barterer than a farmer and always returned from his sojourns to Bethel Hill with more supplies than his family could use. "My father lived on a farm," the merchant would later recall, "but he was really more of a hunter and trader."[16] In 1946 L. L. Bean would reveal a bit about how he'd come by his entrepreneurial spirit, telling a writer from the *Saturday Evening Post* that his father, who "was more successful as a preceptor than as a provider" was

> what Maine people called a "hoss jockey"—in other words, a congenital trader. He was always buying and selling horses, cows and almost anything else at hand, and when he took a trip out to Bethel Hill to lay in supplies, he would haul back eight or ten barrels of sugar, a barrel of molasses, and similarly large stocks of other staples for trading with the neighbors. He enjoyed that more than farming. "There were five of us boys," L. L. says, "and I guess we were all the same way. Didn't any of us ever put on overalls."[17]

Young Leon's entrepreneurial side began developing at about the same time as his love for the outdoors. Around the time he turned eleven, L. L. asked his father to buy him five steel traps to use on their property. He also wanted to go to the cattle show at the county fair eighteen miles away in Norway. When he was told that he could have the traps *or* go to the county fair, he took the traps and that fall managed to catch five mink (which he sold for $1.25 each), as well as five large muskrats (eight cents apiece) and three fox kits (five cents apiece). "That looked pretty good to me," he recalled later.

Shortly after L. L.'s twelfth birthday, his world was turned upside down when both of his parents died within four days of each other, but again, the exactness of the merchant's memory doesn't match up with other published accounts of the event. In his autobiography, there's a photo of the family's farmhouse, under which the caption reads, in part, that his family lived there until "my father and mother died, Nov. 18, 1884 and Nov. 22, 1884." Three pages later, he recalls that his parents died at the "ages of 43 and 41, respectively." It's important to remember that these facts are from a book L. L. Bean wrote largely from memory in his late eighties.

It's easier to have faith in the information contained in the Beans' obituaries, which were published as a single item in the *Oxford County Advertiser* on November 28. "Mr. B. Warren Bean," it said, "who has been hopelessly sick for some time, died at his residence in Bethel Nov. 13th. Mr. B possessed a strong constitution and was confined to his bed but a few days, resisting the sickness which brought him low in death with the same courage and firmness that marked him as an extraordinary man in everyday life." The obituary continued, "Death had marked Mrs. Bean for its own, and all the tender care and precious hope which clustered within the group of six lovely children and many kind friends could not save her. Her sister [Martha Brooks] remarked that 'she seemed like a tired child, anxious for a much needed sleep.' The earthly pilgrimage of Sara [*sic*] S. Bean ended Nov. 17th."

It's possible that the differences between the newspaper's obituary and L. L.'s recollection of the dates of his parents' deaths could be explained by the fact that they passed away on the 13th and 17th of November and their funerals were conducted on the

18th and 22nd. As for the correct age of his mother at the time of her passing, Sarah Swett Bean was born on March 9, 1846, which, as the obituary correctly reported, would have made her thirty-eight years old at the time of her death, not forty-one.

Part of the introduction to the first section of a scrapbook L.L. Bean, Inc., published for its employees and friends in 1987 reminds us of the influence Benjamin and Sarah Bean had had on Leon and his sister and brothers: "In keeping with the times and place where they lived, L. L.'s parents imparted a love of the outdoors and strong beliefs in family solidarity, hard work, concern for others, and ethical values derived from the Golden Rule. The lessons were not wasted on 'L. L.' He made them the center of his business philosophy and extended the principles into every detail of his business relationships."[18]

"The home which the parents have taken so much care to make," said their obituary, "is not to be broken up, if it can be kept up after sustaining such a loss." Friends and family pitched in to do what they could to keep the Bean brood more or less together. While it seems that the couple's three oldest children—Henry, who was almost twenty, Otho, seventeen, and Inez, sixteen—were able to fend for themselves, the three youngest—Leon, twelve, Ervin, seven, and Guy, six—were "farmed out" to live with friends of the family. In his autobiography, L. L. notes that he lived "for about a year" with the family's next-door neighbors. The share of their parents' estate that each of the six orphaned Bean children received amounted to about $225.

After that, he lived in South Paris, probably with his mother's older brother, Benjamin Swett, because it's around this time he begins going on hunting trips with his cousin "Louvie" (L. P.) Swett, who, by the 1920s, would become a well-known automobile dealer in the Bangor area.

In the fall of 1885, just after he turned thirteen, L. L. Bean became a genuine Maine outdoorsman when he went on his first hunting trip and shot his first deer with a defective rifle borrowed from his brother-in-law. After taking the train from South Paris to Gilead, he and Louvie hiked three miles south to Hastings, where they spent the night. The next morning L. L. shot a small deer, but it kept going, and he had to adjust his rifle with a small screwdriver so he could get off the second shot and "finish the job." Exhausted, L. L. was forced to leave his deer in the woods and return for it the next afternoon.

The following year Louvie and fourteen-year-old L. L. returned to the Wild River Valley (in what is now Beans Purchase in the White Mountain National Forest) and hiked up the Wild River Logging Railroad, where they stayed in an old office building at a logging camp. The day after Louvie shot a deer and went home, L. L. shot a deer that he soon sold to a pair of luckless hunters for twelve dollars. After returning to Hastings to stock up on provisions, he set out a string of traps and caught four sables and a wildcat. Ten days later, L. L. returned home with the pelts and most of the twelve dollars.

When he was about fifteen, L. L. Bean set out on his long, circuitous journey from Oxford County to his eventual home in Freeport. His first residence outside of Oxford County took him only about eight miles to the southeast, when he began working for his uncle in 1887. Sylvanus Bean's West Minot farm was just across the line in Androscoggin County, and only a few miles from Auburn. There, the young L. L. Bean was paid twelve dollars a month for the two years he worked for Uncle Sylvane. Perhaps it was the lure of more money that made him pick up and move a few miles away to W. H. Berry's East Hebron farm back in Oxford County, where he worked until 1890 for sixteen dollars a month.

During his stay in the area, Leon Bean was said to have attended nearby Hebron Academy, but didn't graduate. Longtime Hebron Academy archivist Dave Stonebraker conducted a thorough search of the school's records and could not "confirm with any original documentation that Leon Leonwood Bean attended Hebron Academy in the years 1889 or 1890." Stonebraker also checked "an older Register . . . kept by Nellie Whitman, longtime preceptress of the school. Her [researched] entries account for members of classes during the terms of instruction from 1882–1988. She seems to have tracked members of the classes and made notes on who graduated from the Academy. The Register is in her hand, and again, the name Leon Bean does not appear." Stonebraker concluded the summary of his search with: "The closest I can come is Bracey Bean of Hebron who enrolled in 1897, and there are numerous children, mainly girls, of the Bean family from Minot." Still, W. H. Berry's grandson recalls his grandfather telling him that the main reason L. L. Bean went to work on his East Hebron farm was so he could attend Hebron Academy for free.

JUST AS THE YOUNG L. L. BEAN was continuing to grow and change, so was the town of Freeport—almost as if it were preparing for the arrival of the merchant who'd soon become its most famous resident. At about the same time Leon Leonwood Bean was discovering the Maine woods during the mid-1880s, E. B. Mallet was discovering the town of Freeport. It's safe to say that Edmund B. Mallet, Jr., was an early version of L. L. Bean; had he not invested heavily in the town when he had, it never would have grown to the point where it would have attracted shopkeepers such as the Bean brothers. Freeport had fallen on hard times. The advent of the railroad following the Civil War had caused not only the loss of the town's shipbuilding industry but also the decline of maritime commerce at Mast Landing and Porter's Landing. ". . . [T]he railroad laid its track and established the Freeport depot here, thereby dealing the Landings a death blow commercially."[19]

Porter's Landing had been so named because it was where Seward Porter had begun his shipbuilding company in 1782. In its heyday, Porter's Landing served as the primary port for Freeport and cities as far inland as Lewiston. Before the yard was taken over by Rufus Soule about fifty years later, it had turned out several fine ships, the most notable of which was the privateer *Dash*, a fast topsail schooner built around 1812 for Seward Porter, Jr., and his brothers, Samuel and William. ("Privateers were privately owned vessels commissioned by the U.S. government to seize [armed and unarmed] British ships during the war, imprisoning their crews and keeping the booty they found."[20]) Eventually *Dash* was lost at sea with all sixty hands, including three of the Porter brothers: John, Jeremiah, and Ebenezer.

Mast Landing, at the head of the Harraseeket River, was named after the "King's Pines" that were shipped from there to England for the construction of ships for the king's navy. (All white pine trees greater than 24 inches in diameter a foot from the ground were marked with the "Broad Arrow" to show that they'd been reserved for the use of the king of England.)

The train station in Freeport was located on what's now Depot Street, just down Bow Street from Main Street. (The unusual shape of the intersection of Main and Bow Streets is due to the space required for teams of oxen from Durham and Pownal to safely swing their loads of huge timbers as they turned down Bow Street toward the shipyards at the landings.)

To say that E. B. Mallet, Jr.'s investment in the town's business and industry single-handedly rescued Freeport from its dire economic straits and returned the town to prosperity is certainly an understatement. Upon the 1884 death of an uncle in New York, thirty-year-old Edmund B. Mallet, Jr. (some accounts spell his name "Mallett") had realized a windfall of somewhere between $340,000 and $750,000—he never revealed the actual amount. The Pownal resident (who was driving a coal cart at the time of his good fortune) told his friends, "Well, boys, the next time you see me, I'll be driving six white horses."[21]

He then borrowed his train fare to New York City to collect his inheritance, which he wisely invested in neighboring Freeport, where he soon purchased a handsome home and then set about reviving the foundering town. Soon Mallet had built two large shoe factories, which would provide local people with jobs for much of the next century.

While obtaining stone for the foundation of the first factory, which reportedly cost $20,000 to build, Mallet's workers found some very high-quality granite half a mile from the center of town. The young tycoon promptly started the first of a pair of quarries, with the second one coming three years later at Mallet's Station, a mile from town on the Maine Central Railroad line.

Next, Mallet built a gristmill at a cost of perhaps $15,000, then he put up a sawmill. By the time he'd added a brickyard and a lumberyard to his holdings, E. B. Mallet had succeeded in bringing prosperity back to Freeport. Such was Mallet's interest in helping out the town and its people, it's said that once he even asked "for an increased valuation on his own property, which would tend to reduce the taxes of others less fortunate."[22] To help with housing for his 250 employees, he built six cottages and three double tenement houses, reportedly on Dennison Avenue and Oak Street. It is said that within six years of Mallet's arrival, 180 new houses had been built in town.

> Another undertaking was that of a business block on Main Street, one hundred feet by seventy-four feet for a wholesale and retail general store, having a plate glass front and heated by steam. The first floor, used for dry and fancy goods, was one hundred by thirty-eight feet, while the grocery and provision department was ten by thirty-six feet. . . . It has been said by one who is a competent judge of merchandising that this store was the best to be found east of Boston.[23]

The "wholesale and retail general store" was built mainly to supply food and clothing to Mallet's workers and their families. One story says that halfway through the store's construction, Mallet heard that a company in Portland was also building a store 100 feet long. Since he wanted his to be the biggest store in the state, he told his foreman to add another foot to the building. The (Bangor) *Industrial Journal* called the store "one of the largest and finest in Maine . . . teams [of horses] can be driven right through the basement."

Festivities held on the Fourth of July, 1889, celebrated the one hundredth anniversary of the town's independence from old North Yarmouth and were "opened with a salute of thirteen guns, possibly fired from a pair of brass guns, which were relics of the old artillery companies."[24] Early in its second century, Freeport continued to grow quickly: in 1891, the town's selectmen authorized Mallet to dam Frost's Gully Brook, build a brick pumping station, erect a standpipe on Maple Avenue, lay 14,400 feet of water pipe in town, and maintain eighteen hydrants.

Such progress set the stage for even more manufacturing jobs like those held by nearly one hundred local women and girls who sewed men's and boys' clothing from material shipped from Boston and New York. Mallett Drive (as it's currently misspelled on the street sign and on some of the businesses there), which marks the northern end of the town's shopping district, was so named to honor Freeport's original business tycoon. (It's where McDonald's restaurant is currently located.)

With prosperity returning to the town, Freeport's centennial had been a generally happy affair—for most people. For E. B. Mallet, though, it was a different story:

> Mr. and Mrs. Mallet did not live together following a disagreement in 1889. The disagreement was the result of Mrs. Mallet's refusal to be hostess at a luncheon at the Mallet residence in honor of the Governor of Maine [Edwin C. Burleigh, a Republican] and the dignitaries who were attending Freeport's centennial celebration of its separation from Yarmouth to become a town. Mr. Mallet and two of his [four] sons moved out of the family home into another, which he had bought and extensively repaired.[25]

BY NOW LEON L. BEAN had turned eighteen, tired of working as a farmhand, and set off into the world to seek his (eventual) fame and fortune. The events of the next three years of L. L. Bean's life not only illustrate his desire to further his education but also demonstrate his quickly developing knack for salesmanship. In 1891 he attended Kents Hill Commercial College in Readfield, where he took a "commercial course" in the school's Department of Actual Business Practice.

He initially paid for a year of schooling by selling a new brand of soap to area housewives—asking them to try half a box on a trial basis. Throughout the summer, he worked at persuading local grocers and wholesalers in Portland that they could sell a lot soap—until they had committed to buying a whole "carload." The money he made from this scheme helped with many of his expenses, but he still had to go to work in Bangor, in a butter factory.

Even though he "came out pretty well" in his soap-selling venture, it would be another twenty years before L. L. Bean would take his next big gamble, promoting his new hunting boot. In the meantime he continued to lay the groundwork for his success, first by financing his education at Kents Hill and then by honing his sales skills in the retailing of footwear and clothing. A listing on page 67 of Cannon & Co.'s 1891 *Directory of Bangor and Brewer* shows "Bean, Leon, butter maker, b. 6 Garland," perhaps indicating that he boarded at 6 Garland Street. It's interesting to note that Bangor's shoe industry, driven by firms like Parker and Peakes, and E. A. Buck, was booming at the very time Leon was toiling in the butter factory, and no doubt had a lasting effect on the impressionable young laborer.

Having secured the funds necessary to continue his education, L. L. Bean returned to Kents Hill, where his studies in business included algebra, first analysis, second analysis, language, rhetoric, spelling, bookkeeping, arithmetic, third analysis, geometry, and Latin. Shortly before his graduation in 1893, Leon created the first "business" to bear his name, the fictional Bean & Co., as part of his course work. Some of the inventory for his imaginary shop gives a sneak peek at Bean's penchant for dealing in dry goods, yard goods, and men's furnishings. The list included, among other things: elastic web, buttons, silk, flannel, and baleen, thin strips of whalebone used to stiffen corsets.

In the rosy glow of retrospect, Kents Hill would publish a brief account of the school's former student in the October 1956 issue of the *Kents Hill Bulletin*, being sure to emphasize the institution's role in his success. The piece, entitled "Kents Hill's Horatio Alger— L. L. Bean, '93," so impressed the Freeport merchant that he would dedicate a full page to it in his autobiography.

Chapter 2

L. L. Bean finally got sick of returning home
from a day of tramping around the Maine woods
with his feet cold, wet, and sore

In 1893, after his graduation from Kents Hill (and possibly following another brief stint of working in Bangor where his cousin and frequent hunting partner Louvie Swett now lived), Leon L. Bean went to work in the shoe store of his older brother Otho.

While L. L. was working for Otho in Yarmouth, the town of Freeport was continuing to evolve, almost as if it were preparing for his imminent arrival. In 1883 John Thomas Oxnard built the Oxnard Block on the west side of Main Street, directly across from Bow Street. (Some accounts have the building being constructed by E. P. Oxnard six years earlier, but most agree on the later date.) The big change to the town, and the one central to the story of L. L. Bean in Freeport, occurred the following year as a result of the Fire of '94. One history of Freeport recalled the inferno:

> [T]he Brewster Block [was] destroyed by fire in 1894. Sparks carried by the wind ignited the Congregationalist church, which was on rising ground, overlooking the Square, and that structure, a landmark since 1819, was totally destroyed. The church and the Brewster Block occupied the space where the L. L. Bean block and the stores to the north of it now stand.[1]

With the land adjacent to the Oxnard Block now available, J. T. Oxnard seized the opportunity to erect another building of similar size next to it. Oxnard christened it the Warren Block, after his wife's maiden name. The Warren Block, which in its early days had a "play-acting theater" on the third floor, stood about where the front of the current L.L. Bean store meets the sidewalk, and was the company's home until the sagging old structure was torn down in 1977. A cryptic handwritten note dated "1/9/75" in the Freeport Community Library has this to say about the Warren Block: "Front section two floors and a loft built in 1893—(Tax Records). Mildred Pettingill attended socials in the loft during her high school days from 1893 to 1901—(F. H. S.)—" It's signed "E. M. C." (In 1962 L. L. Bean would purchase the aged Oxnard Block, which had become a fire hazard, and demolish it for parking and green space early the following year.) One of the tenants of the Brewster Block had been the post office, which would later return to the site and remain downstairs from L. L. Bean's factory and store until 1962.

Now Freeport and L. L. Bean were ready for each other, and in 1895 the young retailer arrived in town to run Bean Brothers, a men's clothing store owned by his brother Otho. Though Leon spent just six or seven years in Freeport before moving to Auburn for a while, he made the most of his time there, including getting married. Upon arriving in town, he began courting Bertha, the daughter of Charles U. Porter, a carpenter, and his wife, Charity Ann Davis Porter. The Porters had played a leading role in the town's shipbuilding industry and were still one of Freeport's more prominent families.

At the time the two were courting, L. L. wasn't earning much money and was reduced to renting a horse and carriage to take out Bertha, who'd previously worked as a teacher and in a dry goods store. Longtime L. L. Bean assistant Ethel Williams would later recall, "On Sundays the young men would take the young ladies out on buggy rides. They had their own buggies and own horses. He didn't have a buggy, and he had to hire one from the livery stable and it was an old nag, I guess. He wasn't too proud of that."[2] When they were wed on September 27, 1898, Leon Leonwood Bean was twenty-six years old and Bertha Davis Porter was thirty-three. Since Bertha's father had passed away two years earlier, her mother lived with the couple in a rented farmhouse on Hunter Road just south of town.

There's a rumor from this time that L. L. Bean was involved in a scheme to lend money to American soldiers during the Spanish American War. Often soldiers running low on funds would need a few dollars to hold them over until they got paid. The story goes that L. L. Bean would advance them what they needed on the condition that it be repaid the following payday along with 10 percent interest. This scenario seems unlikely, since L. L. was a struggling newlywed in 1898 and there's no record of him serving in the military. (He would, however, serve as a civilian consultant to the War Department in Washington during World War II.) It is worth noting that his younger brothers, Ervin and Guy, reportedly served in the Maine Militia's First Infantry Regiment during the conflict with Spain. (Records at the Maine State Archives show that Ervin served in Company D of the Maine Militia's First Infantry Regiment from May 2 through November 1, 1898, while Guy's obituary says that he served three years in the same outfit.)

As L. L. Bean was beginning his new life in southern Maine, others were also discovering the state's rural allure, and its great outdoors was beginning to become big business. Nearly two decades earlier, the state legislature had realized that it was becoming necessary to police the activities of those who used the state's woods and inland waterways for recreation and, in 1880, created the Maine Warden Service. Among the state's best-trained and most-trusted law officers, game wardens were originally charged with enforcing its fish and wildlife laws. Over the years their responsibilities have grown to include such diverse activities as enforcement of snowmobile and ATV laws and searching for lost people, duties they must carry out in all weather conditions. The Maine Warden Service, which tries to keep about a hundred game wardens in the field, is currently Maine's second-largest law-enforcement agency after the Maine State Police.

By 1891, Maine's commissioners of Fisheries and Game had taken notice of the increasing number of sports "from away" (out of state) and had released a report that outlined the benefits they brought to Maine in their quest for recreation and trophies. The report emphasized the importance of the state's fish and game, writing of "the many sportsmen they bring here who spend their money freely" on farm products, hotels, and rail transportation. The authors, Henry O. Stanley and E. M. Stilwell, go on to point out that sport in the state "supports many a poor man in our backwoods who acts as a guide."

But Stanley and Stilwell also urged caution in protecting Maine's fish and wildlife, noting that they were sought not only by visitors but by the state's resident sportsmen as well. "If rightly managed we can always have plenty of fish and game. . . . But we are sorry to say in many localities the laws are not properly respected. We have the best code of laws of any state in the Union, which if lived up to would always keep up the supply of fish in our streams and game in our forests." This concern for the state's natural resources would eventually lead to the issuing of hunting and fishing licenses to out-of-state sportsmen and later to Maine residents. A more immediate remedy to the problem was the licensing of Maine's guides beginning in 1897.

The following paragraphs, probably written in 1901, show the thought that Maine's lawmakers had put into developing guidelines for the licensing of the first Maine guides, and just how popular these licenses quickly became:

The Legislature of 1897 enacted a law requiring every person who engages in the business of guiding either in inland fishing or forest hunting to cause his name, age and residence to be recorded in a book kept for that purpose by the commissioners, and procure a certificate from them setting forth in substance that he is deemed suitable to act as a guide and providing for a penalty for those who guide without being registered. The fee for such registration is $1.00 for residents and $20.00 for nonresidents.

The registration of guides was a great undertaking, involving a vast amount of work. The registration has been as follows:

In 1897, 1,316 guides were registered;
In 1898, 1,464 guides were registered;

In 1899, 1,780 guides were registered;
In 1900, 1,824 guides were registered.[3]

Most people probably think that the realm of the registered Maine guide has traditionally been that of the male and that the advent of the female Maine guide is a relatively recent phenomenon. Nothing could be further from the truth. Maine's first licensed guide was "Fly Rod" Crosby (1854–1936), a woman. The following piece from *The Maine Professional Guides Association Directory* tells the story of this fascinating lady:

On March 19, 1897, The Maine Legislature passed a bill requiring hunting guides to register with the state. Maine registered 1,316 guides that first year. The honor of receiving the first Maine guiding license went to Cornelia Thurza Crosby, or "Fly Rod," as she was affectionately known to friends across the country.

Crosby first discovered her love for the wilderness when, on the advice of her doctor, she left her job in a bank to seek "a large dose of the outdoors." This prescription brought her to Rangeley, Maine. . . . She became friends with the local guides, and from them she learned the lore of the woods and the pleasures of camping, hunting, and fishing.

In 1886 a friend presented Cornelia with a five-ounce bamboo rod. She became so adept at fly-fishing that she once landed 200 trout in one day. She began to write up accounts of her fishing adventures and submitted them, under the name "Fly Rod," to O. M. Moore, editor of the *Phillips Phonograph*. "That's mighty good stuff!" responded Moore, "Send some more right away!" "Fly Rod's Notebook" became a widely syndicated column appearing in newspapers in New York, Boston, and Chicago, and the new name stuck.

Although she shot the last legal caribou buck in the state of Maine, "Fly Rod" Crosby's most remarkable and enduring contribution to her native state happened far from the North Woods. In addition to being its first licensed guide, she was

Maine's first public-relations genius. She arranged an elaborate hunting display at the First Annual Sportsmen's Show in New York's Madison Square Garden, starring herself, rifle in hand and wearing a daring, knee-length doeskin skirt.

Her sensational appearance at the Sportsmen's Show, together with the popularity of her column, helped to attract thousands of eager would-be outdoorsmen—and women—to the woods and streams of Maine.

Even L. L. Bean, Maine's consummate outdoorsman, would hire registered Maine Guides to accompany him on many of his hunting and fishing adventures—once he made enough money to afford them, that is. When L. L. got around to writing his book on outdoor skills in the early 1940s, the State of Maine would recognize two classes of guides, Class A (formerly known as general guides) and the less-proficient Class B (formerly local guides). By then, L. L. Bean had enough experience in the out-of-doors to know that he wanted his guide to carry a full-size axe instead of a gun, and enough food for three meals—in case the two got lost.

By THE TURN OF THE CENTURY, the Bean Brothers store had set up shop in the Warren Block, where the L. L. Bean retail store now stands, and was called E. A. Bean after Ervin, who was managing the operation. The Beans boasted that they had men's suits "in nobby mixtures. Plaids, the new stripes, blacks, browns, and all the rest." They even offered "custom suits" starting at nine dollars. According to some accounts, the store was funded by older brother Otho, who worked as a traveling salesman for Cohen, Goldman & Company, and sold "gents' furnishings, hats, caps, boots . . . shoes and rubbers."

Business must have been pretty good, and L. L. and Bertha wasted little time in increasing the numbers of their family by two: Lester Carleton "Carl" Bean was born at 1:00 P.M. on Monday, August 20, 1900. (Carl would graduate from the University of Maine, marry Hazel Haskell in 1924, and take over the company upon his father's death in 1967, only to die later the same year.)

Charles "Warren" Bean arrived soon thereafter, on Monday, November 11, 1901, at 7:00 in the morning. The musically talented "Warnie," as he was also known, would graduate from Brunswick's Bowdoin College in 1923, marry Hazel June Turner in 1940 (the couple would divorce in 1951), and live to the age of seventy.

A 1902 newspaper ad for the E. A. Bean store proudly proclaims, "ALL GOODS SOLD, GUARANTEED TO GIVE SATISFACTION OR MONEY REFUNDED." Though this could have been L. L.'s idea, and the beginning of his famous 100 percent money-back guarantee, it also appears that he'd already moved on, at least temporarily. At some point during the early 1900s, Leon L. Bean had moved north to Auburn.

There's little doubt that L. L. was working in W. H. Moody's shoe store at 74 Main Street, Auburn, in 1902; the question seems to be when—if ever—did he actually move to Auburn? There is some evidence that the young salesman, who still lived on Hunter Road, may have commuted to work. Ethel Williams, who later worked for L. L. Bean for thirty-eight years, recalled that "he walked down to the tracks and took the . . . trolley to Lewiston and stayed up there during the week." Possibly L. L. commuted to work while he looked for suitable living arrangements for his growing family since, according to his autobiography, he eventually did move his family up to Auburn: "In 1902 we moved to Auburn, Maine, where I went to work in a shoe store. . . ." Merrill & Webster's Auburn business directory of 1900 includes the following listing: "Bean, Leon L., clothing 74 Main, bds 8 Goff." By 1904 the business was called "Bean Brothers" (L. L. and Ervin), and L. L. was living at 292 Court Street.

The Bean Brothers' Auburn store would continue in business for almost a decade: from 1906 through 1909, it was run by Ervin and Otho (with Ervin living on Court Street, sometimes with his brother Guy, who's listed as an insurance agent). From 1910 through 1913, the Beans' store was operated by Alton O. Howard and Harry Wood. For the record, other Auburn Bean listings of interest are Henry W., of 274 Court Street from 1893–96, who worked first as a shoemaker and then as a traveling salesman, and

Ervin, who worked as a grocer from 1926 through 1929. He had a home at 347 Sabattus Street and a "sum res Belgrade Lakes."

Once established in his new position, L. L. quickly realized that he wouldn't be able to get by on his meager twelve-dollar weekly wage, so he struck a deal with Mr. Moody, who let him have a counter to sell pants that he bought from Otho. This new arrangement worked satisfactorily enough to allow the young entrepreneur to purchase his own enclosed C-cab carriage and have it lettered with "The L. L. Bean Pant Store" and his business address at Mr. Moody's place. (At the time, L. L.'s competitors included one of Maine's largest department stores, J. J. Shapiro & Bros., located just down the street at Shapiro's Corner in New Auburn. Often compared to the Macy's store in New York, Shapiro's claimed to have the lowest prices of any store at any time.)

During L. L.'s absence, Freeport continued its economic growth thanks in large part to the railroad. In 1903 alone, the town's still-thriving shoe industry, started two decades earlier by E. B. Mallet, accounted for much of the freight being shipped to and from Freeport station. The big shoe factory, now under the ownership of A. W. Shaw, received an estimated 475,000 pounds of leather annually and shipped away about 300,000 pairs of shoes. Even the smaller factory of the Davis Brothers received about 50,000 pounds of leather from which they made and shipped "thousands of cases of shoes yearly." The town's aptly named lumber dealer, Mr. Woodman, "received some 8 or 10 carloads of building lumber, beside 5 or 6 cars of shingles during the year."[4]

Of course the rails were capable of bringing more than just cargo to Freeport, which prompted Amos Gerald of Fairfield to capitalize on the notion of developing the rustic town's tourism potential. Around 1902 he constructed an electric railway between Brunswick and Yarmouth, where it connected with the line that ran to Portland. The new line, which charged five cents for a three-mile ride, passed through Freeport center, where there was an "Electric Waiting Room" in the Harraseeket House, and through South Freeport where, on the highest point of land, Gerald had erected a grand hotel called the Casco Castle.

According to one local history, the wooden castle, which charged $3 a day (or $12 a week) for a room and meals, was complete with a "draw-bridge, postern gates, portcullis, and everything consistent with a Norman feudal castle. . . ."[5] While its grounds also contained an amusement park, a ball field, and a zoo, the hotel's most notable and longest-lasting feature would be its 100-foot stone tower, constructed by Benjamin Franklin Dunning, and accessible from the Casco Castle's main and fourth floors via footbridges.

Freeport continued to chug along in other ways as well. In 1904 Augustus Derosier opened a little "convenience" store, which is still in business on Main Street today, and the Bean Brothers clothing store reappeared. The town also received its first telephone service that year.

The newfangled mode of communication, first installed in the A. W. Shaw & Company shoe factory, caught on quickly; in just a few days, the number of telephone subscribers in town had jumped to around fifty. By 1907 even L. L. Bean, who'd returned to Freeeport in the meantime, would be listing a telephone number ("TELEPHONE 6-7") in his ads. The town also saw the construction in 1905 of the Carnegie Building, which would house Freeport's B. H. Bartol Library for nearly a century.

Another noteworthy event of this period was the birth in 1904 of Jack Gorman, future husband of L. L.'s daughter Barbara.

Before Leon L. Bean could begin his empire in Freeport, he'd first have to move back there, which he did in 1905. (L. L. recalled that he moved back to Freeport in 1907, but that date appears to be incorrect.) Although a store called L. L. Bean Clothing and Shoes opened on the second floor of the Warren block in 1905, the young merchant, who was selling items such as Walk-Over shoes ("$3.50–$4.00") and Sweet-Orr work pants, was probably still in the employ of his brother Ervin. In 1907 L. L. was selling shirts for 39 cents apiece, and earning $12 a week at a time when Maine Guides commanded $4 for a day of their services.

Aside from financing the occasional hunting or fishing trip, most of L. L.'s income went toward the support of his family, which continued to grow with the arrival on June 8, 1907, of L. L. and Bertha's third and final child, a daughter, Barbara. (Barbara would marry Jack Gorman in 1929 and the couple would raise three sons together. The youngest, Leon Arthur, born in 1934, would become president of L. L. Bean, Inc., in 1967 following the deaths of his grandfather and his uncle Carl.)

On July 24, 1908, Ted and Gertrude Goldrup put $5 down on a $45 White Family rotary sewing machine (serial number 174014) at the shop of W. W. Fish, the local furniture salesman and undertaker who frequently did business in the same building as L. L. Bean. The Goldrups made two more payments on the machine—$5 on October 27 and $10 on December 19—before paying off the balance on January 2, 1909. In just a few short years, their purchase would have a major impact on the future of a certain neighborhood clothing salesman who was, no doubt, very familiar with the town's still-thriving shoemaking business.

The wee hours of December 28, 1909, were clear, still, and very cold. By 3:00 in the morning, when the urgent barking of Linwood Porter's dog had awakened several townspeople, the temperature in Freeport had plunged to ten degrees below zero. What was it—besides the cold—that could have caused Dewey to make such a commotion in the middle of the night? First to arrive on the scene was the night watchman from the A. W. Shaw shoe factory, who discovered a blazing fire in the rear of the Curtis and Morton grocery store on Main Street. He also noticed the door of the store's safe was wide open, and word spread quickly that the fire must have been started by a burglar.

Feeding on the building's old, dry timbers, the flames spread rapidly. Soon the Clark Hotel and sixteen other businesses between Bow and Mechanic Streets had been destroyed, resulting in losses totaling $57,300. The *Portland Evening Express* called the fire "the greatest conflagration in the history of Freeport and one of the most serious ever experienced by any town." Most of the flattened shops had been located in the adjoining H. E. Davis Block, which had recently been the home of E. B. Mallet's giant general store.

When the severity of the situation was realized, a call went out to Portland for assistance. The city's Engine No. 3 and its crew, led by District Chief Burneam, were quickly dispatched to Freeport via special rail car. That afternoon's Portland paper reported that, "an engine was sent out from that City, arriving at about 6 o'clock, and rendering very valuable service." The article went on to state: "It was the splendid work of this steamer, coupled with the training and discipline of its crew which saved the town from almost complete destruction."

Not everyone concurs with the reported heroic efforts of Engine 3; decades later, an elderly woman would recall in a letter on file at the Freeport Community Library that the fire engine from Portland had been sent up on a train that made so many stops along the way, it arrived at 6:00 A.M., after the fire was out—but just in time to have its picture taken for the newspaper. One thing that had played a key role in containing the fire was the brick wall of Lewiston Trust and Safe Deposit Company on Mechanic Street. Had that wall not been there to impede the blaze's progress, many people believed that it would have ruined many more buildings farther up Main Street in the direction of Brunswick.

Across the street from the Clark Hotel, the Oxnard and Warren Blocks had also sustained considerable damage; water the firefighters had trained on the Warren Block broke out the building's front windows, resulting in damage to both W. W. Fish (undertaker) and L. L. Bean (boots, shoes, and clothing). Even before the fire was completely out, many of Freeport's displaced merchants were overheard negotiating for new shop space and are said to have secured other nearby locations for their businesses, many as soon as the following day. Once it became apparent that the burned-out buildings could not be saved, townspeople pitched in to remove items from the doomed businesses and much was salvaged, including the stock from A. W. Mitchell's variety store in the Clark Hotel and records kept by town clerk Robert E. Randall in the law office of Randall & Keene. All of the businesses destroyed in the fire quickly secured other premises in town and were conducting business again within a few days.

Verde C. Morton, one of the owners of the store where the fire started, refuted the burglar theory saying that the safe had probably been left open the night before and that the blaze began in a seldom-used part of the basement. "Perhaps a tramp got in," theorized Morton, "and carelessly or otherwise started a blaze."[6] Despite the scale of destruction to the town, the 1909 fire would end up having a silver lining: "In the end, however, the town benefited through this misfortune, for modern brick blocks soon took the places of those destroyed, thus providing better business quarters."[7]

Proving that L. L. was already becoming popular, if not yet famous, Lewiston's *Daily Sun* ran a brief mention of the merchant's travails the following day: "The gents furnishings store of L.L. Bean, Freeport, was damaged to the amount of $400 by the fire at that place this week. Mr. Bean formerly had a store on Main Street, Auburn."

Fire wasn't the only challenge shop owners in Freeport—and elsewhere—currently faced. An article in the March 11, 1908, edition of the *Daily Sun* carried an ominous warning of a new plague that could devastate small businesses:

The story of the rise of the so-called mail-order business is an interesting chapter in our commercial history. The spread of the craze—for it must be classed as such—resembles that of an ordinary epidemic against which no precaution is taken. The disease has until very recently been allowed to spread without even quarantine regulations. But from present indications its decline will be as rapid as was its rise.

The idea of selecting goods from a catalogue containing pictures of articles and then ordering the articles thus selected by mail was the direct result of the failure of the business end of the Grange movement—the Grange store.

By 1910 Henry E. Davis and Joseph C. Clark rebuilt their burned businesses even though there had been initial speculation that the Clark Block might be rebuilt as retail space since the hotel had reportedly "never been a great success." (In a very strange bit of irony, it would be the 1981 fire set by a burglar in Leighton's 5 & 10—located in the very same Clark Block—that would create the space for the Dansk kitchenware store—the one that's usually held responsible for starting Freeport's outlet boom.) Many of the burned-out merchants returned to the rebuilt Davis Block, and L. L. Bean and W. W. Fish even moved across the street to join them. Bean would move back across the street to the Warren Block, site of his famous store's current location, in 1917, and would purchase the building in 1920.

Now conducting business in his new quarters, L. L. Bean probably would have remained content to live in Freeport, make enough money to support his family, and go on the occasional hunting or fishing trip. In his autobiography, L. L. reveals that he was much more interested in hunting than in retailing. He also was on the lookout for a decent pair of boots. On yet another of his many hunting trips, L. L. Bean finally got sick of returning home from a day of tramping around the Maine woods with his feet cold, wet, and sore. Determined to do something about it, he went back into the woods the next day wearing a pair of old rubbers and three pairs of socks. The heels of the rubbers, which would later be filled with cork, initially used pieces of felt to fill the void and provide some cushioning. This solution worked fairly well, but L. L. found that his feet were still weary because of the lack of support around his ankles and lower legs. His solution to this problem would prove to be the key to his success.

"I took a pair of shoe rubbers from the stock on the shelves," he said, "and had a shoemaker cut out a pair of 7 1/2[-inch] tops. The local cobbler [named Dennis Bibber] stitched the whole thing together." Several accounts of the creation of the boot that would become known as the Maine Hunting Shoe say that the first pair was sewn "by a local woman." While it's true that the Goldrups helped in the manufacture of many of L. L. Bean's early boots—Ted Goldrup cut the "light weight Tan Elk" uppers while his wife, Gertrude, stitched the leather pieces together on the White sewing machine they'd purchased from W. W. Fish back in 1908—the boots' uppers were joined to their rubber bottoms by Bibber.

The Goldrups' grandson, Fred Goldrup, remembers, "I do know that Dad, when he was about ten, I guess, would take the leather uppers of [Bean's] Hunting Shoes up about three miles on Route 125, and my grandmother had a White sewing machine, a treadle machine, and she sewed those uppers on that machine. And then he would take them back downtown. Acoss the street was a cobbler, who sewed on the rubber bottoms. Sometimes Mr. Bean would give my father a nickel for his errand, and he would give it to his mother. And that's the story of the Hunting Shoe, actually."

In September of 1911, L. L. made a pair of his new boots for Edgar Conant, a local breeder of fancy Holsteins to whom he'd "quite innocently praised" his shoes, to try out. "From his recommendation," L. L. later wrote, "I decided I had struck the right thing in the great hunting ground in the State of Maine." Following some field testing of prototypes in the woods that fall around his Haynesville camp—during which Bean, his cousin Louvie, uncle Benjamin Swett, and friend Levi Patterson shot four deer and three moose—the merchant from Freeport felt confident enough of his creation to bring it to the market.

Copy written for the L.L. Bean catalog in 1975 by L. L.'s grandson Leon Gorman would show how well the boots, whose basic design had changed little from their original inception, had stood the test of time:

> Mr. Bean developed this boot in 1912. He was tired of coming home with wet and sore feet from wearing the heavy leather woodsman boots then in common use. Rubber boots were clammy feeling and too clumsy for all-day walking. He decided to combine lightweight leather tops with all-rubber bottoms, incorporating the best features of both types of footwear and doing away with the disadvantages. He called his new boot the Maine Hunting Shoe.
>
> The practical advantages of this design were readily apparent to hunters and woodsmen. For bare ground walking, it was

light in weight, snug fitting, had a cushioned innersole, and a non-slip, chain-tread outersole. For wet going and walking on snow, the waterproof bottoms were ideal. Mr. Bean invented the split backstay to prevent chafing and by keeping all the parts as light and flexible as possible he had a boot that could be used all day in perfect comfort.

The Maine Hunting Shoe was an immediate success.

Almost.

Chapter 3

Soon he had scraped together $18.75, enough to place a few small ads in **National Sportsman**

Certain that he'd hit upon a product that would fill the needs of outdoorsmen everywhere, L. L. Bean set to work in the basement of the store he and his brother maintained in the Davis Block. From this space 25 feet wide and 35 feet long, L. L. Bean sent out the first hundred pairs of the Maine Hunting Shoe, which he offered for sale at $3.50 a pair, postpaid—including a repair kit.

He promoted his new product with an enthusiasm previously reserved only for his own hunting and fishing activities, with the marketing of his boot quickly becoming a "consuming passion": he'd send an ad "to every man's name I could get ahold of." L. L. Bean took the names on what would turn out to be the first of his many mailing lists directly from the list of out-of-state sports who'd recently purchased hunting licenses from Maine's Inland Fisheries and Game Department. In September of 1912, L. L. sent 1,000 of his fellow sportsmen a three-page circular (which was really nothing more than a folded sheet of paper) featuring a small black silhouette of the Maine Hunting Shoe and some promotional information about the new boot. "It really had four pages," said L. L., "but I didn't have anything to put on the last page so it was blank."

As gregarious as he was in person, L. L. Bean was indeed a man of few words when writing, and the first two pages of his new circular contained only a page and a half of information. The first page had a one-inch illustration of the boot in the upper left-hand corner, next to which was written, "Weight Only 31 Ounces (the pr.)." The body of the text, which followed the capitalized heading "MAINE HUNTING SHOE," extolled the virtues of Bean's creation:

Outside of your gun, nothing is so important to your outfit as your footwear. You cannot expect success hunting deer or moose if your feet are not properly dressed.

The Maine Hunting Shoe is designed by a hunter who has tramped Maine woods for the past eighteen years. They are light as a pair of moccasins with the protection of a heavy hunting boot.

The vamps are made of the very best gum rubber money will buy. The tops (7½ in. high) are soft tan willow calf that never grow hard by wetting and drying. Leather inner soles keep the feet off the rubber and prevent "drawing" that is so objectionable with most rubber shoes. Skeleton cork-filled heels keep the shoes from slipping and make them much more comfortable to one accustomed to wearing shoes with heels.

For those hunters who go just before the first snow it is next to impossible to find footwear that is adapted to both bare ground and snow hunting. The Maine Hunting Shoe is perfect for both. For bare ground, its extreme light weight and leather inner soles keep it from drawing the feet while the rubber soles keep it from slipping. For snow, by using a heavier stocking, you have warm, light, dry footwear that is ideal for still hunting.

The second page continued:

The light weight friction lining makes them easy to dry as a dish. Just roll down the leather tops, set them where it is warm and they are dry in ten minutes.

With every pair we give a small repair outfit that we warrant to mend a cut or snag in five minutes.

For all-round hunting purposes there is not a shoe on the market at any price equal to the Maine Hunting Shoe. See guarantee tag that is attached to every pair.

Price $3.50 delivered on approval anywhere in the U. S.

It was signed, "L. L. BEAN, MANUFACTURER, FREEPORT, MAINE."

The third and final page of the initial circular consisted of a letter dated September 1, 1912, from Edgar Conant, Bean's first boot purchaser, praising his fellow Freeporter's footwear. Mr. Conant, who owned the Village Centre Farm (it really was located right there in the village), evidently was a disciple of the same school of writing as L. L. Bean, because the body of his letter was as brief and to-the-point as was the merchant's ad copy:

Am sending you the pair of Maine Hunting Shoes I bought of you last fall. I wore these shoes two weeks moose hunting last October and then put them right into hard service on the milk farm right up to the first of March. They are now in almost perfect condition except the soles are worn so thin I want them revamped. This is the first winter I ever got through without two or three pairs heavy buckle rubbers.

Your shoe is not only O.K. for hunting, but is the lightest and best wearing farm shoe I ever had.

The first circular ever sent by L. L. Bean was printed in the same Cheltenham typeface that is still used in the catalog today. In October, Bean sent the circular again to all those who'd not responded to his initial mailing, and this time the previously blank fourth page contained a typed follow-up letter which emphasized six reasons why they should try his new boot:

Freeport, Me.
Oct. 5, 1912.

F. N. Sawyer
31 Chestnut St.
Wakefield, Mass.

Dear Sir:
Recently I sent you a circular of my Maine Hunting Shoe. As I have not received your order, I take the liberty of again calling your attention to my shoe. I am receiving so many compliments from all over the states that I am sure the shoe would please

you, and am willing to send you a pair on approval. Below are some of the good points not to be found on any other hunting shoe.

L. L. then reiterated his boot's six strong points:

1st. Weight, lightest shoe made.
2nd. Leather innersoles.
3rd. Made in whole and half sizes for both men and women also in F and H[?] widths.
4th. Cork filled heels that keep them from slipping.
5th. Price, lowest of any sporting shoe on the market.
6th. A printed guarantee with every pair.

L. L. closed his letter with, "I enclose order blank and envelope for your convenience."

L. L. was now committed to making and selling his boots, so he ramped up his marketing efforts. Soon he had scraped together $18.75, enough to place a few small ads in *National Sportsman*, which was then edited by William Harnden Foster, who summered in South Freeport.

One writer claimed that L. L. Bean's statement about using the hunting-license list as a mailing list couldn't possibly have happened until after the 1917 fall hunting season, "when Maine instituted its first licenses." The fact of the matter is that while Maine didn't issue nonresident *fishing* licenses until 1917, it had been issuing nonresident *hunting* licenses since 1903, and it was the holders of those who had received Bean's first circular. (Maine would begin issuing hunting licenses for Maine residents in 1919.) L. L. may have been a few years off in recalling some of the dates in his autobiography, but when it came to the date of his first mailing list, he was right on the money.

But despite all his hard work in manufacturing and marketing, L. L. Bean's first attempt at selling his new Maine Hunting Shoe to the public proved a dismal failure. Anyone who reads anything about the history of L. L. Bean's outdoors empire will no doubt stumble across the often-repeated story about ninety of the hundred pairs of boots being returned because of defective stitching that caused the rubber bottoms to separate from the leather tops. (The actual cause of the problem, according to L. L. was that "the rubber was not strong enough to hold the 'stitched on' tops" and tore away from the stitching.) L. L. Bean hastened to honor his ironclad, 100 percent money-back guarantee, leaving himself in pretty good standing with the customers whose footwear had failed them. It also left him in quite a bind, because now he had no reliable boots to sell and no money with which to fund his plan for improvements—a plan that centered around the U.S. Rubber Company in Boston.

The U.S. Rubber Company had been formed when nine small rubber companies consolidated in 1892. The firm employed a process developed by Charles Goodyear called vulcanization, using heat to bond rubber to cloth or other rubber components. Prior to vulcanization, shoe companies used a cold sealing process in which glue or cement held the pieces together.

In the fall of 1912, L. L. Bean borrowed $400 from his brother Otho, and went to Boston to try to convince the management of the U.S. Rubber Company to manufacture a lightweight rubber bottom that was strong enough to have a leather top attached to it. When he was told that that type of last would be very expensive to manufacture, and that he'd need to place a much larger initial order, L. L. returned home and raised more money. U.S. Rubber would continue making the rubbers for Bean's boots, often telling him that he was their largest single customer for rubbers, until the mid-1960s when the company ceased production in the Boston area and, indeed, much of the country.

As L. L. strove to improve the quality and durability of his footwear, he was also becoming more and more embedded into the fabric of Freeport. He shared space with W. W. Fish in the H. E. Davis Block at 15 Main Street, where, according to a Portland-area directory of the day, he sold "clothing." The big news for L. L. Bean's store that October was, according to the *Six Town Times*, "a large turnip in his window which was raised by Mr. Herbert Talbot that is 3½ feet around and weighs 26 pounds." Earlier that year, to accommodate his family, he bought the former Fred W. Nichols house just off Main Street at 6 Holbrook Street. The building now houses the L.L. Bean company archives.

His soon-to-be-famous Maine Hunting Shoe (which a hunter, Bean would later boast, "might like better than his wife") was about to transform this small town clothing salesman into the mail-order mogul from Maine. "My life up to the age of forty years was uneventful, with a few exceptions," L. L. Bean would write in his autobiography. Well, he was about to turn forty and his life was about to become very eventful; Leon Leonwood Bean was on the verge of becoming one of the country's most famous self-made men of the twentieth century. Within ten years, products sold by L. L. Bean would be featured on the cover of *National Sportsman*— after Talbot's turnip had long been forgotten.

IF "LUCK" IS REALLY PREPARATION meeting up with opportunity, then L. L. was indeed lucky in 1913. As he prepared the more reliable incarnation of his design, the final piece for the beginning of L. L. Bean's mail-order empire fell into place when the post office provided the opportunity for him to ship his product all over the country at a reasonable rate. The parcel-post rate was approved by Congress on August 24, 1912, and on November 30, 1912, Postmaster General Frank H. Hitchcock signed order number 6685, which read, "The accompanying regulations for the conduct of the parcel post system shall take effect on January 1, 1913, superseding all regulations in conflict therewith."

While other mail-order companies such as Sears, Roebuck and Montgomery Ward would be slow to warm up to the government's new shipping rate, L. L. Bean jumped on it with both feet, to the point of calculating how much it would cost to ship a given item to the nation's various postal zones. Maine writer John Gould would later recall a time when Mr. Bean enlisted the help of his friends (as they came in for their "regular forenoon howdies") in selecting which one of twenty-seven axes scattered around his office should be included in his next catalog. Gould wrote that the merchant partially based his final decision on the fact that the axe had to be light enough to carry in a pack and "light enough to be mailed, as Mr. Bean was careful about pounds and ounces and parcel post zones and 'What be I goin' to get from it?'" At the time, L. L. would have spent 8 cents to ship a 3¹/₂-pound axe to a customer in his local zone, but it would have cost him 48 cents (". . . twelve cents for the first pound and twelve cents for each additional pound or fraction thereof") to mail the same axe to a customer in Alaska, which was located in Zone 8.

Prior to the introduction of parcel post, a shipper's options had been limited; second class mail had no weight limit but was restricted to "newspapers and other periodical publications," while first, third, and fourth class mail was limited to four pounds—with the exception of "a single book" for fourth class. At the time, anything sent within the United States or "to Canada, Cuba, Mexico, Panama, and the United States postal agency at Shanghai, or to officers and crew of United States war vessels" qualified for domestic rates.

Fittingly, the very first package to be shipped via parcel post from Freeport, Maine, was mailed by "L. L. Bean, Manufacturer." The problem is, L. L. says he mailed the parcel-post package on January 1, 1912, exactly one year *before* the post office began offering the service. And he has a photograph of the receipt in his autobiography to back him up. There it is, plain as day on page 154, a slip signed by L. T. Patterson attesting to the fact that "United States Mail insured parcel No. 1" was indeed mailed in Freeport, Maine, at 8 A.M. on January 1, 1912.

The existence of this slip raises two questions. First, how was L. L. able to get the United States Post Office to open on a national holiday? And why is the receipt dated a year ahead of time? The answer to the first question lies in the fact that the L. T. Patterson who worked at the post office is probably Levi Patterson, one of L. L.'s hunting buddies who'd helped him test prototypes of his new boot in Haynesville. Or maybe L. L. went in the next day and, since it would do no harm, asked his friend to backdate the receipt.

The answer to the second question also seems fairly straightforward. As is the case with most of us in early January, probably Mr. Patterson simply forgot to change the year before he stamped the receipt. His mistake should in no way cast any doubt upon L. L. Bean's claim of having mailed the first parcel-post package from Freeport, Maine. (Patterson, it seems, was a good enough hunter, but couldn't cook to save his life. "One Fall I went to Hastings, New Hampshire," L. L. would write in his later autobiography, "and took along a fellow by the name of Levi Patterson, who knew so little about cooking that his wife said he would starve to death in a grocery store." When it was his turn to fix breakfast, Levi served the hunting party the cold leftovers of a boiled dinner that L. L.'s brother Otho had prepared for supper the previous evening.)

Something else to consider is the fact that, right next to the photo of the receipt, L. L. writes that a pair of Maine Hunting Shoes were in "the first parcel post package mailed from Freeport when that service began in 1912. (See receipt at left.)" The problem is, you'll recall, that L. L. didn't send out the first circular for his new boots until September of that year.

In the fall of 1914, the majestic Casco Castle seaside hotel burned to the ground. The fire completely consumed the main building, which was made of wood, leaving just the "picturesque gray stone tower rising majestically above South Freeport's cottages and wharves," according to a 1930 book about the town. "Today," the book continues, "the rock-fishermen and lobstermen guide their courses by the tower, which is on the highest point of land along the coast of South Freeport."[1] It was a dark day for the trolley company, which owned the hotel, but the rest of Freeport continued to hum along, including the business of one L. L. Bean, who was very close to finding the beginning of his path to prosperity.

He continued to refine the Maine Hunting Shoe, which would help to establish the company that would, in turn, be financed first by the sale of the boots and soon by other hunting-related goods. At first L. L. offered his new boot either with or without a heel and with a crepe sole or a gray rubber one, your choice. As far as Ken

Stilkey—who would start working for Bean in 1924—was concerned, any style of the boot was okay. He couldn't see any advantage (or disadvantage) one way or the other.

L. L. MUST HAVE FIGURED that if he could sell his boots to the public, then why not socks since they tied in perfectly with his footwear? The first socks he offered for sale were hand-knit by his acquaintance Emma Tooney up in Unity (which isn't far from other patriotically named mid-Maine towns such as Washington, Jefferson, Union, Liberty, Hope, and Freedom). The new socks quickly became very popular—too popular, in fact. Emma could only knit just so fast, so she recruited some of her friends into the sock-knitting business. But even they couldn't keep up with the soaring demand.

Before long, L. L. was selling more socks than Mrs. Tooney and her friends could produce, and he had to resort to offering machine-knit socks in his catalog. As was his style, he personally tested the new socks to make sure they were up to snuff. Boots and socks were soon followed by the Maine Hunting Coat which sported seven pockets, including an extra-large one built into the double-layer back for carrying small game the hunter may have bagged.

Around this time, L. L. saw the growing potential of his new business and realized that he'd need help with all the cutting and shipping and packing, so he made Ted Goldrup his first official employee. Ted and his wife, Gertrude, you'll recall, had moonlighted for Bean, cutting and sewing the Maine Hunting Shoe's leather uppers in the evening after their regular jobs at a local "shoe shop" (as the Maine footwear factories were usually called). A few years later, L. L. Bean would hire the man he'd call his second employee, but it seems that, unofficially at least, that title should go to Ted's wife, who'd been stitching the uppers together at home since 1912.

By 1915 L. L. was supremely confident of his newly refined boot and had worked up a rather clever print ad. The ad's photo showed a pair of his boots perched atop a small scale, its pointer moved only slightly from the top of its round face, with the accompanying copy proclaiming that the Maine Hunting Shoe was "Light as a moccasin (only 33 oz.), with the protection of a heavy hunting boot." The advertisement promised that the boot was "Made on a swing last that fits the foot like a dress shoe. Warranted to stand the hardest test. Best waterproof tops and rubber vamps money will buy. White rolled soles and leather innersoles."

Who could refuse an offer like that? For only $4 delivered you could own an eight-inch-tall pair of genuine Maine Hunting Shoes ($5.60 for the fourteen-inch model)—and that still included a repair kit. But don't just take L. L. Bean's word for it, the reader was then urged, "Send for a circular and guarantee tag, also free sample of rubber and leather used in this shoe." The ad concluded with bold-face type again emphasizing "Weight Only 33 oz.," the two-ounce increase no doubt reflecting some much-needed improvements over Bean's defective initial offering. One of the enhancements of this time appears to have been an arched innersole, which was such an improvement it put the boot "in a class by itself."

Even though the Maine Hunting Shoe had achieved a level of reliability acceptable to even L. L. Bean, that didn't mean he was happy with it. Old-time employee Ken Stilkey recalls that there was a year when the company came up with a sole that had ribs running across it. The new design worked well for walking forward, but didn't prevent the wearer from sliding sideways. The following year, the chain-link tread pattern appeared on the sole but not the heel, and so on, until the boot eventually evolved into more or less what it is today.

Having settled on the basic design for his timeless Maine Hunting Shoe, which was perfectly serviceable for hunters and other "sports," L. L. Bean next turned his attention to the manufacture of footwear that would hold up to the punishment of the state's loggers and guides, who toiled long hours, day in and day out, in Maine's rugged forests. To meet the needs of this hearty breed, Bean "added a line of heavy leather-top rubbers for lumbermen, together with other specialties." This heavy-duty boot, or one similar to it, survived for at least the next decade. Featured as the

Maine Cruising Shoe in the 1921 catalog, it was described as having dark red vamps and soles, "the same as used in high grade automobile tires," and had a top made of "the toughest tan leather money can buy."

"This shoe," the copy continued, "is intended for Lumber Cruisers, Guides, and Choppers, who want a good fitting shoe that will stand the hardest kind of usage and don't mind a little extra weight." These boots may have been the ones that were renamed Maine Guide Shoes and offered for sale in the 1926 L. L. Bean catalog. Stilkey remembers that the regular Maine Hunting Shoe was a little lighter, but both boots would last a long time, even if they were worn on rocky surfaces. "Wear, wear, wear," he said.

Although L. L.'s footwear remained top notch, the truth is his strength was in marketing as opposed to actualy making the boots, and this fact once led the Maine merchant to a near brush with inferior quality, at least as Fred Goldrup remembers things: "Once, a leather salesman came to the factory and tried to sell L. L. a different kind of split leather for the uppers. L. L. liked the stuff and wanted to try some, but my grandather, who was Bean's leather buyer and cutter, looked at it and didn't like it. L. L. said, 'Well, we ought to try a roll and see how it works out.' My grandfather told him, 'If you buy that leather, I won't cut it.' L. L. didn't buy any."

Never mind the fact that he'd been successful with his new line of boots and other goods for only a few years, people were already starting to take notice of the merchant of the Maine woods. The editors of the new edition of the *Portland Directory*, which just three years earlier had listed the nature of L. L. Bean's business as "clothing," changed the category of his offerings to now read "Maine Hunting Specialties." As word of his business spread, it quickly outgrew L. L.'s manufacturing and storage facility in the basement of the Davis Block, forcing him to commandeer space in the back of the store he shared with his brother Guy for use as an office and shipping room.

By 1916 recreation in the Maine outdoors had become a flourishing business, not just for L. L. Bean but for the state's guides as well, to the point where the commissioners at the Fisheries and

Game Department felt it necessary to further refine the regulations governing their licensing:

> The commissioners may "license as guides such nonresidents *as reside in territory contiguous to the state* under such conditions as are herein provided for the registration of resident guides." The fee for nonresident guides was $20.00.

The previous year the commissioners had stipulated that

> No person shall engage in the business of guiding . . . until he shall have filed with the Commissioners of Inland Fisheries and Game a certificate and affidavit signed by the municipal officers, or a majority thereof, of the town or plantation within which the applicant resides (or the nearest town or plantation) setting forth in substance that the applicant is a person of good moral character and sobriety, and is deemed by them to be a suitable person to receive a certificate as a guide.

Also in 1916, the management of a thriving U.S. Rubber Company, manufacturer of the bottoms of Bean's Maine Hunting Shoes, decided it was time to consolidate its more than thirty brands of rubber-soled footwear under a common name. When the executives at U.S. Rubber learned that their first choice for a name, Peds, had already been taken, they went with their second choice, calling the line Keds. The following year, advertising agent Henry Nelson McKinney coined a word for the company's canvas-top footwear based on its stealthiness, calling it the "sneaker."

Reflecting some of the recent additions to his line of goods, L. L. Bean's first small advertisement in *Forest and Stream* magazine was for an article of clothing. The ad, placed in the September 1916 issue, was for the Maine Safety Hunting Coat, which was described as being all wool and 36 inches long. Available in "red and black and green and black plaid," L. L. concisely stated that the coat, which he would personally model in upcoming catalogs, was waterproof and was the "best coat made for Maine deer hunting."

Surely a bargain at "$8.75, delivered free on approval." At the bottom of the ad, the prospective customer was urged to "send for circular and free sample, also list of what to wear on Maine hunting trips." This list no doubt included such items as Maine Hunting Shoes and Bean's own comfy socks. As his business grew, L. L. Bean continued to emphasize his commitment to quality. To make sure that everyone was aware of this, he published the following in one of his 1916 circulars:

NOTICE

I do not consider a sale complete until goods are worn out and customer still satisfied.

We will thank anyone to return goods that are not perfectly satisfactory.

Should the person reading this notice know of anyone who is not satisfied with our goods, I will consider it a favor to be notified.

Above all things we wish to avoid having a dissatisfied customer.

While peace and relative prosperity reigned in the United States at this time, most of Europe was embroiled in the Great War, and L. L. Bean did his small part to help out by sending dozens of pairs of socks to the relief effort in France. For this act of kindness, Monsieur Bean received a letter in early May from *L'Assistance aux Dépôts d'Éclopés* in Paris thanking him for his "very welcome and most generous gift of 150 pairs of socks. . . ." The letter, a copy of which he included in his autobiography, concluded by telling him, "Your gift brings physical comfort and will bring to our sick and wounded men, in addition, the moral support of sympathy and good wishes from our sister Republic."

In early 1917 Central Powers leader Germany announced that it would resort to unrestricted submarine warfare against all shipping to Great Britain. This move would draw America into the fray two months later, and many Freeporters would serve under General John J. Pershing as members of the American Expeditionary

Force in France, where most saw fierce fighting. Three men from town would be lost in the war.

Townspeople supported the Allies and the Associated Powers by turning out shoes for the troops and buying war bonds. Eighty-four years later, Maine writer John Gould would recall, "I saw my first 'aeroplane' in 1917, when a biplane flew over promoting war bonds. It was a miracle."[2] The war effort in Europe also brought about a temporary revival of the local wooden shipbuilding industry in the form of the Freeport Shipbuilding Company, which turned out two Ferris-type steamers at the former Soule Brothers yard. By the end of the war, the Allies were building new ships faster than the Germans could sink them, thus ending Germany's plan to force the British into surrendering by cutting off their supplies.

The town's role in wartime manufacturing stimulated the local economy, which certainly didn't hurt the business of L. L. Bean. Realizing that he'd gotten all he could out of the 25- by 35-foot space in the cellar of the Davis Block (which he kept for storage), he moved his business across Main Street to the company's present location in 1917—though he leased "only the top floor" (2,355 square feet) of the three-story, 7,065-square-foot building. The block's ground floor housed the post office, and its second floor was divided into two "housekeeping" apartments.

The move, which took place in June, put L. L. Bean in the War-ren Block—where the retail store still stands today—for good. At about this time, L. L. began using cash registers supplied by NCR, and "The first year he was in his new quarters . . . saw sales of $23,245." The store directly across the street in the Davis Block became known as L. L. and G. C. Bean, and would continue until at least 1927, when it was known as Guy C. Bean & Co.

As business picked up steam, so did L. L.'s marketing efforts, which took two different tacks. The first was to increase the number of display ads he ran in *Forest and Stream* magazine during 1917. His timely ads were for the Maine Trouting Boot in May, the Maine Fishing Shoe in June, the "Maine Arched Inner-sole" ("takes away that flatfooted feeling so as to make your Hunting Rubbers and Moccasins feel the same as your everyday shoes") in September, and the Maine Duck Hunting Boot in the magazine's October and November issues.

"In 1917, he took the step that was to lead to the name L. L. Bean becoming synonymous with sporting goods throughout the world. He put all his items together in a mail order catalog."[3] Now armed with a more-or-less real catalog that showcased his wares, L. L. Bean once again added to the list of sports who received information about his latest offerings via the U.S. mail. The latest group of potential customers available to L. L. came from the list of sports who had recently purchased one of Maine's new nonresident fishing licenses (previously, L. L. had marketed his goods to holders of nonresident hunting licenses).

With his advertising efforts paying off, the corresponding upswing in business necessitated L. L.'s hiring more help to make and ship his boots and the other goods he now offered. A photo in his autobiography, *My Story*, shows two elderly men engaged in the manufacture and shipping of Bean's Maine Hunting Shoe. The caption of the 1959 photo says it is of "Winnie Given and Ben Stilkey," Bean's second and third employees. Both men—then in their mid-seventies—had started with the company in 1917, and were still there in 1960. (Given's real first name was Winfield, and everybody except L. L. seemed to call him Win.)

Secure in the knowledge that his business was headed in the right direction, L. L. felt the need to start giving something back to his adopted hometown. One of his first undertakings was to oversee the construction of Freeport's new high school in 1917, when he was the acting chairman of the school committee. Once the building was completed, L. L. assured the town that it had a first-class facility with modern heating, lighting, ventilation, water, and sewage systems for its 237 students—and the whole thing had been done with $7.49 left over from the original budget of $28,600.

Maine writer John Gould remembered entering the school as a fifth-grader "when it was spanking new" in 1918. He recalled receiving an entirely adequate education there despite the school's meager resources: "Our school library," he wrote, "was a windowsill with a dictionary and a set of *Stoddard's Lectures*." One warm November morning he arrived at school only to be told that classes had been canceled because Germany had surrendered. After marching in an "impromptu celebration parade," Gould and his friend Johnny Snow went out hunting for "pa'tridges." "We got three, and Mother made us a pa'tridge pie."[4] Evidently, John Gould's mother made everything from scratch, including bread; according to one old-timer, she was "about the last person in town to accept sliced bread. 'I guess I can slice my own bread,' she used to say." (The Continental Baking Company would begin slicing Wonder Bread during the 1930s, but would temporarily stop the practice during the Second World War, when there was no steel available for the knives.)

The ten-year-old Gould also sold live ducks to L. L Bean to use as decoys when he went to his duck-hunting camp on Merrymeeting Bay at the confluence of the Kennebec and Androscoggin Rivers. "One evening he walked to our house," said Gould, "rapped on the door, and asked for me. He said he'd heard that I had tollers. I did—a nest of wild mallard eggs had been found, brought home, and hatched by a broody hen." Gould recalled how he came to do business with Freeport's leading merchant:

> Unlike other wild ducks, mallards will domesticate, so I was keeping some as part of my 4-H poultry project. Back then live birds could be legally used as decoys, or tollers. I did not hunt ducks, but I was not averse to letting Mr. Bean borrow a pair. He came to the duck pen with me and we stuck a duck and a drake in two old socks, which is the way to carry ducks, and off they went a-quacking. Mr. Bean always gave me $1.50 per mallard. Ninety years ago, things looked good up ahead.

Sometimes L. L. would be obliged to make an occasional return visit during the season, thanks to his brother Otho (or "Ortho," as Gould called him). "Ortho was inclined to be clumsy," noted Gould, "and had a knack for shooting the decoys, so during the duck season, L. L. would come back to renew his decoys and usually say a few words about Ortho's marksmanship."

Attached to an anchor in the water by a leather strap on one of their legs, these live decoys were known as tollers because their quacking attracted wild ducks just as a tolling bell calls the faithful to church. John Gould recalled that he quickly came to count on L. L.'s business every fall, when the Maine merchant would stop by his house to purchase three mallards, two hens and a drake, for a dollar apiece.

Later the price for live decoys increased and Gould recalled that the $1.50 he received for each bird "was some old good in them days. Mr. Bean would select a pair and use them at his waterfowl 'camp' at Merrymeeting Bay. I'd keep my breeders and then caretake his ducks until he wanted them." The use of live decoys would remain legal in Maine until 1934. "It was a sad business day for me," said Gould, "when the law was changed to outlaw live ducks as tollers." While they were legal, L. L. and his brother Otho would show up at the Gould household every fall and take their pick of ducks from the youngster's 4-H flock. ("It might be," added Gould, "that somebody will be interested that I was the first to exhibit wild mallards in a poultry show. The judges weren't sure how to judge them, but gave me a blue ribbon anyway.")

The money young Mister Gould had received from L. L. Bean for his barnyard mallards happened to be just about the same as Mr. Bean charged "Johnny" Gould for a pair of boy's Maine Hunting Shoes. "I had a first pair of L. L. Bean's Maine Hunting Shoe, which cost $3. Mr. Bean told me never to pay more than $3 for a pair of shoes, as the best ones could be made to sell for that."

THE SAME YEAR THAT L. L. BEAN moved his business to its new home in the Warren Block, a company that would turn out to be one of his major competitors for many decades was also relocating to much larger quarters in New York City. In 1917 Abercrombie & Fitch moved its sporting-goods store from its midtown location just off Fifth Avenue to a twelve-story building on the corner of Madison Avenue and 45th Street, where Ezra Fitch had a sign put up proclaiming that this was "Where the Blazed Trail Crosses the

Boulevard." Entire floors of the building, which even had a rifle range in the basement, were dedicated to specific sports. The big store's six floors of outdoors clothing even included a large women's selection, which had been added in 1913, more than forty years before L. L. Bean would deem it necessary to open a lady's department in his store. There was even a country setting on the roof that included a fly-fishing pool and a log cabin!

The Manhattan-based business had gotten its start on June 4, 1892, when David T. Abercrombie, a designer of tents, rucksacks, and other camping equipment, decided to open a store on Water Street—not far from Wall Street—in lower Manhattan. Abercrombie was joined by Ezra Fitch in 1900, the same year that the business relocated to 314 Broadway. In 1904 the name of the company was changed to Abercrombie & Fitch, but David Abercrombie would resign in 1907 following several heated arguments about which direction the business should take (foreshadowing—by more than eighty years—the rift between Leon Gorman and Bill End that would result in End's sudden departure from L.L. Bean, Inc.). Ezra Fitch wanted to expand the business, while Abercrombie, much like L. L. Bean in his later years, was happy just to let business take its course. Fitch wisely chose to keep his company's name as it was and, in 1909, he mailed to 50,000 of his best customers a catalog of an amazing 456 pages—a tome the scale of which L. L. Bean probably never even dreamed, even in his later years. In 1939 A&F would adopt the slogan, "The Greatest Sporting Goods Store in the World," but overeager expansion during the fifties and sixties caused the business to falter financially. In 1977 Abercrombie & Fitch was bought by Oshman's but continued to struggle until 1988, when it was purchased by The Limited, Inc. (owner of brands such as Victoria's Secret), and became what it is today.

It wasn't long before L. L. Bean's catalog business was so good he needed to work at it full time. "By the next January [1918] business had grown to such proportions that I sold the [Davis] retail store [to Guy] in order to devote my whole time to the mail order business I had built up." Newspaper ads from 1918 and 1919 show that the store in the Davis Block was still called L. L. & G. C. Bean, and Mrs. Mortimer's silent movie theater, the Nordica, showed a short animated ad for "L. L. & G. C. Bean, Walk-Over Shoes" before every feature. (The theater was named after Lillian Norton, an internationally known opera singer from Farmington, Maine, who performed as Madame Giglia Nordica, or "Lilly of the North," who died in 1914; her ghost is said to haunt Merrill Hall, the oldest building on the University of Maine's Farmington campus.) When Guy wasn't busy running and promoting his business, he found the time to coach Freeport High School's tennis team, on which L. L.'s son Carl played in 1917.

As the war across the Atlantic drew to a close in 1918, L. L. kept up his marketing efforts through the mail and in magazines that catered to outdoorsmen. He ran an ad in the November issue of *Forest and Stream* for "Hand Knit Hunting Stockings" which bragged that they were made of "heavy Maine wool with legs 4 in. longer than ordinary socks so as to come by the knee and not slip down." Surplus socks originally intended for shipment to France, perhaps?

As business picked up, L. L. knew that he had the manufacturing and shipping sides of things pretty well covered, but realized he was going to need a good assistant in the office. To fill this new position, L. L. needed to look no further than the home of his loyal employees Ted and Gertrude Goldrup. He hired their daughter Hazel, who took to her new job like a duck to water. Hazel's importance to the growing business cannot be overstated, and L. L. gives her much well-deserved praise in his slender autobiography, writing that she was his company's bookkeeper, cashier, auditor, and boss of the office, who took care of things whenever he went hunting. Hazel Goldrup Day worked for L. L. Bean for more than fifty years, retiring in 1971; she was replaced by the equally capable Ethel Williams.

Another employee with whom L. L. would soon trust the place while he was away attending to other matters was Raymond Stowell, "an American Legion man who saw service in France." While Hazel was taking care of things in the office, Raymond would be seeing to it that everything was running smoothly in "the selling and shipping department." Usually everything in the selling and shipping department did run smoothly, but not always. L. L. would later recall an incident that took place about this time that proved his system for filling orders still had some wrinkles that needed to be ironed out.

What happened was that a customer had sent in an order for a pair of boy's Hunting Shoes, but the order was lost. Several weeks later, the customer sent another letter inquiring about the status of his order. It was also misplaced. After a few more weeks, Bean's received a registered letter from the irate customer "in which he told us plenty," recalled L. L. The company replied, saying that they would send a pair of boy's Hunting Shoes right out if the man would tell them what size he needed. The man fired back, saying that he had ordered a pair of boy's Hunting Shoes size 5, but now the lad was all grown up and needed a pair of men's size 6.

Though L. L. Bean's young enterprise was going strong, the same could not be said for some of his fellow manufacturers around Freeport. In 1918 the now-defunct A. W. Shaw shoe factory went on the auction block to help satisfy its creditors, and was nearly sold to a Portland company for scrap. With an eye toward saving the building, L. L. Bean and business associate Roland Kimball raised $20,000 through public subscription to purchase the structure, and then got the town of Freeport to abate the taxes on the property. Freeport Realty then invested in two other shoe shops, which flourished and expanded greatly, providing steady jobs for hundreds of area workers, even through the darkest days of the Great Depression.

The big factory in town at the time was operated by Sears, whose shoes were shipped in boxes made at Ike Skillin's Freeport Box Shop. The word among the locals was that one of Ike's boxes would likely wear longer than the shoes that came in it.

In between his many business dealings, L. L. made sure he stayed in good practice for his hunting trips. Occasionally he'd get together with his brother Otho and some of their friends for target practice at the shooting gallery in the basement of the Davis Block, which Otho shared with W. W. Fish, the local undertaker. The targets, surrounded by sheets of heavy steel, were located at the street end of the basement, which meant that the practice sessions could be clearly heard up on the sidewalk. Unwitting passersby who inquired about the sound of gunfire coming from the vicinity of the undertaker's shop would be told that the mortician was "just making sure they're dead." Actually, Will Fish didn't take part in the shooting but he did step around the corner to watch the proceedings from time to time.

One shooter who soon joined the group in the basement was a young John Gould, who, upon the occasion of his twelfth birthday, had received from his father a "Winchester single-shot .22 rifle." Decades later, he'd recall his experiences in the *Christian Science Monitor* column he wrote to recognize the mail-order company's ninetieth anniversary:

> Hearing of my happiness, Lin Bean invited me to the shooting gallery in the basement of the Bean Bros. Clothing store to shoot targets, learn marksmanship and gun safety, and enjoy the fellowship of the Freeport Rifle Club. In the archives of L.L. Bean, Inc., you'll find a target I shot there at age twelve, and for open sights off-hand that isn't bad.[5]

By 1919 L. L. Bean's sales had jumped to $57,389.80, and he'd taken over the second floor of the Warren Block for his factory and added a storage room. His ad budget had grown to about $3,000 annually, and that year he mailed approximately 35,000 catalogs printed in two colors and containing sixty-three illustrations. Another part of his advertising money also went toward the year's four *Forest and Stream* ads for seasonal L. L. Bean footwear. Some of the funds were earmarked for additional postage, since he was able to again add to his mailing list when the Inland Fisheries and Game Department issued the state's first resident hunting licenses. For the sum of 25 cents, a Mainer could hunt, in season, until he or she "ceases to become a bona fide resident of Maine."

One of those sixty-three catalog illustrations was of the brand-new, all-leather Bean's Engineering Shoe. "[W]e are placing on the market," touted L. L.'s copy, "the best heavy leather shoe that can be made. . . . All sewed, not a tack or nail in them." It had been developed by L. L. "for Civil Engineers, Contractors, and general outdoor workers where the best as well as the most comfortable shoes are required." (In 2007 L.L. Bean, Inc., would reintroduce the Katahdin Iron Works Engineer Boots, as it now called them, with the catalog copy assuring the reader that they were "still made by the Chippewa Factory in El Paso, Texas," and featured "a classic Munson last and premium Goodyear® welted construction for exceptional support and durability." While the price of the 1919 version was unavailable, Bean's updated version was going for $149.)

Another fortunate occurrence for Bean's business in 1919 was the completion of the "black-surfaced road" between Portland and Brunswick. The new road passed through Freeport and brought out-of-town customers right to the factory, which, until then, had been patronized largely by local people. Now visitors from points south could drive right to the L. L. Bean shop to try on and purchase boots of all heights and sizes, with heels and without, to get the most comfortable fit.

Longtime Bean employee Ken Stilkey remembers that, in the beginning, customers could purchase Maine Hunting Shoes with or without heels. His recollection is verified by a page dedicated to Maine Hunting Shoes in the 1919 catalog, which proclaimed at the bottom, "All shoes come with or without heels."

Booming business at L. L. Bean's place pushed the hunting season payroll for both the day and night crews to better than $1,000 per month. (There was no Christmas rush at L. L. Bean for the company's first several decades; back then, Bean's customers were concerned primarily with hunting and fishing and tended to make their purchases according to the current sporting season.)

But while business may have been great during 1919, it wasn't all roses for L. L. Bean; that year he suffered the loss of his sister, Inez. She was L. L.'s only sister and, at four years older, was the sibling to whom he was closest in age. Inez Bean Cummings was fifty-one when she passed away. In his 1960 autobiography, L. L. shares the following information about his sister and her family: "Inez Alice [Bean], b. Aug 23, 1868, m. Eli Eugene Cummings, son of Moses of Bird Hill. She died March 1919. Children: 1. Florence Cummings, b. Nov. 6, 1891, m. Walter Bailey. 2. Frances Cummings, b. Oct. 15, 1893, m. Howard Laselle."

Chapter 4

*"If you drop in just to shake his hand, you get home
to find his catalog in your mail box"*

L ife in Maine was good as the new decade commenced. The state
was preparing to celebrate its 100th year of independence from
Massachusetts, and business was booming for Mr. Bean's manufacturing facility in Freeport. By now, L. L. was mailing out two editions of his basic catalog, one issue in the spring, the other in the
fall. Items in this year's "catalog"—which was really a circular consisting of little more than sheets of legal-size paper grommetted at
the top to heavy blue construction paper—included a pair of
Heavy Duty Lumbermen Boots (which commanded the princely
sum of $14.75) and Bean's own Summer Outing Shoe. Available in
either brown or white duck, a heavy, plain-weave cotton fabric, the
Outing Shoe looked very much like an old-time canvas high-top
sneaker.

With his circulars now reaching customers far beyond the state's
borders, Bean's business grew tremendously, eventually making
Freeport's small post office one of the busiest in Maine, to the point
where it had been upgraded first to a second-class post office, and
then to a first-class one. The local high school yearbook noted that,
in 1920, "Mr. Bean's mail at present makes up about 37 percent of
the entire business handled thru the Freeport Post Office."

At the same time as L. L. Bean was becoming established in
Freeport, Maine, another outdoorsman was cutting his retail teeth
on the other side of the country. Twenty-year-old Eddie Bauer,
who'd worked in a local sporting-goods store since the age of thirteen, opened his own shop in Seattle, Washington, where he strung
tennis rackets using a special vise of his own design. In 1936 Bauer
would create the product that, like Bean's boot, would become the

catalyst of a retail empire. After nearly dying from exposure in 1936, Bauer made himself a quilted down jacket, which he patented, along with a sleeping bag, the same year. "I knew the value of down," he would say later. "But not until I had hypothermia and nearly died on a steelhead fishing trip did I do anything about it." His down jacket would become immensely popular following World War II, during which he provided down-filled flight suits to American pilots. Eddie Bauer wouldn't issue his first catalog until 1947. (After having been fierce competitors in the mail-order game for nearly six decades, L.L. Bean, Inc., would come very close to purchasing Bauer's company in 2004.)

As word of L. L. Bean's business continued to grow, so did his income. Though not yet wealthy, even by the day's standards, ample funds were available for him to swing the purchase of a new automobile, a 1920 Reo. (A decade earlier, Henry Ford's new assembly line allowed him to produce a new $850 Model T every ninety minutes. By the early 1920s, American auto makers would be turning out about three million cars a year.) Since it was L. L.'s first car, he even saw fit to include a picture of it in his autobiography. The picture shows the whole of L. L.'s new car with him sitting proudly behind the wheel and a black bear that he'd trapped in Haynesville tied to the front fender. Sitting there, L. L. appears to be more proud of that car than he is of his trophy.

Just as his business was beginning to grow, so was L. L.'s reputation as a merchant and an outdoorsman—at least locally. In its 1920 edition, Freeport High School's yearbook, the *Clarion*, included a thumbnail sketch of the town's best-known entrepreneur, recounting how he'd come to invent his boot eight years earlier, and how his business had grown since. Even though it was just five paragraphs long, the piece in the *Clarion* is the earliest known published account of L. L. Bean's mail-order business. But in a couple of decades, his burgeoning company would become the subject of articles in nationally known magazines such as *Life* and the *Saturday Evening Post*.

Now successful, L. L. Bean was mindful of those less fortunate than himself. When Dr. Charles S. Curtis, L. L.'s friend and administrator of the Grenfell Mission in St. Anthony, Newfoundland, told him about the poor-quality sealskin boots with which the children had to make do during the region's long, cold winters, and asked for donations, L. L. didn't hesitate. He shipped to the mission cartons of various sizes of his famous rubber boot bottoms, to which the women there attached knee-high leggings they'd made from sealskin. Their warm, rugged footwear reportedly made the home's seventy boys and girls "the envy of the community."

Despite his catalogs, car, charity work, and *Clarion* write-up, what had to be the biggest event in L. L. Bean's life in 1920 was his purchase of the Warren Block and adjoining land, or, as he'd later recall, "I bought the building and added to it." What he added to it was a separate storehouse and more space to his freight shed. At the time, Bean's manufacturing operation took up half of the building and he rented the rest of it to the post office, the printer, a barbershop, and a restaurant. As stated in his autobiography, L. L. bought the Warren Block on January 26, 1920, for $7,983.64 by putting $100 down "to bind the bargain. The balance was paid as follows:

February 7	Check for	$ 200.00
March 1	Nine Liberty Bonds	2,424.98
March 1	Cash	5,184.71
March 1	My Note	50.00
March 5	Balance in Cash	23.95
	Total	$7,883.64

Ironically, the Warren Block, which was located on the very spot where L. L. Bean's giant flagship store is today, wouldn't have a proper customer showroom for at least another twenty years. "I suggested a retail store to him once before he was ready to think about it, " said Maine writer John Gould, "and I might as well have suggested he take ballet lessons." It isn't that customers weren't welcomed there (visitors would often be treated to a yarn or two from L. L. himself if he wasn't out hunting or fishing), it's just that it was easy to get lost in the place, which "was about as efficient," said Gould, "as a wet sponge at opening a beer bottle." On more than one occasion, a disoriented visitor, usually "from away," would surprise a bootmaker busy in his or her cubbyhole by asking for directions to the flannel shirts, or even how to get out of the place. According to Gould:

> The factory was an improbable makeshift in the original opry-house of the community. There was no effort in those days to carry on a retail store, so no arrangement was provided to greet the occasional tourist who wandered in. The theater's stage was storage for hides; fishing flies were tied in a one-time dressing room. If unaccustomed to the Bean layout, you could wander around for an hour trying to find a way out. You'd come upon ladies stitching canoe shoes, and upon men putting buckles on snowshoe harnesses. In what, I think, was the ticket booth.

For all the effort they'd expended to get to the factory—and then find their way out—these intrepid customers weren't even given a discount on their purchases; according to Gould, L. L. "said it cost as much to handle a customer in person as it did by mail." But at least they could tell their friends that they'd been to L. L. Bean's in Freeport, Maine. (Before long, it would become even easier to get lost there as the factory expanded to rambling proportions via Maine's typical "add-on" type of architecture, which L. L. Bean would elevate almost to an art form.)

In his introduction to L. L.'s 1960 autobiography, Gould recalls a later visit to Bean's factory in great detail:

> The building hadn't been built for him, and he had grown into it deviously. The outside stairway went up three floors from the sidewalk, and having mounted it you would arrive all a-pant in a little room that smelled of oil-tanned leather and rubber cement, and you had to look around to see where to go. If you persisted, you'd startle various employees hidden away in random cubicles pursuing some manufacturing task like a dedicated neophyte. Whoever it was, he'd look up surprised that

you found him, as if only the initiated could gain admittance. He would gladly direct you to Mr. Bean's office, usually through the mailing room, stitching department, and fly-tying department. You would perhaps arrive to hear a spirited discussion going on between Mr. Bean and assorted Freeporters, as to the relative merits of the .30-.30 and the .32 special.

One of the first big events of the 1920s—back in a time when towns went all out to mark the observance of such occasions—was Freeport's celebration of Maine's centennial anniversary. The State of Maine had been admitted to the Union on March 15, 1820, when, as part of the Missouri Compromise, it was separated from Massachusetts to form the twenty-third state.

Held as an Old Home Week from June 21 through 26, Freeport's observance of the state's hundredth birthday proved to be an ambitious undertaking. B. Frank Dennison was the celebration's honorary chairman, while prominent Freeport citizen Edmund B. Mallet worked as its active chairman. (This is the same E. B. Mallet whose businesses had revived the town's lagging economy more than three decades earlier.) Publicity for the event was handled by L. L.'s youngest brother, Guy, who still ran the Walk-Over shoe store in the Oxnard Block just across the street from L. L.'s manufacturing facility. For the big occasion, the town was decked out in red-white-and-blue bunting, "and every effort was made to welcome visitors and make them feel at home."

On Monday, June 21, visitors were formally received and entertained by pictures and dancing at the Nordica Theater. Tuesday there was a ball game with open house at the Nordica. On Wednesday the stores closed and a merchants' picnic was held in Mallet's Grove, where a free clambake and coffee were provided. Field sports followed and a ball game. Thursday the old time players gave an exhibition of playing and on Friday High School girls played a ball game with the boys, and in the evening Donald B. MacMillan, the Arctic explorer, gave a lecture in the Baptist Church.[1]

While the weather had been less than ideal earlier in the week, it had turned quite nice for the celebration's grand finale on Saturday. The day's festivities commenced in the morning with a parade, which "was a mile long," then a picnic dinner at Mallet's Grove, followed by a baseball game. At 4:30, Governor Carl Milliken addressed the crowd in the town square from a bandstand constructed at the front of the Oxnard Block. During the afternoon and evening, all were entertained by the "Yarmouth Band of twenty-five pieces," and at dusk the town square was closed to traffic, with all vehicles being detoured onto Mill, Middle, and School Streets. Fireworks and a big street dance were part of the "carnival which lasted until those taking part felt they had sufficiently celebrated the occasion."

One of Saturday's best-remembered events took place next door to the Oxnard Block at L. L. Bean's Warren Block. Well, actually it took place *on* the Warren Block, to the top of which the crowd's attention was directed by none other than L. L. Bean himself, whose normal "foghorn-level" voice was amplified even more with the help of a megaphone for the occasion. Bean informed the rapt crowd that a certain Professor Landsdown "would defy the force of gravity and would leap from the roof of the Warren Block to the street, three stories below, without the aid of any safety device." Here, John Gould picks up the story:

> Due time was allowed for effect, and then Ike Skillin pushed Prof. O. C. Howe E. Landsdown, who was a stuffed dummy, off the roof and he came end over end towards the sidewalk. But Ike miscalculated, and the dummy hit a utility wire on the way down and got hung up in great embarrassment to the perpetrators. The remains of Prof. Landsdown were afterwards removed by the firemen.

THOUGH IT HAD PROVEN to be very successful for nearly a decade, L. L. Bean continued refining his boot, and in 1921 took out two United States patents and one Canadian patent "relating to the back seam and the reinforcement in the tongue." L. L. submitted his ideas to the Canadian Patent Office in Ottawa in early 1921, and to the U.S. Patent Office in Washington at about the same time. (Though L. L. reports the date of the patents as 1918 in his auto-biography, the drawings submitted to the patent office bear the date 1921 and prove him wrong on this one.) He also sought to patent "a Felt Sole and Heel construction with short metal calks that will prevent slipping" for use on the bottoms of waders used by fishermen.

An ad in the January 1921 issue of *Forest and Stream* magazine puts the price of one version of Bean's Maine Hunting Shoe at $3.60. By September, his catalog would list the price of a 5-inch men's boot (measured from the floor to the top of the leather) at $3.75.

By now, L. L. Bean had learned that there was good money to be made by simply offering different versions of his famous boot—and by charging extra for options. A pair of Bean's Maine Cruising Shoes, heavy-duty versions of the Hunting Shoe, cost a lot more ($9.25 for the 14-inch model) but were probably worth every penny since they were guaranteed "to outwear three pairs of ordinary leather top rubbers." At the time, heels, black vamps with white soles, and shipping west of the Mississippi would each have set the customer back an additional 25 cents. Adding "snow-shoe loops" (which prevented the straps of your snowshoe harnesses from sliding off your heels) to a pair of Maine Hunting Shoes cost an extra dime.

Customers could also order the "Maine Arched Inner-Sole" separately for their new footwear. Bean also offered, for $6.85, a 14-inch Maine Trapping Shoe, which looked very much like the Hunting and Cruising Shoes but was entirely "made of high grade gum rubber." (You can usually determine the height of your Bean Boots without using a ruler by simply counting the pairs of eyelets and adding two—for example, the author's 10-inch Maine Hunting Shoes from the early 1990s have eight sets of eyelets.)

One person who felt that Mr. Bean's footwear was more than up to any task that could be put in front of it was Donald B. MacMillan (1874–1970). An alumnus of Bowdoin College in nearby

Brunswick, Captain MacMillan (who'd later attain the rank of admiral), had first traveled to the Arctic with the 1908–09 North Polar Expedition led by American explorer Robert E. Peary, and would return to the polar regions twenty-seven times over the next forty-five years. In 1925 he would direct a polar expedition to Greenland with the aid of U.S. Navy commander Richard E. Byrd. For his immediate need in 1921, MacMillan outfitted his arctic expedition team with Maine Hunting Shoes, for which he'd have high praise when ordering Bean's improved boot for his next expedition two years later: "My men are very enthusiastic over their experience with your foot equipment on our last Arctic Expedition," he'd write, "finding it extremely practical, especially for fall and spring work."

By 1922 L. L. Bean's fame and fortune had grown to the point where they had reached major milestones. First the fortune: it was in the early 1920s that the annual sales receipts of L. L. Bean, Manufacturer, achieved the $100,000 mark—a substantial amount at the time, even for a good-size business. Just a decade old, L. L.'s business was now a going concern, with the bulk of the company's out-of-state orders coming from "sports" in New York, Massachusetts, Pennsylvania, and Ohio—in that order. L. L. was also said to have personally seen to the needs of "the chief game warden of the United States, George A. Lawyer."

There were also "orders on file from Corea [sic], China, Hawaii, Belgium, England, Canada, and Alaska." (In the above list of far-flung locations, Bean obviously means the nation of Korea, not the coastal Maine town of Corea, which lies roughly twelve miles due east of Bar Harbor.) Because of his new notoriety, L. L. Bean would often receive prompt delivery of letters, requesting something or other from his inventory, which arrived at the post office downstairs in envelopes addressed simply to "Bean, Maine," or even to "Sporting goods house in a small town in Maine."

But don't for a minute think that the early success enjoyed by L. L. Bean's new company was a happy accident. He worked hard at it, coming up with some very clever ways of making darned good and sure that he got the most out of every one of his marketing dollars. For example, the small display ads he placed in *Forest and Stream* magazine weren't just pitching items such as Maine Hunting Shoes, Guide Shirts, and Winter Sports caps; they also contained an ingenious tracking system L. L. had devised so he could accurately figure how many sales each ad generated. An ad in the magazine's October 1922 issue listed his address as 101 Main Street, while the ad in the July 1923 issue said he was located at number 103. (For the record, when L.L. Bean, Inc., officially moved its offices down Route 1 to Casco Street in March 1984, the "Change of Registered Office" form the company filed with the State of Maine listed the address of the retail store as 95 Main Street.)

And of course L. L. continued to lavish much attention on his beloved catalog, the mailing list for which he maintained with a passion that bordered on obsession. His employees worked under the standing order to get the names of whoever happened to venture into Mr. Bean's mazelike domain. "If you drop in just to shake his hand," wrote John Gould years ago, "you get home to find his catalog in your mail box."

And John Gould should know about Mr. Bean's catalog; he often worked after school with the man who printed it. In a January 2004 *Christian Science Monitor* article, published four months after his death, Gould recalled the process involved in printing the L. L. Bean catalog, including an elusive insect that was said to be responsible for typos and various other printing mistakes:

It was in 1922 that I first saw a type louse. Mr. Putney was foreman at the Freeport Press, and he printed the first catalogs for L. L. Bean. He did this on a Golding letterpress. When Mr. Bean wanted color, I was hired to come in after school at 10 cents an hour to slip-sheet the color inserts. As Mr. Bean needed only 2,000 copies, I was earning 20 cents an afternoon.

When Mr. Putney put the picture of the canoe shoe on the wrong page and had to reprint that signature, he said, "It's them exasperatin' type lice again, I'll have to spray." (It was no small matter; the signature was eight pages.) So then, wishing to inform me on all matters concerning graphic arts, he took the trouble to show me a type louse.

The fall issue of the catalog carried a date of September 1, 1922, and contained numerous articles of clothing such as a Guide Shirt ($4.85), the Maine Outing Shirt ($5.50), and the Maine Hunting Shirt ($8.25). On the previous page could be found the "1922 Maine Hunting Coat." This coat, which had a total of nine pockets, was "designed, made, and sold," bragged the accompanying copy, "by one who has hunted Maine deer for the past twenty-four years." Modeled in the catalog by L. L. Bean himself, the coat retailed for $15.00 (or $23.00 with a pair of matching plaid pants). All of the above garments were made of wool.

Nearly two pages of the catalog were dedicated to Bean's bread-and-butter item, his famous boot. But just because it was already a big success didn't mean that L. L. was finished tweaking it. He wasted no time in putting to use his recently approved patent for a new backstay, "which," read the catalog copy, "we shall use on all our 1922 Hunting Shoes. . . . The split backstay is a positive protection against heel cord chafing . . . and makes the shoe very much stronger at this particular point. To the experienced hunter I need not say more." There was even a photo of the new backstay with a caption proclaiming that it had been "Pat'd Jan. 11, 1921."

Other improvements to Bean's boot included his making it available in five widths (C, D, E, F, FF) and adult sizes from 2 to 12 ("Whole Sizes Only"). The boot was now available in seven heights (6 1/2 inches and 8 through 18 inches in 2-inch increments), with prices running from $4.50 to $13.75. The shorter boots could also be had in "Boys' sizes 2 to 4" and "Misses' and Youths' sizes 8 to 1." Included with each pair of boots was a free twenty-cent "repair outfit" consisting of a "can of Water-proof Dressing and Rubber Repair Patches, with cement for applying same." A guarantee tag attached to every pair assured the purchaser that his or her new footwear would stand the test of time:

We guarantee this pair of shoes to give perfect satisfaction in every way. If the rubber breaks or the tops grow hard, return them, together with this guarantee tag, and we will replace them free of charge.
[signed]
L. L. BEAN. Freeport, Maine.

As L. L.'s fortunes were increasing so was his fame. Around this time, several of the products he offered were featured in a painting that would become the cover of the January 1922 issue of *National Sportsman*. The 1921 oil painting entitled *The Moose Hunter*, by William Harnden Foster (1886–1941), who also happened to be the magazine's editor, depicts a hunter on a snowy trail about to take aim at the snorting bull moose glaring back at him. Everything worn by the hunter—his cap, coat, knapsack, mess kit, pants, boots, and snowshoes—was made either by or for L. L. Bean (but his rawhide-laced wooden snowshoes wouldn't appear in L. L. Bean's catalog for another three years). Only a decade earlier, L. L. Bean had placed some of the first ads for his now-famous footwear in *National Sportsman*, paying $18.75 for a one-inch ad that had run in three issues.

William Harnden Foster lived in Concord, Massachusetts, but summered by the ocean in South Freeport, where he was a member of the local artists' colony. Besides being the editor of a successful magazine and an accomplished outdoors artist, Foster was also an avid bird hunter. Actually, to say that he was an avid bird hunter is an understatement. He was obsessed. So obsessed, in fact, that, when he wasn't able to go out in the Maine woods and scare up the partridges (ruffed grouse) he loved so much to hunt, he'd hone his skills with a few rounds of skeet shooting, a sport he invented while in Maine.

While a partridge sitting in the middle of a dirt road is an easy target for almost anybody with a shotgun, shooting one in flight is an entirely different matter. Once startled from their concealment on the ground, partridges can just as quickly disappear into the tangle of branches and brush that are the Maine woods. For this reason, skeet shooting involves firing birdshot at clay birds launched by two separate machines from eight different positions around the skeet field—mimicking the trajectory of partridge flushed suddenly from the underbrush. W. H. Foster built the world's first skeet field in Freeport, Maine.

By early 1923, word of L. L. Bean's growing business began to spread beyond Freeport when a Lewiston newspaper carried an article about it—one of the first publications outside of town to do so. The piece, which appeared in the January 12 edition of the *Lewiston Evening Journal*, ran under the headline: "'Hobby' Which Started a Maine Man in Business." In the largely accurate piece, the writer (who wasn't given a byline) came up with a thumbnail sketch of L. L.'s childhood, how he developed the Maine Hunting Shoe, and how his business had grown since then.

One thing the unknown reporter failed to do, it seems, was interview L. L. Bean himself, since the piece doesn't contain a single quote from the well-known outdoorsman turned merchant. It ends with praise for Bean and a plug for Maine and the many opportunities it holds for its youth:

> Freeport is proud of Mr. Bean and his family and his business. He is a fine type of the red-blooded, kindly, out-of-door men that Maine breeds. His success should be an encouragement to the boys of Maine to stay right at home and develop the resources and industries of Maine. There are great possibilities right at our doors—all that is needed is the vision to see the opportunity and the grit to work that vision into a reality.

The year that was turning out to be a good one for L. L. Bean would be the last one for Freeport's first entrepreneur, E. B. Mallet, who died on September 17 at the age of seventy. Born in 1853 aboard the ship *Devonshire* in the English Channel, Edmund B. Mallet, Jr., was the son of a sea captain from Warren, Maine, and the former Sarah E. Thornton of Pawtucket, Rhode Island. Four decades earlier, Mallet had taken a large inheritance from his uncle and invested it in Freeport, turning the struggling town into a busy center of industry. He died from an "infection of the right hand and forearm" three days after badly burning his finger. Mallet, whose occupation was listed as "gentleman farmer" on his death certificate, is buried in Freeport's Woodlawn Cemetery.

During the winter of 1923, L. L. took his brothers Guy and Otho to his camp, the "Dew Drop Inn," where they combined their vacation with some product testing. They had taken along several pairs of wooden snowshoes to try out over the rugged terrain of eastern New Hampshire's Wild River Township, where L. L. had hunted as a boy with his cousin Louvie Swett. When they'd finished their informal test, the trio concluded that the Maine style of snowshoe was the one best suited to be included in Bean's upcoming catalogs. The Maine snowshoe, which is a sort of bear paw with a tail, is widest at the ball of the foot, tapers to the nose and back, and has a tail for tracking. While they were at the camp, the brothers also wanted to find out how deer lived during the winter. They found that the deer followed the woodcutters and fed off the tops of the fallen trees.

In his later years, L. L. Bean would say that of the nine camps he'd had during his life, the Dew Drop Inn on New Hampshire's Wild River was his favorite. In his autobiography, he recalled that he had tried to purchase the camp from the lumber company in 1901—they wouldn't sell it to him, but did allow him to fix it up and keep using it. In 1925 the federal government, which had owned the land for more than a decade, ordered him to move the camp—even though he probably still didn't own the place—or they would, and that was the end of that.

The lumber company to which he was referring was the Hastings Lumber Co., which, you'll recall, had sold its Wild River parcel to the government in 1914 when the feds were acquiring land for the White Mountain National Forest.

Though L. L. and his brothers were limited to testing snowshoes in New Hampshire, his rugged boots would again be going to the Arctic, where they'd be put through what would have to be the ultimate torture test for outdoor footwear. During the latter

part of June, L. L. Bean had received from Admiral MacMillan a letter ordering "7 pair Maine Hunting Shoes with Non-Slip sole for
myself and crew." MacMillan praised the Bean boots he'd taken on
his last expedition and said that he expected the new model to perform even better:

> I believe that the new crepe sole Hunting Shoes which we are
> ordering this year will be even more popular with my men, if
> such can be possible.
>
> The rocky frozen ground of Ellesmere Land, where we are
> planning to winter within twelve degrees of the Pole, is the
> very hardest kind of a test on the wearing qualities of foot gear.
> You may look for an interesting report upon my return home in
> the fall of 1924.

If the soles of any of the boots he'd ordered had worn out
through normal wear and tear (and he could have somehow gotten
them back to Freeport), the admiral could have had new bottoms
attached to them for a nominal fee. "Why throw out a perfectly
good—and broken-in—pair of leather uppers," Bean figured,
"when you can have new bottoms put on for about one third the
cost of a new pair of boots?" His ad in the July issue of *Forest and
Stream* magazine, which carried the headline "AS COMFORTABLE AS
AN OLD SHOE," reminded its readers that

> Old shoes are old friends—DON'T throw them away. Send old
> leather top rubbers (any make) and—we will attach our 1923
> HUNTING RUBBERS, repair and waterproof tops—new laces and
> return post-paid for only $3.40 (with heels $3.65). Same guaran-
> tee as new shoes. Do this NOW before you forget.

His reasoning would prove to be right on target; in just a
few years, the workers at L. L. Bean, Mfr., would be kept busy
updating dozens of pairs of Maine Hunting Shoes every day. (Now,
well into the twenty-first century, L.L. Bean, Inc., continues to offer
this service.)

In 1924 L. L. Bean introduced the first modern version of his catalog. It still featured the familiar Cheltenham font but was now bound in the small, nearly square format that the company continues to use. Another holdover is the catalog's organization, or lack thereof. The items inside are currently grouped by categories such as Footwear, Outerwear, Women's Apparel, Home, Travel Gear, Outdoor Gifts, etc. And there's no index, either—necessitating the catalog's recipients to leaf through the entire catalog in order to find what they want. The omission of the index was yet another shrewd idea L. L. had come up with to help improve the bottom line, and his successors have continued to use it.

While the offerings in recent catalogs had become increasingly diversified—Bean already offered accessories such as the all-wool Maine Outing Shirt ($5.50) and Bean's Winter Sports Cap ($1.75)—it would be a coat introduced for his bird-hunting customers that would prove to be L. L. Bean's breakout item of 1924. Bean's Field Coat was made from heavy cotton canvas and was "built to withstand the briars and branches of the thick Maine woods." Meant to be worn over a midweight sweater, this durable, practical garment would go on to become a classic, still commanding a full page in the company's Christmas catalog more than eighty years later.

By now L. L. Bean's manufacturing company employed twenty-five full-time workers, each of whom was paid about $25 a week, which made the business's monthly payroll nearly three times the $1,000 it had been just five years earlier. Of course the increase in Bean's sales had more than kept pace with his increased payroll; in only two or three years the company's annual sales had jumped from $100,000 to around $135,000.

And there was another cause for celebration in Freeport—this was also the year that L. L.'s oldest son, Carl, twenty-three, got married to eighteen-year-old Hazel Haskel in Augusta.

For 1925 L. L. Bean continued to expand his product line, which now included items such as Bean's Sport Oxfords and a Lambskin Boot, both of which were featured that year in small ads placed in *Forest and Stream*. Also featured in the recently revamped catalog, the first full-size edition of which was reportedly mailed to customers in 1925, were two distinctly different types of "shoes." The fall version of L. L. Bean's 1925 catalog featured on its cover William H. Foster's 1921 wintertime painting, *The Moose Hunter*, which was appropriate because it was one of Bean's first circulars to include snowshoes among its offerings.

These snowshoes were constructed of ash and rawhide, and were probably made by Tubbs in Norway, Maine, before the company moved to Vermont in late 1932, leaving as its successor the recently established Snocraft Company. (Norway is right next to South Paris, where L. L. Bean had spent much of his childhood following the deaths of his parents.)

While they were of very high quality, L. L.'s accompanying copy made the snowshoes sound almost mythical, telling his readers that "we now offer the best that can be made." His description then went on to tell of "a secret process" and "perfect balance":

> The frames are especially selected; State of Maine, second growth white ash butts, seasoned so they will not warp.
>
> The filling is the very best cowhide, cured by a secret process that positively prevents sagging. The workmanship in every detail is so well done that it gives the shoe a perfect balance.
>
> Our liberal guarantee applies the same as to our other goods.

The men's model of the Maine Snowshoe was 48 inches long, available in widths of 12, 13, or 14 inches, depending on the weight of the user, and cost $9.75 east of the Mississippi. There were also two narrower, longer ladies' sizes for $9.50. For an additional 60 cents each, the customer could order decorative wool tassels or have their initials added to the snowshoe's toe bar. (Could this have been the first "monogramming" offered by L. L. Bean?)

In 1926 John Gould, along with twenty-five others, graduated from Freeport High School, a couple of years after Barbara Bean, L. L.'s youngest child. Sixty-four years later, he'd write a column for the *Christian Science Monitor* about a recent class reunion, wherein he recalled, among other things, the town of Freeport before L. L. Bean's company got big. Really big. Some of his 1990 recollections of 1926 are:

Now and then, we members of that class are asked if we knew L. L. Bean, and we say no—that L. L. Bean knew us. His daughter, Barbara, was in high school with us, but not in our class.

It is interesting that only one of our class ever worked for L. L. Bean and stayed in Freeport.

Even after 1926, Freeport "corner," the business section, still had hitching posts.

Today Freeport has everything else, but in 1926 it still had trolley cars. A cross-country electric railway between Yarmouth and Brunswick had a car each way every hour—they passed in Freeport square, the "corner."[2]

It was about this time, or perhaps a few years earlier, that L. L. Bean had given young John Gould a nearly new reflector oven, the type used for baking by a campfire. "Mr. Bean had used it a couple of times," said Gould, "and gave it to us." (L. L. liked to use the reflector oven by his campfire so much that he'd dedicate Chapter 32—the whole page—to "How To Use [a] Reflector Baker" in his forthcoming outdoor skills book.) Johnny Gould and his pal Eddie Skillin took it with them whenever they went on one of their days-long "exploration expeditions" through the Maine woods. "Unless we camped near a home," recalled Gould, "we didn't need to ask permission. This was long enough ago so possessiveness hadn't really hatched. Anybody who said no to two polite youngsters was an old grouch, and we passed on the other side."

At this point L. L. Bean could well afford to give a used reflector oven to a teenage boy; the fall edition of his recently revamped catalog was featured in *Forest and Stream*'s September review of new items, and received high praise from the magazine's editors:

A novel and attractive catalogue has just been issued by L. L. Bean of Freeport, Maine. In it are listed everything the hunter, trapper, and guide might need in the line of footwear and clothing. Mr. Bean has long been known as a manufacturer of outdoor apparel and has established an enviable reputation by his policy of supplying articles that are correct for the purpose recommended.

A copy of this interesting catalogue may be obtained free by writing L. L. Bean, Freeport, Maine.

A couple of items worthy of note in Mr. Bean's interesting catalog were a canoe and a certain kind of blanket he offered. The canoe was called "The Maine," a 16½-foot outboard motor canoe upon which L. L. lavished even more praise than he'd heaped upon his nearly perfect snowshoes. For $129, the customer could own "the most remarkable boat of its class ever designed," boasted the copy. "A marvel for beauty, speed, and comfort." The 125-pound canoe certainly was sleek, and its sponsons, the craft's buoyant appendages at its gunwales (which, Bean pointed out, "add to its appearance and make it next to impossible to capsize"), were painted green to contrast with its red body and small gray bow deck.

The inside of the craft, from the gunwales down, featured natural wood ribs, a floor rack, and a toolbox under the stern seat, all sealed with varnish. For a small additional fee, the purchaser could have "The Maine" or any other name lettered onto one or both sides of the bow inside the green stripe. "In a word it is a de luxe, comfortable craft," Bean summed up, "that is the equivalent of a motor boat at a fraction of its cost."

Since it was a wood and canvas canoe, similar in construction to a traditional Maine Guide canoe (probably built with white cedar ribs, red cedar planking, and heavy-duty No. 6 or No. 8 canvas), but with a transom added to its truncated stern, the craft may have been made for Bean by the Old Town Canoe Company in Old Town, Maine (or possibly by the nearby E. M. White Canoe Company). Interestingly, beginning in 1920, the Old Town Canoe Company featured in its catalog cross sections of the eight models of canoes it offered, one of which was a "16 ft. 'Square Stern Sponson' Model." (Old Town is about 10 miles north of Bangor, where a young L. L. Bean had worked briefly as a butter maker.)

The blanket L. L. offered was the Hudson Bay Point Blanket, which was a trendsetter of sorts in his catalog. The story goes that L. L. had tried to get the Hudson Bay Company to make a version of its comfortable, long-wearing wool blanket for him so he could sell it under his own name. Hudson Bay Company refused. Since the blankets, which have been around since 1779, were of such high quality and fit his product mix so well, L. L. relented and included them in his catalog under their own name.

Hudson Bay Point Blankets are still available in a variety of color and stripe combinations, but what makes them unique are the "points" found on the edge of each blanket. These short indigo lines represent the original price, in beaver pelts, for each size blanket; a four-point blanket fits a double or twin bed, while an eight-point blanket fits a king-size bed. This was probably the first time that a product had been afforded such status in Mr. Bean's catalog. Previously, the names of nearly everything sold by the merchant had started with either "Bean's" or "Maine." L.L. Bean, Incorporated, continues to carry many items made for it by other companies, while many other items sold there now carry their own brand names.

L. L. Bean probably wasn't too concerned about whose name was on the blankets he sold; he had a business to run—and business was good. Here's a brief summary, in L. L.'s own unique, to-the-point style, on how his year had gone:

Eighty-five thousand [catalogs] were printed—the campaign covering the last four months of 1926. Postage used, $950; total cost of campaign including catalogs, magazine advertising, and postage, $9,734.29; inquiries received, 11,102; sales resulting, $172,540.17. You will note from my catalog that my goods are marketed direct-by-mail to the consumer and that the total cost of the campaign figures about 5$1/2$ percent of cash sales. We have a record of each individual sale, the day it was received, and whether customer sent check, money order, or had the goods mailed C.O.D.[3]

Nearly $5,000 of Bean's advertising budget had gone into magazine ads, primarily in publications targeted toward the outdoorsman, such as *Forest and Stream* and *Outdoor Life*.

Successful though it was, Mr. Bean's catalog was still a pretty slender one; all the goods contained in his spring 1926 offering could be listed on just twenty-one lines of its order form:

Maine Hunting Shoes
Maine Hiking Shoes
Maine Guide Shoes
Pr. Maine Camp Slippers
Pr. Maine Fishing Shoes
Pr. Maine Trouting Boots
Pr. Maine Engineering Shoes
Pr. Indian Moccasins
Pr. Summer Outing Shoes
Fishing Coat
Pr. Lastic Knickers
Maine Hunting Blouse
Outing Shirt
Bean's Leather Blouse
Hudson Bay Blanket
Maine Outboard Motor Canoe
Bean's Sweat Shirt
Duffle Bag
Pr. Gloves
Rain Shirt
Rain Pants

Financially secure, L. L. Bean took what very well may have been his first out-of-state hunting trip. He even left the country! Bean, along with his brothers Ervin and Guy and their cousin Louvie Swett, traveled all the way to Quebec's Gaspé Peninsula, just to the north of Maine and its eastern neighbor, New Brunswick, to hunt caribou. The trip was so memorable to the merchant that there are two photographs of the hunters and their prey included in

L. L.'s autobiography. The caption of the first one reads, "L. P. Swett of Bangor, Maine, and myself, with two Caribou shot the winter of 1926 at Gaspé Peninsula." The second reads, "My first and only Caribou, shot on the spot where the picture was taken. Gaspé Peninsula, Canada, 1926."

This hunting trip—for which each man had forked over $25 for a nonresident hunting license—was a far cry from the first one he and Louvie had gone on in 1885, when they'd traveled by train from South Paris to Gilead and then hiked into New Hampshire's Wild River area in search of whitetail deer. A November article in the *Bangor Daily News* focused on L. P. Swett, who was now a successful auto dealer in the area, and chronicled the quartet's adventures:

> Mr. Swett made this fascinating trip in company with E. A. Bean of Belgrade, G. C. Bean and L. L. Bean of Freeport, manufacturers of the Maine hunting shoe, the party journeying by way of St. John and Moncton, N.B., and Campbellton, crossed the Bay of Chaleur and proceeded 200 miles to Gaspé, Quebec, one of the least known parts of Canada, then 32 miles up York River to Dartmouth Lake, with its virgin forests, a land of real delight to sportsmen who care to undertake a hard journey.
>
> The party enjoyed two weeks of sport there, each man securing a caribou. This is considered to be the last stand of the caribou in the east, their nature not permitting them to remain where there is anyone about to disturb them . . . caribou having migrated from Maine many years ago.

In March of 1927, L. L. Bean's close attention to his prized catalog earned him an award from *Postage* magazine. The publication, which billed itself as "A Monthly Magazine for Users and Producers of Direct-Mail, Printing & Letters," awarded Bean its prize for "Best Booklet" in the competition's largest class, which was for booklets weighing less than two ounces and mailable for one cent. John Howie Wright, the magazine's editor and publisher, appeared to be a man of even fewer words than L. L. Bean (if that's possible);

the entire body of his letter congratulating the merchant on his award consisted of two one-sentence paragraphs:

> It gives me great pleasure to send you the enclosed $25.00 in gold for the Best Booklet.
> Full details about all the prize-winners appear in our March 1927 number.

L. L. was so proud of the award that he gave an entire page of his autobiography to a copy of the actual letter. No doubt Bean agreed wholeheartedly with Wright's philosophy stated in the magazine's tag line: "Anything that can be sold, can be sold by mail." (Delivery of items from the catalog would be free until 1991, when rising costs would prompt L.L. Bean, Inc., to start charging its customers for shipping.)

Since L. L. was justifiably proud of his award-winning catalog, it's not surprising that 1927 was also the year he started keeping an archive of his catalogs, probably beginning with that year's spring edition. In keeping with the changing times, L. L. Bean's early 1927 "supplement," as he then called the semiannual versions of his catalog, featured on its cover a picture of a majestic, rocky mountain in the background and a camping area in the foreground upon which dozens of sports had descended in their automobiles. It was an appropriate cover for the time because more and more people were coming to depend on the increasingly reliable automobile as a way to fulfill their wants as well as their needs.

Coincidentally, it was around this time that the last copy of Mr. Bean's catalog was printed by the Freeport Press. Beginning in 1928, the catalog would be printed by the Dingley Press, a printer of marine hardware catalogs, which had purchased the Freeport Press and would continue to operate downstairs from Bean's manufacturing facility in the Warren Block for many years. (Dingley Press, now located in Lisbon, Maine, would continue as the primary printer of L. L. Bean's catalogs until late 1980 when the retailer would switch the bulk of its business to printing giant R. R. Donnelley & Sons.)

The fishing and camping items that had started appearing in the catalog a few years earlier were now becoming firmly established in the product mix, and of course, L. L. Bean was again the only expert to whom his customers needed to turn. For example: "It is no longer necessary for you to experiment with dozens of flies to determine the few that will catch fish," his copy assured his readers. "We have done the experimenting for you."

The fly-tying room at L. L. Bean, Manufacturer, was yet another one of those happy accidents that happen when success begets success. At first, Bean needed a few flies tied just to fill the orders for those that were out of stock. Then the darned thing just kind of took on a life of its own. Before long, there would be color inserts in the catalog to show the flies in all their glory. Then there was an actual fly-tying department, which would eventually be headed up by his good friend and frequent hunting partner George Soule, and would eventually employ as many as "sixteen girls," the first one coming on board in 1936. (L.L. Bean's 2007 Fishing Catalog would offer a selection of over 200 individual fresh- and saltwater flies—plus a selection of 84 just for eastern trout alone.)

But just as Bean's Maine Hunting Shoe was still his primary product, hunting would remain the primary focus of his business for the foreseeable future; the four ads L. L. Bean ran in *Forest and Stream* in 1927 all appeared in the magazine's September and October issues, just in time for sportsmen to have their orders filled before the start of hunting season.

In addition to Bean's footwear, another type of "shoes" offered by mail in 1927 were Bean's Official Horseshoes, which "weigh 2 1/2 lbs. per pair, and come in two colors, red and black, marked 1 and 2." For only $3.25 for "One Set of Four Standard (size M) Pitching Shoes" and rules, plus $1.65 for a pair of 30-inch-long stakes, L. L. Bean assured his customers of a total-body workout: "Every muscle of the body," he wrote, "is brought into play in throwing shoes and walking from one stake to the other." In order to grease the skids just a bit, L. L. reminded his catalog's readers of the genuine article's scarcity—"since official shoes [are] so hard to get we could not resist listing them," he wrote, implying that his was one of the few companies to have them. "Put a pair of stakes out near your camp or cottage," advised Bean's catalog copy, "and note how quickly your place becomes popular."

A true believer in the benefits of pitching horseshoes, L. L. noted in his autobiography, "I always kept horseshoes at my hunting and fishing camps." A frequent competitor with his younger brother was Otho Bean, who soon excelled at the game, often prevailing in tournaments that included the best players in the area. As writer John Gould noted, Otho (whom Gould always called "Ortho") had more ways than just competing against his brother to keep his game sharp:

> Freeport always had a merchants' picnic on the Fourth of July. The storekeepers said thanks to the townspeople for a year's trade and everybody had clams and lobsters. The horseshoe-pitching contest was always won by Ortho Bean, L. L.'s brother, who had a court in his cellar and could pitch all winter.

Although it's a bit repetitive, Gould gives us another look at the town's horseshoe pitching contest in one of his many books about Maine (in the book's foreword, he says that "personalities and places have been disguised, but sometimes not too well," and it's clear that it's Otho he's writing about):

> The horseshoe-pitching contest was usually won by Herman Potter, who pitched horseshoes all summer in his back yard, and then moved down cellar and pitched all winter. He could win a game with seven ringers, and usually did. This made it far more significant, in our town, to win second, and it was my fame one year to win it. I had good luck, and a little twist that Herman showed me. The prizes for all the contests were donated by the merchants.[4]

Perhaps the prize "Herman" won came from his brother's store.

WITH L. L.'S EXPANDING COMPANY now offering a line of fare that varied widely from his original footwear, he had to assure his customers that he'd stand behind every single item, be it a cap or a boat. The solution was simple: L. L. Bean extended the 100 percent ironclad guarantee he offered on his Hunting Shoes to everything he sold. A piece in the 2002 edition of *L.L. Bean, Inc., Outdoor Sporting Specialties: A Company Scrapbook* notes that the cornerstone of Bean's is "a liberal return/repair/reuse policy that has been in effect since 1927." However, in the not-too-distant future, a certain item would put L. L.'s liberal return policy to the test:

> Back in the early days of the L.L. Bean mail-order business, when a lah-di-dah element first began to appear north of Ogunquit, Mr. Bean condescended and offered a waterproof, foulweather cape that had the usual unconditional Bean guarantee and came in an oilskin pouch about the size of a man's wallet. Tucked in a pocket, it weighed little and took little space. The thing did have a fault. If a shower came up, the unfolded garment kept the customer dry as advertised, but when the sun reappeared, there was no possible way to refold the thing and put it back in the little pouch. The packing secret was known only to the manufacturer. Try as he did, every customer either left his L.L. Bean rain gear hanging on a spruce limb somewhere beyond Lily Bay, or stuffed it in a hundred-pound feed bag and sent it to Freeport to get his money back. Mr. Bean's unqualified money-back pledge cost him dearly, and the item was not in the next catalog.[5]

As for the "repair/reuse" policy, in coming decades, the company would employ large numbers of skilled workers whose jobs were to repair the stitching and zippers on products such as jackets, backpacks, and sleeping bags. But at this point in its history, the primary product L.L. Bean refurbished in Freeport remained the Maine Hunting Shoe, which could still be completely rebuilt for less than four dollars.

Longtime L.L. Bean employee Ken Stilkey clearly recalled

workers resoling as many as 200 pairs of boots a day in the late 1920s, waterproofing, lacing, and shipping out the finished boots each morning. In the afternoon, they would receive as many as 200 more pairs of boots in need of repair, and begin removing the old rubber bottoms to make way for their new replacements.

IN 1928 L. L. BEAN'S PRESTIGE among outdoorsmen received another boost when the famous author Ernest Hemingway recommend Mr. Bean's Maine Hunting Shoes to a friend, possibly after having worn a pair while hunting big game in Africa. It was around this time that Hemingway, who'd recently published *The Sun Also Rises* and *Men Without Women*, began spending long periods of time in Africa, Spain, and Key West, Florida. In 1935 he would publish *Green Hills of Africa*, his accounts of big-game hunting. (Fifty years after that, a writer for *Sports Illustrated* would recall that the prose of Bean's first catalog "was pure L. L., as distinctive as early Hemingway: 'Outside of your gun, nothing is so important to your outfit as your footwear.'")

In 1928 and 1929 L. L. Bean, still looking to sell his wares to the hard-core sportsman, ran a total of fourteen ads in *Forest and Stream* magazine, the most interesting of which appeared in the August 1928 issue. It offered, for anyone taking the time to write to Bean's (which, that month, was located at 133 Main Street), a free catalog that would be coming "off the press Aug. 12." The catalog's cover featured a bull moose standing among the reeds, head held high, snorting and sniffing the chilly autumn air. Inside his autumn offering, interested sports would find such diverse items as Bean's Maine Duffel Bag, Bean's Wool Camp Mattress, and Bean's Sleeping Bag, all of which the happy camper could put inside his new Maine Guide Tent.

The tent, "made of 10-ounce water-proof olive drab duck, size 7 x 9 feet," sounds as though it may have been an army surplus item. His reputation for offering rugged, reliable outdoor gear had reached the point where it was not at all unusual for L. L. Bean to be able to sell all manner of leftover government gear through his catalog (this would be especially true following World War II).

He'd do this by pointing out the virtues and practicality of each item, praising everything from cans of dehydrated potatoes to down sleeping bags as much as he could without misrepresenting them. (Wouldn't it be ironic if the $18 surplus sleeping bag being sold by Bean after WW II had originally been made for the government by Eddie Bauer?) By informing his customers that his Maine Guide Tent, with its two doors, two windows, and "sewed-in insect proof" floor, "is proving very popular and is the best value we ever offered," he could, in good conscience, charge $22.85 for a canvas tent that may or may not have been left over from the Great War.

For the adventurous and non-adventurous alike, L. L. introduced his Leatherette Shirt in 1928. Like his famous boots and Field Coat (and eventually his venerable Boat and Tote Bag), this shirt would still be one of the mainstays of his product line decades later. Four years after its introduction, Bean would begin calling it the Chamois Shirt. In its first catalog appearance after the name change, he would opine:

> Looks and feels like high-grade chamois leather. Absolutely will not shrink and is more durable than wool. The longer it is worn, the more it feels and looks like chamois leather.
>
> This is the shirt I personally use on all my hunting and fishing trips.
>
> The best value in a shirt we ever offered.

It cost $1.75. Even though the 2010 price of the shirt, which is still called Bean's Chamois Cloth Shirt, starts at $34.50 (and goes up to $44.50 if you're a tall politician whose favorite color is plaid), it's somehow comforting to think that nearly eighty years later, people are still wearing that chamois shirt when heading out to the woodpile or to get the newspaper.

In spite of the haphazard way his manufacturing facility was laid out, Bean was very careful to get his money's worth out of every piece of fabric or leather he purchased. Many of the products in his ever-expanding line—such as tents, duffel bags, and briefcases—could be made by utilizing not only the materials that were already on hand, but also the same skills and machines his workers were already familiar with. It's been said that L. L. was so careful of his inventory, he even got his employees to produce belts and neckties out of the longer pieces of scrap material.

And of course there were still the boots, which were being turned out by the dozens with rubber bottoms provided by the now-ailing U.S. Rubber Company. U.S. Rubber had recently been acquired by the Du Ponts, who wasted no time in turning the operation over to their dependable manager, Francis Breese Davis, Jr., who quickly set about streamlining the company's production methods. But Bean's boot rubbers would continue to come from U.S. Rubber in Boston until the company ceased production in the mid-1960s.

At least one former employee, Kippy Goldrup, recalled that the company also received boot rubbers from a manufacturer named Hood, at least for a while during the late 1920s, and figured that most of the wood from the shipping crates ended up part of many area homes. Goldrup also remembers that all the Hood boxes came stenciled with the Freeport company's name misspelled as "Beane."

THE BEGINNING OF THE GREAT DEPRESSION notwithstanding, L.L. Bean, Inc., made $251,951.91 in 1929, which proved to be a year of change in Freeport. This was the year that L. L.'s daughter, Barbara, married John Thomas Gorman (1904–59) of Passaic, New Jersey. The wedding took place on September 21 in Nashua, New Hampshire. Only about six years old when her father invented his famous boot, Barbara Bean grew up right alongside his company. She had graduated from Freeport High School in 1924 and from Wheaton College in 1928. Next, according to her father's autobiography, "she took the Katherine Gibbs one-year course for college graduates at the Boston school. Before marriage she was secretary to the assistant editor of *House Beautiful Magazine*."

As it turned out, the cover of Bean's 1927 catalog, with its car-clogged campground depicting America's love affair with the automobile, was almost prophetic. The Portland and Brunswick Street

Railroad, which traveled right down Freeport's Main Street with a stop at Morse Street next to Bean's, had steadily been losing riders to the automobile. By 1929 the line, which had come to Freeport in 1902, had lost so much business to America's new favorite mode of transportation that it was abandoned.

Chapter 5

*"It's not just the knife that's being sold; it's the honesty,
know-how, and practicality of an experienced fisherman
that is firmly on display"*

An early 1930s promotional booklet put out by the Freeport
Chamber of Commerce notes among its meager listing of
Freeport's industries, "L. L. Bean, manufacturer of Maine Hunting
Shoes, has a mail order business which has grown remarkably in
the last ten years. Starting with the Hunting Shoe, he now outfits a
complete camping or hunting expedition."

The main reason—besides, of course, the quality of his products—that L. L.'s young company would manage not only to survive the darkest days of the Great Depression but even flourish
was Bean's image as the consummate outdoorsman. All that consummate outdoorsman needed to do in those difficult times was
convince other people that they needed what he was selling. And
what better way to make sure that lots of people knew they needed
what he was selling than to take his wares directly to them in
Boston's Mechanic's Hall in the back of Lee Soule's Model T Ford
truck. (Designed by William Gibbons Preston, Mechanic's Hall was
built in 1881 on Huntington Avenue, not far from Copley Square. It
was demolished in 1959 to make way for the Prudential Center.)

Right from the start, L. L.'s appearance at the midwinter Boston
Sportsmen's Show was a big success. Not only did he achieve his
goal of collecting hundreds of new names for his carefully culti-
vated mailing list, his woodsy exhibit also quickly became a de
facto advertisement for the Great State of Maine to boot—a fact that
pleased the people at the Maine Publicity Bureau.

The cast of characters assembled at Mr. Bean's booth evidently
included several real Maine Guides who kept Bostonians and

sports alike entertained with demonstrations of the proper way to call a moose or cast with a fly rod—when they weren't too wrapped up, that is, in telling fish stories and other tall tales. While L. L. Bean and the Maine Guides were the state's featured attractions, they were far from the only natives of the Pine Tree State to make the annual trek south to the other Beantown. According to Maine writer John Gould, in any given year "half of Freeport would go to the show."

Then, one year, L. L. just decided that he was done with the Boston Sportsmen's Show. Gould remembers that, as upsetting as it was to both the show's organizers and the Maine Publicity Bureau—which considered L. L. Bean "a strong right arm"—for him to stay home, he had his reasons. Chief among them was the fact that it was the same people who went to the show every year, and he already had their names on his mailing list. So he stayed home and spent $10,000 for a list of "professional people" in Ohio instead.

Now a recognized authority in his field (as well as the woods), L. L. Bean had become a trusted source of information for everyone not exactly sure of how to conduct his or her outdoor adventure. Hunters, campers, and explorers of all types felt comfortable asking him for advice on what to take and how to use it, even if their trips would find them in conditions much harsher than those ever found in Maine. One longtime employee recalled that, on more than one occasion, "callers would give L. L. an outline of where they were going and confidently rely on him to select the necessary items and ship them off."

One such adventurer might have been the fellow who wrote to L. L. Bean in 1930 to thank him for the equipment he'd used on an Alaskan dog sled trip, which covered 1,600 miles of wilderness and frozen tundra. The intrepid explorer was especially pleased with the two items that protected him from the region's subzero temperatures and polar winds whenever he made camp: Bean's Arctic Sleeping Bag and Bean's Pine Tree Poleless Tent.

Since Eddie Bauer's creation of the down-filled sleeping bag was still a few years away, outdoors enthusiasts of the time were still making do with the heavy, cumbersome models that relied on thick wool and cotton blankets for insulation. The sleeping bag used by our Alaskan musher reportedly weighed in at a hefty 11 pounds—which, at the time, was actually quite light for a bag of that warmth—but featured a revolutionary new closing system: a "hookless fastener" (a zipper).

No more fumbling with a row of fussy snaps which left cold spots—now all a weary camper had to do was get in the bag and zip it up. In a 1929 magazine ad for a similar sleeping bag, which cost $21.50, Bean had gushed about the new innovation. "Another strong feature," he wrote in his distinctive shorthand, "is the automatic fastener on side that opens and closes bag in a second." The new hookless fastener caught on quickly and in 1930 also supplanted the snap fasteners atop Bean's Sportsman's Kit Bag, a small duffel bag.

The tent the Alaskan adventurer took along with him on his trek across Seward's Icebox proved to be equally as revolutionary. His high-tech Bean's Pine Tree Poleless Tent cost a hefty $42.50 in 1930 dollars, and tipped the scales at just under 50 pounds. The company's official timeline states that it was 1957 before one of Bean's first "pole-less" tents was added to the spring catalog, with the later one (the New Poleless Tent) costing $71.25 and weighing in at a svelte 11 pounds.

As his business continued to prosper, L. L. Bean enjoyed his success by creating a lifestyle that combined business with pleasure. He no doubt spent many a winter's evening watching the industrial league basketball team he sponsored, the L. L. Bean Sportsmen, which was made up of a dozen local athletes, but he probably spent most of his free time at one of the several camps he owned throughout Maine. It was at one of these remote locations where he could often be found testing new products or making refinements to existing ones.

Bean's refuges ranged from his handy duck-hunting camp on Merrymeeting Bay near Brunswick to the new Dew Drop Inn in remote Haynesville in Aroostook County. (The first Mainer to utter the now-overused phrase, "You can't get there from here," was probably trying to give someone directions to Haynesville.) L. L.'s other Maine camps were located on Sebago Lake, in the Belgrade Lakes area, in Kingfield, and near Freeport on Lane's Island in Casco Bay—not to mention his admitted favorite, the now-gone original Dew Drop Inn in the Wild River area of New Hampshire.

For the convenience of his valued customers, Bean had also purchased a private pond in Freeport where he would allow them to test his latest lines of fishing equipment. Located about a mile up Route 1 from Bean's manufacturing facility, tiny Pratt's Pond proved to be the ideal location for his customers to try out all types of fishing gear—from fly rods and reels to hip waders and lures—before selecting their purchases.

One of L. L.'s fishing-related items they might have considered buying during the early thirties was "a new 10-inch leather trimmed canvas top rubber designed for early boat fishing, stream fishing, and fall hunting. Weight only 33 ounces per pair. Same high quality rubber as used in our Maine Hunting Shoe but lighter throughout. Lowest price ($3.85) and most practical 10-inch sportsman's shoe we have ever made."

No matter how much financial success L. L. Bean was enjoying at the time, nothing could have brought him more pleasure than the arrival of his first grandson, John Thomas Gorman, Jr. (1930–2010), on May 25 in Nashua, New Hampshire. Tommy, as he would come to be called, was the son of L. L.'s daughter, Barbara, and John Gorman, Sr., and would go to work for his famous grandfather after graduating *cum laude* from Fairfield University in 1954.

As the decade progressed, change came to the State of Maine in two distinctly different ways. In 1931 the black-surfaced Route 1, constructed in 1919 between Portland and Brunswick and now extended northward, was replaced by one made of cement. The original asphalt road had brought more and more cars through Freeport with the obvious result being an increased number of garages and filling stations. Its replacement only served to bring even more travelers through town, and even more filling stations were constructed—"until one almost wonders if Main Street will become a solid mass of such stations, for now there are nine from the overpass to just beyond school street"[1] (a distance of just over half a mile).

WHILE CONCRETE WAS REPLACING asphalt in southern Maine, something very different was happening in the northern part of the state. Percival Proctor Baxter had loved the Katahdin region from a very young age and gradually became determined to make the area into a massive state park for the people of Maine to enjoy in perpetuity. The only problem was that the expansive forest lands surrounding Maine's highest peak were owned by timber companies that used the trees for lumber and to feed the state's many paper mills.

As a state legislator, Baxter had first tried unsuccessfully in 1917 to convince the state to purchase the land surrounding mile-high Mount Katahdin for use as a state park. Undeterred by his initial failure, Baxter tried again, this time while serving as Maine's governor between 1921 and 1925, when he tried to get legislation passed that would allow the state to purchase the land. Again he failed.

His setbacks only made him more determined to secure the land for a park, and after his term as governor ended, he set about raising money for the purchase. This time Baxter's efforts were met with great support, even from some who had opposed his idea while he was in office. By 1931, after fifteen years of planning and negotiation, Percival Baxter had raised enough money to purchase the park's first 6,000 acres, which included Katahdin. In all, he would secure nearly 113,000 acres—in thirty-two parcels—surrounding the great mountain. By 2005 Baxter State Park would be about 12 miles wide and 24 miles long, consist of more than 200,000 acres, and cover eight townships (a Maine township generally measures six miles square). In 2006, seventy-five years after Percival Baxter's initial purchase, his original vision for the park would finally be realized with the state's purchase of the 6,016 acres surrounding Katahdin Lake for $14 million. Baxter's vision had always included Katahdin and Katahdin Lake, which he considered one of "the most beautiful of all Maine lakes."

Percival Baxter had long realized that "as modern civilization with its trailers and gasoline fumes, its unsightly billboards, its radio and jazz, encroaches on the Maine wilderness, the time yet may come when only the Katahdin region remains undefiled by man."[2] With that in mind, he decreed that "the said land shall forever be used by said State for *State Forest, Public Recreational Purposes, Shall Forever Be Left in Its Natural Wild State, and Shall Forever Be Kept as a Sanctuary for Wild Beasts and Birds*," and that it be used as a state park and for recreational purposes. Toward this end he established a trust fund to provide operating income to ensure the park's future. "Man is born to die," wrote Baxter. "His works are short-lived. Buildings crumble, monuments decay, and wealth vanishes, but Katahdin in all its glory forever shall remain the mountain of the people of Maine."[3]

So taken was L. L. Bean by the effort and accomplishment of Percival Baxter that he would dedicate the final, "long" chapter of his slender 1942 book to the man and the park he'd created in Maine's North Woods. "Here in the heart of Maine, 145 miles north of Bangor," Bean would write, "this modest man has realized a long cherished ambition to preserve in its primeval ruggedness the State's natural heritage of rugged beauty in the Katahdin region, which embraces 30 or more mountain peaks including the lofty Katahdin range." (Actually, the park's southern Togue Pond Gate is about 90 miles north of Bangor.) "Here," he continued, "you may see beaver dams making lakes of 50 acres or more. In truth more wildlife can be found here than in any other part of Maine."

Justin Williams, one of L. L.'s longtime employees and a frequent hunting companion, confirmed that his friend's views on conservation were more than mere lip service, noting that some people would continue to hunt or fish even after getting their limit early in the day. L. L. always stopped when he was supposed to.

While Baxter is by far Maine's biggest state park, it wasn't the first. That distinction goes to Aroostook State Park in Presque Isle, which was established on 100 acres of donated land in 1935, the same year the Maine Legislature established the state park system.

With his Freeport business continuing to chug along nicely, L. L. Bean decided it was time, in 1932, to take the next big step, and he began drawing up plans for an addition to the Warren Block. While many companies were cutting back on production, his factory continued expand to the point where an addition was needed—a real, well-planned addition, not just another makeshift ell or storage room. It would nearly double the size of his factory upon its completion in 1934.

The reasons behind the nonstop growth of L. L. Bean's enterprise continued to be the gradual, well-thought-out introduction of new products and the steady sales of core items such as his boots and popular Leatherette Shirt, which had just been renamed Bean's Chamois Cloth Shirt. Most of Bean's new offerings were still geared toward his primary customer, the outdoorsman, but one of this year's new products was not. Like it or not, the success of his mail-order company had turned L. L. Bean into a businessman, at least some of the time, and this may have been part of the reason he felt the need to introduce into his catalog what was, for him at least, a fairly unusual product.

Bean's Brief Case was targeted toward the executive or even the traveling salesman. Given his proclivity for making his products sound outdoorsy, it almost seems strange that he elected to call the satchel Bean's Brief Case and not something like Bean's Sportsman's Attaché. As was (and continues to be) the case with everything his employees made in Freeport, Bean's Brief Case was made with materials and machinery his workers were already very familiar with—in this case, a zipper, black leather, and a commercial-grade Singer sewing machine.

Along with his business, L. L.'s extended family also grew when daughter Barbara gave birth in Portland, Maine, to his second grandson, James Warren "Jimmy" Gorman, on May 29, 1932. By the time L. L.'s autobiography, *My Story*, was published in 1960, Jimmy would be a mechanical engineer, married with two small sons, and living in Kingston, New Hampshire.

Diagonally across Main Street from L.L. Bean sat the squat, dark-green Patterson Block, which housed Cole's Drug Store and

Miss Caldwell's Ye Green T-Kettle gift shop. In 1933, Mr. Cole had hired recent high school graduate Franklin Gould to work as his soda jerk for a dollar a day. One hot morning in early August young Mister Gould (no relation to John Gould, the writer) spied a shiny new Cadillac pulling up in front of the post office right below L. L. Bean's factory. Leon Leonwood Bean was about to receive one of the first of his many famous customers: Eleanor Roosevelt, Mrs. FDR herself, who, along with a friend, was followed closely by a pair of very attentive Secret Service agents in a second car. Gould alerted the gift shop's clerk, Miss Strout, and everyone else in the building to what was happening across the street, but no one there seemed to much care that the nation's first lady was only a few yards away. They were all Republicans and probably still smarting from Roosevelt's victory over President Hoover.

"She and Mr. Bean make a good pair, I would say," a customer commented. "He's switched parties, you know."

"Switched parties! That's putting it mild," Miss Strout retorted. "Ever since I can remember, he was chairman of the Republican Town Committee."[4]

A woman of Mrs. Roosevelt's stature surely was escorted to the Warren Block's secluded shopping area, otherwise she'd have had quite a time finding Mr. Bean's "showroom" which, at the time, was located in a small space at the rear of the third floor. Franklin Gould (who became the editor of the local 6 *Town Times* newspaper when it debuted in late 1945) recounted the first lady's visit in a 1998 magazine article:

> To get there, a customer had to climb an open stairway on the outside of the building (the south side, on the left) to a second-floor entrance and pass through the cutting room, redolent of leather and rubber, to an internal stairway to the third floor. Here arrows led through the sewing room and the shipping room and past a glass-enclosed office overlooking Main Street where one could usually view Mr. Bean himself, a large, leonine man with a wide face, broad hands, and a booming voice.[5]

About half an hour later, L. L. stuck his head out the window and hollered for Freeport's police chief, Bill Bailey. One of the Jordan boys said that the chief was over at Leighton's garage and he'd go and get him. Chief Bailey appeared in the street almost immediately. "There you are, Bill. Good," said L. L. "The president's missus is coming down. See that she gets out of town all right." Chief Bailey duly stopped traffic while Mrs. Roosevelt and her escorts backed out of their parking spaces, and then the two sleek convertibles drove away, heading north on Route 1 toward Lubec. Once there, the first lady and her entourage would take the ferry to Campobello Island in Canada. (The Roosevelt International Bridge, which spans the swift tidal currents of the Lubec Narrows, would not be built until 1962.)

Mrs. Roosevelt's 1933 visit seems to be the same one recalled "a few years" later by Dorothy Gluck in the June 1940 issue of *Yankee* magazine. In that piece she stated that L. L. Bean "ran to the front window and bellowed at Freeport's one policeman," whose name she recalled as "Joe." "'It's Mrs. Roosevelt,' he yelled, pointing. 'Mrs. President Roosevelt! Hey Joe! Take good care of Mrs. Roosevelt! There she goes!'" Mrs. Roosevelt, noted Gluck, had stopped at Bean's factory in hopes of buying the president a pair of fishing boots but, unable to find any that suited her, she "finally . . . emerged without the boots." On its website, L.L. Bean's official timeline lists the date of the first lady's visit to Freeport as 1938, but it seems clear that Mrs. Roosevelt visited Mr. Bean's establishment more than once. It's also not unusual for 3s and 8s to look very similar on old documents.

Another version of what seems to be the same visit was also later recalled by L. L.'s daughter, Barbara, who remembers her brother Carl trying to quietly inform his father that Mrs. Roosevelt was there while she was standing right behind him. When Carl finally managed to get through to his father, who'd been concentrating on the newspaper, that Mrs. Roosevelt was there to see him, L. L. bellowed, "Who? What? Which Mrs. Roosevelt?" before standing up and shaking hands with her. He then gave her a trout knife to take back to the president before hollering out the window to the policeman.

Writer John Gould also recalled being introduced to Mrs. Roosevelt by L. L. Bean when "one day as I appeared in his doorway, he called, 'Come in, John! I got somebody here wants to meet you!' It was Eleanor Roosevelt."[6] Gould didn't mention what year he met the first lady. What he did recall was the fact that L. L. Bean always saw it as an honor when a famous person climbed those creaky old stairs to meet him. He didn't realize that they were the ones honored to meet him. "I think he has never quite accepted the simple truth," wrote Gould, "that he is a famous person."[7]

Though the first lady may have left without the boots, a note L. L. received a few days later shows that she had indeed delivered his gift to her husband:

THE WHITE HOUSE
WASHINGTON
August 5, 1933
My Dear Mr. Bean:
I am grateful to have the knife, which I shall keep on my desk. It was very kind of you to send it to me.

   I hope that next year if I stop in South West Harbor on my cruise, I shall have the pleasure of seeing you.
Very sincerely yours
[signed]
Franklin D. Roosevelt

Mrs. Roosevelt's visit notwithstanding, most people still mailed in their orders and, if the volume of mail passing through the Freeport post office was any indication, they usually received the requested items promptly. According to figures he provided to one local newspaper, in 1933–34, L. L. Bean, Manufacturer, spent $25,021.35 on postage, which amounted to 74 percent of the total business of the post office in the fiscal year ending July 1, 1934 (the previous year, the price of a postage stamp for a one-ounce first-class letter had increased from two cents to three cents). The seasonal nature of Bean's business put the town's post office "into a first class position," making it even bigger, at times, than the Brunswick post office just up the road. By the time he penned his autobiography in 1960, Bean would be able to brag that, because of his company, "a clerk in the Freeport Post Office can quote mail rates to any place on the globe." Business at the town's post office was so brisk, in fact, that a Freeport Chamber of Commerce's promotional booklet of the era refers to Bean's building as the "Post Office Block" (but has less than glowing praise for Clark's Hotel across the street):

> The square is the town's natural center of interest and activities. The hotel is better than average and the same may be said of the stores, which represent various lines of business. Here are the bank, the library, movie theater, and five garages.
>
> L. L. Bean's Hunting Shoe Factory and mail order business is located in the Post Office Block, and campers or hunters often stop here to purchase equipment to use in big game country farther up state.[8]

Though it would continue to allow him to hobnob with the rich and famous for the rest of his life, L. L. Bean rarely took advantage of his fame. One of the few times he did so was in rural Maine so he and some buddies could go hunting. The story goes that he and a group of friends took a deer-hunting trip to northern Maine where the tract of land on which they wanted to hunt was owned by a man who didn't allow trespassers. As they neared their destination, the others became increasingly concerned that they'd be turned away and their long trip would have been for nothing. But when they arrived at the gate, the landowner "received them with open arms." Only on the way home, after each hunter in the party had bagged a deer, did the merchant reveal to his pals that he'd had the situation well under control all along: "I knew he'd let us in," Bean said. "He buys his boots from me."

IN 1934, TWO THINGS HAPPENED that would ensure the continued success of L. L.'s company. The first event, that which would have an immediate effect on his business, took place on November 16, 1934, when "L. L. Bean, Manufacturer" became "L.L. Bean, Incorporated," and shares of stock were issued. (This is a good time to clarify that "L. L. Bean," with a space between the initials, refers to the man who founded the mail-order company, while "L.L. Bean" refers to the company itself. Obviously, the names can sometimes be used interchangeably.) The amount of capital stock was $200,000, or 2,000 shares of common stock with a par value of $100. The officers elected were: L. L. Bean, President and Treasurer; Carl Bean, Vice President and Assistant Treasurer; Jack Gorman, L. L.'s son-in-law, Vice President and Clothing Buyer; and his son Warren Bean, Clerk.

All the stock, said L. L., was held in the family with the exception of ten shares given to three of his employees. (Some shares, including those given to the employees, must have been parceled out at a later date, since a document on file in Augusta shows that Leon L. Bean and his sons, L. Carl Bean and C. Warren Bean, all of Freeport, each received one share of common stock, as did (employee) Raymond W. Stowell also of Freeport. The "number of shares in treasury unsubscribed" was 1,996.)

Stock in L. L. Bean's company immediately became very popular and would have sold extremely well except for one disappointing fact—it has never been made available to the public.

The year's other big event was the birth on December 20, 1934, of Leon Arthur Gorman in Nashua, New Hampshire. Why was the arrival of L. L. Bean's third grandson in five years a bigger event than the births of the first two? At the time, it wasn't. But in about thirty-five years, Leon Gorman would make the difference between L.L. Bean, Inc.'s living and dying.

Another noteworthy happening in 1934 was the completion of the factory addition that nearly doubled the size of the Warren Block, which was now made up almost entirely of additions. "The new addition," reported the *Brunswick Record*, "was designed by production engineers, and gives the manufacturer advantages long needed. The business has increased regularly every year—last year's was the largest ever—and if the expected increase comes this year, even this new space will be none too large."[9]

Renovations included the addition of an elevator, which seemed to have been installed more for the sake of freight than for people. No longer did two men have to lug a large wicker basket full of outgoing packages down two flights of stairs to the post office, which now shared the Warren Block's ground floor with the *Freeport Press* newspaper. The new lift not only made Mr. Bean's workers happy, it also pleased the postmaster, who'd often complained to L. L. about the condition of some of the packages that arrived downstairs.

The L.L. Bean catalog kept pace with the building and had grown to an impressive fifty-two pages, requiring 20 tons of paper for the printing of August's fall catalog alone. The mailing list for Bean's semiannual offerings now exceeded 100,000 names, "a roster of Bean customers who actually write in if they do not receive the catalogs!" During this period, the catalogs' covers featured pictures that were similar to the realistic, often humorous portrayals of everyday life painted by Norman Rockwell (1894–1978) for the covers of magazines such as the *Saturday Evening Post, Look,* and *Ladies' Home Journal.*

A painting by W. H. Foster on the cover of Bean's 1934 fall catalog depicts a duck hunter lifting his quarry into the boat only to realize that he'd just bagged another hunter's toller (live decoy) when he spots the dead duck's leather leg strap. The cover of the previous year's spring catalog featured an illustration entitled *The Silver Hook.* The picture, done by an artist whose identity has been lost to history, shows a barefoot boy—with a stick for a fishing pole—selling his day's catch to a luckless fly-fisherman. (Remember that in 1886 L. L. Bean had sold the second deer he ever shot to a pair of unsuccessful hunters for $12.) As was his nature, L. L. got maximum mileage out of the artwork he purchased for his catalog: nine years later he would reuse *The Silver Hook* painting—along with the admonition, "By following directions in my book, you can get your trout without resorting to this method" pasted in the upper right-hand corner—in his *Hunting, Fishing, and Camping* book. Nearly four decades after they'd originally appeared, the company would dust off some of these old covers to use during its sixtieth anniversary in 1972. (*The Silver Hook* would also appear on the cover of the Spring 2007 catalog during L.L. Bean's ninety-fifth year.)

On August 13, 1934, L. L. Bean decided to try his hand at writing something longer than the brief but glowing descriptions of items in his catalog. In the piece, which appeared in the fall catalog below a photo of his recently renovated Freeport factory, L. L. talked about the addition to his building and how he got where he is today. The newspaper in Brunswick even picked up on Bean's literary efforts and ran an article about his business ten days later. Considering its source, L. L.'s catalog editorial is quite lengthy:

I have just completed a large addition to our factory and thought a short sketch of the business might be of interest to customers.

This last addition increases our floor space 91%, giving us a total floor space of 13,497 square feet.

We have two shutes [*sic*] running direct from our shipping room to the post office, which carry all our letters and packages.

In 1912 our business was in a basement 25 x 35 and our catalog was size $5^1/2$ x 8" with four pages, which took less than 100 pounds of paper. We now publish two catalogs a year, which require over 35 tons of paper. Last year our business required $25,021.35 worth of postage stamps, which amounts to 74% of the total business of the Freeport Post Office year ending July 1, 1934.

I was born in Maine and have always lived here. At the age of eleven I was put on my own resources through the death[s] of both my father and mother.

Hunting and Fishing is my hobby. In fact I personally test out practically all our new specialties before offering them for sale.

It was about 1911 that I was unable to find a Hunting Shoe that suited me. I took an ordinary rubber and sewed on a light weight Tan Elk Top. Even this crude shoe was a big improvement over anything on the market at that time. In fact I am using the same Tan Elk to-day in my Maine Hunting Shoe. From this small start we have developed other practical specialties. While our factory is too small to make all the articles we sell, we do design practically everything shown in this catalog. They are all made according to our own specifications and carry our own guarantee. Four of the specialties we manufacture are patented in the United States and Canada.

For years all my profits were spent in advertising. The results have proved my judgment was correct.

Everyone is welcome to call for advice on where to hunt or fish and make a purchase if they see fit.

Our factory is right on the cement road 19 miles east of Portland, Route #1.

Our catalog not only goes to every state in the Union but to every civilized country in the world.

I wish to take this opportunity to thank you for your patronage and goodwill.
Sincerely, L. L. Bean

One of the new items featured in his 1934 fall catalog was Bean's Trout Knife, which sold for 75 cents or was "given free with $20.00 order" (or if you happen to be the first lady of the United States). Seldom, if ever, has so much been written about so small a knife, a fact which, given the publicity it generated, would have tickled L. L. to no end. It almost seems as if he planned it that way. For a long time, you see, Bean's Trout Knife had been just that— a knife for cleaning fish and "for general camp and home use." As L. L. described it in the fall 1934 catalog:

For some time we have been perfecting a knife for cleaning game fish. This is the result.

The cutting blade is 4 1/2" long and extends full length of large walnut handle fastened with three brass rivets as shown. The handle is so long (4 5/8") that the hand does not come in contact with the fish. Once used you will never again use a jackknife that is more work to clean than the fish. . . . If kept in the genuine elk leather case as shown, which completely covers knife, you will always have a clean sharp knife.

A modern version of Bean's Classic Trout Knife is still available in 2010. It features a durable 4-inch stainless-steel blade, which does not extend the full length of the handsome 4¹/₂-inch rosewood handle fastened with two brass rivets. It sells for $29.

In the mid-1980s, things got interesting when one biographer used the knife to illustrate the point that L. L. Bean wasn't selling just cutlery, he was selling an image:

> . . . only L. L. Bean would have the nerve to take a small boning knife, sew up a leather blade cover for it, and call it a Knife for Cleaning Trout. It is this self-centered audacity that separated Bean from his contemporaries, that absolutely incredible ego, that sense that he could do no wrong, have no bad ideas, that made him the personal discovery of his customers.[10]

A few years later, author and longtime Bean employee Carlene Griffin would give her take on the subject by reproducing the catalog copy in her book and asking her readers to decide for themselves. "It's not just the knife that's being sold; it's the honesty, know-how, and practicality of an experienced fisherman that is firmly on display. Read [the copy], then ask yourself if you would even consider buying any other trout knife."[11]

L. L. seemed to have anticipated this whole thing in his 1960 autobiography, which allowed him to have the last, brief word on the matter. "No doubt," he wrote, "a chief reason for the success [of] the business is the fact that I tried on the trail practically every article I handle. If I tell you that a knife is good for cleaning trout, it is because I found it so." Imagine, all this publicity from a nine-inch boning knife (not to mention the fact that the whole thing is also being recounted yet again in *this* book). L. L. Bean would have loved it. And he was right about the jackknife.

As the mystique surrounding L. L. Bean began to grow, more

and more people wanted to be associated with him, even if that connection was only by mail. Those wanting his attention ranged from everyday Mainers to famous athletes—very famous—one of whom was New York Yankees slugger Babe Ruth. A frequent Bean customer, the Sultan of Swat sent the merchant a baseball and an autographed photo, which he'd signed: "To L. L. Bean—A hunter's delight. Sincerely Babe Ruth. June 1st 1934."(Ruth would play one more season with the Yankees before being inducted into the Baseball Hall of Fame in 1936.)

Among Ruth's correspondence to L. L. was an earlier handwritten note in which he thanked his friend for some recently purchased hunting gear—maybe items he'd had shipped to New York after stopping at the Freeport store the previous Thanksgiving:

BABE RUTH
New York
Jan. 2, 1934
Dear Mr. Bean:
Received hunting clothes and they fit perfectly. Have been working very hard on radio records. I have been so busy that this is the first chance I had to write and thank you for those wonderful shoes, they fit perfect.
Thanking you again,
I remain your friend.
Babe Ruth

Among the not-so-famous people who wrote to L. L. Bean that year was John R. Perkins of Wayne, Maine, whose letters from L. L. Bean he donated to the Maine Historical Society in Portland. (Mr. Perkins is probably the same John Perkins, a Maine game warden, who is shown on page 46 of Bean's company scrapbook taking charge of a confiscated live moose with the help of fellow warden Adelbert Piper.) It seems that Mr. Perkins had been dissatisfied with the fit of the gun case he'd recently received from the company and had returned it. A response dated October 3, 1934, asks for his assistance in the matter: "Before we send you another Gun

Case we wish you would send us an outline of your gun drawn on the paper we are enclosing. This will ensure a proper fitting case." Later that year, Perkins was less than happy with the blanket he'd ordered from Freeport and evidently suffered no compunction in saying so. On December 13, he received this reply from Bean's:

> We are sorry that you are not satisfied with the quality of the Camp Blanket we have sent you.
>
> Please feel free to send it right back for your money.
>
> We realize these blankets have not been going through as good as formerly but we still consider them a good value at the price. If you send yours back be sure and write us at the time.

Once the company's daily customer-service issues had been resolved—probably in the morning so he could get away in the afternoon—L. L. would often steal away from his makeshift factory for a little recreation, such as duck hunting. A few years later in his book, *Hunting, Fishing, and Camping,* L. L. would impart the following bits of wisdom on bagging your limit of ducks:

> Present restrictions make duck and goose hunting much more difficult than it was a few years ago when you could use live decoys.
>
> For ducks I recommend a 3 shot 12 gauge Automatic Shot Gun. Use a long range load with number 4 shot.
>
> I use about fourteen removable head decoys. Make your set about 100 yards off a point of land in an open spot with grass enough around you so you can scull quite close without ducks seeing you.
>
> When you see birds coming, keep very still until they light in. Lay very low in your gunning float until you are within range. Don't try to kill the whole flock. Pick out the nearest duck and stay with it until it drops before trying for a second bird. Go where the wild rice is plentiful, if possible, and get your decoys out by daylight.

While L. L. may have recommended using a three-shot rig, this hardly seemed to have been his own weapon of choice for shooting at birds. As good as he was at shooting deer (at one point he claimed to have shot thirty-two deer in thirty-one years), L. L. was far less proficient at hitting a bird on the wing. Back when he was able to handle the thing, said Bean's hunting buddy George Soule, L. L.'s "old smokepole [was] a great heavy 12-gauge Remington automatic fitted with a nine-shot extension magazine."[12] Soule remembered that L. L. wasn't shy about pulling the trigger, either, recalling one time that L. L. kept shooting at a duck as it was flying away, certain that he'd hit the thing on the seventh or eighth shot.

When the State of Maine outlawed live tollers in 1935, the wooden decoys L. L. Bean put in his catalog were made by his best friend, George Soule. The difference in their ages was about forty years, but L. L. didn't hold Soule's lack of experience against the youngster; he knew a good bird-hunting guide when he saw one. Soule probably first endeared himself to L. L. Bean, who by this time was well over sixty, when they went partridge hunting together and Soule saw to it that, more often than not, his old boss actually shot a bird. As was his habit, Soule had studied his prey and was familiar with the wary bird's tendency to begin and end each and every day in or near the very same tree. He then parlayed this wisdom onto a hunting style that made it almost easy for L. L. Bean to shoot a partridge. A friendship was born.

Under Soule's tutelage, L. L. Bean became enough of an expert on hunting partridge that he'd even include a chapter on it in his upcoming book. But that still didn't mean that he was actually very good at shooting the darned things—especially the ones around Freeport. According to L. L.:

> There are two kinds of grouse in Maine—smart and foolish. The latter are so tame that they can be shot on the ground or on the limbs of trees with a pistol or a rifle. These are the birds found in the big woods. They are identical in every way with those found in the settled areas except that they have no fear of humans.

The grouse of the inhabited sections are much smarter than their backwoods brethren. We don't shoot them with rifles or pistols; we don't always hit them with a shotgun. They have been well-termed "the smartest upland game bird that flies."

What George Soule was really good at, though, was duck hunting. Every once in a while, during the season, L. L. would stop by the shipping room, or wherever Soule happened to be working at the time, and say that it looked like a good day to head out to the duck blind. "George," he'd announce in his normal, public-address-volume voice, "let's you and I go duck hunting—don't bother to punch out." Soule was more than happy to oblige, and off they'd go with their shotguns and decoys, in the direction of Casco Bay toward the vicinity of Lane's Island and Blind Point. At first the pair made do with L. L.'s dilapidated set of round-bottom decoys "that skittered, bobbed, and pitched like seagoing rocking horses in the slightest chop."

Pretty soon Soule, whose hobby was woodworking, spoke up and told L. L. he could make much better decoys, and that's exactly what he did. The first decoys George Soule made—out of cork he'd salvaged from an old refrigerated truck in Portland—were crude but they worked well and L. L. Bean told George Soule that he'd put his decoys in the catalog. By 1967, L.L. Bean would be handling about 35 percent of Soule's hunting decoys. The reason, said Soule, that the first dozen rudimentary black-duck decoys from his basement were so successful was because "they had flat bottoms and keels, and they looked pretty natural on the water."

Eventually Soule also began making duck calls for the catalog after L. L. saw firsthand what they could do. In the late 1930s, Justin Williams (another longtime employee of Bean's, for whom Justin's Way next to the retail store is named) was out duck hunting with L. L. and decided to use his duck call. It was an old one but a good one, and Justin was highly skilled at using it. After a few calls, the result was nothing short of amazing. When the sky filled with ducks, L. L. vowed that he'd have duck calls in his catalog the following fall—duck calls patterned after the one

Williams used, and made by George Soule.

It's said that Soule's Coastal Duck Call was patterned after those made by Tom Turpin (1872–1957) from the 1930s until 1949, at which time he turned his turkey- and duck-call business over to his brother, Inman. (In 1957 Inman would sell the turkey-call business to Roger Latham and the duck-call business to Melancon.) Soule made his duck calls out of walnut and rosewood, and was said to have played them like musical instruments, causing a duck to turn back, right over the blind. *Sports Illustrated* once reported that "Soule's call is a Turpin made in Louisiana, and, once one hears him chirp into it, one wonders why he needs decoys at all."[13]

"I love to call ducks," Soule once said. "I'd rather call ducks than shoot them any day."

But the decoys remained his bread-and-butter items. In its heyday, Soule's company, Maine Coastal Decoys, turned out as many as 15,000 ducks and geese a year. The wooden birds featured Maine pine heads while their specially processed Portuguese cork bodies were made sixteen at a time on a shaping lathe originally used in making furniture. Once the heads and bodies had been joined together, the flat-painted birds were sent out to a half dozen or so local housewives and young mothers who added the decoys' features—an olive bill and blue wing patches on the black ducks, for example. Just as Bean did with his products, Soule personally saw to the quality of his decoys, many of which ended up being sold through Bean's catalog.

George Soule changed with the times; when the demand for oversized decoys increased, he and his business partner, Sewall MacWilliams, adjusted their production accordingly, becoming the first carvers to make the modern ones commercially available. When demand for working and oversized decoys started to dwindle, they increased production of the decorative decoys, the kind people like to use to decorate their Bean-inspired living rooms and dens. Regardless of what kind they were, George Soule's decoys will always be the standard against which other duck decoys are measured. "Except for God," as one admirer put it, "nobody makes a duck like George Soule."

IN 1935, L. L. BEAN did it again. Literally. The editorial he'd penned for his catalog a year earlier had gone over so well with his customers that he couldn't resist the urge to write another the following fall. Having said just about everything he'd wanted to say in his previous missive, Bean's brief text this time consisted of but four paragraphs below five photos of him and his factory.

The page's photo layout, presented under the heading "Interior Views of Factory of L.L. Bean, Inc.," centered around an ovate snapshot of a much younger Mr. Bean ("L. L. Bean, Pres."), which had been cropped from a portrait of him and his brothers, Guy, Otho, Ervin, and Henry. (It had probably been taken sometime in the teens.) Surrounding L. L. were four regular photos ("Corner of Shipping Room," "Section of Cutting Room," "Part of Stitching Room," and "Another View of Factory"), angled toward him. The space between the photos was filled in with basic line drawings showing a hunter, a fly-fisherman, and the white-pine cone and tassel, Maine's official state flower. The whole display had the look of the flag of a small country showing how everything revolved around its president. In a way, this was actually becoming the case in Freeport, Maine.

In his brief message at the bottom of the page, L. L. assured his customers that his business was continuing to flourish:

> Last fall we received so many favorable comments on our "Editorial Page" that we have decided to continue this page in each of our fall catalogs. We hope this page will bring us in closer touch with our customers.
>
> Our business for the year ending July 1, 1935, showed an increase of 29% over the previous year.
>
> We have just broken ground for a large addition that will be shown in our 1936 fall catalog.
>
> Everyone is welcome to call for advice on where to hunt or fish and make a purchase if they see fit.
>
> Our factory is right on the cement road 19 miles east of Portland, Route No. 1.
> Sincerely, L. L. Bean

L. L. liked the editorial's photo spread so much that he included it, sans text, on page 34 of his 1960 autobiography. Just as he was careful to let not a scrap of material go to waste in his factory, L. L. Bean made just as sure he got all the mileage he could out of practically every photo ever taken of him. A case in point is the 1935 John Gould picture of L. L. posing with a moose he'd bagged in Canada. Not only does he use the photo in 1942 as the frontispiece of his first book, *Hunting, Fishing, and Camping,* as well as in a full-page catalog spread for it, the picture also takes up all of page 35 in his autobiography. (A different picture, published in the Brunswick newspaper, shows L. L. and his friend Levi Patterson, each standing next to the moose he'd bagged on the trip. The photo caption says that Patterson's trophy weighed about 700 pounds, while L. L.'s prize came in at about 600. It also notes that their hunting companion, Heiman Merski, didn't get a moose but did shoot a nice doe.

By now L.L. Bean, Inc., employed about fifty people, one of the newest of whom was his first cashier, an eighteen-year-old named Carlene Groves Griffin. Carlene (so named because her father, Carl Groves, had wanted a boy) would end up working at Bean's for more than seventy years. When she started, L.L. Bean, Inc., had one bookkeeper, one telephone, three people to open the mail, and one NCR cash register located in the salesroom next to the freight elevator that L. L. usually rode to his third-floor office.

According to a *Portland Press Herald* article that was published in 2009, a year after Carlene had retired at the age of ninety-one, "Griffin got the job at the Freeport store through luck and relationships. Her cousin, who was friendly with L. L.'s daughter, got Griffin an interview in 1935, during the height of the Depression. She felt fortunate just for the chance for the interview, and was ecstatic when an offer of work followed."

In her early years at Bean's, it would often be Carlene's job to walk down Bow Street to the train station on Depot Street and pick up the four or five orders customers had sent to L.L. Bean via telegraph. Griffin recalls walking down the hill to where "a little old man sat behind the counter, tapping out Morse code on the telegraph." (Telegrams peaked in popularity in the 1920s and 1930s because it was cheaper to send a telegram than to place a long-distance telephone call. After more than 150 years of service, Western Union would deliver its final telegram on January 27, 2006, completing its transition from a communications company to a financial services company.)

Carlene's first stint with the company lasted only about a year "because there wasn't enough work." She returned to the company for five years beginning in 1942 before again leaving, this time to raise a family, but resumed working at Bean's in 1952—this time for good. During her lengthy career with the company, her duties would include doing pretty much whatever needed to be done, ranging from repairing used hunting boots to mailing out catalogs to occasionally updating Mr. Bean's prized mailing list on a typewriter. By the late 1990s, Carlene's job would be to oversee the fax machines at Bean's corporate headquarters down the road on Casco Street. Griffin remembers that in 1935 the starting wage for an untrained eighteen-year-old female was eighteen cents an hour. In 1992 she published her memoir, *Spillin' the Beans*, wherein she recounts her time with the company through a collection of anecdotes and interviews of other longtime employees. She was still with the company when retired Bean president Leon Gorman (who was less than a year old when Griffin started working for L. L.) published his own memoir in 2006.

While future competitor Eddie Bauer was more or less just getting started with his first product—a down-insulated jacket—exactly twenty-five years after L. L. created his hunting shoe, Bean's company was forging ahead. In 1936 the company's sales had reached an impressive $540,000, thanks in part to the addition of products such as Bean's Blucher Moccasin to the catalog. (This style of footwear, in which the vamp overlaps the shoe's top from the sides, creating a place for the eyelets, is named after Gebhart Leberecht von Blucher [1742–1819], a Prussian field marshal.) The men's version of the shoe, which originally sold for $2.75, would cost $48.00 in 1987 and $69 in 2010, by which time they had become part of the much more diverse line of Bean's Handsewn Moccasins.

L. L.'s 1936 catalog copy said that these shoes had "all the comfort of the Indian Moccasin," a statement repeated almost verbatim in Bean's catalogs through 2007.

Also new in 1936 was Bean's magnificent Double L Bamboo Fly Rod, the simple use of which was evidently sufficient to have the most tranquil of effects on any angler lucky enough to own one during the Great Depression. In 2005, L.L. Bean would introduce a $1,495 re-creation of the rod, and relying on a heavy dose of nostalgia, describe it as follows in the catalog: "When the Double L Bamboo Rod was introduced in 1936, life moved at a slower pace. The relaxing state induced by the act of casting a handmade bamboo rod was at the heart of the fly-fishing experience." (You could get even more relaxed in 2007 by using one of Bean's twenty-five 95th-Anniversary Double L Fly Rods with W. A. Adams reel—$2,995 for the set.)

In the fly-tying room, Frances Stearns provided L.L. Bean with another first that year when she became the first female to work there. Frances, whose skills would earn her national recognition, tied all the specialty fishing flies for Leon Leonwood Bean. Eventually she became so proficient at her craft that she was able to tie certain flies in as little as ten or fifteen minutes, though some of the more complicated ones could take her an hour or even two to complete. Frances, who also taught L.L. Bean's first fly-tying classes, had learned to tie flies from her brother-in-law, George Soule. "L. L. never used any fly other than what my mom tied for him," said her son Cody. "She got feedback from L. L. and George and their fishing buddies and was always willing to change things—a different size hook or a different feather."

In 1950 Frances would be diagnosed with breast cancer and, at the age of thirty-two, told she had six months to live. She fought back by taking up meditation and enduring multiple surgeries. She used her work to keep her hands busy and take her mind off the pain. "She was very strong," said her daughter-in-law, Susanellen Stearns of Freeport, "and would never tell anyone if she was in pain. She just knew that it would go away." Frances Lee Stearns would live until May 10, 2003, reaching the age of eighty-five.

Once, recalled John Gould, those flies nearly got the famous outdoorsman in trouble with the law:

> Did I ever tell you about the time L. L. Bean and his brother [Otho] were going up to Goddard Brook to "try out" a trout fly George Soule had just invented? As they were getting into the automobile, loaded down with angling specialties from the Bean catalog, Ern Morton, the Freeport Tax Collector, happened by, and he called, "Got your fishing licenses?"
>
> And by the George Harry, neither one had a license! They had to wait until Town Clerk Bob Randall came to open his office, and Ern's timely reminder about a license probably spared L. L. Bean the unpleasantness of a fine for angling without a license.
>
> The next morning, Ern Morton got a free pair of Maine Hunting Shoes and a personal letter from [Bean's secretary] Hazel, signed by L. L. Bean.[14]

Bean's Brook Trout Flies, Blucher Moccasins, and everything in between went out through the company's bustling shipping room. A mid-1930s photo of the room, with its posts and beams, bare lightbulbs, and exposed sprinkler system shows at least eight men hard at work amid dozens of various-sized cardboard boxes. As usual, all of Bean's packages and mail continued to pass through the Freeport post office on the first floor, but this year something down there had changed—there was a new postmaster in town. L. L.'s youngest brother, Guy, assumed the position of Freeport's postmaster in June and would shepherd what many referred to as "L. L. Bean's government-subsidized shipping department" through one of its most profitable periods. Guy held the position of postmaster for twelve years, until his retirement in September 1948 at the age of seventy.

According to some accounts, the size of L. L.'s business quadrupled during the thirties—despite the Great Depression. Or maybe because of it. Not only did Bean's merchandise provide good value for the money, his customers could have their Maine Hunting

Shoes changed over to moccasin bottoms for $2.85 in the spring, and then have them changed back to rubber in the fall for the same amount.

WHILE THE 1930S IN GENERAL were good to Mr. Bean's business, 1937 in particular would turn out to be a watershed year. This was the year that L. L. Bean's company turned twenty-five. It was also the year that the sales of L.L. Bean, Inc., passed the $1,000,000 mark for the first time. (On June 15, 1937, it was unanimously voted to increase the capital stock of the corporation from $200,000 to $400,000.)

While the rest of the country had been reeling under an unemployment rate as high as 25 percent during the Great Depression, the town of Freeport seems to have made out relatively well. Or maybe the people of Maine had just become accustomed to working and having little to show for it. Of course the town's perceived prosperity had more to do with genuine financial factors than with the fact that most Freeporters were oblivious to what was going on around them. And the town's biggest single factor (benefactor?) was, of course, L. L. Bean.

By now Bean's business required ten or twelve women to handle its data processing. All the women, each at her own desk, worked in a very large room with two tall windows. The volume of mail generated by Bean's enterprise was sufficient in 1937 to give his brother's post office permanent first-class status. According to Guy Bean, the Freeport post office showed receipts of $56,500, contributed $12,200 in salaries to the town, and led all first-class post offices in Maine in per capita sales of savings bonds.

For the packages that needed to be shipped by rail, Mr. Brown's truck was their ticket to the train station just down the hill. Full to the point of being almost overloaded, the truck would wobble across Main Street and proceed slowly down Bow Street to the Maine Central Railroad depot with a Bean employee walking behind the truck to watch for any packages that fell off. "We had to do this every time," recalled Carlene Griffin, "yelling at him to stop when a package tumbled to the street, and he'd get out of the truck and put the errant parcel on the front seat."[15]

With L. L.'s business doing relatively well, he didn't forget other people of Freeport who weren't so fortunate, and sometimes hired entire families to work for him. Often he'd buy worms he'd never use from local kids for a penny apiece. When job seekers came to town and he didn't have any work for them, L. L. would send them across the street to Collins' Restaurant, where they were given a free meal. Often when he was out fishing and saw youngsters using makeshift rods to try to catch some fish for the evening meal, he'd give them real fishing equipment.

It's important to note that during the depression, L. L. Bean wasn't concerned with just the prosperity of his business and employees, or performing random acts of charity. He was also very involved in looking out for the well-being of Freeport as a whole. Along with Roland Kimball, he'd started Freeport Realty Co. in 1918 in order to save the bankrupt A. W. Shaw shoe factory, serving as the company's president during the 1920s and again from November 22, 1937, until July 9, 1947. During his tenure, Freeport Realty leased two vacant shoe factories and converted the old high school into a third one.

The three buildings had a combined floor space of 79,276 square feet, and were fully equipped with everything needed for the "economical manufacture of shoes." (There was also a fourth, separately owned, shoe factory in town, the old H. E. Davis building on West Street.) For most of the decade, the shoe shops of the Freeport Realty Company would have a total weekly payroll ranging from $14,000 to $27,000, depending on the season. According to one history of Freeport, "the Freeport Realty Company [is] a local corporation whose stock is held by many of the townsfolk." The Town of Freeport helped out by abating taxes on the properties.

All of this investment in the town was paying off handsomely; a headline in the *Portland Evening Express* at the end of the decade would proclaim, "Freeport Makes Enviable Record for Employment." While Portland, Maine's largest city, was "more nearly paralyzed than any of the large cities of the country," the paper reported that "the town of Freeport points to as many as 1,450 persons employed in peak seasons and approximately 850 on the payrolls at all times." At the end of the article, the reporter praised the town for its economic progress during the current hard times:

> The Freeport town government also has reason to be proud of its record during the recent lean years.
>
> The records show that the debt has been reduced by $36,671 since 1933 and is now but $20,000; that the valuation has increased more than $100,000 in the same period, and that the tax rate is but $3 more per thousand than it was in 1933. Freeport has unquestionably kept its feet on the ground.[16]

L. L. Bean had by now become such an astute businessman that one might be inclined to think he'd received his education at Harvard. In fact, someone there actually did think that he'd graduated from the university in 1937, and included his name on a list of award recipients sent to the *Boston Globe*. The June 7, 1989, edition of the paper reported that, along with Watergate prosecutor Archibald Cox, philanthropist Walter Rothschild, and others, L. L. Bean was going to be awarded a special medal during Harvard's commencement ceremony from the Harvard Alumni Association for "extraordinary service" to the university.

The next day the *Globe* ran a corrected version of the article in which "clothing and camping entrepreneur L. L. Bean, a 1937 graduate" had been replaced with "retiring Radcliffe president Matina Horner." It's safe to say that L. L. had not been a member of Harvard's Class of '37. By then he was almost sixty-five years old and had children who were in their mid-thirties. (In an interesting bit of irony, L.L. Bean, Inc., would be the subject of seven case studies done by the Harvard Business School between 1965 and 2004.)

Longtime friend Paul Powers, a Freeport attorney and fellow past master of the town's Masonic Lodge, once recalled that the experiences drawn from a lifetime of fending for himself had served L. L. Bean better than the degrees of many highly educated people who, it turned out, just weren't all that intelligent. "L. L. was extremely ambitious. For a man who had little formal education, [he] had one of the finest minds I've ever seen. He's my living example of the man who could be extremely successful—who could be self-educated in his own way without a college degree, as opposed to a man with a Ph.D. degree who doesn't know how to change a flat."[17]

As we'll see later, however, L. L. Bean would get an advanced degree, of sorts, in the summer of 1951 when journalists William A. Hatch and Richard A. Hebert would award the seventy-nine-year-old merchant an honorary D.S.D. (Doctor of Sportsmen's Dif ficulties).

One Chicago-based peddler of the day recalled how he and his fellow traveling salesmen "made Marshal Field rich" only to be put out of business when people in rural areas discovered they could get just about anything from one of the country's many mail-order houses. Mail-order houses would in turn, he lamented, soon be "put out of business by the automobile." While this sad fact may have been true of many catalogers of the period, it didn't apply to a certain mail-order merchant in coastal Maine who continued to sell durable goods that people really needed. Not only was L. L. Bean continuing to ship an ever-increasing number of packages to his loyal customers during each and every year of the Great Depression, they were also coming to him—almost literally beating a path to his door.

So much traffic continued to stream through town on Freeport's recently improved Main Street that, by 1937, it had become necessary to install a stoplight at the intersection of Bow and Main Streets, right in front of L. L. Bean's store. "This proved to be a great convenience," noted one historian, "for thousands of cars from all parts of the country and Canada pass along Main Street, and without an automatic halt in traffic it would be difficult at times to cross the highway or for a car to enter from Bow Street." Back then, the residents of Freeport couldn't have begun to imag-ine what Main Street would look like after the town's crop of fac-tory outlet stores had taken firm root fifty years later.

Business as usual in 1938 consisted of L. L.'s seventy-five employees (which rose to as many as 100 during busy periods) shipping out an estimated 700 tons of merchandise to every state in the union and several foreign countries. One recent hire at Bean's establishment was son-in-law Jack Gorman, whose job was that of clothing buyer. He got along okay with L. L., according to his son Leon, but probably wasn't crazy about his job.

New that year was the federally mandated minimum wage, which guaranteed that every worker would earn at least 25 cents for each hour worked. As long as he ran the show, L. L. Bean usually managed to stay a few pennies ahead of minimum wage as it increased over the years. It's a pretty good guess that Mr. Bean's son-in-law was started at a somewhat higher salary. Not long after Jack Gorman's son took over as president in 1967, he'd begin to make the company's wages and benefits much more competitive.

A new item for that year was Bean's Business Man Shirt, the result, the catalog informed its readers, of an eighteen-month-long examination process of "about every semi-dress shirt manufactured east of the Mississippi River." Since he needed to tie in a semi-dress shirt with the rest of his product line, L. L. stated its purpose as giving his customers "something out of the ordinary to wear going and coming from their hunting and fishing grounds." A good fit was assured since, when ordering, the buyer had to "send us your weight, height, collar size, and sleeve length and we will send you a Shirt that fits, no matter how stout or slim you are, and at no extra charge."

Bean also promised his customers that his $1.95 shirts (or "3 for $5.35 postpaid"), with their collar stays and "strongest money will buy" three-hole pearl buttons, would "compare favorably with any $2.50 shirt on the market." The shirts were made of broadcloth, chambray, or madras, and available in a variety of blue stripes and solids, any one of which was virtually guaranteed to make the wearer look "well dressed" or "the smartest." Maybe both.

On another page of the catalog, L. L. gave his readers "Seventeen Reasons Why Fish Leave Home." Did they drop out of school? No, they were lured away by one of Bean's distinctive salmon or trout flies. The page, which appears to have been a glossy color insert since it notes that "prices and description [are] on page 16," shows detailed pictures of nine of Bean's Brook Trout Flies and, right below them, eight of Bean's Salmon Flies, which were intended for landlocked salmon and also for lake trout. The Black Gnat, Silver Doctor, Royal Coachman, and Hackles of both the Brown and Gray varieties were included among the selection of tiny trout flies, while the assortment of salmon flies included the Lady Doctor; the Brown, White, and Red & White Bucktails; and, of course, Bean's Special.

At the bottom of the page, the merchant was able to assure his customers that every fly was "Tied By L.L. Bean, Inc., Freeport Maine," since around this time the company already employed two or three people who did nothing but tie flies.

Also new was Bean's Zipper Duffle Bag, which had replaced the Sportsman's Kit Bag. Once outfitted with all of the above items, the sportsman could arrive at his camp, change into his fishing clothes, and store his Bean's Business Man Shirt in his Bean's Zipper Duffle Bag until it was time to change again for the trip home.

The last year of the decade would turn out not to be a very good one for L. L. Bean. In 1939 he'd suffer a pair of personal losses as well as a downturn in business. At first glance, everything seemed to be proceeding according to plan; the 200,000 people on Bean's mailing list were continuing to receive their spring and fall issues of his four-color catalog, which now took 80 tons of paper to print and was even mentioned in *Three Centuries of Freeport*, a recently published history of the town:

> The latest issue of this catalog was an edition of three hundred thousand copies of sixty-eight pages each, listing all kinds of hunting and fishing supplies. Every item contained in the catalog has been tested in actual service by Mr. Bean and found to be satisfactory before being included.
>
> A large block on Main Street, with adjoining storehouses, is occupied by this enterprise, which employs seventy-five to one hundred hands. Much of the business is mail order but sportsmen passing through stop to supply their wants from the store, which is open twenty-four hours a day.

The postage from this one business exceeds $48,000 per year.

While most of the townspeople seemed to have no problem with Mr. Bean's use of the town post office—which leased space in Bean's building—as his shipping department, at least one Freeport resident saw things a little differently. On July 27, 1938, Mr. A. P. Winslow wrote a letter to the editor of the *Brunswick Record* to complain about several of the existing post office's shortcomings:

> First, the only door by which the patrons enter or leave opens in; how he has gotten away with this so long beats me. How about the desk room? Many smaller offices nearby are equipped with glass-top desks. Let three people try and write at the same time at the desk now in the present post office, and how much privacy have they? Also, measure how much room there is between the entrance door and the patrons' window.

The response to Mr. Winslow's letter came quickly in the form of a petition that was signed by "every business man" in Freeport as well as ninety-one others, and stated that relocating the post office would be a great injustice to Mr. Bean, adding that he stood ready to enlarge and improve the current facility, making it the envy of any town the size of Freeport. As a result of this outpouring of public support, and L. L.'s soon making good on his promise to expand the post office, he would be able to write in 1960, "The Post Office is still on the ground floor of our factory."

The size of L. L. Bean's building now stood at 36,000 square feet, and even the stairs on the side of the building had been enclosed, which made climbing them in the winter a much less risky undertaking. L. L. maintained an office over the stairs on the third floor, and dictated letters to his secretary in the main clerical office through what had been, until recently, an outside window. Improvements such as these enticed more and more people to visit the L.L. Bean, factory despite the fact that it evidently still lacked a proper showroom.

As noted above, 1939 was also the year that L. L. began experimenting with the concept of staying open twenty-four hours a day—he probably figured if the sports were going to drive all night to get to their camps or hunting grounds, he might as well be open so they could stop in on the way. "L. L. Bean, in the beginning," noted George L. Moses in the *Cape Cod Standard-Times*, "opened his place at all hours in self-defense. . . . Hunters and fishermen from out-of-state do most of their traveling on Sundays. Vast numbers of them, actually, thus roll through Freeport on a Sunday and often late at night and early in the morning. In the old days, having come so far, they felt somewhat free to thump on L. L. Bean's window and get him up to trade."

Actually, it probably wasn't L. L. the hunters had rousted at 3:30 in the morning but his oldest brother, Henry, who worked the graveyard shift as a sort of night watchman. Henry sold them their shoelaces, left their money by the cash register, and mentioned the event to his brother later in the morning. According to John Gould:

> The next day there was a push-bell on the building, with a little night-light and a card that said, "Push once a minute until clerk appears." Henry was the clerk, and as he made regular rounds to inspect the building he was often out of hearing of the bell. I rang one night, and it took 25 minutes to bring him. Henry looked and acted so much like L. L. that hundreds of customers, in those earlier days, thought L. L. himself stayed on duty all night.

But Bean's first shot at staying open around the clock lasted only about a year. By 1940, the store's operating hours had been cut to twenty, and by the end of the World War II the building was closed between 1:30 and 7:00 A.M. (The current twenty-four-hour system wouldn't be implemented until 1951.) Even though the bulk of his business was still done through the mail, L. L. Bean was more than happy to welcome walk-in customers.

The size of Mr. Bean's building may have been steadily growing, but it seems that, at the end of the decade, the amount of his sales was actually shrinking. According to a 1992 L.L. Bean calendar (probably prepared as a handout for the firm's employees), in 1939, L. L. employed eighty-five people and had $743,990 in sales—quite a nosedive after the company had reportedly hit the $1 million mark just two years earlier. (A photo taken on August 28, 1939, during a clambake at "Burnett's" shows L. L. surrounded by about fifty employees and their family members.)

If Bean's business had in fact slowed, it wasn't because people were pinching pennies, recalled Carlene Griffin. "Nobody had any pennies," she said. "There was absolutely nothing." Maybe everybody figured they had everything they needed by then or they were just "making do" until the economy improved. As the country was recovering from the Great Depression, Bean's busy time remained November's deer-hunting season, as hunters were looking to put meat on the table, but even then they bought only what they needed to help them in their quests for food—a new pair of boots, perhaps.

In spite of his advancing age, L. L. Bean still enjoyed being active in the outdoors. Photos from the summer of 1939 show him shooting skeet and with some friends on a fishing trip at Moosehead Lake, but life's everyday activities were becoming more difficult for him as he approached seventy. The first medical problem to pop up around this time was the loss of sight in one eye, probably as the result of a cataract.

L. L., apparently undaunted, forged ahead in spite of his bad eye. "I can still see plenty out of the other," he reportedly told people, and even continued to go duck hunting with a specially made shotgun. According to his grandson, Leon Gorman, Bean's double-barreled Parker shotgun was made with the stock offset to the right so the barrels would fall under his good left eye. Another concession he made to having only one good eye was the fact that the shotgun was a twenty-gauge, which was safer to use than his old twelve-gauge, which had more of a recoil, or "kick." The gun was bored tight for a duck-hunting choke.

Interestingly, L. L. Bean himself twice states that he lost the sight in his other eye. A photo caption on page 50 of his autobiography reads: "1940. Right after I lost the sight of my left eye," while the caption of another photo on page 78, showing him and his second wife on a fishing trip, reads, in part, "She was my nurse a few years ago, when I lost the sight in my left eye."

But L. L. Bean's biggest loss would come in the spring. In his autobiography, he wrote simply, "Bertha Porter Bean, mother of my three children Carlton, Warren, and Barbara, died in May 1939, at the age of seventy-three." Suffering from acute bronchial asthma, which caused "acute circulatory collapse," Bertha passed away on May 22. L. L. and Bertha had been married for forty-one years.

At his age, L. L. was having to rapidly accept loss, in one form or another, as a fact of life—and the death of his wife and partial loss of vision, which had befallen him in quick succession, were only the beginning. A photograph from November of 1939, probably taken at Thanksgiving and showing the five Bean brothers all wearing suits, would probably be the last one taken of Henry, Otho, L. L., Ervin, and Guy all together.

Chapter 6

. . . at the age of seventy-four, he realized that
he was famous—really famous

Throughout the 1940s, L. L. Bean's fame and the fortunes of his bustling business continued to grow despite the facts that another world war was looming on the horizon and L. L. himself was in his late sixties as the decade started. In June 1940, Dorothy Gluck's article about Mrs. Roosevelt's visit to Mr. Bean's establishment ran in *Yankee* magazine, prompting regular folk and perhaps even a few more well-known people to undertake a trip to L. L.'s outdoors emporium. Sometimes their journeys to Mr. Bean's establishment were for shopping, but often their reason for traveling to Freeport was just so they could meet the man behind the persona.

As the size of Bean's product line and marketing budgets increased, so did the frequency of his catalog drops. Beginning in the 1940s, Bean's regular catalogs, hundreds of thousands of which were now being mailed out each spring and fall, would be joined by the occasional summer camping and winter supplements. But just because L. L. Bean kept adding more and more Bean-branded gear to his catalog (the Hudson Bay Company blankets were still the only items sold under another vendor's name), it didn't necessarily mean that the thrifty Yankee wanted his fellow sports to buy more gear than they actually needed.

Often the contrary was true, with L. L. appearing determined to make sure that his customers got just what it took to do the job—no more than they needed and certainly no less. By the spring of 1940, L. L. and his buddies were sure that they'd narrowed down the number of flies any bass fisherman could possibly need to six, and he wasn't shy about saying so. Under the heading "Bean's Big Six Bass Flies," L. L. confidently stated:

After considering dozens of bass flies, we have decided to eliminate all but the six shown below.

You don't have to experiment with dozens of flies to find the ones that will catch bass. We have done that for you. If bass won't take one of these flies, the chances are one hundred to one they are not rising. Tied on a No. 3 sprout hook with turned down eye or short gut.

Price 25¢ each. All six in sheepskin roll same as shown on page 4, $1.45 postpaid. Price with spinner 35¢ each, 6 for $2.00.

For the record, Bean's Big Six Bass Flies were: Col. Fuller, Parmacheene Belle, Scarlet Ibis, Montreal, Brown Hackle, and Gray Hackle. L. L. made a similar listing for Atlantic Salmon Flies, but since he didn't think he knew a lot about this particular aspect of fly-fishing, he compiled this ranking by conducting a survey of fishermen who did. Their top six choices, in this order, were: Silver Doctor, Jock Scott, Black Dose, Dusty Miller, Silver Gray, and Durham Ranger. (Previously, L. L. had decided that "nine flies in two sizes are all that are necessary" for brook trout, while it took only "twelve flies in two sizes" to be successful in catching land-locked salmon. As spare as his selection of flies already was, the frugal Bean was able to winnow his selection of lures even further, concluding that for both types, as he later told *Saturday Evening Post* writer Arthur Bartlett, "four or five will answer nicely.")

Another item that would soon take its place in Bean's catalog alongside the fishing tackle and hip waders were shoes for nurses.

While business was good, it was also a time of great loss for L. L. Bean. On top of having lost his wife, Bertha, and the sight in one eye the previous year, L. L. would suffer, in quick succession, the loss in 1940 of two of his four brothers. Ervin, L. L.'s next-to-youngest brother, died in Belgrade Lakes of apoplexy (stroke), following a brief illness. The death certificate lists Ervin's "Usual Occupation" as "Merchant, General Store." In his autobiography, L. L. writes that his brother had been born on January 15, 1877, married Inez White of Belgrade, and worked as a merchant. Ervin Bean died on August 7, 1940, at the age of sixty-three.

Several weeks later, Henry passed away following a lengthy stay in the Freeport Hospital. Though the immediate cause of death is given as "uremia due to staphylococcus," Henry also suffered from "prostate obstruction." His occupation is listed as "Traveling Salesman, Sporting Goods." Of this brother, L. L. wrote that Henry was born on February 17, 1865. He married May Brackett and was a shoe salesman. He had two sons: Earle Henry Bean of Belmont, Massachusetts, and Norman Stuart Bean of Florida. Henry Warren Bean, the eldest of the five Bean brothers, died on October 15, 1940, at the age of seventy-five.

Two of the few bright spots in L. L. Bean's personal life that year had come in July, first on the 3rd, when his younger son, thirty-eight-year-old Warren, married twenty-year-old Hazel June Turner in Bowdoinham (the two would divorce in 1951), and again toward the end of the month, when the sixty-eight-year-old merchant married Lucille "Claire" Boudreau, a forty-six-year-old registered nurse in Belmont, Massachusetts. She had been one of L. L.'s nurses during his recent series of eye operations, which explains the sudden appearance in his catalog of such an uncharacteristically Bean item as nurses' shoes. It was always L. L. Bean's nature to sell what he knew.

THOUGH HE'D REACHED A CERTAIN AGE "and could have slacked off," according to a company-published scrapbook, "'L. L.' remained in active control of the company." At least while he was in Maine, that is. Maybe his new wife had something to do with it or maybe L. L. just realized that it was time to slow down a little bit and enjoy life. Whatever the reason, by the end of 1940, L. L. had come to the conclusion that it was time to start spending a good part of Maine's long, cold winters in warm, sunny Florida. During the month or so he spent in the Sunshine State, L. L.'s business affairs were seen to mostly by his son Carl and somewhat less by his other son, Warren. Eventually, L. L. and Claire would spend as many as three or even four months in Florida each winter.

"When L. L. started spending his winters in Florida," recalls Carlene Griffin in her memoir *Spillin' the Beans*, "he was deprived of the deep Maine woods and northern lakes and bays, so he threw himself wholeheartedly into deep-sea fishing. In time, it became as much a passion for him as traipsing through the snows of Maine on the trail of deer or bear, and he often sent photographs and letters back to the company full of enthusiastic accounts of his new hobby." Ironically, during the winter of 1940–41, the first one the Beans spent in Florida, it was Claire, not her famous sportsman husband, who reeled in the couple's first sailfish on February 14, 1941. Was it beginner's luck? Probably, since Claire had never fished before marrying L. L., and caught a fish on her first cast.

The photo caption of the smiling Claire next to the big fish published in the *Portland Sunday Telegram* of February 23, 1941, tells us even more:

> Mrs. L. L. Bean of Freeport established a boat record for the season when she landed this eight-foot sailfish on a light rod while fishing with Mr. Bean and Capt. C. O. Savage 20 miles north of Palm Beach, Fla. last week. In reporting the catch, Mr. Bean said the fish jumped clear of the water almost immediately after being hooked and fought furiously for more than 45 minutes before Mrs. Bean finally brought the trophy to gaff. Mr. and Mrs. Bean are at the Royal Poinciana Apartments at Palm Beach for several weeks and doing considerable fishing off the Florida coast.

The following May, Claire's sailfish would be entered in the 1941 National Sportsman Hunting & Fishing contest, which had a $3,000 first prize. L. L. believed the fish had a fine chance of winning a major prize in the sailfish division. L. L. wouldn't catch his own first Florida sailfish until the following winter.

As nearly as anyone can remember, it was around 1940 that L. L. "put in a hospital plan for his employees," years before the idea had even occurred to most other businesses. Later would come Christmas cash, and that would be on top of profit sharing and an annual bonus. No doubt, L. L. liked to look out for his employees but maybe, just maybe, all this generosity came about because a little holiday cash for his loyal employees could help assuage L. L.'s guilt about leaving them back in snowy Maine far better than any tacky postcard or crate of oranges—which he sometimes did send north along with grapefruit and other "Florida specialties."

One time, L. L. did send something from Florida that boosted the morale of his workers quite a bit—but it happened sort of by accident. One year, two weeks before he was due to arrive back in Maine, L. L. shipped up a beautiful smoked sailfish he'd planned on keeping for his own personal dining enjoyment. There was a mix-up with the shipping orders and, instead of being delivered directly to L. L.'s home a block away on Holbrook Street, the fish ended up on the desk in his vacant office, where human nature eventually took its course. After a few days, some passerby could resist temptation no longer and took a piece of the fish. More pieces quickly disappeared until one side of the sailfish was gone. After that the other side quickly followed.

When L. L. arrived home and went looking for his fish, everyone in the place could remember seeing it on his desk a while ago, but no one could seem to recall who'd eaten the thing. "L. L. wasn't as much angry about it," recalled Griffin, "as he was disgusted. 'Just plain disgusted,' as one of his close associates put it with a twinkle in his eye."

In case one fish story wasn't enough in 1940, L. L. Bean would soon add a few more—as well as hunting stories, camping stories, and lists of equipment. "That was the year," according to John Gould, "that he got the writing bug." Maybe, now that he'd started to slow down ever so slightly, he had more free time—enough perhaps to write a brief book. In the introduction to *My Story*, Gould noted that:

> . . . one day in a sales conference there came up the question of an outdoors book. A book they could list in the catalog, and would be the kind of authentic wildlife book nobody else had. Bean mentioned it to his author friends, and they told him he ought to write it. He spoke to me about it, and I handed him a

picture I had—the one of L. L. and the moose which [would become the book's] frontispiece. . . . I made the negative in 1935 when he brought the damned thing home from Canada.[1]

Another generally accepted reason L. L. Bean decided to finally write a book about hunting, fishing, and camping was simply that he'd grown tired of dispensing the same pieces of advice over and over. It had reached a point where so many people had taken him up on the offer in his earlier editorials saying "everyone is welcome to call for advice on where to hunt and fish," that he was now spending as much time on the telephone as he was running his business. And then there were the letters, so many, in fact, that a catalog ad for his book would include the sentence, "This book on how to Hunt, Fish, and Camp is the answer to hundreds of letters asking for information on these subjects." Why keep repeating himself, he figured, when he could put all that wisdom into a book and make a profit to boot.

It had already become readily apparent from his "interesting" descriptions of the items in his catalog, that L. L. Bean would never earn a place among the state's literary elite—and at least one major publisher had already told him so. (After the war, another scribe would remark that L. L. "often does considerable violence to academic English.") No one was more aware of his limitations as a writer than L. L. himself, but he still wanted to write the book, and when he decided to do something, who was going to stop him? Gould recalled that "one author, experienced in the sadder aspects of belles-lettres, told him anybody with a press could print a book, but it took a sales organization afterward to make the difference. That settled it, for best of all Bean knew selling. Half the people in Alaska were on his snowshoes and satisfied, and now for a book."[2] Though the seed had germinated, it would be another two years before L. L. Bean's first literary effort would bear fruit.

IN 1941 L. L. BOUGHT THE LAND across Morse Street and started construction on a three-story building that would expand his company's total floor space to 63,000 square feet. Bean's new 27,000-

square-foot building would be located just across the way, to the rear of the neighboring Oxnard Block, because L. L. had been unable to purchase any more land behind his existing factory. The new structure, which would be connected to the Warren Block via an enclosed walkway over Morse Street, wouldn't be completed until 1942. But once it was finished the new Gorman Building would put L.L. Bean, Inc., in a class by itself.

"Bean to Have the Largest Building in Town," proclaimed the headline in the June 20, 1941, edition of the *Freeport Press*. And it would be the largest by quite a bit, no mean feat considering that the town still had four operating shoe factories at the time. According to the article, the new building would house the following businesses:

> The Dingley Press, formerly of Portland, will occupy the entire first floor. This concern has a contract with Mr. Bean for printing all his semi-annual catalogs for the next ten years as well as continuing their marine hardware catalog printing.
>
> The top floor will be used by Geo. Soule in his fishing-fly business and the manufacture of other fishing goods.
>
> The middle floor will house the stitching room where many of Bean's products will originate.

In the second paragraph, the reporter mentions George Soule's fishing-fly business, for which he and his associate, Sewall MacWilliams, rented space from L. L. before the two decided to try their hand at decoy-making. The article failed to mention the fact that the Freeport post office would be expanded to take up all of the first floor at its present location in the Warren Block—at no expense whatsoever to the taxpayers. An artist's conception of the entire Bean complex at the time clearly showed its impressive size but omitted the Oxnard Block, replacing it with green space. Also, in what may have been a misguided attempt to emphasize the factory's proximity to the ocean, the picture also shows the Atlantic just behind Bean's buildings to the north when it's really two miles away in the other direction.

Bean's growing concern was beginning to attract a lot of attention; his business had already been the subject of articles in the January 4 edition of the *Portland Press Herald* and in the article "Keep It Quaint" by Lester C. Walker in the June 1 issue of *Forbes* magazine. In December, *Reader's Digest* would also run "Bean, the Happy Hunter" by Webb Waldron. But the first big national exposure L. L. Bean's company would receive came on October 13, 1941, his sixty-ninth birthday, when that week's issue of *Life* magazine featured a four-page photo spread about the Yankee merchant and his mail-order empire. (Mrs. Gluck's recent article in the regional *Yankee* magazine had vividly recounted the First Lady's unannounced visit to L.L. Bean, but hadn't really said much about his business.) By L. L.'s own estimation, it would have cost him about $48,000 had he purchased those same four pages for advertising, but it's probably just as well that he hadn't—any momentum the piece generated in November, when the orders started arriving in the mail, stalled right after the Japanese attack on Pearl Harbor.

Though the timing of the *Life* article proved unfortunate, that wouldn't really be much of a problem for L. L. Bean, whose company now sent out 300,000 of its 80-page catalogs twice a year. Nearly 90 percent of the company's business was done through the mail, which meant that the cataloger accounted for nearly 80 percent of the business at the Freeport post office. "The mail is so heavy (500 outgoing sacks on rush days)," reported the piece, "that recently when the U.S. Government offered to build Freeport a new $85,000 post office, Mr. Bean countered by spending $25,000 of his own to enlarge the existing post office on the ground floor of his store." L. L.'s subsidization of the post office not only amazed the bureaucrats in Washington, it also made his brother Guy, who was still Freeport's postmaster at the time, famous in postal circles as the only postmaster in history ever to refuse an appropriation.

After the war, Washington would again suggest that the town needed a new post office, "but L. L. finds it hard to believe," according the *Saturday Evening Post* in 1946, "that even the Government would be so un-Yankee as to upset the present ideal arrangement just because it has some money to spend and the old post office is a bit antiquated." By then, Guy had established a "government-controlled space" in a room on the same level as the factory, into which L. L.'s workers sent packages by means of a conveyer belt. The mail then dropped down a chute to the post office below. The Freeport post office would remain in the Warren Block until 1962, when it moved north to its present location on the same side of Main Street—all of 700 feet away.

The post office wasn't just the company's primary way of shipping packages in '41; it was also L.L. Bean's main method of communicating with its customers. Most of the orders for products came through the mail and, increasingly frequently, it was becoming necessary for the company to correspond with a purchaser in order to straighten out a problem or two. To help streamline this process, L. L. or one of his assistants came up with the idea of developing a form letter, an early example of which was mailed (with a three-cent stamp) to regular customer John Perkins, who'd also corresponded with the company in 1934. Below the company's letterhead, which still proclaimed "Manufacturer, Leather and Canvas Specialties," the body of the letter looked like this:

Dec. 29, 1941
John R. Perkins
Wayne, Maine
Dear Customer:
As we are unable to purchase certain materials, we are obliged to cancel your order for Norwegian Type Moccasin (come one width only). We could furnish the regular Indian Moccasins with sole at $3.50.
Enclosed find refund for $2.25 sent for Camp Moccasins.
Yours truly,
LLB:D
L.L. Bean, Inc.
Encl. $2.25

The materials for the moccasins had probably become unavailable due to the recent outbreak of hostilities with the Germans and

Japanese. Apparently the amount returned to Mr. Perkins turned out to be insufficient and, on January 20, 1942, he received a pre-printed card with which he was refunded an additional 30 cents.

Evidently the start of the war hadn't been sufficient to deter former baseball great Babe Ruth (1895–1948) from doing a little hunting, as shown in a recent photo he'd sent to L. L. The picture shows the smiling Bambino, reportedly clad in L.L. Bean hunting clothes and boots, holding his trophy, a pheasant, in his right hand and a shotgun in his left.

Early in the new year, L. L. Bean chartered a boat from Palm Beach's Inlet Dock, and finally managed to equal his wife in the big fish department. Justifiably proud of his accomplishment, L. L. would later include a photo of himself and the boat's skipper flanking his catch in his 1960 autobiography. Probably because of his success, L. L. would see fit to include a chapter about saltwater fishing in his new outdoors how-to book.

No doubt he'd previously done some fishing off the coast of Maine in the Bailey Island area, but the chapter in his book was probably inspired by his fishing trips in Florida and he just tweaked it to apply to the bluefin tuna, striped bass, and mackerel found along the coast of Maine. The section on saltwater fishing, which also included a few lines about surf casting and fly-fishing, was the book's final sporting chapter, appearing just before a long one about Baxter State Park.

Though it was far from the scale of Percival Baxter's effort, L. L. would make his pitch for conservation in his soon-to-be-published book, *Hunting, Fishing, and Camping*, penning a whole chapter on "How To Prevent Forest Fires." He starts by citing some recent statistics about forest fires in Maine:

In 1941 about 31% of the forest fires in Maine were caused by careless smokers and campers.

The fire hazard in Maine, with its 16,270,000 acres of forest land, has become a serious matter.

Maine issued 163,641 hunting and fishing licenses last year (1941). This army of hunters, fishermen, and campers can be a great help to prevent forest fires.

In 1941 forest fires in Maine burned over 40,353 acres. The opportunities for recreation, sport, and other out-of-door activities, as offered in certain sections of this State, will no longer be available if fires are allowed to claim their heavy toll.

Bean goes on to list eight rules for making sure that a campfire doesn't get out of control, then concludes the chapter by noting that even curved pieces of glass from a broken bottle can "intensify the rays of the sun shining on them to the point where fire can ignite the dry leaves, duff, or humus beneath. The best time to stop a forest fire is just before you start it. A Fire-Proof forest demands one-hundred percent public cooperation. Wild Life depends on the forest. Keep Them Green."

No one seems to be sure, really, exactly when L. L. Bean tired of seeing famous folks and fly-fishermen alike making their way through his factory—following directions on makeshift cardboard signs before eventually finding their way to his tiny, cluttered shopping area—and finally decided to open a proper merchandise showroom. Reports such as "the . . . firm didn't get around to opening the salesroom until about 1940"[3] are countered by other assertions that the showroom definitely opened in 1945.

Some clues as to just when the first showroom actually opened came from L. L. Bean himself when he decided to list the two decades-worth of additions he'd made to his business since buying the Warren Block in 1920:

> I made additions to the building as follows:
> 1922 Stitching Room Addition:
>   3 floors 12' x 57'. Total   2,052 sq. ft.
> 1934 Salesroom Addition:
>   3 floors each 2,140 sq. ft. Total   6,420 sq. ft.
> 1935 Back Stitching Room and Fly Room
> Addition:
>   3 floors 43' x 46'. Total   5,934 sq. ft.
> 1936 Employees' Stairway and My

Office Addition:

    3 floors 8' x 41'. Total   984 sq. ft.

1937 Clothing Room Addition:

    3 floors 41' x 69'. Total   8,487 sq. ft.

1939 Accounting and Buyers' Office and
Addition to Salesroom:

    3 floors 26' x 68' (5,304 sq. ft.)

    1 floor 26' x 26' (Bridge, 676 sq. ft.)

        Total   5,980 sq. ft.

1942 Gorman Building Addition:

    3 floors 79' x 114'. Total   27,018 sq. ft.[4]

From this list we can see that L. L. Bean had what *he* thought of as a showroom as early as 1934, but that he probably didn't open what everyone else considered a showroom until around 1942, when the just-completed addition to his factory finally provided him with the space for a proper display area. Then again, maybe he waited for a sure sign that the war was about to end soon. Whenever the showroom eventually materialized, it was open twenty hours a day, until 3:00 A.M., and proved to be a big improvement over the cramped quarters in which Bean's 200 or so daily customers had previously found themselves. "People wandered through the factory," said longtime employee Mel Collins. "We'd fit 'em right in the factory. They'd look around, see if anyone was lookin', and try on pants right there in the aisle."[5]

When he was back in Maine, his company's use of form letters and other small steps toward efficiency, along with the help of a capable staff, still left the seventy-year-old L. L. plenty of time for fishing He could head for nearby Pratt's Pond, which he owned and kept well stocked with trout, or take off on a fishing excursion to Canada, where his day's salmon catch reportedly set records.

Ever mindful of the value of capitalizing on his sporting achievements, L. L. sent a photo of himself and his mid-June haul to the *Portland Sunday Telegram*, which printed the snapshot with the following caption: "Taking five salmon in a single day, L. L. Bean of Freeport Saturday broke the record for the famous Plaster

Rock pool on the Tobique River in New Brunswick. Mr. Bean, shown above with his record day's catch, also set another unusual record by taking each fish on a different pattern of salmon fly. The fish, which weighed from $8^1/_2$ to $9^1/_2$ pounds each, were all landed on a $5^1/_2$-ounce rod."

Just prior to the start of the war, L. L. Bean had decided that he wanted to buy a pleasure boat. (Longtime employee Wid Griffin remembers that L. L. actually had two such Chris Crafts, one at South Freeport and another at his camp on Sebago Lake. This story is about the one up at Sebago.) But just because L. L. had been lucky enough to get a big boat around the time of the war didn't mean that he was actually lucky; L. L. would find out the hard way that shortages of both manpower and materials were already beginning to affect the quality of consumer goods.

Since he usually kept his boat at his camp on Sebago Lake, he must have figured that he needed a big boat for big lake. "[I]t was about twenty feet long," George Soule remembered nearly fifty years later, "and he was having it delivered to one of the launching ramps at Lake Sebago." (If the nearby canoe in a photo of L. L.'s boat is a 20-foot Maine Guide model, then Bean's "Cabin Boat" is actually about 28 or 30 feet long.) "When the boat arrived, L. L. got a bunch of us from the shop to unload it, and after we finished, L. L. sort of sidled up to me and said, 'George, these other fellows are going back, but we ought to try this boat out.'"[6]

Shortly after the two got underway in the new craft, several spokes fell out of the steering wheel. After they'd been replaced, the flywheel fell off the engine. Soon, the pair drifted ashore at a vacant camp, where they found some tools and made a temporary fix to the engine. The flywheel stayed on long enough to get them almost back to L. L.'s camp before it fell off again. After they had once again drifted ashore, L. L. called the engine manufacturer who sent a mechanic up the next day to fix the problem. L. L. had the mechanic stay around to make sure everything was in proper working order, and it's a good thing he did—no sooner had they gotten underway than the flywheel fell off a third time. The mechanic then promised L. L. they'd change the engine and have his new boat ready to go in a couple of days.

A few days later, the man called and told L. L. that the new motor was running just fine and the boat was ready to go. L. L. hurried to his camp, eager to finally take his new craft out for a spin, only to find it sunk at the dock. "The new engine didn't line up just where the old one did," said Soule, "so they had to bore four new holes in the hull. The trouble was they forgot to plug the old holes." Once he'd gotten the bugs worked out, L. L. was as proud of his boat as he'd been of his first car, that 1920 Reo, even featuring a picture of the craft in the book he was working on. The photo caption read, "Fishing party, with guides and a string of canoes, starting for Spencer Bay, Moosehead Lake, Maine. On reaching their destination each guide will take one or two fishermen in a canoe. (The Author's Cabin Boat is in the foreground.)"[7]

Around this time, L. L. started taking his grandchildren out on his boat for some of their fishing expeditions. According to Leon Gorman's recollection of one outing, a good time was *not* had by all:

> I remember trolling with L. L. when he had a place on one of the Belgrade Lakes in Maine. He'd take us fishing up there when we were little, but he didn't have a lot of tolerance for kids not catching fish. They weren't fun times. He just couldn't sit back and see us foul up the landing of a trout or a bass or whatever. After a lot of yelling, he'd eventually take the rod away and land the fish himself. We were either letting slack in the line or reeling too fast. I know that makes him sound mean, but he really was a good guy. He just couldn't contain himself. L. L. was almost always good-natured and affable. I can't imagine anybody not liking him. Even when he was upset about something, he was upset in kind of a humorous and likable way.[8]

Did L. L. ever take him hunting? "Only once," Gorman says.[9]

DURING THE SUMMER, L. L. also found the time to finish writing his book on outdoors skills, which had come about, he said, so he didn't have to spend much of his day giving advice to greenhorns over the phone and in letters, and "to put all the answers between two covers and let 'em pay for 'em." The Dingley Press printed the first edition of L. L. Bean's first book, *Hunting, Fishing, and Camping* (the title of which was sometimes strangely punctuated as *Hunting-Fishing and Camping*, as if L. L. viewed hunting and fishing as one thing and camping as quite another). The first 5,000 copies of the book, which was priced at a dollar, sold out almost immediately and were quickly followed by 10,000 more. A 1944 copy of the book, already in its fourth printing, consists of 43 chapters and a total of 104 pages.

But wait. There's a reason—besides the fact that "the instructions are so condensed"—that the introduction says "the reading time of the whole book is only 85 minutes." It's because the book is really only 88 pages long (the text starts on page 7, and ends on page 94). This makes its average chapter almost exactly two pages long, including photos and small illustrations, of which there are a total of 114—plus a table on fly rods. The book's final ten pages consist of reprints of Chapters 3, 4, 14, 15, and 16 ("How to Dress a Deer," "How to Hang Up a Deer," "Signals for Hunters," "How to Use a Compass," and "How to Find a Lost Hunter") for the sport to cut out and keep with him. (John Gould reported that "Mr. Bean has never lost a reader.") These reprints are followed by six blank pages, which Bean called "memorandum pages," so the sport can make notes about his own outings.

The very first line of the book's introduction stated in no uncertain terms that the author's intention was "to give definite information in the fewest words possible on how to Hunt, Fish, and Camp," and to dispense with tall tales of his own many outdoor experiences. And that's exactly what he did. "To make this book as brief as possible I am dealing only with major information," he continued. "Minor details are easily learned by practice."

John G. Mock, outdoors editor of the *Pittsburgh Press*, concurred, writing that L. L.'s book "lacks all the flowery expressions and gives only the meat. It's nicely illustrated and gotten up in a style which immediately appeals to all outdoorsmen." He went on to describe the basic layout of the book, after which he concluded his review by noting: "It is obtainable direct from the author, L. L. Bean, Freeport, Maine. Inquiry will be welcomed."

And it was available *only* from Freeport. After the book had been on the market for about fifteen years, recalled fellow writer John Gould, "a publisher wanted to buy copies in quantity, and Bean told him he could buy copies the same as anybody else, by mail, postage prepaid, at list price." From time to time, bookstore owners would approach L. L., asking to sell his book in their shops, but would always leave disappointed after L. L. told them his terms. "More bother 'n it's worth,"[10] he would say.

For retail purchasers, according to Gould, "If requested, he'd autograph copies with a rubber stamp." He also noted that "it had a vinyl cover so a rain shower wouldn't hurt it." (He's probably talking about the first edition L. L. had given him as a gift: "He gave me the first copy of *Hunting, Fishing, and Camping*, inscribed 'From one author to another,' and he has the word author in quotes." Other editions of the book are known to have had red covers or green and black covers, among other probable colors, which were "cloth bound.")

By the fall of 1942, L. L. had already made some minor adjustments to the book, which would be printed in several incarnations throughout its long life. A full-page ad for Bean's "Improved Revised Book" on page 46D of that season's catalog made sure everyone knew that the latest issue would be "off the press September 15th." The book would sell consistently, five to ten thousand copies a year, for the next two decades.

To ensure the continued profitability of his tiny tome, he'd send free copies to boys who'd written to him. "The boys' fathers see 'em," he reasoned, "and I get orders for more," not to mention orders for sporting equipment. (In an interesting aside, it's around this time that the letterhead of L.L. Bean, Inc., changed to reflect the company's emphasis on sporting goods. The tag line below the logo now described the business as "Manufacturer of Hunting and Camping Specialties" instead of "Manufacturer, Leather and Canvas Specialties.")

As for the profitability of Mr. Bean's book, here's a breakdown from John Gould of just how well L. L. made out on his first foray into the world of publishing. The following comes from the *New York Times Book Review* of June 9, 1957:

On the first printing, Bean's net cost, delivered to the customer, was 32 cents a copy, but the second printing dropped to 22 cents. It leveled off at 25 cents for a long time, but gradually went up until the fifteenth printing hit 50 cents. In the meantime, he has advanced the retail price to $1.25. Authors will be interested to observe that his net accrual is now 75 cents on a $1.25 sale; whereas in 1942 he made only 68 cents on a $1 sale.[11]

In addition to providing his fellow Freeporter with the photo of him and his moose, John Gould would also pen a lengthy introduction to Bean's second "major" literary effort, his slender 1960 autobiography, as well as mention him in several of the weekly articles he'd write for the *Christian Science Monitor* over the next sixty years. Coincidentally, 1942 was the year that Gould got his start writing for the *Monitor*, after sending some of his work on speculation to the newspaper's editor, Erwin Dain Canham (1904–82). Gould's first article appeared in the paper on October 21, 1942.

As America ramped up its involvement in the Second World War, there were shortages of just about everything. L. L.'s company would have to make do despite shortages of commodities such as rubber, paper, and metal. L.L. Bean, Inc., would especially miss the rubber, a photo caption in the company's 1987 scrapbook noting that "the bottoms of the Maine Hunting Shoe were made of a black synthetic material. Because the bottom material was not the 'real McCoy,' 'L. L.' changed the name to Leather Top Boots and returned to the old name after the war." Compounding the shortage of rubber and other vital materials was the government-imposed wartime ban on hunting and the sale of hunting equipment. In light of these shortages and regulations, Maine Hunting

Shoes would officially be known by their new name until the release of the spring catalog in 1947.

Even L. L. Bean was prone to the occasional slip-up; though he was mindful of the government's ban on the sale of hunting equipment, the fact that his boot bottoms were now made of synthetics occasionally slipped his mind—like the time he listed "one pair 12 (in.) Leather Top Rubbers" as his footwear of choice for your next deer-hunting trip in the 1944 edition of his book, which, incidentally, continued to use the word "hunting" in its title.

A later article in the *Saturday Evening Post* would also refer to them as "leather-top rubbers." (Even though the war had been over for more than a year by then, the boot wouldn't be called the Maine Hunting Shoe again for several more months.) Whatever their technical name, the government placed a large order for Bean's boots to issue to soldiers and sailors serving overseas, thanks in large part to L. L.'s first stint as a cold-weather gear "expert" with the War Department in Washington.

In the fall of 1942, L. L. traveled to Washington to work on a special committee whose objective was to recommend cold-weather apparel for the army. When it came to selecting footwear for the troops, there was a lot of disagreement within the group about the appropriate height of their leather-top boots. Experts from the west and the south favored boots as high as 18 inches, but L. L., knowing from experience that footwear that tall would cause a soldier to tire quickly, lobbied for a 10-inch version. He also pointed out that a typical soldier walking seven miles a day in the taller boots would lift the extra eight ounces 18,480 times, or a total of 4,620 extra pounds. Manufacture of the shorter boots, he noted, would also use less elk hide, which was both scarce and expensive. A compromise was reached when the committee decided to specify a 12-inch model that was based on L. L.'s famous boot.

> Similar boots were used aboard ship, on wet and icy decks, and as it was necessary at times for a man to get out of them in a hurry before he went into the water, they asked for ideas on a "quick release" fastening. Many elaborate schemes were

devised, but my son, Carl, came up with a very simple idea—instead of lacing the five eyelets from the bottom up, a small loop was made in the laces, and they were laced from the top eyelet down. In an emergency a man grasped the small loop at the top and the laces came out, leaving him free to kick off the boots.[12]

The naval version of Bean's footwear, which featured a non-slip sole for use on aircraft carriers, did eventually feature Carl's lacing system, but not until L. L. had proven to the navy that it was better than the system they'd had in mind. L. L. countered the navy's system by sending two pairs of boots down to Washington so they could do a test of their own to see which ones could be gotten out of faster. One pair was laced the navy way and the other pair the Bean way. Shortly afterward, the navy began ordering the Bean version of the boot.

In *In Search of L. L. Bean*, his mid-1980s history of the company, M. R. Montgomery would spend an entire page of the book attempting to explain and then replicate Carl's esoteric lacing arrangement. But Carl's system wasn't a mystery to everyone; in fact Carlene Griffin recalls chatting with an old friend who used to be pretty good at it. "Bean's," she wrote, "made many 'navy boots' (similar to the army version), and Mary Dyer remembers lacing them in the special way devised by Carl."

Despite the war, sales remained steady in Freeport. All the gear Bean sold to the government probably offset whatever income he lost on the sporting side of his business, and besides, L.L. Bean, Incorporated, was really small potatoes when compared to other wartime suppliers such as the Ford Motor Company. L. L.'s boots and briefcases, while important to the war effort, were hardly on the same order as Henry's Jeeps and B-24 Liberators. (Ford's specially built new plant at Willow Run, one of five production lines to build the heavy bomber, turned out several versions of America's most extensively produced wartime aircraft, rolling one off the assembly line every sixty-three minutes.) But then L. L. Bean didn't need a small army of managers to run his business. Nope;

his sons, son-in-law, and a few trusted others were sufficient to keep track of the company's growth, which in 1942 included the completion of the Gorman Building just across Morse Street.

L. L. also continued to go on his annual summertime Canadian fishing trip, a trip he would take until reaching the age of eighty-four. But the maladies of old age were beginning to hamper him in both his sporting endeavors and the activities of daily life. L. L. Bean's eye problem had been gradually joined by hardness of hearing, a problem he remedied by having Brice Roberts install an amplifier in his telephone, and by speaking to others in an increasingly loud voice. Bean's grandson, Leon Gorman, once told a reporter, "He was slightly deaf, so his voice boomed, and you could hear him a hundred yards away."[13]

"L. L. always talked as loudly as he could," remembers Gorman. "Being partially deaf, he seemed to assume everyone else was similarly impaired. The windows were always open, and so every presentation or discussion with L. L. was conducted with an audience of ten to twenty people listening to every word. . . . I'm sure my first conversation with L. L. was broadcast companywide in a matter of minutes."[14]

L. L.'s friend John Gould recalled how about half the men of Freeport would go to the post office every morning when the weather was warm just so they could stand below the merchant's open window and listen to his conversation with his stock broker. The system worked quite well, Gould said, until it began to get chilly and L. L. closed his window, leaving his fellow investors out in the cold until spring.

Kippy Goldrup said that he thought L. L. Bean had no use for Mr. Edison's invention at all, once telling Carlene Griffin, "He didn't need a telephone to call Portland [18 miles away], he just had to open the window!"

"You could hear him all over the world," Griffin once told a TV news reporter. "And he really didn't care much what he said either, you could hear it all."

Just as L. L. Bean's health was beginning its long, gradual decline, so too was his business's longtime home, the Warren

Block, which was nearing its fiftieth year. The tired old building's ground-floor structural members were beginning to fail, necessitating an elaborate system of exterior trusses, which became known around town as a "beam corset," to support the structure. Though the support system was probably meant to be a temporary fix, it would help to delay the Warren Block's demise until February 1977.

By the middle of the war, L. L. Bean was doing quite a bit of traveling around North America, heading to Canada for pleasure and Washington for business. At this point in his life, it almost seemed that L. L. continued to pursue his outdoorsy lifestyle not only because he enjoyed it, but also because he seemed to feel it was necessary to be out there in order to uphold his image as North America's preeminent sportsman. By now his wife, Claire, had become his hunting and fishing companion, and it was she who accompanied him on his annual fishing trip in New Brunswick in 1943, catching a record 22-pound salmon on the Restigouche River.

L. L. was recalled by the navy 1943 to help design a large briefcase for officers in training to carry their charts in. L. L.'s recall came in early July, when the War Department reappointed him—at $25 a day—to work as a "Departmental Expert" for the Office of the Quartermaster General's Military Planning Division Research and Development Bureau.

Once the government had settled on the briefcase's size and the number of pockets it should have, L.L. Bean, Inc., received an order for 40,000 of them. While it had been Carl who'd devised the quick-release lacing system for the navy's boots, it was L. L.'s other son, Warren, who designed their briefcase. "Warnie" decided to base the bag on an earlier design ("same as # 9 bag except for a few construction details"), and came up with a detailed plan for a briefcase that was 17 inches long and 14^1/$_2$ inches tall. The *Freeport Press* was tapped to print "U S N" on the side in 1^1/$_2$-inch letters located 4 inches from the top. L. L. learned later that the officers had carried the briefcases all over the world after their training was completed.

He also designed an axe for the army, which generated several small orders and still appeared in his catalog two decades later.

There's no doubt that L.L. Bean, Incorporated, designed and manufactured the boots and briefcases they supplied to the government, but the axes were probably made for Bean by the Snow and Nealley Company of Bangor, Maine, just as they had been for several years. (Snow and Nealley is now located across the Penobscot River in Brewer.) Founded by Charles Snow and Edward Bowdoin Nealley in 1864, the company was soon producing the axes and mauls that would become the cornerstones of their business.

After the Great War, Snow and Nealley had grown to meet the needs of the ever-expanding middle class, and in 1920, Edward's son William met with L. L. Bean to see about having his axes sold through the outdoorsman's catalog. It was the beginning of a relationship between the two companies that would last for decades. (In 1997 Snow & Nealley would sell its professional logging equipment division in order to focus on garden tools, woodworking equipment, and axes, including their signature Hudson Bay axe with its 24-inch hickory handle. The same head on an 18-inch handle is called the Penobscot Bay kindling axe.)

But L. L.'s time in Washington wasn't all work and no play. Fortunately for L. L., who was a big fan of our national pastime, he found time to take in several Washington Senators games while serving his country in our nation's capital. According to his grandson, Leon Gorman, L. L. spent about half his time in Washington at the ballpark. "He was quite a baseball fan." That year (1943) the Senators finished second, thirteen and a half games behind the division-winning New York Yankees, but ahead of L. L.'s beloved Boston Red Sox, who struggled to a seventh-place finish, twenty-nine games out.

The Pentagon had been dedicated on January 15, 1943. The 29-acre main building, which consisted of five concentric pentagons and seven levels (there are two below-ground levels under part of the building), was built at a cost of $49.6 million. Due to the wartime shortage of steel, it had been constructed almost entirely of concrete, which required 680,000 tons of sand and gravel dredged from the nearby Potomac River. The entire Pentagon complex had cost a total of $83 million. The groundbreaking ceremony for the building had been held on September 11, 1941.

During a cab ride back into town from the recently completed military headquarters, L. L. got the chance to pull a fast one on an unnamed army officer as they shared the cab. After the war, the story of L. L.'s encounter with the general was recounted by writer Arthur Bartlett at the beginning of a lengthy article in the *Saturday Evening Post*. It all started when L. L. happened to mention that he was from Freeport, Maine, while conveniently "forgetting" to introduce himself. The general took the bait:

> "Freeport?" he said. "That's L. L. Bean's town."
>
> "Ay-yah," the man from Maine agreed. "'Tis."
>
> "There's a man I'd sure like to meet," said the general. "L. L. Bean. I discovered him four or five years ago, and I've been buying from him ever since. By George, it's wonderful the way that man figures out just what you need for hunting and fishing. You hunt or fish?"
>
> "Ay-yah," said the Freeporter, "do a lot of it. Always use Bean's things too. Now, you take Bean's duck hunting coat. . . ."
>
> The conversation had hit high gear and continued, an exchange of hunting and fishing experiences, well interlarded with tributes to the equipment and clothing sold by the mail-order house of L. L. Bean, all the way to the hotel where the civilian was getting out. As he stepped from the cab, he extended his hand. "Pleased to meet you, general," he said. "My name's L. L. Bean."

Upon its publication in late 1946, the *Post* article would lead to another brief exchange during a WPOR radio interview with Freeport's own George Hunter:

> Q. [Quoting from the *Saturday Evening Post*] Was the general surprised when you told him your name was L. L. Bean?
> A. I'll say he was. It was almost another Pearl Harbor.

IN 1944, JOHN H. FIGI, JR., began pulling a little red wagon around Marshfield, Wisconsin, to deliver cheese. Three years earlier, Figi, a federal cheese grader, had begun his business, the Wisconsin Cheese Club, by mailing out cheese he'd dipped into melted wax on the family's kitchen stove. Proving he was every bit as resourceful as L. L. Bean, whose second item—wool socks—was a tie-in to his boots, John Figi was soon buying thousands of center cuts left over from the manufacture of wooden toilet seats, which he had silk-screened with his company's logo and sold as cutting boards.

Eventually his Wisconsin Cheese Club would grow into the multimillion-dollar Figi's Gifts in Good Taste, which now sells meats, cheeses, nuts, and candies worldwide through the mail. What in the world does John Figi's budding food gift business have to do with L. L. Bean? Nothing yet, but in about thirty year's time Figi and his seasonally utilized computer system would play a big part in maintaining the mailing lists of L. L. Bean, Inc.—as well as those of some of his rivals.

Though L.L. Bean, Inc., did continue to publish its "72-page" catalog during the war, it was about 10 percent smaller than the company's previous 72-page offering had been. Due to the unavailability of some merchandise, wartime versions of Bean's catalog simply omitted pages 7 through 10 and 63 through 66. While some attribute the abridging of Bean's booklet to a shortage of paper, L. L. himself explained the catalog's odd page-numbering system to his customers by means of an insert saying that many of the items on the missing pages were simply no longer available. "Suggestions that he go to the expense of renumbering the other pages made no impression on him. 'No use trying to gloss it over,' he declared. 'Folks will like it better if we don't.'"[15]

One new item L. L. was able to squeeze into the 1944 edition of his catalog was his handy Bean's Ice Carrier, which measured 10 inches by 15 inches on the bottom, was 13 inches high and constructed of builders' canvas. Catalog copy of the day noted that the bag, with its sturdy canvas handles, "is offered for those who have found difficulty in carrying ice from car to ice chest," and also "serves as a basket for wood, garden vegetables, fruit, etc." The Ice Carrier sold for $3.00 but would eventually disappear from the catalog only to be reincarnated in the 1960s as Bean's bestselling Boat and Tote Bag.

Though paper, like most everything else, was in short supply during the war, it was still plentiful enough that L. L. was able to replace the aluminum picnic plates he usually sold with paper ones he called Bean's Compartment Grill Plates. L. L. assured his customers that these plates were "Manufactured for us from State of Maine new spruce logs and thoroughly sterilized during every process of manufacture. Everyone who . . . enjoys picnics should own a quantity of these plates."

There was also sufficient paper to feed the presses, which continued to churn out updated editions of his outdoors skills book, samples of which L. L. mailed out to prospective customers. It arrived in their mailboxes in a large envelope bearing the following statement:

NOTICE

This envelope contains 16 pages of the L. L. Bean book entitled "Hunting-Fishing and Camping."

We hope this cross section will help you decide whether or not you would care to own a complete copy.

The new Improved Revised book has 43 chapters, 114 illustrations on good paper, cloth bound, 108 pages including memorandum pages with headings for making notes on 10 outing trips.

Price $1.00 postpaid anywhere in U. S. or Canada.

Restrictions on hunting appeared to have eased somewhat in late 1944, and L. L., his brother Guy, and their old friend Levi Patterson took the opportunity to go hunting that fall up at L. L.'s Haynesville, Maine, camp. From the looks of the game that's draped over the back of their sedan in a photo from that excursion, the trio appears to have bagged three deer and a black bear. (After losing his original Dew Drop Inn in New Hampshire to the expansion of the White Mountain National Forest in 1925, L. L. began spending more and more time at his cousin Louvie Swett's Haynesville camp, which he bought from Louvie in 1930 and christened the new Dew Drop Inn. Every fall, L. L. would head north to the camp, where he'd hunt, fish, and test new equipment for his catalog. When the camp burned to the ground in 1948, he had it rebuilt the same year.)

WHEN THE WAR ENDED, it was soon back to business as usual in L. L. Bean's 63,000-square-foot facility on Main Street. Sales of Mr. Bean's items quickly rebounded to the point where the company's annual postage bill totaled about $80,000, most of which came from shipping merchandise and mailing out catalogs, which now featured the photography of Freeport native Clifford Merrill "Mel" Collins (1909–96). Collins had studied photography at the New York Institute of Photography and would be the official photographer of the L. L. Bean catalog from 1944 until 1949, when he left the company for a while, and again from 1955 until retiring in 1974.

"The first studio we ever had," said Collins, "was downstairs where they used to tie catalogs [in bundles for mailing] and right next to the maintenance department up in the old building. The ceiling was so low that you couldn't get the lights high enough. Every time the clicker [leather cutter] upstairs came down, the dust would come down, and if you had a white shirt, it was a sight! So I got the boys to put up insulation to catch the dust."[16] Eventually, Collins's little studio would move upstairs and finally down the road to an air-conditioned room in the Taylor Building. "Nice place to work," recalled Collins.

Collins's 1996 obituary stated that "he served in the Army as a sergeant during World War II, then went to work for L. L. Bean as the company's 17th employee." (In 1939 a *Portland Evening Express* article had already put the number of Bean's employees at "about 75 persons with 100 on the payroll in peak seasons," but it's entirely possible that Collins had previously worked for L. L.—perhaps right after graduating from Freeport High School in 1927.)

On 19 December 1945, L. L. Bean received a letter of "appreciation and commendation" from Brigadier General Georges F. Doriot in recognition of his service to his country during the war. The letter praises the Mainer's "excellent work and technical assistance in connection with such important items for the soldier as winter footgear, more specifically Shoe Pacs, are fully recognized and greatly appreciated by the entire Quartermaster Corps." The general's letter concluded with

> I personally want you to know that your many contributions will long be remembered and recognized by the Quartermaster Corps as playing a vital part in the total effort to help bring victory to our country. It is hoped that you will continue to be interested in our post-war program of improving existing Quartermaster items and in the development of new ones.

Another perk of having served his country in Washington—one that probably meant as much to L. L. Bean as the praise he'd received from a senior military officer—was the system of connections he'd made which would enable him to purchase the several war surplus items he'd soon put to good use. Some of these leftover supplies were repackaged and found their way into Bean's famous catalog, while others would be used as raw material for the manufacture of other doodads. But they all had two things in common: these were things L. L. was certain that, with the right amount of persuasive copywriting, he could convince his loyal customers they just couldn't do without; and, thanks to his knack for knowing what to sell and when, all of them would turn a profit in one fashion or another.

One such item to catch L. L.'s eye was a government-issue toiletry organizer that was made of cotton duck and had eleven pockets that snapped shut. L. L. swore by the Ketchall, as he called it, even going so far as to list the items he put in it when he went hunting, and noting that he also used it in his cottage and boathouse. Empty, Bean's Camp Ketchall sold for 45 cents postpaid, or it could also be had "partly filled with the following items: Waterproof Dressing, Gun Oil, Whistle, Chap Stick, Drag Line, 63-inch Leather

Shoe Laces, 10 packages Waterproof Matches, Cards, 2 packages Fire Kindler, and 2 bottles Lunch Tablets" for $2.75.

Another new item that probably came from the government's war surplus stockpiles was Bean's State of Maine Dehydrated Potatoes, which would still be offered in the catalog in 1949. L. L.'s descriptive powers rose to great heights as he detailed to his readers this latest achievement in tuber technology:

> Dehydrated Vegetables are comparatively new to the general public. The potatoes we offer are the finest Maine potatoes and are the same as have been used in making dehydrated potatoes under strict government regulations.
>
> For campers these are a great advantage over bulky bag potatoes. For example, one peck of potatoes weighs 15 lbs; when dehydrated they weigh only 2 lbs and are packed in two small packages.

He went on to point out that this breakthrough in technology would be especially appreciated by "cottage and apartment dwellers" who were short on storage space and needed only to immerse the amount of dried potatoes required for that evening's meal in cool water before departing for work in the morning. Containers of Bean's potatoes could be had in three convenient sizes: a 4-ounce resealable can for 16 cents, a sturdy 8-ounce box for 26 cents, or "four pounds in a handsome pail" for $1.96. By the way, L. L. thought the pail, which was painted to resemble a wooden bucket, would make "a nice gift package," especially since it could also serve as "a handy container [such] as a water pail, waste basket, etc." when empty.

While L. L.'s bargain-hunting instincts were as sharp as ever, that didn't always mean the items he picked would become big winners in terms of sales. For example, shortly after the war, L. L. chose to carry an army surplus packboard instead of an aluminum pack frame recommended by his employee William "Wid" Griffin. The army one, remembers Griffin, was "made of molded plywood and had a thousand straps and things on it. And 'L. L.' looked at it and said: 'That's what we want!' So that went in [the catalog] and he cut off half the straps on it and made dog leads out of them." At the end of the first year, said Griffin, "the volume of sales [was] six or seven hundred dollars and 'L. L.' went: 'Boy that's really good!'"[17] (After a few years the aluminum pack frame Griffin had initially recommended finally made it into the catalog, and, at the end of its first year, had made ten times as much money as the plywood packboard had.)

"I remember, right after the war," an unidentified former clerk told Bean biographer M. R. Montgomery, "he bought all these damn old worn-out leather flight jackets—the fleece-lined ones. I can't remember all the things we used to make out of them. Innersoles for boots. Hat bands to hold trout flies. Stuff like that. Not catalog stuff, just little damn things that laid around on the counters and people would buy them."

Though it wasn't exactly government surplus, another item L. L. Bean sold after the war was the Grumman Aluminum Canoe, which was built by the Grumman aircraft company, whose naval architects had designed the hull portions of the fuselages for the company's Goose, Duck, and Widgeon amphibious aircraft. (Grumman had also built Hellcat fighter planes and TBF torpedo bombers during the war.) The canoes, which weighed anywhere from 38 pounds to 74 pounds, were available in lengths from 13 to 18 feet and cost between $143 and $174. "When the canoe is swamped," stated the catalog copy, "it will support people sitting on the inside or on the gunwale and will not turn bottom up." This remarkable buoyancy, noted the catalog, was "because of the two built-in watertight air chambers, one in the bow and the other at the stern."

Taking a break from this recent spate of product promotion, L. L. led a small party on a fishing trip back to Plaster Rock on the Tobique River in New Brunswick during 1945. A photo from the trip shows L. L. with his wife, Claire, and son-in-law, Jack Gorman, posing behind their catch of nine salmon and nine trout laid out neatly on a board. The snapshot would eventually become the cover of Bean's spring 1946 catalog, once again reinforcing L. L.'s image as a topnotch sportsman even as he approached his seventy-third birthday.

For most of 1946, not too many events of note seem to have happened in Freeport, Bean-wise. In June, L. L. took yet another fishing trip to Plaster Rock, this time in a party of four comprised of L. L. and his wife, Dr. A. Mackay Frazer, and Brooks Shumaker of Boston. The group spent a week at a sporting camp and fished the Tobique River, from which its members caught twenty Atlantic salmon totaling 140½ pounds. A photo of the smiling L. L. shows him holding by the tail a 19-pound salmon that reaches from his waist almost to the ground. (Later L. L. would reveal in a radio interview that "Canada gives both Mrs. Bean and myself complimentary fishing licenses.")

Most of the rest of the year was fairly uneventful; L. L. tended to his steadily growing business and got on with the routine that made up his life in Freeport. But late in the year, L. L. managed to score two advertising coups in about a month's time, the first of which was getting a sign pointing to his business erected on top of the rebuilt Clark's Hotel building across the street, which had been damaged in a recent fire.

The fire had started in the basement of Kimball's Pharmacy, and was discovered shortly before 6:00 A.M. on June 6. According to reports, twenty-four residents of Clark's Hotel had to be rescued, including several by ladder, and the upper rooms of the building sustained smoke and water damage. The pharmacy and the Gould-Curtis clothing store were destroyed in the blaze, and several other businesses on Main and Bow Streets were damaged. It took four hours to put the fire out, and assistance from the Brunswick and Yarmouth Fire Departments was required. Freeport Fire Chief Guy Rowe estimated that damages could total $150,000.

In a 2008 interview with the author, Earle G. Shettleworth, Jr., recalled how Mr. Bean had handled the sign negotiation with his father, who had purchased the block after the fire:

> Mr. Bean had tried, on several occasions, to get that sign on the building prior to my father's ownership, but it was the classic

small-town situation where the previous owner didn't want to do that, didn't want to cooperate.

Not long before the [December] opening, L. L. Bean, who I don't think my father had previously met, came over to introduce himself and to welcome my father to Freeport. And, at the same time, he asked my father if he would consider putting a sign on the top of the Clark Building that would point to L.L. Bean's across the street. You would not, in those days, have seen L.L. Bean's, which of course was located in, I believe people called it, the Post Office Block, and of course, as we know, it was a fairly low-key operation as far as the public was concerned, especially then, back in the forties. . . .

I can remember [in the early 1950s] walking up that big flight of stairs—that rather steep flight of stairs—to the second floor. Then, the showroom was the second floor . . . and, of course, it was a kind of rambling interior space. Part of it, at least, was pine-paneled, and I can remember, as a child, being impressed with the large number of taxidermy specimens that hung from the walls—all of those fish or other creatures that L. L. Bean or his friends had bagged over the years. Some of them are still on display, which is fun.

L.L. Bean's was a very different-appearing place then, in the forties, than it is today. . . . With Route 1 still going through Freeport (the bypass had not yet been built, Interstate 295), you can understand how important it was for people to be directed to Bean's. You can't imagine that today, but it certainly was an issue then.

So L. L. Bean posed the question to my father: Would he consider allowing Mr. Bean to put a sign on top of the building pointing to his building, just simply an arrow with the words "L.L. Bean"? And my father immediately said, "Yes." And so then, Mr. Bean said, "How much will this cost me?" thinking that my father would probably charge him monthly or yearly rent, maybe, for putting the sign on.

And my father said, "Nothing, it's to our mutual interest," because my father recognized that Bean's was an important drawing card, and that it was definitely valuable as a location for him to be across from Bean's as much as it was for Mr. Bean to have the sign.

Mr. Bean didn't say anything, he just kind of said good-bye, pivoted on his heel, and went back across the street. The next day he came back, laden with two big Hudson Bay Blankets, and they were both in these beautiful cardboard boxes, I can remember the boxes as a child. You know how Hudson Bay Blankets had those wonderful colored stripes on them? These boxes, in color, reproduced the blanket on the cover of the box, so just the boxes alone were beautiful. And these, in their time, were very expensive blankets. So he brought two, one in each hand, handed them to my father and said, "One for you, and one for your wife—this is for the sign." And so that's how he paid for the sign.

But the sign on the roof of Clark's Hotel would turn out to be small potatoes compared to what would happen next. On December 14, 1946, the *Saturday Evening Post* came out with a four-and-a-half-page story (including four color pictures) entitled, "The Discovery of L. L. Bean."

L. L. Bean's sudden windfall of publicity—which he figures would have cost him $53,000 if he'd had to purchase the same amount of space in the magazine—had come about because a writer with the *Portland Sunday Telegram* had decided to take a shot at breaking into the big time. Norway, Maine, native Arthur Bartlett (1901–63), a graduate of nearby Bowdoin College in Brunswick, submitted a story about L. L.'s outdoors emporium to the *Saturday Evening Post*, which at the time was the country's leading weekly magazine with over five million regular readers. "Mr. Arthur Bartlett, writer for the *Saturday Evening Post*," said Bean, "spent days in my factory getting material for this story, and Mr. David Robbins took over a hundred pictures to illustrate the article. I was not allowed to change one word of the story, or to select a single photograph." Decades later another *Telegram* writer, business columnist Harold Boyle, would recall the success that

Bartlett's story brought to both Bartlett and L. L. Bean:

> Much to his surprise, the *Post*, then under the editorship of George Lorimer, accepted the Bean story and sent him a check for either $12,000 or $15,000 upon publication.
>
> It started him on a free-lance career that got him into the leading publications in the country. Bartlett's good fortune rubbed off on Bean.
>
> A week after the *Post* article appeared, Bean wrote him a letter that went something like this: "Dear, Mr. Bartlett: I want you to know that I got 1,700 letters up to yesterday from customers and friends who told me how much they liked my writeup in the *Saturday Evening Post*. I thank you.
>
> "On the theory that you are a single man, I am sending you one of my best blankets.
>
> "If you are a married man, let me know and I will send you another blanket. Again I thank you."
>
> Bartlett always treasured that letter which, he said, reflected the down-to-earth character of the rugged L. L. Bean.[18]

When the article appeared, it caused quite a stir in Freeport and much of southern Maine. The publicity generated by the piece and its accompanying color photographs was immense and immediate. On December 11, 1946, the same day that the *Post* started hitting newsstands across the country, L. L. sat down for an interview with George Hunter, "The Big Man From Freeport," on the recently inaugurated Freeport Grain Broadcasting System. (In his later autobiography, L. L. would mistakenly write that the interview took place on October 11, 1947.)

L. L. showed up at 7:30 in the morning in his Sunday best all set to talk with Big George, who conducted the interview in a work shirt and overalls. The broadcast of the program on WPOR in Portland was delayed by technical difficulties until that afternoon, when Roscoe Bigelow made it in to fix the transmitter. Once all the bugs had been worked out and the interview finally got underway, L. L. talked about how he ran his business ("I . . . try to furnish [sportsmen] the things they need, and also discourage them from buying things they do not need") and, of course, about how grateful he was for the publicity that the *Post* article had given his company:

> I am in hopes that this story will be of interest to my many thousands of customers and friends throughout the United States and Canada.
>
> I particularly want to thank Arthur Bartlett and David Robbins for this wonderful story and the very appropriate photographs.
>
> I have been a reader of the *Saturday Evening Post* for a great many years and consider it tops, both in reading matter and advertising. During all these years I have never noticed a single liquor or questionable advertisement.

Once the news of L. L. Bean's newfound fame got out, the awards and accolades began rolling in, with the first coming from the Town of Freeport. On Wednesday, December 11—the same day as L. L.'s radio interview—"the selectmen of the town of Freeport passed by unanimous vote a resolution designating Monday, December 16th, 1946, as 'L. L. Bean Day.'" On the evening of that special day, Leon L. Bean was fêted at a dinner held at Stoney Maynard's International Red Door Restaurant on the Yarmouth Road. Since the facility was small, seating was "limited to the business men of the town" and a few special guests, including Governor Horace A. Hildreth. (Shortly after leaving office, Hildreth would start Maine's first television station, CBS affiliate WABI, Channel 5 in Bangor.) Also in attendance were Harold Schnurle, a representative of the Maine Development Commission, and Fred H. Goldrup, one of L. L. Bean's original employees.

All the to-do about the *Post* article seemed to finally change the way L. L. Bean saw himself. Finally, at the age of seventy-four, he realized that he was famous—really famous. "I don't think he was publicity-conscious in the beginning," said John Gould, "and then all at once the *Saturday Evening Post* had a story about him and he realized that he'd achieved something. . . . There was a little change came over him because of that." When he finally got around to writing his self-published autobiography in his late eighties, he called himself "the world-famous Yankee hunter and fisherman" who "turned his love of outdoor life into a multi-million dollar success story."

During the evening, L. L. Bean was presented with the clay mockup of a plaque that would soon be cast in bronze and hung, said L. L., "in the building in which I started with a few borrowed dollars and a hunting shoe." Mounted on a square piece of varnished oak, the plaque reads, "In esteemed recognition of his many contributions to the welfare of the town of Freeport. Presented by the citizens to L. L. Bean, Dec. 16, 1946." (It is now on display in the Taylor Building down the road from the store.)

And of course there were speeches. First Mr. Schnurle spoke, saying there was no way the government could have afforded to publicize Maine to the extent of the windfall of favorable information included in the *Post* article, estimating that the write-up could be worth as much as a million dollars to the state. When Governor Hildreth's turn to speak came, he echoed the sentiments of Mr. Schnurle, and figured that the 600,000 copies of Bean's catalog printed that year served as a pitch to sportsmen worldwide to come to Maine.

And the governor was right. But just because, as *Boston Globe* writer M. R. Montgomery would observe nearly four decades later, "Bean's, once fashioned in the image of Maine, had itself become the public image from which Maine could profit,"[19] it didn't mean that L.L. Bean, Inc., would profit much from all this publicity—at least not in the short run. But it did bring about one unexpected development: L. L. started hearing from long-lost descendants of an uncle who'd moved west years before. The cards and photos they sent helped L. L. assemble a "nearly complete" family album.

Just as the attack on Pearl Harbor had torpedoed any increase in sales from the 1941 *Life* article, the timing of the *Post* feature (most people had already ordered their items for Christmas) also negated much of its potential positive effect. Bean seemed to view this setback as a minor inconvenience, since the article had gotten his name out there in the nation's number one weekly, and besides, his business was doing just fine, thank you. Twice a year, the company sent out roughly 300,000 of its randomly organized catalogs which generated nearly all of its $1.5 million in sales—all this based on a boot whose popular 12-inch model now cost $8.75.

That's not to say that customers weren't still beating a path to his door in Freeport. The showroom was open eighteen hours, six days a week, and there was a phone number tacked to the door that people could call if they needed something on Sunday. There's even one report that says it was about this time that L. L. started handing out annual bonuses to his hundred or so hardworking employees. Even the town of Freeport got in on the act and revived the board of trade, which had lain dormant since before the war.

The day after the testimonial dinner was held, Henri A. Benoit, who ran A. H. Benoit & Company, a men's clothing store in Portland, sat down and composed a letter of congratulation to Bean, who'd started out in Freeport selling a similar line of merchandise. Benoit's letter read as follows:

Dear Mr. Bean:
Governor Hildreth and Mr. Schnurle at the Testimonial Dinner tendered you in Freeport Monday evening admirably expressed our sentiments. Your contribution to Maine is invaluable—it cannot be expressed in mere words, not measured in cold dollars and cents.

As a business firm—we can well appreciate—that the integrity for which the name L. L. Bean stands—all over the world—did not come about by chance. By your efforts and straightforward "down to earth" way of doing business, you have not only brought success to the firm of L. L. Bean, but you have added prestige to the State's business and industry from which all will benefit.

Again, please add our sincere and hearty congratulations to the hundreds you have already received.
Sincerely yours,

A. H. Benoit & Company
[signed]
Henri A. Benoit, President

A brief overview of the *Saturday Evening Post* article shows that it touched on the many facets of L. L. Bean and his homegrown company. After opening with the anecdote about L. L.'s taxi ride with the general, Bartlett went on to tell his readers about Bean's customers who, be they average hunters, campers, and fishermen or famous actors, athletes, and politicians, all believe "that Bean is a personal discovery, to be cherished as a rare and rich curiosity." Next he focused on the passion that the aging Bean still had for the kind of work he'd chosen for himself: "'Gosh, I like it,' he says explosively, 'My job's not work! The days ain't long enough.'"

After dedicating a paragraph to L. L.'s invention of his famous boot, Bartlett explained how he came about his love for the out-of-doors by examining his childhood in western Maine. The last half of the article concerned itself with L. L.'s rambling production facility and his equally rambling catalog before concluding with a review of Bean's outdoors book, which by now was in its sixth printing.

While L. L. Bean had apparently been successful in giving one of his fine wool blankets to Mr. Bartlett, he wasn't as fortunate in his attempt to give some to the publisher of the *Post*, who had a summer home in Bar Harbor. His attempt to make a gift of the Hudson Bay Blankets was rebuffed, and L. L. Bean received payment for the full price of the blankets.

L. L. carefully tracked his company's increase in business as a result of the *Saturday Evening Post* article, noting that, for the last ten days of December, inquiries about his catalog more than doubled. For the first twenty days of 1947, the inquiries numbered 19,000—nearly three times as many as the previous January. He knew exactly how many inquiries the piece had generated because of the help he'd had keeping an eye on just how much bang he was getting for his free publicity. "I remember the *Saturday Evening Post*," said former office worker Idalyn Cummings. "Oh! Every day we'd have to keep track. Every day he'd want to know how many [letters] he got."[20]

More than two months after the appearance of the *Post* article, the Maine merchant continued to receive kudos from his friends and peers. In February, the Cumberland County Fish and Game Association put on "L. L. Bean—and Old Timer's Night" in Portland. During a dinner at the Falmouth Hotel, L. L. was presented with a plaque which was actually a framed copy of the association's resolution that had been signed by more than 100 members and guests. The resolution deemed it "fitting and proper to pay special tribute to [the association's] many outstanding fishermen and hunters, notably, L. L. Bean—and its Old Timers," before concluding with

> Now, therefore it is resolved—That the Cumberland County Fish and Game Association designates and sets apart Thursday, 20 February 1947, as L. L. Bean—and Old Timer's Night as an expression of recognition of the contributions made by L. L. Bean—and its Old Timers, to the welfare and prosperity of the Association and the State of Maine.

Eventually the spotlight on Freeport began to dim and life around town began to return to its normal pattern of business as usual. L. L., his sons, and his son-in-law returned to running the company, and the elder Bean inched ever closer to semiretirement. On July 9 L. L. Bean ended his nearly ten-year tenure as president of the Freeport Realty Company. From now on, the real estate with which L. L. Bean would be primarily concerned would be his own, and in 1947 he built a one-story, 3,800-square-foot warehouse to accommodate his continually expanding business. A photo caption in his autobiography says that the structure was made of aluminum and was located a quarter-mile from the factory, but lists its size as only 3,100 square feet.

Now that L. L. Bean was a (self-)published author, another local writer, Henry Milliken, looked to him for help, asking the Maine merchant to write a brief introduction to his own slender volume called *Hunting in Maine*. The fact that the 186-page book was published by L. L. Bean, Inc., explains why L. L.'s name appears on the book's title page in type the same size as the author's name. This also helps to explain why there's a formal photograph of Bean in the beginning of the book and none of the author, who's shown only in the rudimentary drawings of one E. H. Pike.

Though the book contained all the "personal yarns and experiences" with which L. L. had promised not to bore his readers in the introduction to his own book five years earlier, he nevertheless manages to praise the book as highly as his well-developed sense of Yankee self-restraint and knack for catalog copywriting would let him. A sample of the book's introduction sounds characteristically Bean at his concise best:

> In this book will be found informative and entertaining stories of trips afield and into the deep wilderness to hunt white-tailed deer, black bear, raccoon, red fox, ruffed grouse, pheasant, woodcock, snowshoe rabbits, and bobcats.
>
> I like this book because it has the flavor of the Maine woods. It is good reading, but it is also packed with hundreds of hunting facts, which the author learned by actual experiences.
>
> Henry Milliken, tall and lanky, has spent many months in the woods and along the waterways of Maine. He is a Down-Easter and he writes in a dry, humorous way.

This was probably the same Henry Milliken who would later write a lengthy article about Freeport entrepreneur E. B. Mallet for the June 5, 1971, edition of the *Lewiston Journal*.

AS MEMORIES OF THE RECENT WAR gradually faded, more and more signs pointed to the normalcy of prewar days. Bean's catalog no longer had any missing pages and the prewar version of the venerable Maine Hunting Shoe was set to make a comeback. A page in Bean's Spring 1947 catalog carried an "Important Announcement" that trumpeted the return of the Maine Hunting

Shoe, "the same as our 1941 Prewar Hunting Shoe."

The "new" old Bean Boot had had its wartime black synthetic bottoms replaced with the classic "non-slip pure rubber vulcanized sole. It will not wear smooth, is more durable, and weighs 4 ounces less than our war shoe." A much later newspaper article stated that the boot's "chain tread sole [was] added in 1947," and copy from the '47 catalog seemed to bear this out, describing the Maine Hunting Shoe as having tops "of soft, Brown waterproof Elk Leather," while the "vamp and sole are extra high grade gum rubber . . . dark red with brown crepe chain sole."

Completely new to the catalog that fall was an item that was destined to become another Bean classic: the Field Coat, which L. L. designed for "any sportsman who does duck hunting, bird shooting, or fishing." Still available today, the abrasion-resistant cotton-canvas coats go for $89 to $149, depending on the type of lining. A refined version of the coat (made of British Millerain canvas with an 80-percent-wool "button-out liner vest") can be found more than sixty years later in the company's trendy L.L. Bean Signature catalog at $185 a pop.

Maybe the success of Bean's boot-driven venture was noticed by another purveyor of outdoors gear who also decided to expand into the mail-order business, since it was around this time that future Bean competitor Eddie Bauer decided to launch his own mail-order catalog on the other side of the country. Thanks to his new catalog, which was spurred by the popularity of his wartime down flight suits, Bauer's business, like Bean's, would flourish.

While Eddie Bauer's catalog was just getting off the ground, L. L. Bean's publication continued to be the quintessential wish book for sports from all walks of life. A chapter about Bean's company in the 1949 edition of Tom Mahoney's book *The Great Merchants* mentions an order "from a man in St. Mary's, Pennsylvania. The sportsman wrote that it would take 'too damn long to fill out the list he wanted,' and instructed Bean to send him every item in the catalog on pages 8 through 64 inclusive!" Well, maybe not *every* item; in his autobiography, L. L. recalled that the order was for 51 items from page 7 to page 64, the catalog's last page.

The customer enclosed a check for $426.40.

Of course not everyone was interested in outfitting himself for a major outdoor adventure; some people just wanted the shoes that they'd ordered more than two months earlier. Around Christmas L.L. Bean, Inc., received the following cryptic letter from Mukwonago, Wisconsin:

Dear Sir:
Send for shoes; 4 weeks pass, no shoes. Write letter, 6 weeks pass, no shoes. Write another letter, next day shoes come. Shoes O.K. Me O.K. Hope you O.K.
S. Larson.

After September of 1948, any packages, late or otherwise, mailed out from Bean's would no longer pass through the post office under the watchful eye of Freeport postmaster Guy C. Bean. Guy, who, one writer would note, "was one of the few Democrats in Maine," retired as the town's postmaster, a position he'd held since June of 1936. Unfortunately, Guy Bean's retirement was a brief one; he'd die at the age of seventy-two just a few years later.

As the decade drew to a close, the continued prosperity of L.L. Bean, Inc., necessitated the purchase of a neighboring property to facilitate expansion, and in 1949 the company bought the Winslow Building on the corner of Main and Morse Streets. Reportedly, in the late 1700s, a front room in the two-and-a-half-story building had served as Freeport's first post office before it moved across Main Street to the Holbrook Block. (The Winslow Building, also known as the O. G. Morse Block, along with the Nevin's Block just behind it, would be demolished during March 1967 in order to expand Bean's parking lot. Bean's purchasing of adjacent properties is one indication of its growth, which continues to this day.)

By now, L. L.'s down-home business had evolved sufficiently to warrant its own chapter in Tom Mahoney's *The Great Merchants*. Being included by Mahoney was "no small achievement," according to the company scrapbook, "since the book studied the greatest of American retail companies." In the ten pages he dedicated to L.L. Bean, Inc., Mahoney first described a few of the "several hundred items for the sport, dress or comfort of hunters and fishermen," that could be found in the Freeport store. He then retold the time-honored tale of L. L. inventing his boot and how the business grew as "he began to add related items, of similar quality and utility, starting with socks."

Mahoney attributes the success of L. L.'s company to the values instilled in its owner when he was a child, such as giving people value for their money and treating them the way he'd want to be treated. "When Bean says in his catalog that the hook disgorger on Bean's Pocket Fish Knife 'is the best I have ever tried,'" Mahoney wrote, "fishermen know Mr. Bean himself has given it a workout." To emphasize L. L.'s philosophy that more was not always better, Mahoney then trotted out the old saw about Bean admonishing his readers that "nine flies are all anybody needs for brook trout."[21]

And he couldn't overlook the lack of organization that defined both L. L. Bean's catalog and his maze-like facility: "Shoes are scattered from one end of the catalog to the other, listed under twenty-two different categories and separately from Oxfords." On the rambling layout of Bean's building, Mahoney observed that "the arrangement is actually not as inefficient as it seems at first glance, and the hillside location permits trucks to deliver to the upper as well as lower floors." In spite of this cluttered approach to retailing—or maybe because of it—said the writer, famous people from Mrs. Roosevelt to Ted Williams flocked to Freeport. Mahoney also noted that Bean kept all the famous autographs alphabetically in his letter file and that he "makes no capital of names in selling his merchandise."

Chapter 7

"Outside of my wife, this is the handiest
piece of equipment a man could take into the woods"

In 1950, L.L. Bean, Incorporated, took in $1,848,000. By the time the Maine Central Railroad made its final parcel-post run from Freeport that September, Bean's shipments of packages had grown to the point where it had become necessary for the railroad to drop off a baggage car down the hill from the factory to accommodate all of L.L. Bean's freight.

L. L.'s business also benefited from the sale of nonresident hunting and fishing licenses. Though he regularly sold more than anyone else in the state—$45,736 worth this particular year—he also made no secret of the fact that he was losing money on the 25 cents he received for each $20.25 permit sold. Five years later, he'd tell a writer that his "commission didn't even cover salaries for the girls who tended our bank teller windows 24 hours per day that [November]." But he wasn't complaining. The license-selling business was a good thing and L. L. Bean knew it; by 1954, about 5,100 people would buy their licenses in his store, and once they were there, very few of them left without purchasing some or most of whatever else they needed for their particular adventure. In all, he figured they spent another $60,000 on gear and supplies.

Although the growth of the company remained steady, it was going slowly—very slowly. Granted, the business would continue to grow, doing somewhere in the neighborhood of $4 million dollars a year by the time L. L. died in 1967, but actual growth barely outstripped inflation. One expert even noted that, in terms of real dollars, the company was probably losing money during the late 1950s and early 1960s. L. L. Bean was slowing down as he aged, and so was his company.

While the nearly nonexistent growth of his business seemed not to concern Bean in the least (one of his most frequently quoted statements from the period was "I get three good meals a day and I couldn't eat a fourth"), the passage of time was proving to be a lot more troublesome for L. L. and his immediate family.

On June 6, 1951, L. L.'s younger brother Guy died from a coronary embolism after spending a week in the Brunswick hospital. He had also suffered from arteriosclerosis. The two remaining Bean brothers were now L. L., who was nearly seventy-nine, and his brother, Otho, eighty-four.

Guy Chester Bean was born on August 5, 1878, and married Mary McArdle, who was born on February 26, 1880. The two had no children. Later L. L. would recall the time that, when Guy was a baby, he had been knocked down by a large rooster that drove his spur into Guy's forehead, leaving a lifetime scar. Guy Bean was seventy-two when he passed away.

ACQUAINTANCES OF L. L. BEAN had always known that he was most interested in selling his goods to people who hunted and fished because those were the things that *he* enjoyed doing. Sure, he was concerned about running a profitable business and keeping his loyal workers employed, but he just wasn't motivated to see how much he could grow his business. So it's not surprising that L. L.'s recent attempts to drum up business were modest at best—one he'd even attempted a dozen years earlier without much success. But this time the world was ready for his revived idea of staying open all night.

One bit of publicity on which L. L. Bean might have capitalized was the fact that his famous Maine Hunting Shoes were again being pressed into service, this time in Korea, by at least one very important soldier. The Bean Boot-wearing GI was Lieutenant General Matthew Ridgway, commander of U.S. forces in Indochina. (General Ridgway had taken over in April of 1951 for General Douglas MacArthur, who had been relieved of his command by President Truman for fear that MacArthur's aggressive strategy for fighting the North Koreans could escalate the conflict into a full-scale war with China and the Soviet Union.)

Two times a year, the Dingley Press, still housed in one of the company's buildings, spent nearly five weeks printing each season's supply of L. L. Bean's 380,000 catalogs, which, by the way, made his directory of goods the largest circulating of any Maine publication. Everyone who made a purchase from Mr. Bean's outdoors wish book remained on his mailing list for another five issues. Those who didn't order were removed after receiving just three more issues. The three hundred items in each of those catalogs generated most of the $2 million worth of goods the company sold every year, necessitating the help of about a hundred full-time employees during a time when much of southern Maine had fallen into a postwar period of economic stagnation.

During the summer, the five-page article "L. L. Bean, D.S.D. (Doctor of Sportsmen's Difficulties)," by William A. Hatch and Richard A. Hebert of the Maine Publicity Bureau, gave some of the merchant's dedicated workers a break from the anonymity of their everyday labors. The piece detailed L. L.'s "personally [filling] out a typical order . . . for his midwestern friend, a doctor," following him as he confidently strode through his sprawling factory, all the while being sure to face the camera. During his travels through the plant, L. L. first checked in with four of his "mail 'girls,'" who were busy sorting, checking, and routing the morning mail. (One photo from the period shows ten women sitting at two rows of desks with the caption saying, "Two women would type the name, address, date, and the amount of money received, then items were handwritten on forms to instruct the shipping room what to include in the order.")

Next, L. L. checked in with tackle buyer Bill "Wid" Griffin and with Richard Houle, who was hand-sewing moccasins, before stopping to chat with salesroom manager Dick Stilkey and veteran leather stitchers Charles Stilkey and Hilda Wheeler. The spread's next page shows the boss discussing the doctor's needs with Sewall MacWilliams, head of the company's "fly-tying" shop, and with company auditor Dan Snow before he personally lugged the completed order over to the wrapping "assembly line," where the bundle's postal fees were quickly computed. The package was then "chuted" down the conveyer belt to postal employees Philip Hatch and Richard Wade in the "first class" Freeport post office. Only when he was sure that the completed order was safely on its way to the doctor did L. L. stop to conduct a staff meeting with Snow, Griffin, shoe manager Ralph Hall, and hardware manager Ernest Griffin.

Though the whole thing was obviously set up for the camera, it did serve to illustrate the point that the "Doctor" was still in, and still capable of diagnosing and treating the difficulties of any sportsman, no matter how serious. While L. L. Bean may not have had any fancy college degrees, he knew everything he needed to know to pull himself up by his bootstraps. And besides, you can't teach someone common sense.

The ninth edition of L. L.'s *Hunting, Fishing, and Camping* book and what passed for a booming mail-order business in 1951 were certain to attract all sorts of loyal customers to Bean's rambling old store on the Maine coast. And come they did. From hard-core sports to the merely curious, hundreds were soon making the trek to Freeport, often arriving there at all hours of the day and night. While their business was certainly appreciated, the commotion some of them made wanting to gain entry to L. L.'s store in the middle of the night frequently wasn't. Many was the night that saw L. L. Bean rousted from a sound sleep by the bell from his store a block away to get up and make a sale, which he was happy to do. But, at seventy-eight, he wasn't getting any younger. One story about Bean's second attempt at staying open all the time has it that, when the night watchman he hired found the rambling old building a little too spooky to suit him, L. L. had to hire another man to watch the place and to take care of any customers who stopped by.

This arrangement worked out so well that L. L. Bean decided to do something he hadn't tried since just before the war; he decided to keep his showroom open twenty-four hours a day, seven days a week. While his motivation for keeping the store open all night may have been merely an act of Yankee practicality, he wasn't about to pass up the opportunity to garner a little more publicity from the change, making sure that everyone who needed to know was aware of the fact that "I threw away the latch key!" Except for funerals, a fire, and a brief brush with a local blue law, L. L. Bean's Freeport store has been open for business—or just browsing—ever since. "We never know," said L. L., "what time our customers might be passing through town on their way to an upstate fishing stream or hunting lodge. We never know what they might need." And just so there was no confusion, he even had a neon sign hung over the sidewalk pointing to the entrance.

While the importance of L. L.'s decision to keep his outdoors emporium open 'round the clock might have been lost on most people at the time, loyal Bean employee Carlene Griffin sensed its significance right from the start, recalling for a TV news crew, "A night watchman had to sweep the floors and pick up after and haul trash away and what-have-you. But he never had time because the customers would come in. And finally he told them, you know, 'I can't get my work done because I'm always answering the door.' And I happened to be there the day they took the key and threw it away. My desk was here [pointing] and the door was here, and I said to myself, seriously, I says, you know, 'This is the beginning of something.'"[1]

But soon it would take more than a glowing sign to help Bean's devotees find their way to his store. On November 12, 1951, the state would open the "Freeport Three and One-Half Mile By-Pass," as L. L. called it in his catalog, which took much of the through traffic off Route 1—Freeport's Main Street—and shuttled it around the town's business district. Today that bypass is part of I-295, and the reason L. L. Bean mentioned it in his catalog was to tell people headed north how to get off the darned thing so they wouldn't also bypass his store in their rush toward the Great North Woods. The man whose catalog was printed in the Cheltenham font was going up against the road whose signs were lettered in Highway Gothic. He even included a detailed map of the stretch in question on page 3 of his spring 1952 catalog, along with a classically logical Bean argument as to why the weary travelers should make the effort to pass through town:

The new road around Freeport is longer and slower. There are three lights on the By-Pass and none on the straight U.S. 1 Business Highway through Freeport Village, as shown on the above map.

The By-Pass takes the truck traffic around Freeport, making the route through Freeport faster, safer, and allows ample free parking. Even if you do not intend to stop, the route through our pleasant village will give you 5 minutes' relaxation from heavy traffic strain.

Coming by toll road, Freeport is the first shopping center east of Boston. Those who visited us last year will be surprised and pleased with the new atmosphere of quiet, easy shopping conditions.

Keep right on the Black Top Highway.

Nowadays it takes much longer to drive through town than to bypass it, especially during the summer. I-295 is the fast way north while the traffic on Route 1 slows to a crawl due to all the preoccupied outlet shoppers and the three or four stoplights between Bean's company headquarters and the McDonalds about a quarter mile past the retail store.

THE SECOND HALF OF 1952 was a time of life's milestones, both good and bad, for the extended Bean clan, beginning with the June graduation of L. L.'s youngest grandson, Leon Gorman, from Portland's Cheverus High School. According to one newspaper report, Gorman, who grew up in the nearby town of Yarmouth, "was an ardent Boy Scout in Troop 35 that his father led and just missed earning his Eagle Scout's badge because he never did the required bird study."[2] After graduating from Bowdoin College in Brunswick and serving four years in the navy, where he was stationed on a destroyer escort, Leon would show up at the family business in 1960 looking for a job.

On November 19, 1952, L. L. Bean lost his last surviving sibling when Otho died at the home of Guy's widow on Morse Street, near the factory. Otho Bean died of a cerebral hemorrhage and had been suffering from pulmonary tuberculosis for two years. His passing was attended by Dr. A. L. Gould, one of L. L.'s longtime fishing buddies. Otho Ralph Bean, born January 7, 1867, had been predeceased by his wife, Annie Merrill Bean. The couple had no children. Otho was eighty-five.

Through the clarity of hindsight, it may have been obvious to many who knew him that this was about the time L. L. began to slow down and become complacent about the growth of his business. But since he was still able to go to the factory and on the occasional fishing trip, L. L. was able to hide any physical decline from most outsiders, especially the writers and reporters who still made occasional pilgrimages to Freeport to write the stories that added to the myth of the merchant from Maine.

The most recent of these writers was Augusta, Maine's, own Earle Doucette, who'd just completed a nice piece about Mr. Bean and his Freeport business for the June 1953 issue of *Coronet* magazine. By now, it had become customary for someone in southern Maine to write a piece about every major write-up on L. L. Bean, and on May 28, Bill Hatch of the Maine Publicity Bureau continued that tradition with this five-paragraph press release about the *Coronet* piece just out:

> To sportsmen the world over, L. L. Bean and the State of Maine are synonymous. Few outdoor enthusiasts would consider their outfit complete without a liberal supply of Bean's famous products.
>
> The Horatio Alger-like story of how L. L. Bean started life as a penniless orphan and built a multi-million dollar industry, through a practical application of honesty and Yankee know-how, is told in this month's *Coronet* magazine in an article entitled, "The Super-Salesman of Freeport, Maine," by Earle Doucette of Augusta.
>
> Earle describes Bean as "an oracle to whom the secret of the outdoors is an open book," and attributes his phenomenal success to the fact that "everything that he sells has been given a grueling test by himself or one of his staff."

According to *Coronet*'s article, Bean's own business axiom is simple: "Sell good merchandise at a reasonable profit, treat your customers like human beings and they will always come back for more."

This basic business formula has resulted in sportsmen spending over two million dollars annually for merchandise with the distinctive Bean label.

Doucette's article relates many homely anecdotes about the down-east philosophy and Yankee ingenuity of Maine's own L. L. Bean, and reveals the little-known fact that the L. L. stands for Leon Leonwood.

More than forty years after he'd started his company, Maine's super salesman began sharing the wealth with his workers when he started a profit-sharing program in 1953, but this didn't mean that Bean's workers were wealthy—or could even afford to retire, for that matter. They often continued working into their seventies and eighties, and since L. L. was then in his late eighties too, he thought nothing of having "younger" workers around with fifty or sixty years of experience. The profit-sharing funds were distributed to eligible employees based on their pay and the number of years they'd worked for the company, and had to be calculated on an individual basis. There was no pension program.

All the publicity he'd been receiving assured L. L. Bean of maintaining at least a steady stream of catalog orders during the fifties, but at least one interesting sale in 1954 might have been generated by a personal connection left over from his wartime duties in Washington. It's hard to tell which, since L. L. simply shows a copy of the customer's letter in his autobiography without any further explanation:

3 November 1954

Dear Sir:

I enclose herewith my check for $1.95 for one of Bean's Crow Call to be sent to the following address:

Admiral Robt. B. Carney, U.S.N.

Chief of Naval Operations
Navy Department
Washington 25, D. C.

I think you would be interested to know that I am getting this call for our very distinguished Secretary of State John Foster Dulles.

Very Sincerely,
Robt. B. Carney
Admiral, U.S. Navy

Not all the correspondence received by L. L. Bean, Inc., contained only orders for merchandise. A note arriving at the company that same year from one Ellis A. Nelson of Minneapolis included an order along with a rather interesting personal observation:

Enclosed find check for which please send me one Bean's Pack Basket and one Pack Basket cover.

Outside of my wife, this is the handiest piece of equipment a man could take into the woods.

Another correspondent wrote to change an address and thank the company for helping him find true love:

For several years Miss Jean Hulbert, 606 Oakmont Ave., Erie, Pa., and Otto Fred Loeffler, 305 Poplar St., Erie, Pa., have been receiving your semiannual catalogues quite regularly.

Effective today, kindly remove Miss Hulbert's name from your mailing last, because she is Mrs. Loeffler now. The common interest in the items listed in your catalogue helped greatly to bring us together.

I heard of your reputation to solve the almost impossible requests from your patrons, but did you ever play cupid before? There is a first time for everything.

The company still receives fan mail and letters thanking it for the extra effort or personal touch of an employee.

L. L. Bean probably gained quite a few more fans in 1954 when he finally decided to open a department that was dedicated to the women who also loved the outdoors. One account says that L. L. opened the women's department in the salesroom "at his wife's insistence," while others give much of the credit to his daughter-in-law Hazel (Carl's wife) for urging him to make his popular Chamois Cloth Shirts and Maine Hunting Shoes available in ladies' sizes. Whoever was behind his doing so, L. L. had soon added "a line of stylish sportswear," and that fall, the L. L. Bean catalog featured sweaters, boots, socks, shoes, and coats for the lady of the house alongside the old standby, long underwear.

According to Leon Gorman, who would begin working at his grandfather's store a few years later, the two Bean women collaborated on the project. Sort of. L.L. Bean's women's department, which was then run by Hazel, had been opened at the urging of L. L.'s wife, Claire, "to give the women something to do while their husbands browsed." The problem was, remembers Gorman, Hazel refused to display most of the items from the catalog with her "trendier sportswear assortment." Generally Leon and Hazel got along quite well, but their opinions about what was "appropriate sportswear for the L.L. Bean woman were far apart. Hazel was an attractive, stylish lady and liked attractive, stylish clothes. That's what we got, and that was the beginning of the ongoing debate about who the 'Bean woman' was, a debate that persisted long after Hazel and me."[3]

The *Wall Street Journal* noted that Bean's ladies' department accounted for only 2 percent of the company's total sales by 1972, but it was a step in the right direction since, according to Hazel Bean, "wives formerly 'stayed down in the car' while their husbands shopped because 'there was nothing up here to interest them.'"[4] Back then, "It was a man's world, you know," remembered longtime employee Carlene Griffin. Whosoever idea it actually was, Griffin finally got it off the ground when she set up a table to sell the 200 pairs of red, white, and blue Bermuda shorts that Jack Gorman had recently picked up in Portland. Two days later, most of the shorts had been sold, making L. L. Bean a firm believer in carrying women's clothing.

Worthy of note is the fact that L. L. Bean had not been totally oblivious to the clothing needs of his primary customers' better halves. As far back as 1922, he'd included a women's Maine Hunting Shoe in his catalog, and even noted that a wool coat he offered "makes a handsome coat for ladies." Regardless of who actually talked him into opening his women's department, L. L. was more than happy to take much of the credit for its promising start.

By 1955 he was already telling an interviewer that it was particularly important for women to order the right size clothing: "Most of them are so style conscious," he noted, "they like to change their clothes every time they cross the street. Naturally, when they're getting outfitted for a hunting or fishing trip, everything must fit just so." The previous October, one customer's clothing order had included the puzzling statement, "I want to outfit my wife for shooting this Fall."

In his autobiography a few years later, Bean, who'd by then been won over by the growing sales of his new department, elaborated on his earlier point of view, saying that a man dresses for comfort when he goes fishing, and doesn't care what he looks like. A woman, on the other hand, wants to look stylish—whether she's at the beach or going fishing or dancing. L. L. concluded that there was "a great future in [women's clothing]" for his company, and it should be paid attention to. (Though L. L. was quick to take credit for the modest success of his fledgling women's department—it was his business, after all—he wouldn't see the need to include a ladies' version of the popular Chamois Cloth Shirt in his catalog until the fall of 1958, when he'd declare the new item to be "an extremely smart model.")

Though Bean's ladies' department contributed only a tiny part to Bean's total sales in 1954, his company remained a big fish in the small pond of Maine, continuing its slow, steady growth to the tune of $2.25 million in sales, 78 percent of which was through the mail. Of the nearly $500,000 customers had spent in his store, purchasers of fall hunting licenses had accounted for about $60,000, including "$3.75 for postage stamps in our 'open all night' dispenser." (In

1954 the price of a first-class stamp was still 3 cents, but by early 1956 President Eisenhower would call for the price to be increased to 4 cents, claiming that the Post Office Department was losing $1,000 a minute.)

Besides hunting, fishing, and running his business, L. L. Bean remained a big fan of America's pastime, and even sponsored a local Little League team. A photo of the squad in Bean's soon-to-be-(self-)published autobiography shows coach Ken Stilkey (1929–84), a longtime Bean employee, and a dozen unnamed, shiny-faced boys posing for the camera in their "L.L. Bean, Inc." uniforms. The uniforms included a large capital B on the caps, which were undoubtedly well received by local Boston fans.

L. L.'s passion for the intricacies of the game was such that he developed a simplified scoring system for Little League baseball. Maybe the idea had come to him while he was taking in a Washington Senators game during the war, or maybe it arrived as a brainstorm like many of his ideas for new products or improvements to old ones. In typical L. L. Bean fashion, his name appeared twice on the cover of the little comb-bound book. It read: "*L. L. Bean's Simplified Baseball Score Book. Especially Adapted for Official Little League Baseball. L. L. Bean, Freeport, Me., Originator and Author.*"

During the summer, he also ran spots on the radio, taking care to get the most coverage he could for his advertising dollar by placing ads on WLAM in Lewiston/Auburn, WPOR in Portland, and Boston's WBZ, among others. Not surprisingly, L. L. Bean decided to have his ads air during broadcasts of Boston Red Sox games, to which the majority of New England radios were probably tuned on any summer afternoon. L. L. even shared with writer Dan Callahan "one of the scripts we've prepared for the one-minute spot we use before the broadcast of every Red Sox game" (even though it takes only thirty seconds to read aloud):

Are you planning to fish or go hunting during your vacation? Then let L. L. Bean choose the equipment you'll need. He tests practically every piece of fishing and hunting equipment sold at his Freeport factory. He knows what you'll get with his equipment. Write to L. L. Bean at Freeport, Me.

He'll send you his free catalog. Or better still, visit L. L. Bean's factory salesroom in Freeport. The latchstring is always out at L. L. Bean's.

In a nod to the increasing diversity of his customer base, L. L. continued to purchase advertisements in outdoors-oriented magazines such as *Sports Illustrated, Field & Stream, Outdoor Life,* and *Sports Afield,* but he also placed them in *Vogue, Esquire,* and the *New Yorker,* among others, to make sure he reached the people—male and female—who didn't necessarily live for the great outdoors. By now he'd even revived the very same system for tracking the effectiveness of his ads that he'd first used in 1922:

Now Freeport isn't a very big place and we're known by everybody in town—particularly the letter carriers who work out of the post office downstairs in our building. So they don't pay any attention to the street number on a letter requesting one of our catalogs. But we do! It's our way of checking pulling power of publications in which we advertise. By the way, the average request cost us 34 cents for advertising last year.

Having sold more than 1,250,000 pairs of Maine Hunting Shoes to date, Bean's business became the subject of two more magazine write-ups in 1955, first in the January issue of *Fortune* and then by Dan Callahan in the September 1 issue of *Sales Management.* The *Fortune* piece opened by stating:

Next to Montgomery-Ward's Sewell Avery, the best-known person in the U.S. mail-order business is probably Leon Leonwood ('L.L.') Bean, sporting-goods merchant of Freeport, Maine. Like Avery, Bean is in his early eighties, runs his company with a firm hand, and is a staunchly conservative man of business. . . .

Unlike Avery, Bean personally designs over half his products, writes his own catalogue, and even occasionally helps wait on the thousands of customers who stream through his rambling retail store each week. Even more unlike Avery, L. L. Bean is famous because of his popularity with customers, who view his flavorful, discursive, sometimes ungrammatical catalogue captions as the next-best thing to a hunting or fishing trip to the big woods.

The *Fortune* article proceeded to report that "to accommodate his catalogue readers, Bean once tried to reclassify his stock into distinct categories, but he soon abandoned the notion. 'The catalogue is thrown together. People tell me they have to look through all 104 pages to find what they're after and that they like it,' he says. 'The way I look at it, nobody ever won an argument with a customer.'" Bean's point that his haphazard catalog worked extremely well, thank you very much, was driven home by the simple fact that "his company earned $80,000 before taxes last year on $2 million worth of sales, and it owes not a cent to anybody."

Naturally, it wasn't just the business magazines that were interested in Mr. Bean's business; twice in late 1954 he'd been featured in articles in *Sports Illustrated*, which dedicated a lot more space to hunting, fishing, and camping at that time than it does today. The first of these articles, "Woodland Stoplight" (November 8), was about the safety benefit of a vest made of the "day-glowing, fluorescent red [material] developed by Joe and Bob Switzer of Cleveland for the Army Signal Corps." The vest which "shines brightly in early morning, late evening, or during overcast—times of most accidental shootings"—was available from L.L. Bean for $1.90.

Maine would not require hunters to wear "hunter orange" until the regular firearms deer season in York County—the state's southernmost county—in 1967, and in the rest of Maine beginning in 1973. The following statistics show what an important role hunter orange and hunter safety courses have played in reducing hunting fatalities in the state: Between 1948 and 1972, an average of more than eight hunters died each season. Between 1973 and 1983, that figure had dropped to three. In 1984 there were no hunting-related fatalities in the state for the first time. And since 1984, there has been fewer than one death per year.

Two weeks later, Bean's 12-inch Maine Hunting Shoe ($12.85) and an assortment of camping gear (which "can be assembled for under $60") were included in *Sports Illustrated*'s "Christmas by Mail" feature.

L. L.'s business probably could have been a lot more profitable if the old factory on Main Street hadn't been so easy to steal from. We're not talking petty shoplifters here, either; a lot of stealing was done by a few of Bean's overnight employees who knew the lay of the land. One former clerk remembers just how bad it was, and even though his numbers may not correspond with those from the *Fortune* article, he still makes a good point, saying that L. L. didn't care about money. Back when the company was doing $2 million in business, most of the profit would be going right out the door— sometimes "by the pickup load," if there's any truth to the story about the guy who worked the graveyard shift and his two cohorts fresh out of the Maine State Prison at Thomaston.

In the subsequent Callahan interview, L. L. provided readers with even more insight into the seeming lack of organization of his famous catalog:

> Well, it is organized—our way. And it works. So why should we change it?
>
> You see, there are so many new items coming along, we've found it advantageous to print the catalogs right in our own factory. To keep the printers working year-round, we give them from four to eight pages a week—filling each page with what- ever pictures and copy we have ready. At the last minute, we fix up an index.
>
> This system has its advantages. For example, if a customer wants to see what we carry in the line of flies, the index tells him we feature 24 kinds. These are listed on 11 pages of the catalog.
>
> By the time he's seen our 24 flies, he's also looked at 62 other items on the same and facing pages.
>
> Then, too, he's bound to see a few other things as he turns

from one page to another.

Self-service supermarkets operate the same way, don't they?

"As I see it," figured Bean, "our catalogs prompted over 90% of the $2,246,000 we took in last year. And I attribute $1 million of this to impulse sales." He then went on to note that "since we went into business 43 years ago, over seven million people have taken the time to request catalogs. Of this number, 400,000 are still customers." In 1955, L. L. Bean's 104-page catalog contained 420 items (all of which, according to the local *Freeport Press*, could be purchased for a total of $3,242).

L. L. concluded his catalog seminar by explaining why products didn't carry stock numbers. "We've never numbered the items in our catalogs. I don't believe in simplifying the bookkeeping to the point where a product loses its identity. What's the point in giving a name to an item if you don't use the name?" (A few years after Leon Gorman took over following L. L.'s death, Bean's items would get stock numbers.)

However L. L. saw fit to organize his catalog, the continuation of its printer was assured when, in 1955, Alexander R. (Sandy) Fowler (1921–2004) purchased the Dingley Press from Walter F. Dumser, who'd occasionally picked up a few extra dollars by taking on outside printing jobs "when not busy with Bean work," which accounted for about seven-eighths of his business. Fowler decided to buy the press when the business he'd been working for moved to the Midwest. Relocating there would have left Fowler, an expert sailor, just a little too far from the Atlantic Ocean to suit him.

Every once in a while during the course of their business relationship, Sandy Fowler would get a break on the price of paper (which was purchased by L. L. to save on taxes), and the two would agree to split the savings fifty-fifty. "Here's what you would normally pay," Fowler would tell L. L., "but I've gotten these guys down by three or four hundred dollars. What say we split it? He'd say, 'Fine. Good deal.'" The Dingley Press would stay in the L.L. Bean factory until it moved across town in 1972, and would print Bean's first all-color catalog in 1979. Dingley would continue to print all of the merchant's catalogs until Bean switched to printing giant R. R. Donnelley & Sons Company beginning with the summer 1981 catalog. Fowler once made the telling remark that "'L. L.' was not interested in expansion at the time, so the number of Bean catalogs printed didn't change much until Leon Gorman took charge of the company."

Besides giving readers an inside look at the workings of Bean's mail-order house, the *Sales Management* interview with Dan Callahan was probably at least partly responsible for L. L.'s largest and last literary effort, the story of his life. The release of L. L. Bean's autobiography—which would turn out to be every bit as disorganized as his catalog—was still five years away, but the interview had ignited a spark. A few years later, L. L. would begin writing his autobiography.

One of the "tales" he'd include in the telling of his life story is actually the lengthy caption of a photo originally published in the May 1955 issue of *Fur-Fish-Game*:

> An outstanding catch, one of the largest ever landed off the Palm Beach Inlet, was the 7-foot 10-inch white marlin whipped on February 24 by Mrs. L. L. Bean of Freeport, Maine. It was brought in on a nine-thread line (27-pound test) after a play of 54 minutes with more than eighteen jumps, and a big shark in pursuit. Shown with Mrs. Bean and her catch is L. L. Bean (left), the noted sportsman-manufacturer, and Captain Al Luthander, skipper of the charter boat *Robert L,* from which the catch was made.

Then there's the one that got away. Not included in L. L.'s upcoming book would be a story about President Eisenhower's June fishing trip to Maine—in which the eighty-two-year-old L.L. Bean didn't participate. During his excursion to the Pine Tree State, Ike had enjoyed the company of a dozen businessmen and politicians, all Republicans, and about seventy reporters and photographers. Not even Maine's newly elected governor, Edmund S. Muskie, a Democrat, had been invited to accompany the president on his late-June fishing trip, which took him to Parmachenee Lake and Rump Pond, and Little Boy Falls and the Riffles on the Magalloway River. During the trip the president reportedly used a split bamboo rod that had been presented to him by "state leaders" in Vermont. All L. L. Bean could do was send a gift, for which he received the following thank-you note:

THE WHITE HOUSE
WASHINGTON
July 1, 1955
PERSONAL
Dear Mr. Bean,
When I was in Maine recently, Senator Payne gave me the leather picnic bag, with accessories, that you so kindly had made for me. I am delighted to have it—and I know Mrs. Eisenhower will find many occasions on which we can use it.
    I am more than grateful for your thought of me.
    I truly enjoyed my all too short visit in your beautiful state.
With best wishes,
Sincerely,
[signed]
Dwight D. Eisenhower

While L. L. included lots of fishing gear in his famous catalog, one thing Bean's customers wouldn't find in it were souvenirs. And they most definitely wouldn't find them in his store either. The article, "It Takes a Sportsman," in *Fortune* emphasized that he refused "to have anything to do with 'foolish gadgets,' even if they are supposed to fit into his line," and went on to recount the story of how one salesman had recently tried to sell Bean a gag fish scale that was calibrated to increase the weight by two or three pounds. "That was just plain silly," remarked L. L., "and I wouldn't stock it—although I know I could have sold hundreds of them. I just don't want that type of trade." Another item that L. L. wouldn't tolerate in his store was a certain metal ashtray—at least not once he realized it was there. According to one former employee:

We had these pewter ashtrays in the salesroom. Kind of cute, had a buck's head and a mallard duck on it, and we sold a million of them at $2.85. Well L. L. came through one day and noticed them for the first time and wasn't he bullshit when he saw them. He didn't want any goddamn souvenirs in his place. I mean that. Just threw them out in the trash. "You don't buy souvenirs at L. L. Bean's store!"

That's what he was yelling while we were hauling them out. Things are different now.⁵

Twenty years after the telling of the clerk's ashtray story, L.L. Bean still carries the finest equipment and clothing for hunting, fishing, and camping, but there are also enough gadgets, knick-knacks, and doodads scattered around the flagship store to do justice to any Route 1 gift shop.

BUT LET'S BACK UP TO LEARN about Leon Gorman's entry into the company. Just a few miles up Route 1 in Brunswick, L. L.'s grandson Leon graduated *cum laude* from Bowdoin College in 1956 with a B.A. in liberal arts. A survey conducted by the *Portland Press Herald* found that the class of '56 "face[d] the best job prospects in history," with graduates of Colby, Bates, Bowdoin, and the University of Maine being interviewed by representatives of some 400 businesses and industries. "Starting pay," noted the paper, "ranges from $350 to $400 a month with some scientific and technical positions offering even more." (At the time, when the federal minimum wage was a dollar an hour, the Maine legislature killed a bill to raise the state's minimum to 75 cents.)

But Leon Gorman wasn't sure what he wanted to do with his new degree. Preoccupied with college and not looking to the future, he found himself wondering, "What do I do now?" once his studies concluded. While he was scrambling to get in a law-school application and take the foreign-service exam, a flurry of job interviews landed him briefly in Boston as a merchandise trainee at Filene's department store. Although his stay at Filene's lasted only about six months, it was there that Leon Gorman would begin his real education, the one that eventually would help him build his grandfather's tired mail-order business into a retail empire.

The whole time he'd been going to job interviews, Gorman knew there was always the option of going into the military; a friend of his had recently graduated from Naval Officer Candidate School, so it seemed like a good option. In January 1957 Leon Gorman joined the navy, where he was soon attending OCS himself. After completing OCS, Lieutenant Gorman served out his stint as commander of the Combat Information Center on a destroyer. It was another valuable learning experience where, at age twenty-two, he was put in charge of an operations division and the thirty-five sailors assigned to it. By his own admission, Lieutenant Gorman was unable to be highly directive with his men or chew them out. It was the beginning of a management style—focusing on "successful outcomes"—that would serve him well.

Later on, Leon Gorman would reflect that it was around this time—the late fifties or early sixties—that his grandfather really began to slow down, and started to lose his business acumen. Bean's sales had reached the $2 million mark during the late fifties, and pretty much stayed there throughout the early sixties. (Gorman, who'd become the company's president in 1967, wouldn't take the chance of losing his touch as he aged and would step aside when he was sixty-six.) In a 1981 speech given to the Newcomen Society of North America, he would sum up the problems that ailed his grandfather's business at the time:

> Like many great entrepreneurs, however, "L. L." had never been able to delegate any responsibilities or plan for any future beyond his own. During the fifties and early sixties his company was suffering from a lack of management and direction. His product groups were right, but the specific products were getting out of date and there were lapses in quality. Service was becoming erratic and the catalogs and advertising were repetitive and losing their effectiveness. The company's atmosphere was congenial, but the staff was aging and without motivation. Profit margins were disappearing.[6]

Unaware of the company's emerging problems, national publications continued to print lengthy profiles of L. L. Bean and his coastal-Maine business. This time it was *Sports Illustrated*, which again dropped in on Mr. Bean to see if he had any advice on striper fishing. Notice how L. L.'s expression changed when he discovered that the reporter was there to talk about fishing, and not about L. L. Bean:

The investigator did not expect to find Mr. L. L. Bean himself at the store. If half the tales told in the catalog were true, he would be well into his 80s and probably retired.

"I would like," said the investigator to the receptionist, "to see Mr. L. L. Bean."

"Mr. Bean," said the girl, "is out for his coffee break. Please have a chair."

In a few moments Mr. L. L. Bean himself bounded up the stairs, tall and straight as a beanstalk and jolly as Santa Claus. At his invitation, the investigator followed him into his office and stated his mission.

The smile faded from Mr. Bean's merry face. He looked a little sad. Then he reached down and pulled out a drawer of his desk. He drew out a book, picked up his ballpoint, and autographed the flyleaf. He handed it to the investigator.

"All I know about fish," he said softly, "is in this book. Take it with my compliments."

The investigator took the book and got up on his feet.

"Is there anything," he said slowly, "about the striper in here?"

Mr. Bean shook his head.

"I am an Atlantic salmon man."

There was even a fine piece included in the October 1956 edition of the *Kents Hill Bulletin*. The school, from which L. L. Bean had graduated sixty-three years earlier, had evidently decided that it had waited long enough to take some of the credit for L. L. Bean's success. The *Bulletin*'s write-up picked up on the Horatio Alger angle from Earle Doucette's *Coronet* article from a few years earlier. Here's part of the brief article, which was titled "Kents Hill's Horatio Alger—L. L. Bean, '93":

> Back in 1891 a Kents Hill student, Vernon Swett of South Paris, persuaded his young cousin, Leon L. Bean, to come to school on the hill. Orphaned and left with two hundred dollars in his pocket, the youngster arrived in due course, finished his studies in the commercial subjects at Kents Hill, then joined his brother in a small clothing store in Freeport, Maine. From there on his story is well known. The L. L. Bean mail-order house catalog is familiar to every hunting and fishing enthusiast from coast to coast. His two-million dollar business in Freeport has been written up in *Saturday Evening Post*, *Life* Magazine, *Pine Cone*, and *Down East*, and as recently as August 27, 1956, *Sports Illustrated* carried an account of an interview with Mr. Bean.
>
> However, we are concerned not so much with the phenomenally successful business, as with the boy who came to Kents Hill who today credits the school with a sound preparation in business methods that helped him become established later on.

But all the glowing write-ups in the world couldn't change the simple fact that L. L. Bean was losing his touch and sales were slumping.

ITS LEADER'S DECLINING KNACK for doing business wasn't the company's only immediate problem. The old saying, "You do your best business on Main Street," couldn't have rung more true for the first forty years of Mr. Bean's business. But that pesky bypass, the one that had first reared its ugly head four years earlier (now part of Interstate 295), was continuing to take its toll on the foot traffic at L. L.'s store. It was whisking thousands of potential customers quickly around Freeport, depriving Bean of many of the impulse shoppers who weren't specifically seeking out the Maine merchant—the "Hey, look, L. L. Bean! Let's stop here!" crowd.

While the mail-order end of the business had at least remained steady, the store's bottom line was taking a direct hit. Before the new road started taking business away, the showroom had been taking in about half a million dollars annually. By 1956, that figure had dropped to $411,000. By 1958 it would be $395,000. L. L. Bean again struck back on page three of his catalog, but this time instead of the map he'd used in 1952, he printed a photograph of the exit sign, which showed the good folks "from away" just how they could get to: "Route U.S. 1," Falmouth Foreside, Yarmouth, Brunswick, and of course, Freeport. Naturally, the photo was accompanied by the usual Bean argument as to why the happy vacationers should detour through downtown Freeport:

> Our Factory Salesroom is open 24 hours a day, 365 days a year. There are many items in our Salesroom not listed in our Catalog.
>
> We are located 18 miles east of Portland on U. S. 1 Business Highway. Coming from Boston on the Maine Turnpike take Exit 9 at Falmouth for Rte. U. S. 1 as shown.
>
> The mileage from Freeport to Augusta by U. S. 1 non-toll road is less.
>
> Plenty of free parking near Salesroom entrance.

When they did find their way there, the tourists would arrive at Bean's increasingly sprawling complex, which had recently grown to include a small shoe factory. In his autobiography, Bean noted his recent acquisition by saying only that in 1956 he bought a small "running shoe factory" across the street—and by "running," he meant "operating," since the shop produced moccasins, not running shoes. The reason L. L. bought the Small-Abbott moccasin factory was so he could have Bean's own hand-sewn moccasins made "in house"; this was still a point of pride with the old man. It would turn out to be a good investment, since hand-sewn footwear remains one of the company's premier products—although much of it is now imported.

The moccasin factory wasn't big, only around 3,200 square feet (about the size of the warehouse L. L. had built in 1947), but combined with his rambling factory and salesroom, it brought the total size of his operation to 70,000 square feet. This was the only time in its history that L.L. Bean, Incorporated, purchased another operating business. Maybe L. L. figured if he couldn't increase his sales, he'd grow his company by buying a smaller one. Interestingly, though, Small-Abbott Co., Inc., wouldn't officially be consolidated with L.L. Bean, Inc., until August 1970.

Probably not coincidentally, in 1956 L. L. decided to do something about all the waste his company was generating, and installed an incinerator. The new furnace could burn a day's worth of boxes, paper, and envelopes in less than three hours, meaning that the company no longer had to haul its waste to the town dump, about three-quarters of a mile away. In his autobiography, there's a picture of L. L. standing in front of his new incinerator, which was very high-tech at the time.

Another indication that L. L.'s mind was more on rest and recreation than on retailing was the increasing amount of time that he and his wife had been spending in Florida every winter. By 1957, when the average income of an American family was $4,970, the Beans were able to have a new home built in Miami Shores. The low, modern-looking ranch-style home, where L. L. and Claire were now spending as many as three months a year, appears to have been designed to include all the latest amenities, such as an attached garage, an in-ground pool, and, next to it, what seems to be an area for L. L.'s favorite game, horseshoes. In *My Story*, L. L. notes that he and his wife had been going to the Florida East Coast for two or three months every winter since 1941.

In June, L. L.'s old friend, Maine writer John Gould, came up with a piece for the *New York Times Book Review* that talked about L. L.'s old standby, his *Hunting, Fishing, and Camping* book, which "has steadily sold from five to ten thousand copies a year, year in and year out since 1942. (Mr. Bean expresses the amount in M's, the usual State o' Maine symbol [thousands of] for board feet, axe handles and boxes of fish.)" Gould noted that by this time Bean's book, which he sold through his catalog for $1.25, "went over the hundred-thousand mark long ago and [Bean] expects to be well on the way to his 200,000th copy after one or two more printings." He went on to report that Bean's catalog designer "says there is no likelihood of deleting it in the foreseeable future." Gould also gave a good example of how, fifteen years earlier, it had been easy for L. L. Bean, the author, to be interrupted by L. L. Bean, the salesman:

> In a fascinating account of some hair-raising woods experience, he will insert a plug for woolen socks, but in the next paragraph you are back on the trail of a bobcat along the Allagash, with dogs howling and hot biscuits browning by an open fire. Mr. Bean would rather hunt than read. Recognizing this as a common trait among the species, he boasts in his preface that he has so condensed his material that the entire book can be read in 85 minutes.

Three months after John Gould recounted the tale of L. L.'s first book, the town's newspaper ran a headline proclaiming "New Book Compares L. L Bean with Avery of Montgomery Ward." The book in the headline was *Adventures in Small Business*, due to be published in September by *Fortune* magazine, and if the comparison to Ward's Avery seems familiar, it's because the *Freeport Press* article was a word-for-word copy of the one that had run in *Fortune* almost three years earlier. In fact, from the sound of it, the book most likely was no more than a collection of articles that had previously appeared in the magazine.

The company wasn't completely stagnant during the late fifties, and as if to make that point, Bean introduced its "New Poleless Tent," an innovation that L.L. Bean, Inc., still touts on its company timeline ("1957—L. L. Bean adds one of the first pole-less tents to catalog"). According to the copy in the spring catalog, this new high-tech marvel was "the lightest weight and easiest erected small tent we have ever listed. Made of the finest light weight Egyptian tent cloth of light green color. No poles are required and except in high winds ropes and stakes are not necessary." The tent, which the catalog claimed could be set up in less than two minutes, measured 5 feet wide by almost 8 feet long, weighed 11 pounds, and cost

$71.25 postpaid. (The company overlooked the fact that it had carried a similar item in 1930 when it sold its 50-pound "Bean's Pine Tree Poleless Tent" for $42.50.) The 1957 model looked kind of like a forerunner of the present-day self-supporting dome tent, but without the rain fly.

As L. L.'s age climbed to the point where hunting all day was no longer an option, he seemed to spend more and more time pursuing the less demanding sport of fishing. The rewards of this form of recreation were twofold: not only was it something he could do with his wife, but his passion for angling also netted him yet another write-up in yet another outdoors magazine. This assured the continued growth of his status as a household name, even as his physical abilities and the sales at his store continued to decline. The piece, which appeared in the January 1958 issue of *The Fisherman*, was written by Jack Denton Scott, and both praised the creative Mainer and promoted his business:

> L. L. Bean, perhaps the most famous character in the State of Maine, is probably known to as many sportsmen as any other individual in the world. He has made his Freeport, Maine, postmark famous throughout the civilized world.
>
> Freeport, an unhurried little town of 3,000 lying on U.S. Highway 1, eighteen miles north of Portland, is one of those fortunate communities that undoubtedly owe much of their existence to the American fisherman. Day and night for forty-five years, they have made their way there to buy boots, rods, reels, lures, rain wear, and other outdoor gear from L. L. Bean. Although his business is primarily a mail-order enterprise, so many customers beat their way to his front door that he threw away the key to his store, and now maintains a 24-hour service, giving his more than a hundred employees alternating time schedules.

Somewhat ironically, it was at about this time that L. L. Bean sold his camp at Belgrade Lakes, probably preferring to fish in Canada in the summer and Florida during the winter. In his autobiography, L. L. shows photos of the two Belgrade lakes cottages—the large one for summer vacations and the small one for guests.

Despite slumping sales at the store, Bean's semiannual catalog drops continued to generate strong sales, maybe even enough to compensate for the slowdown in local business. The new catalog, L. L. noted, would be Bean's biggest ever: "We've had to shorten our index in order to make more room for all the new items that we have this year." The July 17, 1958, edition of Freeport's *Weekly News* even ran a full-page spread of the process, showing Sandy Fowler and his workers at the Dingley Press as they readied 406,000 copies of "the virtual bible of the sporting world" for its August 7 release, "and already orders are pouring in faster than the clerks can handle them." Borrowing from the *Fortune* article, the piece wrapped up by noting that "the catalog is the key to Bean's much vaunted business. He personally designs over half of his products, writes his own catalog, and stresses to make it the next best thing to a hunting or fishing trip to the big woods."

In those simpler times, when a man's haircut still cost a dollar, L. L. was so proud of his mail-order catalog that he even included a photo of the printing process of his fall 1959 circular in his soon-to-be-released autobiography. The photo, showing one of the catalog's 32-page signatures coming off Dingley's web offset press, gives an intriguing glimpse into the "organization" of Mr. Bean's publication. The product mix on some pages makes perfect sense; shoes are shown with boots while fish and game plates are shown with matching cups and mugs. But other pages feature such disparate pairings as ladies' moccasins alongside "Bean's Maine-woods Soap," or a "Folding Door Franklin Stove" adjacent to a pair of pup tents.

A photo of Bean in the August 13, 1959, edition of the *Brunswick Record* showed him looking over a copy of his latest fall and winter catalog, and the text noted that even though the Maine merchant was "now 86 years old, [he] still puts in a full day in the store in addition to finding time to write his life story." Soon, the use of color in L. L. Bean's catalogs would increase as fast as the Dingley Press could keep pace with the evolving technology.

Just as the decade had started with the deaths of L. L.'s brothers, Guy and Otho, it would end with another loss for the Bean family when L. L.'s son-in-law, Jack Gorman, died suddenly on December 15 at his Yarmouth home. He was fifty-four. A brief biographical sketch in the company's scrapbook has this to say:

> Jack Gorman, the son-in-law, rounded out the second generation (along with L. L.'s sons Carl and Warren) engaged in the business. Trained as a forester, he turned his talents to managing the apparel line, earning the respect of all his associates for his capable performance. Jack served as a vice president and director of the company. He was a precision marksman, avid deer hunter, woodworker, and viola player for the Portland Symphony Orchestra.

John T. Gorman, Sr., was survived by his wife, Barbara, and sons John Jr. (Tommy), James, and Leon. His position as L. L.'s clothing buyer would be filled by his former assistant, catalog photographer Mel Collins—at least until Leon joined the company.

For a while in the early 1900s, L. L. and his brother Ervin had a store in Auburn. Maine. Their sign is at the center of the photograph. Courtesy of the Androscoggin Historical Society

An early picture of the Oxnard Block in Freeport shows the Warren Block, to the right, where L. L. would move his store in 1917. Courtesy of the Freeport Historical Society, Babe Walsh Collection

Freeport Square—also known as Post Office Square—on a busy summer day in the early 1900s. COURTESY OF THE MAINE HISTORIC PRESERVATION COMMISSION

The Oxnard and Warren Blocks are shown in this 1909 photo, taken from behind the smoldering remains of Clark's Hotel. COURTESY OF THE MAINE HISTORIC PRESERVATION COMMISSION

Artifacts from L. L. Bean, Manufacturer's early days. The sewing machine and the boots at the scale are from the very beginning— 1912. COURTESY OF THE FREEPORT HISTORICAL SOCIETY, MEL COLLINS COLLECTION

Opposite: This map of the White Mountain National Forest shows the approximate location of L. L. Bean's first Dew Drop Inn, which backed on Dewdrop Brook. The hunting camp was owned by a lumber company and removed by the government eleven years after it took over the land in 1914. MAP DRAWN BY DEAN BENNETT

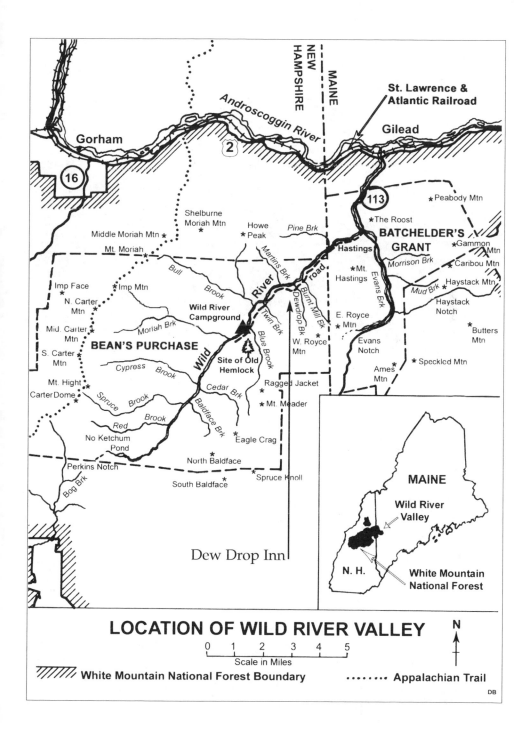

LOCATION OF WILD RIVER VALLEY

N

0 1 2 3 4 5
Scale in Miles

White Mountain National Forest Boundary

Appalachian Trail

DB

Freeport's Casco Castle and Amusement Park in its heyday. The building would burn to the ground in 1914, leaving only the stone tower on the left (still standing today). Courtesy of the Freeport Historical Society, Babe Walsh Collection

A view of Freeport's Post Office Square in the 1920s. There are still trolley tracks running down Main Street. Courtesy of the Maine Historic Preservation Commission

FALL
CATALOGUE
1927
L. L. BEAN, Manufacturer
FREEPORT, MAINE
Dept. 222. Please send your free illustrated CATALOGUE showing Deer Hunting Shoes, Duck Hunting Boots, Leather Hats and Caps, Clothing for Deer and Duck Hunting, Rain Suits, Duffle Bags, etc. Also brief extract of new Maine Game Laws and other information.
Name
Street
City
State

The disturbing cover of Bean's fall 1927 catalog, shown in an advertisement in the October issue of *Sun-Up: Maine's Own Magazine.* COLLECTIONS OF MAINE HISTORICAL SOCIETY

Admiral Donald B. MacMillan (center) and his pilot Charlie
Rocheville (left) are both wearing Bean's Hunting Shoes in this
photo taken at Battle Harbor, Labrador, in 1931. COURTESY OF THE
PEARY-MACMILLAN ARCTIC MUSEUM, BOWDOIN COLLEGE

Many of L. L.'s employees take time off to enjoy a clambake at
Burnett's in August 1939. L. L. Bean is in the center of the group.
COURTESY OF THE FREEPORT HISTORICAL SOCIETY, MEL COLLINS COLLECTION

This artist's drawing of a proposed expansion of L. L.'s factory in the early 1940s incorrectly shows the ocean *behind* the complex!

L. L. Bean supplied boots for the war effort but was also asked by the navy to design an officer's briefcase for carrying charts. The final version was designed by L. L. Bean's son Warren.

Shortly after World War II, the Warren Block needed shoring up
with an external brace. The building would stand until 1977.
COURTESY OF THE FREEPORT HISTORICAL SOCIETY, BABE WALSH COLLECTION

By 1950 the town had installed a traffic light at the intersection
of Main and Bow Streets. (There is no stoplight there today.)
COURTESY OF THE MAINE HISTORIC PRESERVATION COMMISSION

Thanks to E. G. Shettleworth, whose store occupied the first floor
of the Clark's Hotel building, L. L. Bean's rooftop sign points
across the street toward Bean's business in the late 1950s. Drivers
approaching the square from the south had a clear view of it.
COURTESY OF THE MAINE HISTORIC PRESERVATION COMMISSION

Packers hard at work in Bean's shipping room, probably in the 1960s.
COURTESY OF THE FREEPORT HISTORICAL SOCIETY, MEL COLLINS COLLECTION

By the mid-1960s, the Warren Block (right) had been added onto several times and was on its last legs. Courtesy of the Freeport Historical Society, Mel Collins Collection

L. L. Bean's factory and store looked rather bland in the late 1970s. The Warren Block used to stand in front of the section to the right. Courtesy of the Freeport Historical Society, Mel Collins Collection

This issue of the *Boston Globe* featured an article by M. R.
Montgomery. He reported that Bean's marketing research
showed that advertisements in the *New Yorker* and the *New York
Review of Books* actually drew more orders than those in *Field &
Stream* or *Sports Afield*. PHOTOGRAPH BY JAMES L. WITHERELL

In 1984 shoppers flocked to L.L.Bean's new trout pond. The black duck carvings are by Ted Hanks of Jefferson, Maine. Courtesy of the Freeport Historical Society, Mel Collins Collection

L. L. and his exploits were frequent subjects of Maine writer John Gould, shown here with his daughter Kathy in 1988. Courtesy of the Freeport Historical Society, Mel Collins Collection

A look at the 1989 construction shows the entrance to the Mobil station once owned by sometime-author Henry Milliken. Bean's Bike, Boat, and Ski store occupies the site today. Courtesy of the Freeport Historical Society, Mel Collins Collection

Although the newly renovated store had opened in May 1989, workers were still busy finishing the waterfall in June. Courtesy of the Freeport Historical Society, Mel Collins Collection

Leon Gorman made headlines often as the man who modernized his grandfather's company and turned it into an international retailer and catalog business. COURTESY OF THE FREEPORT COMMUNITY LIBRARY

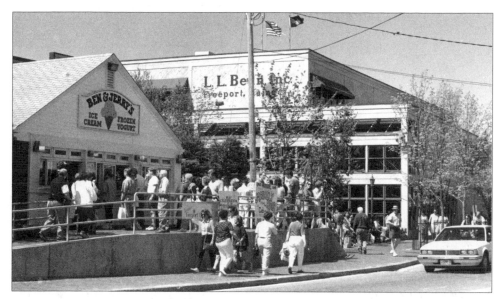

Although L.L. Bean, Inc., purchased the little building and the land on which it sits (shown here in the early 1990s), Ben & Jerry's is still serving ice cream into 2011. Courtesy of the Freeport Historical Society, Mel Collins Collection

The new L.L. Bean outlet store is part of the Freeport Village Station outlet mall, across the street from the flagship store. Photograph by James L. Witherell

This building across Morse Street from the flagship store has been the L.L. Kids store, then Hunting and Fishing, and now the Home store featuring home furnishings. PHOTOGRAPH BY JAMES L. WITHERELL

The Final Charge features two bull moose with locked antlers, on display at the flagship store. PHOTOGRAPH BY JAMES L. WITHERELL

The new Hunting and Fishing addition to the flagship store features timber-frame construction and a big fieldstone fireplace on the landing. PHOTOGRAPH BY JAMES L. WITHERELL

Your pick of logos: the Bean Boot on a polo shirt, above, or the sunrise-over-Katahdin logo on the vest below. PHOTOGRAPHS BY JAMES L. WITHERELL

A display of catalog covers in the flagship store. Photograph by
James L. Witherell

The women's section features the new L.L. Bean Signature line at
Christmastime, 2010. Photograph by James L. Witherell

The author's well-worn boots. Photograph by James L. Witherell

The giant Bean Boot statue outside the flagship store's main entrance is sixteen feet long and fourteen feet tall. Photograph by James L. Witherell

A bust of Leon Leonwood Bean in the Discovery Park at the flagship store in Freeport. PHOTOGRAPH BY JAMES L. WITHERELL

Chapter 8

*"To a great extent, it was the secretaries
that really ran the business"*

Mirroring the turbulence of the times, the 1960s would also be a period of milestones and major changes for L.L. Bean, Inc. During the next ten years, the venerable Freeport company would endure an extended period of stagnation which would ultimately end with the passing of its legendary founder. But the end of one chapter of the company's storied life would inevitably lead to the start of a new one, one that would see the emergence of a visionary new leader who'd turn out to be a lot hungrier than his grandfather, the man content to get three good meals a day.

As it had for most of the preceding decade, Bean's company continued to chug along to the tune of about $2.5 million in annual sales, much of it generated by his Maine Hunting Shoe. As they'd been from the beginning, the boots' rubber bottoms continued to be supplied by the U.S. Rubber Company of Boston. On the whole, L. L. seemed to be well pleased with his relationship with U.S. Rubber, and was no less happy about his standing with them as well, since they told him many times that he was their biggest customer for boot rubbers.

At the time, L. L. Bean's business consisted of about 70,000 square feet of floor space and "about one acre" of parking. The salaries that L. L. and Carl drew for running the place totaled about $80,000, which was reportedly about twice the company's slowly declining profit for an entire year, while Bean's average worker earned about $5,000. The more skilled stitchers, who sewed L. L. Bean's boots and shoes, fared slightly better than the rest: they could earn as much as $7,000 in piecework wages. In fact, the wage Bean paid his 115 employees was one of the many secrets to his success that he'd reveal later that year in his autobiography, writing that since his company was located in a small town, living expenses were low, so "good wages here would be small in a city. Our prices are made accordingly."

But not all of his workers saw things the way Bean did. One former clerk in particular, a man who'd worked his way through college at Bean's, took issue with L. L.'s belief that the wages he paid were "good":

> I liked him. You know, if you worked for Bean's you didn't work too hard. And you didn't get paid diddly-squat. I never did understand him about that.
>
> He'd get grumpy sometimes, and he'd come down to the salesroom and yell at us and tell us he could replace us all in fifteen minutes. And I guess he could. He'd give you these incremental wage increases; I guess he would hear about what was going to happen, because you'd get a raise and a few days later the minimum wage would go up and you'd be making exactly a nickel over minimum.[1]

By this time, L. L. Bean was in his late eighties and in declining health. As the years went by, the amount of time he spent at his winter home in Florida had gradually increased from a month or two to its present "three or four." So it had come to pass that, for the last several years, the factory and store in Freeport had meandered along under L. L.'s part-time guidance while the day-to-day operations of L.L. Bean, Inc., were really being managed by his sons, Carl and Warren, with most of the day-to-day decisions being made by Carl—when he wasn't off playing golf or hunting for antiques, that is. "To a great extent," opined Leon Gorman after becoming the company's president, "it was the secretaries that really ran the business."

And this was not a case of overstatement or exaggeration on his part. Ethel Williams and Jessie Beal were, technically, the respective secretaries of L. L. and his son Carl. But in fact, said Leon Gorman, they were much more than that to the company. Jessie oversaw the company's order entry, mailing list, and personnel matters, while Ethel looked after Bean's advertising program and catalog production, and also dealt with the buyers. At the time, the best way to get something done at L.L. Bean was to go through either Ethel or Jessie.

But just because L. L. Bean was wintering for longer and longer periods in sunny Florida didn't mean he'd given up work altogether in favor of fishing or pitching horseshoes. He still personally approved the spring edition of his semiannual catalog, which was "printed on the premises" (on the first floor of the three-story warehouse and shipping building), on four Swedish presses "in our quarter-million-dollar printing plant"—which was really Sandy Fowler's Dingley Press. Since revisions from one issue of his catalog to the next were usually minor, and all the changes were personally approved by Bean himself, it would continue to bear his unique style of writing right up until his death.

Time magazine would report that Bean's "spare, disarming style has been used in advertising textbooks as exemplary of what direct-mail selling should be. Sample: 'Most hunters and fishermen smoke. For a long time we searched for an outstanding pipe. This pipe is the result.'" Not only had the piece finally made L. L. Bean's familiar writing style famous, it also served to illustrate the selling power of his recommendations, since the pipe he plugged in his catalog was reportedly nothing more than a garden-variety Dr. Grabow item that could be purchased at any drugstore. (L. L. Bean did not smoke.)

Distributed to 410,000 of his best customers, each of the semiannual editions of L. L. Bean's 1960 catalog consisted of 116 pages and required over 175 tons of paper to print. Some of the highlights of this year's catalog included oversize duck decoys for "$142.00 per dozen" and 124 different styles of shoes. "As we fill orders the same day received," noted Bean, "we are obliged to carry over 24,000 pairs of shoes in stock the year 'round. We manufacture about one-third of them. The balance is made to our order by Maine and Massachusetts factories."

SINCE REVIEWING THE CATALOG was probably a routine task that L. L. could complete rather quickly, he still had plenty of time to finish that autobiography on which he'd slowly been working for the past few years. ("A while back a feller came in the office and offered me $2,500 to let him write the story for me. Then when we got into it I found out I was doing most of the work so I decided to try it on my own."[2]) In 1960 he would finally publish *My Story: The Autobiography of a Down-East Merchant*, the seed for which many people believe had been planted in L. L.'s brain during his 1955 interview with *Sales Management*'s Dan Callahan. Bean's second book, which sold for $3.85 postpaid, bears a striking physical resemblance to his first, the perennial "bestseller," *Hunting, Fishing, and Camping.* The slender volume originally consisted of 163 pages—not very many for a man who'd lived so long and accomplished so much (the book's second edition is 157 pages long, and subsequent editions are even thinner), but that's not to say he didn't *try* to write more.

L. L. started out with every intention of writing a traditional autobiography. Once he got going, he actually wrote about nine of the book's first twenty pages. But after that, his compact writing style and years of coming up with word bites for his catalog caught up with him. Around page 27, he began to fill his book with a mixture of photos from the Bean family album and some of the many letters of praise and thanks he'd received during his long career. A total of about twenty-five pages is all the actual writing he could muster, and that's if you count a copy of the first page of his original catalog. In the end, *My Story* ends up looking more like *My Scrapbook,* but it's still interesting reading if you can manage to find a copy and have some sense of the actual sequence of events in the long, busy life of L. L. Bean.

He tapped longtime friend John Gould to write the introduction for *My Story*, which would turn out to be nearly as long as the total amount of text that Bean himself was able to manage. (Maybe in a move to save paper, L. L. didn't include Gould's introduction in every edition of his book; the text in a copy at the Curtis Memorial Library in Brunswick is just 104 pages long and starts after only an eleven-line foreword by L. L.) One facet of Bean's growing celebrity that Gould touched on his introduction was how it never ceased to puzzle the famous Freeporter that while he could understand why people would want to buy his boots, "the rest just doesn't make sense."

But it wasn't merely humility on L. L.'s part that kept him from telling his story in more detail. It was also his never-evolving, scattershot style of writing: he seemed to put down his thoughts pretty much in the order that they occurred to him. Another writer, M. R. Montgomery, devoted more than two pages to the disorganization of L. L. Bean's second major literary effort, using the example of Bean writing about the incorporation of his company in 1934, and how he then "continues on without a break, or a pause, or any apology, back to the 1890s."

Mixed-up or not, in 1960, when L. L. Bean was in is late eighties, he finally got to tell his life story in his own words, and he got to once again use P. B. Parsons' painting, *The Old Country Store*, this time on the book's dust jacket. L. L. liked the painting so much that, after missing his chance to buy the piece in 1915, he used its likeness on five of his fall catalogs between 1930 and 1952. The company would use it again on its sixtieth anniversary catalog in 1972 (where we'll learn more about the artist and his painting).

Since both books written by L. L. had been self-published, there weren't very many reviews of his literary efforts. (Even Bean's friend John Gould hadn't reviewed the merchant's 1942 *Hunting, Fishing, and Camping* until 1957.) Maybe L. L. had a subscription to *Yankee* magazine at the time and sent in a copy of his latest work for review, since Geoffrey Elan has these few words to say about it in the "Books Received" section of the magazine's November 1960 issue:

My Story by L. L. Bean, 163 pages, profusely illustrated, from the author, Freeport, Maine, $3.85 postpaid.

Those who know Mr. Bean were not surprised when, a few years ago, the *Saturday Evening Post* came out with a full-color feature on him and his activities. Now, in his eighties, Leon

Leonwood Bean takes his story from 1881 to date, with a top dressing by John Gould you cannot fail to enjoy.

LEON GORMAN WAS HONORABLY discharged from the U.S. Navy on May 3, 1960, after serving as a line officer on destroyers for three years, the last one being spent on the USS *Tills* (DE 748), a destroyer escort training ship home-ported out of Portland, Maine. Since he was discharged in nearby Brunswick, home of his alma mater, Gorman decided to stop in at Bowdoin College on his way home for some advice. Sam Ladd, the college's placement director, suggested that he see his grandfather on the way home. "Sam saw a lot more opportunity there than I did, and perked up my interest. Maybe L. L. had something for me to do."[3]

When Gorman showed up for the job interview in his uniform, his grandfather seemed genuinely glad to see him, and happily hired Leon at a starting salary of eighty dollars a week because, after all, he was L. L.'s grandson, and L. L. had always "had a soft spot for unemployed relatives." Since L. L. had interviewed Leon in his usual conversational tone of voice, everyone on that floor probably knew Leon was coming on board before he did.

L. L. had hired his grandson but hadn't told him what to do, so Gorman wandered around the office until he found a place to sit down—which happened to be at his father's old desk, so he "sat down and did the job that went with the desk." That made Gorman Bean's clothing buyer. (A 1979 Leon Gorman résumé of unknown origin on file in the Freeport Community Library lists his first position at Bean's as "Assistant to Vice President" Carl Bean.) Whatever his first official title there, upon his arrival at L.L. Bean, Inc., Leon Gorman found his granddad's business to be a particularly sleepy one; his undergraduate degree from Bowdoin made him the only college graduate in the whole place.

But buying clothes was only his official job duty. Back then, if you worked at L.L. Bean, you did a little bit of everything, and Gorman, who was the third son of L. L.'s daughter Barbara, got the full education, just the same as L. L.'s. sons, Carl and Warren, had received when they started working at the family business. Leon's hands-on learning experience covered all aspects of a successful mail-order business, starting with taking customers' orders over the telephone. From there, he learned the rest of the system. He picked orders in the warehouse, learned how to pack them properly, and finally, shipped them out to the waiting customers. Sometimes he even helped paste up L. L.'s cherished catalogs. One thing Leon Gorman didn't know much about back then was accounting, which was a good thing considering that the company's entire profit at the time was a paltry $42,000. Gorman once recalled that, if he had known Bean's situation, he would have gone to work for the phone company.

Almost as soon as he'd arrived in Freeport, Leon Gorman tried to improve the efficiency in Bean's creaky old business-as-usual office, where L. L. and Carl were more interested in paying their personal bills and socializing than running the company. As it was, Bean's massive mailing list had to be retyped on three-by-five cards every time a new catalog was mailed out. While this provided job security for the two dozen or so women in Bean's sizable secretarial pool—and evidently quite a few of the town's other typists—it was far from the best way to run a business of this size. Customer purchases were kept track of on the cards, with the names of those not placing regular orders being deleted from the list.

Not long into his tenure at Bean's, Leon Gorman suggested that they use a Chicago company to streamline the catalog-mailing operation. L. L. was aghast. What would his customers think if they began receiving L.L. Bean catalogs that bore a postmark from the Windy City? Gorman's idea was quickly vetoed.

Probably L. L. had been genuinely concerned about the image problem of his famous catalog being disseminated from the Midwest, but there was also another reason for his reluctance to the idea: money. If the company needed a new desk or filing cabinet, Carl would go to Portland and buy a secondhand one. Getting a new pickup truck almost took an act of Congress. The "company" copier was the one in its lawyer's office across the street, and a friend in the shoe industry once told Gorman that L. L.'s manufacturing area looked like a Singer sewing machine museum. About the only concession L. L. and Carl ended up making to modernization was the purchase of electric typewriters for the clerical staff.

One of the few battles Leon Gorman did win during his early tenure at Bean's was the approval of his idea to at least have a copy of the company's valuable mailing list kept in another location in case the tired old Warren Block caught fire some night. Any sizable blaze in the aged timber-frame structure would surely have made it a total loss, taking with it the priceless list of names and addresses that L. L. Bean had worked a lifetime to amass, and which accounted for $1.8 million of the company's annual sales.

On October 13, 1960, L. L. Bean celebrated his eighty-eighth birthday, no doubt with the customary trappings of cards, cake, gifts, and guests. But this year there was more. That very same day, the *Enterprise* in Lisbon Falls printed an entire page of congratulatory notes and letters from well-wishers ranging from old friends to some of Maine's most prominent politicians, thanks to the paper's publisher, one John Gould. Praise for L. L. on his eighty-eighth came from Governor John H. Reed, U.S. senators Margaret Chase Smith and Edmund S. Muskie, as well as outdoors writers Bud Leavitt of the *Bangor Daily News* and Gene Letourneau of the *Portland Press Herald*, among others.

In his brief note, Leavitt summed up the wishes of all the others, writing, "Mr. Bean is one of America's greatest Americans and merchandisers. In my time, I would like to know, exactly, the number of sportsmen who have reiterated, 'I stopped at L.L. Bean's last night . . . ' before coming to camp. No other man in our time has done more for the outdoor cause of Maine."

Another of the notes was from George Hunter, who'd interviewed L. L. on the radio the day the big *Saturday Evening Post* article came out in 1946:

L. L. may be 88, but I was talking to him the other day and he seemed about as he did when I was a boy around Freeport and we both wondered if the other would ever amount to anything. I suppose Freeport was the last place in the world that realized

L. L. Bean had become famous! I'm sure I realized it only when I grew up and moved around, and when I said I came from Freeport people would ask me if Mr. Bean was all right. It was a distinction to come from Freeport, but it gave me great respect to be able to say I knew him well. I hope I can continue to say that for many long years to come.

It had taken way too long, but Freeport—and the rest of Maine—finally realized what a treasure they had in L. L. Bean.

Perhaps it was this milestone in L. L. Bean's life that prompted former Red Sox slugger Ted Williams to make this rather unusual pitch to the aged merchant late in the year:

November 9, 1960
Dear Mr. Bean:
As you know, my career as an active ball player is over and it is now my intention to devote more time to my fishing tackle business.

With this in mind, we are planning to expand our operations to include other sportsmen's items.

As I have visited your plant and used your products, I am familiar, in a way, with your company, hence the reason for this letter.

I would appreciate your advising me if you would be interested in merging with Ted Williams, Inc., or, if not, would you consider the outright sale of your company, and if so, on what terms.

If either of the above propositions interests you, kindly advise me at your earliest convenience.
Looking forward to an early reply, I remain very truly yours,
TED WILLIAMS, INC.
[signed]
Ted Williams
President

The fact that Mr. Bean respectfully declined Mr. Williams's request was probably of little consequence to the Splendid Splinter since, only seven weeks later, he'd sign a lucrative consulting deal with Sears. For about $100,000 a year, he became the head of the "Ted Williams Sears Sports Advisory Staff," a group of athletes who field-tested, endorsed, and helped market sporting goods for the largest department store chain in the country. Williams was in charge of hunting, fishing, and baseball. His name went on rods and reels, shotguns, and bats, balls, and gloves.

"He tested them, too," basketball Hall-of-Famer Jack Twyman says. "He'd make the buyers cry. They'd have some new product and he'd say, 'This is just a piece of crap.'"[4]

If they had agreed to do business together, L. L. Bean and Ted Williams probably would have gotten along famously.

IN ITS FEBRUARY 6, 1961, ISSUE, *Newsweek* took notice of L. L. Bean when it mentioned the imminent release of his spring and summer catalog and the immediate flood of orders it would elicit. "Judging from past performances," reported the piece, "the return rush of orders will pour back into Bean's crazy, maze-like store in the little village of Freeport, Maine (population: 4,055), at the rate of around 1,500 a day—seven days a week, 52 weeks of the year." (During Bean's busy season, the company received up to 5,000 letters a day.)

So taken was the writer of the article by Bean's unorthodox catalog and factory, he tried to describe them to his readers as best he could: "Bean's catalog now lists more than 400 items, but it has no index. The Bean store itself is equally mystifying. It originally occupied the second floor over the village post office, but as Bean needed more space, he simply added a floor here, and a wing there, and the store's 65,000 square feet now spill over onto a dozen different interconnecting levels."

Late the following year, *Time* magazine concurred with its rival's description of the rambling L.L. Bean factory: "The Freeport factory expanded steadily but haphazardly, and today it looks like a cross between Grandma's attic and a broken roller coaster,"[5] the article noted. "Dumbwaiters hesitantly carry materials from floor to floor through a mazelike production line. Mailing labels are typed and pasted by hand, and requests for catalogs are filed in shirt boxes."

But inside L. L.'s labyrinth, the confusion was organized to the point that the company was able to manufacture more than half of the items listed in the L.L. Bean catalog that year. (L. L. figured that each page in his circular was worth about $10,000 in sales, which helped to explain the absence of a space-wasting index.) More than 350,000 copies of his latest catalog were sent directly to those on his mailing list, and L. L. figured that the remaining 60,000 would either be handed out over the counter or sent out to people who'd written in for one. At any rate, they'd all be gone by February, just about when the next edition was due out.

In the spring Leon Gorman had been able to enlarge the company's retail store by working around his uncle Carl, whom he once described as "unpleasant" to work with. Since Carl couldn't be bothered to climb the stairs to the store's third-floor showroom, Leon was able to put out all the sizes of a particular item and arrange the space in a more logical layout. Before the makeover, the retail area had had just one sample of an item on display, necessitating the clerk's running to the stockroom to retrieve a different color or size.

Newsweek noted that Bean's "research and development" in his outdoor laboratory (the Maine woods) had led directly to the creation of many of the products he sold, including "the Bean 'Toter and Deer Carrier' (a stretcher-like device that is pushed along on one wheel), a coat without sleeves, a vest with sleeves, and a fur-lined bottle holder (to keep bottles from breaking under rough handling)." All those other doodads were nice for the bottom line, but still king among Bean's offerings was his Maine Hunting Shoe ($11.35 to $23.85), of which he'd sell some 16,000 pairs that year. "We know how important those boots are to a man," said L. L. "He might like them better than his wife." Bean's second most popular item, especially around Christmastime, was his Chamois Cloth Shirt.

In November 1961, Leon Gorman was recalled to service by the navy, which required the pleasure of his company until the following August. (The reason for Gorman's return to active duty was the second recommissioning of the USS *Tills*, this time from October 1, 1961, until August 1, 1962. By 1969 the *Tills* would be deemed unfit for service, used for target practice, and sunk off the coast of Virginia.) During his deployment, Gorman served aboard the destroyer escort, which was sent to Guantánamo Bay, Cuba, from where it patrolled the Windward Passage in the Caribbean.

During his time away, he no doubt had a lot of time to reflect on the goings-on at the family business, and certainly didn't like what he had seen there. At sixty-two years younger than his famous grandfather, Gorman was able to see how modern management and production techniques could transform the company from a diamond in the rough to one of the crown jewels of mass marketing. But it almost didn't happen. While he was gone, Bean's board of directors—which was more or less controlled by L. L. and Carl— became aware that Leon had been able to get a few new products into the catalog. In order to nip this practice in the bud, the board voted—in Leon's absence—that no new item could be put into the catalog without the unanimous approval of the board. Since both L. L. and Carl were opposed to change of any kind, the vote almost guaranteed that no new products would be approved for the catalog.

If the vote had been taken before he was recalled, said Gorman, "I would have had to leave the company."[6] (Gorman wouldn't actually learn about the vote until forty years later—after he'd retired as Bean's president and CEO!)

Aging and frail, L. L. was more than happy to let things be. Years later, Leon Gorman would tell a writer for the now-defunct *Maine Times* newspaper that, in the early sixties, "Things had deteriorated. It was a place of benign neglect." Specifically, he put the blame for Bean's failure to grow on the poor performance of its ad agency, slow service, and the company's outdated jumble of products, such as outdated fishing tackle and the war-surplus items that L. L. continued to put into the catalog.

And customer service was no better, with Bean's buyers often debating with customers—by mail—over the validity of their right to a refund. Despite the fact that L. L. had instituted a thirty-six-hour standard for order fulfillment back in the thirties, orders placed during the Christmas rush often took more than two weeks to process. Twenty-five percent of customer orders were being back-ordered or canceled. According to the *Maine Times*:

> "No one was really working to make the business a success," [Gorman] said; even L. L. . . . was too old and tired to care. Gorman said Bean's was carrying obsolete equipment, such as heavy, paraffin-coated tents. There were long delays in meeting customers' needs; and the company's advertising firm, A. E. Ellis in Boston, "had finally run out of ideas, to put it mildly."
>
> Ellis was using its $100,000 Bean advertising budget to place ads in the customary fish and game magazines and the *New Yorker*. But there was no market testing, no demographic studies of customers' whereabouts, no aggressive efforts to improve business. Bean's was, until that time, living on L. L.'s legacy, Gorman said.

One of the first things Leon Gorman would do after becoming president would be to replace A. E. Ellis with Barton, Church and Golf of Providence, Rhode Island, before later settling on the direct-mail specialists at Sawyer Direct.

Most of Bean's employees were as antiquated as his business. The average Bean employee was sixty-seven years old at a time when "retiring" in Freeport meant going to work for L.L. Bean, Inc. The old man paid his hourly workers so little that no one there could afford to retire; they just kept showing up for work every day and turning out ever more Bean-branded shoes, boots, and ice carriers (which would soon become Bean's popular Boat and Tote Bags). The good news in all this was that they received an annual bonus. "Pay is so modest," noted *Time* magazine, "that each change in the federal minimum wage law has required an adjustment of the whole salary schedule. But Bean's 115 workers also get an annual bonus, which [in 1961] amounted to 30% of wages."

Gorman saw his grandfather's company as too labor-intensive and years behind the times, but he would later look back on these rustic days as the beginning of the company's second period of development, one of transition. (According to Gorman, the first part of the company's development had been the period from L. L.'s beginnings until his death in 1967, with the transitional part partially overlapping the first, running from 1961 to 1975. The third period of development would be Bean's rapid growth after 1975.) It's also notable that 1962 was the year Leon Gorman started taking two business courses per semester at the University of Maine in Portland (now the University of Southern Maine).

In 1962 L.L. Bean, Inc., would mark its fiftieth year in business. This was because Bean had chosen as his starting date 1912, the year he sold his first batch of Maine Hunting Shoes, and not 1917, when he'd moved to the Warren Block, or 1920, when he'd purchased the building. (The L.L. Bean anniversary celebration has sometimes been held in September—for example, the party for the company's eightieth anniversary was held during the weekend of September 19 and 20, 1992—but the company's ninetieth and ninety-fifth anniversary bashes would coincide with July 4th.) At the midpoint of its first century, L.L. Bean employed 120 people and did exactly $2,539,315 in business.

As he approached his ninetieth birthday, Mr. Bean's condition had deteriorated to the point where he now got around with the help of a walker. Even so, he still insisted on going to work, even if his workdays were considerably shorter than they used to be and often consisted of little more than taking care of personal matters. "[T]hey'd come down in a Cadillac each morning and pick him up and then about 2 in the afternoon they'd bring him back home," fifty-two-year-old Freeport native Ken Mann would recall in 2000. "That was when I worked at my father's gas station, right [across the street]."[7] Feeble though he was, L. L. was still mentally alert (even if his attention span had decreased noticeably) and still had his famous booming voice. He celebrated his company's milestone by writing the following brief letter, which appeared in his fall 1962 catalog. It seems, given the letter's economic style, that he actually wrote it himself, instead of handing the task off to an assistant:

> For fifty years I have been sending catalogs to sportsmen all over the world. I wish to take this opportunity to express my heartfelt gratitude to the many friends I have made and the many hunters, fishermen, and campers who have seen fit to trade with us over these years.
>
> I have always greatly enjoyed hunting and fishing and can honestly say it has been a pleasure helping others enjoy these wonderful sports.
>
> In 1912, the first 4-page catalog illustrating my Maine Hunting Shoe was mailed out. The shoe is still with us. The catalog has grown to 116 pages. I believe the success of our catalog has been that everything we offer is guaranteed to be practical for its purpose. We never hesitate to return a customer's money, no questions asked, and intend to follow this policy for the next fifty years.
>
> I should like to remind everyone who comes to Maine that the latchstring is always out at L.L. Bean, Inc.

As usual, Bean's famous factory store remained open twenty-four hours a day—at least until early March, when one of New England's famous blue laws threw a monkey wrench into the works. Dating back to colonial times, these puritanical edicts forbade certain practices we now take for granted, especially drinking or working on Sunday. Late in the winter of 1962, Bean's store fell victim to such a regulation when a law passed in September by Maine's 100th Legislature mandating Sunday as a universal day of rest went into effect, forcing L.L. Bean to close its doors on March 4th and 11th. (In 1960 the Lewiston City Council had technically violated the blue law, voting five to two to allow Gus Tramer's Midway to open at the Lewiston Fair Grounds on a Sunday, as long as there were "just rides for the kids" and no gambling or "girlie shows.")

While the new law did allow L.L. Bean to continue selling hunting and fishing licenses on Sunday, the twenty-five cents he took in on each one wouldn't have covered what it cost him to staff the counter, even if the store did sell one-fourth of all hunting and fishing licenses issued in Maine. Since it was pointless for L.L. Bean to stay open just to sell licenses, for those two Sundays in March, all who arrived at the store's usually welcoming door, with "Salesroom Entrance, L.L. Bean, Inc." lettered on the glass, now saw a piece of paper saying, "Closed All Day Sunday" taped to the lower left-hand corner of the window, near the door handle.

Before the law had gone into effect, someone at the Lisbon, Maine, *Enterprise* newspaper (most likely John Gould) spoke up and gave the Maine legislators the verbal beating he felt they deserved. "This points up, of course, an absurdity of making laws without stopping to think what you're making laws about. Freeport," he continued, "may well be expected to give L. L. Bean the permission he will be obliged to ask for—but will naturally have to do so in a blanket fashion, which means that in order to open L.L. Bean legally on Sundays, they might have to open some places they wouldn't otherwise want to."

The new law stipulated that "no person shall on the Lord's day, Memorial Day, July 4th, November 11th, and Thanksgiving Day, as proclaimed by the Governor, keep open his place of business to the public except for works of necessity or charity." After listing more than forty exemptions, the law continued to allow that

> In any city or town that shall vote as hereinafter provided, it shall be lawful to keep open to the public on the Lord's day and aforementioned holidays, other places of business not exempted under Section 38. This provision shall not be effective in any municipality until a majority of the legal voters, present and voting at any regular election, so vote.

Later that March, the voters of Freeport expressed their support by giving Bean permission to open on the Sabbath, not just because almost everyone in town loved the old guy and had a great deal of respect for his business, but also because of the store's "mainte-nance of a twenty-four-hour fire alarm system" for the community. The next time Bean's store would close would be in November 1963 for President Kennedy's funeral.

In August 1962 Leon Gorman returned from the navy to his desk at his grandfather's factory, this time with the title of "Assis-tant to Vice President & Clothing Buyer," a title he'd keep until March of 1967. Around this time Gorman probably decided that his future was in Freeport and he'd better learn to hunt and fish. "If I were in another business," he told the reporter from *Time*, "I probably wouldn't care much about hunting or fishing, but I'm learning fast."

In fact, Leon Gorman's introduction to fly casting had come rather hastily on the warehouse roof when a salesman, who figured Leon already knew how to fly-fish, invited him on a fishing trip. Wid Griffin took Leon up to the roof of the warehouse, where there was nothing in which to tangle the line, and worked with him until he could cast well enough to maybe catch fish. The fishing trip was a success, with Gorman even catching some trout. Before long, he'd be first in line to get one of those new ferrule-less Fenwick fly rods when they came out.

It was also around this time that he proposed streamlining things in the office by either buying or renting one or more Addres-sograph machines, whose aluminum blanks could be embossed with the customers' names and addresses, greatly speeding up the mailing process. His idea was shot down immediately. L. L. wouldn't hear of fixing something that, in his opinion, wasn't even close to being broken. Not only were the clerk/typists perfectly adequate, Bean thought, but he wasn't about to lay off anyone who'd given him years of loyal service. Besides, the extra hands came in handy for picking and packing orders during the busi-ness's busier times.

In fact, L. L. Bean was so proud of the nimble digits of his office staff that he even bragged about how his company's incoming orders were handled somewhat as at Sears, Roebuck and Com-pany. Through the magic of carbon paper, one of Bean's "girls," he said, could fill out three copies of an order, an address label for the shipment, and an address card, which was checked against the mailing list, the maintenance of which was equally labor-intensive.

Mr. Bean's distaste for automation would even make it into that December issue of *Time*: "Bean rules his board of directors—two sons and two grandsons—with a firm hand and brushes aside suggestions from his heir apparent, Grandson Leon Gorman, 27, that the company 'automate' by buying an Addressograph. 'Why expand when you're 90 years old?' demands Bean." L. L. then repeated his mantra about getting three good meals a day. (Shortly before his death a few years later, he was again asked if he had any plans to expand his business, to which he replied, "Yes, we have some suspenders in the catalog." These could be the same braces worn by baseball legend Ted Williams when he dropped by the store bright and early one mid-November morning in 1972 "wearing a pair of Bean's heavy-duty red suspenders and left with two more.")

Carlene Griffin would tell the *Portland Press Herald* shortly after her retirement that she "was among a group of women who typed up carbon copies of the store's early modest mailing lists, 33 names to a page—three columns of 11 each. The original labels went on the spring catalog, and the carbon copies went on the fall catalog." No, L. L. Bean wasn't about to have any of his gals replaced by one of those fancy Addressograph machines.

The future of L. L.'s company remained a mystery to many people, including Leon Gorman. Years later he'd be given bank records from the early sixties that did not paint a rosy picture of the company's future: Bean's accountant Shailer Hayes had told Leon Gorman that L. L. had no will, and refused to even discuss the continuation of his company after his passing. L. L. Bean was fine with things the way were—so the latest sign of progress to come to Freeport might have bothered him just a bit.

FOUR YEARS EARLIER, PRESIDENT EISENHOWER had asked Congress to approve a $2 billion post office modernization program under which 2,500 government-owned post offices would be renovated or replaced and another 12,000 leased buildings would be remodeled or replaced. On Monday September 17, 1962, the Freeport post office officially opened in its new location 700 feet up Main Street from its old home in L. L. Bean's Warren Block, where it had been located for as long as most townspeople could remember. The new 4,971-square-foot building, which was owned by the North Berwick Lumber Company, was leased to the Post Office Department for $10,890 a year. A unique feature of the new post office was that the service lobby had an open counter in place of the customary screened-in windows. A dedication ceremony for the new building was held on September 29 and featured talks by acting postmaster John R. Lavers and Earl F. Bagley, the Post Office Department's real estate officer for the State of Maine.

The main reason that the Freeport post office had been conveniently located downstairs from Bean's business for as long as anyone could recall was because L. L. had tried his best to keep it there. Back in 1941, you may recall, L. L. had even countered the Post Office Department's proposal to build the town a new $85,000 post office by spending $25,000 of his own money to renovate the existing facility downstairs from his factory.

But the post office wouldn't be completely gone from Bean's for many years to come. Since the company sent out more than 200 large sacks of mail each day, accounting for almost two-thirds of the Freeport post office's annual receipts, L.L. Bean would retain the wire-enclosed parcel post unit located on its second floor. From the shipping room, all of Bean's outgoing packages went down a conveyer belt to this area, where they were sorted by post office personnel and loaded into mail trucks bound for Portland.

On July 1 of the following year, the Post Office Department would introduce the Zoning Improvement Program, or ZIP Code, with the Freeport post office being assigned 04032. At the same time, the post office began using standardized two-capital-letter abbreviations for all the states, for example, "ME" would replace "Me." on mail coming to Maine. (By March 1976 L.L. Bean, Inc., would still be doing so much business through the mail that the company would get own ZIP Code, 04033, which would go into effect with the mailing of that year's summer catalog. Finally, in the early 1980s the U.S. Postal Service would implement its ZIP-plus-4 program. For many years, you could send your order to: L.L. Bean, Inc., Freeport, ME 04033-0001, but in 2007 the company briefly added a PO Box (1912, the year of the company's founding) to its address before relocating its mail order processing center out of state. The address as of 2011 is: "L.L. Bean, Inc., PO Box 1205, Albany, NY, 12201-1205, USA."

ON OCTOBER 13, 1962, L. L. BEAN turned ninety. The headline of the article in the next day's *Portland Sunday Telegram* proclaimed, "At 90, L. L. Bean's Still Boss of Famed Freeport Firm," even though his health had deteriorated to the point where he was no longer able to visit his employees at his factory and store just up the street. Without saying as much, the end of the piece gave several hints as to the merchant's actual condition:

> His staff of 115 men and women who think of their "boss" with affection and respect, remembered him Friday with a gift and several bouquets of flowers, delivered to his home.
>
> Mrs. Bean, who advised [his employees] in the choice of a gift, brought the tokens of affection in to Mr. Bean, one at a time, and reported to the staff that "he was overwhelmed."
>
> L.L. Bean, Inc., employees work hard twice a year to find the right birthday and Christmas gift for the man they call "not only our boss but our friend as well."
>
> "I'm not 16 any more," Mr. Bean says these days, but he is an unusually alert and capable 90-year-old.

Two months later, L.L. Bean, Inc., bought the neighboring Oxnard Block (also known as the Garnet Block after a more recent owner). The run-down, rain-damaged seventy-year-old building would be quickly demolished to make room for some much-needed parking next to the factory showroom. (The 27,000-square-foot annex Bean had added to his factory in 1941 had been built behind the Oxnard Block.) In an interview given just before the building was razed in January 1963, Leon Gorman said its disposal was more for aesthetic value than economic, noting that the cellar hole would be filled in and then either planted with grass or made into a customer parking lot. The parking option quickly won out.

The urgency with which off-street parking was needed in Freeport was becoming greater all the time. Within three years after the newly extended interstate had bypassed Bean's, sales at the retail store had plunged by more than 20 percent, to just under $400,000. The reason was simple: without the convenience of easy parking, many harried tourists just gave up looking for a spot by the store and headed back to the interstate to continue their journey northward. But, according to Bean biographer M. R. Montgomery, once the old building was gone and Gorman's parking lot was finished, "Store sales increased immediately, and carried the company in the black for the rest of the decade." In fact, noted Montgomery, Leon Gorman's management of the store was about the only thing that stood between Bean's and insolvency during much of the sixties:

> The year the parking lot went in, 1963, store sales bounced from 1962's $456,000 up to $527,000.
>
> The next year, when word got around, they jumped again, to $609,000. Gorman was managing the store, and the sales were increasing by 12 to 15 percent a year, while the company as a whole was growing by 1 or 2 percent. Without the increase in store sales, Bean's would have been losing ground in absolute terms, and was, in fact, losing ground in constant dollars, discounting inflation.[8]

From 1963 through 1966, L.L. Bean, Inc., would stay the course with any news from the Freeport merchant requiring something less than a banner headline. The next big news item about L. L. Bean would be reports of his death in early 1967. Until then his business continued to soldier on with one of the company's "highlights" for the early sixties consisting of little more than Leon Gorman convincing the board to increase the annual advertising budget to around $50,000. It's also around this time that L.L. Bean, Inc., started mailing out four catalogs a year: spring, summer, fall, and Christmas.

Gorman had noticed that there was an obvious gap in the company's "merchandise cycle" between its fall and spring catalogs—Christmastime. With the help of L. L.'s assistant, Ethel Williams, Leon convinced his grandfather to send out a thirty-two-page Christmas catalog in 1963, and Gorman was at last able to include several new items he had been trying to get into Bean's regular publications. Fortunately for Gorman and his new products, the Christmas catalog was a success.

At this point Bean's catalogs required a total of 225 tons of paper a year. It's said that Bean's catalogs were so popular then that people would spend three or four dollars on a toll call to Maine just to request one. One blind man, who was having them translated into Braille, received all the changes from Bean "to keep him up to date." L. L. no longer wrote the catalog, of course, but the deadline for each one was "advanced" ten days so he could completely rewrite and revise each issue, which he did right up until the end.

WHILE L.L. BEAN WAS SPINNING its wheels, rival Eddie Bauer was surging ahead on the publicity he garnered from helping to equip Norm Dyhrenfurth's expedition to Mt. Everest. One of the team's members, thirty-four-year-old Jim Whittaker of Seattle, would become the first American to reach the top of the 29,028-foot peak. Members of the expedition reached the summit on May 1, 1963, and again on May 22, when they used the previously unattempted West Ridge route to the top of the mountain the Tibetans call *Chomolungma* or *Qomalangma*, "Goddess Mother of the Universe." Whittaker would later start his own outdoors-related business, Recreational Equipment, Inc. (REI).

At the time, the managers at L.L. Bean had no interest whatsoever in mountaineering, preferring instead to keep the company's focus on its core sports of hunting, fishing, and camping. Even ten years later, the *Wall Street Journal* would report that "Bean leaves the market for gear used on highly technical expeditions like rock climbing to such outfitters as Eddie Bauer of Seattle and Eastern Mountain Sports of Boston." Gorman explained it this way: "We cater to the average guy who likes to enjoy the outdoors. Most of us are average sportsmen ourselves. We know what works and what doesn't."

It wouldn't be until 1990 that L.L. Bean, Inc., would become involved with an expedition to Everest when it sponsored the Peace Climb in observance of the twentieth anniversary of Earth Day. The expedition party would be made up of climbers from China, the Soviet Union, and the United States, and Jim Whittaker (then sixty-one) would be one of the expedition's three leaders.

While Eddie Bauer had built his company on goose down, L. L. Bean had initially scoffed at the idea of selling $70 eiderdown parkas, saying that "hunters would only be wasting their money on a coat that expensive." But by 1964, he'd relented and included Bean's Down Filled Parka in his fall catalog. The long (42-inch) coat was filled with "100% pure 10 oz. northern waterfowl down," cost $52.90 postpaid, and was available in any color customers wanted, as long as it was dark green. Now that he'd seen the light and embraced the warmth of down, Bean's sluggish sales inched ahead. For the year, his company would post a $70,000 profit on about $3 million in sales.

The company's fortunes improved somewhat again the following year, with a Bean spokesperson reporting that "'65 is well ahead of last year," thanks to a large increase in the sales of equipment to campers who, he noted, "don't spare the expense once they get serious about it. Also, fall vacationing is causing an increase in hunting, fishing, and camping specialties."[9]

Of Bean's 120 employees, nearly a third of them were engaged in the production of many of the nearly 1,000 items (11,000 when all the items' sizes and colors were figured in) that were helping to pull the company out of its recent slump. Two of the products introduced in 1965 that remain very popular today are Bean's Boat and Tote Bag and Bean's Insulated Hunting Shoe. In its initial catalog appearance, the Boat and Tote Bag was described as "a handy tote bag for the boater or camper. Sturdily constructed from extra heavy white duck." The tote bag was hardly a new idea; it had actually existed at L.L. Bean since at least the 1940s, when its main use was for carrying blocks of ice—which explains its generous proportions of 8" x 17" x 16" high. When it was introduced in 1965, the $4.75 bag came only in basic white with the bottom and handles available in either red or dark blue. Today Bean's Boat and Tote Bag is available in several sizes, styles, patterns, and colors. A large 2010 version of the bag measured 15"H x 17"W x 7^1/$_2$"D and started at $24.95.

"As a result of many customer requests," L.L. Bean had developed an Insulated Hunting Shoe whose rubber bottoms featured a layer of Ensolite insulation that "will not lose its insulating properties even when punctured." And of course it had been thoroughly tested in the Maine woods: "A Maine Trapper tested this for us last Winter," according to the catalog, "and reports it very warm." Back then, the price of a pair of 10-inch Bean's Insulated Hunting Shoes was $20 postpaid. In the 2010 Bean catalog, the 8-inch Thinsulate version went for $94.

It was a good thing that business had picked up in 1965, because that August the company became the subject of Case Study Number 366013, the first of seven case studies to be done about it by the Harvard Business School. The thirteen-page report by Charlie Leighton and Frank Tucker, which would be revised in late 1987, studied the "development and operations of a small manufacturing and mail-order company doing $3 million in sales." According to Bean biographer M. R. Montgomery, "When, in 1965, the Harvard Business School wrote up a case study on L.L. Bean, Inc., Gorman gave them a copy of the [1946 *Saturday Evening*] *Post* article, and it was reprinted almost in its entirety as the main body of the case study." In the seventies, the *Wall Street Journal* would note that, despite Harvard's interest, "Bean was more of a curiosity than a successful business."

Validating Leon Gorman's less than glowing assessment of the company's situation at the time, the case study reads, in part: "Gorman had recently made several recommendations that he thought would improve efficiency, cut costs, and increase sales, but they had been turned down by the company's two top officers. His grandfather and his uncle felt that since business was increasing there was no reason to make changes, even though Gorman's recommendations might have merit."

Regardless of all the attention from Harvard, much of Bean's success at the time could probably be attributed more to its introduction of a few new products just as the country's interest in camping was beginning to grow, rather than to any real change on the company's part. In fact, the researchers probably wondered, at least to themselves, how L.L. Bean, Inc., could continue to forge ahead while still clinging to such outmoded production and business practices. Leon Gorman was still a very frustrated young man. According to the Harvard case study, "he was told by 'L. L.' and his uncle Carl, 'to wait for the day he became president, and then he would be able to institute whatever changes he felt were needed.'" He wouldn't have long to wait.

That L. L. Bean himself had little if anything to do with his company's reported upsurge in sales was readily apparent since he'd hurt his back the previous year and was now more or less confined to his home and failing fast. Shortly after his company had sent out nearly 435,000 fall catalogs, L. L. celebrated his ninety-third birthday "quietly, at his own request, with just his family calling on him for short visits. Although his traditional birthday visit to his store was not made this year, the founder of Maine's best-known store still makes an occasional call on his employees and oversees much of the Bean advertising."[10]

As people's interest in outdoor recreation went, so went L.L. Bean's bottom line. In just two years, Bean's total sales had seen a substantial jump, from $3 million in 1964 to $3.8 million in 1966. (For the sake of comparison, Sears, Roebuck and Company had sales of $5 billion in 1963. In 1967 Sears would sell $1 billion worth of goods in one month.) While Bean's overall business was helped by an article in *Grit* in February 1966 and another in an October issue of *Yankee* magazine, the company's net profits still languished at a mere 2.2 percent of sales, or $85,000.

This lackadaisical feeling seemed to be shared by all of Freeport, which was mired in similar economic doldrums. Former resident Earle Shettleworth, Jr., whose father owned the store across the street from Bean's, remembered the town's situation in an interview with the author:

> My father bought the [Clark] building in '46 for $32,000, and when he decided to sell it in the mid 1960s, to Paul Powers, the local attorney who was a good friend of his, it was reappraised and the irony is that between '46 and, say, around '65, '66, Freeport had remained so static economically, and had even lost ground with the loss of the shoe factories and so on, that my father could no more than get his money back for that building— $32,000. That building is now [in 2008] valued at $7 million for tax purposes.

Though L. L. was no longer running his business on a day-to-day basis, it was very much in the company's best interest to keep this fact from the public. One such case of this public relations sleight of hand appeared in an edition of the *Lewiston Journal* when a certain photo of the company's directors accompanied an article that ran on May 21, 1966. The picture, which may have been provided by the cataloger or might have come from the newspaper's files, showed L. L., his sons Warren and Carl, and grandsons Tommy and Leon, along with accountant Shailer Hayes, sitting around a desk. It carried a caption saying that this was a meeting of the firm's "Management Today." Technically the caption was correct, since all six men were still with the company, but L. L. rarely came to the store anymore and the same photo appears in a later edition of L. L.'s autobiography with the caption: "L.L. Bean, Inc. Directors' Meeting, August 23, 1961," making the group photo almost five years old when it was printed in the *Journal*.

Whoever was actually running things at L.L. Bean, Inc., was doing a good job—sales were steady enough so that the Freeport post office, through which most of the company's catalogs and mail still passed, was now the state's seventh largest, surpassing even the volume of those located in much larger cities such as Brunswick and Westbrook. Largely responsible for the crush of mail to and from all fifty states and every "civilized" country (sixty-nine in all, according to the company) were the L.L. Bean catalogs, which featured a revised—and much more profitable—product mix. This fresh inventory helped both Bean's sales and its mailing list nearly double between 1960 and 1967. Now the company was growing at an annual rate of 20 percent.

On February 5, 1967, L. L. Bean died peacefully of "a heart ailment" at his winter home in Pompano Beach, Florida. News of his passing quickly circulated through Freeport and around the country. Besides being carried by the local media, L. L. Bean's obituary appeared in *Time* magazine and every major newspaper in the country. News of the merchant's death even received lengthy coverage on the *NBC Evening News* with Chet Huntley and David Brinkley. At L. L.'s factory and store, the news fostered feelings of both sadness and trepidation among his loyal workers. Carlene Griffin clearly remembers that L. L.'s employees—all 145 of whom called him a friend—took the news of his death very hard. They also wondered about the future of the company for which most of them had worked so long.

As it turned out, the company's management wasn't all that sure about the company's survival either, at least not at first. Leon Gorman was at a sporting-goods show in Chicago when his grandfather died, and remembers how traumatic L. L.'s passing was for all of his employees—and customers, too. Even Gorman wondered if L.L. Bean, Inc., could survive the demise of its namesake, on whose powerful personality it had depended so much.

Before launching into a short sketch of his life and times, the *Portland Press Herald* ran the following brief obituary of Leon Leonwood Bean:

FREEPORT—Leon L. Bean, 94, founder, president and treasurer of L. L. Bean, Inc., world famous sporting goods and clothing mail order firm here, died Sunday in Pompano Beach, Fla.

He leaves his second wife, the former Claire Boudreau of Belmont, Mass., whom he married in 1940; two sons, Lester Carl Bean and Charles Warren Bean, both of whom are associated with the Bean firm; a daughter, Mrs. John L. (Barbara) Gorman of Yarmouth; five grandchildren, six great-grandchildren, two nieces, and two nephews. His first wife, the former Bertha Porter of Freeport, whom he married in 1898, died in 1939.

The funeral will be held at 2 P.M. Thursday at the Congregational Church, Freeport. Interment will be in the Webster Cemetery, Freeport, in the spring.

Early the following year, the Town of Freeport honored its late benefactor by putting his picture on the cover of the town's 178th annual report and eulogizing him on the first page:

Leon Leonwood Bean, who passed away February 5, 1967, has been a part of Freeport's history since he first came here in 1895 to manage his brother's shoe and men's furnishings store.

An ardent sportsman, he designed a boot to his liking in the early 1900s. His Maine Hunting Shoe was an immediate success and in 1912 he started a mail order sporting goods business. By hard work and Yankee honesty, he spread the names of L. L. Bean and Freeport, Maine, across the country and around the world.

When he died, Mr. Bean left a thriving business in Freeport and a lifetime of participation in town affairs. He showed what one man can do with confidence in his abilities and the courage to act. We can all share the pride L. L. Bean had in his name and in his community.

This year's Town Report is dedicated to Leon L. Bean. He made Freeport a better place in which to live.

With L. L. gone, leadership of the company passed to his elder son, Carl, who became president of the company in March, while Leon Gorman became Bean's new vice president and treasurer. Under the pair's leadership, business continued with the razing of two more buildings on Main Street, the O. G. Morse Block, which was being removed to provide more customer parking, and the neighboring Nevin's Block because it was in "poor shape." The employees generally seemed to like Carl, who possessed the same inventive mind as his father, and was always finding little ways to improve the firm's manufacturing systems.

A brief background of Carl in the company's scrapbook simply describes him as "an avid hobbyist and antique collector," but Ken Stilkey, another longtime Bean employee, has high praise for the man, recalling that Carl was one of the nicest people he ever met, and always saw the good in everyone.

But not everyone who knew Carl remembered him as fondly as Ken Stilkey. One unnamed former employee didn't have much use for him at all, recalling an idea Carl had come up with to prevent some local women from shoplifting— and a not-so-pleasant side of his disposition:

> Carl had this idea we'd put a one-way mirror in the women's room. I thought that was a hell of an idea and said I'd do the watching, but we never did it. That was about Carl's speed. I mean [L. L.] wasn't the sharpest thing going, couldn't spell worth a damn for one thing, but Carl. Lord.
>
> Carl had to have the big office. L. L. would just sit out in the middle, but Carl had the big office [which was accessed by way of a secret panel in the stairwell]. My God, Carl would talk so slow it would take him a month to get a sentence out. He had this lump on his head. Like a growth or something. When he got mad, got his blood pressure up, that lump'd turn bright red. You saw him coming with that lump all red, you'd look around quick for something to polish or a place to hide.[11]

Who else didn't especially care for Carl Bean? Leon Gorman, for one. According to Bean biographer M. R. Montgomery, Leon and Carl had "a cordial relationship, on the surface, although anyone asking Leon Gorman what he thought of Carl is likely to be greeted with a shrug of the shoulders, a roll of the eyes, and a look, in an unguarded moment, of distaste. But Carl was sixty when Leon Gorman came on board, and Leon planned on waiting."[12]

In the end it really wouldn't matter how Leon felt about Carl, because the two wouldn't have long to butt heads in L. L.'s absence. Less than nine months after the death of his father, Lester Carleton Bean died early in the morning of Saturday, October 14, 1967, a few days after being admitted to the Osteopathic Hospital in Portland. Below the incorrect headline "Carl L. Bean of Freeport Dies at Portland," the *Lewiston Evening Journal* ran a brief obituary on page 16 later that day:

> FREEPORT (AP)—L. Carl Bean, 67, who headed a nationally known sporting goods store here, died in a Portland hospital today.
>
> He had been president of L.L. Bean Co., Inc. since his father and its founder, Leon Leonwood Bean died in Florida last February at the age of 94.
>
> Bean's store, which keeps open 24 hours daily throughout the year, serves sportsmen all over the nation, mostly through its mail-order business.
>
> Carl Bean had been vice president from 1938 [*sic*] until his father's death.
>
> He leaves his widow, Hazel, and a brother, C. Warren, both of Freeport, and a sister, Mrs. Barbara Gorman of Yarmouth.
>
> The funeral will be in the Freeport Congregational Church at 2 P.M. Monday.

(Actually, Carl had become vice president and assistant treasurer upon the company's incorporation in late 1934.)

That summer, Carl's secretary, Jessie Beal, told Leon that a nurse had confided to her that Carl had been suffering from a terminal illness for several years—"Probably much of the time I was at odds with him," said Gorman.

WITH CARL'S PASSING, thirty-two-year-old Leon Gorman became the third president of L.L. Bean in nine months, but he'd stay at the helm of the company for the next thirty-five years. During that time, he would transform the business his grandfather started from a sleepy $3.9 million mail-order house with four annual catalogs to a thriving $1.1 billion retail powerhouse with more than fifty different catalogs. This was Leon Gorman's chance to begin the gradual implementation of his ideas that would change his grandfather's quaint little company forever.

The copy of Leon Gorman's 1979 résumé on file in the Freeport Community Library notes his latest promotion with simply "Oct. 1967 L.L. Bean, Inc. President." Actually he was voted president of L.L. Bean, Inc., by its board of directors on October 18, four days after Carl's death. Gorman's promotion received barely a mention in the *Portland Press Herald*, but it didn't matter—Leon Gorman was finally free to run the company without having to answer to his grandfather and uncle.

The most important thing Leon Gorman knew early in his tenure as the company's new leader was how much more he had to learn about running it. So he got to work. From the day he'd walked into the business, Gorman recalled later, he'd been a student of L. L. Bean, learning well the business principles his grandfather had practiced for more than fifty years:

> His deep-rooted beliefs in practical, tested products for outdoors people, and in giving complete customer satisfaction were accepted by me as the only way to run a business. His catalog production methods, his style of writing copy, his advertising techniques for getting new customers, and his conservative financing became the basis of my business education.
>
> Anyone who'd ever worked for "L. L.," as I was fortunate enough to have done, could not help but be permanently influenced by his strong personality and fundamental honesty.[13]

While fiscal conservatism and fundamental honesty were the basic principles one needed to run a successful company, Gorman also knew that if he wanted L.L. Bean to grow the way he'd envisioned, he'd need a more formal education in the matters of big business. The process was one of total immersion; he studied old catalogs, took business courses, got involved with as many out-door activities as he could, and—most importantly—he talked with his employees and his company's vendors. For a long time, Gorman signed every check that went out so he could be sure he knew exactly where every penny was going. He had a clear vision of where he wanted the company to go and just how he was going to get it there—so much so that upon his retirement as president in 2001, Gorman would be recalled as a man who had a reputation as a "soft-spoken but headstrong leader."

While many of L. L.'s business practices should have been put out to pasture years before, some of his traditions were pure gold, and, as progressive as he was, Leon Gorman knew enough to keep those things as unchanged as possible. One such keeper was his grandfather's laconic, get-to-the-point style of catalog copywriting, which made such an impression on Gorman that he'd still be using it to sell the company's number one product nearly ten years later. In 1975 he'd pen a piece about the Maine Hunting Shoe that one Bean executive, chief merchandising officer Tom Sidar, would describe as "a more general style, not quite so first-person and still sound[ing] like L. L. Bean. . . ."[14] Here it is:

Bean's Maine Hunting Shoe
Mr. Bean first developed this boot in 1912. He was tired of com-ing home with wet and sore feet from wearing the heavy leather woodsman boots then in common use. Rubber boots were clammy feeling and too clumsy for all-day walking. He decided to combine lightweight leather tops with all-rubber bottoms, incorporating the best features of both types of footwear and doing away with the disadvantages. He called his new boot the Maine Hunting Shoe.

The practical advantages of this design were readily appar-ent to hunters and woodsmen. For bare-ground walking it was light in weight, snug fitting, had a cushioned innersole and a non-slip, chain-tread outer sole. For wet going and walking on snow, the waterproof bottoms were ideal. Mr. Bean invented the split backstay to eliminate chafing, and by keeping all parts as light and as flexible as possible, he had a boot that could be used all day in perfect comfort.

The Maine Hunting Shoe was an immediate success. Over the years, continuous improvements have been made. The best top-grain leathers from improved tanning processes are adopted. New developments in rubber compounding provide longer-wearing bottoms. But the basic design of Mr. Bean's boot has yet to be improved for all-weather and all-purpose outdoors comfort. Today the Maine Hunting Shoe is the most widely used sporting boot in the world.

"Changes in the catalog copy," noted M. R. Montgomery, "indicated the passing of the founder: the past tense replaced the present, and the chamois shirt became the 'shirt Mr. Bean always wore on his hunting and fishing trips.'"[15] Leon Gorman had quickly realized that the most important part of L. L. Bean's legacy and enduring appeal was the power of his personality and honesty that had made his customers remain so loyal to the company. What he needed to do, Gorman knew, was to keep that legacy alive.

"We were very sensitive to the legend," said Gorman. "We were all focused on not only telling the L. L. Bean story but embellishing it wherever we could."[16] (Interestingly, while his grandfather's legacy would live on through Leon's copywriting, the same couldn't be said for L. L.'s first book, *Hunting, Fishing, and Camping*, which went out of print at about the same time its total sales reached somewhere around the 200,000 mark.)

In the spring 1968 catalog, Gorman included Bean's first guarantee statement, which was based on that of Sears and stipulated that any returns had to be new and unused. Though the statement was vague about what the company would do with any used products being returned, the guarantee was unconditional. Once the new policy took effect, the company discovered that most people were more than fair and honest about the items they were returning. In 1969, L.L. Bean broadened its guarantee to make it unqualified, and in 1970 it would be printed in boldface type.

Leon Gorman might have wanted his late grandfather's style of writing emulated for the catalog, but that was where many of the similarities between the two ended. While L. L. had been drawn to the outdoor life at an early age, Leon had to learn how to hunt and fish after coming on board so he could do more than merely talk the talk when it came to the passions of his company's core group of customers. As for the business side of things, that was an area in which Gorman and his granddad couldn't have been more different. While L. L.'s idea of growth was to stick a few new products in the catalog each season to see how they'd do, Leon was keenly aware that his liberal arts education from Bowdoin and a brief stint as a Filene's merchandise trainee hadn't come close to preparing him to run a multimillion-dollar company.

For those worried about the company's short-term future, there was little to fear: in 1967 L.L. Bean had sales of $4.75 million, sent catalogs to 600,000 customers, and employed 200 people. The company's annual growth rate of 25 percent meant that L.L. Bean would double in size every three years. Sales were already outpacing the cataloger's order fulfillment and inventory management facilities, both of which Carl had refused to update. Now Leon Gorman could. That December, Bean's employees received a 30 percent cash bonus and a 15 percent profit-sharing contribution.

DURING THE LATE SIXTIES, progress at the cataloger manifested itself in disparate ways. On August 15, 1968, the same year rival mail order firm Eddie Bauer went public, L.L. Bean's certificate of incorporation was amended as follows: "That the capital stock of the corporation consists of EIGHT THOUSAND (8,000) shares of the par value of ONE HUNDRED DOLLARS ($100) for a total capitalization of EIGHT HUNDRED THOUSAND DOLLARS ($800,000)." According to records on file in Augusta, the last time the company had changed the value of its stock had been in June of 1937 when it had been "unanimously voted to increase the capital stock of the corporation from $200,000 to $400,000." The document creating this latest change was signed by L. L.'s remaining son "C. Warren Bean,

Clerk of L. L. Bean." As remains the case to this day, virtually all of the company's stock was held by the extended Bean clan.

At the annual shareholders' meeting, L. L.'s widow, Claire, was elected to the board, and the benefits of being on her good side were not lost on the company's new president. Since Claire now voted the majority of the company's stock, Leon and his assistant, Ethel Williams, spent a lot of time making sure that Claire's every need was being met, and eventually, Leon Gorman gained her "full confidence" in his judgment.

Another sign of progress, of a sort, came when noted writer Nathaniel Benchley (1915–81) deemed the fictitious details of a couple's shopping excursion to L.L. Bean, Inc., worthy of an article in *Holiday*. "A Long Day's Shopping at L. L. Bean," which appeared in the magazine's December 1968 issue, took the form of a one-act play featuring a character called "HUSBAND" who learns the nearly complete tale of L. L. Bean's life and times from a very knowledgeable "CLERK" who seems to have memorized nearly every salient fact of the merchant's long existence. Occasionally, the "WIFE" drifts in and out of different scenes throughout the store. The following exchange is typical of the informative banter between the HUSBAND and the CLERK:

CLERK (Smiling): Well, Bean's likes to know what it's selling. Mr. Bean used to say he'd never sell anything he hadn't tried first.

HUSBAND (Looking around the salesroom): He must have done a lot of trying.

CLERK: He got so he let the staff do some of it. But look at this pocket knife here. He tried every kind of pocket knife and couldn't find one he liked, so he had this one made up special. It does everything you need. But it's so thin you can barely feel it in your pocket.

HUSBAND: I guess I'd better have one.

CLERK (Producing the knife): You won't regret it. That'll be two ninety plus tax, which is, uh——

HUSBAND: Just hold it. I may be getting some other things.[17]

The following year, progress came in a form that caused more consternation than most of the changes in Bean's management or business practices ever had: Leon Gorman had carpet put on the stairs. Maybe it says something about Yankee stubbornness and resistance to change, or maybe it was just the times, but you'd have thought the world was coming to an end when L. L.'s grandson ("Barbara's boy") decided to cover up those creaky old stairs leading up to the showroom, which also got carpeted. (The real reason for the carpet was the simple fact that the old wooden floors and stairs had been sanded down so many times, there wasn't enough wood left to sand, so the place needed to be carpeted.) Not too long afterwards, the rickety old stairs to the salesroom would be replaced "for safety's sake."

Of course the carpet was more than just mere renovation; it represented, as one writer put it, "the outward and visible sign of a new era" at L.L. Bean. Just because Freeporters had to accept progress didn't necessarily mean they had to like it, and to most of them that rug represented change. Since this was a change they could see, one that stared them in the eye every time they needed a fly-fishing lure or a box of shotgun shells, this latest change proved none too popular with most of Bean's regular customers who, out of necessity, wearily trudged up the old staircase once or twice a week. "Not going to put in a computer, are you?" [one old-timer] asked. "I remember '69 when you put the rug on the stairs. Place hasn't been the same since."[18] He was right: computers weren't far off.

ALONG WITH THE NEW CARPET came myriad other changes to the venerable Freeport company, which was about to begin a long period of stunning growth. Coupled with a convergence of outside factors—such as the increased availability of skilled shoemakers as more and more of Maine's shoe companies began sending work overseas, and the recreation boom of the late sixties and early seventies—was Leon Gorman's vision for the company, a vision upon which he was ready, and now able, to act. He started laying the groundwork for the company's explosive growth by making use of modern technology wherever he could, beginning with "those computers." In 1969 L.L. Bean converted its mailing list from a hand-typed operation to a computerized application. More precisely, according to the *Bean Bulletin*:

In October 1969, Flexowriters from Singer were introduced to L.L. Bean. The primary purpose was to replace the typing of catalog labels by putting the customer names and addresses on the computer.

This was accomplished through a local bank. The initial effort included converting the manual file of about 750,000 records and then keying the name, address, order value, and source code for all orders and inquiries to update the file. Priscilla Leavitt was in charge of order processing, while Jane Brewer led the group responsibile for the mailing list. Nancy Marston was hired for her experience with Flexowriters.

Thanks to Carl Bean's aversion to new technology, L.L. Bean, Inc., had gone straight from hand-typing its mailing list twice a year to a keypunch paper tape, skipping over a couple of other systems that had come and gone in the interim.

Sales of goods to the people on Bean's mailing list, each of whom now received two 104-page catalogs and two 40-page supplements per year, continued to climb. Throughout the Christmas rush, the company would send out more than 3,500 packages a day. During all of 1969, the sub-post office in Bean's building would handle 335,500 pieces of parcel post. This was in addition to the packages that were sent out via UPS, Railway Express, and freight. By the end of the sixties, L.L. Bean had sold a grand total of 1,550,000 pairs of Maine Hunting Shoes, employed roughly 200 workers, and had $7,388,496 in annual sales. In another ten years, the Freeport merchant would employ 1,200 people and be doing about $73 million in sales.

Chapter 9

*"Why, it flies in the face of everything L. L. stood for.
Quality, dependability, durability. Not fashion"*

For much of the sixties, Leon Gorman's ambitions for the future
of the company had been stifled by the stubbornness of his
grandfather and uncle, both of whom had been quite content to
maintain the status quo. Now, with L. L. and his like-minded son
gone, Gorman was free to shoot for the moon, and he wasted little
time pulling the trigger.

On August 3, 1970, L.L. Bean filed notice with the State of
Maine that, effective August 28, it intended to officially bring the
little moccasin factory it had purchased into the company fold.
Specifically, it intended to complete a "joint plan of merger and
agreement of merger between L.L. Bean, Inc., and Small-Abbott
Co., Inc., with L.L. Bean, Inc., as surviving corporation." The cataloger had owned the Small-Abbott moccasin factory, the only operating business it would ever purchase, since 1956. During 1970,
Bean would actually sell slightly more moccasins—26,800 pairs in
30 styles—than Maine Hunting Shoes (26,500 pairs)!

Leon Gorman's plan for growth must have been a grand one
almost from the start. First, to help organize Bean's voluminous
mailing list, had come the Flexowriters, with much of the groundwork for the business's imminent explosive growth soon to follow.
One of the company's first major expansions on Gorman's watch
came in August 1970, when he moved Bean's manufacturing operation to the 13,000-square-foot E. E. Taylor hand-sewn-shoe factory,
where the company's manufacturing operations were combined.
There, sixty-five Bean employees would make boots, moccasins,
and canvas equipment. Lasted shoes and moccasins were then sent

to a new drier where up to 540 pairs at a time would spend an hour in its 150-degree chamber.

The Taylor Building had originally been part of Casco Laces Company, which was, appropriately enough, located on Casco Street about a mile south of Bean's old facility. In 1970 Leon Gorman made the decision to commit to even more growth deciding that, in a few years, L.L. Bean, Inc., would expand the Taylor Building and construct a massive Distribution Center there. Two years after that, the company would move most of its offices down Route 1 to the Taylor Building. To this day, the company's headquarters are located on Casco Street in Freeport, Maine. (A note on file at the Freeport Community Library says that the offices and warehousing of E. E. Taylor remained in the building along with Bean's stitchers until 1972.)

In 1974 L.L. Bean, Inc., would buy the Taylor Building and its surrounding land, which would soon become the site of Bean's Distribution Center (or "DC," as it's known around the area), the company's first major construction project since the completion of the 27,000-square-foot Gorman Building in 1942.

The space vacated by the employees at the old Bean facility on Main Street was quickly taken over by expanded offices. With Bean's manufacturing force now moved down the road, the accounting department moved into its new home in late summer. Under the direction of Everett Bucklin, the quarters had been transformed from a cutting room into a modern office area, complete with carpeting and new paneling.

The company's offices weren't the only areas to get spruced up at the time. Since it was still responsible for about 20 percent of Bean's annual sales, the salesroom also received a moderate makeover. "Early in 1970 the showroom was remodeled and enlarged, providing a new area for the Footwear Department. The counters were restyled and rearranged to be more attractive and functional."[1] Updated the salesroom might have been, but the simple fact was that not much could be done with the basic layout of the tired old Warren Block. In a 1970 *Down East* magazine article, writer Lew Dietz's description illustrates how little things had actually changed in the old building in the past forty years:

> The selling floor, storerooms, offices, workshops, shipping and mailing rooms, and a post office substation are housed in a great rambling frame building and connected by labyrinthian passages that would daunt a speleologist. The selling floor, achieved by conquering twenty-five steps, is as casual as a Maine clambake and every bit as cluttered as the Bean catalog.[2]

(Decades after the demise of the Warren Block, both floors of the current retail store still feature departments on several different levels, thanks to a combination of surviving sections and many additions of varying vintages.)

But more shoppers created a new problem, one that would continue for the next several decades. Customer parking became a bigger and bigger problem, so L.L. Bean bought a pair of apartment buildings on Main Street with plans to demolish them in order to create more parking space. "This purchase also included a sizable lot of land to the rear of these buildings," reported the company's newsletter, "that will be developed for customer parking. When this lot is completed, we hope to have access to Morse and Nathan Nye Streets."[3]

Manufacturing's recent move to the Taylor Building and subsequent renovation of the old Warren Block on Main Street hadn't come close to feeding Bean's increasing appetite for space. The company also leased 20,000 square feet in the Davis Building, a warehouse on nearby West Street, and purchased a "small business block north of the factory on the corner of Main Street and Cushing Avenue" for future development. But Bean's biggest expansion was down the road a way. About three miles down the road.

LATE IN 1970 THE COMPANY PURCHASED an eighty-acre blueberry farm on the south side of Desert of Maine Road from L. L.'s widow, Claire, for an undisclosed amount of money. (The Desert of Maine Road is immediately west of I-295, and is commonly referred to simply as "Desert Road.") Gorman said he planned to use the land, "but not within five years or so," as a site for a new building "for shipping and packing" because of its proximity to the interstate highway.

Desert Road gets its name from the natural phenomenon that lies at its end a couple of miles from the interstate. What is now the Desert of Maine started out in 1797 as the 200-acre William Tuttle Farm, where the family raised crops of hay and potatoes for many years. But, according to the Desert of Maine brochure, "failure to rotate crops thereafter, combined with massive land clearing and overgrazing by sheep resulted in severe soil erosion that exposed this hidden Desert. As the spreading sand grew uncontrollable, the Tuttles surrendered, leaving the Desert to its destiny."

By 1903, 75 acres had become useless for agriculture, and by the 1920s, the Desert of Maine had become a roadside attraction with each car entering the parking lot being "provided with a long placard, which is attached to the bumper and carries the title 'Desert of Maine.'" The brochure makes it clear that "no, we didn't dump it here," saying the sand that makes up the desert had been deposited by a glacier during the Pleistocene Epoch, 11,000 years ago. The Desert of Maine is open from early May to mid-October and offers, among other attractions, tours, a campground, a gift shop, and a museum in the farm's original 40' x 78' 1783 barn.

All the big projects and plans Leon Gorman had in mind would take a while to construct and implement. In the short term, he would grow the company simply by doing more of what his predecessors had done, but doing it more efficiently than they could ever have dreamed. Gorman stuck to what he knew. His commitment to concentrating on catalog sales instead of opening more stores around the Northeast would pay huge dividends. To meet the burgeoning demand for the latest high-tech outdoor gear, such as cross-country skis and recently added Raichle hiking boots, he made sure that Bean's product lines boasted both depth and quality.

Great gear was one thing, but Gorman also had to make sure that enough of the right people knew about Bean's new and improved offerings to make his plan work. To do this, the company launched a customer acquisition campaign that included more modern catalogs—including many with color pages—smarter placement of advertisements, and the increased utilization of rented mailing lists.

At the time, an ad appearing in several national magazines was generating 700 to 800 catalog requests a day. Unofficial Bean historian M. R. Montgomery hit the nail on the head when he observed that

> These were fascinating years, as Leon Gorman made the company grow, but managed to make it grow without fundamental changes. It was the era of "more of the same." There was no real change in the product mix in the catalog, or the method of getting new customers—display advertising in national magazines and high-circulation newspapers. But, simply by working the old system harder,
>
> Gorman would increase sales from $3.8 million in 1966 to $20.4 million in 1974. By keeping an eye on the store, including cutting employee theft and improving inventory control, Gorman pushed net profit from $85,000 (2.2 percent of sales) in 1966 to $1.3 million (6.5 percent of sales) in 1974. The old system of assessing inventory by visual inspection ended in 1969, when a local accounting firm was hired to keep track of it.[4]

Actually it wasn't all business as usual. By now L.L. Bean was using its Flexowriter computer to handle all of its catalog-mailing and order-processing needs. A machine then labeled, bundled, and tied the catalogs in stacks presorted by ZIP Code. With the help of technology, what once had been the most labor-intensive operation in the company could now be performed by only four people.

ONE OF THE FIRST PEOPLE to get in on the ground floor of the new era of L.L. Bean, Inc., was Leandro "Lee" Surace (1938–2001), previously with Blue Cross and Blue Shield of Maine, who was hired by Bean's recently hired controller, Dan Lord, in October 1970. Surace would join L.L. Bean as chief accountant and eventually rise to the position of senior vice president and chief financial officer. He'd earn a business degree from the University of Southern Maine in 1973 and an MBA in 1981, eventually serving as chair of the USM School of Business Advisory Council and participating in reviews of the accounting curriculum to ensure that course work met the needs of graduates and businesses. Upon Lee Surace's passing in 2001, the Gorman family would endow the L.L. Bean/ Lee Surace Chair at USM to allow the university to recruit and hire a senior faculty member in accounting.

Gorman knew that just adding new upper-level personnel to the company wasn't going to get the job done. Soon after taking over, he realized that in order to achieve the results he envisioned, he had to upgrade the caliber of all his workers on a companywide basis. And he was willing to invest whatever it took. In order to attract and retain better people, Gorman completely overhauled the company's personnel policies. Wages were increased to a competitive level, and a job-rating system and performance bonus were added. Pension and savings plans were added, as was group life insurance. The changes worked; when Gorman had joined the company in the early sixties, the average age of it workers had been in the sixties; soon it would be in the forties.

At the time, the company's payroll was being handled by the computer, while all other accounting matters were still being performed by hand.

A November 1970 article in the *Portland Press Herald* quoted Leon Gorman as saying that "L. L. Bean's business is about 25 percent ahead of last year's with increases in all items." According to a later calendar put out by the company, by the end of the year, Bean had sold about $12.8 million worth of goods to people who loved being outdoors—or at least wanted to look like they did. It offered for sale more than 6,000 items (when all the different sizes and colors were figured in), and employed 300 people at Christmastime, 50 percent more than the rest of the year.

For the second consecutive year, L.L. Bean purchased the entire back cover of the January issue of *Down East* magazine (which had arrived in subscribers' homes well before Christmas) to advertise its holiday gift ideas, the same four items as the previous year: Bean's Maine Hunting Shoe ($16.00–$21.85), Bean's Chamois Cloth Shirt ($7.25), Bean's Insulated Hunter's Hat ($4.35), and Hudson Bay Point Blankets ($37.00). The ad also included an order form that could be mailed in with the customer's check or money order.

Ten "operators," as they were then called, took hundreds of orders a day, many of them by long-distance before Bean implemented its toll-free ordering number. At the time, upgrades to the telephone system consisted only of a WATS line installed to help control the cost of the company's outgoing long-distance calls.

In the midst of all this growth, the company still offered its customers the service of rebuilding and refurbishing worn-out Maine Hunting Shoes, saving their owners anywhere from $3.50 to $14.00 over the price of a new pair.

Improved revenues at the house of Bean obviously translated into good fortune for much of Freeport, not the least of which was the U.S. Post Office. While many post offices around the country were losing money and being supported by taxpayer dollars, the one just up the street from L.L. Bean, Inc., expected its income for 1970 to be somewhere in the area of $800,000. A newspaper article of the day quoted its postmaster, Ervin D. McCluskey, Jr., as saying, "We're one of the few money-making post offices in the entire system," adding that, of the nation's 34,000 post offices, Freeport ranked in the top 1,000 in revenue returned to the treasury.

"L.L. Bean," said the article, "is the greatest single reason for the postal profit in Freeport." In the postal unit on the second floor of Bean's factory, three clerks scurried to fill the 245 sacks hung on the walls for outgoing mail. During an average day, the cataloger shipped out about 4,500 packages, but McCluskey estimated that 100,000 Bean packages would pass through his department during the Christmas rush. For all of 1970, the Freeport post office would handle 463,000 parcel post packages from L.L. Bean.

It didn't take long for Bean's booming business to attract the attention of the *New York Times*, which included the company in a January 1971 article about shopping by mail. After noting that the recent economic slowdown "has affected mail order, as well as the rest of the economy," reporter Joan Cook noted that

> One specialty store that has no reason to complain is L.L. Bean,
> Inc., of Freeport, Me., which marked Dec. 7, 1970, as the day it
> received the largest amount of mail in its 68-year-old [sic] his-
> tory, 10,398 pieces.
>   A backwoods bonanza founded by the late Leon Leonwood
> Bean in 1912, Bean sends its catalogue to 750,000 readers in
> every state and more than 70 foreign countries.
>   Bean's, which is still family-owned, does an annual busi-
> ness of more than $6 million according to Mrs. Ethel Williams,
> its advertising manager.[5]

"[T]he next best thing to swapping stories on the premises,"
Cook concluded, "is taking a vicarious trip through the catalog."

It wasn't too long before Leon Gorman realized he needed a
way to keep the workers informed as to all the changes and other
goings-on at the suddenly jumping Bean's. To this end, he facili-
tated the March 1971 launch of *You Name It!*, a monthly corporate
newsletter for which employees were encouraged to submit ideas
for a permanent name. Many of the articles in the first issue of
Bean's house organ were about things that had happened during
the previous year: one told about Bean's "Sportsman's Paradise"
float honoring Maine's sesquicentennial, which had taken prizes in
several parades, while another welcomed Lee Surace "our chief
accountant" to the company. Among the newsletter's more timely
pieces was an open letter from Leon Gorman explaining the company's recent growth to all Bean employees—and telling them to
expect more:

> TO OUR EMPLOYEES
> As you know, there were numerous changes made in expand-
> ing our operations during 1970. There will be more in 1971.
>   I would like to tell you why we have to make these changes,
> because I realize they are disruptive and not to be made with-
> out good reason.

The reason is simply *growth*. And the changes are healthy symptoms because companies, like any living thing, have to grow to remain strong and vigorous.

Furthermore, companies can only grow because the people in them grow—no more, no less. Because you have grown in your individual abilities, we have grown together as a company. Consequently, you have played the major role in forcing us to change. And I hope you feel the justly deserved satisfaction from your jobs well done that have made this growth possible.

I also think this opportunity for individual development and job satisfaction is the most important thing a company can offer. It's an opportunity not only to achieve your own goals, but to achieve them in working with others and enjoying the many satisfying personal relationships.

I hope you are looking forward to the challenges of our continued growth in 1971, and I request your active participation in the changes we will have to make.

Leon A. Gorman[6]

The permanent name of *You Name It!* would soon become *The Bean Scene.*

Another addition to L.L. Bean that year came in the person of John Walling. During his tenure with the company, Walling would see the opening of the company's first factory outlet store in North Conway, New Hampshire, in 1988, and the Freeport factory store moving out of the company's original location and into the former Eastland Shoe building the following spring. By the time he retired in 2002, Walling would be in charge of fourteen outlet stores. He recalled that when he arrived at Bean's, the retail store was still "an old country operation" where employees still wrote down orders on notepads.

AFTER FIFTY-THREE years with the company, Hazel Goldrup Day finally decided it was time to retire. Much more than a secretary, Hazel Day had been L. L.'s assistant and office manager long before those titles became fashionable. When he was away on one of his many hunting or fishing trips, it was Hazel who saw to it that everybody pulled their weight while the boss was gone, and, though it was mentioned earlier, it bears repeating that Mrs. Day received high praise from L. L. in his autobiography, where he wrote that "Miss Goldrup" deserved more credit for the early success of his mail-order business than any other person. She was replaced by the equally capable Ethel Williams, who also recognized the accomplishments of her predecessor. "No question," said Williams, "the whole plant ran smoother because of her. She had her finger on the whole thing."[7]

An even bigger loss than the retirement of Hazel Day came on September 10, 1971, when L. L.'s younger son, Warren, died at Brunswick's Parkview Memorial Hospital. He would be remembered as the person who designed many of the company's specialty items such as luggage, cases, and sheaths made from canvas and leather. (It was Warren, remember, who'd designed Bean's popular briefcase for naval officers in 1942.) "Warnie" graduated from Bowdoin College in 1923, and was well known locally as a talented piano player. Divorced since 1951, he left behind two grown daughters, Linda, twenty-nine, and Diana, twenty-five.

Other recollections of Warren don't usually have a whole lot to say about him except to note that he was musically inclined and frequently imbibed. Even his death certificate seems to indicate that Warren was far less involved with his father's company than older brother Carl had been, listing his usual occupation as "Clerk—L.L. Bean, Inc." Charles Warren Bean was sixty-nine. With Warren's passing, Leon's mother, sixty-four-year-old Barbara Bean Gorman, was now L. L.'s only surviving child.

THE 100TH ANNIVERSARY of L. L. Bean's birth coincided in 1972 with the 60th anniversary of the company he'd started after a too-long day of hunting had taken a toll on his big, flat feet. Much of the business continued to be housed in the Warren Block, the sagging wood-frame building that had been the home of Bean's business since 1917. It was also in 1972 that the Dingley Press, printer of millions of Bean's classic catalogs over the past several decades, decided to vacate the premises, and moved its thirty-one employees out of the Gorman Building to a larger facility located across town at 10 Hunter Road. Soon Bean's labeling operations and personnel also relocated to the Dingley plant.

At the rate it was growing, the mail-order firm must have made good use of the vacated space—at least for as long as the Warren Block remained standing. Before the end of the decade, the tired old building would be put out of its misery by the wrecking ball. The Dingley Press would continue to print the L.L. Bean catalog through the spring of 1981, after which the flourishing mail-order company would simply require a printer with better equipment and more capacity.

In just two years, Bean's total sales had jumped from $12.8 million to exactly $15,784,094, requiring the company to employ a permanent, full-time staff of about 300. One newspaper piece from the day, entitled "L. L. Bean Dusts Off Old Covers," notes that the company would issue nearly 1 million of its 120-page fall shopping guides, which would require 800 tons of paper to print. The article begins with these observations:

> A bit of nostalgia marks L.L. Bean's celebration of their 60th year as they blew the dust off several old files to discover a library of old catalogs.
>
> These were the mail-order catalogs that for years enabled sportsmen throughout the world to shop, to dream and to better enjoy their hunting, fishing and camping adventures.
>
> In them was a variety of outdoor clothing, footwear, and sporting equipment, all tested by L. L. Bean or his staff and fully guaranteed.[8]

The publicity surrounding the anniversary edition of Bean's catalog made the cover of that one issue the most famous ever to be mailed out of Freeport. The fall 1972 issue of the company's circular featured the rustic *The Old Country Store* painting by American artist Philip Brown Parsons (1896–1977). The work depicts a hunter standing in the middle of an old general store demonstrating, sans rifle, exactly how he shot the unfortunate fox lying on the floor in front of him. The overcoat-wearing hunter has the undivided attention of the storekeeper and an old man seated on a crate, while the hunter's dog, lying behind him, seems to be more interested in the fox. L. L. had always said that it was one of his favorite paintings, but the company's offer to purchase the piece for its 75th anniversary in 1987 would be declined by the painting's owner, the Harvard (Massachusetts) Public Library.

Born in West Medford, Massachusetts, P. B. Parsons loved the outdoors as much as L. L. Bean did, and also made his living doing what he loved, illustrating no fewer than sixty covers for the likes of *Hunting and Fishing, National Sportsman,* and *Outdoors* magazines. Besides his association with Bean, Parsons had another connection to coastal Maine in the person of Freeport summer resident William Harnden Foster, whose 1921 painting *The Moose Hunter* had appeared on the cover of Bean's fall 1925 catalog. Parsons studied under Foster as well as at the Boston School of Painting and MIT. In addition to L. L.'s favorite painting, five other Parsons works also graced the covers of his catalogs between the late 1920s and the early 1940s.

Besides featuring works of art on its catalog cover, L.L. Bean was also becoming fashionable in other respects as well. For some unknown reason, Mr. Bean's practical, $28 to $30 Maine Hunting Shoe had suddenly become a popular item among women living in cities and the suburbs. "We were inundated with orders," Leon Gorman told the *New York Times*, "some of which had to be custom made because they were for size 5 feet."

It goes without saying that the whole thing "caught Bean's by surprise," since, "if anything, the 60-year-old company had always disdained passing fashions," according to Rita Reif in her article, "A Rustic Store That Became Awfully Chic." To make her point, Reif pointed out that the company's "only other near-fashions—the Norwegian or Icelandic sweaters at $15 to $45—seem about as chic as Bean's 'guaranteed itch-free' long underwear, or the watertight and baggy 'Bean's Boot Foot Waders.'"[9]

So business was good at L.L. Bean. A little too good perhaps, with the cataloger suddenly finding itself less and less able to keep up with the ever-increasing demand for its wares. The unpopular (at least within the company) solution to Bean's current dilemma was to bite the bullet and attach a stock number to each item in its circulars. This would make things a lot less informal for all of Bean's loyal customers, who'd been used to ordering Bean's Chamois Shirt on page 16 or the new hammock on page 73. In the end, the company's consternation would be much concern about nothing. Bean's customers were already used to dealing with stock numbers when ordering from places like Sears and J. C. Penney. An added bonus was that any ordering snafus could be blamed on the computers that the company was installing to manage the new system.

Now that the company could no longer deny its desperate need to computerize, Gorman eased everything into gear in his usual methodical manner. He "hired a data-processing expert to plan the system," says M. R. Montgomery, "and started to worry about the employees' ability to shift over from the shouted instructions and handwritten orders to keypunching and printouts. Simultaneously, he hired Portland industrial psychologist Jim Mahoney to give aptitude and personality tests to prospective supervisory employees, and to conduct interviews with potential senior-level managers and department heads."[10]

Except for the company's need to increase the number of Flexowriters (to fourteen) required to keep up with growth, not much else would happen on the computer front at Bean's until 1974. That's when the firm got its first computer for managing inventory, an IBM 3/10. The following year, the company's computer system would look like this: operators keyed orders into IBM 3742 data entry devices from which floppy discs were fed into an IBM 370/115 computer which, in turn, validated information such as stock numbers and selling prices, and generated a printout containing the customer address, order number, part number, size, quantity, price per item, extended totals, batch number, order number within the batch, and a six-digit (warehouse) location code. The computer also updated the sales and inventory files as well as the customer's buying record.[11]

By 1977, the company planned to acquire "cathode ray tube (CRT) terminals," which would enable Bean's sales personnel "to interact with the computer on a real-time basis, thereby further enhancing both customer service and inventory control." Pretty high-tech stuff for the mid-seventies, but it didn't always work as expected; when the company tried to run accounts receivable "using CRTs which were at the offices located at the store, the computer was not fast enough and the accounts receivable were backlogged almost two months."[12]

Progress also had other drawbacks. With its Distribution Center, computers, and other improvements (such as a letter-opening machine that could unseal 30,000 letters an hour), L.L. Bean, Inc., was becoming a marvel of efficiency—but at what cost? Initially Leon Gorman was concerned about the effect that all this new technology was having on his company's folksy image, but soon concluded that growth was okay as long as it didn't change the "character" of L.L. Bean.

One thing Leon Gorman wouldn't have to worry about for long was how his workers would cope with all the changes that were about to come their way. While the vast majority of Bean's employees then may not have had much in the way of formal education beyond the high-school level, their inborn intelligence and Yankee ingenuity enabled most of them to quickly adapt to whatever new piece of equipment they were confronted with—even if they didn't much like the whole idea at first. Carlene Griffin recalled one longtime member of the clerical staff, whom she calls "L. D.," who wasn't about to budge from her trusty typewriter:

> Look, I learned how to use a typewriter when the only thing I knew was how to milk cows. I learned how to sort out a mailing list and keep everything in order when the only experience I'd ever had was at a table in the kitchen making out milk, cream, and butter bills. It was a big deal when we added eggs; I had to redesign the whole system.[13]

But eventually even she learned to love her new computer. "L. D. left the company several years ago, and the last time I saw her she was humming a tune to herself as she was wiping the dust off her monitor."

ON OCTOBER 6, 1973, which happened to be Yom Kippur, Israel's holiest fast day, Egypt and Syria attacked Israel in an attempt to regain the territories they had lost in the Six-Day War of 1967. Israeli forces—fighting fiercely against Arab forces financed by Saudi Arabia and Kuwait, and using sophisticated Soviet weapons—soon found themselves in need of aid from the United States and other Western nations. In retaliation for this support, the Arab oil-producing states soon instituted an oil embargo against Israel's allies, forcing Americans to severely limit their driving. This decrease in travel caused such an increase in telephone orders to L.L. Bean that the company needed to hire ten full-time operators more than a decade before the introduction of its toll-free ordering number.

Late in the year, Israel purchased some of the cold-weather gear it needed for the Yom Kippur War from L.L. Bean. Included in the three major purchases for the Israeli Army, the Maine company sent "at least 200 pairs" of "Bean Boots," among other things, which evidently also included heavy socks and several pairs of snowshoes for use in the mountainous Golan Heights. One order alone consisted of 80 pairs of the Maine Hunting Shoe, 200 pairs of inner socks, 300 pairs of ragg socks, and 100 green chamois shirts. "Winters in the Golan Heights," said an Israeli spokesman, "are very, very cold and raw."

According to the *Portland Press Herald*, "The first two orders, [Bean advertising manager Ethel] Williams said, were paid for by U.S. citizens. Winter clothing, along with snowshoes, were ordered by telephone and shipped to a warehouse in Pennsylvania, she said." The third order, said the paper, "was made by an Israeli who visited the store's showroom with a well-thumbed Bean's catalog." His order, the one that included the 200 pairs of boots, was reportedly about twice the size of the first two orders.

For 1973 L.L. Bean would achieve its $20,403,226 in total sales with the help of 350 hardworking employees, a number that swelled to 425 during peak season, with the additional employees working in Bean's tent room. With the posting of figures like those, it's not surprising that the business writers at the prestigious *Wall Street Journal* took notice of the company's impressive growth that year. In "Homey Hustlers," which the paper ran in its December 5, 1973, issue, staff reporter Thomas Ehrich brought his readers up to speed on just how efficient the company had become under its latest president: the Freeport firm now shipped 650,000 packages a year, sales were climbing 25 percent annually, profits had risen to 6 percent of sales (from just 2 percent under L. L.), and it was all due, in great part, to Leon Gorman's trebling the advertising budget to $150,000 a year.

Another reason that L.L. Bean, Inc., was now doing so well was because of the company's competitive pricing structure on its durable merchandise. "Prices seem reasonable," Ehrich wrote, giving the following examples:

> The Maine Hunting Shoe, for example, starts at $18.50 a pair. The Trap and Skeet Shoe made by Bass fetches $25. Abercrombie & Fitch calls the same shoe a Safari Boot and sells it for $32. Bean lists Stanley vacuum bottles at $14.80 to $21.60. Abercrombie prices the same bottles at $19.25 to $28.
>
> Scattered through the catalog are items like the popular $8.85 chamois-cloth shirt, wool shirts, unusual caps, trout flies, axes, animal traps, duck calls, tents, and many others. Few cost more than $50 each. The most expensive, a canoe, is $375.

Of course, it bears keeping in mind that the Abercrombie & Fitch store with which Ehrich was familiar was located on Madison Avenue in Manhattan, while L.L. Bean was perched on a small hill beside Route 1 in Freeport, Maine—but then L. L. had already given his "good wages here would be small in a city" speech to a reporter more than a decade ago. Even with recent improvements in pay and benefits for his workers, Leon Gorman certainly had many fewer business expenses than did his competition in the big city. (Two years later, a writer at the *Washington Post* would call L.L. Bean "the people's Abercrombie & Fitch.")

But Ehrich took care not to reduce the L.L. Bean experience to mere numbers: "In a retailing world of plastic, neon, and the get-with-it sell, Bean's rambling wooden store remains a reassuring haven of durable wool, hand-stitched leather, and no-nonsense styling," where, notes Ehrich, customers still had to "walk up two creaking flights of stairs to a merchandise-packed salesroom decorated with snowshoes and mounted trout." In spite of the old wooden stairs and the cramped display area—or maybe because of them—most summer nights found the place packed "wall to wall until three or four in the morning," according to Bucky Arris, the store's second-shift manager. "Every year it gets more amazing."[14]

In December, Bean's bootmakers in the Taylor Building produced their 50,000th pair of Maine Hunting Shoes for the year. On page 111 of the company's scrapbook, there's a picture showing four proud workers standing behind a hastily made cardboard sign in honor of the achievement. The sign proclaims, "50,000 Pair, 12/10/73, Time 1:48 pm, Boot Dept., We're No. 1, LOOK! And that's the truth." The caption of the photo reads, "Pride in craftsmanship has always characterized the workforce at L.L. Bean. In 1973 Jerry Arris, Scott Brown, Bob Stewart, and Emile Sylvain celebrate the production of 50,000 pairs of Maine Hunting Shoes within a year." (An entry in the company's 2002 information packet erroneously stated that the occasion marked a "milestone: 50,000 pairs of Bean's Boots sold to date." According to *Down East* magazine, the company had already sold about 1.55 million pairs of the famous footwear by 1970.)

As the Freeport company became more well known, so too did its president, Leon Gorman, who'd become enough of a minor celebrity to make an appearance on the television game show *To Tell the Truth*, where he attempted to stump a panel of better-known celebrities who tried to guess his occupation. The program, which was hosted by Garry Moore, aired on NBC affiliate WCSH, Channel 6, in Portland on January 18, 1974, according to the *Bean Scene* newsletter. There was no word on whether or not Gorman managed to stump the New York panelists.

The Bean Scene also noted that in late 1973 the L.L. Bean Horseshoe League's tournament could not be completed after being moved to rocky, frozen ground. Why the move? Because, at the original site of the contest behind the E. E. Taylor Building, ground was being broken for Bean's massive new 110,000-square-foot Distribution Center, which the company would begin using the following August. Completed at a cost of more than $1 million, the all-steel, insulated building would measure 328 feet by 290 feet and stand 30 feet high (think of a football field with 30-foot bleachers).

Shortly after Dan Lord had hired Lee Surace in 1970, the pair projected the company's growth conservatively for the next five years, and told Leon Gorman that he had to build a new distribution center. He hired an industrial engineering firm and an architectural firm to help with the planning, design, and construction of the mammoth structure.

Inside the new building were 640 of a possible 880 racks, each nearly ten feet wide and 22 feet tall, allowing inventory to be stacked to a height of 26 feet. Upon its completion, the DC would house approximately 1,400 line items in 16,000 sizes, styles, and colors worth more than $7 million. All this modernization enabled L.L. Bean to accomplish a 24-hour turnaround on virtually all of the nearly one million orders it received each year. By now only about 30 percent of the company's shipments were going out via the U.S. mail; most were now being shipped by UPS.

The new Distribution Center began operating in August 1974. Its horseshoe layout allowed goods to be received, warehoused, moved to ready stock, picked and packed, and then shipped back out the door they'd come in. With such a commitment to major growth, Leon Gorman now realized that he'd never again have the option of "pulling our horns in" if things didn't work out the way he'd planned. (Five years later, the DC would be expanded again.)

Enough people had recently discovered L.L. Bean so that the firm's sales were just about doubling every three years. According to the *New York Times*, the company's sales increased 24.5 percent a year through the end of the decade (Leon Gorman puts that figure at a less-meteoric but still-impressive 19 percent during the recession in '74 and '75). With well over a million customers, as many as 450 workers, and a gross of $29 million, the company was one of Freeport's biggest employers, along with the Eastland Shoe Company.

The following spring, L.L. Bean would send out "1,470,000 catalogs (first class mail, 80 cents a whack)"[15] and ship out 18,521 packages during one day in December—enough to fill about five tractor-trailer trucks. The company kept no fewer than three clerks on duty in the salesroom from 11:00 P.M. until 7:00 A.M., even though most nights' sales weren't sufficient to cover their wages. "The cost doesn't matter," said Gorman. "It's service we're willing to pay for. We'd need a night watchman anyway, and staying open all the time provides good public relations, although we didn't plan it that way."[16]

Amid all of the amazing growth of L. L. Bean's company, it's important not to lose track of some of the people who'd been an important part of his life. Claire, L. L.'s second wife, passed away in 1974 at the age of eighty. She must have felt secure in the knowledge that her late husband's company had not only survived his passing but was now thriving beyond his wildest dreams.

ON A MORE UPBEAT NOTE, L. L.'s old friend and hunting partner George Soule received some of the recognition he deserved when he was featured in "Duck-Hunting Secrets of the Decoy Master," an article in the September issue of *Sports Afield*, which accurately informed its readers that

> No one is more aware of the requirements of the modern duck hunter than George Soule of South Freeport, Maine. Best known as the man who designs and manufactures the duck decoys and duck calls sold by L.L. Bean, Soule has probably done more to assist the modern duck hunter than anyone else. The excellence of his decoys has become the standard against which other commercial duck decoys are compared. Though he

does not take credit for inventing the oversize duck decoy, he was the first to make the modern variety commercially available. He is also the designer and first to promote the use of the new oversize *stand-up* decoys.

Carved from cork processed especially for him in Portugal, and with heads hand-crafted from Maine pine, Soule's decoys are all made under his personal supervision in a little shop heated by a wood stove next to his house on the shore of Casco Bay. Last year he turned out more than 15,000 goose and duck decoys.

In 1975 L.L. Bean, Inc., entered what Leon Gorman has called the third period of the company's development, probably referring to its entry into the era of high tech. Business was booming; orders were pouring in one end of the Distribution Center, and goods, 20 percent of which were still made by Bean, were flying out the other. The company would do about $30 million in sales in 1975.

That same year, L.L. Bean established a customer service department in order to respond "promptly, accurately, and courteously" to the hundreds of inquiries the firm received each week. Leon Gorman actually looked at the recent doubling of Bean's return rate as a good thing; by taking back products that its customers were not happy with, L.L. Bean, Inc., was "developing an extremely loyal customer base for the future."

With the latest in computers, warehousing, and shipping facilities, the merchant was now lacking just one thing—a modern management team. For much of his tenure at the top, at least until the arrival of Dan Lord and Lee Surace in 1970, Leon Gorman had pretty much tried to manage the place with a pencil and paper, and it just wasn't working anymore. No matter how many sixteen-hour days he put in, Gorman simply was no longer able to run things without the outside help L.L. Bean needed to become a more professionally managed company. What he was specifically seeking was a merchandise manager to "be in charge of all buying and buyers for our catalog and retail store, as well as product development, retail store operations, and marketing planning."

So Leon Gorman put out the call, but not before a lot of reflection about bringing in someone from outside to help run the business. Still wondering if he could afford to bring in a professional, and whether or not that person would prove too disruptive at his family-run business, Gorman settled on a candidate. Bill End would prove conclusively to the company that it couldn't afford not to hire the best people if it wanted to continue to grow.

William T. End was a twenty-six-year-old Harvard MBA from Milwaukee. For the past four years he'd worked as a product manager for the Gillette Company in Boston, where he was reportedly responsible for the product development of Right Guard, Foot Guard, and Soft 'n' Dri. End was just the kind of person Gorman was looking for—capable, with a "low-key personality" so as not to detract from L. L.'s legacy. On the one hand, Leon was looking for someone who had "an avid interest in hunting, fishing, and the outdoors," but on the other hand, "if there was a genuine L. L. clone out there," observed Bean expert M. R. Montgomery, "Leon Gorman didn't want to meet him."[17]

Bill End was born in 1950 in Fox Point, Wisconsin, and attended Boston College before doing his graduate work at Harvard. "I answered an ad in the *Wall Street Journal*," he replied when asked how he got the position at Bean's. "There were a lot of qualified people. I think I got the job because I liked the outdoors and had some experience there."[18] Leon Gorman would call End "extremely bright and highly energetic." Besides developing several new products, he'd soon bring his enthusiasm to bear on Bean's marketing strategy by renting mailing lists from other outdoor suppliers—such as Eddie Bauer—for $40 per 1,000 names (a move that would pay off handsomely since the average order per person was about $40 at the time). Bean's new man would also supplement the company's presence in traditional outdoors periodicals with "test" ads in as many as eighty publications which ran the gamut from *Grit* to *Parade* to *Mother Earth News*.

During his next fifteen years with the company, Bill End would advance through the management ranks to the point where he seemed well positioned to succeed Leon Gorman as Bean's next president and CEO even though Gorman had made it clear at the outset that End would act only "as my understudy, being capable of running the business in the event of my death or disability. I am thirty-nine," he continued, "so there is no guarantee that he will succeed me—only that he should have the ability to do so if something unforeseen happens to me."[19] (At this point, it's important to start keeping in mind that the quiet Gorman could also be very stubborn and wouldn't always see eye to eye with members of his upper management team.)

By March 2, 1976, L.L. Bean, Inc., had grown to the point where the United States Postal Service issued the company its own ZIP Code. The government decided that Bean's was deserving of its own number, 04033, about the time its volume reached "more than 2.2 million mail orders." (Later, even as the firm approached its 100th anniversary in the age of toll-free numbers, faxes, and the Internet, a mail-in order form—complete with fit charts and contact information—would still be included in every catalog.)

Another manifestation of the company's growth was the changeover of L. L.'s original location from a combination of store and offices to one of all retail in November 1976, when any remaining administrative offices at the firm's original town square location were moved down Route 1 to Casco Street. There they shared space in the newly expanded Taylor Building with the company's manufacturing and distribution arms. According to newspaper reports of the day, "The retail store of the sporting goods concern moved across the hall to a newer wing, still three flights up from the ground floor, but in an area about 3,000 square feet larger than the old store."[20] Maintenance supervisor Everett Bucklin noted that patrons of the extensively remodeled new store would be better served because of the move. (In its never-ending quest for a better retail store, the company would remodel the remaining structure several more times, beginning in the eighties.)

With the move of the administrative offices and retail store, the Warren Block, into which L. L. had moved his fledgling company in 1917, was now completely empty. By the fall of '76, Chief's Barber Shop had vacated the premises, Freeport Variety had moved across the street to the Davis Block, and the post office had already been gone from the building for more than a decade. "The old structure was just not suitable anymore," said Bucklin. "There were some real problems with the ground floor structural members . . . and we had outgrown the old store anyway." The Warren Block, original home of L.L. Bean, Inc., would be torn down a few months later.

With Bean's downtown location now completely dedicated to retail, Freeport's business district was beginning to become a desirable shopping destination. The first person to make the connection between the number and type of shoppers L.L. Bean attracted and the potential for sales in her own shop was Nan Kilbourne-Tara, who organized Praxis, a crafters' cooperative that sold relatively expensive items such as pottery, jewelry, and textiles.

By locating her business near Bean's, Kilbourne-Tara was at least five years ahead of the curve at a time when most of downtown Freeport's main street was still populated by the fixtures of small-town Maine life: the B. H. Bartol Library, Leighton's Five and Dime, a gas station or two, and the Knights of Pythias Hall. "I felt Bean's was a drawing card for the right clientele," she said of her original plan. "This was a beautiful environment." (By 1983, her business would have practically doubled every year, and the factory outlet stores had begun to spring up around her. "The discount mentality is the absolute antithesis of what we stand for," she said then. "Is this going to become another North Conway?")[21]

DURING 1976 L.L. BEAN would once again become an icon of style when the outdoors retailer was the subject of an article in the June 2 issue of the trend-setting *Women's Wear Daily*. In her article entitled "Spilling the Beans," Lois Pershetz observed that those mounting the stairs to Bean's salesroom included "hunters, campers, backpackers, monied ladies from Boston suburbs looking for gardening gear, college students after just comfortable clothing, and an increasing number of fashion-conscious customers fulfilling their latest fantasies with good-looking, practical, rugged outdoor clothing." But that was just the beginning.

In September the company would be the recipient of the Coty American Fashion Critics Award. "A fashion award, for crying out loud." wrote a *Cleveland Press* reporter who clearly reveled in the irony of the situation. "For a company that outfits hunters and trappers, hikers and anglers for their treks into the woods, this could be disheartening. Why, it flies in the face of everything L. L. stood for. Quality, dependability, durability. Not fashion."[22]

But Leon Gorman took the award in stride; after all, this was the second time in just the past four years that L.L. Bean had become haute couture, but it was still big news to some people from away, most notably the people at NBC's *Today Show*, who set up a mid-September interview with Bean's boss. Reporter Cassie Mackin's first question was, "Mr. Gorman, how do you explain L.L. Bean suddenly finding itself in fashion?" He was at something of a loss for an answer:

> Well, it's kind of difficult for me to explain . . . not knowing anything about the fashion business. I've been thinking a little bit about it in the past few days since, you know, since we're getting so much publicity on the different garments, and I have an idea it goes back to where the young people started getting into backpacking and the outdoors and adults were also taking up camping and more outdoor activities and necessarily they started wearing, you know, functional apparel and gear and learned to like it and started wearing it for casual wear as well, and I think this trend has just, you know, continued since the late sixties to the point where it's recognized by those in charge of fashion and so forth, and here we are.[23]

Ms. Mackin next asked him if being a Yankee businessman who was now "radical chic" was a strange position to be in, and Gorman replied, "It's the first time I've ever been called radical, and I'm not sure what 'chic' is either." He seemed to be truly embarrassed about the fact that the sturdy, practical clothing his company had been producing for years occasionally crossed paths with the latest American fashion trends.

(Three decades later, Leon Gorman would write, "I made an eleven-minute appearance on NBC's *Today Show*. I remember the producer telling me in the waiting room that a live audience of more than eight million people was watching, and that my interviewer Cassie Mackin was new at the job and nervous. If she started to get off track, he said, I was to take over the interview. I was not even sure whether my own voice would work, and I was being asked to manage the interview. The segment went well. . . .")[24]

Some of the items cited by the fashion press as being responsible for the award were Bean's Allagash Hat ("Australian style" with a "wide 3-in. brim," $13.25); Trail Model Vest ("Filled with 3.5 ounces of prime Northern Goose Down," $23.50), and Bean's Gumshoe ("Three eyelet version of our famous Maine Hunting Shoe," $22.50). "'The Bean look' or 'the survival look,'" noted the Associated Press, had now become "as fashionable for a stroll down Fifth Avenue or Wilshire Boulevard as for climbing Katahdin or canoeing the Allagash."

BESIDES ALL THAT BUZZ about fashion, another big reason for Bean's continuing growth was its acceptance of credit cards beginning in the fall. The idea, said the cataloger, was to make shopping more convenient for its customers. It worked. The amount of an average sale went from around $40 to $45. At the same time, L.L. Bean had also begun to include little memos in the catalog encouraging its customers to order by phone. "When we put in credit cards," said Bean's John Findlay, "that's when the phone business went up." It's no coincidence that 1976 was also the year that the firm stopped having its night clerks work the floor and the phones and hired its first group of "phone representatives." By 1981 phone orders would account for 25 percent of the company's catalog sales—even though toll-free ordering wouldn't be implemented until 1986—and credit card purchases would account for 50 percent of Bean's total sales volume.

If wearing things bearing the L.L. Bean label was once again trendy, then there were a lot of fashionable people out there. As the company now processed 4,000 orders on a typical Monday—and as many as 40,000 a day at Christmastime—it was becoming increasingly apparent that L.L. Bean would need more sophisticated telecommunications, computer, and order-fulfillment systems. Making sure that the company's needs were met in these areas became the responsibility of thirty-four-year-old John D. Findlay, who'd recently joined the company from Automated Data Processing in Clifton, New Jersey.

As Bean's vice president of operations, Findlay was responsible for seeing to it that everyone's needs were met, be they trendy urbanites in Boston who requested hats and down vests, or snowbound workers in Buffalo who required boots and long johns that winter. (At this point, 45 percent of Bean's customers lived in the Northeast and mid-Atlantic states.) So the firm could concentrate on other priorities, L.L. Bean sent its list-processing work to Figi, meaning that Bean's 128-page fall catalogs were mailed out to the 2.6 million customers on mailing lists maintained by John H. Figi's Gifts in Good Taste of Marshfield, Wisconsin. (Figi also maintained mailing lists for Eddie Bauer, and others.)

While John Findlay was gearing up to process orders, Bill End was prospecting for more customers. As Leon Gorman would later note:

> Our most important marketing efforts were in the areas of list acquisition and list activation. In 1976 we made extensive market surveys among our customers to determine their age, education, and income demographics to assist us in our media selection. We also wanted to learn how our customers really felt about L.L. Bean so we wouldn't change anything they liked but could improve any areas where we were weak.
>
> In acquiring new buyers, we carefully analyzed our costs in order to determine how much we could afford to invest in new names. . . . We also developed extremely accurate methods for measuring results.[25]

Toward the end of 1975, shortly after his arrival in Freeport, Bill

End tried a number of approaches to increase the number of buying customers. One was renting a list of 400,000 outside names, a move that proved so successful that by 1980 the number of outside names the company rented would approach 5 million. End left no stone unturned in his quest for new customers—or old ones, for that matter, even going so far in 1976 as conducting a test where the company mailed catalogs to former purchasers who hadn't ordered from Bean's in at least three years. "We found this 'rejuvenated' segment," said End, "to be by far the best list we tested."[26]

Another large component of the approximately $3 million L.L. Bean spent on marketing expenses that year went to the company's new advertising agency, WRK. Formerly, the merchant had used Sawyer Direct, an expert in advertising for mail-order companies, until Sawyer's parent company, Batten, Barton, Durstine, and Osborne divested itself of the agency. "When Bob Sawyer went with Wunderman, Ricotta and Kline in New York," reported the *Maine Times*, "Bean's chose to do business with that agency in order to maintain its good working relationship with Sawyer. It meant a $400,000 chunk of advertising from Bean's." Working with Lee Bois, head of Bean's one-woman advertising department, WRK placed ads in such formerly un-Beanlike magazines as *Seventeen*, *Glamour*, and *Vogue*.

The end of an era came in early 1977. Around the middle of February, the Warren Block was razed by a large crane from Crooker Construction of Brunswick. The work started on Tuesday afternoon, and "we expect the area to be leveled and clean by Friday afternoon," said Bean maintenance supervisor Everett Bucklin. The site, noted Bucklin, "would be 'leveled and landscaped,' that some parking might be added but the company wanted to 'add some green out there if we can . . . we don't want it to look like an asphalt jungle.'"[27] Bean's ever-growing need for additional parking spaces would again quickly win out.

The iconic old Warren Block had been living on borrowed time for decades; just after the war it had to be shored up by external beams. Recently Bean's complex had been briefly closed after management feared it might collapse under the weight of a heavy snowfall. Mike Perry, who had just been hired for Bean's shoe department, remembered that day well:

I remember once in my early years, when I was working in shoes, Bill End came by the store—we had a wicked snow-storm, fifteen inches of wet, heavy snow—and he says, "Well, we gotta close the store down for a couple hours," because you'll always hear about the only time the store closed was for L. L. Bean's funeral.

I'll never forget Bill coming up to the store and looking around. He and the managers talked and said, "Yup, we're closing the place down." I don't know where all the shovels came from, but we were all up on the roof—that was before we abutted out onto Main Street, there was a parking lot down there—and there were employees out in front, not letting people in because the doors didn't lock. We shoveled furiously for a couple hours, getting the snow off because it was a flat roof. Finally Bill was satisfied that we'd gotten the majority of the snow and weight off, and they reopened the store. It's a wonder we didn't fall off the roof. This day and age, OSHA would never let you do that. We all ended up with sore backs.

A few days after the last pieces of the Warren Block—which had outlived L. L. Bean by almost exactly a decade—had been cleared away, CBS News dispatched Dan Rather, one of its top reporters, to chilly coastal Maine to film a feature about L.L. Bean for its new documentary program, *Who's Who*. Rather began the segment by talking with *Vogue* magazine editor Grace Meribella, who explained that last year's Coty Award had gone to the company in the "special award category for gear," adding that "it was the most natural idea, it came so naturally from [all the voters], because 'gear' really is what it is, it's clothes to wear in the elements, clothes that you hack, and clothes that you work with, and clothes that don't pretend to be anything but honest the way sneakers are honest."

Then, after speaking briefly with Dr. Joyce Brothers about what purchasing the company's handmade goods constructed of natural materials "tell[s] us about ourselves," Rather then interviewed Leon Gorman in the retail store (which was in the midst of yet another remodeling), asking him to comment on the company's success. "I don't think it's going to any of our heads and that sort of thing," said Gorman. "I think we're still committed to doing what we've always done, and I think Maine people just naturally try to do the best they can and don't get carried away by, you know, success or whatever." The boss also revealed a possible tweak to the design of the venerable Maine Hunting Shoe: "Charlie Carter said that if they skive this down [pointing] a little more," Gorman said, "it will bring that seam in so it won't make the boot look quite so long."

"How long's it going to take to get that finished up?" asked Rather.

"It's a fall item."

"1977?"

"'77, yeah."

Rather said that the piece would probably air in about three weeks in the program's Tuesday 8:00 P.M. time slot, which it did, running opposite an episode of ABC's *Happy Days* and the series premiere of *Eight Is Enough*. The television listings in the *New York Times* listed the eleventh episode of *Who's Who* as follows: "8:00 (2)•WHO'S WHO: Interview with James Earl Ray; Profile of former New Dealer Thomas Gardiner Corcoran; Report on L.L. Bean, Inc., a mail order company." A typed transcript of the L.L. Bean segment is on file in the Bartol Room of the Freeport Community Library.

An article in the *Portland Press Herald* told about Rather's visit and also noted that the *60 Minutes* co-host and former White House correspondent was not impressed with President Carter's first month in office. "Quite honestly, I don't think too much of his start," said Rather while in Freeport. "The modern presidency certainly needs heavy doses of planning, organization, and competent management,"[28] said the reporter, traits that had characterized the Democrat's campaign but were so far lacking in the early days of his administration.

SPEAKING OF POLITICS, the Dickey-Lincoln hydroelectric project marked the first time in L.L. Bean's sixty-five-year history that the company became actively involved in a political matter when Leon Gorman sided with Chris Herter, executive director of the Natural Resources Council of Maine, in his opposition to the proposed dam on the St. John River. "My company's efforts in the past on lobbying and getting along in Augusta have been sporadic, inconsistent, and often ineffective,"[29] the Bean boss told other business leaders at the Associated Industries of Maine annual meeting.

But Gorman's opposition to Dickey-Lincoln had a laser focus, and this time none of those adjectives would apply to his efforts. During the first half of 1977, an L.L. Bean letter-writing campaign to more than 50,000 of its customers would account for more than $17,000, or 40 percent of all the money raised by the NRCM. "Save the St. John" petitions in the retail store netted nearly 33,000 signatures, 57 percent of those collected by the Council. "There are likely to be other issues in the future on which we'll take stands," said Gorman, whose subsequent forays into politics would be opposing the closure of the Maine Yankee nuclear power plant in 1980 and coming out against casinos in 2003.

The hydroelectric project, originally proposed by the Army Corps of Engineers in 1965, called for a two-mile-wide, twenty-seven-story dam to be built across the St. John River in the northern Maine town of Allagash Plantation, and would have cost as much as a billion dollars to construct. Had the dam been built, it would have been bigger than Egypt's Aswan Dam, and would have flooded 88,000 acres of timberland to create a reservoir 57 miles long. (Nearly a third of the land involved was owned by Canada's Irving Pulp and Paper Co.) The project's chance of succeeding took a serious hit when environmentalists discovered 200 specimens of the endangered Furbish's lousewort in the dam's flood zone.

Furbish's lousewort would be to Dickey-Lincoln what the three-inch-long snail darter fish had been to the Tennessee Valley Authority's Tellico Dam. The plant (*Pedicularis furbishiae*), thought to have been extinct for thirty years, is a yellow, three-foot-tall wild snapdragon that was named after Brunswick botanist Kate Furbish (1834–1931) and the "erroneous belief in medieval Europe that a related species transmitted lice to cattle."[30] Section VII of the 1973 Endangered Species Act expressly forbids any federal agency to take any action that jeopardizes the continued existence of an officially endangered species. Opponents of the project also claimed that in the summer, when the river is low, the dam would be capable of generating electricity for only two and a half hours a day. Following a protracted battle over the project, Dickey-Lincoln would never be built due to lack of federal funds.

OVEREAGER EXPANSION PLANS had recently put L.L. Bean's rival, Abercrombie & Fitch, in dire straits financially, and it was purchased by a competitor. (Despite the takeover, A&F would continue to struggle before being purchased by The Limited in 1988, quickly evolving into a Gap-like fashion Mecca for the younger set.) Its Maine-based competition was having no such difficulties. Bill End was continuing to mine the mailing lists (by making use of the best mailing lists, Bean increased its customer base by about 32 percent in 1977), while also exploring other avenues of advertising for new customers. He also had three men working for him who did nothing but develop new products or tweak profitable Bean classics. Among the new offerings at the time were the L.L. Bean Canoe and, of course, a new knife, the L.L. Bean Trapper's Knife.

End's efforts, when coupled with the recent trend toward comfortable clothes and the fact that competitors' prices had soared to the point where it now cost only a bit more to purchase items 100 percent guaranteed by L.L. Bean, all boded well for the Freeport company. The addition of a sixth circular to the company's catalog drops helped push its annual sales from 1976's $41.5 million up to $58 million the following year, and the 415,000 New England names included on the firm's massive mailing list represented 11 percent of the region's households—the upscale 11 percent.

As the company continued its rapid growth, management realized it needed a way to ensure the continued high quality of the products Bean's offered its loyal customers, who'd come to expect nothing less. Quality control, which had consisted of spot checks of incoming merchandise, became more formalized with the hiring of an assistant manager who, along with three other workers, continued the spot checking process "at a small work station" in the Distribution Center. Two years later, L.L. Bean would hire a full-time manager for its renamed and greatly expanded Quality Assurance Department, which would soon number more than thirty people.

"In 1977 we automated backorders!" exclaimed the *Bean Bulletin*. "No longer did we use rulers to measure backorders. No longer was the manual status board in the warehouse needed for checking each order prior to sorting for picking. We could now ensure shipping the oldest backorder first when merchandise arrived. We could also distinguish between demand (what the customer wanted) and sales (what we shipped)." Also in 1977 the company implemented an inventory management system to help it maintain the highest in-stock level of products possible.

While formal quality control measures at the company may have been just getting off the ground, proof that the basic design of most of its products was sound was shown when other retailers started copying Bean's more popular items, such as the Chamois Cloth Shirt and the Maine Hunting Shoe. One of the first companies to make a knockoff of L. L.'s famous $29 boot was K-Mart with its $20 offering. "We got one, tore it apart, and analyzed it," said Gorman. "It was nice but didn't have the Bean quality. . . . Virtually every shoe manufacturer now has a hunting boot in their line."[31]

Success begets success, and L.L. Bean continued to succeed in the new year. Growth for 1978 included the beginning of a $4.5-million expansion that would soon create a 72,000-square-foot building for Bean's Freeport manufacturing operations, and add another 200,000 square feet to the Distribution Center. Work on the project, according to an article in the *Brunswick Times Record*, was "scheduled to begin around the middle of June and is expected to be completed by July of next year." The piece also noted that "a crossing guard currently directs employee traffic at the Casco and Main Street intersection between 4 and 5 P.M. each weekday—quitting time for most employees. That practice, [Town Manager Bruce]

Benway said, will continue after the expansion, and a traffic light that could be turned on during peak traffic may be installed at the intersection."

Another small but significant change at L.L. Bean that year was the retooling of the company's corporate logo. Gone was L. L.'s old "Hunting, Fishing, and Camping" tag line, replaced by "Outdoor Sporting Specialties," which reflected the company's emphasis on human-powered, noncompetitive outdoor activities, and harkens back to L. L.'s belief that we enjoy the outdoors "to forget the mean and petty things of life."

In November the company opened a second, smaller store in Freeport that catered to a very exclusive clientele—L.L. Bean employees. At the Davis Warehouse, which the company would purchase two years later, the firm's legion of employees—600 permanent workers and just as many seasonal ones—could rummage through tables, racks, and bins of returned merchandise deemed not pristine enough to sell at the retail store. Most of the items offered for sale there could be had for pennies on the dollar. (By knowing exactly what he needed and spending a couple of hours digging through hundreds of parts in an old apple crate, the author once pieced together a $300 Thule roof rack system for $30.) The price of admission to this exclusive establishment was a valid company I.D. shown at the door.

With L.L. Bean, Inc., opting to concentrate on its core business of mail order in lieu of opening any new retail stores, the $7 million invested in marketing—the rental of names and advertising—was paying huge dividends. As luck would have it, the late seventies were the golden age of renting mailing lists, such as the ones Bean had recently procured from the likes of Eddie Bauer, Orvis, and even the Burpee Seed Company.

Realizing that at least a third of the company's $78 million in sales for 1978 would come during the two-month Christmas season, management was sent scurrying to secure more help. When Bean advertised the 500 job openings for its peak winter season, well over 2,000 people eventually showed up. "The response was phenomenal," said director of personnel Robert Skladany. "In the first day after advertising in the newspapers, 223 people showed up. The problem then became how to graciously tell 1,600 people that there weren't enough jobs."[32] The following year, the company would accept no more than 1,400 applications.

Of the 500 or so temporary workers who were hired, about 200 would work in the Distribution Center while another 110 would supplement the company's normal staff of 20 operators. Since the firm's volume of telephone orders was growing twice as fast as its mail orders, these 130 smiling voices could expect to answer as many as 12,000 calls a day, a task they prepared for by undergoing three days of training at a total cost of $15,000 to the company.

The first two Mondays in December are usually when Bean's phone lines are the busiest. Interestingly, while most of the company's other operations were being done on computers, taking orders over the phone still involved pushing a pencil. One reporter noted that Bean's "operators must be reasonably well-educated, write clearly, and have a satisfactory telephone manner." (It's also noted that flannel sheets were a very popular item that season.)

The company's computer technology continued to keep pace with its staggering growth. In 1978 Bean initiated on-line corrections for order processing and "the first financial package—General Ledger (which included budgeting)." But, according to the *Bean Bulletin*, that would pale in comparison to what would come next:

> 1979 was a big year. The inventory planning system (item forecasting), which required over five man-years of effort, was implemented. This was our largest effort to date and required a lot of support from the merchandising people and especially Dick Leslie. We also implemented a batch Picking System to analyze the orders and sort them into the most efficient picking sequence for the Distribution Center. Accounts Payable was implemented as well.[33]

Given the company's recent increase in computing power, it somehow seems fitting that L.L. Bean would choose 1979 to join forces with Japanese electronics giant Sony, which sold selected items from the Freeport company in its Sony Plaza Stores. For many years now, the Maine firm had been receiving an increasing number of orders from Japan due in large part to the nation's interest in American products and a favorable exchange rate. The cataloger saw that now was the time to capitalize on this situation. Though the association with Sony, which L.L. Bean has since called "a small-scale experiment," would eventually end, the Maine firm would continue its presence in the Far East by entering into a joint venture with Seiyu, Ltd., and Matsushita Electric Industrial Co., Ltd., in 1991.

Closer to home, the Main Street store had undergone more improvements, both physical and electronic. On the ground floor, a permanent "Sale Room" had been set up where irregulars and closeouts in men's and women's clothing and camping items were on display. "The Sale Room concept," reported the *Bean Scene*, "worked very well during the midwinter and summer sales this year and should prove an asset to the retail operation and a convenience to our customers." Upstairs in the main salesroom, Customer Service had moved "to a new counter behind the former hat wall in the men's department. The C.S. representatives now have their own cash register; transactions at the Customer Service counter—exchanges, refunds, shipping, discount purchases, etc.— now can be completed there. Customers no longer must seek a check-out counter to finish their transactions."

The rest of the salesroom was being similarly modernized, starting with a review of its inventory and cashiering systems by the retail consulting firm of Coopers & Lybrand. The goal of this review was to ensure that the store always maintained the right amount of stock in the right sizes for the customers. "The information necessary to achieve this balance," said the *Bean Scene*, "will be gathered at the 'point-of-sale terminals'; store personnel probably will still call them cash registers."

And the sprucing up at Bean's store wasn't limited to just the sales areas. Outside, the company demonstrated its support of Freeport's new Townscape plan through both beautification projects (such as paving the parking lot) and a sizable donation. In

April, L.L. Bean, Inc., contributed $10,000 to the Freeport Town Council to launch the project. According to Bill End, vice president of marketing, Bean's participation in the Townscape project was good for both the firm and the town. "L.L. Bean is one of the largest merchants, employers, and taxpayers in Freeport. We have an obligation to work with the town on matters of mutual importance and to make any improvements we can. . . . The thing to remember about the Townscape is that this is not a historical restoration or beautification project. The long-term intent of the Townscape plan is to stimulate existing business, and attract new business to a financially viable downtown area."[34]

These new ventures were supplemented by major improvements to the company's most basic sales tool, the L.L. Bean catalog, which was being converted to a full-color format as fast as Sandy Fowler's Dingley Press could keep pace with the evolving technology. By 1979 all the company's catalogs had been converted to four-color printing, making them more attractive and easier to read while retaining their traditional style. (In the early days, you'll recall, about the only color to be found in one of L. L.'s catalogs were the occasional pages of fishing flies, inserted one at a time by a young John Gould.) The new catalogs, which were now being printed in seven different versions and mailed out a total of 20.3 million times that year, served only to accelerate the company's already meteoric growth to the point where it reached the $94 million mark.

The company made only about 20 percent of the items it sold, but that was still a staggering amount of stuff. In 1979 L.L. Bean completed its 72,000-square-foot manufacturing building, tripling the company's manufacturing capacity. The new building also allowed the company to store all its materials under one roof, helping keep inventories at more acceptable levels. The new facility opened on May 1 at 7:00 A.M., when the ribbon was cut by Edna Hawes, who'd worked in manufacturing at L.L. Bean since 1950. All the women received corsages. "We wanted our building to be on a quality level with you people who work in it," Gorman told the assembled workers, "and on the quality level with the products that you make. I think the building has achieved these results."[35]

Unusual for a manufacturing building, the structure was far from a typical prefab steel box. It was constructed of twelve-inch insulated concrete blocks and featured ten home-sized boilers as well as air filtration systems. High shelves were eliminated so everyone could see out the windows, which actually opened, and larger windows in the lounge area looked out toward the DC and the grove of trees to the east of it. The building also included individual shops for all the maintenance trades. "It may be the best manufacturing building in the State of Maine," Gorman asserted. It also allowed L.L. Bean to return to Maine the manufacture of its classic Boat and Tote Bag, which at the time was being made in Pennsylvania. The following year the industrious workers at L.L. Bean, Inc., would turn out 175,872 pairs of Maine Hunting Shoes, 164,339 pairs of hand-sewn footwear, and about 200 other "leather or canvas specialty items" totaling 528,524 pieces.

One big problem accompanying Bean's huge increases in sales was the inevitable lapse in the quality of some items. The company began a major effort to rectify the situation in 1979 when it hired Don Thacker to head up its new Quality Assurance program. Between the two of them, Thacker and supervisor Dave Holt oversaw four groups of workers: two shifts of quality assurance inspectors; a general lab that also tested, fit, and evaluated samples; a return/disposition department; and "100 percent inspection."

Under the program, all new shipments were subject to Bean's "Acceptance Sampling Procedure," which was based on the Defense Department's "Military Standard 105D 'Sampling Procedures and Tables for Inspection by Attributes.'" This sampling plan, explained the company, was widely used by industry, and the acceptable quality level at L.L. Bean had been set at "an exacting 4 percent." If a new shipment failed two sample-inspections, it was put on hold and then rejected or subjected to a 100 percent inspection since as much as 90 percent of it might have been good and the merchandise was needed to fill customer orders. Other possibilities were that Bean could fix the problem and charge repairs to the vendor or reject an entire shipment and send it back.

In order to keep pace with this productivity, L.L. Bean completed its "all new" Distribution Center in August of 1979. The new DC wasn't actually "all" new, but a 200,000-square-foot expansion of the company's five-year-old facility. As had been the case with the manufacturing facility, the new design enabled the company to keep under one roof stock that had previously been kept in Portland and at the Davis Warehouse. By shifting the flow of goods through the building from receiving on Casco Street to shipping on Double L Street, the new design also alleviated congestion on Casco Street, which had previously been used for both activities. Inside the 310,000-square-foot building, merchandise moved along on a mile-long system of conveyor belts costing half a million dollars. "Picking, packing, and shipping benefited from imaginative and advanced data processing applications. The total system complemented the workers' skills and raised productivity."[36]

Other improvements to the DC included new shelving hung cantilever-fashion from the back, which not only eliminated external posts for easier access, but also held 20 percent more inventory. The pickers selected their assigned items from two-tiered "flip-top" cartons and then sent everything up to the packing line on new compartmentalized rolling carts, which had superseded the company's five-year-old rolling-rack-and-tote-bin system. During the peak season, L.L. Bean was shipping out 33,000 packages (and using 70 pallets of cardboard for boxes) every day, with the company's manpower requirements increasing accordingly. The previous year, Bill End had estimated that Bean's 600 permanent workers would "swell to about 1,000 by August of 1979," when the expansion was completed. (Bean's workforce had been steadily growing by about 15 percent in each of the preceding four years.) The company's phenomenal growth would only continue.

Chapter 10

. . . at Bean's, "hard times" was a relative term

The 1980s would prove to be a real roller coaster ride for L.L. Bean, with a short spurt of phenomenal growth being followed by an uncharacteristic dry spell. By the end of the eighties, the company would find itself still searching for just the right formula for maintaining an extended period of sustainable growth. The ups and downs of the decade began on a somber note for the family with the passing on February 16 of Carl's widow, Hazel, at the Freeport Nursing Home. Hazel Haskell Bean was seventy-four.

As the last members of the previous generation passed on, Leon Gorman found himself wrestling with a problem created by modern technology—nuclear power. Throughout his tenure as head of L.L. Bean, he had championed many environmental causes, but that didn't mean that his views always sat well with environmentalists. Gorman's most controversial stand came in 1980 when he supported keeping Maine Yankee, the state's only nuclear power station, open, an opinion he'd probably been expected to express since he also served on the board of Central Maine Power Company, which owned the eight-year-old facility.

In his 2006 memoir, Gorman again emphasized that he thought his conclusions and subsequent actions on the nuclear issue had been correct, but wasted no time admitting that his position had not been especially good for business. He felt that nuclear energy was a clean and efficient source of electricity, and that shutting down Maine Yankee would be detrimental to the state's economy. He also knew that he was dealing with a touchy subject, one that raised strong feelings on both sides of the issue. L.L. Bean received thousands of letters criticizing its pro-nuclear stand, some of them advocating a boycott of the company. So Gorman, "having been burned" by his support of Maine Yankee, vowed to avoid political issues, a promise kept until coming out against casinos in Maine in 2003.

Though the people of Maine did vote to keep the plant open, the 900-megawatt Maine Yankee nuclear reactor would be finally shut down in 1997 due to ongoing maintenance problems. Demolition of the facility would begin in 1999 and continue through 2004, when its 150-foot containment dome was imploded.

In fairness to Gorman, he did have the names and addresses of anti-nuclear organizations printed in the company newsletter so his employees could get the other side of the issue if they wanted it. In 1985, when a dam would be proposed for the West Branch of the Penobscot River, Gorman, still smarting from the Maine Yankee controversy, "simply gave each side equal space in our retail store to tell its story and let the public decide for itself."

Prior to the November nuclear referendum, syndicated columnist Jack Anderson had written, in Gorman's words, "that our company threatened to withhold funding from a Maine 'environmental coalition' if it supported the anti-nuclear referendum. This statement is entirely false with absolutely no factual basis of any kind. The falsity of Anderson's statement," Gorman noted in his October 6 letter to the editor of the *Portland Evening Express*, "can be verified by the leadership of the Natural Resources Council of Maine. . . ."[1] And it was, in the editorial page's very next letter.

"Jack Anderson's claim that the L.L. Bean company threatened to withhold funds from an environmental organization," wrote NRCM executive director Rob Gardiner, Jr., "is simply not true." He went on to clarify that "while the Natural Resources Council of Maine was not specifically named in the column, there is no question that he was referring to this organization."[2] When Gorman had been awarded an NRCM conservation award in June, Gardiner explained, the Bean president had joked that he hoped the organization wouldn't want it back when L.L. Bean came out with its pro-nuclear stand the following week. Several weeks later, when the NRCM came out in favor of closing Maine Yankee, Gardiner said that Gorman had "expressed regret that we had taken a position and that our effective environmental coalition which was united against Dickey-Lincoln and other issues might be badly split on the referendum question."

At the time, L.L. Bean contributed 1.5 percent of its pretax profits to environmental and community causes. Forty percent of that amount was directed toward environmental organizations with the primary recipients being Maine Audubon, the Natural Resources Council, the Appalachian Mountain Club, and the Chewonki Foundation. L.L. Bean had also donated $36,000 to the Maine Audubon Society, where Gorman was serving as an advisory trustee, so it could retrofit its recently acquired Falmouth farmhouse as an alternative energy center. L.L. Bean had also adopted a nineteen-mile stretch of the Appalachian Trail.

Perhaps not coincidentally, this was also the year that L.L. Bean, Inc., undertook another new endeavor, but this time it wasn't one that was aimed at increasing sales—at least not directly. The firm's Public Clinic Program was launched when then-assistant store manager John Walling and camping clerk Mike Perry worked with Outward Bound to set up a winter camping clinic that Perry was hosting for the merchant. Walling recalls that things took off from the January 26 presentation when Leon Gorman said that the event went well, but thought that L.L. Bean could take the lead on similar events—the idea was, after all, to show its customers that L.L. Bean was "the store that knows the outdoors."

Having spent a grand total of $241 on advertising—$145 for black-and-white posters for area supermarkets and $96 for "media space" (newspaper advertising)—for the clinic, Walling and Perry weren't sure what kind of turnout they'd get. "Gosh, we had sixty people show up," recalled Perry in a recent talk with the author, "on a January night, no less! That was a good number, so John said, 'You know, there's a real potential here to interact with customers and show them that the store employees really do stuff in the outdoors.' Soon I was working twenty hours on the sales floor and twenty hours behind the scenes in what was then called the Public Clinic Program—descriptive name!" Within a year, Perry was managing the program full time, and before long it had a part-time secretary. (By the time Perry left L.L. Bean in June 1996, the Outdoor Discovery Program, as it's been known since 1991, had ten full-time employees.)

One of the main points of the program, besides teaching skills to the public, has always been to impart a basic respect for the outdoors by demonstrating principles such as the Leave No Trace ethic. "We don't beat people over the head with an environmental message," said Perry. "If we do the things that need to be done, people will get the message in an understated way." Although the Outdoor Discovery Program probably does translate into some additional sales for the company, it isn't a big moneymaker. The program, asserts Perry, measures its success "in smiles, not sales."

Though the program is now a huge success—offering all types of outdoor experiences in its glossy 24-page catalog—some of the program's early clinics, said Perry, had required a little last-minute improvisation.

One January we had a cross-country ski race coming up at the Desert of Maine on the weekend. The Friday before the race it [the race course] was boilerplate [ice], just boilerplate, and we didn't have any grooming equipment to chop it up and make tracks. We had relied on having nice powder and just sending the folks out when the gun went off, figuring they could make their own tracks!

Well, I'm a can-do kind of guy, and I used to work with a guy named Phil Savignano, and Phil's a can-do guy too, and we're thinking, "God, what are we going to do?" One of us came up with the idea to call one of the local construction companies and rent out one of their tractors. So we called some local contractor whose response was, "You want to do what?" We wanted a bulldozer to go around the course and the tread would rip up the snow. We had this guy out there on Friday just going round and round backwards, chopping it up—so instead of being solid ice, it was like plates of broken glass, but at least nobody was going to die!

We just made it happen. We didn't have a big budget, but

we weren't going to be denied. That was typical.

Another funny story is about one of the cooking classes we used to have with Alex Delicata. Alex was a great chef with game, and he had a rabbit-cooking class for about sixty people scheduled for one evening at 7:30. We were setting up the chairs at about 6:45 and all of a sudden he gets this panic-stricken look on his face and says, "Oh, my God! I forgot the rabbits!" He lived in Durham [about five miles away]!

Alex bolts out the door, gets in his pickup truck, and races down to Durham to pick up the rabbits.

I'm doing a wicked long introduction stalling for time, and he comes sashaying in at 7:35, about five minutes late, with the rabbits, and no one was the wiser.

More good publicity for the Freeport merchant came from Suzanne McNear's "The Annals of Marketing, Part II: L.L. Bean: Putting the Great Outdoors in High Gear," which appeared in the March 1980 issue of the *TWA Ambassador* in-flight magazine. It must have brought a collective smile to the faces of all who worked in the Freeport company's Public Affairs Department. The first two lines of the article read: "The story of L.L. Bean is an American story about a dream that did not go wrong. It is a story about honesty, reliability, promises kept, guarantees made good even after twenty or thirty years or more." How could she miss? Bean's management thought so highly of Ms. McNear's essay that they would include it, in its entirety, in the company's seventy-fifth-anniversary scrapbook seven years later.

WHILE MS. McNEAR'S thoughtful article was something for her readers' minds, Lisa Birnbach's little book would be something for Bean's (and her) bottom line. One of the Bean Boot's all-time biggest boosts came in the form of a little 224-page book with a plaid-trimmed cover: *The Official Preppy Handbook*, edited by Birnbach (Workman Publishing, 1980, $3.95). While it must be said that the tiny tongue-in-cheek tome about everything "Prep" (which evidently must always be capitalized) was not solely responsible for the company's phenomenal growth spurt during the early 1980s—that's also when the firm's direct-mail budget increased 38 percent, from $2.6 million to $3.6 million—its importance certainly can't be underestimated.

In this case, it was a matter of Bean's relentless preparation for growth happening to mesh perfectly with the increasing buying power of the country's college kids, be they actual Preppies or merely those wanting to look the part. "The fashion trend came to us, landed on our doorstep, and drove us crazy,"[3] Bill End would later tell the *Maine Times*. Preppies were helping the Freeport merchant move $100,000 worth of flannel sheets each fall, and sales of penny loafers were up 22 percent. The fact that people were rediscovering outdoor activities and becoming more aware of environmental issues probably didn't hurt the company's coffers either.

Leon Gorman later recalled that Birnbach's book was "a well-done caricature" of the well-heeled teenagers and their parents who used his company's products, adding that its demographics were similar to those on the company's mailing list. The handbook called the company "a Down-East extravaganza, the Bean catalog is the biggest seller of the rugged New England Prep look. Never mind that you don't really need a game pocket in your back-to-school Field Coat. Home of the ubiquitous rubber moccasins and the Norwegian sweater. Let that label show!"

On the book's "must-have" footwear front, Bean's makes out very well, with its boots and rubber moccasins just edging out the Blucher mocs for number of mentions. Coming in a close second to its footwear was the L.L. Bean Norwegian Pullover ("the nearest thing to a Prep membership card"), which appears in the little book three times. Honorable mentions go to Bean's Chamois Shirt, the Field Coat, and the Hudson Bay Blanket.

Just so nothing is missed in the quest for ultimate Preppiness, Birnbach notes that many fashion necessities for women can come from actual men's clothing lines "or near imitations," and may include "anything from L.L. Bean." To help the terminally fashion-conscious in their pursuit of everything Prep, she even gives the location of the store, which, she gushes, "is nothing less than a Prep

Mecca," and emphasizes that "a middle-of-the-night pilgrimage here is one of the Prep rites of passage." Unfortunately, the address she lists in the book for the retail store is actually for the company's business offices and Distribution Center down on Casco Street.

In addition to the book's many references to Bean's, the Pine Tree State merits at least another ten mentions, which run the gamut from relatively interesting to fairly crude. Two of *The Official Preppy Handbook's* more unique perceptions of Maine are the placement of Bowdoin College in Brunswick ("SATs: V550, M570" and Leon Gorman's alma mater) at Number 2 on its list of "Top 10 Drinking Schools," and its inclusion of "anything in Maine where you have to dispense with your bodily fluids out of doors" among its "most sought-after" summer camps for Preppy fledglings. (In the interest of fairness, Maine's Bowdoin, Colby, and Bates Colleges are among the best small colleges in the country, each ranking in the top twenty-five of *U.S. News & World Report's* prestigious annual listing of liberal arts colleges. In the magazine's 2010 survey, the trio came in at sixth, twenty-first, and twenty-third respectively.)

According to senior vice president for marketing Bill End, Bean's had done $94 million in sales the previous year. Thanks to the 2.2 million orders the company received in the mail that year, plus another 500,000 by phone, Bean was set to improve upon that by 31 percent, which means it would end 1980 with sales totaling $121.5 million—all of which translates to a profit of $7.6 million for an average of about 6 percent after taxes for the past few years. Making this growth possible, besides Gorman's almost obsessive commitment to modernization and 1,406 loyal employees in the trenches, was L.L. Bean's ever-expanding team of managers.

When Gorman started with his grandfather's business in 1960, he was the company's only college graduate; now the company boasted that it paid the salaries of no fewer than sixty-six college graduates, including fifteen MBAs who made it possible for Gorman to say things like, "Between 1975 and 1980 we had a compounding growth rate of 30 percent." By the end of the decade, many of Bean's top executives would have come to Freeport from the likes of Gillette, Spiegel, Sears, and other top national companies. "They've had years of experience," George Burman of the Boston-based DM Management Co. told the *Washington Post*, "so they're good with the fundamental blocking and tackling. There's a backwoods aura to that company, but there are plenty of MBA types walking around there."[4]

Back in 1975, when L.L. Bean was doing about $30 million in sales, the company's forecasters predicted it'd be doing about $60 million in sales by 1981. The actual figure would turn out to be more than $172 million (but then, how do you predict something like the Preppy phenomenon?). In 1977 the company's three- to five-year planning had included trying to forecast what its energy cost would be in 1980. Given its track record at the time, Bean's attempted energy prediction probably missed the mark by quite a bit. But the fact remains that the cost of energy was increasing along with the costs of labor, raw materials, inventory (in which Bean's had $30 million tied up), and shipping, to name just a few. The bottom line was that the company had to find ways to cut costs.

WITH THE CATALOG STILL ACCOUNTING for more than 80 percent of the company's business, it was imperative that it be printed and distributed in a very timely manner, since any delays could cost Bean's millions in lost sales. R. R. Donnelley & Sons of Chicago, L.L. Bean's new printer, could offer the firm thirty-four rotogravure presses in five locations, which "will protect us," said Bean's employee newsletter, "from fire, equipment failure, or any other catastrophe that might occur and interrupt the printing schedule." The Dingley Press had one location and used web offset printing. Donnelley could also print the addressee's name and address on the catalog and the enclosed "ordervelope," and save the cataloger money on postage by presorting the mailings by postal carrier routes. Some estimates put Bean's savings over the life of the first three-year contract with Donnelley as high as $4 million.

In 1980 the forests of Maine provided L.L. Bean with 10.5 million pounds of paper—enough to print over 26 million catalogs, enabling the Freeport company to mail nine separate catalogs to its best customers. The 400,000 mailing-list names L.L. Bean had tested in 1975 led to its renting 5 million names by 1980. Bean's marketing expenses had grown from $3.1 million to $10.5 million in the same five-year period, yet remained the same percentage of its sales.

Back in 1979 the Dingley Press had printed L.L. Bean's first full-color catalog, but the small Maine printer found itself struggling to keep up with the cataloger's escalating needs for both quality and quantity. When L.L. Bean switched to R. R. Donnelley, marked improvements in clarity, color registration, and consistency were immediately obvious.

But what was good for L.L. Bean, Inc., was bad for the Dingley Press. At first it was very bad. Donnelley printed its first L.L. Bean catalog, the summer 1981 edition, in March. The Freeport firm had advised the Dingley Press of its upcoming departure so the printer would have time to land other printing jobs, but since the company's presses were kept busy filling Bean's orders right up until the end, it didn't even have time to look for, much less print, any catalogs for anyone else (the company had never done business with any of Bean's direct competitors). No longer having the Freeport merchant as a customer meant that the Dingley Press, which had printed Bean's catalogs since 1928, had lost 95 percent of its business and was forced to lay off thirty of its seventy-two employees.

Christopher Pierce had bought the printing company from Sandy Fowler just seven months before the contract with Bean's expired. "We were like baby birds getting shoved out of the nest," said the press's new owner, "and we had to learn how to fly on the way down. We did." Not only would Pierce land on his feet, he began rebuilding right away. He started by sending out 2,000 marketing letters accompanied by a letter of recommendation from Leon Gorman. This netted Pierce fifty-five responses but only five printing jobs.

Despite the slow start, Dingley's business soon began to snowball, and by August 1982, the printer's customer list had grown to twenty, replacing 70 percent of its lost business, and by 1985, Dingley's thirty-five clients would have it back to its former $6 million sales mark. By 1993 Dingley's presses would be running twenty-four hours a day, the printer's sales would be more than $22 million, and it would be looking at its second expansion in five years. To make sure it didn't take another hit like the one it took in 1981, the Dingley Press, now located in Lisbon, Maine, was printing catalogs for more than fifty different firms.

THE PREPPIES THAT BEAN was about to gain because of *The Official Preppy Handbook* weren't the company's only new customers of the period. Since 1975, Bean's had doubled its number of female customers, who now accounted for half of its sales. While some of this increase was because of Preppy women purchasing men's products—college women who'd become loyal Bean customers down the road—the company was also courting other women who'd never been near a Prep school.

The driving force behind getting more women's items included in the L.L. Bean catalog was Charlie Kessler, vice president in charge of product and one of those Harvard MBAs who'd recently come on board. It was about this time—when Bean had just three clothing categories: footwear, outerwear, and underwear—and only after a long, hard fight, that he'd managed to get the corduroy shirtdress ("a practical dress for Fall wear. Made of soft, narrow wale, 81% cotton, 19% polyester corduroy") into the catalog. By Christmas more than 5,000 of the $29 dresses were on backorder. Next he got the women's wool blazer into the catalog. (For what it's worth, Bean's corporate timeline notes that 1980 is also the year it introduced dog beds to its product mix.)

Thanks to women, Preppies, sports, and even the company's "worst" customers (more on them later), Bean's sales for fiscal year 1981 would skyrocket to $172.3 million from 1980's $121.5 million, an increase of a staggering 41.8 percent, the company's largest ever. (Bean's fiscal year concludes at the end of February, after all the holiday returns have been processed.) Mail-order sales had accounted for $146 million of the company's income. Helping

Bean's achieve this lofty growth were 1.4 million "buyers," as the company calls its customers, from the 10 million people who'd received the firm's 32 million catalogs that year. Thanks to the continuing Preppy movement, L.L. Bean, which now employed a total of 1,472 salaried, hourly, and seasonal workers, also received its second Coty fashion award in five years.

L.L. Bean was also noticed for a third time by the researchers and students of Harvard Business School, who were producing case studies of companies around the world at the rate of about 600 a year. The June 1 study done by Hirotaka Takeuchi and Penny Pittman-Merliss focused on how L.L. Bean had grown to its present size from a $3 million company in 1967. At twenty-six pages, Case Study Number 581159 was exactly twice as long as the first one the school had done with Bean's sixteen years earlier. "Cases have become longer over the years," explained Harvard marketing professor Walter J. Salmon, "mainly because the business world is more complex."⁵ As a service to businesses, Harvard Business School Case Services would then sell these reports, each averaging about twenty pages and costing $10,000 to produce, for five or ten cents a page.

Once he'd signed a release card allowing the school to use the case in its curriculum, Leon Gorman was invited to attend a class in which the case was being taught. Noting that the students were quite insightful, an obviously impressed Gorman said the discussion gave him a new perspective. Still, in the late eighties the *Maine Times* would report that, despite Gorman's involvement, "after the study in 1981, the year that L.L. Bean, Inc.'s, growth exploded, Bean shut the door on Harvard."⁶ (The Freeport firm would fling the door wide open again beginning in 1992, with Bean and Harvard teaming up on four more case studies between then and 2004. In 2006, Leon Gorman would collaborate with the school on *L.L. Bean: The Making of an American Icon*, a memoir about his time with the company.)

With all of L.L. Bean's recent success, it was becoming increasingly difficult for even the reticent Gorman to stay out of the limelight. In March, the *Maine Times* newspaper had named Leon

Gorman one of "The Ten Most Influential People in Maine," and on July 17, 1981, after Harvard had come calling, he was fêted at a Free Enterprise lunch in Brunswick that was put on by the Newcomen Society of North America. As guest of honor and speaker that day, Leon Gorman delivered a speech entitled "L.L. Bean, Inc.: Outdoor Specialties by Mail from Maine," which would later be published as a 23-page book. (If the title of Gorman's speech sounds familiar, it's because it's very similar to that of the chapter about the company, "L.L. Bean, Inc.: Sporting Goods by Mail from Maine," in Tom Mahoney's *The Great Merchants*.)

One of the newspapers covering the event was the *Maine Paper*, the conservative, Hallowell-based publication of Leon's cousin, Linda Jones. Though the paper would survive for less than three years, it would set the stage for Jones, the daughter of Warren Bean and granddaughter of L. L., to make unsuccessful Republican runs for Maine's 1st Congressional District in 1988 and 1992.

L.L. Bean's continuing success forced the company to keep expanding. In October, Gorman announced plans for a $2 million two-story addition that would add 40,000 square feet to the company's existing 60,000-square-foot office building on Casco Street. Bean's also purchased the Fogg House, a gray-and-white Cape out on Desert Road, which the company planned to use for meetings and seminars and for its fly-fishing school. The year before, Bean's had purchased the Davis Warehouse on West Street, which it had been renting for about a decade.

Also the previous year, two of the town's dentists had purchased the William Gore House situated on the corner of Main Street and Mallett Drive. The pair, who'd converted the building into dental offices and apartments, received kudos from *Down East* magazine for "preserving the outward appearance of the Greek Revival-Italianate house . . ." at least until a couple of years later, when rumors began to circulate that a fast-food restaurant was coming to that location. Along with Bean's fantastic growth, the town had been undergoing a gradual transformation, one that was already happening too quickly to please many people in town.

Soon things would change even faster. September 23, 1981, is a date that will live in infamy—at least in Freeport, Maine. At first the apartment building fire seemed like no big deal; probably the only reason it merited even a brief mention in the next day's edition of the *Boston Globe* was because it had occurred across the street from L. L. Bean's famous retail store. The entire article, under the headline "L.L. Bean aids at Maine apartment fire," consisted of just ninety-four words:

> A fire at the Midtown Apartments in Freeport, Maine, left 32 families homeless yesterday and forced L.L. Bean, Inc. to turn customers away for the first time since its founder, Leon Leonwood Bean, died 14 years ago. The firm, specializing in outdoor gear, is noted for being open 24 hours a day, 365 days a year. The store kept its restroom facilities open to firefighters and gave away chamois shirts to firemen and driven-out apartment tenants. Fire Chief Dwight Libby said there were apparently no serious injuries.

News of the store's closure, which had lasted about six hours because fire equipment in the street had blocked access to the parking lot, caused concern among many of the company's loyal customers. Three weeks later, L.L. Bean, Inc., was still receiving calls and letters from people wondering about the fate of the company. "Ever since that fire in September," said Bean spokesperson Kilton Andrew, "we've gotten calls and letters from people concerned that we've been burned out. We are assuring people that business is on as usual." The main reason for the confusion, he explained, was a picture that had appeared in several newspapers with the caption "'Fire Closes Bean's,' which was true," said Andrew, "but it's being misinterpreted."[7] The store had reopened the day after the fire even though Main Street remained blocked off for about three weeks.

The real story of the blaze is that it had been set downstairs from the apartments by a local man who was trying to cover up traces of his burglary of Edgar Leighton's five-and-dime (formerly

Shettleworth's) in the old Clark's Hotel building on the corner of Main and Bow Streets. The building is the very same one that had been gutted by fire in 1946, and was the location at which the 1909 fire, which had burned almost everything on that side of Main Street, had started. Three days after the fire, police would arrest twenty-seven-year-old Severn P. Denyer, Jr., of Freeport and charge him with arson, burglary, and theft. "I recall that he pled guilty, and was sent to [the Maine State Prison in] Thomaston," said Freeport Police Chief Gerald Schofield in a telephone interview nearly thirty years later.

While L.L. Bean had been able to manage the situation relatively quickly, the immense impact the fire would have on the quaint town of 5,800 wouldn't be felt for a couple of years. Before long, a Boston developer would buy the building, rebuild the burned-out shell, and raise the rent.

THE SAME MONTH AS THE FIRE, Bill Riviere (1917–2005) (along with the staff of L.L. Bean and Bruce Willard, an assistant product manager for apparel, who acted as a liaison between the company, the publisher, and the author) published *The L. L. Bean Guide to the Outdoors* (Random House, $15.50, illustrated by J. Nicoletti). The result of ten years of work by Riviere, a writer and retired Maine Guide living in North Berwick, the 299-page book, including appendices and index, was the company's first real attempt to update L. L.'s venerable 1942 work, *Hunting, Fishing, and Camping*. Riviere had actually completed a rough draft of the book's fifteen chapters in fall 1978, but the incorporation of comments and suggestions by Gorman, Bill End, and director of product management Charlie Kessler, among others, would add another three years to the time required to complete the text. *The L. L. Bean Guide to the Outdoors* would end up having eleven chapters and five appendices.

With L. L. gone and the technology of camping and related equipment continuing to evolve, Riviere had first approached Bean president Leon Gorman in 1971 with the idea of updating L. L.'s classic 1942 woodcraft guide, *Hunting, Fishing and Camping*. Nothing came of the writer's proposal until "a couple of years later" when publishing giant Random House approached Gorman with a similar idea. Once Riviere got down to work on the project, he realized just how long a process it would become.

Since his book was to focus on outdoors equipment, Riviere would have to consult with dozens of experts both from outside the company and within. Because of the need to get everything just right, finishing *The L. L. Bean Guide to the Outdoors* would take the writer another seven years. The decade-long delay between the book's inception and publication would give it a lag time exactly twice as long as that of L. L.'s 1960 autobiography, *My Story*.

Reviews of Riviere's ninth book were generally good (the *Globe* headline proclaimed, "Bean outdoor guide right on the button"), and tended to describe the book's content, which, in turn, described all sorts of the latest outdoors equipment. But not everyone was so kind to the efforts of Riviere, et al., notably Bob Cummings, the *Maine Sunday Telegram*'s environmental reporter. He really liked Riviere's first chapter about weather forecasting in the field—which happened to be an expanded chapter from one of his earlier books, *Pole, Paddle, and Portage*—but not too much else:

> But it isn't really a guide to the outdoors. It's a guide to outdoor equipment—some outdoor equipment. It talks about clothing, boots, sleeping bags, tents, backpacks, skis, snowshoes, canoes, compasses, and pots, pans, and stoves.
>
> These are things everyone needs to know about. The outdoors, however, is more than backpacks, tents, and other equipment.
>
> It's also about hunting and fishing, mountains, glaciers, hiking, rock climbing, bird watching—yes, even all-terrain vehicles and snowmobiles. And these activities—and the specialized equipment they require—are largely ignored.
>
> A better title might be, "A guide to outdoor equipment sold by Bean's."
>
> But even this wouldn't wholly solve the dilemma. Bean sells fishing poles, lures, reels, and other essentials, none of which are included in this book.[8]

Despite his criticisms, Cummings eventually conceded that "the Bean book isn't just a promotion for the things Bean sells. . . . It really is an impartial guide to outdoor equipment," even acknowledging that "the information can be extremely valuable if you have to purchase something new and are faced with hundreds of possible choices." Even if not everyone liked it, any well-turned-out project with the L.L. Bean name on it was bound to generate interest far and wide, and the book got a big boost when *Today Show* personality Willard Scott stopped by to interview Riviere in Bean's book department. By the end of October, the book would already be in its second printing, with a total of 150,000 copies.

Leon Gorman explained that the new book focused on equipment because "there has never been a greater assortment of high-performance and reliable equipment. At the same time, there has never been a greater assortment of poorly designed and generally inappropriate products."9 Gorman also said he thought Riviere's work was the most authoritative book on outdoors gear "since Horace Kephart's *Camping and Woodcraft* in 1917."

But only about 20 percent of Kephart's classic book deals with outdoors gear. As good an outdoorsman as he surely was, William A. Riviere would have to go some to rival the information accumulated by Horace S. Kephart (1862–1931), the "Dean of American Campers," who'd lived a Thoreau-like existence for the last twenty-five years of his life in western North Carolina's Great Smoky Mountains. Volume I of his manual, *Camping*, covers 394 pages in 23 chapters, while *Woodcraft*, the book's second volume, contains 469 pages in another 23 chapters.

Though the book's copyright date is 1917, at least thirty-six editions of Kephart's masterwork would see print, beginning with 1906's *Book of Camping and Woodcraft: A Guidebook for Those Who Travel in the Wilderness* and concluding with *Camping and Woodcraft* in 1974. In 1921 his efforts were first combined into the two-volume classic whose later version would be reproduced in 1988 and include a lengthy introduction by Kephart biographer Jim Casada. Testifying to the enduring popularity of *Camping and Woodcraft* original editions, Casada noted that

. . . it is today quite difficult to locate a copy in good condition. Almost invariably when one encounters a survivor it is dog-eared, with well-thumbed pages, turned-down corners and an unmistakable aura of having been well and truly "used." . . . Far from being relegated to comfortable obscurity in some gentleman's library, as a handsomely-bound prisoner in a glass-fronted cage, it was instead a book to which one could return time and again. If one classified it according to Francis Bacon's inimitable description—"Some books are to be tasted, others to be swallowed, and some few to be chewed and digested"— *Camping and Woodcraft* certainly would have fallen into the latter category.[10]

Because of the company's popularity and spiking profits, the value of Bean's stock soared. Under normal circumstances, this would have led to a rush to buy Bean. But just like the company, there was nothing normal about its stock either, and, as Harold Boyle explained in the *Portland Press Herald* in November of 1981, anyone who went to his broker trying to purchase some shares of L.L. Bean stock went away disappointed:

Thousands of Maine people heard one of their old-line companies cited on the popular "Wall Street Week" Channel 10 [Maine Public Broadcasting] show a week ago.

"What was one of the best mail-order stocks to own?" a viewer asked the guest financial expert on retail merchandising stocks.

Without any hesitancy, he said, "L.L. Bean."

But he was quick to add that the stock in the nationally known Freeport concern is not available to the public. It is owned 100 percent by the Bean family, and is known as a "closed corporation," which is unlike stock in Sears, Roebuck, J. C. Penney and other mail-order companies whose shares are traded on the New York Stock Exchange.

Every so often, rumors spread in Wall Street that "L.L. Bean is going public," which means that the Bean family has decided to sell some of its stock to the public.

First reaction to that rumor is, "Who was the lucky buyer and how did he do it?"

Best opinion is that buyers would line up overnight like rock fans to try to buy a few shares of this Maine concern in any public offering.

Gorman continued to perpetuate the L.L. Bean mystique throughout the 1980s, and his plan worked well—especially in terms of the free publicity it generated. Stories about the company appeared in *Reader's Digest*, the *Boston Globe*, the *New York Times*, *U.S. News & World Report*, *Sports Illustrated*, *Forbes*, *People*, and *Time*. One story, "It's Not Just Folksiness at L.L. Bean, Inc." by William Cockerman, appeared in the October 11, 1981, edition of the *Hartford Courant* and was reproduced in twenty-two other newspapers over the next six weeks.

One of the *Globe* articles was probably the one that ran in the December 27, 1981, *Boston Globe Magazine* entitled "The Marketing Magic of L.L. Bean" by M. R. Montgomery, who would reveal Bean's "magic" to be nothing more than good, sound marketing research which saw the company carefully tracking the success of its various ad buys. By doing this, Bean's management discovered something they never would have expected—the *New Yorker* and the *New York Review of Books* turned out to be better sources of new customers than, say, *Field & Stream* or *Sports Afield*. The management of Bean's wasn't doing anything different than L. L. had done when he'd put phony addresses in the magazine ads he'd placed during the 1920s to see which ones generated the most responses from all the "sports" out there. Now, wrote Montgomery, they were just doing more of it, and doing it better than L. L. ever could have hoped to.

"So how did Bean's run past every competitor?" he asked. "The answer is deceptively simple: It mailed more catalogs." Montgomery's 5,600-word article would become the basis for his 1984 book, *In Search of L. L. Bean*, a work of which the company was never particularly fond, especially at first. (Interestingly, four months later, on April 25, 1982, the *Maine Sunday Telegram* would run an article about L.L. Bean by Bill Caldwell called "The Midas Touch," which shares many striking similarities with Montgomery's piece.)

By reminding us that "A sport is the parent of a Preppy," Montgomery was able to explain almost instantly any increase in Bean's sales that hadn't been attributable to Lisa Birnbach's best-selling little guidebook. "At L.L. Bean," he noted, "the core product is L. L.'s Maine Hunting Shoe, that leather-topped, rubber-bottomed contraption you see both in Maine, on real hunters in pursuit of authentic deer, and in Harvard Square, on Preppies of both sexes."

The key words here are "both sexes." Long after L. L. had okayed a ladies' department in the fifties, sufficient numbers of women had discovered the merchant's outdoorsy fashions to make that part of the business a very successful one. In 1981, the women's clothing area of L.L. Bean's Freeport store was pulling in $1,500 per square foot compared to $250 for an average urban department store. Accounting for more than $22 million during fiscal year 1981, the sales of women's clothing at L.L. Bean was right up there with the income generated by the company's famous boot, prompting Leon Gorman to remark, "We have seen the emergence of women to their proper role in society." (Even Bean's "'worst' department, fishing and hunting gear," noted Montgomery, "generates $400 worth of business per square foot annually.")

He emphasized that the growth of Bean's retail store exactly paralleled its catalog sales, which, ironically, were about to reap the benefits of some good old Maine thriftiness. Leon A. Gorman knew the value of a dollar, a trait no doubt inherited from his grandfather, who, you'll recall, had reportedly paid his help the minimum wage plus a nickel. While wages and benefits at Bean's had improved considerably since L. L.'s time, Gorman still saw to it that he got his money's worth from every one of his company's dimes. It was this trait, claims the Boston writer, that led directly to even more growth when, one day, Bean's president found himself sitting on a few extra catalogs. One and a half million to be exact.

In an effort to keep the company's growth at a manageable rate,

Gorman had the printer, R. R. Donnelley, mail out 7.5 million Christmas catalogs instead of the originally planned 9 million. Instead of letting $420,000 worth of catalogs expire in a warehouse somewhere, wrote Montgomery, "they went out to a list of Bean's 'worst' customers. People who hadn't ordered for a few years, people who didn't order very much when they did order; essentially marginal customers were given a chance to reacquaint themselves with Bean's, in hopes that they would buy just a little bit, and hopefully after Christmas."

The experiment was an unmitigated failure, only adding to the "avalanche" of orders Bean received during the holiday season. In his later book, Montgomery says that the company should have expected such a spike in sales since Bill End had achieved the same result when he'd sent catalogs to a similar "rejuvenated" segment five years earlier. While he conceded that the mailing could have been a "genuine mistake," Montgomery also theorized that it could have been "an in-house ploy" to increase sales without letting operations or customer service executives know what was coming.

L.L. Bean's Christmas 1981 sales figures looked like this: On a single day in December, Bean's retail store did 5,542 transactions, operators in the phone room took 14,241 orders, and the Distribution Center shipped 43,221 packages by either Priority Mail or UPS Blue Label service. In one week before Christmas, L.L. Bean shipped 225,000 packages, issued 12,740 gift certificates, and answered 99,447 telephone calls. And the retail store topped $1 million in sales. For the entire year, a quarter of the company's catalog orders had been phoned in, and credit card purchases accounted for 50 percent of Bean's sales volume. (And the stitchers of L.L. Bean, Inc., produced nearly 250,000 pairs of Maine Hunting Shoes.)

In 1982 Bean's retail store in downtown Freeport would be visited by 2.5 million people, with about 40 percent of them making a purchase. The 30,000-square-foot store would generate nearly $30 million in sales, or roughly $1,000 per square foot, five times that of a regular department store. The company estimated that during the spring about 80 percent of its expansive flagship store's shoppers were Maine residents, while the summertime crowd, in turn, consisted of about 80 percent out-of-staters, with the mix about 50-50 during the Christmas season. Among that many patrons, there are bound to be a few bad apples, and every year L.L. Bean was losing hundreds of thousands of dollars worth of camping gear, shoes, and clothing to shoplifters, especially during tourist season and the Christmas rush.

In February the company's security staff sought ways of making its job easier when Bean's security supervisor, Russell Dyer, a retired colonel in the Maine Warden Service, traveled to the state capitol in Augusta to testify in favor of a change to Maine's seven-year-old shoplifting law, hoping to convince lawmakers to allow store security personnel to detain suspected shoplifters. Previously, only the owner, manager, or a supervisor could detain a suspect, but only with probable cause and then for just half an hour.

L.L. Bean's policy at the time called for one of its seven plain-clothes security staff to apprehend suspects outside while still on store property. "Our concern is with the customers," said Dyer, "so we want to do it outside. We don't want to use uniformed people, either. The only obvious security person," he said, "is the customer service person at the front door, who checks for untagged merchandise."

The merchandise for which Bean's did receive payment during 1982 would total $224.3 million, meaning that its sales had nearly doubled over the past two years. While the growth itself was welcomed, it revealed a number of problems within the company and prompted Bean's president to deliver "A Message From Leon," an L. L.-like address about the company's issues in the February *Bean Scene*. On the one hand, according to a recent "formal attitude survey," things were going pretty well, said Gorman, but there was still a lot of room for improvement:

> It was very gratifying to learn our morale is quite superior to most companies and our job satisfaction is generally high. Most of us enjoy working at L.L. Bean and share a great deal of pride in the company. We identify with our products and our customers. We have a high commitment to quality. By and large,

we like our jobs, our compensation, and our working relationships. We are optimistic about the future.

On the other hand, there are some very definite things that we are not so happy about. We've got some problems with our Job Evaluation System and our pay structure. Advancement opportunities aren't what they should be. Some of our management practices aren't sufficiently sensitive to our human needs. We've got some dull and boring jobs. Upward communications need improvement. A lot of us don't know what those people over there are doing and they don't seem to care.

"Our next step in the process," said Gorman, "will be a series of small group meetings. . . . This is where we can all give our input as to the causes behind the problems. We can further give our specific ideas to help correct them."[11]

One of the ideas that arose as a result of these meetings was the "Bean's Best" strategy, meaning that the company wanted to be able to verify that it was the best resource to its customers among its competitive group. To that end, Bean's management developed monitoring systems to ensure that it excelled in the areas of product, service, and communication. This strategy would serve the company well until the end of the decade when, despite strong growth, productivity would be on the decline.

As L.L. Bean's meteoric growth continued unabated, the company's renewed success allowed Leon Gorman to make donations to worthwhile causes other than the environmental groups to which the firm usually contributed. The previous fall, Gorman had been approached by Bowdoin College for donations to fund a chair in environmental sciences, and by Colby College, which was looking for contributions to its $25 million capital campaign. In early April Bean's gave both colleges, as well as Bates College in Lewiston, $250,000 each.

According to the *Maine Times*, "All three schools termed the contributions 'very substantial' for a private company, especially since the only condition set by the company is that the money be used for scholarship aid to Maine students." Interestingly, the donations to Colby and Bowdoin Colleges were the company's first gifts to the schools, even though Leon Gorman had graduated *cum laude* from Bowdoin in 1956, and with Bill End, had presented a case study of the company at the Colby College Institute for Management in 1980. In 1981 Bates had received a small donation from the Freeport company to help fund its new athletic facility.

In April 1982, L.L. Bean hired its first catalog copywriter, Toby Lee Soule, who was offered the position after recently completing an oral history of the Freeport company. A talented writer and artist who'd painted decoys made by her father, George V. Soule, Toby would retire from L.L. Bean in 1996 and die in Portland in 2001. Until Ms. Soule came on board, most of the catalog writing had been handled by Leon, who'd even rewritten some of his grandfather's copy in order to give the catalog "a more consistent and straightforward voice." By looking at his catalog from the point of view of a customer, and coming up with copy that fell somewhere in between his own "long copy" and his grandfather's short, get-to-the-point style of catalog writing, Leon had tried to keep the myth of L. L. alive without copying his voice.

Coincidentally, one of those Toby Soule had interviewed for her oral history project was Freeport native Mahlon "Babe" Walsh, the man who'd cut L. L.'s hair from 1926 until just before the merchant left for Florida for the last time in 1966. In his interview, Walsh clearly recalled the target range that L. L. and his brother Guy had set up below their clothing store before L. L. came up with his boot. "Guy Bean run the store, I guess with L. L. when they first started, and they had this shooting gallery downstairs. . . . Well I wasn't in on it, I was too young, but Carl, L. L.'s son, and I used to go down there and I think once in a while they let us shoot. There was somebody down there most of the time practicing, like Levi [Patterson], or I can remember Marion Chase's father was there, had a gun, a twenty-two. They made quite a lot of it." Babe Walsh died in 1982 at the age of eighty-one.

In addition to being the subject of everything from Harvard case studies to oral histories to books on popular culture, another outside indication of L.L. Bean's success came when an increasing number of business authors began using the company as examples in their books. The first of these citations was a brief paragraph about the steadfastness of L.L. Bean president Leon Gorman in Terrence E. Deal and Allan A. Kennedy's 1982 book, *Corporate Cultures: The Rites and Rituals of Corporate Life*:

> L. L. Bean's Maine Hunting Shoe spawned a multimillion-dollar mail-order business, which now has a real hero to protect it. L. L. Bean's grandson, Leon Gorman, refused to remove a Maine Warden Jacket from the Bean catalog even though none had been sold for many years. Why? Gorman understands that, in the face of a throwaway culture, long-lasting, even permanent, products have built the corporate reputation. And so he is reluctant to drop old items or add new ones. Unlike his unfortunate competitor, Abercrombie & Fitch, Gorman never moves far from the Maine Hunting Shoe, or the Warden Jacket. Employees and customers can depend on the culture of L.L. Bean.

While many stories about the company see fit to include the above quote from *Corporate Cultures*, few bother to put it in its proper context. It comes from the book's third chapter, "Heroes: The Right Corporate Stuff," which says that there are two types of corporate heroes: "Born Heroes" and "Heroes Who Are Made." Born heroes, explain the authors, are people like Henry Ford, John D. Rockefeller, and William Kellogg, who built huge empires from scratch. (L. L. Bean himself probably would have been included in this category if he'd only been as focused on growing his business as his grandson would become.) The chapter then goes on to point out that there are two types of made heroes, the first being the "situational hero," who arises from a particular situation within the business. The second type is the "compass-hero," who, like Gorman, takes charge of a company "in a situation where things have to change and there are no role models for the change." He then sends the message that "in the future, business will be done either more aggressively or more courteously" Or, in the case of L.L. Bean, Inc., both.

Abercrombie & Fitch, soon to be reborn as a trendy young people's clothing store, had gone bankrupt about five years earlier and was eventually acquired by The Limited, which owned the Victoria's Secret and Express chains. According to writer M. R. Montgomery, the original incarnation of A&F had failed because, during the Preppy phase, it had gone heavily into women's clothing and lost its core customers: fishermen. In other words, exactly what *Corporate Cultures* would have predicted. Leon Gorman said he was sorry to see them go.

As for the drab green, multi-pocketed Maine Warden Jacket mentioned above, its eventual removal from Bean's catalog would garner mixed reactions from the higher-ups at the Freeport company. "Leon wanted to keep the Warden Jacket," said Charlie Kessler, vice-president in charge of products. "It took me three years to get it out of the catalog. The customer was telling us he wasn't interested."[12]

But the jacket had been an L.L. Bean staple for years. It had given millions of customers pause to stop and daydream every time they stumbled upon it while thumbing through the latest edition of Bean's circular. "As a longtime customer who never ordered a Maine Warden Jacket," wrote Montgomery, "I also miss it. I didn't want one. I didn't need one. But I got used to seeing it and thinking, well, maybe someday I'll need a heavy wool jacket with lots of pockets. Midlife career change or something."[13]

"Never should have dropped it," said senior vice president Bill End. "I wish it was still in there. All it needed was some redesign. You can't knock things out just because they aren't paying their way. I just believe that we wouldn't sell the casual clothing if we didn't have duck decoys in the book. We are walking a very fine line."[14] Many people were still interested in the Maine Warden Jacket, and just because they never ordered one didn't prove otherwise. But soon enough, it would enjoy the last laugh—sort of.

"The easiest thing to do," End predicted with uncanny accuracy, "is get into women's clothing and make a zillion. But I think that would be a short-term profit bonanza at the expense of the company. If you want a guaranteed disaster, continue the shift towards women's apparel."[15] Look what it did to Abercrombie & Fitch—not to mention the situation in which L.L. Bean, Inc., would find itself with its ill-fated Freeport Studio line twenty years down the road, when most women couldn't or wouldn't believe that "fashion" could emanate from a company known for its hunting boots and down vests.

NOT ALL WRITE-UPS OF THE COMPANY were as welcomed by those at Bean as its recent mention in *Corporate Cultures*. According to the introduction of his 1984 book, it was around this time that M. R. Montgomery informed Leon Gorman that "the article they liked so much" the previous year "was about to become the size of Babe the Blue Ox." Gorman, said the *Maine Times*, "threatened to contact M. R. Montgomery's publisher to block the book, *In Search of L. L. Bean*. 'He wrote a rather stiff letter,' said Montgomery, but Gorman dropped the matter." Not only was Bean's itself involved in publishing a couple of books with Random House (*The L.L. Bean Guide to the Outdoors* and *The L.L. Bean Game and Fish Cookbook*) at the time, said Gorman, he also stressed that "our customers see the company as having a certain 'mystique' that will be difficult to maintain as more and more information about the company is reported to the public."

Montgomery rebutted Gorman's "mystique" argument with: "Anybody who puts 28 million catalogs in the public mail every year is open to public comment." And he wrote his book. Nevertheless, Montgomery said he "basically heeded [Bean's] request not to 'come up sneaking around Freeport.'"[16] (Interestingly, just a year later, Leon Gorman would be telling a reporter that "most people are surprised at how big we are," and that Bean's policy was "to be as open as we possibly can about this business. And that has given us a flood of favorable coverage.")[17]

According to Gorman, the Freeport merchant's current self-perception is much different than the image it told Montgomery it was trying to convey. When the company built its giant Distribution Center, for example, Leon Gorman worried that Bean's customers might begin to see the company as just another big retailer. (Remember that Bean's had delayed introducing stock numbers into its catalogs for exactly the same reason.) But before long, Leon Gorman realized that "what we stood for didn't depend on having or not having a big warehouse or a big computer."[18]

By the 1990s, Leon Gorman would be forced to admit that the company's ability to change while continuing to convey its traditional Maine values had begun to work against it. People expected the latest L.L. Bean catalog to contain the same old active wear it always had, and didn't even bother to open it. Gorman would later comment that L.L. Bean changed so subtly it appeared to stay the same.

Some twenty years on, L.L. Bean, Inc., had sort of come to terms with Montgomery's unauthorized story of Mr. Bean and his business, even going so far as to include it in the second edition of its company-issued scrapbook: "[L. L.'s] story . . . was picked up by the local press and eventually the national media. Continuing interest in the man and his company led to an unauthorized biography by M. R. Montgomery (1984), as well as the inclusion of L. L. in *The Dictionary of American Biography* (1988) and the *American National Biography* (1999)." Montgomery's *Globe* article and subsequent book are also two of only eight works cited in the bibliography of Leon Gorman's 2006 book about his days at the company.

As for the aforementioned cookbook, it was released in late 1985 and received this write-up in the (Lewiston, Maine) *Sun*:

> The legendary L. L. Bean may have known how to wield a fly rod or hunting rifle, but even his closest companions acknowledge that his skills as a camp cook left much to be desired. So there's probably no doubt that the late founder of the world-famous outdoors outfitter in Freeport would have benefited from the cooking tips contained in a new book that bears his name. With nearly 500 recipes ranging from moose bourguignon to mallard Millinocket, *The L.L. Bean Game and Fish Cookbook* is a comprehensive guide on how to convert the

bounty of the field and stream into a culinary masterpiece.

Just before Labor Day 1982, Dansk Kitchenwares opened its newest outlet store in the former Clark's Hotel building directly across from L.L. Bean. But it wasn't the first new store to settle on Main Street recently. Even before the September 1981 fire, the owners of upscale shops and family-oriented restaurants had already figured out that Bean's great big store located smack-dab in the middle of downtown Freeport was the perfect "anchor store" for what would eventually turn out to be Maine's largest outdoor shopping mall. In July 1981 Deering Ice Cream had opened on Main Street just after Praxis established its crafters' co-op, and Steve and Judy Brown opened their goldsmith shop down on Mechanic Street, but still before the fire. After Leighton's burned, other companies were quick to jump on the bandwagon. Edgar Leighton would later reopen the business he'd run since World War II, on a side street, a block back from Main Street.

But not just any store would qualify for occupancy in Freeport. Bean's attracted a certain type of clientele and so too would the new businesses—referred to as "Bean sprouts"—that would soon spring up around the retail giant. Bean maintenance supervisor and Freeport planning board chairman David Thompson and others said they didn't want a bunch of cheap discount stores that would give the place a "tourist trap" reputation. This attitude was more than just snobbish elitism on the part of the new outlets; it actually reflected economic reality: with rents so high there, only shops charging higher prices for their goods would be able to make a go of it in what was becoming Freeport's increasingly trendy downtown shopping district.

The cheap discount stores would be priced out of the area, but then so would most of the stores from which the town's residents had purchased their necessities for years and years. "If you want a hundred-dollar pair of shoes, it's okay" said Dick Wagner, the fourth generation of his family to operate Derosier's Variety Store on Main Street, "but if you want groceries or clothes for the kids, you won't find them here anymore."[19]

Even L.L. Bean was paying a price for its success. When the firm wanted to get underway with its latest retail store expansion, it found its neighbors willing to sell only if the price was right. Recently the company's executive vice president, Bill End, had confirmed to the *Wall Street Journal* that the estimated $260,000 Bean's had paid for a small house nearby "was in the ballpark. . . . We typically have to pay two times what the property is worth,"[20] he conceded. The cataloger must have considered it money well spent though; sales at the retail store had grown 20 percent per year over the past decade. By 1982 it was generating $30 million a year, or $5,000 for every man, woman, and child living in Freeport. (Soon the owners of homes worth $50,000 a few years earlier would be asking $200,000, and in 1990, writer John Gould would report that "a man just sold his house for a million dollars and saw it torn down to make a parking lot.")[21]

Just before Memorial Day 1982, the Jameson Tavern opened for business next to L.L. Bean in a 200-year-old building that had served as a law office, a private residence, and a gymnasium. It's also a widely held belief that the papers giving Maine its independence from Massachusetts had been signed there in 1820, although some historians dispute the accuracy of that claim. Regardless of just how historic the building actually is, one thing's certain: it's in an excellent location for a restaurant. Soon after opening, co-owner John Rasmussen would be serving 2,000 meals a week to many of Bean's 48,000 weekly visitors. The average price of a meal in the new eatery was about $15. "It's like having the hot dog franchise at Fenway Park," Rasmussen told the *Wall Street Journal*.

Nearby, George Denny opened his Cole-Haan shoe store in the beautifully remodeled Knights of Phythias hall, which, until recently, had been home to the town's Western Auto store. Denny had purchased the two-story wood-frame building for $150,000 and poured another $150,000 into upscale renovations. "Upscale," in this case, meant that shoes in the main showroom started at $130 for women's styles and $165 for men's, but some women's boots went for as much as $350—and then there was the occasional $600 "specialty item." Discontinued shoes and discounted seconds starting at $40 for women's and $60 for men's were—and still are—located in the basement.

"When I saw the Mercedes Benzes and BMWs parking at Bean's lot," Denny recalled later, "I said, 'Those are Cole-Haan customers.'"[22] He would soon complete the remodeling of two neighboring buildings into four more stores for other outletters who felt the same way he did: his tenants included a sheepskin shop, a ladies' clothing store, and two gift shops. "Any building in the shadow of L.L. Bean does a lot of business," he observed. "Freeport wouldn't be Freeport without Bean, and those stores wouldn't be there without Bean." Other outlets in that area include Nine West shoes and Polo-Ralph Lauren. It looks like Dick Wagner knew what he was talking about.

In July 1982 Hathaway Shirts opened in what had been, until very recently, Roger Downs's grocery store, the last one in town. (It would be nearly twenty-five years before Shaw's would open a supermarket in a shopping center just south of town on Route 1.) Located on Water Street in Waterville, Maine, the C. F. Hathaway Co. was the nation's oldest shirt factory. Regrettably, the 165-year-old factory would close its doors in October 2002 due to offshore competition and the loss of a big contract with the U.S. Air Force.

Even though Cole-Haan and Hathaway had opened their Main Street outlets a couple of months before Dansk, it's usually the Danish kitchenwares store that's singled out as having started the "malling" of Freeport, probably because it was the first of the big national chains to establish itself in town (Cole-Haan was from nearby Yarmouth and Hathaway from Waterville), or maybe because its origin could be traced to a single catastrophic event—the recent fire. But back in early June, three full months before Dansk opened its doors, the headline on the front page of the *Maine Times* was already asking, "Why is Freeport becoming a boomtown for classy discount stores?"

Since each and every one of these small newcomers would owe whatever success they achieved entirely to the fact that they were riding on L.L. Bean's very long coattails, it behooved them to seek the blessing of the town's retail patriarch. Hathaway would have "never gone in without [Bean's] blessing," said Robert Joly, one of the shirtmaker's VPs. Even Dansk sought and was granted an audience with the town's premier retailer, and was told by Bill End that the catalog giant would be happy to help with the revitalization of downtown Freeport as long as the town's planning board could keep the growth in check. It was (and still is) a good idea to stay friendly with L.L. Bean, especially if you wanted to do business in the community where that one company paid 14 percent of the town's property taxes—$265,000 at the time.

Since all the outlet stores wanted to come to Freeport because of Bean's success, and Bean's current hot streak could be largely attributed to *The Official Preppy Handbook*, could the whole outlet thing be put on the shoulders of its editor, Lisa Birnbach?

Once the outlet ball started rolling, it didn't take long for it to gather a full head of steam. According to local businesswoman Karen Haskell, everyone quickly realized what had been obvious all along. "Here L.L. Bean was," she said, "sitting in the middle of nothing in southern Maine, drawing 2 million people. They said, 'Gee, maybe I can cash in on some of this traffic.'"[23] Executives at Dansk emphasized that they'd been interested in the Leighton's location even before the fire, after having read the recent Harvard case study of L.L. Bean. "We feel that it is a terrific location for us," said Dansk's vice president at the store's opening. "We hope to capitalize on the flow of traffic into L.L. Bean's."[24] The location would work out as well as they had hoped; according to store manager Elaine Lospennato, just five weeks after opening, the Dansk cash registers would be ringing up 200 sales a day. (But, in the land of outlet stores, nothing lasts forever and even trailblazers eventually move on. Just before Memorial Day 2006, Dansk would be holding a clearance sale to make way for a new tenant, Lenox China. Lenox would close its doors in late 2007, only to be replaced by a Tommy Hilfiger outlet, which still occupied the space in 2011.)

In order to accommodate the anticipated influx of shoppers, Freeport's planning board seriously considered rerouting traffic, according to its chairman, David Thompson. The most viable option, he said, would be to change the traffic flow of the short section of U.S. Route 1 that runs through town into one-way. Not only would this alleviate the town's anticipated traffic woes, noted *Maine Times* reporter Phyllis Austin, "it would also create more prime business sites." (Nearly three decades later, a few more stoplights will have been installed, but all the summertime traffic on Route 1 still flows both ways, in fits and starts, right through the middle of downtown Freeport.

DOWN EAST MAGAZINE SAID it "looked deceptively like the outdoor catalog mailed out by a certain Maine outfitter." *Newsweek* simply called it "the paperback decoy." "It" was *Items from Our Catalog* (Avon Books, $4.95), a cleverly conceived spoof of the venerable L.L. Bean catalog—thought up by Manhattan writer/actor Alfred Gingold, with photography by Dan Nelken. At first glance, Gingold's book looked just like the Freeport merchant's fall catalog, until the reader noticed that the dog on the cover (designed by Deborah Bracken and illustrated by Tom Beecham) was wearing a camouflage Pet's Camping Bra (36B-BOWWOW, $7.75 ppd.) and sitting next to a blind duck decoy (ALMS, $7.75 ppd.) Still, many people were fooled, and, convinced that it was a real catalog (of some sort), actually tried to place orders by calling the number for bulk book sales listed inside.

And just what, pray tell, were they attempting to order? Perhaps it was the sexier, sequined version of the Pet's Camping Bra (36C-VAVOOM, $11.25 ppd.) they fancied. Or how about Swiss Army Earrings (actual little knives, CUKU 4, $.03 ppd.) or a Solar Watch Cap (SOL, $65.75 ppd.)? Or maybe the Gum Shoe (three flavors: spearmint, cinnamon, and bubble, GTTNU $43.75 ppd.) or even a Real Rag Sweater—that was actually made of rags (One Pattern: Heather Garbage, SHMATA, $41.25 ppd. Food stamps accepted for this item).

And then there was the "YOHO Shoe Boat, $392.50 ppd." Shaped like Bean's Handsewn Moccasin (left foot), the Shoe Boat came complete with a flag on the bow and a tiny outboard motor astern. Dimensions for the imaginary size 9 boat were: "Length 9'2", Beam 4'8", Weight $91^1/_4$ lbs." The opulent from away could even purchase the entire State of Maine (about 32,562 square miles, LLBN, $76,000,000 plus $3.20 pstg.). With its December 1 release, *Items from Our Catalog* piggybacked on the popularity of Bean's 1982 Christmas catalog to become one of the hottest books of the season. By January, Gingold's effort had gone through seven printings (730,000 books) and displaced a Garfield cartoon book at the top of the trade paperback bestseller list.

Items had gotten its start when Gingold assembled the twenty or thirty items he'd written as gags to send to friends into a short article that he eventually sold to Avon. When asked why he was "attacking" L.L. Bean, he explained that he wasn't attacking anybody, he was spoofing catalogs in general; it's just that Bean's was the easiest one to parody. "It has good clean writing," he told the *Brunswick Times Record*, "and appears as though it was written by one person." Gingold stressed that he was "'an avid reader and purchaser' of the catalog for over eighteen years, and from his experience, he believes L.L. Bean carries quality clothing at a good price. 'They sell terrific stuff,' he said."

Capitalizing on the success of *Items from Our Catalog*, Gingold would follow it up with *More Items from Our Catalog* in October 1983. He especially liked the company's use of "pant" to describe a pair of trousers or slacks instead of "pants." (In 2007 Dear Abby would respond to a young reader's query as to why he had a pair of shoes, a pair of socks, and a pair of pants by explaining: "Technically, a 'pant' is the leg of a garment. Two pants (legs) make up a 'pair' of pants." In 2006 a Lewiston newspaper columnist would write about her day of shopping in Freeport, including a stop at the "L.L. Bean Outlet—Where comfort is queen. A pant sale offered various styles originally $89 and under for a mere $9.95.")

The folks at L.L. Bean had probably expected another skewering of their popular circular at some point—it had been nine years since *National Lampoon* had published its "Eddie Bean Down-Filled Camp and Trail Catalogue" parody—and took the ribbing in stride. "If you're something of a national institution," said Bean spokesperson Kilt Andrew, "it's inevitable that someone would do a parody." At the time, Andrew said, "It's freedom of the press, what the heck?"[25] but declined to comment on the quality of the 84-page send-up of his employer's catalog. In the rosy glow of retrospect, L.L. Bean would come to accept, if not appreciate, Gingold's effort, even including it in "Parodies Without and Within" in the company's scrapbook, saying that "[in 1982 Avon] Publishing released the now-classic *Items from Our Catalog*, complete with a cover that featured a Pointer in a camouflage bustier." The Freeport company said that *Items* "featured a host of clever pages, all making full use of Bean's traditional language and layout styles." The article even included a copy of *Items*' YOHO Shoe Boat ad.

BACK IN THE REAL WORLD of catalog sales, Bean's brain trust was doing its best to keep up with its latest growth spurt. Realizing that the best way to do that was to have employees who were both happy and healthy, Bean's concentrated on taking care of them. Programs like a one-third discount on purchases, tuition reimbursement, and an annual bonus that would average 22 percent for the decade of the eighties helped to take care of the "happy" part. The company also took a multifaceted approach to the "healthy" component of the equation by becoming one of the first companies in the country to offer its workers an on-site fitness room, where, at the time, health promotion specialist Helen Quigley worked with about ninety-five people a day. Earlier in the year, the firm had completed a mile-long jogging trail through the woods adjacent to its offices and distribution complex.

But what has to be Bean's most popular employee perk is located about 115 miles north of Freeport. In 1982 the company bought a sporting camp on the western end of Rangeley Lake, "a premier cold-water lake," said Gorman, "in an exceptionally pretty part of western Maine." Besides the quality of its trout and salmon fishing, the area is also famous for its many hiking, camping, and winter sports activities. The cabins at the sporting camp, which is two miles from Oquossoc, are named after popular fishing flies and range in size from the two-person Parmachene Belle, to the ten-person Royal Coachman. To provide more room, part of the camp's main lodge would later be divided into the Kennebago

Wulff and the Gray Ghost. Year-round demand among employees for spots at the sporting camp was so great that Bean's had to set up a companywide lottery to allocate usage, the first of which was held on May 14, 1982. In 1984, the former Westshore Camps would get a permanent caretaker in the person of Roger Verrill.

During the late nineteenth and early twentieth centuries, many city dwellers with the means spent much of the summer enjoying the tranquility of Maine's hundreds of sporting camps, traveling first by train and then by steamboat, wagon, or canoe to reach their destination—often bringing with them a considerable amount of their belongings. "A mystical Maine Guide," notes one sporting camp brochure, "was the central figure in the guest's activities and took the 'sports' to the secret spots for fishing, hunting or observing wildlife."[26]

The camps, which usually consist of a central lodge where guests dine and socialize and a dozen or more guest cabins, are generally situated on a remote pond or lake where an ample supply of versatile Rangeley boats waits at the dock. There are now about fifty sporting camps remaining in Maine (for a brochure, contact the Maine Sporting Camp Association at HC 76 Box 620, Greenville, ME 04441, or at www.mainesportingcamps.com or info@mainesportingcamps.com). Much more about the history of these rustic retreats can be found in Alice Arlen's books, *In the Maine Woods* (1998) and *Maine Sporting Camps: The Year-Round Guide to Vacations at Traditional Hunting and Fishing Lodges* (2003), both from Countryman Press.

Those interested in Rangeley's rich outdoor sporting history can visit the 3,500-square-foot Rangeley Outdoor Sporting Heritage Museum at the corner of Routes 4 and 17 in Oquossoc. The welcome center of the museum, which opened on August 14, 2010 following ten years of planning, fundraising, and hard work, has "an authentic 1890s log sporting camp interior."

BY 1983 THE NUMBER OF NEW restaurants and shops that had moved into downtown Freeport over the previous two years now totaled more than a dozen and included newcomers Canon Towels and Frye Boots. Barbizon Lingerie was located where Mel's Sporting Goods used to be. And that apparently was only the beginning; because of recent zoning changes, there was the real possibility of another two dozen or so new stores coming to town within a year. The recent influx of shops was enough to make Bean's Bill End wonder aloud if they could "make enough during the seasonal peak (July through December) to carry them for the whole year and whether Freeport can support 10 retailers or 15 retailers or 20 retailers remains to be seen. I think it's too early to tell."[27]

One longtime local businessman called the interlopers "jackals," while another worried that "if this becomes discount city, the good stores could suffer." Still, at this point, the majority of people seemed to favor the growth these new businesses were bringing to the downtown area. Until June, that is, when they got wind of something that would quickly galvanize the community in its opposition. What they smelled were hamburgers—McDonald's hamburgers.

"It's a given," End had told the *Wall Street Journal* late the previous year, "we'll have a McDonald's here before long." He was right. When word got out in June that McDonald's might be planning to raze the historic William Gore House (c. 1855) to build a restaurant, it was clear that that time was drawing near. Freeport sprang into action. Townspeople had already organized the Freeport Residents Association, headed by John and Barbara McGivaren, which had successfully blocked the construction of a heavy equipment dealer on nearby Route 136.

But this was different. What many Freeporters wanted was a concerted effort aimed squarely at McDonald's. Concerned townspeople quickly called a meeting at the high school where "The Freeport Mac Attack" was formed on the spot. The group had T-shirts made and circulated a petition that was signed by 1,200 residents. "We sent it to the president of McDonald's, registered mail, return receipt requested, along with a T-shirt and everything we could think of,"[28] said Gordon Hamlin, a Mac Attack leader.

The petition affirmed the group's "unyielding opposition to the McDonald's Corporation's locating at the corner of Main Street and Mallett Drive and its firm commitment to the preservation of architectural integrity of the North Main Street Village Zone." It wasn't that the group's members were opposed to McDonald's in principle; they were opposed to the idea of losing the Gore House, located next to what was then the town's only traffic signal.

Even town officials had hoped to convince Ronald McDonald and his crew to set up shop elsewhere in Freeport so the part of the large Gore property that was set back from Main Street would be available for a new supermarket. But there was little even the planning board could do to stop the Golden Arches from coming to the edge of downtown Freeport; as town manager Dale Olmstead pointed out, "We have a very strong zoning ordinance. Quite frankly, what has happened on Main Street is exactly what the town council and planning board wanted. The zoning ordinance was developed primarily to attract business to the village commercial area."[29] And, just a few months earlier, they had changed a zoning rule that would have kept fast-food franchises out of that area. When McDonald's finally did move into the Gore House, the townspeople had no one to blame but themselves.

On the bright side, the historic Gore House stayed where it was with McDonald's fitting its restaurant inside. Anyone who eats there might even find the seating area at the front of the house to be somewhat charming. Large framed photos of the town's past decorate the walls, and in its early days the restaurant's tables even had white linen tablecloths (protected under a piece of Plexiglass), though they've since been eliminated. Outside the building there are no giant plastic arches, and customers using the drive-through are greeted by a sign informing them, "We have no audio. We can hear you. Please speak into the monitor. Town ordinance."

But L.L. Bean, the company whose success had been primarily responsible for the town's sudden growth, would find itself falling on hard times in 1983. The Preppies stopped buying from Bean, and Leon Gorman's sunny 1980 prediction to the *New York Times* that he thought the company could "continue a 20 to 25 percent growth rate per year for the foreseeable future" was now nothing more than a fading memory. It's not that the company found itself on the ropes; at Bean's, "hard times" was a relative term. Think of it as more of a little slowdown.

Okay, a big slowdown. Gone were the unrealistic 40 percent and 30 percent sales increases of 1981 and 1982. (For the 1982 fiscal year, L.L. Bean had distributed $5.3 million in bonuses and profit sharing—or 19 percent of its earnings for more than 1,400 eligible employees.) For the fiscal year 1983, L.L. Bean's sales increase barely outstripped the rate of inflation, growing a meager 6 percent. It was the first time that the company's growth had stalled under Leon Gorman's tenure. It wasn't that the company had changed its products and values in order to become fashionable, it was just that for two heady years the paths of function and fashion had converged in Freeport (or, to paraphrase the old Abercrombie & Fitch motto, "the blazed trail had crossed Route 1"—if only for a while).

Leon Gorman was eventually forced to concede that much of Bean's recently skyrocketing sales had been attributable to the fickle fashion tastes of the college crowd and not the company's revamped catalog. He later summed up his company's current situation in an address at the University of Vermont:

We found in 1983, however, that our success was due to more than our own efforts. A phenomenon called "the Preppy boom" emerged in the late 1970s. It was best characterized in Lisa Birnbach's 1980 publication of *The Preppy Handbook* which prominently featured our company. Our functional value product line, oriented toward outdoors people, had become fashionable. L.L. Bean was perceived as "Preppy," and many people, while buying our products, were buying them for the wrong reasons.

Fashionability is neither consistent nor reliable. In 1983 the Preppy bubble burst and our sales increase fell to 5.9% [to $237.4 million]. In 1984 it more or less stabilized at 6.7% [$253.7 million]. I was frankly glad to see this happen. I had become increasingly concerned that we might be losing sight of the business we were in, that we were starting to chase fashion instead of function.[30]

The irony of the situation is that, by all accounts, it was the company's commitment to basic, rugged clothing that had led to its temporary belt tightening. Bean's just wasn't "hip" anymore. Even more ironic is the fact that the company's rededication to, and tweaking of, that same staid product line would eventually become its salvation. Bean's management team went back to the basics, starting with two very important policy decisions: the "concentration" decision and the "market standing" decision. These were then included in the firm's formal purpose statement along with the basic sentiment of L. L.'s original Golden Rule: "Sell good merchandise at a reasonable profit, treat your customers like human beings and they will always come back for more." All these policies and rules were then combined to form Bean's new purpose statement: "To market high quality recreational products of the best functional value directly to the outdoor-oriented American consumer with the kind of superior personal service we would like to receive."

It was this steadfast dedication to its basic product line, said the *Economist*, that enabled L.L. Bean to compete with other catalogers on the cost of its items to consumers. "Though it pays its 1,400 Freeport workers above par—partly to keep out the unions—it says it can compete with rivals on price because it does not have to worry about one of the most costly phenomena of the clothing business: obsolescence. It simply keeps producing the same practical stuff. That policy has allowed it to forge enduring bonds with loyal customers."

L.L. Bean, Inc., was changing, but gradually, its stable product lines lending themselves to continuous improvement with the deletion of unpopular products and the addition of new ones. Leon Gorman compared his company's gradual evolution to the Volkswagen Beetle of the day, saying that it was continually improving while managing to appear pretty much the same.

"Our decision to 'stick to the knitting,'" said Gorman, "was based on the belief that our fundamental positioning strengths were still valid. Our core product line continued to provide superior functional value with relevant and broad consumer appeal to outdoors-oriented American consumers."[31] (Despite the homey-sounding knitting metaphor, just as the *Washington Post* had noted a few years earlier, the *Economist* also pointed out that Bean's "management is far more sophisticated than its folksy catalogue and refusal to advertise on television suggest. In the past few years, Mr. Gorman has recruited a dozen executives with degrees from America's top business schools.")[32]

"No matter what we did then, we were right," recalled Gorman. "We thought we were real clever. It was a humbling experience for all of us when the day of reckoning came."[33] When the Preppy trend ran out of gas, Bean's growth lurched to a sudden stop.

Boston Globe writer M. R. Montgomery, writing at the time without the benefit of hindsight, reported that Leon Gorman had intentionally put the brakes on Bean's growth when he saw his company getting too big too quickly. "His decision to slow down in 1983–1984," wrote Montgomery, "was not explained to his staff, not talked out in meetings. 'Leon looked at all the numbers,' an insider remarked, 'but it wasn't the numbers. He makes intuitive decisions, and he decided he didn't like what he saw happening to the company.'"[34]

While Leon Gorman would no doubt agree with the "intuitive decisions" remark, he seemed to be addressing Montgomery's mysterious insider directly more than twenty years later when he firmly asserted that he'd had no control over the L.L. Bean's sudden slowdown. "Some people in the company said that I deliberately slowed sales. I was glad to see the slowdown in 1983, but we didn't pull sales back on purpose. The customers took care of that."[35] Maybe surprisingly, his company's recent slowdown didn't really bother Gorman; too many customers, he said, had been buying Bean's products because they were fashionable, not because they were functional.

Gorman's statement clearly shows his determination to keep

L.L. Bean's position as a source for those who actively enjoyed the outdoors, a tenet to which he would hold very firmly—but that in no way meant he wanted the whole thing to stop in its tracks. (In 2006, when asked by Forbes.com what the then-revived Preppy movement meant for his company, his answer revealed that his opinion of the fad hadn't changed a bit over the ensuing twenty-five years: "I personally don't like it. I didn't like it in the eighties. It happens to coincide with us by chance. It's part of the fashion cycle, but we don't aspire to it."[36]) The slowdown had happened all on its own and in spite the fact that the company was spending ten times as much on marketing ($33 million) as it had eight years earlier. Bean's management also expected that the number of its now 1,600 permanent workers would increase by 10 percent to 15 percent in each of the next three years.

While Bean's management had seen the writing on the wall for some time now, most of the rest of the fashion world must not have realized that the Preppy boom had gone bust, and even included L.L. Bean among the fashion houses chosen to design outfits for the world tour of Charlie Brown's faithful dog, Snoopy, and his sister, Belle. The pair of pooches outfitted by Bean traveled in the company of about a hundred other Snoopys and Belles who were clothed in designs by the likes of Oscar de la Renta and Diane von Furstenberg. According to Leon Gorman, Bean's Snoopy sported Bird Shooting Pants, Bean Boots, and a Chamois Shirt, and carried a rucksack, while Belle was attired in Chinos, a button-down Oxford shirt under a Norwegian Sweater, and Blucher Mocs. She also carried a Boat and Tote Bag. Gorman would even include a photograph of the pair—which one writer had described as "dressed to the canines"—in his 2006 book.

Before landing in Sacramento in late 1985 to celebrate Snoopy's thirty-fifth birthday, the pooches had already been on display in Europe and the Far East. While Peanuts creator Charles Schultz said he was delighted with his characters' fashion tour, it didn't go off without a few glitches; some of the designers had felt the need to give Belle a tummy tuck or even a bust line, while another had the pair—who are brother and sister, remember—getting married.

The designer dogs then departed California for a six-month tour of Australia.

Even with its previous Preppy sales volume, the firm had continued to top the customer satisfaction survey of a major consumer publication, a fact that was not lost on other journals. The *Harvard Business Review*, in its article, "Quality Is More Than Making a Good Product: It's Also a Matter of Keeping Close Tabs on Changing Customer Values and After-Sale Servicing" (July 7, 1983), used two companies as good examples, L.L. Bean, Inc., and Caterpillar Tractor Company, both of which, the piece said, "have developed successful customer-driven quality programs" and "enjoy an enviable reputation for high quality." As for the Maine-based business, the article noted that some 96.7 percent of 3,000 customers L.L. Bean had recently surveyed said that quality is the attribute they like most about the company. Bean executes a customer-driven quality program by

> Conducting regular customer satisfaction surveys and sample group interviews to track customer and non-customer perceptions of the quality of its own and its competitors' products and services.
>
> Tracking on its computer all customer inquiries and complaints and updating the file daily.
>
> Guaranteeing all its products to be 100% satisfactory, and providing a full cash refund, if requested, on any returns.
>
> Asking customers to fill out a short, coded questionnaire and explain their reasons for returning the merchandise.
>
> Performing extensive field tests on any new outdoor equipment before listing it in the company's catalogs.
>
> Even stocking extra buttons for most of the apparel items carried years ago, just in case a customer needs one.

Customer satisfaction is all well and good, but it doesn't pay the bills, and the company was forced to temporarily put one of its major projects on hold. In February L.L. Bean had bought a golf course on Desert Road, next to the land it had purchased from

L. L.'s widow, Claire, in 1970. After purchasing the course for the usual "undisclosed price," the company then leased it back to former owner, Ronald C. Coffin, to run for two years with no guarantee of what would become of it after that. The nine-hole, 171-acre course, said Bean spokesperson Kilt Andrew, was to serve as a "buffer zone" for the giant Distribution Center the company planned to build there in 1985. Andrew noted that probably no part of the new facility would be located on the golf course, but said that "aesthetics are a real consideration here. You want to site the building at a very respectable distance from Desert Road."[37]

The plan for the Desert Road site had called for the construction of a giant distribution facility that would enable the firm to keep pace with its recent phenomenal growth. When the slowdown hit, the company took stock of its situation and, on September 30, 1983, issued a press release announcing that the planned construction of its new Distribution Center on Desert Road had been put on hold. News reports of the day said that the company was postponing construction of the $25-million, 350,000-square-foot facility "until next year," but the delay would turn out to be far longer than that.

But it wasn't just Bean's finances that plagued the Desert Road project; residents opposed to the merchant's plan complained of a potential conflict of interest because the town planning board included two Bean employees. (Townspeople would raise similar concerns when the company decided to go ahead with the massive project nearly a decade later.) Earlier in the year, some townspeople and members of the planning board had also expressed reservations about the firm's expansion plans for its downtown retail store, to which Bean executive VP Bill End responded, "I think it's completely at arm's length. We don't have anyone we're beholden to and no one is beholden to us."[38]

While they found the concept to be "basically sound," several Freeporters had issues with the height of the retail store's new addition and its copious use of glass. Robert McNair of project architects Symmes, Maini & McKee addressed the height issue at the February 2 planning board meeting by saying that the addition would be the same height as the existing store, but the roof along Main Street would slope down to just 34 feet. Concerns with potential traffic, parking, and pedestrian safety problems were also raised, with End responding that the company planned to increase its number of downtown parking spaces. By the end of April, L.L. Bean's expansion plans had been passed by the planning board after the firm agreed to an additional five-foot setback and traffic signs along Cushing Avenue (now Justin's Way).

While construction at Bean's retail store was beginning in May, the company was addressing its parking issues by razing the former Loree Shoe building across Main Street. Though the store's expansion would cost Bean's 54 parking spaces in the "immediate vicinity" of the store, the company would realize a net gain of 112 spots (from 334 to 446) by adding 63 spots by the store in the area of Nathan Nye Street (formerly Bond Street) and another 103 at the Loree site. Demolition of the massive old shoe factory was being done by Harry C. Crooker & Sons of Brunswick and was expected to take about two weeks.

Just because it wasn't the best time for L.L. Bean to build its huge warehouse in the countryside didn't mean that the family-owned company was in trouble. Far from it. At the time, the company was able to add two stories onto its offices at the Taylor Building as well as make a significant contribution to the state's largest hospital. L.L. Bean's $1 million contribution to Maine Medical Center toward its expansion prompted the 109-year-old hospital to name the five-floor addition the "Leon L. Bean Memorial Wing." The new wing would house an operating suite; ambulatory surgery facilities; special care, burn, and dialysis units; delivery rooms and neonatal intensive care units; and blood bank, supply, and food preparation services.

"We are extremely pleased that the hospital's expansion will be named after our founder," Leon Gorman told 140 people at a fundraising dinner. "To many people, Leon L. Bean and his company were, and continue to be, representative of the quality of life in Maine."[39] Bean's donation helped the hospital exceed its $11.2 million goal by $2.4 million. Other major contributors to the cause were: the hospital's staff, $3.2 million; philanthropist Elizabeth B. Noyce, $1 million; and Hannaford supermarkets, $350,000; among many others. The cost of the total project, which would include improvements to existing buildings, would be $54.5 million. The L. L. Bean wing would be dedicated on August 6, 1985, bringing the facility's number of operating rooms to 19 and beds to 598.

But probably one of the best investments L.L. Bean, Inc., ever made, albeit on a much smaller scale, was the one that got the shoe on the road. Bean's involvement in community activities has always been one of its core values. That meant that the Freeport firm often took part in local parades, which, in turn, meant that the company's workers were obligated to come up with a new float every year. In early 1983, one employee suggested that the company should build a permanent float. "I liked the idea of a permanent float and the president of the company liked it,"[40] said Kilt Andrew, Bean's assistant manager for public affairs, "so I got to work on finding someone to build it." What to build was a no-brainer; of course it would be a giant Maine Hunting Shoe, a Bean Boot, "size 14" (its length in feet). But finding someone who could actually build the thing was no easy task. After much searching, Andrew settled on the 101-year-old Portland School of Art (now the Maine College of Art) to construct the float.

Work on the project started during spring break in March at the Portland school's sculpture department, where a small crew of artists put in a week of thirteen-hour days. Those were then followed by six weekends of construction in a nearby garage on Brackett Street. The 12-foot-tall boot was constructed of canvas over foam that was then glued to chicken wire attached to a spruce framework. It was built in four sections (trailer, shoe, ankle, and a top that's detachable for storage). It has an entry hatch that's hidden by the "Maine Hunting Shoe" label.

The trailer was made by welding a Datsun (now Nissan) axle to a flatbed. The "leather" part of the boot was painted with acrylic house paint, while the lower "rubber" part of the boot was polished with butcher's wax. The boot's giant shoelace isn't a leftover from the Casco Laces Company, which had previously occupied Bean's headquarters, but rather a length of ferry anchor rope donated by the Casco Bay Island Transit District. When it was completed, the authenticity of the huge Hunting Shoe was verified by Bean's bootmakers, who inspected the float during their breaks. To make it roadworthy, the big boot was outfitted with taillights, a license plate, and even a spare tire.

A rolling testament to Yankee ingenuity and thrift, the $6,000 "Das Boot," as its builders had come to call it, would make its debut in Freeport's Fourth of July parade, and was featured in a book produced for the National Governors' Conference, held that summer in Portland. *Sports Illustrated* photographer Bill Eppridge would photograph Leon Gorman in the top of the boot, leaning on its tongue, for a lengthy article about the company by John Skow in its December 2, 1985, issue. The L.L. Bean president liked the photo so much that he included a full-page color copy of it in his book twenty-one years later.

BY FAR THE BIGGEST OF THE PROJECTS the company went ahead with in 1983 was the expansion and modernization of its Main Street retail store. "The goal: to provide the best customer service at the best outdoor specialty store in the USA," read the opening line of the April *Bean Scene* article. "The effort: to plan and build a 25,000-square-foot addition in one year. The result: more display area, more pleasant shopping, better customer service, and more sales."

Since the existing store already generated $1,000 per square foot annually, the question was, "Will our expansion," asked the piece, ". . . add $25 million in sales? Probably not." The main thrust of the addition was not to make more money for the company, said the article, but to make shopping at Bean's a more pleasurable experience. And besides, the family-sized tents and the sea kayaks that were then displayed in an outside courtyard would take up a lot of floor space in the proposed addition's solar tent room—not a good way of improving the "dollars-per-square-foot" figure. The roomier store, which would have its grand opening in May 1984, would also make it easier for employees to restock the shelves and racks. Though a 25,000-square-foot addition was going onto a 30,000-square-foot building, the new-look store would actually boast just 50,000 square feet of retail space with the remaining 5,000 square feet to be used for storage. One thing that the article didn't mention was the estimated cost of the project: $3.5 million.

The construction aspect of the store expansion seems to have been up to Leon Gorman's expectations; management of the store during renovations, not so much. According to M. R. Montgomery, Leon Gorman had fired the manager of the retail store, which had been producing an impressive $800 per square foot annually, because he "just wasn't up to speed . . . on managing the renovations."

Accounts of the man's professional death were not exaggerated; in early April, an announcement carried in the Portland newspaper said, "Thomas C. Nannery, who joined the Bean staff last year as assistant manager of the store's retail sales, has now taken over as store manager. In another store-related promotion, John W. Walling, who came to the store as a sales clerk in 1972, has been promoted from assistant to operations manager of the store." The piece also notes that in March, "it was announced that William T. End, who had been senior vice president, had been promoted to executive vice president of the outdoor sporting goods establishment."[41]

Maybe it was a good thing that Chris McCormick joined L.L. Bean when he did. Not only would the man who'd go far within the company find out right away that L.L. Bean wouldn't always be basking in the glow of double-digit growth, he'd also be able to draw on lessons learned during the company's future downturns. McCormick graduated from Connecticut's Fairfield University in 1977 and spent the next six years as media buyer and then marketing manager with Garden Way, Inc. When he saw an ad in the *Boston Globe* for an assistant advertising manager at L.L. Bean, he sent in his résumé. The cataloger called him three days later. Thereafter, he'd earn a promotion roughly every other year, becoming vice president of advertising and direct marketing by 1991.

A couple of years earlier, Leon Gorman had told a reporter, "It is far-fetched that the children in this generation will be capable of managing the company in five or ten years [because it will be so large]. We want to ensure that there is some stability to management," he said, referring to his handpicked successor, Bill End, whom he'd hired in 1975. (Back then, no one could have foreseen the rift that would develop between Gorman and End, one that probably had its origins in the Preppy bust of '83.)

The company's sluggish streak would continue through the 1984 fiscal year. When it mercifully concluded in early 1985, Bean's figures would reveal that sales of the Freeport firm had "grown" just another 6.7 percent to the $253.7 million mark. That level of growth was unacceptable, said Bill End, recalling that any time Bean's business slowed, "there was consternation" and all the managers would scramble to get things going again. Bean's senior vice president of operations, John Findlay, thought that the company's previous meteoric growth used to "cover up many ills."

Eventually those ills—and a lot of animosity—would become very apparent. With the independent presentations they'd given at the Colby College Institute for Management back in 1980, Leon Gorman and Bill End had verified that they were on the same page as far as the future of the firm was concerned, their separate presentations perfectly complementing each other.

But by 1984, 1980 would seem like ancient history. The company wasn't recovering well from the Preppy crash, and it was here that the difference in Gorman's and End's philosophies about the future of L.L. Bean began to emerge. In a nutshell, Bill End advocated carrying more apparel and branching out into retail stores, while Leon Gorman was determined to grow the company's active outdoors image through its existing mail-order model. These differences of opinion would grow and fester for the next several years, eventually concluding with End's departure from the company.

Claiming that he had never seen another retailer who had successfully operated both stores and a catalog division, Leon Gorman was opposed to expanding into retail because it was a completely different animal and required different sets of logistics, merchandising skills, and corporate cultures. And besides, he reasoned, not only did no one in the ranks of Bean's management have any experience in retailing, none of them even really understood the basic differences between mail-order and retail sales.

He was also strongly opposed to having the company focus too much on casual apparel, since a focus on "fashiony" clothing would compromise Bean's character and move the company away from its outdoorsy image and more toward one as a glorified clothing store.

But the era of casual dress in the United States had begun, and other catalog companies such as Lands' End and Eddie Bauer had been quick to capitalize on the trend—especially Lands' End, which had also realized significant growth during the Preppy period. But L.L. Bean, Inc., was more like the recently departed incarnation of Abercrombie & Fitch had been, an established company with its roots firmly planted in its outdoors tradition. While Abercrombie & Fitch would eventually be reborn as a fashion house for the younger crowd, the original version of the company had tried to make the transition into casual apparel and failed. In spite of his opposition to carrying casual clothing, Leon Gorman would be forced to admit that the increased capacity at his rapidly growing business had also increased its dependence on the sale of women's casual apparel.

With Bean's two top executives wanting the company to take very different paths, it wouldn't be long before the managers working under the pair began to feel the strain. Vice president of advertising and direct marketing, Bill Henry, recalls the strain of being caught in "this schizophrenia" that was going on inside the company; all the growth was in the area of casual wear, but Leon Gorman stubbornly wanted L.L. Bean, Inc., to retain the rugged image of its namesake.

Determined to return his company to a more solid footing while still retaining its traditional image and character, Leon Gorman began laying the groundwork for Bean's rebound. Helped by an improving economy and aging baby boomers who'd begun pursuing all sorts of outdoors interests, he adopted an "outdoors lifestyle merchandising" strategy which he spearheaded with a series of specialty catalogs, each targeted at the established buying habits of an appropriate segment. The company was undertaking "a massive project," Gorman noted, "'to get a specific lifestyle activity interest on each of our customers.' In order to properly target the specialty catalogs, 'Bean's data processors are compiling files on product purchases.'"[42] Among the few who realized just how high-tech the Freeport firm had recently become was, in fact, *Down East* magazine, which noted that "apart from values, the Bean's of the 1980s is hardly old fashioned."

The five new catalogs targeted the areas of fishing, hunting, summer sports, fitness, and home and camp furnishings. Now, instead of dedicating a lot of pages in the main catalog to fishing, which may not interest a lot of people, Bean's could cut its exposure from thirty-two pages to four—just enough to pique the interest of anglers who'd then be encouraged to request the firm's new fishing circular. Included in each specialty catalog was a hotline people could call with questions, meaning the company "got some real stumpers." One fisherman wanted to know which type of fly would work best on a specific stream in Montana. Bean's staff tracked down an expert in the area and got the man his answer.

In addition to targeting customers with specific interests, the specialty catalogs served another purpose—making room in the main catalog for more profitable merchandise. In the case of fishing, for example, the fishing customers would receive a catalog dedicated exclusively to fishing. Future specialty catalogs would include fly-fishing, winter sports (such as cross-country skiing and snowshoeing), hiking, camping, cycling, and canoeing.

M. R. Montgomery probably summed up Bean's new approach best:

> In the spring of 1984, Bean's test-marketed an all-fishing, all-camping, all-outdoors catalog. At the same time, everyone on the mailing list got a small book titled "Weekends." Both books were a success, and the pattern was set. In the fall of 1984, there

would be an all-shooting, all-hiking, all-outdoors book in which the dominant pattern was camouflage clothing, and the regular fall catalog would continue to expand into the dressier sports clothing, the upscale household items. The world had gone in two directions and L.L. Bean was not about to leave a road untaken.

Even though L.L. Bean was still on the rebound financially, it managed to continue its support of worthy causes. When Leon Gorman had learned that most companies allocated about 1 percent of their pretax earnings to corporate giving, he decided to contribute 2.5 percent, with the bulk of it going to human service agencies and outdoors and conservation organizations. One beneficiary of Bean's generosity was the Appalachian Mountain Club, the nation's oldest outdoor recreation and conservation organization, which received $500,000 from the Freeport company. Tom Deans, the AMC's executive director, called Bean's donation "incredibly important" to his organization. L.L. Bean also donated $200,000 to the Portland Museum of Art.

Though not exactly qualifying as a donation, L.L. Bean did "outfit" the twenty members of the State of Maine's delegation to the 1984 Republican National Convention. "We called it the 'I'm from Maine and don't you forget it' outfit,"[43] delegate Charlie Cragin joked of the $55 ensemble, which consisted of a cap with a lobster patch, a red or green shirt with the outline of Maine silkscreened on the breast, and a brass "leaping salmon" belt buckle. Cragin conceded that the outfit was "kind of Preppy." (In the interest of bipartisanship, Bean's extended the same offer to the Democrats, who reportedly turned it down.)

JUST BEFORE MEMORIAL DAY IN 1985, L.L. Bean unveiled the latest addition to its downtown retail store. Far from the ells, rooms, and sheds that L. L. had tacked on to the Warren Block out of necessity back in his day, this latest expansion was big, modern—and planned. There was an atrium and the granite paving was from Deer Isle. The customer service area had been enlarged, and there was room to display the company's expanded range of merchandise, which now included saltwater fishing gear, sea kayaks, and bicycles. While the factory outlet store had remained in the building, it was moved to roomier quarters upstairs, where bargain hunters could browse at their leisure through the floor samples, factory seconds, and slightly irregulars marked as much as half off. The exterior of the building was done in barn boards with its always-unlocked entrance framed in brick. Permanent staff at the store was expected to increase from 140 to 150, and seasonal staff by 30 to about 250.

The centerpiece of the revamped store, said Gorman was "a trout pond (with fifteen healthy Maine brookies)." Well, eventually. Actually, the store opened with only eight trout—and they liked to hide in the shadows. The other seven would be added a little later. "They'll be easier to see," said a store manager, "when there are more of them." The first sign of trouble with the fish, which Bean's had gotten from Mineral Springs Trout Ponds of East Vassalboro, Maine, had come back in February when eighteen of them died within three or four hours of being introduced into the 8,500-gallon pond. Some adjustments were made to the pond's filters, which remove chlorine from 65 gallons of the 54-degree water every minute, and the pool was ready for occupancy again. Eighteen months later, the average length of the brook trout had reached 17 inches.

"One wedding was held by the trout pond the first year," said Gorman, "and a Connecticut woman had the pond replicated for her new home." While there's no further information about the lady from southern New England, details of the store's first wedding would appear in a *Down East* magazine article a year later:

[The store's] new ambiance is undeniably appreciated by a couple from Lewiston. Last New Year's Eve Bob Gillam and Susan Greene strolled in about 6 P.M. accompanied by a justice of the peace who married them in two minutes flat on the landing over the trout pond. Sales clerk Bob Hart served as a witness, shoppers gathered around, but the happy couple hastened away before the press could arrive.

A piece in *Sports Illustrated* said the couple had "committed matrimony."

The tradition would continue in a more formal manner in 1991 when another couple would tie the knot on the landing over the trout pond. This time the couple, Russell Pomeroy and Shirley Summers of Arlington, Virginia, asked for and received permission to get married in the store on September 1 as long as the ceremony was a brief one. "We're not a chapel in the woods," said Bean spokesperson Catharine Hartnett. Pomeroy would wear a tuxedo and Summers a traditional long gown for the 8 A.M. wedding. Pomeroy said he was serious about the marriage, but felt that the ceremony didn't have to be a solemn occasion. "This is a union," he told a reporter, "not a sentence."[11]

Besides the occasional bride and groom, the area above the pond is populated by a small flock of flying black ducks ("puddle ducks") carved from basswood by Jefferson, Maine, decoy maker Ted Hanks in 1984.

Weddings notwithstanding, this remodel of the company store had to be the most talked-about change to the place since Leon Gorman had that green carpet put down back in 1969. The changes were so great that they had even Gorman, who'd approved the plans, feeling a little nostalgic, saying it was "almost a complete break from the past. But what most upset me was that it seemed to change the personality of the store from a comfortable and woodsy, uniquely L.L. Bean environment to one that was starting to feel like other stores." One change to the store that would be universally approved of that summer was the addition of air conditioning.

Another plus to the revamped store was that it provided a modern backdrop for the publicity Bean's was about to receive from the late-October visit of humorist and writer Erma Bombeck, who was in town to film a cooking segment. The piece, which featured Bean employee Alex Delicata preparing an omelet, was being recorded for a future broadcast of ABC's *Good Morning America* program.

It's unlikely that the latest doubling of the size of L.L. Bean's retail store had had any impact on the number of outlet stores, which now surrounded it on three sides. They would have just kept on coming to Freeport anyway. And every one of them wanted to be near L.L. Bean. "The whole development machine was driven by the economy," Freeport tax assessor Joseph Downey told the *Washington Post*, "and the economy was the number of bodies coming to shop at L.L. Bean's."[45] At the time, there were more than two dozen building permits waiting for the approval of the planning board. According to the *Post*, land was valued at $1.2 million an acre in the commercial zone, which made up 2 percent of the town but accounted for more than 30 percent of its tax revenues.

With so much going on in Freeport, even L.L. Bean was beginning to feel squeezed for space. Of the company's peak 1984 workforce of 2,580 employees (versus 1,450 permanent workers), 430 were temporary operators (versus 115 permanent ones), who were charged with accurately and courteously recording each and every one of the 2.6 million customer orders the firm would receive by phone that year. While the cataloger had had little trouble procuring seasonal order-takers, it had no place to put them—at least not in Freeport. Bean solved its seasonal seating dilemma by opening one of its first out-of-town facilities.

By early August many of the firm's operators had been relocated to the former Ames department store located between WGME-TV and Laverdiere's drugstore in Portland's Northport shopping center, allowing the company ample time to train its seasonal hires. The new out-of-town call center would do much to alleviate the overcrowded conditions the firm had suffered through the previous holiday season, when it had been forced to set up 180 temporary call stations in its conference rooms, training rooms, and classrooms. Even before the Northport facility opened, Kilton Andrew had told a reporter that even though "I don't think the [Freeport phone system's] capacity's ever been computed, it's reputed to be the greatest of any single facility in the country."[46] For a while, L.L. Bean also had rows of workers at sewing machines repairing returned items in the 73,800-square-foot facility, which the company had initially leased for three years.

A few months prior to having relocated many of its operators to Portland, the company had also moved its offices out of downtown Freeport, at least on paper. On March 7 L.L. Bean, Inc., filed papers with the Secretary of State's office saying that it was officially changing the location of its registered office from 95 Main Street to Casco Street. The change came about ten years after the firm had moved most of its offices down Route 1 to the E. E. Taylor Building. (A document filed with the state eight days later listed the company's eight directors as Leon A. Gorman; Norman A. Poole; John T. Gorman, Jr.; William T. End; John D. Findlay, Jr.; Linda Bean Jones; James W. Gorman; and Hazel J. Dyer.)

BESIDES ITS SPACE PROBLEM, another encountered by L.L. Bean in 1984 was the surge in the number of publications that were either about the company or featured it prominently. While two books would prove to be more of a distraction than anything else, the third item, a magazine parody of L.L. Bean, would see the Freeport company pursuing the matter all the way to the Supreme Court.

First there was that paperback book that parodied just about everything in the state. "The acerbic humor of the *Uncensored Guide to Maine*," noted Bean's *Company Scrapbook* in its only reference to the tome, "was not aimed squarely at L.L. Bean but made ample reference to the company." And to the town of Freeport. The book's many essays ran the gamut from clever on one page to callous on the next, often landing somewhere in the middle.

One timely item in *The Uncensored Guide* declared "Freeport— A Trade Zone for the Rich," and "reported" that "it is rumored that the town fathers and mothers of Freeport may soon pass an ordinance prohibiting Maine natives on the streets between 8 A.M. [and] 8 P.M. It is also rumored that dozens of young men and women from New Jersey have been hired to wear L.L. Bean clothing and impersonate Maine people during these hours."

Another of the book's pithy pieces defined the Bean Boot as "a specially designed boot with a built-in pouch for carrying beans.

The sweat from the foot cooks the beans and makes them tasty and tender for the campsite supper." *The Uncensored Guide*'s alternative tourist stops to L.L. Bean's store included Pushard's shoes on the Kennebec River in South Gardiner and Povich's on Front Street in Bath (both of which are now long gone). When the catalog giant refused to sell the book in its flagship store, the publisher wasted no time in slapping a large red-and-yellow rectangular sticker on the cover proclaiming: "Banned by L.L. Bean." Ironically, the Freeport firm's brief mention of the book was kinder to it than the book's own publisher, Augusta's Lance Tapley, had been to his authors, Mark Melnicove and Kendall Merriam. In his tongue-in-cheek "Publisher's Disclaimer," Tapley explained his dilemma:

> Don't get me wrong. I like seagulls, clamshell ashtrays, L.L. Bean's, and fir balsam pillows as much as anybody. I didn't want to make fun of Maine. . . . I'm only the publisher. The authors are the people to blame. They wrote this. Everybody knows writers are crazy. One of them is from away, so what does he know? The other was born in Rockland, and that's even worse! They're poor, ungrateful writers, for God's sake, which means they can't even keep a nine to five job—mere barnacles on our stately ship. I'm sure somebody will scrape 'em out of state after this book appears. Probably a reviewer from *Down East*. Good riddance. If they go far enough away, I won't have to pay them royalties.

Late in the year, M. R. Montgomery published *In Search of L. L. Bean* (Little, Brown and Co., 242 pp., $16.95), the unauthorized L.L. Bean history for which he managed to obtain a lot of information about the family-owned company through careful research and by talking to several of its employees, both past and present.

Reviews were generally good. *Maine Sunday Telegram* writer Bob Cummings, who, a few years earlier, had had faint praise for *The L.L. Bean Guide to the Outdoors*, took a somewhat kinder view of *In Search of L. L. Bean*, observing that "it seems to be drawn from reliable sources: interviews he did with the company as a reporter for the *Boston Globe*, reports compiled by the Harvard Business School, and L. L. Bean's own books *My Story* and *Hunting, Fishing, and Camping*. . . . This is a fascinating account of the birth and development of L.L. Bean, Inc.," he says, "a tiny country clothing store that grew into one of the giants of the outdoor equipment business."[47]

Toward the end of his review, Cummings stated that *In Search of L. L. Bean* "is a good book that should be read by anyone interested in Maine biography, Maine business, and Maine's dream of attracting tourists and out of state industry." This was right before he took Montgomery to task for the several geographic errors his book contains—such as placing New Hampshire's Mt. Adams in Maine's Oxford County, and saying that the state has a Caribou Mountain Range—leading him to conclude that "it would have been a better book had Montgomery consulted a map before beginning to write."

Cummings pointed out some other errors Montgomery made about the locations of places in Maine, but missed the one he made about L. L. Bean shooting his first deer near the Moose River in the Jackman area. In his book, Montgomery wrote:

> The first time I went into the big woods, looking for the spirit of L. L. Bean, it was west of Jackman at Holub [*sic*] Pond. . . .
>
> Until 1960, one would have come into the Moose River by Maine Central, hitching a ride on the work train from Jackman, the schedule set entirely by the railroad's good offices. It was on that line, farther northwest, that little Lennie Bean and his cousin caught a ride to the camp where young L. L. killed his first deer.

In searching for L. L. Bean near Holeb Pond and the Moose River, Montgomery was more than a hundred miles off course. Little Lennie Bean, you'll recall, had actually bagged his first deer by New Hampshire's Wild River after he and cousin Louvie Swett had taken the train from South Paris to Gilead. The pair then walked three miles south to Hastings, Maine, where they spent the night at a boardinghouse before heading into New Hampshire.

In his review, Cummings committed his own faux pas, writing that "70 percent of [Bean's annual sales are] in ladies' street clothes." The line from Montgomery's book actually reads: "From 1978 to 1984, 70 percent of Bean's new customers were women."

Christopher Lehmann-Haupt, the book reviewer for the *New York Times*, also seemed to like Montgomery's work, saying that he found it "edifying." Still, he said he preferred the part of the book about L. L. Bean, the old man, to the part about L.L. Bean the company. "But what exactly it is you've got hold of here is not easy to explain," wrote Lehmann-Haupt. "[It] is sort of a company history of the Freeport, Me., sports outfitter, though it is by no stretch of the imagination an authorized one. The subject of L. L. Bean gets Mr. Montgomery, an outdoor sports columnist for the *Boston Globe*, into several other matters, which he pursues with a verve and wit not often encountered among company historians."[48]

While the company had dealt with both *The Uncensored Guide to Maine* and *In Search of L. L. Bean* at the time by pretty much ignoring them, that was not something it could do with the third publication to make reference to the Freeport merchant that year. On August 29, the October 1984 issue of *High Society* magazine hit the newsstands. Normally, the monthly installment of "America's Hottest Sex Magazine," as the publication called itself, would have gone largely unnoticed in Freeport, but this month was different. This month's edition of *High Society* included a two-page parody of the famous Bean catalog titled "L.L. Beam's Back-to-School Sex Catalogue," which featured "nude and partially clad men and women posing with sporting equipment being used in various sexual acts."

The Freeport firm, whose official color is Bean green, saw red, and on September 25, L.L. Bean, Inc., sued New York's Drake Publishing, Inc., publisher Gloria Leonard, and fifteen other magazine employees for $1 million in compensatory damages and $15 million in punitive damages. The case, which was filed in U.S. District Court in Bangor, charged the magazine with intentionally using Bean's "typographical and layout style, including its Cheltenham typeface." The complaint went on to say that "The 'Sex Catalogue' in itself creates a sense of disgust and revulsion in the reader. Any reader will thereafter associate the depravity of the defendant's magazine with the plaintiff's products, resulting in . . . injury of the plaintiff's business reputation and acceptance with its customers."

On October 5, U.S. District Court Judge Conrad K. Cyr ruled against L.L. Bean's request to have copies of *High Society* removed from stores pending the company's lawsuit against the publisher, saying it had not shown that "the company would have suffered irreparable injury if the restraining order were not granted." Drake's attorneys argued that the restraining order could have been seen as a violation of the publisher's First Amendment rights to free speech. (Ironically, the issue had originally been scheduled for removal from the shelves on September 27.)

The folks from Freeport would get their win in court fifteen months later, when U.S. District Court Judge Gene Carter ordered Drake Publishing not to further distribute its catalog parody and not to publish a facsimile of the L.L. Bean trademark again. Judge Carter ruled in Portland that the *High Society* parody had undermined the good will and reputation of L.L. Bean under a 1981 Maine "trademark dilution" law. Earlier in the case, Bean spokesperson Kilton Andrew had said that the company had always been concerned about parodies of its famous catalog, but this was different. "It's an instance," he said, "where we had to take action." While L.L. Bean had won the most recent legal battle with Drake, the war was still far from over. The dispute between the Freeport cataloger and the New York publisher would drag on until mid-1987, when the matter would finally be settled by the United States Supreme Court.

One publication the company obviously had no problem with in 1984 was its own *L.L. Bean Fly Fishing Handbook* (Nick Lyons Books), written and illustrated by expert fisherman Dave Whitlock.

Five years earlier, in the days when the Preppy phenomenon was just beginning to build a head of steam, L.L. Bean's bean counters had forecast a 1985 profit of about $22.7 million based on $344.3 million in sales. Obviously that projection had proven to be an optimistic one. Two slow years had put that goal out of reach, but with the company putting 20 different catalogs into the mail 68 million times, the firm's resulting 4 million orders gave Bean's a growth spurt to $303.8 million. That figure translated into a one-hundred-fold increase in sales since Leon Gorman had taken the reins of L.L. Bean, Inc., in 1967.

During the mid-eighties, "our profitability and productivity ranked in the 75th percentile of American industry,"[49] reported Leon Gorman, which may have been one of the reasons, besides community spirit, that L.L. Bean decided to make a contribution of $100,000 to the local school system. In March 1985, Leon Gorman gave the first of four annual $25,000 checks to school committee chair Elyse End. The money, which would be matched by local tax dollars, would enable the school system to hire a full-time computer coordinator, said superintendent Eve Bither, as well as upgrade the schools' existing computer hardware, software, and reference materials. (In 1981, L.L. Bean had helped the Freeport schools get their first computers with a $7,000 grant.)

Bean's booming workforce was continuing to grow to the point that the company finally had to split its hiring and human resources departments. One reason for the split was the company's need for more operators—it had recently unveiled a toll-free "800" order line that would soon go nationwide. For years, L.L. Bean had resisted the trend among catalogers toward offering their customers a free call, and besides, at the time, L.L. Bean still offered free shipping on everything it sold, except for Federal Express orders and oversized items. "One of the reasons we decided not to go to toll-free calls," a customer service executive had confided to M. R. Montgomery, "is that the customers spend so much time just chatting with the girls when it's *their* nickel. We don't mind talking about the weather up here, but I think it would get out of hand with a free telephone line." Shortly after Montgomery typed those words, L.L. Bean would have a change of heart that would reward the company with nearly 3 million incoming calls and a phone bill of $5.3 million.

The company's newly renovated flagship store continued to

hold its own in Bean's revival with its three million annual visitors accounting for about 15 percent of the firm's sales. In the week before Christmas alone, the retail store's three dozen NCR 2152 terminals would process more than 40,000 transactions.

While Bean's massive Distribution Center was undergoing its second major expansion since being built in 1974, three leased trucks each made two round trips per shift to another warehouse in Lewiston, 18 miles away. Upon their arrival, workers would unload articles for storage in Lewiston and send the trucks back to Freeport with items needed to replenish the DC's ready area. Soon the company would also lease space in Lewiston for another manufacturing facility, where workers would attach tops to the bottoms of Maine Hunting Shoes and then pack them for shipment.

But not all of the firm's facilities were on the scale of its retail store or its large warehouses. On March 18, 1985, the company opened the Fogg House, the Desert Road farmhouse it had purchased from Merrill O. Fogg in 1981, as a training facility. The same year, L.L. Bean also purchased the Downing house near the retail store, officially saying little about the acquisition beyond "private home purchased in 1985."

After two slow years, L.L. Bean grew 20 percent in 1985. Layoffs had been avoided, and the question of opening retail stores was off the table—at least for the time being. With the L.L. Bean ship now back on its charted course, apparent harmony returned to Freeport. Senior VP John Findlay was fine with the status quo; he already had his hands full, he said, and with the growth now at "$70, $80 million a year," why would they want to expend more time and effort expanding into retail?

A *Sports Illustrated* interview later that year would reveal that even Bill End seemed to be on board with Leon Gorman's current plan of attack—at least for the time being. "No, Bean should not expand by starting a chain of retail stores. Retailing on a nationwide scale is a tough business and not Bean's specialty. 'We should stick to what we know,' [End] says," echoing Gorman's earlier sentiment. This December show of unity may have come about as a result of the company's first formal planning session, which had been held at the Bethel Inn in May, or perhaps during a four-day camping trip two months later, when ten of the company's top executives hiked forty miles in the nearby White Mountains of New Hampshire.

THE FIRM'S EFFORTS TO RECOVER from the effects of the recent Preppy bust included more than just a few specialty catalogs and a rededication to the product lines it had sold for decades. It was time to break out the big guns—or at least a few long guns. So, in August of 1985, L.L. Bean began selling shotguns. "L. L. dabbled in firearms himself," noted Bean spokesperson Kilton Andrew. (Leon L. Bean was said to have owned several guns including a twelve-gauge Browning-style automatic, a twenty-gauge Parker, a .35 Remington rifle, and a .25-caliber rifle, also probably a Remington. The Parker hung on Leon Gorman's office wall for years.)

Still, it's ironic that the company bearing his name would choose to sell shotguns; while L. L. Bean had been very proficient with a hunting rifle, bagging a deer every fall for nearly forty years, his skill with a shotgun left plenty to be desired. L. L.'s Remington shotgun "had a great big tubular magazine," recalled one old hunting buddy. "I think you could put a dozen shells in it. People that hunted with L. L., they remember him firing off the whole clip at a duck more than one time."

The reason, said Andrew, that Bean's was just now starting to sell guns was because it hadn't previously been able to provide repair services. And service is an important component in the sale of firearms. Executive VP Bill End noted that when the firm had first started testing shotguns to include in its product line, every one from a certain Spanish manufacturer had failed. "After 10 days of shooting," reported *Sports Illustrated*, End said, "'not one of the five guns we bought was still functioning.' Bean chose an Italian manufacturer."[50]

The company didn't expect the sales of firearms to generate a lot of revenue. Since it couldn't sell shotguns through the mail, they could be sold only in Maine and New Hampshire, a contiguous state (Maine is the only state that borders just one other state).

Still Andrew felt selling shotguns would be good for business, at least image-wise. "We're doing it now because there has been some clouding of our outdoorsness. You got the feeling when the *Official Preppy Handbook* came out that perhaps we had lost some [customers] who believed we were not in the outdoor business. This is a clarification [that we are]."[51] Nevertheless Bean's shotguns would serve the same purpose as its decoys had—to help sell clothing.

Because of federal laws and shipping restrictions, the management of L.L. Bean realized it wasn't feasible to sell guns from the catalog. Leon Gorman decided his company should carry them in the store since Bean's not selling shotguns and rifles, he said, "was like running a restaurant without selling main courses." According to the *Maine Times*, once the firm began carrying guns, its menu of firearms included a variety of twelve- and twenty-gauge models "including well-known Remingtons, Winchesters, Brownings, Fabio Zamottis [*sic*], and Barettas [*sic*]. The Remingtons, the least expensive of the guns, cost several hundred dollars, while the Barettas [*sic*] run up to $2,400."[52] (The twelve-gauge Fabio Zanotti L.L. Bean offered in 1985 cost $2,150. In 2007 the most expensive shotgun in Bean's Hunting and Fishing store would be the double-barreled Merkel 147 EL twelve-gauge priced at $5,995.)

Several years later, L.L. Bean would introduce its New Englander, an over-and-under shotgun designed by the firm's staff along with SIG Arms, and handmade by Rizzini in Italy. According to the company, it was "considered by journalists to be one of the finest guns ever produced." Despite the company's decision to start carrying guns, some hunters still saw L.L. Bean as abandoning them and turning its back on its roots by selling out to the Preppies and other purchasers of the company's clothing lines, which continued to expand.

The company was currently carrying a far broader selection of hunting and fishing gear than L. L. ever had—yet it still amounted to a small percentage of total sales. With no easy solution, the firm's management would struggle with this difficult image problem for many years.

On a lighter side of the issue, there is absolutely no indication that L.L. Bean's decision to begin selling firearms was in any way influenced by a few lines from the previous year's *Uncensored Guide to Maine*, which had carped that L.L. Bean doesn't "make enough of their own stuff. Nor do they dirty their hands by selling guns. This would bring the real sportsmen a little too close to the nonsports who make up most of the clientele. The Casco Bay Shirt wouldn't look good," the book said, "on the typical bear hunter."

Okay, so the Casco Bay Shirt is out for bear hunting. One item the typical bear hunter *would* have found useful was Bean's Thinsulate Maine Hunting Shoe, which, according to the company, was the first Maine Hunting Shoe to be "absolutely waterproof up to the top line" thanks to its Gore-Tex sock liner. The new boot, which featured 200-gram Thinsulate insulation, was introduced twenty years after Bean's first Ensolite-lined boot, and sold for $96—nearly five times as much as its predecessor.

Another piece of outerwear introduced that year would also prove successful only after some early bugs with its construction had been worked out. A set of first-generation Gore-Tex jackets that product testers used on the St. John River (in 1984) "just leaked like a sieve,"[53] said Gorman. "We were all wet for a week."[54] Once the problems had been fixed, Bean's Gore-Tex Stowaway rain jacket would prove to be another long-term winner.

The company worked hard to keep its active lines relevant. If the hunters were still skeptical of Bean's commitment to the traditional outdoorsman despite the fact that it was now selling firearms, they must have really been left scratching their heads over Bean's other new-for-'85, big-ticket category—bicycles, which Gorman saw as one of the ways the company could offset what he called "positioning drift." At the top of the firm's new three-bike lineup was Bean's Touring Bicycle, a $595 variant of the recently introduced ST500, the first bike produced by the fourteen-year-old Cannondale company of Bedford, Pennsylvania. A Bean brochure for the bicycles sounded like it could have been written by L. L. himself, proclaiming "Fly Like the Wind" on its cover and promising that "almost without effort, you will ride faster than ever before, and in complete control. The miles will fall behind you as you enter a strong, steady rhythm. At the end of your ride, you'll step off feeling refreshed, invigorated. . . .

"Aluminum is stronger than even Reynolds 531 steel," said the copy, "lighter and much stiffer, allowing the most efficient transfer of energy from pedal to wheel. You will ride farther, faster, and with less effort." Besides the touring machine, Bean also offered two $395 models, one for fitness riding, the other for exploring country roads. All three of the Ned Kitchel-designed bikes used Cannondale's then cutting-edge frames made of oversized TIG-welded aluminum, and featured an eclectic mix of mid-level components from the United States, Japan, and Europe.

Recently, the company had also taken a chance on another unusual product that would turn out to be one of its holiday staples—Christmas wreaths. But getting his company's goods into the L.L. Bean catalog hadn't been easy for Morrill Worcester, who courted the Freeport firm with sample after sample and letter after letter. Early on, he was turned away because "the catalogs have been paginated and all the terms they use like that," he said. "It really was the better part of two years convincing them."[55] Finally, persuaded that he could meet the demand, L.L. Bean put Worcester's wreaths into its 1984 Christmas catalog. That first year, more than 30,000 customers ordered Bean's fresh Maine-made balsam Christmas wreaths "sight unseen." By 1994 Worcester's company would be turning out one decorated wreath every five seconds—70 percent of them to be sold through L.L. Bean.

But just because Worcester already had his wreaths in the catalog didn't mean it would be easy for him to convince the firm to carry his other balsam creations. "I must have worn holes in the carpet," he said, "marching in there with the ideas that I've had rejected."[56] The Worcester Wreath Company of Harrington, Maine, would remain the cataloger's sole supplier of holiday wreaths until the two businesses would part ways for "financial reasons" in early 2009.

Another avenue the outfitter explored for enhancing its image as the outdoors authority was the introduction of its "Outdoor Video Library," a series of basic how-to videos that were taped throughout Maine. The first two "lessons from the masters" the company released were the "L.L. Bean Guide to Outdoor Photography" with Lefty Kreh and the "L.L. Bean Introduction to Fly Fishing" with Dave Whitlock. The 55-minute Kreh tape came with the *Kodak Pocket Guide to Outdoor Photography*, while the 70-minute Whitlock video included a copy of his *L.L. Bean Fly Fishing Handbook*. Each video cost $29.95 postpaid.

Soon, two more tapes would be added to the collection, the "L.L. Bean Guide to Bicycle Touring" and the "L.L. Bean Guide to Canoeing," each of which also came with a related handbook. All four tapes could be purchased or rented from the company and were available in either VHS or Beta format.

On top of the company's own foray into the world of media, L.L. Bean continued to be featured in major publications. One article, which appeared in the August 8 edition of the *Christian Science Monitor*, was written by Pulitzer Prize-winning journalist John Hughes and may have been one of the paper's few stories about the company not penned by L. L.'s old friend John Gould. In it, Hughes said that he was comforted by the consistent quality of the products found in the firm's fall catalog. He opened the piece by mourning the loss of a couple of mail-order catalogs he'd known over the years, then continued:

> And so it has been reassuring to get the familiar catalog in the mail from Freeport, Maine, and learn that nothing is changing in the world of L.L. Bean.
>
> It is full once again of the things that I will probably never buy, but which conjure up pictures of simple woodsmen, warm wool plaid against their chests, out with their dogs in the forest, beyond the reach of recorded telephone messages, computer printouts, and music they don't like with lyrics they can't stand.

A November issue of *Time* magazine took a different tack, devoting more than a page to "The Offspring of L.L. Bean," the outlet stores that wanted to be near the firm's flagship store like a school of pilotfish swarming around a shark.

"[His] long article gives one of the best overviews of the company," is what L.L. Bean thought about John Skow's *Sports Illustrated* essay, "Using the Old Bean." "In the past couple of years," observed Skow, "Bean's commitment to outdoor sports has reached a level so intense as to almost suggest Caspar Weinberger brooding about the Soviets." This retrenchment, he continued, had been due to Leon Gorman's realization a couple of years earlier "that Bean was in danger of being seen by its new customers not as a sporting goods dealer, but as last year's fashion house."[57] Two years after Skow's eleven-page article appeared, the company would include part of it—the part about its current recovery from the Preppy hangover—in its *Company Scrapbook*.

Also that year, *A Passion for Excellence*, the bestseller by Tom Peters and Nancy Austin about running a successful business, used the Maine company in many of its examples of excellent customer service. A sequel to the best-selling *In Search of Excellence*, the book mentioned L.L. Bean eight times and included a full-page photo of the firm's "Golden Rule" advertisement. Also reproduced in the book is Leon L. Bean's "What is a Customer?" maxim, posters of which are still prominently displayed throughout the company:

What is a Customer?
A Customer is the most important person ever in this office . . . in person or by mail.

A Customer is not dependent on us . . . we are dependent on him.

A Customer is not an interruption of our work . . . he is the purpose of it. We are not doing a favor by serving him . . . he is doing us a favor by giving us the opportunity to do so.

A Customer is not someone to argue or match wits with. Nobody ever won an argument with a Customer.

A Customer is a person who brings us his wants. It is our job to handle them profitably to him and to ourselves.

But not all mentions of the company that year were necessarily good publicity. In late June, L.L. Bean was mentioned in a story about a group of "drunken teens" who'd pelted the tour bus of singer Willie Nelson with bottles after he made a 3:00 A.M. stop at the store following a concert in Augusta. Bean's security staff called the police after members of Nelson's entourage clashed with the teens, sending one of them to the hospital. The article noted that "the incident occurred as the bus was headed back to the highway."[58]

On top of that, there was the Dear Abby Spruce Gum Incident of '85. The whole thing started innocently enough in mid-June when Abigail Van Buren (aka Pauline Phillips) printed a letter from Rhode Island's Richard Coia, who'd responded to an inquiry from one of her readers saying that Bean's Freeport store stocked the concoction, which "keeps the mouth moist and has none of the drawbacks of chewing tobacco." Soon the store had received nearly 1,000 orders for its hard-to-find gum. The only problem was, L.L. Bean hadn't carried spruce gum for about a year.

Most of those who ordered the spruce gum probably wouldn't have liked the stuff anyway. Former hard goods buyer K. C. Putnam says that spruce gum was an "acquired taste," and most people who tried it found it so repulsive that they would spit it out on the floor of the store. That foul flavor may have been the reason L. L. himself used to delight in walking around his store passing the stuff out to unsuspecting customers. "[It] tasted like hell," said longtime employee Carlene Griffin with a chuckle, "but he loved it."[59]

In the end, the matter would be resolved with a simple explanation from L.L. Bean spokesperson Kilton Andrew, who admitted that the whole misunderstanding had been the Freeport firm's fault. With spruce gum now "scarcer than hen's teeth," the company, said Andrew, sent a postcard to each prospective customer explaining that "Dear Abby checked with us before writing her column and she was told in error that we carry spruce gum." Andrew asked the advice columnist to let her readers know that "our spruce gum supplier went out of business but we're looking for another. We'll let you know if we're successful."

For ages the terrible-tasting gum had been furnished to L.L. Bean by the Kennebec Spruce Gum Company, which had been run for years by Gerald F. Carr (1917–99). Carr, who also worked for the Maine Central Railroad, had taken ownership of the Kennebec Spruce Gum Company from the family of his wife, Virginia Anley Carr, and operated the business until the mid-1970s. The company had also supplied the gum to Bean competitor Lands' End.[60]

ON APRIL 26, 1986, EDDIE BAUER'S family disclosed that another of the country's pioneering outdoorsmen and merchants had passed away a week earlier. Bauer, who'd been issued a patent for his down parkas and sleeping bags in 1936, suffered a heart attack just two weeks after his eighty-two-year-old wife, Christine, had died of cancer. With the death of Eddie Bauer, Leon Gorman had lost a worthy competitor and fellow outdoorsman, but he'd endured a much more personal loss the previous December when his mother, Barbara Bean Gorman, passed away at a Portland nursing home. The last surviving child of Leon and Bertha Bean, Mrs. Gorman was seventy-eight.

IN 1986 IT WAS BUSINESS AS USUAL in Freeport, but this year some of L.L. Bean's business pertained to preliminary preparations for the company's seventy-fifth anniversary celebration to be held in September of the following year. One of the matters the company wanted to address for its celebration was the acquisition of what had always been L. L.'s favorite painting, *The Old Country Store*, by Massachusetts native Philip B. Parsons (1896–1977). So fond had Leon L. Bean been of the painting of the hunter spinning the tale of how he'd bagged the fox at his feet, that he'd used it on the covers of five of his catalogs and again on the dust jacket of his compact autobiography. He had even tried to buy it decades earlier after seeing it on the cover of *National Sportsman* magazine, but he was beaten out by just a few minutes by another bidder, Philip Babcock, a Harvard, Massachusetts, fruit grower.

More than seventy years later, L. L. Bean's heirs would still be trying to purchase that painting. Babcock had donated it to Harvard's town library, which is why, try as they might, the current owners of L.L. Bean, Inc., were still unable to acquire the painting. The library's trustees were unwilling to part with the art more because it had been a gift than because any of them particularly cared for it. Former trustee Jerry Heywood said he liked it best when it had been wrapped up and stored in the library basement during renovations.

When he gave the painting to the library, Babcock said in a letter that it reminded him of a time when Harvard was "a town that once had its own old-fashioned country store, its fox hunters and its silent, snow-enshrouded, sleigh-tracked hills from which to listen to the winter music of hounds." (The library's directors would lend the painting to L.L. Bean for its 75th anniversary celebration before donating the work to the Freeport firm in 1991. It's now kept in L.L. Bean's climate-controlled archives.)

In spite of the fact that the Freeport company had been making steadily increasing use of computers over the past decade (and maybe because of all the to-do about P. B. Parsons' bucolic painting), several current and recent newspaper articles still described L.L. Bean, Inc., of Freeport, Maine, as "low tech," "reverse chic," and even "rustic." Kilton Andrew had no problem agreeing with those labels. "We don't intend to be at the front edge at all. We don't want to be the biggest. We simply are aiming at being the best at what we do. Those products aren't intended to be avant-garde in any regard,"[61] he said. One writer concurred, saying, "It's easier to find frump than fad at L.L. Bean." Leon Gorman must have been very pleased when he read that.

One recent article related the tale of an Alaskan family whose order had to be "delivered" to them by parachute. When the package couldn't be located, they called Freeport and L.L. Bean sent out a duplicate order, free of charge. When the original shipment turned up after the spring thaw, the satisfied family kept it and sent Bean's another check.

IN THE MIDST OF ALL THIS Down East rusticity, a funny thing was happening half a world away—the sale of L.L. Bean's products started to take off in Japan. The company's sudden success in the Far East was totally unexpected. "Lo and behold," said Bean's international VP, Richard Leslie, "without the slightest attempt on our part to foster growth, we had miraculously developed a substantial and fast-growing customer base in Japan."[62] The strong support of Bean's Asian customers would spur its continued growth—sometimes even accounting for *most* of the Freeport company's growth—through the mid-1990s.

The partnership L.L. Bean had entered into in 1979 to sell a few select items, such as Bean Boots and fishing tackle, in Sony Plaza Stores in Japan would last until 1986. In 1992 Bean would partner with Seiyu, Ltd., and Matsushita Electric Industrial Co., Ltd., to operate a few stores throughout the country before acquiring them from its partners late in the decade. Seiyu would later partner with Wal-Mart and operate the Bentonville, Arkansas, company's Japanese stores under the Seiyu name.

But it wasn't just Japanese consumers who were interested in L.L. Bean. In recent years executives from several of America's top companies had visited Freeport for a VIP tour of Bean's still-expanding Distribution Center. Companies such as Xerox; Time, Inc.; IBM; J. C. Penney; and even Bean competitor Eddie Bauer all sent members of management to the coast of Maine to see how workers at the Freeport firm's 315,000-square-foot facility managed to send out the 5.8 million packages generated by the firm's 75 million catalogs. The company's secret weapon would turn out to be its people.

A few days after Christmas 1985, *Dallas Morning News* writer Jim Wright penned a response to a *New York Times* article about the executive tours, saying that all those executives could have saved themselves the trip to Freeport. "Bean has never made any attempt," he wrote, "to conceal its recipe for success, which is simply to treat its people—both customers and employees—like human beings instead of a disposable commodity."[63] Sure, the technology was very impressive but, as impressive as it was, it was only there to enable the staff to do their jobs more efficiently.

"Here is a conventional warehouse," remarked Xerox's Robert

Camp, "that is very efficient and only semi-automated." That fact shouldn't have come as a surprise: L.L. Bean has long been known for the quality of its people. "Our technology has never been state-of-the-art or cutting edge," said senior VP John Findlay. "To a certain extent, some of us hate equipment. . . . Because people don't break down."[64] During the 1985 holiday season, the staff at the Distribution Center alone doubled to 700 hourly workers.

If the executives had come in August of 1986, they'd have seen a bigger and even more impressive facility, as a 250,000-square-foot addition to the DC was nearing completion. (At 115,000 square feet when it was built in 1974, the DC had already had a 200,000-square-foot addition put on in 1979.) In the middle of the month, L.L. Bean ran the first test of its amazing tilt-tray sorter that scanned the bar codes of outgoing packages and instantly slid them into the correct mail bin. The company was also installing a computerized scale that would verify that a package contained what it was supposed to. What was in all those packages could have been almost anything. At the time, the cataloger had about 13,500 stock keeping units, or SKUs (a size 44 red Chamois Shirt would be one SKU, for example).

With 90,000 new square feet on the front of the building for reserve storage, the number of Bean's SKUs could soon increase to 60,000. The remaining 160,000 square feet, which were being added to the rear of the facility, were dedicated to shipping operations and "will allow the return processing and alterations departments, now located at the Northport Plaza in Portland, to return to Freeport."[65] (Returns would come back to Freeport in September, while customer service had moved to Northport on July 16, the day before the company's Beanery cafeteria opened at the Freeport DC.) Bean's latest expansion of its Route 1 DC had eased the need for the company's delayed Desert Road facility, though that option remained on the table while management monitored sales trends.

One problem with Bean's new giant-sized warehouse was the giant-sized tax snafu the company would run into because of it—one that would take a change in Maine law to resolve. It seems that in 1978, the state had passed a law allowing businesses that invested at least $5 million and created at least 200 new jobs to deduct from their taxes 10 percent of their investments in annual increments of $300,000. Since its new facility had cost $13 million and created 250 new jobs, L.L. Bean took the money off its taxes in 1986 and would do so again in 1987. Eighteen months after the firm's first deduction, the state's Bureau of Taxation ruled that the cataloger didn't qualify for the deductions because its new addition didn't meet the mechanical requirements used to test how many jobs had been created, since it had been in operation for only the last four months of the year.

The Bureau of Taxation ordered L.L. Bean to repay its initial $300,000 plus $38,500 in interest. But that wasn't the worst part of the problem. Since the law required businesses to meet its criteria in the first year of operation or lose any chance at the tax credit, the Freeport firm stood to lose a total of $1.3 million in tax deductions. L.L. Bean's dilemma would finally be resolved in September 1988, when the state's lawmakers voted to restructure the statute retroactively, making the company qualified for the lucrative tax break.

Another thing working in L.L. Bean's favor was the sales trend of its signature product, the Maine Hunting Shoe. Sales of the famous boot surged to 250,000, an astonishing 100,000-pair increase over 1985. But not all of Mr. Bean's famous boots were *outbound* from Freeport; in 1986 alone, customers would send back or bring in more than 17,000 pairs of their beloved Maine Hunting Shoes for some attention from the company's busy rebuild service. "For $22.75," noted one writer, "a customer in Hickory, North Carolina, receives a new rubber sole and other repairs to a 14-year-old pair of boots that now sells for $64.75."[66]

And remember the Maine Warden Jacket, the drab green, multipocketed coat that had been so unceremoniously dumped from the L.L. Bean catalog a few years earlier just because it wasn't selling? Well, it was back. Sort of. More than just getting "some redesign" like Bill End had thought it needed, the outdated, heavy wool coat was reborn in 1986 as the Maine Warden's Parka, a high-tech, breathable, down-filled clothing equivalent of the Humvee, advertised to keep its wearer warm to about 40 degrees below zero. And it was available in four conservative colors. By 2011 the "Maine Warden's 3-in-1 Parka with Gore-Tex" would still be available ($299 or $319 for tall), including a removable hood. Now M. R. Montgomery, John Hughes, and millions more just like them could once again thumb through their L.L. Bean catalogs, pause at the page with the Maine Warden's Parka, and dream.

IN 1986, L.L. BEAN, INC., made the *Forbes* magazine list of the 400 biggest privately held American companies. The only other Maine company to make the list was the Bath Iron Works shipyard. With the return of growth to his firm, Leon Gorman found himself in demand for speaking engagements, one of his most notable being with the University of Vermont's class of '86. In his address, the L.L. Bean president talked about the company's fortunes during the decade so far, including the rise and fall of Preppy-related sales—and reiterated his commitment to continuing growth through Bean's catalog-based business model as opposed to expanding into the retail store channel.

With things once again going swimmingly in Freeport, one would think that the relationship between Leon Gorman and heir-apparent Bill End would also be fine. One would be wrong. The problem now was not so much how and where L.L. Bean would sell its products as it was just *what* L.L. Bean should be selling in the first place. Because of "lifestyle positioning issues" he saw, Leon Gorman decided that he needed to remain actively involved in the product selection process. Many people at the company thought he was *too* involved.

Chief among those was, of course, Bill End, who used the example of two dressy shirts to make his point. On one hand, Gorman considered a pinpoint Oxford shirt to be "too fancy" a fabric for a catalog item. Oxford cloth was acceptable, remembers End, but not pinpoint Oxford. "Leon drew that distinction and gave up a chunk of the business."[67]

With End going for the increased profits that would come with casual clothing lines and Gorman dedicated to maintaining the company's sporting image, the other managers remained caught in the middle of a situation that would only continue to deteriorate. Sometimes, recalled John Findlay, directives from Leon Gorman and Bill End would directly contradict each other, leaving subordinates complaining on a daily basis. Bill End "would be telling them one thing," says Findlay, "and Leon would be telling them another."[68]

In 1987 L.L. BEAN OBSERVED the seventy-fifth anniversary of the first sale of Leon Leonwood Bean's crude, cobbled-together rubber and leather Maine Hunting Shoe. The company's low-key celebration of its diamond jubilee included tours of its recently upgraded Distribution Center for 200 invited guests. At a reception following the tours, President Leon Gorman said that if L. L. Bean could see his company today, he'd be pleased "that we're still selling good merchandise and we still treat our customers like human beings." Maine Governor John McKernan and L. L.'s old friend John Gould also addressed the crowd.

When asked what he thought the business would be like in twenty-five years, Gorman replied, "Probably a little bigger, but otherwise much the same." He said that he expected Bean's to double in size over the next five years. Two years later, Bean's president would reveal in an unusually candid interview something the governor had said that day: "Whether Maine is Bean or Bean is Maine," had started him thinking. "It really made an impact on me," said Gorman. "I think that periodically, the public ought to know what's going on and what our future is."[69]

On Sunday, September 13, two days after the tours, 5,600 of the company's employees, retirees, and guests flocked to Freeport's oceanfront Winslow Park. The celebration included face-painting and contradancing, featured a variety of well-known Maine entertainers including humorist Tim Sample and musicians Rick Charette and Schooner Fare, and generally "went off well in spite of the rain." The festival's celebrants "feasted on chicken, baked beans, and local products including Jordan's hot dogs, Tom's chips and Deering Ice Cream."[70] And of course there was the "massive" Bean Boot–shaped birthday cake.

The same day as the big celebration, Clark T. Irwin, Jr., wrote an anniversary feature for the *Maine Sunday Telegram*. Irwin chose not to recount the obligatory story of how L. L. had come to invent the Maine Hunting Shoe seventy-five years earlier and how ninety of the first one hundred pairs were returned for a refund—a tale with which most adult Mainers had long ago become all too familiar. He chose instead to interview Boston University marketing professor—and Bean devotee—Ronald C. Curhan. "'I have to tell you, we love Bean's,' Curhan said. It's the only place where he can find a good wool sweater with a zipper in the front, 'and if you call up, as we do, you frequently get referred to someone who really knows something about the product instead of a generic person who just takes orders and doesn't know whether it's in stock.'"

Throughout his article, Irwin sprinkled several statistics that served to illustrate the company's size and its success under Leon Gorman's command, talking about everything from the number of Bean's permanent employees (2,300), to the number of pages in its latest Christmas catalog (72), to the number of Bean Boots manufactured to date (3.5 million pairs). The piece also included a box that featured more than a dozen interesting facts about the company's history, some of which were: L.L. Bean paid $50 million in wages during 1987 (an average of $18,500 per employee), purchased $21 million worth of Maine-made goods for resale (70 percent of it from its own manufacturing facility), spent $15 million to ship 9 million packages, and sold 85 percent of its goods to out-of-staters. Bean had also made $43.9 million in capital investments in buildings and equipment over the previous five years.

Keepsakes of L.L. Bean's seventy-fifth included T-shirts, brass paperweights, and a thirty-panel quilt made by several employees, but "the most visible mark of this year's anniversary," noted one account of the celebration, "is a scrapbook-type history book published by Bean and distributed to employees and suppliers." The brainchild of Leon Gorman himself, *L. L. Bean, Inc., Outdoor Sporting Specialties: A Company Scrapbook* originally consisted of 163 pages plus a four-page introduction by John Gould, who told a local reporter, "The thing about Bean is that it's kept its character, as much as Freeport has lost its character."[71]

In the scrapbook's foreword, its authors state that they "have selected material that, in our opinion, best reflects the life of 'L. L.' and the history of the company." They also concede that "in true scrapbook fashion, some photographs and illustrations are directly related to the written material nearby, while others are merely 'stuck down' where space was available." Still, the work is a treasure trove of information for anyone with a basic understanding of L.L. Bean's chronology.

Comprised of hundreds of pictures and dozens of articles about the Freeport company, the scrapbook was assembled by book designer Bruce Kennett and noted Maine historian William David Barry. It was printed on Patina paper made by the S. D. Warren Paper Co. of Westbrook, Maine, in an edition of 10,000 copies by Portland's Anthoensen Press. The scrapbook's newspaper and magazine articles were composed in Times New Roman while the rest was printed in Bean's signature Cheltenham type. An expanded second edition of Bean's company scrapbook would be published in 2002 for the company's ninetieth anniversary, and would include an additional seventy-seven pages of text and pictures. Another L.L. Bean book project appearing during the company's seventy-fifth year was Judith Jones's *L. L. Bean Book of New New England Cookery* (New York, Random House).

A highly visible symbol of the anniversary was the colorful new label Bean's had introduced earlier in the year to complement the firm's traditional product tags. The older labels consisted of the L.L. Bean name in dark green on a sandy beige background. (Actually the company had about forty different labels at the time, but they all looked pretty much the same and were usually hidden inside the products they were attached to.) Designed to be used on Bean's "active products," the new one was "obviously a label designed to be worn on the outside of a product," said Bean's assistant product manager of trousers and sweaters, Rod Lane. "We have some sleeping bags, packs, and other items, and some apparel in the fall book that sport the new outside label," said Lane. "The apparel," he added, "carries our regular label in the collar."[72]

Leon Gorman called it the "Spirit of 75" insignia. Most people just called it something like "Sunrise Over Katahdin." Whatever you called it, Bean's bright new label featured Maine's highest peak looming over the state's dark forests and the West Branch of the Penobscot River, all framed by a yellow and red sunrise. At the bottom of the whole thing, in the foreground, was "LLBean" in big white letters trimmed in red. The label frequently included the phrase, "An Outdoor Tradition Since 1912."

Previously the Freeport firm had preferred to let its products speak for themselves, but now decided the new label helped it distinguish itself in the marketplace. To Gorman the message of the new label mimicked his perception of L.L. Bean: Katahdin (whose name means "the greatest mountain" in Abenaki) always seems to remain the same despite small daily changes. In typical Bean fashion, the new label would soon beget a more subdued version, featuring only three colors in addition to the company's name: blue (for the sky and water), green (for the trees and foothills), and purple (for the mountains and borders of the letters).

Though it was turning seventy-five, Bean's practical take on apparel still resonated in at least some areas of the fashion world. One of those places was a new quarterly magazine called *Ricochet*. Named after the French child's game of skipping stones on a pond, the new periodical purported to mimic the stones' path and "follow the migratory path of new ideas which skip over boundaries, rebound and come to rest in unexpected places in Europe and North America." An article in the magazine's premiere issue described how European designers had been inspired by American companies such as L.L. Bean, Brooks Bros., and Sebago, Inc. An interesting policy of the magazine was to print each feature article in English as well as the original language of its author.

Though it wasn't part of his company's seventy-fifth anniversary celebration, Leon Gorman accomplished his own noteworthy feat in 1987 when he climbed Mt. Rainier in Washington State. Gorman, who'd met Jim Whittaker in 1980 when the two men were inducted into Woolrich's Outdoors Hall of Fame, was invited by the mountaineer to join a small party attempting to climb the 14,410-foot peak. It was by far the toughest climb Gorman had ever attempted; high winds blew over the climbers' tents and they had to slog through nearly waist-deep snow to reach the summit. Once there, the adventurers were rewarded with a crystal-clear day that afforded them a spectacular view including the smoking remains of Mount St. Helens on the horizon. (Mt. St. Helens is 50 miles southwest of Mt. Rainier.)

During the trip, Whittaker pitched the idea for an international "Peace Climb" of Mount Everest. The climb was a Herculean task that would take three years to come to fruition in time for the twentieth anniversary of Earth Day. The president of L.L. Bean jumped at the chance to be part of what promised to be a groundbreaking expedition. It meshed perfectly with the company's image, and it would give the entire town of Freeport something to get behind. Putting his money where his mouth was, he saw to it that L.L. Bean, Inc., backed the effort with gear, clothing, and a $100,000 grant. In 1990 he'd even join three others from L.L. Bean on the slopes of the world's highest peak, following a preparatory ascent of Tanzania's Mount Kilimanjaro in 1989.

BEGINNING ITS SEVENTY-FIFTH YEAR of operation, L.L. Bean boasted an annual sales figure of $368.5 million for fiscal year 1986, giving the resurgent Freeport company sales averaging a million dollars a day. This latest growth spurt bumped Bean's average growth rate to 15 percent over the past five years (a period which included the last year of the Preppy boom and the two lean years following it). And the news was going to get better, with revenues continuing to soar to the point where the company would go on to finish 1987 with an increase of a whopping 33.9 percent, to more than $493 million in annual sales.

In March 1987 the New York mail-order tracking firm Maxwell Sroge Publishing, citing "total 1985 sales," ranked L.L. Bean seventh, behind such catalogers as Spiegel, Sears, J. C. Penney, and Lands' End, with "sales of $219.6 million," a figure the company had surpassed back in 1982. (Bean's actual 1985 figure had been $303.8 million, which would have moved it into fifth place on the list, ahead of Lands' End and Brylane, Inc.) In December 1987,

Forbes got it right by ranking L.L. Bean 323rd among the nation's 400 largest private firms with 1986 sales of $368 million and 2,300 permanent employees. The only other Maine company to make Forbes's list that year was again Bath Iron Works, which was 185th with annual sales of $622 million and 7,700 workers. On a related note, researchers at the Harvard Business School issued an updated version of the original case study they'd done on the Freeport company in 1965.

L.L. Bean was also recognized by the readers of *Consumer Reports*, who rated the mail-order company number one over forty-seven other catalogers in an August survey. According to the magazine, "More than nine out of ten respondents said they were satisfied with the company's products. L.L. Bean won first place in every category where it had a product."[73]

A story that illustrates the company's level of service very well was related in a letter from "L. S." to the *Seattle Times* during its "Rate the Catalogs" survey, in which the Freeport company also placed first. When he was injured in a fall, L. S. had to have the sleeve of his favorite chamois shirt slit open by a nurse who needed to take his blood pressure. "A couple of weeks after I got out of the hospital," L. S. told the paper, "I mailed the shirt to L. L. Bean with a letter telling them how pleased I was with how well the shirt had stood up to everything—except the emergency-room shears. L.L. Bean mailed me a brand-new shirt and reimbursed me for postage for the one I had sent back!"

But not all aspects of Bean's seventy-fifth year were particularly memorable. The company continued to battle Drake Publishing to the conclusion of its lawsuit over the 1984 *High Society* "L. L. Beam's Back-to-School Sex Catalogue" parody. When we last left the fight in 1986, U.S. District Court Judge Gene Carter had ordered Drake Publishing not to further distribute its catalog parody and not to publish a facsimile of the L.L. Bean trademark again. So far, so good.

But the case would sour for L.L. Bean in 1987, beginning in February when Boston Appeals Court Judge Hugh H. Bownes overruled Judge Carter, writing that "although parody is often offensive, it is nevertheless deserving of substantial freedom as entertainment and as a form of social and literary criticism. It would be anomalous," he continued, "to [diminishing] the protections afforded parody solely because the parodist chose a famous trade name rather than a famous person."[74]

L.L. Bean was unwilling to settle for such a ruling. Determined to see the case—which had now passed through the courts of Bangor, Portland, and Boston—through to the end, the Freeport firm decided the matter was headed to Washington and appealed to the U.S. Supreme Court in early March. Few lawyers thought L.L. Bean could win, even if the Supreme Court did agree to hear the case. University of Maine Law School professor David D. Gregory weighed in on the matter by observing that "the law on prior restraint of First Amendment freedoms all comes from cases decided by the United States Supreme Court, so the chances of reversal are small."

In late June, Professor Gregory would be proven correct when the Supreme Court let stand the lower court's ruling that Maine's trademark law could not be invoked to suppress the *High Society* parody of Bean's catalog, saying that "using a state trademark law to squelch satiric material would violate freedom of speech." In early October L.L. Bean and Drake Publishing reached an out-of-court settlement for the still-pending $16-million lawsuit for an undisclosed sum.

Just as the *High Society* case was winding down, L.L. Bean suddenly found itself in the middle of another legal dustup, again involving the company's famous catalog—only this time Bean was the defendant in the matter. The cataloger's latest legal problems started when someone at the company authorized changes to the artwork Danbury, Connecticut, artist Walt Spitzmiller had submitted for the cover of the firm's fall 1986 catalog without first consulting him. In February Spitzmiller's attorney, William Laviano, filed suit against L.L. Bean in the Bridgeport, Connecticut, District Court seeking unspecified damages, including any profits the firm made from using his painting, and to have the company destroy any copies it made of his work.

Spitzmiller, who'd done all the covers for the company's seasonal catalogs in 1986, accused Bean of giving the bird hunter in his painting a yuppie look by changing the hat he was wearing and removing his beard. L.L. Bean also removed pigmentation from the face of the hunter's golden retriever, Slick. "It's a good thing the dog can't sue them," said the artist, adding that his original retriever had looked like a real dog while Bean's version "looks like something from F.A.O. Schwarz."[75] Spitzmiller, who'd been painting since 1969, alleged in his suit that L.L. Bean breached its contract with him and damaged his reputation, and also violated copyright, artist's authorship, and fair trade practices. *Newsweek* dubbed the matter "L.L. Bean vs. the Preppified Pooch," while a headline in the *Portland Press Herald* succinctly described the artist as "'Yup'-set."

In 1986, L.L. Bean put 75 million copies of its 21 different catalogs into the mail. Though continued growth in both the numbers of titles and quantities of L.L. Bean catalogs sent out were pretty much business as usual for the Freeport company, one interesting new catalog the firm was debuting was its Women's Specialty catalog. "It was a longtime dream for us to do a women's book," said Betsy Kelly, product manager for Women's Casual Apparel. "When we decided to do a Women's Specialty, the merchandising committee gave us a lot of direction, they really wanted to see an active women's book."

Launched in the spring with a standard test book circulation of 500,000, the new catalog featured several new items and colors not found in Bean's regular circulars. "A lot of the uniqueness comes from additional colors," noted Kelly, "brighter and a little more feminine, like the rose and lavender shades we're running in the trail model vest." Did this new direction mean Leon Gorman had softened his stance on casual wear? Probably not—remember, merchandising wanted an "active" book.

WITH ALL THE SALES GENERATED by those millions of catalogs, it was time for L.L. Bean to look outside of Freeport—and even outside of Maine—for places to expand its operations. The company found itself in need of more manufacturing space, more space for its returns and overstocks, more warehouse space and, of course, more room for its ever-expanding staff of telemarketers. One step the firm took to alleviate overcrowding was the stopgap measure of relocating the manufacture of some of its Bean Boots and hand-sewn uppers to a leased factory about fifteen miles away in the Lisbon Falls Industrial Park. In a few years, Lisbon Manufacturing would be absorbed into Bean's new Brunswick facility.

In February 1987 Bean's "signed a 100-day option to purchase an undisclosed site in North Conway, New Hampshire. But the company said that's not necessarily the site it is going to go into."[76] "It" was an outlet store, which would eventually be located in a new mini mall going up in town. By October the North Conway planning board had approved developer Stanley Tanger's plan to construct a 49,000-square-foot mall on Route 16, about a third of which would house the first L.L. Bean Factory Outlet Store. Tanger's site plan passed by a three–two vote despite the group's misgivings about potential traffic problems caused by the nearly 300 cars entering and exiting the mall during peak hours. "I think what carried it," said the board's chairman, William Crowley, "was the threat of a lawsuit if it wasn't approved."[77] The L.L. Bean store, which would share the mall with six to eight smaller shops, would open on April 18, 1988, and carry "rejects and discontinued items" from the company's Freeport headquarters. (As of 2011 the L.L. Bean Factory Outlet Store is still there.)

In April L.L. Bean had announced its decision to locate its second new call center in two years in the city of Lewiston, which had prevailed in the company's selection process over Augusta, the Saco-Sanford area, and Bangor and despite some serious lobbying by the midcoast towns of Rockland and Belfast. While Lewiston hadn't offered L.L. Bean any special incentives for locating there, the cataloger chose the city on the Androscoggin simply because it was the closest to Freeport. Lewiston also offered a very attractive piece of property right in the city's downtown—the former Peck's Department Store, which had sat vacant for much of the past six years. Lewiston Telemarketing would open with many of its 125 permanent workers on June 20, 1988. By fall, the call center would employ as many as an additional 500 seasonal operators.

While Bean's call center in Lewiston was gearing up, more L.L. Bean growth was taking place in Portland during 1987 and 1988—much more. While the company's finance and operations research personnel were still getting settled in from their April move to the firm's new Deering Building, which it shared with Prudential, the company's order entry and control people were relocating to its recently expanded Northport facility nearby. The firm also located its Portland Pallet Facility across town, in the McAlister Farms subdivision just off Warren Avenue. The L.L. Bean warehouse there consists of offices and sixteen loading docks. "PPF people," said the company's *Bean Scene* newsletter, "receive, store, pick, process, and ship pre-pack merchandise."

Two other Bean warehouses, the Annex and CanCo (formerly American Can Co.), are located in another area of Maine's largest city, two miles away on Read Street, just off Forest Avenue. The CanCo building is where merchandise destined for the retail store and new North Conway outlet is "tagged and inventoried," while the green metal Annex across the street is where the cataloger stores cardboard, computer forms, and oversized pre-packs. (The author worked as a bicycle assembler at the Annex in the early nineties; workers there also mounted bindings on cross-country skis.)

Back in Freeport, the company had purchased L. L. Bean's home near the store from his estate. Initially the firm would use its founder's Holbrook Street residence as offices for its Facilities Management before constructing a climate-controlled addition to hold the company's archives, which would be formally established in 1994.

For 1988 L.L. Bean's growth continued at such a pace that it was described as a resurgence, even though the firm had been thriving for the past few years. "Bean's resurgence is all the more remarkable," reported the *Washington Post*, "because it has come amid a slowdown—and perhaps a shakeout—in the once booming catalogue business."[78] While the *Post*'s conclusion was correct at the time it was printed, it would turn out that the Down East retailer was simply lagging behind the curve. As is the case with many trends, the nationwide mail-order slowdown was just taking a little longer to reach northern New England.

For the time being, at least, life was good in Freeport. The company was projecting sales of $500 million for the year, which would put it 20 percent ahead of 1987, when sales had surged 36 percent (Bean would actually end up doing $586 million in 1988). The retail store alone accounted for $70 million in sales, while the 90 million catalogs the company sent out pulled in the other $520 million, at an average rate of $67 for every order taken, filled, and guaranteed by Bean's hardworking staff. And somewhere in there was the $5 million the firm made on its Japanese sales. This all worked out to a return of better than $5.55 per catalog mailed—versus a break-even point of $1.25—in spite of a recent 30 percent increase in the price of postage and a 15 percent jump in the cost of paper.

While success may very well be its own reward, Leon Gorman and his company were no strangers to accolades from others, nor to the notion of sharing some of that success with the community. In December Gorman was awarded the William and Mary's 1988 Business Medallion for representing "the highest standards of professionalism and integrity in the practice of management." During the presentation, he was praised for his "'deep concern for the preservation of the human and old-fashioned commercial values' of the company's founder." Recently, Bean's president had also served as campaign chairperson for the Greater Portland United Way. Also in 1988, Bean's earmarked $1 from each caribou T-shirt sold for a project to reintroduce the animals to Maine, and donated $600,000 to a foundation to raise the aspirations of Maine students.

And even more than twenty years after his death, Gorman's grandfather, Leon L. Bean, showed he was still able to garner an honor of his own, when a sketch of the outdoorsman and merchant was included in the latest edition of *The Dictionary of American Biography*.

In the spring, the Freeport planning board approved the company's plans to expand its retail store for the third time in thirteen years. The $6 million project, said Bean's Kilton Andrew, was designed to allow the retailer to display a wider variety of its merchandise in order to cope with a sharp increase in shoppers at the flagship store. Besides a sizable addition to the front of the store, Bean's plan also called for a brick plaza with a small pond and waterfall feature at what would be the new entrance off Morse Street. "Essentially we're trying to create a village center for Freeport with this plaza," emphasized executive vice president of marketing Bill End. "Our intention with this expansion is not to increase business but to improve the shopping experience."[79]

With the latest incarnation of the retail store giving over the factory store's third-floor space to more room for retail merchandise, the cataloger decided to set up a separate factory outlet down the hill just across Main Street. But with renovation of the 10,000-square-foot former Eastland Shoe building not due to be completed until late the following June, the company was in a bind when it came to finding a space for its late-fall warehouse sale. As for Eastland Shoe, it would continue to operate its larger factory out on Route 1 for another dozen or so years.[80]

Bean's solution to its temporarily missing factory store was to hold a sale in a small warehouse down the street. A week after the sale ended, the *New York Times* reported that more than a thousand people had flocked to the sale's opening day, some of them waiting in the half-mile-long line for up to two hours. With a regional shortage of seasonal workers plaguing the firm, the event was staffed primarily by its salaried employees. "This has been in the spirit of the quilting bee," Kilton Andrew told the *Times*, "or a barn raising."

The sale ran from November 25 through December 11, 8:00 A.M. to 10:00 P.M. with continuous shuttle bus service running between the retail store and Davis Warehouse from 10:00 to 8:00. The company even printed a letter-size map for those choosing to walk to the sale down on West Street. One executive who worked the event's opening day was Leon Gorman, who "quickly found that he would have to overcome his desire for tidy shelves."[81]

But not everybody in town was enthralled with the retailer's recent expansion plans. By October, when construction on the latest addition was already well underway, some homeowners whose houses lined Morse Street, behind the store, began to make their feelings known. "It's lousy," said Dennis Daniel, one of the affected homeowners, whose house sits a hundred feet from the building's entrance. "We're stuck. We've got a piece of property that can't be sold. People who have shown any interest don't want it as a residence." The reason that no one wanted to move into the area, explained Daniel, was because of the traffic that circled through the neighborhood looking for places to park. People have parked in his driveway, he said, camped on his lawn, and even used it as a urinal.

Nine of the street's eighteen residents wanted to have the neighborhood rezoned to allow for commercial development so they could sell their homes and recoup their investments, like homeowners along Main Street had done back in 1983. When Daniel's plight was featured in the *New York Times*, he'd been trying to sell his house for five months. In response to the complaints, the town put up no-trespassing signs, beefed up police patrols, and worked with the retailer to construct a parking lot that would divert traffic away from the homes. As for the rezoning proposal, Freeport town planner Jackie Cohen sympathized with the homeowners' problem but said that she was opposed to rezoning the neighborhood except in the unlikely event that one company presented a development plan for the entire area.

Doing what it could to address its parking problems, in January L.L. Bean had struck a deal with Aero Tech, a manufacturer of wire for furnace filters and finished filters to do a land swap. As its part of the deal, Bean would build a new 34,500-square-foot facility in a Brunswick industrial park at a cost of more than $700,000. Once L.L. Bean took ownership of the parcel at the corner of Mill and Oak Streets in Freeport, the old building would go the way of the old Loree Shoe factory, being razed to make way for a 49,000-square-foot, 187-car parking lot. "Ultimately," said Kilton Andrew, "the Brunswick industrial park property and building will be transferred to Aero Tech."

ALSO PROVING PROBLEMATIC for L.L. Bean in 1988 were the political aspirations of L. L.'s forty-six-year-old granddaughter (and

Leon's cousin) Linda, the older of Warren's two girls. Often referred to by the press as "the L. L. Bean heiress," the conservative Linda Bean-Jones announced in February that she planned to challenge Ted O'Meara in the June 14 primary to see who'd square off against former two-term governor and first-term Democratic Congressman Joseph E. Brennan in November. Though Bean-Jones, a Hallowell real estate agent who'd inherited the bulk of her money following the 1974 death of L. L. Bean's second wife, had never before run for office, she was already well known to many on Maine's political scene.

Described as a "bubbly liberal" when she attended Ohio's Antioch College, her views changed drastically as she got older. Four years after divorcing first husband, James Clark, in 1971, she married Windsor farmer Verne Jones and began her political transformation. In 1979 she started the conservative *Maine Paper* in Hallowell, in which her name appeared as Linda Jones. The weekly tabloid, which she subsidized, lost money and survived for just less than three years. Bean-Jones also formed the Maine Impact Coalition, which helped elect conservative candidates to the state legislature. She had also worked as a fundraiser for the Reagan-Bush ticket in 1980 and 1984, and was a regular at state Republican conventions.

After Jones's paper folded, she helped raise nearly $300,000 to help overwhelmingly defeat Maine's Equal Rights Amendment in 1984. In 1987 she worked with the Hannibal Hamlin Institute to try to defeat the Land for Maine's Future referendum, a $35 million bond to secure public access to land and water, which was overwhelmingly approved by the voters. (More than two decades later, LMF had raised an additional $62 million through two more bonds and protected 444,000 acres of Maine land.) A May 29 article in the *Boston Globe* noted that her eight-page campaign biography listed more than thirty-five groups with which she'd been associated, but made "no mention . . . of her membership in two of the most controversial and high-profile groups of the New Right: Phyllis Schlafly's Eagle Forum and the National Conservative Political Action Committee."

With all this in her past, Jones, "who used to sport brown hair, glasses, and a few extra pounds, slimmed down and emerged as a blonde with contact lenses."[82] She made a point of traveling to Freeport to tell Leon Gorman that she wanted to avoid any conflict with L.L. Bean during her candidacy. "She wanted to sincerely distance herself from us," said Gorman. That was fine with him, but she also hyphenated her last name for increased recognition (becoming Linda Bean-Jones), which caused her opponent, Ted O'Meara, to lament that there were many days when he felt like he'd taken on Maine's best-loved sporting-goods store.

The state's political pundits felt Linda Bean-Jones would have a hard time getting elected to Maine's 1st District congressional seat unless she was able to appeal to more than just the conservative faithful. Loyall Sewall, chairman of the Republican State Committee, said he was "getting out" if Bean-Jones planned to run on "a right-to-life, fundamentalist, Pat Robertson-type of ticket."[83] During her announcement address, Bean-Jones seemed determined to soften her image by promising "to do more hard work, more coalition building, more thoughtful articulating of the issues, more walking and more listening in order to do more for Maine."

In the end, Linda Bean-Jones, who'd spent more than $639,213, including $559,095 of her own money, would end up losing, 49 percent to 51 percent, to Ted O'Meara, who'd raised only about $65,000. At that rate Bean-Jones had spent $42 for each of her 15,195 votes, while each of the 15,507 votes O'Meara received had cost him about $4. This time around, probably the biggest flap Linda Bean had caused was by inserting her maiden name and her money into things. "[Voters] are not very forgiving of heavy spending in a campaign," she observed, "when it so outdistances a challenger." But she would try again in 1992, when she'd make even bigger waves.

AND SPEAKING OF POLITICS, when President Reagan announced the Malcolm Baldrige National Quality Award in 1988, Leon Gorman attended the White House ceremony, and was so impressed by the belief that quality and productivity could go hand in hand, he decided to have his company compete for the award. Gorman saw the competition not only as a way to restore some luster to the L.L. Bean name, but to improve his company from top to bottom in the process. It was a matter of prestige.

The award had recently been established in honor of Reagan administration commerce secretary Malcolm Baldrige, who'd died in July 1987 at the age of sixty-four. (He was taking part in a California steer-roping competition when his horse reared up and landed on him.) The award was created to stimulate increased productivity and superior quality in American industry.

The Freeport firm submitted a 169-page application, which got it into the finals. And then came a three-day visit by Baldrige Award inspectors. But L.L. Bean didn't win a National Quality Award in either of the two categories, manufacturing and service, in which it was being judged. (Companies such as Federal Express and Xerox also failed to receive awards.) Gorman was told that his company was the highest-ranked service company in the competition, and was also judged to be "world class" in its commitment to customer satisfaction—but that wasn't enough. (The Maine Hunting Shoe had recently topped *Fortune* magazine's list of 100 American-made products "considered to be the finest of their kind.")

The problem, said the Baldrige people, was Bean's reliance on fixing problems instead of preventing them. The Baldrige inspectors found the company lacking because it took a reactive "inspection-oriented approach" instead of concentrating its efforts on initial quality. In other words, L.L. Bean was relying too much on its 100 percent guarantee. The cataloger, said senior vice president and COO Bob Peixotto, was spending too much time and money fixing problems with products that had already made it to the customer.

The costs of poor quality to the company were enormous. Noting that Bean's promised 100 percent satisfaction or your money back, the *Wall Street Journal* reported that "the problem is, lots of customers aren't satisfied. [In 1988], they returned $82 million worth of goods, or about 14 percent of Bean's $588 million in sales. The returns cost Bean $18 million in shipping and handling costs—

and a National Quality Award for service from the Commerce Department."[84] The *Journal* went on to point out that most of Bean's returned goods came from people who ordered the same item in two or three sizes or colors and returned the ones they didn't want. Only a small percentage of returned merchandise, it said, came back because of defects.

Instead of fretting over missing out on the award, Bean's president used the situation as an opportunity to implement what he felt were some much-needed changes in the company. Gorman used the critique from the Baldridge people "as kind of the kick-off point to getting into the total quality movement here in Bean."[85]

And he was serious about making changes, even if it meant putting the brakes on Bean's growth for a while. Leon Gorman didn't mind fewer new customers, "as long as we do it right," he said, adding that he would like to see the company grow at a rate of about 5 to 8 percent over the next few years. This was from the company that had realized an average growth rate of 23 percent over the past decade and had had hopes of reaching $1 billion in sales by 1992. "It's a good thing we're not a publicly-owned company," he said. "We don't have to worry about earnings."[86] (Estimates put Bean's 1988 after-tax earnings at about 7 percent of sales, compared to 1986's 6 percent.) The one thing Leon Gorman needn't have concerned himself with was slowing his company's growth—the recession would take care of that part for him. He added that L.L. Bean would spend about $2 million in 1989 and 1990 to improve its service.

Two years after L.L. Bean had finished fêting it's seventy-fifth successful year in the outdoor sporting specialty business, Freeport commenced another celebration, this one a week-long observance of the town's 200th anniversary of independence from North Yarmouth. L.L. Bean's contribution to the town's bicentennial celebration included offering its Casco Street parking lot as a staging area for the parade, and providing personnel and funds to publish the *Freeport Bicentennial Commemorative Journal*, edited by Sarah Wiley.

An appearance by Ronald McDonald—and the fact that he was spared the fate that had befallen the unfortunate Professor O. C.

Howe E. Landsdown at Freeport's observance of Maine's centennial in 1920—provided some evidence that the town was, perhaps, finally coming to grips with its emerging outlet identity. (Professor Landsdown, you'll recall, was the stuffed dummy who'd been tossed off the roof of L. L. Bean's Warren Block during the celebration. He got caught on the power lines and had to be rescued by the fire department.)

In the spring, L.L. Bean finished out the 1980s by being named Cataloger of the Decade at *Catalog Age*'s American Catalog Awards in Chicago. "We were recognized," said Leon Gorman, "for doing a consistently excellent job year after year." Specifically, L.L. Bean, Inc., won the Gold Award for its 1988 Spring Women's Outdoor Specialties, and Gold and Silver in the Sporting Goods category for its 1988 circulars, Hunting Specialties and Spring Sporting Specialties. "Catalogs were judged not on aesthetics but on their 'estimated effectiveness as a selling tool, customer service practices, copy, precise targeting, concept, and user friendliness.'"[87]

The fact that the awards' fifteen judges hadn't ranked the competing catalogs based on their aesthetics probably worked in favor of Bean's entries, since some people continued to view the Freeport firm's circulars as being on the dated side. An uncredited writer for the *Denver Post* opined, "What may be 'hunt couture' to me is still haute couture to millions of fans who in these days of Neiman-Marcus catalog excesses enjoy the novelty of seeing the same bulky, reassuring styles in the same solids or checks with nary a shoulder pad or designer twist in sight." And all of it was still being modeled by Bean's very own employees.

The writer, who probably had yet to see one of Bean's new women's catalogs, continued:

> Inside the world of L.L. Bean, browns, tans, and primary colors abound, just as they did decades ago. At least 20 different styles of the same moccasin/loafer are shown, each with its own special feature.
>
> Dozens of plaid flannel shirts, corduroy slacks, windbreakers, and parkas decorate the pages where so much information

is printed it gives me vertigo.

Titles, sizes, numbers, colors, prices, washing instructions—but the customers love it. No ads, no whopping prices, nothing shocking.[88]

All retailers were feeling the effects of the recently slumping economy, but Bean was one of the ones being singled out by the experts for being more to blame for its situation than the others. Other companies, they pointed out, sell products similar to those offered by Bean, but "in flashier packages." And change, said Paul Shain of Milwaukee's Robert W. Baird & Co., doesn't come quickly to a cataloger the size of L.L. Bean. "It's tough for a company like them to turn on a dime."[89] This perception of the company's wares lingered on in spite of the fact that, according to one report, "about 30 percent of the 6,000-item Bean line comes and goes each year."

One major change the company had made to its catalog acknowledged that not all of its recipients lived in places as white as rural Maine. "There was agreement that doing it would have temporary financial implications," an unidentified former manager told the *Maine Times*. "But the question was whether the company would take a moral position to step into the mainstream of society." Though it had taken two years of discussion to get it done, L.L. Bean finally included an African American in its seventy-seven-year-old catalog. The person selected to appear in four of the company's 1989 publications was Bean employee Cheryl Bascom. Bean spokesperson Kilton Andrew thought there'd be "some adverse comment" but to his surprise, there wasn't any. At the time, blacks made up only 2 percent of the Freeport firm's catalog customers.

One person for whose taste L.L. Bean's catalog offerings had changed too much was curmudgeonly commentator Andy Rooney, who went so far as to pen a piece bemoaning the discontinued availability of his favorite pair of pants:

I bought a pair of khaki pants in Maine from L.L. Bean five years ago, and they're a little tattered now, but they're still my second all-time favorite piece of clothing. My favorite was a pair of flannel pajamas I had when I was eight, which, much to my annoyance, my mother threw out when I was nine. I called L.L. Bean to order several more pairs of those khaki pants, and, wouldn't you know, they no longer have them. That figures. One of the characteristics of a favorite piece of clothing is that it can't be replaced. It doesn't matter that you look for the identical thing in the same store. Either they don't have it, or the second one is not as good.[90]

While the pros and cons of Bean's catalog design and layout remained a very subjective matter, lessons learned from the firm's participation in the Baldrige Awards were being looked at very objectively by the firm's management. Leon Gorman reiterated his commitment to improving his company in the areas of quality and efficiency, even if those improvements came at the cost of growing the business. Improvements in products would now take priority over increases in sales, which were going through a slow period anyway.

L.L. Bean hired Harvard professor David Garvin, author of the recently published *Managing Quality: The Strategic and Competitive Edge*, to help set the company right. What came out of the consultation was the Total Quality program, and the first step in the process would be to get all of Bean's people on board. Once this had been accomplished, the company could focus on the application of tools such as industrial engineering, process measurement, and statistics. In order to cut down on the number of returns, the company also planned to revise its catalogs so the merchandise was depicted more accurately and described in more detail; it would also retrain employees to help them find out what customers really wanted.

The training of Bean's 3,570 permanent employees involved "722 flip charts and lots of facilitation." But for all the cataloger's best efforts, Total Quality was in for a rough road. Two years later, Professor Garvin would say that the company had unfrozen the status quo and was in the midst of reshaping the organization, but, said Bean's Chris McCormick, most of Bean's managers doubted that this was what the company needed to turn its fortunes around. The development of Quality Action Teams, which were meant to solve specific problems, ended up only leading to turf battles among managers. Long after it was over, McCormick said that the Total Quality program died from lack of support. He figured 99 percent of the company's managers at the time "didn't do anything with it."

IN THE FALL OF 1989, nine elected Soviet officials were escorted around Freeport by Senate Majority Leader George Mitchell. In Maine as part of the contingent's mission to study the "positive" aspects of capitalism, the group naturally had to stop at the state's most famous store. During their visit to Bean's, the visitors were given gifts including an L.L. Bean Tote Bag and a T-shirt commemorating the upcoming International Peace Climb of Mt. Everest. The only purchase made by the group was when Senator Mitchell bought a wool sweater for the granddaughter of the group's leader, Yevgeniy Primakov, chairman of the Council of the Union of the USSR Supreme Soviet.

"There are many positive things here," said Primakov. "So of course we want to be good students." But it would not be wise, he added, for his country to "blindly follow" the American experence. The Soviets, he said, shouldn't copy the "negative" aspects of capitalism that are "incompatible with our system."[91] The delegation, which had already visited Washington, would make more stops in Kansas, California, Pennsylvania, and New York. Twelve days after the group's visit to L.L. Bean, the Berlin Wall would fall, marking the beginning of the end of the Soviet Union.

One of the highlights of the Soviets' late-October visit was their tour of the newly expanded retail store, which had held its customary pre-Memorial Day grand opening on May 26. Coming in at 40,000 square feet (including the renovation of 13,000 square feet of the old building), the year-long, $6 million project nearly doubled the size of the store's sales space to 90,000 square feet, with another 6,000 being allocated to storage and offices. "What we're trying to do is simply meet the existing flow," said Bean spokesperson Kilt Andrew. "The project was not in anticipation of growth, but simply to catch up."

All departments gained space in the remodel, Andrew said, especially men's and women's clothing. The revised store also featured much larger camping and sporting-goods departments, and even had a space for maps. "We'd rather have our people there to serve people," said Andrew, "than running to get another size or color from stock somewhere." The new store's decor also included a diorama featuring a stuffed deer, bear, and coyote.

Much of the new addition occupied the footprint of the old Warren Block, which had housed L. L.'s original store and had been razed in 1977. The ledge at the corner of Morse and Main Streets was to be smashed as part of the project's landscaping, a phase that was scheduled to be completed in late May or early June. While the expansion had cost Bean's some of its parking spaces at the front of the store, the company more than made up for them by reworking its Morse Street lot and constructing a new one at Oak and Mill Streets on the old Aero Tech site. Landscaping for the addition included a plaza with plants, benches, and a small water feature. Once that had been completed, the revamped store's main entrance off Main Street was expected to open in July.

"Come right on in, folks, and get a road map; you need it," said Justin Williams as he greeted people at the store's temporary entrance on Morse Street. Williams seemed to be in awe of how big the store he'd known so well had recently become. "The people are just starting to roll in. I retired here ten years ago," said Williams. "I was a regular bridge partner of L. L. years ago."[92] The company was expecting more than 4 million visitors to its store in 1989.

It was also expanding itself out of Freeport. The opening of L.L. Bean's new manufacturing facility on July 17, 1989, would mark the first time in the firm's history that none of its products were made in L. L. Bean's adopted hometown, where he'd perfected his Maine Hunting Shoe in 1912. Like the expansion of the retail store, the 130,000-square-foot plant in a Brunswick industrial park just off Church Street had also cost about $6 million, for which the Finance

Authority of Maine issued SMART-E (secondary market tax exempt) bonds. Nearly 80 percent of the 15-year, 7.7 percent interest bonds were sold in Maine.

The new facility employed 240 workers who'd formerly worked in Freeport and another 40 from Lewiston. By the spring of 1991, many of the 100 employees at Bean's Lisbon Falls leather-cutting plant would be transferred to Brunswick following the consolidation of the two facilities. Bean's new factory featured ergonomic workstations plus an exercise room with rowing machines, stationary bikes, and weights.

But the Freeport firm's expansion plans weren't confined just to Maine's southern coastline. L.L. Bean also had its sights set on a couple of sites farther Down East. The location of the cataloger's newest Factory Store in Ellsworth would be the 12,500-square-foot building formerly occupied by Pat's IGA. The company began a $1.5 million remodel of the twenty-year-old cinder-block-and-steel building in late 1989, again shooting for a pre-Memorial Day opening, which would come on May 25, 1990. The store's High Street location was selected because that street also happens to be busy Routes 1 and 3, the primary road to Bar Harbor and Acadia National Park. This would give the new store a summertime traffic count of 24,000 cars a day. "It's like downtown Manhattan," said Joseph Boulos, president of the Boulos Co., which selected the site. This new outlet store would employ about 25 people and have 150 parking spots.

Bean's Kilton Andrew was quick to point out that the firm's third new outlet store in two years did not in any way indicate a shift toward the retail sector. "This is clearly not a signal of an unfolding series of retail stores for L.L. Bean," he said. "These several facilities are to solve one problem and that's the best approach to liquidating discontinued, irregular merchandise. For the shopper who is intending to find what they're looking for in one stop, Freeport remains it." Andrew added that the mail-order business "is what we always have been and will continue to be. That's our specialty."

L.L. Bean, Inc., had also recently purchased a 234-acre parcel of land on Route 202 in Hampden, right next to Bangor. It was here, in the Ammo Industrial Park, that the cataloger was planning to build its first distribution facility outside of Freeport. The company's plans for the site called for a $50 million Distribution Center that would have been operational by 1992 with as many as 500 full-time employees, but Bean's would eventually abandon the project in favor of its Desert Road facility in Freeport. L.L. Bean never developed the Hampden site, and sold it to the Town of Hampden for $360,000 in 2004.

Not to be outdone by its biggest business, the Town of Freeport had recently given the intersection of Main and Bow Streets, across from Bean's flagship store, an award-winning makeover. Though the improvements to the junction appear to consist of little more than a crosswalk and turning lanes at the end of Bow Street, the project was deemed worthy of an Engineering Excellence award in the Consulting Engineers of Maine competition. The intersection was designed by the Falmouth office of T. Y. Lin International, which conducted the downtown Freeport traffic circulation and parking study for the town.

Given all of L.L. Bean's recent physical expansion, it appeared as if the Freeport firm was enjoying an unprecedented period of prosperity. It wasn't. Though the catalog giant was still far from being strapped financially, it was experiencing another slowdown just a few short years after it had extricated itself from its post-Preppy blue period. As part of his drive toward Total Quality, Bean president Leon Gorman had made a conscious decision to slow his company's growth, but even his modest prediction of $640 million in sales for fiscal year 1989 would prove to be optimistic, with the actual figure turning out to be just $618 million.

As a result of the slowdown, the company's seasonal workers received a Christmas gift of just $20 while the regulars found the amount of their annual gift cut in half to $50. The smaller Christmas gifts foreshadowed the cut that would be made to the company's annual bonus, which would be a far cry from the amount to which Bean's employees had become accustomed.

L.L. Bean's return on equity had fallen from about 30 percent in

1975 to about 15 percent in 1990, with much of the company's decline having taken place in the late eighties. Gorman placed much of the blame for his company's "precipitous decline in profitability" on its increased selling and operating costs, which earlier in the decade had been offset by its double-digit growth rate. Bean's recent switch to lifestyle merchandising had quadrupled the firm's number of stock keeping units to 60,000 (55 varieties of boots alone). Along with all those SKUs came increases in the costs of everything from merchandising to warehousing to returns, and a six-fold increase in expensive catalog mailings. But even with all those additional catalogs, managers were fighting for space for their products. "We were competing with ourselves more than competing with the competition,"[93] said Chris McCormick.

L.L. Bean wasn't alone in the sales doldrums. Longtime competitor Lands' End announced in mid-December that its 1989 net income would fall 13 percent and its fourth-quarter revenue would rise just 4 percent compared to 43 percent a year ago. As a result of the news, Lands' End, which had gone public in 1986, saw the price of its stock drop 16 percent, to $23.75 a share. (In 1986 Lands' End also had to sell 14 percent of its stock to pay estate taxes.) Blaming its current problems, in part, on competitors' deep discounting and look-alike catalogs, the Dodgeville, Wisconsin-based cataloger said it planned more new items and a review of its strategy. As a result of the downturn, the company's 4,200 hourly workers each received a week's pay as a bonus while the bonuses of its salaried employees were cut in half.

For all of their company's recent difficulties, the descendants of L. L. Bean were doing just fine. It had recently welcomed a member of its fourth generation, Leon's son Jeffrey, to Bean's Board of Directors on a rotating basis (in 1988 it had been Linda's oldest son, Jason), and a fifth generation into the world (Leon's grandniece, Maura Gorman). A recent issue of *Forbes* featuring its "richest families in America" list had estimated the family's personal worth at about $400 million, a figure with which Leon Gorman took exception, even writing a pointed letter to the magazine. "He chose not to read the published article," said an interviewer, "and 'hoped it would go away.'"[94] L.L. Bean, Inc., also made another *Forbes* list in 1989, coming in 298th on the magazine's list of the 400 largest private companies in America.

For the record, L.L. Bean, Inc., had seventeen owners in 1989: L. L.'s five grandchildren and ten great grandchildren; Hazel Dyer, ex-wife of L. L.'s son Warren and mother of Linda; and Thelma Snow, whose late husband had been L. L.'s longtime accountant.

Probably one of the most revealing looks at descendants of L. L. Bean by an outside source is Phyllis Austin's July 7, 1989, *Maine Times* piece, "The Beans of Freeport, Maine." (The title is a takeoff on the 1985 novel *The Beans of Egypt, Maine* by Maine author Carolyn Chute.) It gave the Maine public not only its first really candid look at the family, but also one of its first glimpses of the long-simmering conflict between Leon Gorman and Bill End.

Aside from the fact that she refers to L. L.'s sons, Carl and Warren, as his brothers (the piece also includes a family tree that gets the relationships right), Austin's article provides a rare, insightful look into the extended family that owned the Maine business, paying particular attention to the political exploits of Linda Bean-Jones, whose time in the Maine spotlight had not yet completely passed. "In general," wrote Austin, "[L. L.'s descendants] seem to be very ordinary and old-fashioned, with no Ivy League school credentials. Leon Gorman is the only super-achiever since L. L. Friends say that the family has a strong eccentric streak running through it, and that some members are extremely timid."

Two years earlier, *USA Today* had observed, "L.L. Bean is like family—a mildly eccentric but amiable uncle who lives up in Maine and sends us packages." But it wasn't problems with the family in general that were causing many of Bean's capable managers to seek employment elsewhere. It was the ongoing frustration of dealing with their boss's "Leoncentric" (as Gorman calls it in his memoir) way of doing things. Gorman "is like the emperor," former director of manufacturing Charlie Kessler told Austin, "and you're careful not to tell him something he doesn't want to know." At the product meetings, "'he decides what is appropriate,' says

Kessler. Gorman has a quick 'yes' or 'no' on what will go in the catalogues, and there's no room for discussion, according to Kessler. 'Anyone who questions his authority gets kicked.'"

Bean's own climate studies continued to show its managers' discontentment about not having decision-making power. With Leon really running merchandising, a lot of Bean's middle managers were frustrated at being charged with improving profits but not having the freedom to do it. Former managers, said Austin, had described him as "quixotic and bullheaded at times." "'I'm letting people take more of the responsibility for what happens,' he said, 'it's just hard to let go what you're used to doing.'"[95] (Years earlier Leon's mother had said of her father, "He was the one who knew what to do and how to do it. Everybody else could help but not ever take his place. He'd always had to take care of everything himself and he never got over it. No . . . his word was it." His efforts to modernize and expand the company notwithstanding, maybe Leon Gorman was really more like his grandfather than he realized.)

Austin also made note of Leon Gorman's impending divorce from Wendy, his wife of more than twenty years. Just as Socrates had encouraged his fellow Athenians to engage in self-examination, he must also have inspired such reflection in Leon Gorman, who'd studied philosophy as a liberal arts major at Bowdoin College (at the time of the interview, he was reading *The Trial of Socrates*). Austin gives only two lines to the matter, which is probably about as much as Bean's reserved president was willing to share: "Gorman offers that he has had a 'mid-life crisis' and is divorcing his wife. 'My life has not gone unexamined.'"

Another of Gorman's longtime relationships was also on the rocks. Since at least the end of the Preppy boom, his senior VP, Bill End, had advocated for growth through the addition of casual clothing and the opening of new retail stores. Leon Gorman didn't see his company taking that course. He wanted to remain true to his grandfather's vision and the company's catalog and sporting roots. At this point, Bean's president was certain that there would be no new retail stores in the company's immediate future. The

Freeport store, which was doing $70 million in business, was enough retail for now. "We don't see ourselves in the retail business," Gorman told Austin. "We can do what we want through the catalogue and can outperform competition."

Though End tried to be diplomatic about his relationship with Gorman, Phyllis Austin's telling article revealed just how badly it had deteriorated:

> Bill End would discuss dissent only in the context of the annual strategic planning meeting held in the spring at the Bethel Inn in Bethel. The most "aggressive debate," End says, is over "active versus casual wear, male versus female products.
>
> "There's always the temptation to go casual," because that's where the bulk of Bean's profits comes from. But, he points out, L.L. Bean's niche is the outdoors. "It's unique . . . critical to our business."
>
> Regardless of the feedback Gorman receives, ultimately "it comes down to what Leon wants to do," End says. End has a powerful personality, and he and Gorman reportedly have rifts, especially over planning issues. On at least one occasion, the two hardly spoke to each other for several weeks, says an ex-manger who worked with Gorman.

Seven years before his death at the age of ninety-four, L. L. Bean had had no will. He rarely delegated responsibility for running his business except by default, because he had simply lost interest in the whole thing. L. L.'s only succession plan was the assumption that his son Carl would run the place. Leon Gorman wasn't going to let the same thing happen when his time to step aside finally came. Although there were no members of the family being groomed to succeed him, almost from the day he'd hired Bill End, Gorman had made it clear that End would be running the place once he stepped aside, even referring to his protégé as "first among equals." Soon Bill End would be running one of the country's largest mail-order companies, but it wouldn't be the one in Freeport, Maine.

Chapter 11

*The fact that the company hadn't strayed too far
from its roots once again proved to be its salvation*

During the early 1980s, L.L. Bean had run out of Preppies, and spent much of the rest of the decade fighting (sometimes almost literally) its way back to profitability while at the same time struggling to keep its unique identity intact. This time, according to company president Leon Gorman, diagnosing his company's problems was much more complicated than recovering from the Preppy hangover—in the 1990s L.L. Bean seemed to have run out of luck.

Gone were many of Bean's core customers, who had aged out of their love for camping and hiking. Other companies fighting for the same customers had equaled whatever technological edge the Maine retailer may have had. Despite these factors, Leon Gorman was still able to somehow find a silver lining in the overcast that would hang over his company for much of the decade, cryptically writing, "Internally we had a lot of turnover in our management group and a lot of change in our business model. Much of it proved to be good."[1]

Things started going south right away when, in January, the firm announced it would have to lay off 150 of the company's 3,186 people. Consumer confidence, said Leon Gorman, was very low, forcing retailers to battle it out for every dollar. He said that his company was dealing with the situation by "intensifying the effort to know what customers want and don't want," an ongoing process that would lead to the company's Selection for Me research among Bean customers and prospective customers. While the recession, which was responsible for many of Bean's problems, would continue for another three years, Morgan Stanley retail analyst Stacy Dutton hypothesized that the Freeport firm could also be "feeling the effects of success for its catalog competitors, especially the J. Crew line of clothes."

The news wouldn't get any better in March with the not-unexpected announcement that the company's famous annual bonuses would be 5 percent, substantially less than Bean's employees were accustomed to. This meant that a full-time worker making Bean's starting wage of $6.50 an hour could expect a bonus of $676, compared to $2,434 the previous year. The cataloger's sales had gone down but its expenses hadn't. A bad time for retailing in general, 1990 was the worst year L.L. Bean had had in a decade.

Bill End and John Findlay, who was then Bean's senior vice president of operations, saw diversification of Bean's product line and the opening of more retail stores as the only ways out of the company's present situation. But Leon Gorman—who in the past had said he'd consider going the retail route when there were no other options—still nixed the idea. Findlay remembers that he felt almost "betrayed," after he and the other managers had long counted on Bean's branching out into retail when the going got tough.

Even during the slowdown, Leon Gorman resisted taking the path to retail stores, feeling it just wasn't the right thing to do. Obviously, Gorman was operating on more than mere intuition. His concerns about the wisdom of L.L. Bean, Inc., taking the retail path were many and varied: besides not wanting to shift his company's business model during a time of weakness, Gorman also reasoned that his company had neither the merchandising skills nor the logistical systems and operating experience to make an investment into retail pan out.

THE OTHER BOOT DROPPED at the end of August with a press release announcing that Bill End would be leaving L.L. Bean after fifteen years. Feeling that his opinions about which direction the company should take were being disregarded, End discussed the matter with Gorman, and the pair decided it was time for End to leave. During his time at there, End had seen the company grow from one with $24 million in annual sales to one with $650 million.

The problem was that Bill End thought the company had the potential to do $5 billion to $10 billion a year in sales if Leon Gorman would implement his ideas about opening other flagship stores, acquiring other catalog businesses, and developing new businesses.

News stories at the time contained the expected denials of a rift between Gorman and End ("... End's resignation ... isn't the result of a philosophical difference between the two") and the usual quotes about his leaving "to explore other interests." End did allow that his departure "just happened fairly quickly. I'll look at my various options and go from there." He added that he had no offers at the time, and said "nothing really changed" since the previous year when he had told *Maine Times* reporter Phyllis Austin that he expected, one day, to take over for Gorman. Austin followed up on End's exit with a piece about how he was still in the running for Bean's top spot: "Leon Gorman says that when he retires from the job," she wrote, "he will give End a call to see if he's interested in taking over. 'Bill is as viable a candidate as he ever has been,' he said."

As for Bill End, at forty-two he was more than ready to lead a major company; he'd just spent the past fifteen years helping Leon Gorman build L.L. Bean into a retail powerhouse, and knew he had what it took to succeed. It's just that he couldn't look forward to running Bean's anytime soon—Leon Gorman was fifty-five years old and in excellent health. Still, End, who also gave up his seat on the board of directors when he left, said he hoped when Gorman got ready to retire, "he will give me a call." (It would turn out that Leon Gorman would retire as president and CEO of L.L. Bean in 2001, one year before Bill End would retire from his job.)

Coincidentally, Russell Gaitskill had recently been "forced out" of his position as executive vice president of merchandising at Bean's chief competitor, Lands' End, for reportedly wanting "to take a more aggressive path in updating its fashion line." Guess where Bill End would soon end up. By mid-January, four months after he'd left Freeport, End joined the Wisconsin-based Lands' End as executive vice president for marketing and corporate planning—a position similar to the one he'd held at L.L. Bean. (One headline proclaimed: "Lands' End lands End.") A year later he'd be named president and chief operating officer, taking over those titles from Richard Anderson, one of the company's founders. End would share the company's leadership role with recently promoted vice chairman of merchandising, David Dyer, with Anderson staying on as the firm's CEO and vice chairman.

Less than a year after his promotion, Bill End was advanced again, this time to the position of CEO. By 1994, he had increased the Dodgeville, Wisconsin, firm's sales to $870 million. But his tenure as head of Lands' End would last less than two years, concluding late that same year. Bill End resigned after his attempts to introduce a more formal management style conflicted with that of majority stockholder Gary Comer. Lands' End had also recently reported a 52 percent drop in profits for the third quarter, despite a 14 percent increase in sales.

In May of 1995 Bill End returned to Maine as a managing partner of Cornerstone Group, a Portland-based company whose aim was to acquire a number of specialty catalogs. Cornerstone had been founded by venture capitalist Don Steiner, with whom End had worked at Gillette before going to Freeport in 1975. By late 1998, Cornerstone had acquired seven catalogs (including The Territory Ahead, which End had acquired while at Lands' End), and planned to go public. Bill End would become Cornerstone's executive chairman of the board in March 2001, a position he'd hold until June of the following year, when he'd retire. He was also a director of Eddie Bauer Holdings, Inc., and Westbrook, Maine-based IDEXX Labs.

NOT ALL THE NEWS from and about the Freeport retailer in 1990 was about lagging sales and Bill End's sudden departure. In the spring, L.L. Bean had gotten a lot of positive publicity from its involvement in the Mount Everest International Peace Climb. After three years of planning, negotiating, mortgaging his house, and "signing more IOUs than a drunken poker player," expedition leader Jim Whittaker had finally managed to raise the $1.1 million he needed to fund the undertaking. After all the preliminary work was done, he was noticeably relieved to finally be on a plane bound for China in February. "Anyway, you know what they say about mountain climbers," the sixty-one-year-old joked, "the only reason they rope up is to keep the smart ones from leaving." Whittaker had been the first American to conquer the 29,028-foot peak twenty-seven years earlier.

Organized to celebrate the twentieth anniversary of Earth Day, the Peace Climb was designed so groups of Chinese, Soviet, and American climbers could work together to reach the top of the world and then clean up some of the trash left behind by some of the 270 expeditions that had preceded them. The plan for the three-month trip, which officially began on March 10, was to have five teams of three (one person from each nation) make their summit attempts as close as possible to April 22, the twentieth anniversary of Earth Day.

But just getting everybody into the same country proved to be almost as daunting a task as raising the money and climbing the mountain. According to USA Today, which dedicated a full page of its January 21, 1990, edition to a preview of the climb, "The Chinese would allow the Soviets to climb in their territory for the first time in 30 years if they could be sure the Soviets wouldn't snub an invitation. The Soviets would agree to accept an invitation as long as they were guaranteed it would be extended." It took the help of Massachusetts senator Ted Kennedy to get the negotiations rolling.

As the Peace Climb's principal sponsor, L.L. Bean had contributed $100,000 cash to the expedition plus most of its climbing gear and apparel, including specially designed mountaineering suits called Everest 90 System Parkas and Bib Pants. L.L. Bean also used the expedition to test its new Primaloft insulation, which has many of the qualities of down but retains its insulating ability when it gets wet. Not all the equipment they sent along was the latest high-tech stuff; the adventurers also carried old standby items such as boiled-wool sweaters and Stewart Manufacturing Co.'s $4.95 Speedy Stitcher Sewing Awl, which has been around since the 1930s. The Soviets contributed $40,000 worth of titanium oxygen bottles, while the Chinese handled the group's transportation, communications, and climbing fees—and provided the mountain.

As a "trekker," the fifty-five-year-old Gorman would help transport some of the team's 25 tons of equipment as high as Camp III at 21,325 feet. (The expedition's base camp was situated at 17,100 feet, nearly three times the altitude of New Hampshire's Mount Washington.) Accompanying Gorman from L.L. Bean were his older brother Jim, Tom Armstrong, and Mike Perry. Blessed with unusually good weather, the expedition would get fourteen climbers to the top of Mount Everest, six (Steve Gall, Robert Link, Sergey Arsentje, Grigory Lunjakov, Da Cheme, and Gyal Bu) at 12:13 A.M. Eastern Daylight Time on May 7, and eight more two days later. Several years later, Armstrong would look back fondly on his adventure: "I feel very lucky," he reflected, "to have experienced Everest before it became commercialized."[2]

UNLIKE MOUNT EVEREST, Freeport, Maine, had been commercialized for quite some time now—and the trend was continuing into the nineties. By one count, the number of shops and stores in Freeport had grown to 110, at least 65 of which were located in a seven-block area of downtown. Paul and Betty Wentworth were not happy with what had happened to their town, even though they'd sold their Main Street dry-cleaning business in 1984 "for a tidy profit." The streets were so clogged, they said, that sometimes it took half an hour to drive across town. "On a weekend, you might run out of gas driving around trying to find a parking space," said Paul. Another complaint he had was, "They don't sell the products you need for everyday life since this commercial explosion started."[3] In a couple of years, someone would float the idea of valet parking and by mid-decade, some merchants would even be calling for the return of passenger train service to Freeport (as this is being written, it's scheduled to return in 2012).

But the growth wasn't going to go away, and Bean's flagship store was the magnet attracting people to Freeport. And attract people it did—all sorts of people at all times of the day and night. The *Maine Sunday Telegram* even ran an article about all the famous people who came to shop at L.L. Bean, often during the summer in the middle of the night, when things were relatively quiet.

The *Telegram* wasn't the first newspaper to report on the famous who favor the Maine merchant; at least a dozen other articles have made mention of the cataloger's notable clientele. In 1978, L.L. Bean itself had compiled a list of the well known who'd been customers of the company—either in person or by mail. Being careful to note that, "*ALL* our customers are VIPs, but here are a few whose names you might recognize," the company listed the names of dozens of its better-known patrons.

In a very informal count, entertainers—from John Wayne and Katherine Hepburn to Maine singer Jud Strunk—far outnumber (at 51) all the other famous folks who fancy the Freeport merchant's goods. They are followed by politicians (14) such as Calvin Coolidge and Barry Goldwater (plus "every governor of Maine"); newscasters (10) like Walter Cronkite and Lowell Thomas; the wealthy (10) including Henry Morgan and the du Ponts; sports figures (8) such as Babe Ruth and Ted Williams; royalty (5), like Prince Andrew and the King of Nepal; generals (2), Omar Bradley and Matthew Ridgeway; explorers (2), John Glenn and Donald MacMillan; and Supreme Court Justice William O. Douglas. The complete list of Bean's celebrity shoppers is certainly much, much longer. (One recent report even noted that "gonzo" journalist Dr. Hunter S. Thompson had preferred to order his clothing from L.L. Bean, as he felt most of its competitors' products were inferior.)

Sales for the 1991 fiscal year would increase only slightly over those of the previous year (from $617 million to $632 million), while the cost of paying the company's employees (4,000 at peak season) ran the company $82.6 million. Additionally, more competition, increases in shipping and mailing costs, and a bad economy—especially in the Northeast—all combined to result in reduced demand for L.L. Bean's products and lower profit margins.

Another factor was the ongoing perception by the buying public that Bean's product mix continued to be stodgy and stale, even though the cataloger was making efforts to update its reputation for offering "conservative styles and muted color schemes" by adding "brighter hues to its fashion palette."

One perception about L.L. Bean that was accurate was the firm's reputation for consistently providing superior service and products. In October 1991 (and again in 1994 and 1999), Bean's topped a *Consumer Reports* survey of more than thirty mail-order companies. Not only was Bean's rated best overall in each survey, the company also took top honors in every product category in which it competed.

Closer to home, the Freeport firm ran away with top honors in the *Maine Times'* search for the best Maine company, clearly outpacing runner-up Tom's of Maine. "The *Maine Times* readers' choice for top company mirrors the findings of *Consumer Reports*. This month, the consumer guide found L.L. Bean was the best mail-order company when it comes to men's and women's apparel. (Second place went to Bean's chief competitor, Lands' End.) Bean was also voted top mail-order company for linen, tools, gadgets, and camping goods." The only category in which L.L. Bean finished second was mail-order food, "which," the article noted, "is little more than a sideline for the company."

But doing well in surveys didn't necessarily translate into more sales for the Freeport firm, and it was surpassed in net sales by its two major competitors, Lands' End and Eddie Bauer. While both of Bean's rivals had focused on casual apparel, Lands' End stuck with its traditional catalog model and Eddie Bauer opted to open several hundred small stores in shopping malls across the country. L.L. Bean, on the other hand, had persisted with sales of its outdoors-oriented products, primarily through its catalogs. (Bean's wouldn't open its second retail store for nearly a decade.)

Being passed in sales by Bauer was one thing; it had been around since the mid-1930s, and, like L.L. Bean, had been founded by its namesake, Eddie Bauer, an actual outdoorsman. Lands' End, however, had been started in the early sixties by a bunch of guys selling sailing gear and had realized tremendous growth during the Preppy boom a decade earlier. "We used to call it Lands' Envy," said senior VP of operations John Findlay, because no one in Freeport could ever have pictured Lands' End passing L.L. Bean in sales. (By 2002, Lands' End's sales would be $1.6 billion compared to L.L. Bean's $1.1 billion.)

Not only was Lands' End getting bigger than L.L. Bean, Bean's was getting smaller; in 1991 the Maine mail-order house underwent the first-ever downsizing of its workforce. Early the previous year, the company had announced plans to "phase out as many as 150 jobs" during the year, saying it hoped to make the cuts as painlessly as possible, hopefully through attrition. Toward the end of the year, L.L. Bean began laying off "about 70" temporary manufacturing workers from its Lisbon and Brunswick plants. This latest round of job cuts was going to hurt even more.

In February, William Booth, vice president of advertising and direct marketing, and Robert Felle, VP of catalog art and production, both decided to take the company's "fairly healthy" voluntary severance packages and move on "to explore other opportunities." Longtime public relations manager Kilton Andrew also retired after fifteen years with the company. Less than two months later, Tom Day (1947–97), Bean's vice president of strategic planning and Total Quality, announced he would resign after thirteen years with the company to become senior VP of logistics and operations at New Hampshire's Timberland Company. Day had been the principal designer of Bean's distribution and order fulfillment systems, and would later found Day and Associates, which would provide assistance to manufacturing, distribution, and retail companies in the areas of consumer and business catalog operations, direct marketing, and electronic commerce.

Senior VP and COO Bob Peixotto remembers 1991 as the year of Bean's first reduction in force. Mark Fasold, head of inventory management, and marketing's Bill Booth also left the company. This "changing of the guard" in Bean's senior management led to an extended period of instability in the company's upper ranks. (In 2001 Mark Fasold would return to the company as a senior VP and CFO.) Amid all the turnover, the cataloger announced that Chris McCormick had been promoted to VP of advertising and direct marketing.

In light of the cuts, L.L. Bean faced the problems of maintaining both worker morale and productivity as well as its public image. Management decided that, since there were going to be rumors about the layoffs anyway, the best thing it could do was provide its employees with honest information about the situation and help them find other jobs. The company explained that the layoffs would be done according to a rating system based on factors such as a worker's experience, education, and other job qualifications. This up-front honesty helped not only to dispel the rumors, it also helped create a sense of trust among the remaining employees.

To help out its displaced managers, L.L. Bean paid severance packages ranging from eight to thirty-nine weeks' pay, and set up a temporary career center in one of its Portland office buildings. The center, which had sixteen workstations, was run by the Portland employment firm of Drake Inglesi Milardo, Inc. Laid-off manufacturing workers also received severance pay and help in finding new jobs.

A year later the company announced that "about 170 fewer [permanent] employees are sharing in this year's bonus." Still, Bean had held up well during the recession; it had laid off only about 1 percent of its workforce at a time when the Maine economy would lose 37,000 jobs.

By late April, the weekly *Maine Times* realized that the people of Maine were wondering about the extent of the Freeport company's plight, and once again put Bean beat reporter Phyllis Austin on the story. She came up with the following statistics (the list's sales figures, which don't agree with later ones, may have been preliminary):

Inside L.L. Bean

Everyone wants to know how L.L. Bean is doing during the recession. These statistics were provided to *Maine Times* last week by the company. They reflect a slight downturn in business in virtually every category. Total sales of $600 million in 1989 declined to $597 million last year.

The number of catalogs mailed dropped by two million, and year-round employees fell by 250.

The average employee wage, however, was up by $998. Bean's tax bill was also higher.
- 1990 sales: Catalogue sales: $525.5 million
Retail store: $71.5 million
- Catalogues: Number mailed: 144 million
Orders generated by catalogue: 8 million
- Retail store: Number of shoppers: 3.5 million
Shopping space: 90,000 square feet
- Employees: Year-round 3,300 regular and temporary
Christmas season peak: 5,387
- Payroll (including cash bonus): $78.1 million
- Average wage (regular employees only): $22,658
- Packages shipped: 10.4 million
- Postage costs: $21.6 million
- Busiest shipping week: 612,000 packages mailed, enough to fill 181 40-foot trailers
- Inventory: Average on hand: $122 million; Peak: $158 million
- Telephone: Inbound orders 10.3 million; 800 number phone bill: $5 million-plus
- Products: Items stocked: 5,500; From the U.S.: 84 percent; Items with Bean label: 94 percent
- New Maine Hunting Shoe sales: 230,289 pairs
- Resoling and repairs on worn hunting shoes: 28,993
- Percentage of Bean's sales from products manufactured at the Brunswick factory: 7 percent, worth $50 million
- Taxes: Personal income tax: $2.9 million
Property tax: $2 million; State sales tax: $4.2 million
- Capital investment in Maine in the last five years: $71.1 million

—*Compiled by Phyllis Austin*

One thing not mentioned in Austin's unique look at the cataloger was the fact that the company's current circumstances had forced it to abandon its nearly eighty-year-old free shipping policy. For the first time, L.L. Bean's customers would feel the effects of the company's belt tightening—to the tune of $3.50 per order, regardless of how much they purchased. "It's something we've been very reluctant to do," said Bean's Catharine Hartnett. "But the $3.50 charge is still the lowest in the industry."[4]

In an attempt to help automate delivery, the U.S. Postal Service was trying to encourage businesses to use more standard-size envelopes. To this end, it increased the cost of mailing an eight-ounce, presorted catalog from 27.1 cents to 36.3 cents—a 34 percent jump. This meant that L.L. Bean's cost for mailing catalogs and shipping packages would increase from "about $37 million" to "close to $50 million," even though the company would mail out fewer catalogs than it had in 1989. The shipping fee would first appear in the company's summer 1991 catalog mailed in April. (A first-class stamp cost twenty-nine cents at the time.)

The free shipping had been an iffy proposition at the company for quite a while now—even back in the mid-seventies, management had been reluctant to publicize it because they didn't know how much longer they could afford it. Bean-watcher M. R. Montgomery of the *Boston Globe* wrote:

> When the decision was made, the Feb. 25 announcement from the company explained that the need to charge for shipping was due to a steep increase in both Postal Service and United Parcel Service rates. In particular, the UPS charges were the culprit. About 70 percent of Bean's deliveries move in the big brown trucks, and UPS had bumped the charge for delivery to residential addresses up by an average of 55 cents, from $1.93 to $2.48 for packages going from 500 to 1,000 miles, and that's most of Bean's business. The company does about 80 percent of its mail-order business with customers who live between Boston and the Mississippi River.[5]

"The average mail-order catalog purchase [from L.L. Bean]," Montgomery noted, "is surprisingly small, $10 to $12. Many an order is for a pair of socks, a cap, a long-sleeved undershirt, or a colorful bandanna. Bean's total orders for its estimated $600 million in annual sales may have been as high as 6 million separate orders, and at the new $3.50 charge for shipping, that would be an additional $21 million income, almost as much as the pretax profit last year. And the Bean charge would still fit the company's image; it's less than the industry average of $5.25 for shipping."

Even Maine's *Down East* magazine mourned the passing of the Freeport firm's free shipping, noting that the recent 25 percent increase in the cost of sending its goods via UPS "translated into an $11-million jump in operating costs for the outfitter. So instead of cutting back on customer service or quality assurance—two other Bean trademarks—the company has reluctantly introduced a shipping charge for each order. All good things, it seems, must eventually come to an end."[6] (Late the very next year, L.L. Bean would switch from Atlanta-based UPS to Memphis-based Federal Express as its primary delivery company. The switch would cut delivery time in half for customers, said Bean's, while the shipping charges would remain the same. The company would revive free year-round regular shipping to the U.S. and Canada in March 2011.)

The cataloger's ongoing quality-improvement and cost-cutting efforts would soon start to pay off. When the company held its annual planning meeting in mid-1991, its annual sales were $617 million, with a return on equity of 14.6 percent. Management set a goal of achieving sales of more than $800 million by 1994 with a 20 percent ROE. What it would end up with three years later were sales of $975 million and a 25.4 ROE. That year L.L. Bean would pay its employees a 22.5 percent bonus. (In February 1992, Bean's regular employees would get a 15 percent bonus for 1991, plus a 5 percent contribution to their long-term profit-sharing plan. Workers had received bonuses of 5 percent for fiscal year 1989 and 10 percent for 1990, with no profit-sharing either year.)

ONE OF THE SMILING MODELS in one of those eight-ounce catalogs could have been you. Or a friend or neighbor. In mid-May the Freeport merchant held an open tryout at its retail store for anyone who'd ever dreamed of appearing in an L.L. Bean catalog. Over the weekend, the firm's photographers took at least 300 pictures of more than 500 prospective models. Everyone received a free photo as a souvenir, and those selected to appear in the catalog would be notified by June 30. (The author had his picture taken following a bike ride on Saturday but was not selected.) L.L. Bean also put on fashion shows on Friday and Saturday. One person who didn't have to wait in line or wonder if his picture would be used was L. L.'s old hunting buddy, world-famous decoy maker George Soule, whose photo would appear on the cover of Bean's 1991 Hunting Specialties circular.

But Bean's practice of using regular folks (mostly its own employees) in its catalog was coming to an end. Suddenly gone were the awkward, self-conscious "models" of the past, replaced by attractive, smiling professionals—and not everyone liked it. "L.L. Bean has left the back country and set up shop at the mall," wrote Tim Warren, book editor of the *Baltimore Sun*. The models in the catalog, he said, used to have "none of the smirky self-confidence of real Preppies; rather, they appeared to be Bean personnel pulled from the stockroom and placed in front of the camera." Now they're "more attractive and given to striking the standard self-assured poses you see in other catalogs. . . . These folks aren't outdoorsmen, they're lounge lizards"[7]

For better or worse, the way the catalog photos were being shot had changed forever. Only a few short years later, a photo shoot on Martha's Vineyard would involve an eleven-member team and a 34-foot motor home complete with a makeup area and a changing room. At the same time, another team would be at work in Maine's Acadia National Park. Gone forever were the days when Bean employees such as VP Tom Sidar were paid a dollar for two hours of modeling work in the Freeport area. "I'd put up the tent, inflate the inflatable boat, then maybe I'd pose while paddling a canoe," he recalled.

And then there was the writing. That, too, had changed. "It's become both bland and boastful," scolded Warren, "if that's possible. Gone are those evocative descriptions of products, the 'we wear this while hunting for antiques in a rural Vermont town or giving the dogs a brisk run at the shore.' Now it's back to matter-of-fact detail in the copy, with one hideous addition: huge head-lines that amount to just bragging. Take this on the chamois shirt, from page 18 of the 1992 fall catalog: '5 Reasons the Original Is Still the Best—Since 1927.' L.L. Bean always used to tout its products, but its manner was proud but quiet. Now the declarations are in neon." Changing the regular catalog, wrote Warren, was one thing, but it got even worse:

> Even the formerly sacred hunting catalogs aren't immune. The fall one I got last month featured a customer's poem lauding the L.L. Bean hunting boots. They're great boots, certainly, but a poem?
>
> What's next—900 numbers so we can call our favorite models? Or karaoke contests in the local hunting lodge?
>
> What the good people at L.L. Bean obviously didn't take into account was that they aren't selling just products—some dopey items, but also many good and useful ones, I should say—but also an illusion.

The illusion, said Warren, was the idea that reading the catalog used to take you away from the humdrum routine of suburbia and out into the deep Maine woods, a "Thoreau-in-waiting," he called it. Leon Gorman called it an "image" or "the Bean mystique." It was what had happened to M. R. Montgomery and thousands of others every time they read the copy next to the old Maine Warden Jacket. Before, the company had gone out of its way to not appear "slick or sophisticated." By using local folks and employees (and their dogs) as models, Bean's was able to avoid this slickness—as well as the fees commanded by professional models.

But not everyone disliked the catalogs' new look, and some liked it very much indeed. Gorman, for one, cited surveys showing that customers generally liked the fancier layouts and increased outdoor photography in his company's catalogs. "We know in a variety of cases the new creative approaches have doubled, tripled, or even quadrupled demand" of some products, said the L.L. Bean president. Even sales of the venerable Maine Hunting Shoe had increased with the new look. "This feels more solid to me," he said. "It's based more on fundamental strength, not dependent on the Preppy figures."[8]

IN 1992, JOHN FINDLAY decided that he was unhappy at Bean's and it was time to move on. Findlay wasn't alone in his departure from L.L. Bean. By 1992, the ratio of the cataloger's hourly workers to its managers had increased to 18:1 from 1984's 11:1. Bob Peixotto recalls that many managers became frustrated because Leon Gorman was looking for people who could buy into his intuitive way of running the company.

The atmosphere among Bean's higher-ups had deteriorated to the point where that summer's three-day sea-kayaking trip in Penobscot Bay would be the company's last management outing. Participation in the annual or semiannual trips to various parts of Maine, regardless of the season, used to mean that the participant had "arrived" at L.L. Bean. Some of the excursions had been pretty tough. Leon Gorman recalled one backpacking trip the group had taken through the rugged Carter-Mahoosuc range of the Appalachian Trail when the temperatures were in the nineties. Old-timers at the company still remember the hike as "the Death March."

The executive exodus would continue for the remainder of the decade, with seven of L.L. Bean's nine senior vice presidents leaving Freeport between 1995 and the end of 1998. Some of them went to Internet start-up companies, some resigned, and a couple were fired. None of them were replaced; their duties were taken on by subordinates.

IN LATE 1990 MATSUSHITA ELECTRIC Industrial Company, Ltd., had begun running ads in Japan promising to take steps to soothe tensions over the country's whopping trade surplus with the United States. It planned to do this, it said, by importing more goods from America over the next five years. Some of the West's most sought-after products, Matsushita executives determined, were those targeting the Japanese peoples' exploding interest in the out-of-doors and quality brand names, both of which made L.L. Bean, Inc., an obvious prospect as a trading partner. Matsushita planned to handle the importing side of any deal while retail giant Seiyu, Ltd., would be responsible for distribution. "If we wanted to make any measurable dent in Japan," said Bean's international vice president Richard Leslie, "we knew we would have to go retail." Even before the deal was done, Japanese newspaper reports were estimating sales of 500 million yen ($4 million) for the operation's first year.

On March 4, 1992, after nearly two years of negotiations, Leon Gorman signed contracts with Matsushita and Seiyu, giving the pair exclusive rights to sell the Freeport firm's products in a series of stores in Japan. Under the agreement, Matsushita and Seiyu would form a new, independent company, L.L. Bean Japan, to which the Freeport firm would simply supply merchandise and training while still having final say on matters such as product quality and trademarks. Bean's Catharine Hartnett emphasized that the Maine corporation would have "no investment" in the royalty venture.

"Our Japanese customers have become familiar with L.L. Bean products over the last several years, and our popularity has grown. Opening a retail store in Japan will give these customers more exposure to our product and should boost our catalog sales as well,"9 said Leon Gorman. "We're not so much pushing our way into this market," he added, "as being pulled."10

When talks between the parties had commenced in 1990, the American company had been selling about $5 million worth of mail-order goods annually to the Japanese, even though they traditionally preferred to shop in retail stores, which were usually quite expensive. (At the other end of the spectrum were the existing Japanese mail-order catalogs, which were described as everything from "stodgy" to "bargain basement.") Although some Bean products had previously been sold in Japan through Sony Plaza Stores, the problem with this arrangement had been that the goods were sold through middlemen "who have crazy markups," said Gorman at the time.

Even ordering items from America could prove extremely costly for the Japanese; in 1988, one family had reported paying $253 for four pairs of slippers after paying the country's 145 percent import duty on items containing leather.

Matsushita representative Masao Watanabe said that initially, L.L. Bean had told the conglomerate, "No, we won't sell our spirit to Panasonic." (Matsushita, the parent of Panasonic and Quasar—among other companies—was worth $33 billion at the time and had recently purchased MCA/Universal Studios for $6 billion. Seiyu was a member of the $8-billion Saison Group and specialized in running supermarkets and department stores. By comparison, L.L. Bean had totaled $632 million in sales in 1991.) "We had to keep telling them," said Watanabe, "that we did not want to buy the company, just the products." The deal would mark the first time that L.L. Bean retail stores had been established outside of Freeport. Although the plan had initially called for the opening of just five stores in five years, the number would eventually reach twenty-three.

Still, Gorman had managed to resist the overtures of his Asian suitors for quite a while before finally consenting to the relationship; a mere four months before signing with Matsushita and Seiyu, the Maine company had been included alongside Lands' End, Orvis, Gander Mountain, and eight other catalogers in American Showcase, a slick, twelve-in-one test catalog sent to 50,000 potential Japanese customers by printing giant R. R. Donnelley & Sons. "The door to the world's second-largest consumer economy is swinging open," announced Donnelley vice president Jim Stewart. In 1990 L.L. Bean had even started its own five-person international division headed by Richard Leslie, the cataloger's newly minted international vice president.

L.L. Bean Japan opened its first retail store on Sunday, November 8 at 10:00 A.M. Located 6,955 miles from Freeport on the narrow streets of Tokyo's trendy Jiyugaoka district (5-26 Okuzawa in Setagaya-Ku), the store was swarmed like Mecca by the area's Bean faithful, who'd been eagerly awaiting its arrival. Executives had expected about a thousand people to be on hand for the store's grand opening. Three thousand showed up. The Freeport company added to the festivities by flying in fifty-four-year-old Ralph Dehahn to demonstrate his trade of sewing moccasins by hand.

Inside, shoppers found the 492-square-meter (5,000-square-foot) store to be appointed very much like its parent store in Freeport, with granite floors, pine beams, and natural light. They also found the genuine American-made gear and clothing they wanted and expected. Among the items from which they could choose were outdoor and casual fashions, footwear, luggage, and a selection of sporting goods that ranged from fishing gear and camping equipment to mountain bikes. Of course the store also stocked fleece jackets, Boat and Tote Bags, and the famous Bean Boot. (Tote-bags are especially popular with the Japanese, who are big users of mass transit.)

"Until now, the Japanese outdoor market has been centered on outdoor sports, focusing mostly on mountain climbing and fishing," said L.L. Bean Japan president Katsuhiro Fujiseki. "L.L. Bean Japan intends to take advantage of the recent outdoor boom in Japan by introducing an essentially American total outdoor lifestyle, including products for everyday casual living."[11] Even though the store's prices were substantially higher than those in the States ($57 for a sweater that cost $27 in Freeport, $81 for a $55 sleeping bag), they were still a bargain by Japanese standards.

After only its first quarter of operation, sales at the firm's first overseas store were running at least 40 percent ahead of projections, requiring steady shipments from Maine to keep the shelves from going bare. "I spend a lot of time urging Freeport to send more, more, more of almost everything,"[12] said Koji Minobe, director of the Japanese operation.

It was already clear that Bean's venture into Japan was a success, and in early July of the following year, L.L. Bean Japan would open a second store in the southern-Tokyo section of Shinjuku. The size of the second store was 11,000 square feet, twice the size of the first but still a far cry from Bean's 90,000-square-foot flagship store. Despite its size, the Shinjuku store still drew about 10,000 people to its grand opening weekend.

At the time of L.L. Bean's first foray into Japan, the country was in the throes of a recession. But far from hurting the new venture, the downturn in the economy actually helped it by making Japanese consumers more price-conscious. While sales in the pricey Japanese stores were off some 20 percent, a favorable exchange rate and Bean's relative bargain prices made the cataloger's goods very attractive to consumers there. Going hand-in-hand with the effect of the recession was the fact that "a somewhat austere look is now considered appropriate," especially among the younger generation, which tended to be more casual than its elders.

Another emerging Japanese trend that worked in Bean's favor was that the nation's workers were quickly cutting back to five-day workweeks, giving them more time to pursue leisure activities. Japan was entering the era of the outdoors. The country's recent interest in leisure activities had arisen not only from the people themselves but also from the government's attempts to make a course correction to the nation's burgeoning trade surpluses by shortening work hours and "expanding domestic consumption." Though his country's people were not yet completely weaned from their workaholic ways, said Matsushita's Akihiro Tanii, "The Japanese lifestyle is changing, with more leisure time, and the Bean's image suggests nature and adventure."[13] L.L. Bean's total sales to the Japanese would account for two-thirds of the company's $100 million in international sales by 1993, and in 1995 the company would open a distribution center and a customer service phone center in Japan. Eventually the catalog there would be printed in Japanese.

At the time the company opened its Shinjuku store, Japan had been Bean's second-largest foreign mail-order market, after Canada. A few months later it would pass Canada, and by late 1995, when the company was opening its fourth new store, in Kobe, Japanese catalog sales would account for 88 percent of L.L. Bean's international mail-order sales. (Canada came in second with 7 percent, and the United Kingdom was third with just 1 percent.)

At the opening of the Kobe store, one man, already dressed head to toe in Bean gear he'd ordered through the mail, approached the visiting dignitaries at the ribbon cutting and beseeched them (in excellent English), "As your most loyal L.L. Bean customer in the Kobe area, it would give me greatest pride if you would grant me the honor of being the first to enter your new L.L. Bean store." His request was granted and he was personally escorted inside by Mrs. James Gorman, Leon's sister-in-law.

THINGS MIGHT HAVE BEEN GOING very well in Japan, but much closer to home there was "Trouble in Beanland," at least if you subscribed to *Forbes* magazine. It seems that in an early July issue, the periodical painted the Freeport firm as being mired in its old ways, saying that Leon Gorman had been "slow to expand product lines, slow to automate, slow to seize international opportunities." *Forbes* had arrived at this conclusion in spite of the fact that Bean's Japanese effort would see substantial growth in the next few years and its Distribution Center was viewed by many as state-of-the-art. (In a dissenting opinion, *Ernst & Young, Inc.* magazine and Merrill Lynch had named Gorman New England's top "master entrepreneur" at an annual awards dinner a week earlier.)

Bean spokesperson Lynn Gallagher said, "Much of the [*Forbes*] information is not substantiated. We feel it's one media source's opinion of us." She also said that Leon Gorman had declined to be interviewed for the article. One person who *was* interviewed for the piece was *Maine Times* reporter Phyllis Austin, who described "the Bean family members as somewhat old-fashioned and eccentric. Linda Bean isn't mentioned."

Forbes may not have mentioned Leon's cousin, but, in 1992 almost everyone else did—including Leon. Linda Lorraine Bean was once again running for Congress and creating quite a stir in the process. Just days before the opening of his company's first Japanese store, Leon's conservative cousin had been soundly defeated (66 percent to 34 percent) by Tom Andrews (D-Portland) for the state's 1st District House seat. During her losing campaign, Linda Bean, as she was now calling herself, managed to make even more waves than she had back in 1988. This time the Bean heiress, as she was still called by the press, attracted even more scrutiny, spending an estimated $1 million of her own money and ending up as the subject of at least fifteen Portland-area newspaper stories, eleven of them on the front page, and none of them particularly flattering.

Problems with the Bean candidacy (she was now married to Donald Folkers) had begun almost immediately. For her June primary battle against Tony Payne and John Purcell, she had chosen to film a campaign spot inside the L.L. Bean factory in Brunswick, where she walked through the boot-stitching room telling viewers

This year at L.L. Bean we gave each worker a 15 percent bonus. Why? Because they deserved it and because that's the way my grandfather would have wanted it. In the same way, he wanted me to make my own way in life. It meant raising three children as a single parent, waitressing at night, learning real estate by day, to make ends meet. That's why I'm fighting for people like Bobbie Mason, who has to work nearly five months just to pay her taxes. And this family, struggling to save their farm while the big spenders in Washington can't balance their checkbooks. I'm fighting to end the waste, cut the taxes, and return to people the power to live their own lives. This isn't an idle dream, it's what your grandfather—and mine—were all about.

Her choice of location for the spot did not sit well with company president Leon Gorman, who shared his feelings on the matter with Phyllis Austin of the *Maine Times*:

Republican Linda Bean's new television ad shows her inside a L.L. Bean, Inc., boot plant, and president Leon Gorman doesn't like the political implications at all.

"I didn't know [the filming] was happening. I was upset it implies a company connection," says Gorman, adding that the ad was filmed while he was vacationing in New Zealand. [On May 24 Gorman would marry his traveling companion, Lisa M. Davidson.] "I have been trying to call her and find out what's going on."

Bean hadn't returned Gorman's call when *Maine Times* spoke with him. Gorman adds that as a major stockholder and director of L.L. Bean, Inc., Linda Bean "has some prerogatives. Still, there's no endorsement of her candidacy on the part of L.L. Bean. She has a right to run and a right to say what she wants. [But] that particular ad is upsetting to me."

Will Gorman ask his cousin not to use the L.L. Bean connection in future ads? "I can't comment on that," he says, adding that the company has had a longstanding policy against political endorsements. "She's familiar with our policy."[14]

Within a week, Gorman had penned a letter to the editor of the *Portland Press Herald*, which had also run an article about the ad, to reiterate what he'd told the *Maine Times*:

In view of the May 11 article, "Bean fights battle of TV ads by herself," I would like to clearly state L.L. Bean's position on Linda Bean's candidacy for Maine's 1st District congressional seat.

Linda Bean is a candidate who happens to be a family member, a stockholder, and a director of the company. However, the company does not endorse any political campaigns and the company never makes any contributions to political parties or candidates.

While L.L. Bean admires anyone who devotes time and energy to government and community affairs, it does not endorse any political candidates, either philosophically or financially.

I appreciate the opportunity to clarify our position.
Leon A. Gorman
President
L.L. Bean
Freeport

"I wouldn't bet on her winning [against Andrews]," said University of Southern Maine political science professor Oliver

Woshinsky after the June primary, "but I would bet on her degrading the atmosphere of politics. This will be a really bitter, knock-down, drag-out kind of a race. These two are as far left and right as you can get in American mainstream politics."[15] Many in her own party thought she should try to soften her image, but Bean said she would not moderate her views in an attempt to broaden her appeal.

The fact that Leon mentions Linda in his 2006 book only once—when he lists the five family members on Bean's seven-person board of directors—speaks volumes about the continuing nature of the cousins' relationship. At about the same time as his book was being published, Gorman would tell Tara Weiss of Forbes.com, "I think the fact that our family relationship's more cordial than close means that personal issues don't get in the way of business." Leon Gorman and Linda Bean are two very different people who just happen to be related.

The company's image problem became widespread in late July when the *New York Times* carried an article about Bean's campaign under the headline, "Heiress to L.L. Bean Champions Conservatism in Race for Congress." It really wasn't even necessary to read the article, since a caption below a photo of Bean described her as "an outspoken conservative opposed to abortion rights, gay rights legislation, and gun control." The piece's text noted that "she believes in Ronald Reagan's program that tax cuts will spur economic growth and lower the deficit." Two weeks later the *Times* ran a letter from Leon Gorman in which he emphasized the points he'd made in his missive to the *Portland Press Herald*. Still, fallout from the *Times* article was immediate.

A postmortem to her campaign noted that it had "proved something of an embarrassment for the company, which had to augment and train its telephone order staff to handle hundreds of angry customer phone calls after national news stories appeared on Bean's conservative views." In early September, the company had confirmed that it was indeed considering fielding a special team to handle the reaction to Linda's campaign. "We're in the process of hiring over 1,600 telephone representatives for the temporary season," said Catharine Hartnett, "and it's our aim and goal to make sure every customer gets consistent information from a person who understands the issue and not from a temporary person who just came on board."[16] In the meantime, L.L. Bean created a form letter to explain its position on the matter and had its service reps transfer concerned callers to the firm's four-person public affairs department.

Despite the company's best efforts, however, a few people still expressed their displeasure with the family-owned business; the Purple Panthers, for example, called for a "gaycott" against the company "to protest the funding of ultraconservative causes by an L. L. Bean heiress and board member."

Between May and November, the Portland newspapers chronicled a lengthy list of alleged irregularities during Bean's campaign, which the paper labeled "bizarre." In May, John Purcell, the more conservative of her primary opponents, claimed that Bean had offered him a job on her campaign if he'd drop out of the race. In September, the *Maine Sunday Telegram* reported that she'd hired the Virginia-based ad agency of Fabrizio, McLaughlin and Associates—the agency that had created the "Willie Horton" ad to help defeat Michael Dukakis in 1988—to work for her during the stretch run against first-term congressman Tom Andrews. Andrews said Fabrizio and McLaughlin promoted themselves as character assassins. His spokesperson, Dennis Bailey, called them "the political equivalent of a drive-by shooting."

After she'd lost the November election, the *Telegram* summed up Bean's candidacy:

Welcome to the world of Linda Bean's campaign for Congress, one of the most expensive and bizarre campaigns in Maine history.

It was a campaign run like a Pentagon war room, based on secrecy, distrust, and paranoia.

It operated a secret campaign office that supporters were told not to talk about.

It wouldn't disclose where Bean campaigned, her birthdate, or who was managing the campaign.

That information was to be kept from "the enemy," Andrews' campaign.

It was a campaign where workers wondered if their phones were bugged, or who among them were Democratic spies.[17]

In October, an entire article in the *Portland Press Herald* had looked at several "significant and unexplained changes" to four campaign spending documents she'd previously filed with the Federal Election Commission. "In April Linda Bean told the federal government that her congressional campaign had repaid $22,000 she had loaned to it," reported the piece. "In August, she changed her report, and the loan was back again. Sometime in that same period, more than $21,000 in small contributions vanished from Bean's campaign reports." The piece also noted that "James W. Gorman [Leon Gorman's brother], an executive at L.L. Bean, is Bean's campaign treasurer."

Two years after the election, those paying close attention could still hear faint echoes of Linda Bean's defeats. In November 1994, political columnist Al Diamon, while giving out his Jasper Award in the *Bangor Daily News*, listed some of the award's past winners, including "Linda Bean, Libby Mitchell, Linda Bean Jones, Joe Brennan, Linda Bean Folkers, and Plato Truman." (Diamon's award, which is given to "political figures whose ambitions exceed their expertise," is named for Republican Jasper Wyman, whose 1988 Senate bid netted him just 19 percent of the vote against Senator George Mitchell, a new low for a member of a major political party.)

LONGTIME L.L. BEAN EMPLOYEE Carlene Griffin provided the company with some much-needed positive publicity with the publication of *Spillin' the Beans*, a look back at her forty-eight years with the Freeport firm. Though not much thicker than her late boss's 1960 autobiography, Griffin's book gives a good look back at how the business grew, just as L. L.'s book did, but does so with a lot more stories. Some are her own recollections of interactions with coworkers or famous customers; some are in the form of interviews. All are interesting and sincere.

A Freeport native, Griffin started working at L.L. Bean in 1935 for eighteen cents an hour. She left a year later because there wasn't enough work to do, but returned for five years beginning in 1942. After she took another five years off to raise a family, Carlene Griffin returned to L.L. Bean for good in 1952. In a 1998 interview, the eighty-one-year-old grande dame of L.L. Bean would tell a reporter that she fully expected to celebrate the new millennium with the company. She made it easily; in his 2006 book, Leon Gorman would recall the time when she was "our regular cashier," noting that "she's still with the company" at eighty-nine. (She would retire in 2008.)

In spite of all the distractions, 1992 would turn out to be a pretty good year for L.L. Bean, Inc. At the end of the fiscal year, the company would find that its quality-improvement and cost-cutting efforts had paid off to the tune of a sales increase of 18 percent, to $743 million, culminating in bonuses of 17.5 percent (totaling $13 million) for its permanent employees. And Harvard Business School was back doing its first case study (number 893003, "Item Forecasting and Inventory Management") on the firm in eleven years. And the cataloger was having a birthday.

L.L.BEAN CELEBRATED its eightieth birthday on September 19 and 20, 1992, expecting about 30,000 people to attend what it billed as "Maine's largest outdoor birthday party." Staffed by 350 Bean volunteers, the weekend's festivities were spread over three sites, with most of the activities and entertainment taking place down Route 1 at the Distribution Center where Saturday's activities concluded with a bean supper and recommenced Sunday morning with a pancake breakfast. Following a performance by Maine storyteller Kendall Morse, L.L. Bean president Leon Gorman welcomed everyone to the celebration at noon on Saturday. His address was followed by performances by Devonsquare and Malinda Liberty and fireworks in the evening. Sunday's events included a bike excursion and entertainment by The Wicked Good Band and Schooner Fare.

Of course, there were also events scheduled in downtown Freeport. At the retail store, participants could take part in everything from fly tying to decoy carving. Outside, twenty local clubs and organizations added to the celebration's county fair atmosphere by setting up food booths all over town to raise funds. "Every time we see a good opportunity to make money for the church," said Mary Jane Krause of the First Congregational Church of Freeport, "we take it. There's no question that Bean is a good neighbor."[18] Other concessions were set up by the Lioness Club, the Middle School Space Camp, and the Maine Audubon Society, among others.

At the company's Outdoor Discovery Center on Desert Road, people could try their hands at archery, fly casting, or clay target shooting, or perhaps watch dog-training demonstrations or try orienteering. For a more relaxing stroll through the woods, guests could return to the DC and walk the nature trail. Tours of Bean's manufacturing and distribution facilities were also on tap. According to one account, "every school bus in town" was pressed into service to shuttle throngs of partygoers among the event's sites. One of the reasons for the large crowd was the fact that each of the 8 million catalogs L.L. Bean had sent out in July included an invitation to the festivities.

As the holiday season approached, changes were in store for the hundreds of permanent and seasonal employees who took orders over the phone. In the spring, L.L. Bean had begun using an early type of caller ID called Automatic Number Identification (ANI), which brought up the caller's name, address, and phone number (but not their credit card information) on the service rep's computer screen. One reporter, who thought the whole thing had a Big-Brother feel to it, discussed Bean's new telephone system with company spokesperson Catharine Hartnett, who explained to him that the cataloger used it "to link customers with proper addresses and phones in its computer system. Verification is faster, and time is money, Hartnett said."[19] Even though the new system improved productivity, enough people thought it was "creepy" when their calls were answered using their names ("Hello, Mrs. Jones") that, after a couple of weeks, Bean's employees went back to just saying "hello" and asking the callers for their ordering information in order to verify it.

Another aspect of the company's high-tech approach to doing business was drawing rave reviews from a different group of people, namely executives from companies such as Xerox, Chrysler, and General Dynamics. What they were doing in Freeport was called "benchmarking," or studying how top companies like Bean can get out as many as 150,000 orders a day while maintaining 99.9 percent accuracy. A recent *Business Week* article had rated the cataloger "one of America's 'World-Class Champs' in customer satisfaction and distribution and logistics." Even before the article appeared, requests to visit Bean's Casco Street facility had been coming in at the rate of about one per day, said Bob Olive, who was in charge of filling orders.

But even high-tech facilities can suffer the effects of everyday problems. Eight days before Christmas the well-being of the workers was put into jeopardy when part of the Distribution Center had to be evacuated after a liquid drain cleaner reacted with alkaline cleaning chemicals causing a noxious gas. According to Deputy Freeport Fire Chief Duncan Daily, the fumes entered the building's ventilation system, causing at least 150 workers to seek medical attention. Twenty-five people were transported to area emergency rooms, where they were treated and released. Though no one was seriously injured, OSHA later announced that it planned to fine the company because it didn't immediately do air testing, didn't have an emergency plan in place specifically for chemical incidents, and hadn't trained its supervisors in evacuation procedures.

Just a week earlier, part of the retail store had been closed to customers because of a similar problem in a third-floor bathroom. The 6:00 A.M. incident, which sent a supervisor to the hospital, happened when the chlorine bleach a cleaning person dumped into a toilet reacted with the residue of a solution used to unclog drains.

IN 1993 L.L. BEAN got down to business in a big way. The cataloger had improved efficiency, found some new products, and generally had made good use of the recent economic slowdown. The fact that the company hadn't strayed too far from its roots once again proved to be its salvation; the era's newly cautious consumers were now looking for sturdy, practical products at reasonable prices—just what L.L. Bean continued to offer. Sales would finish at a very strong $867 million (compared to 1992's $743 million), and bonuses of 16.5 percent (totaling $14.5 million—an average of $3,586 per person) would be handed out (much to the joy of the staff at the nearby Muddy Rudder restaurant in Yarmouth, anticipating some healthy tips). The company would also contribute 5 percent to the profit-sharing plan, and it would embark on a number of innovative and successful ventures, such as a line of kids' clothing.

For much of the past decade, the managers at L.L. Bean had kicked around the idea of introducing a line of footwear and clothing just for children. Bean's main competitor, Lands' End, had been selling kids' clothes since 1987, even coming out with a kids' catalog in 1990. Patagonia and Eastern Mountain Sports were also offering lines of apparel for youngsters, as were The Gap and REI.

When L.L. Bean tested a few children's items in its 1992 summer catalog, the company got nearly four times the number of orders it had expected. "It showed us what we wanted to learn," said Betsy Kelly, who headed up the firm's latest division. In typical Bean fashion, the new downsized line of clothing became integrated into what the company called its "family concept." According to its research, the cataloger found that households with children under eighteen spent 108 percent more on camping equipment than households without children, and 126 percent more on winter sports equipment. "It's not just doing it because we think it would sell,"[20] said Kelly. The idea was for L.L. Bean to make things the whole family could wear or use, she explained, and then eventually teach the whole family about outdoor sports. The company also saw its kids business as a way to "combat" the aging of its "master file."

Initially, Bean's designed the clothes for six- to twelve-year-olds, with about fifty or sixty of the smaller items (sizes 6 to 20) included in the 1993 fall catalog, which was mailed in July. "We're trying to give them all the right things," said Kelly, "all the things to keep you warm and dry." Prices for the children's articles would run about 75 to 80 percent of the cost of a comparable adult item; a Polartec Lite pullover cost $38 for child's sizes, $49 for adults. Smaller versions of the Bean Boot were also "in the works." (While Bean was busy revamping its catalogs, bloated Sears, Roebuck and Co.—which would buy Lands' End in 2002—would stop putting out its money-losing, 104-year-old "big book" catalog in January 1993.)

WHEN L.L. BEAN HAD CELEBRATED its eightieth birthday, about the only things going on out on its Desert Road property were the activities at its Outdoor Discovery Center. A lot can change in eighteen months. In the past year, the company's sales had increased by 18 percent, and by February of 1993, construction on a 126,000-square-foot return center and a 200,000-square-foot warehouse, the first phase of the company's gargantuan warehouse facility on an adjacent site owned by Portland's Wishcamper O'Neil Properties, was well underway. But progress at the site wouldn't come about without some growing pains. The company's plans, unveiled the previous July, called for five acres at the front and twenty acres at the rear of the site's existing industrial park to be rezoned from residential to commercial use. And that would evidently be the easy part.

But it wasn't just the retail giant's plan for building huge warehouses, offices, a returns center, and a maintenance facility in the park that was causing commotion. Nor was it the potential traffic to come from the complex's estimated 850 eventual employees. It was the fact that the 40-acre parcel directly across the road from the industrial park would also have to be rezoned to make the plan work. According to Lyndell "Joe" Wishcamper, his company would need another site for its other "small-scale" (non-Bean) clients when L.L. Bean made public its three-to-five-year plan for a 1.4-million-square-foot facility that would use up most of the site's proposed 78 acres. (Not counting retail space, Bean already had

625,000 square feet of distribution and administrative space in Freeport at the time.)

Clients like Robert Gerber, owner of a Freeport engineering company, wanted to build an office in the industrial park but was "told that property for office development would be available if the parcel across from the industrial park was rezoned."[21] This was where the 40-acre "Hartnett property," which Wishcamper also owned, came in. Though less than half of it was deemed "buildable," it needed to be rezoned from residential to commercial and caused nearly as many problems for the project as had the bigger industrial park.

Concerned residents worried about things like traffic, screening, and light pollution in their bucolic setting. "When I look at this industrial park, at the impact on my life," said neighbor Eileen Peterson, "I'm frightened. I'm very concerned about what it's going to look like and feel like."[22] Because of the hundreds of jobs it would create and the hundreds of thousands of dollars in property taxes it would generate, the Town of Freeport was eager to help see the project to fruition—but not at the expense of the local residents' way of life.

To help spare the Freeport Industrial Park's neighbors from the development's impact, said Bean's Scott Howard, the company was ready to promise in a legally binding document that it would maintain a 100-foot buffer zone around the development and retain the area's rural character by keeping the old Fogg farmhouse that fronts the property. Howard also said that the company would work to keep construction vehicles from residential streets and lower the speed limit along Desert Road.

As far back as 1983, L.L. Bean had considered building a 350,000-square-foot distribution facility on a 120-acre parcel along Desert Road—even going so far as to purchase the abutting 171-acre Freeport Country Club as a buffer—but eventually abandoned the project in favor of a location in Hampden because of Southern Maine's high labor and real estate costs at the time. The company's focus had recently shifted back to the Desert Road site after abandoning plans for the Hampden location, citing high transportation costs and the improving costs of labor and real estate in Freeport.

As Bean's growth continued, so did its need for more merchandise, meaning that an increasing number of the goods to be housed in Bean's mammoth warehouse would be sourced from overseas vendors (by the end of the decade, Bean would be getting its products from sixty different countries). In 1993 the company even opened a sourcing office in Hong Kong to ensure a smooth supply stream from Asia, and by 2006, its fifty-four workers there would be keeping in touch with Maine via phone, fax, and e-mail. (In 1997 L.L. Bean would open a Costa Rican sourcing office that would eventually employ twenty-nine people.)

With all its overseas suppliers, Bean was mindful from the start of the working conditions in its factories. Whenever the company became aware of unacceptable conditions in its suppliers' facilities, it took action. After L.L. Bean terminated a few vendors who were "nonperforming on human rights standards," its other vendors made sure that they were in compliance with the regulations. Not surprisingly, the vendors that were in compliance with the human rights standards were also the ones who performed best in the areas of quality and reliability.

Even before opening its Costa Rican office, the Freeport merchant had been recognized as a leader in the area of workers' rights. In December 1996, when as much as 40 percent of Bean's sales revenues came from clothing manufactured overseas, the company was named to labor secretary Robert Reich's Trendsetter List, a directory of thirty-one garment manufacturers and retailers committed to correcting any violations of labor laws, and the monitoring of suppliers. Aides for Rol Fessenden, Bean's VP of product acquisition, "spy on factories" to make sure the wages and working conditions are meeting the standards.

Just because a wage seems low to us, doesn't mean it's unfair, according to Fessenden, nor are the goods necessarily a bargain by the time they reach the States. Ten or 15 cents an hour (in 1999), Fessenden noted, was a middle-class wage in a place like Bangladesh. "It means clean clothes, absence of disease, food on the table all the time, kids who survive."[23] And, by his calculations, "a typical foreign stitch mill paying employees as little as 10 cents an hour . . . has a cost advantage of barely 25 percent because its tools and processes are so inefficient . . . taking account of quality, reliability, and adaptability—low-wage foreign factories sometimes turn out to be more expensive than those in the U.S."

Closer to home, Bean's production workers were honored when the firm's Manufacturing Division was presented with the prestigious Margaret Chase Smith Award[24] at an October 27 awards dinner. "I was just so excited, and also relieved, when they finally called to tell us we'd won," said Becca McClendon, director of Manufacturing. "I knew the site visit went well, and we were all proud of the work we'd done, but it was sure great to finally know for sure, and especially to have won!"[25] She said all the Manufacturing Division employees deserved credit for their win along with the people in Total Quality, Human Resources, Inventory Management, and Product Development.

Five years earlier, foreign shoe producers had been "beating up" Bean's Manufacturing Division, which was underperforming in the areas of cost, quality, customer service, and morale—problems which had contributed to L.L. Bean's losing the Malcolm Baldrige National Quality Award. Brunswick Manufacturing was Bean's chance to turn things around. The company spent hundreds of thousands of dollars on new equipment and spent hundreds of hours indoctrinating workers in the hows and whys of Total Quality. Soon factory defects were ten times less common and the division was making shoes 300 percent faster, saving $1.5 million a year in that sector of the company alone. In addition, injury rates declined an average of 60 percent a year.

L.L. Bean wasn't hesitant to share the wealth of its returning profitability. Toward the end of the year, the company donated $5,000 to Time and Tide's Mid-Coast Fisheries Development Project to help with its sports fisheries restoration of the shad. The firm was also in the second year of a six-year, $50,000-per-year sponsorship of the U.S. Biathlon Association. And, although he fails to mention it in his book, 1993 was also the year that Leon Gorman and his wife, Lisa, established the Alexis de Tocqueville Society for the United Way of Greater Portland. The society was named after French political writer and statesman Alexis Charles Henri Maurice Clerel de Tocqueville (1805–59), whose 1832 work, *Democracy in America*, was one of the earliest and most profound looks at American life. Gorman named the society after the Frenchman because he'd "admired the American spirit for voluntary effort toward the common good." By 2002 the Alexis de Tocqueville Society would consist of thirty-five families who'd contributed at least $10,000 to the United Way.

Beyond merely doing good things with its money, L.L. Bean, Inc., was also committed to its efforts to save energy and reduce waste. Between 1990 and 1992, the company cut its energy consumption by 4.5 million kilowatt hours and introduced an audit system to identify and eliminate duplicate, unwanted, and undeliverable catalogs. In 1993 alone, Bean "repaired or reconditioned 148,497 items, including boots, shoes, jackets, and bags, to extend their useful lives." Its efforts earned the cataloger the Direct Marketing Association's 1993 Robert Rodale Environmental Achievement Award.

Another notable Bean achievement that year was the fact that the company did 25 percent of its 1993 business during the holiday season: Bean's 3,000 order reps took 200 phone orders a minute— as many as 156,437 calls a day. To keep up, pickers in the company's cavernous 10-million-item warehouse walked an average of 12 miles per shift and the packers sent 200 packages a minute down the conveyer belt to the shipping department. And remember, all this was going on in Maine just as winter was gearing up and a foot or two of snow could keep workers at home and slow trucks to a crawl. "I do watch the Weather Channel," said Scott Bryant, vice president of customer satisfaction. "And I worry a lot."[26]

The weather would turn out to be Bean's ally in the early part of 1994 with a very cold January catching the retailer off guard and increasing its sales almost 30 percent over the previous January. To keep up with demand for its boots, L.L. Bean had to increase production from 1,200 pairs a day to 1,600. The only real downside to the increased demand for all the boots, parkas, and other cold-weather clothing was that the company had just laid off most of its seasonal operators, causing some customers to be on hold longer than usual. "[The cold snap] caught us by surprise," said Catharine Hartnett. "We weren't sure how long it would go on, and we didn't want to staff up for something that turned out to be a fluke."[27] To avoid being taken by surprise again, the cataloger started buying long-range weather forecasts. This jump-start would help Bean's flagship store rack up $114 million in sales for the 1994 fiscal year.

As for its catalog sales, the company was racking up huge savings in postage and paper costs by carefully targeting its mailings. In the fall L.L. Bean generated 10 percent more business on 35 percent fewer catalog pages by, for example, sending its kids' catalog only to those who'd previously purchased children's clothing from them. The 140 million catalogs (in 28 versions) Bean mailed out would lead to the firm's pulling in $976 million overall, good enough for the company to reward its workers with 16.5 percent bonuses averaging $3,774 apiece.

Later in the year, all the company's improvement efforts would be rewarded with its fourth number-one ranking in *Consumer Reports'* customer satisfaction poll in as many surveys during the past eleven years. This time the Freeport firm tied for the top position with Patagonia ahead of forty-three other catalog companies. As a result of the ranking, "We get a lot more people calling for the catalog who have never contacted us before,"[28] said Catharine Hartnett. The ranking was based on a poll of 88,000 *Consumer Reports* readers. Close behind the two winners were Lands' End and REI, Eddie Bauer was ninth, and J. Peterman tenth. L.L. Bean had also topped the magazine's list in 1984, 1987, and 1991.

The Freeport firm sought to further increase its sales by sending a representative overseas to try to tap into the ever-expanding Asian market. The unidentified executive accompanied Senator William S. Cohen and representatives of five other Maine businesses on a week-long trip to Malaysia and Singapore. "They are all seeking to expand markets for their products built in Maine by Maine workers," said the senator. All the traveling expenses of the businessmen were reportedly paid by their companies.

As prosperity rediscovered Freeport, L.L. Bean again found itself sending out more and more catalogs. But paper catalogs alone weren't going to cut it in 1994, when the personal computer was establishing a firm foothold in homes across America and the Internet wasn't far behind. Making sure his company didn't get left in the dust, Leon Gorman named a director of "Media Technologies," whose job was to keep up with the goings-on in the ever-changing word of electronic media, things like CD-ROMs, online shopping, and even interactive shopping on television.

Far from being caught napping, the Freeport firm had been included late the previous year in what was being hailed as "the first major CD-ROM-based shopping catalog." Coming from the marketing people at Apple and Electronic Data Systems, the test-marketed disc, dubbed *En Passant* (In Passing), contained products from 21 companies including L.L. Bean, Lands' End, and Williams-Sonoma (kind of like the 12-in-1 catalog R. R. Donnelley had sent to Japan two years earlier, but aimed at 30,000 owners of CD-ROM-equipped Macintosh computers).

Another way the cataloger made shopping easier for its customers was to launch a free bridal gift registry. A far cry from the highbrow Emily Post–type registries of the society crowd, Bean's Home and Camp registry debuted in the division's spring catalog at the request of its busy customers. "Today's time-deprived young couples have other priorities," said Deb Barney, director of L.L. Bean's Home and Camp. "Accordingly, their preferences tend toward casual dinnerware, or even sporting equipment for their active lifestyles and enjoyment of their limited leisure time together."[29]

BY 1994, EIGHTY-TWO YEARS AFTER L. L. had sold his first Maine Hunting Shoe, his grandson decided it was finally time to organize his company's burgeoning cache of documents and artifacts. Originally housed in a room at the company headquarters, the archives would soon take up permanent residence in a large climate-controlled addition to L. L.'s Holbrook Street home, which he had purchased in 1912. In what seems like a major understatement of the archive's importance, it rates a mere two lines in the first edition of the company's official scrapbook: "The lion's share of the pictures used in the book came from materials in the company archives. The archivist works steadily to preserve the company's heritage and collects interesting bits of lore from all departments of the company."

One bit of lore for Bean's archives was the strange tale of the October theft of a trailer-load of women's clothing en route to the company. All told, the thieves made off with 300 boxes of women's clothing from a New Jersey distributor, valued at $100,000. "This was obviously pretty well planned," said Westbrook Police Chief Steven Roberts. "There were a number of people involved here, not just one or two." The empty trailer was found on a dirt road half a mile from the Roadway Express terminal.[30]

While keeping track of its past, L.L. Bean was also looking to the future. The firm's initial foray onto the Worldwide Web came on September 29, 1995, with the unveiling of http://www.llbean.com. The new site allowed people to go to pages called "About L.L. Bean," "What's Coming," "L.L. Bean Products," or "Outdoor Products." There was also "Park Search," a link that gave them quick access to information about the National Park System. Guests could also click on a "Site Index," "Ways to Contact L.L. Bean," "Free Catalogs," or "Your Opinion."

One thing visitors couldn't do via computer was order something from L.L. Bean—at least not yet. Because of concerns about the security of its customers' personal information, "We're not building any of our shorter range plans on our ability to do full-automated, secure transactions over the Web,"[31] said Dale Moore, Bean's director of new media. Shoppers could look at products on the website but couldn't order them there or by e-mail. Instead they were told how to order their items by phone, fax, or using the order form from the catalog.

With the cost of both paper and postage skyrocketing in the mid-nineties, Bean's management team was willing to consider all types of "alternative media" to supplement the old paper catalog.

Would this coming technology mean the end of the Freeport company's legendary paper catalogs? Quite the contrary. Bean and other retailers would soon realize the value of printed matter when they noticed a strong positive correlation between catalog mailings and a spike in online orders. "You're not supposed to rely on the customer to contact you," said marketing strategist George Hague. "You need to contact the customers." ("The catalog drives people to the Internet," Gorman would tell Forbes.com ten years later.) Well into the new millennium, one of the Freeport merchant's stated goals would be to eventually have sales come more or less equally from its catalog, its stores, and its website. Even online giant eBay would eventually begin mailing out paper catalogs.

A little over a year after the company had launched its website, security in the world of online ordering had improved to the point where L.L. Bean felt comfortable offering it to customers and debuted a small online catalog that consisted of about 300 products. According to IBM executive Keith McCall, the company's new Net.Commerce software would allow L.L. Bean, Inc.'s Internet customers to select items, put them in a "shopping bag" (a virtual L.L. Bean Boat and Tote, no doubt), and then pay with a major credit card. The credit card numbers were then scrambled and sent to Freeport. "It's a big step to be able to offer people their own way [of ordering]," said Bean spokesperson Catharine Hartnett. "We can't just write off a new means of communication because we might be a conservative company."[32]

Besides saving some on the costs of printing and mailing catalogs, Bean also hoped to use the Internet to attract younger customers and those who lived outside the Northeast. In late 1996 L.L. Bean, Inc., received its first Internet order, an event the company made sure it recorded for posterity: "At about 3:23 P.M. on Monday, November 25, 1996, the very first Internet order came through—for a pair of women's Gore-Tex Day Hikers, size 9, shipping to Alaska. Electronic commerce had arrived at L.L. Bean."[33] And its reach had certainly extended well beyond the Northeast. As for attracting younger customers, five years after its launching, Bean's website would be attracting shoppers who averaged about forty, ten years younger than the typical catalog customer.

In 1996 L.L. Bean's sales would reach the billion dollar mark. The company had achieved this impressive milestone eighty-three years after L. L. Bean sold his first few Maine Hunting Shoes and fifty-eight years after first reaching the million dollar mark during the Great Depression. But the impressive figures were misleading. Though the company would end up taking in $1.08 billion, the increase from 1995's $976 million was a relatively small 10 percent, leaving it 8 percentage points (about $90 million) below expectations. When this slowing of growth was combined with the increased costs of postage and paper and the fact that the bottom was about to fall out of Bean's Asian market, senior VP Chris McCormick "thought the sky was falling."

Just as a number of circumstances—both serendipitous and planned—had come together in the early nineties to get Bean's Orient Express up to top speed, an almost equal number of circumstances would conspire to derail it toward the end of 1995, just as L.L. Bean Japan was opening its Kobe store, the first one outside of Tokyo. (The store's opening had been delayed for six months out of respect for the victims of January's devastating earthquake.)

But just as things appeared to be chugging along in good shape, the worsening Asian recession, the weakening yen, other companies' catalogs, and fickle fashion trends would converge to engineer the nearly complete collapse of Bean's Japanese business, which, during the early nineties, had helped to hide the ongoing financial problems in Freeport. The gravity of the situation is best put into perspective by a few facts and figures: in 1995 the $210 million worth of goods L.L. Bean sold in Japan accounted for 20 percent of the company's total sales. By 2000 the value of merchandise sold in Japan had plummeted to only $37 million. During the same period the value of the yen fell 42 percent, causing Bean's total sales figures to remain almost flat for the second half of the nineties.

As profits tumbled, a rift developed with the company's Japanese partners, who wanted to transform the Asian arm of the company into a low-priced sportswear outlet. Just as he'd been firm about the direction of his company's American operations, Leon Gorman was determined to preserve the integrity of the brand in the Land of the Rising Sun, so he bought the retail business from them and combined it with the in-country catalog business, the Japanese website, and the Outdoor Discovery program—and he started rebuilding in Japan.

L.L. Bean would keep plugging away in Japan, even introducing its first non-English catalog in 1996 (previously the company had inserted a Japanese cover sheet containing size and ordering guidelines). It also took advantage of favorable lease terms during the country's recession by continuing to open new stores there. The strategy would start to pay off in late 1998, when sales at the firm's Japanese stores started to pick up. "We've adjusted our budget twice this spring already," said Stuart McGeorge, Bean's general manager of international business in mid-1999. "As long as the yen stays strong, we see sales remaining fairly strong throughout the year."

(The Freeport-based cataloger said it expected its 1999 mail-order and retail-store sales to Japan to increase 5 percent to 10 percent over the previous year. The Maine merchant, which had a 10 percent stake in L.L. Bean Japan compared to Seiyu's 58 percent, would decide to end its licensing agreement with Seiyu on February 28, 2001, in order to establish its wholly owned Japanese unit. In late July, the Japanese Jiji Press reported that Seiyu would dissolve L.L. Bean Japan effective August 7. The cataloger started a Japanese website—www.llbean.co.jp—in June of 2002; by 2011, L.L. Bean would have nineteen Japanese stores, five of which sustained minor damage in that year's devastating earthqake and tsunami.)

THE IMPLOSION OF THE JAPANESE market would have been bad enough had it been an isolated occurrence, but it wasn't; it had come on the heels of an unexpected slowdown in Bean's domestic business. To start the year, warmer-than-normal temperatures around the country were blamed for a drop in the sales of winter clothing. Then, an 18 to 20 percent growth rate during the spring and summer abruptly slowed around Labor Day and stayed at about 8 to 10 percent below projections during the important three-month holiday season, when the cataloger expected to do 40 percent of its business. "It was so sudden," said Catharine Hartnett. "Within seven weeks things went down, and kept going down, at a time when things should be going up."[34]

Nothing seemed to be working; not Bean's 308-page Christmas catalog, not an Internet marketing campaign, not even the 30-second television spots the company started airing in major eastern and midwestern markets could drum up more catalog business. (The company's prior use of television advertising had been limited to ads for the retail store that aired around New England.) The merchant was even considering sending out postcards to select customers to remind them to open their L.L. Bean catalogs. "What we can't get our finger on is this retail softness," said Hartnett. "People aren't buying apparel and we don't know why."[35] (About the only mitigating factor was that the slow holiday sales were not specific to L.L. Bean; thrifty procrastinators were plaguing Bean's mail-order and retail competitors as well, with many of the publicly traded ones seeing their stock prices fall 50 percent over a two-year period.)

But the fact that L.L. Bean wasn't alone in its plight was of little comfort once the harsh realities of the situation began to sink in. While a serious concern, the company's lagging sales were really only exacerbating Bean's real problem; it was also being hit with $25 million in additional catalog distribution expenses due to increases in the costs of paper and postage. As soon as the situation became clear, Bean management took decisive action. Though construction on the Desert Road Order Fulfillment Center would go on as scheduled, management decided in October to delay the planned expansion of the retail store for "at least a year." (When it finally was built, the addition would be less than half its originally planned size.)

The company also put off construction of its kids' store, limited its seasonal hires to 3,700 workers—300 fewer than planned—and froze the number of salaried workers at 740. Autumn departmental operating budgets were cut by 4 percent in September, and another 5 to 10 percent in October. The aggressive revenue budget, explained Hartnett, was designed to compensate for the additional mailing costs.

The company's Desert Road complex wasn't the only project with which it was proceeding in the face of adversity. It was also going ahead with the planned Memorial Day opening of its first store outside of Maine and New Hampshire. Located in Rehoboth Beach, Delaware, the 16,500-square-foot store was designed to provide the cataloger with yet another outlet for its discontinued and returned merchandise. "It clears the warehouse and also gives customers access to some good values," said spokesperson John Lamb. (It also allowed the company to recover 90 cents on the dollar opposed to the 25 cents it would get from selling the leftovers to another company.)

Delaware was chosen as a site for the new store because three previous warehouse sales held in the state had demonstrated strong consumer interest in the company's goods. The new store joined the company's other outlets, in Freeport (opened 1989) and Ellsworth (1990), Maine, and North Conway (1988), Concord (1994) and the one next to the Shop 'n Save in Leon Gorman's birthplace, Nashua (1993), New Hampshire. The company would continue opening outlets, and another Delaware store, this one in Wilmington, would become its ninth in 1998. Bean's Freeport factory store led the pack with sales of $1,000 per square foot, or $10 million annually.

In early 1995, the Worcester, Massachusetts, *Telegram and Gazette* ran an editorial about how "the curious flap over Intel Corp.'s highly touted but flawed Pentium computer chip is a textbook example of botched public relations on a truly massive scale." What happened was, shortly after the new chip's release, Intel engineers discovered a flaw that could cause it to (rarely) make mathematical miscalculations, a detail they initially tried to keep to themselves. Once word got out, Intel's stock price began to fall, forcing the company to run a full-page *mea culpa* in newspapers and offer free replacement chips. The whole mess could have been avoided, said the *Telegram and Gazette*, if Intel had just acted more like L.L. Bean. The paper went on to recount the "hoary tale about Bean refunding the purchase price [$2.85] of a boomerang—long gone from its catalog—because a customer wrote to say that his purchase had failed to return as advertised when he had flung it into the sky decades before."

Ironically, a mere six months after the *Telegram and Gazette* editorial ran, Bean's financial situation would prompt it to revamp its liberal return policy. After eighty-three years, the company quietly began putting realistic restrictions on what people could now bring back for a refund. No longer would they be able to return various and sundry items, some of which L.L. Bean never sold in the first place—like golf clubs or a policeman's hat. Nor would they be able to return things because they needed the money. While L.L. Bean stressed that it would continue to guarantee "100 percent satisfaction" on its merchandise, management told the workers to accept returns only when they're related to the product's performance. "The customer still is always right," said Catharine Hartnett, "except when the customer is not a customer."[36] So you'll probably no longer be able to "return" a boomerang that didn't come back.

While only a few people actually took unfair advantage of the firm's refund policy, a couple of them were L.L. Bean's own workers, who'd devised fairly elaborate schemes to steal from their employer. First Clarence E. Springer, forty-seven, of Zephyrhills, Florida, would plead guilty on March 16, 1996, to three counts of mail fraud for receiving more than $6,000 by creating false return records in Bean's computer system when he worked for the company in late 1994. Two weeks before Springer pleaded guilty, Betty Sanders Seavey, forty-six, of Portland, another employee in the returns department, pled guilty to a separate scam to get money from the company. Seavey admitted to defrauding Bean's of more than $50,000 in refunds and merchandise over a two-year period and was later sentenced to fifteen months in federal prison and ordered to pay restitution of more than $65,000.

As during previous periods of belt tightening, Bean did not forget its commitment to various groups around the state, and even people outside of Maine. First the merchant piqued the interest of prospective visitors when it included a road map and an information packet called "Exploring Maine" with 3.8 million of its June catalogs. (A result of all the publicity was that the tourist industry had to scramble to come up with $45,000 to respond to the unexpected surge in inquires, which would turn out to number about 10,000. "Especially when it's an opportunity like this," said Michael Reynolds, president of the Maine Publicity Bureau, "nobody wanted to let it pass. Nobody could let it pass."[37])

Once the visitors arrived in Maine, they'd find plenty of outdoor recreational activities, thanks in part to Bean's $30,000 donation to pay for additional rangers in Acadia National Park. L.L. Bean also came up with $50,000 to help protect an undeveloped two-mile corridor and 273 acres along Grand Lake Stream, Maine's legendary spot for fly-fishing for landlocked salmon, while another $50,000 was donated to the employees of Polartec-maker Malden Mills in Methuen, Massachusetts, which had experienced a devastating fire on December 11.

The biggest donation of all in 1995 was made in May when Leon and Lisa Gorman gave $2.1 million to Bowdoin College for construction of a marine studies center on Orr's Island. The Coastal Studies Center, which would be located on a 118-acre peninsula donated by fellow alumnus William Thalheimer and his wife, Irma, two years earlier, would definitely help the college attract new students to the state. "There's nothing like it anywhere," said Bowdoin president Robert Edwards.

L.L. Bean, Inc., got some good news to start 1996 when it learned that its founder had been inducted into the Maine Sports Hall of Fame. The *Portland Press Herald* noted that the induction ceremony would honor six living men and L. L. Bean, and would be held on June 1 at Spare Time Recreation in Lewiston. The entry about the Freeport merchant read:

LEONWOOD L. BEAN (posthumously): Founder of L. L. Bean Co., he was a longtime leader, advocate and participant in outdoor sports. Bean's legacy to outdoor enthusiasts is a spirit of preservation as well as participation in Maine's environment.

That spirit flourishes today in the form of informational and instructive clinics in the company Bean founded.

Just two months earlier, hypercorrect language maven William Safire had taken several mail-order companies to task for what he perceived as questionable grammar in their circulars. One, Sears, received a dressing down for saying its "120-pc. mechanic's tool set has more of what you want!"

"Ever met a 120-pc. mechanic?" wondered Safire. "Make that 'Our mechanic's 120-pc. tool set' or 'our mechanic's tool set of 120 pieces.'" Fortunately the Freeport firm fared better than its Chicago counterpart; while riffling through his L.L. Bean catalog, Safire was considering ordering a waffle-stitch knit shirt when he noticed "there was the flat statement from the catalog pioneer: 'All waffle knits are not alike.'

"Would old Louis Bean, in his original clodhoppers," Safire continued, "have insisted that no waffle knits are alike? Hardly. With the lining of his shoes wicking away moisture, he would have advertised, correctly, 'Not all waffle knits are alike.' He knew how to tie a not."[38]

Interestingly, while the preceding pair of news items were good press for L. L. Bean—the man and the company—they each had a problem (besides the fact that puns are lazy writing): both of them got Leon Leonwood Bean's name wrong.

The cold reality of Bean's current situation reared its ugly head in January, when the firm announced that it needed to save $10 million, mainly by canceling raises and offering voluntary separation packages to as many as 400 employees. It was also eliminating for 1996 the worker bonuses it had handed out for at least fifty years. Just three months earlier, Catharine Hartnett had told the press that the company's hiring freeze and budget cuts had been implemented so the company could avoid laying people off later. "We went through a downsizing in 1991," she said, "and we don't want to go through that ever again."[39] But the cataloger couldn't avoid it. Bean's cost-cutting measures weren't enough, and the company would eventually lose 340 people, 186 through early retirement and 154 through voluntary severance packages. All who applied for the buyout programs were accepted. Since the numbers were within the company's expectations, no further cuts would be needed. "There never was a second shoe prepared to drop," said Hartnett.

The firm's workforce reduction came as a surprise to a lot of people, including some economic experts. "[We thought] they were strong. They would grow. We thought this would never happen," said Laurie Lachance, state economist at the Maine State Planning Office. "It's painful to see this occur, because we put them on a pedestal. . . . We are facing the fact that the big companies in the state are all undergoing this kind of self-examination,"[40] she said. The previous year another Maine business giant, Portland's Unum Corp., had been forced to eliminate 280 workers through voluntary means.

"I think it's agreed it could be termed one of the worst retail years in history," said Bob Peixotto, VP of Total Quality and Human Resources. If there was any silver lining to be found in the cloud that hung over Freeport, it was the fact that strong response to a summer sales circular would allow L.L. Bean to rehire 120 temporary customer service workers in June, two months sooner than expected.

Leon Gorman apologized to his employees and told them that he hoped the situation was a one-time event. "It has never happened before during my time at L.L. Bean," he said, "and we do not plan to let it happen again."[41] Though strong Christmas sales and snow in the Northeast turned "a very severe profitability problem" into "a serious one," he said, profitability for 1995 would be about half that of 1994.

Just as it had with L.L. Bean's Preppy-driven success of the early eighties, the press noticed the company's recent slowdown. A writer at *Business Week* took the company to task for virtually everything it had done during its current leader's era, concluding with: "In everything from management to fashion, privately held Bean in Freeport, Maine, is a company firmly stuck in the past."[42]

So much for L.L. Bean's "mystique." But the *Business Week*

piece, which would appear in December 1998, wouldn't be completely correct—not so much wrong as behind the times—because the Freeport firm had been making a concerted effort to change the way it did business for much of the past two years. In late 1996 Leon Gorman had decided it was time to call in some outside experts to take a good hard look at every aspect of the company, from its philosophy to its operations. It was time for L.L. Bean, Inc., to become leaner and more efficient, time to replace its folksy reputation with a reputation for quality and service—and let the mystique fend for itself. Gorman and his top managers wanted an objective look at the way the company had been doing business, a look that challenged the status quo—one from outside the company. The Boston Consulting Group, Inc. (BCG) was selected to conduct the review.

Accepting such basic changes that challenged his deeply held beliefs about the business where he felt like a father would not be easy for Gorman. Though he tried really hard to keep an open mind about the whole review process, it was still a very difficult time for him.

Not surprisingly, the review revealed many weaknesses in the firm's way of doing business. Some—like Bean's huge holiday peak, its increasing costs associated with producing and mailing catalogs, and its recent poor performance in the international sector—surprised no one. The company's other weaknesses—problems with the "growth potential" of Bean's current business model, and competing with "active sports" companies that were much more focused—hadn't been as apparent, at least to Leon Gorman.

After months of hard work by both the BCG and many Bean employees, the Strategic Review process produced five key strategies which Gorman would come to call Bean's "Platform for Growth." They were: Freeport Studio (a women's fashion line), more retail stores, cost reduction (on all levels), brand management (ensuring that Bean's sub-brands, such as L.L. Kids and L.L. Home, shared and reflected the company's core values), and a revamping of "Organization Structure," breaking the company into several distinct SBUs, or strategic business units.

At the time of their unveiling, Leon Gorman was on board with most of BCG's recommendations, even the idea of "fashion," since more and more casual clothing had been finding its way into the catalog in recent years anyway. The one item he didn't wholeheartedly agree with was the review team's identification of the limited growth potential of Bean's catalog-based business model, which pointed toward the long-avoided retail path. However, he decided to go with it because he felt that having a goal "to work toward" would give Bean's employees something to get fired up about.

Since the company's sales were unlikely to improve dramatically during the next three years, it also needed to make $30 million in productivity gains during that period, which is where its giant Desert Road facility could help. In late summer 1993, the firm had opened its 126,000-square-foot returns processing center in the out-of-town location. Working in what one writer called "an intriguing monument to one of retailing's most liberal policies for returning merchandise," the facility's 250 employees could, in their free time, make use of its walking trails and eighth-mile jogging track or eat lunch in a glassed-in cafeteria in a blue corner tower overlooking a small pond. But the spanking new returns center would be just the beginning of Bean's Desert Road campus.

In late June 1996, L.L. Bean, Inc., would unveil one of the biggest expansions in its history with the completion of its cavernous Order Fulfillment Center (OFC), which, with the addition of 330,000 square feet to its 200,000-square-foot warehouse, had become the largest construction project completed in southern Maine during the previous year. When combined with the returns center, the volume of the new facility was staggering:

In 1996 L.L. Bean opened a 650,000-square-foot Order Fulfillment Center. The Order Fulfillment Center, located in Freeport, Maine, is a state-of-the-art distribution facility where employees fill orders placed by customers from around the world. The facility employs [in 2001] over 860 people year-round and approximately 2,000 during the holiday peak season.

The Order Fulfillment Center has the capacity to process 27

million items per year for customer orders and enables most customer orders to be filled within 24 hours. The technology and design of the facility allow L.L. Bean to store over four million units of merchandise and process an average of 50,000 customer orders a day. The facility is one-quarter-mile long and houses three and a half miles of conveyor belts and 25 shipping docks.43

Designing and building the impressive new structure had been a team effort from start to finish. Just as representatives from other companies had visited Bean's Distribution Center for ideas, a group of Bean employees had embarked on its own "benchmarking" tour of competitors' facilities. Their information-seeking sojourn took them to order centers of The Gap, J. C. Penney, Sears, and even a pair of German companies, Otto and Quelle.

For six weeks, workers transferred L.L. Bean's order-filling and mailing operations out to Desert Road from the cramped Route 1 Distribution Center, which would be used as a warehouse. With the new facility, "we're more competitive in a tough retail environment where customers are constantly demanding faster, better service,"44 said Lou Zambello, Bean's senior VP of operations. The company estimated that the new building, with its emphasis on ergonomics, should cut its processing costs by 25 percent while reducing workplace injuries. The OFC's farming-related color scheme, John Deere green, International Harvester red, and Caterpillar yellow, was designed to "make it fit into the surrounding rural landscape."

When Governor Angus King arrived for the $38-million facility's grand opening, he was thinking in terms more advanced than farm implements. "I never knew it was going to be so big," he said. "I drove in here today and I said, 'This is a mistake. This is Boeing here.'" (Boeing's Everett, Washington, aircraft assembly plant is the largest building in the world, by volume.)

Of the four million units kept in inventory at the new facility, the company's seven best holiday sellers at the time were the Original Field Coat, a Bean staple for seventy years; the Northwoods

Flannel Shirt, same price for four straight years; Deluxe Book Pack, a must-have for all school kids; All-Cotton Flannel Sheets, a must-have for chilly nights; Fleece Pulllover, pioneered by Lewiston, Maine, native Yvon Chouinard and Malden Mills' Aaron Feuerstein; Chamois Cloth Shirt, since 1925; and its Maine-made Boat and Tote Bags.

While the company's flagship store in Freeport was doing solid business (including a million dollars in sales the day after Thanksgiving), up the coast in Ellsworth, people weren't so sure about the future of their little outlet store. Rumors had swirled earlier in the year that the retailer was planning to close its High Street outlet store after six years of doing business there. Bean squelched the rumor (which had been started by nearby "For Lease" signs) saying that the location was doing well and that it was committed to the remaining four years of its lease. In fact the company would continue to end up with more than enough merchandise not only to keep all its current outlet stores supplied, but to open new ones in Oregon and in downtown Portland, Maine, as well.

Bean opened its seventh outlet store in Lincoln City, Oregon, "a tourist community not unlike Freeport." L.L. Bean is known as "a real conservative player"[45] in the industry, said Linda Humphers, senior editor of *Value Retail News*, noting that a company the size of L.L. Bean having only seven outlet stores indicated that it was well run with little leftover merchandise. But the opening of Bean's seventh outlet store in as many years wasn't really good news for the Freeport firm—quite the contrary. Consumers feeling the pinch of modest wage increases and mounting credit card debt were opting to put their shrinking disposable dollars into electronics and household goods, not clothing and active gear, leaving the cataloger $33 million worth of stuff to sell off through its outlet stores. (The company gets three to five calls a week from towns asking Bean to build an outlet store.)

One offer the company couldn't refuse in 1996 was philanthropist Betty Noyce's promise to Leon Gorman of a "relatively low" lease for at least five years (and as many as twenty-five) for her space at 542 Congress Street, the former F. W. Woolworth building, recently home to the Portland Five-and-Ten-Cent Store. (Following its downsizing, Woolworth would focus on sporting goods, eventually becoming Foot Locker.) The reason for Mrs. Noyce's generous offer was the fact that an L.L. Bean outlet store in the city's depressed downtown would act as an anchor to attract other retailers to its vacant storefronts. Following four frantic months of renovation, the 15,500-square-foot store would be ready to open just before Thanksgiving.

Minutes after Bean mascot L.L. Bear cut the ribbon, the place was packed with the first wave of the day's estimated 4,500 bargain hunters. In its first two months of operation, the Portland store would exceed Bean's projection by 30 percent. Congress Street was poised for a comeback. (Sadly, in September, while L.L. Bean was still renovating the building, Noyce, who'd been divorced from Intel cofounder Robert Noyce since 1975, died unexpectedly at her Bremen home at the age of sixty-five.)

Even before Elizabeth Noyce had approached L.L. Bean about her Portland location, the company had branched out in another direction, coming to an agreement with Delaware-based MBNA America Bank to offer an L.L. Bean "affinity" Visa card as part of a new Outdoor Advantage Program. (Some of the advantages were free FedEx shipping, special notice of sales, points redeemable toward L.L. Bean purchases, and the right to sign up for exclusive classes and trips.) The card, which featured Bean's seventy-fifth anniversary "sunrise-over-Katahdin" logo, initially carried no annual fee and had an introductory interest rate of 5.9 percent, which rose to 17.4 percent after six months. Though it wasn't just a store card and could be used anywhere Visa is accepted, Catharine Hartnett speculated that it would boost Bean's sales because it would "always [be] a reminder"[46] to shop at L.L. Bean. Customers could also apply for a gold version of the card.

At the time, MBNA was the second largest credit card lender in the world, and had phone centers located throughout Maine in Belfast, Portland, Brunswick, and Orono. MBNA had its regional headquarters in Camden, Maine, and "was a good neighbor of ours," said Gorman. "We liked the fact that its representatives dealing with L.L. Bean customers were all good Maine people with real Down East accents." In 1999 the program would sign up its one millionth member. "It was one of the top ten Visa co-branded programs in the world," said Leon Gorman.

ALL THE EXPANSION the company had undertaken in the past couple of decades might have made some people wonder if L.L. Bean was getting too big for its britches. While that point remained open to discussion, one thing was clear: Bean's britches were actually getting bigger—at least in women's sizes. "Over the past year we have reproportioned our entire line of women's pants and slacks," said Catharine Hartnett in November 1996. In other words, the cataloger had added an inch to the waist of each size (for example, the waist of a pair of size 10 slacks went from 27.5 inches to 28.5). The official reason for the added roominess was that it reflected the trend toward "a more active lifestyle among women," not the fact that the company's aging baby-boomer customers were putting on a few pounds and it was seeing a dramatic increase in returns due to size. Whatever the reason behind the change, "Women are looking for a more comfortable fit,"[47] Hartnett explained.

"It has nothing to do with age. And it doesn't mean women are any less fit," said Jennie Gwilym, Bean's VP for sportswear. "It just means that women have active lifestyles. We're not the same as our mothers—we want to be comfortable, whereas back then our mothers just wanted to look good."[48] It was all proportional, explained Gwilym; the measurements in pants' hips and length were correct, just the waist was too small. "Too small for whom?" wondered AP reporter Victoria Brett. "Women with expanding waists?"[49]

The gradual shift in sizes had even caught Ms. Hartnett off guard at first; after buying a pair of pants in her usual size, she realized that "they fit better than ever. There was definitely more room in the waist," she said. "But I was kind of bummed when I found out why."[50] Men's pants, long sold by waist and inseam measurements, were not resized. Besides, said Hartnett "We already have relaxed-fit [men's] styles."

Speaking of relaxed-fit men's styles, L.L. Bean once again found itself involved in politics (sort of) with the presidential aspirations of Lamar Alexander, whose campaign attire included a red flannel shirt. If he actually won the GOP nomination and defeated President Clinton in the election, humorist Jerry Perisho wondered "whether L.L. Bean will make him a tux for the inauguration." (Interestingly, the favorite footwear of fellow Republican John McCain during his 2000 presidential bid would also come from Bean. Just before a debate in New Hampshire, the candidate hiked up his pant legs to display a "clunky pair of waffle-soled walking shoes." "I've got my lucky shoes on," he exclaimed. "L. L. Bean! I wore them to the first debate and now I have to wear them every time."[51] Another Republican, President George W. Bush, would receive a pair of Bean Boots when he visited the state in 2001.)

But tales of expanding pants and candidate's shirts weren't the only offbeat publicity the Freeport firm would receive in late 1996. A month earlier, writer David Mandel had mentioned the company in an episode of the popular *Seinfeld* sitcom in which Elaine fixes Jerry up with her friend, Gillian, who works at L.L. Bean. At first, Jerry's quite taken with the attractive blonde—until he realizes she has big, unsightly "man hands." As the third show of the eighth season, "The Bizarro Jerry" was episode number 137 and originally aired on October 3, 1996. Ironically, the part of Gillian was played by an actress named Kristin Bauer.

Another odd story involving L.L. Bean emanated from a remark made by its competitor, Lands' End, in January. Late the previous year, Bean's midwestern rival had intimated that its "leading competitor" had removed a supportive steel shank from its boots "to save a few bucks." The Maine merchant quickly responded to this implication by clarifying that L.L. Bean hadn't significantly changed the boot in eighty-four years. Lands' End went too far, said Catharine Hartnett, "and made factual inaccuracies that were basically aimed at our boots." The dig "really got to the heart of our most popular product," she said. "Had it not been the Bean Boot, it wouldn't have been so disconcerting."[52] In Lands' End's next catalog company president Mike Smith penned a sincere apology which appeared inside the front cover. Below the heading "Our Apology to L.L. Bean," he wrote:

> Dear Customer:
> In several of our Fall and Winter catalogs, we made statements about our "leading competitor's" leather-top, rubber-bottom boots. L.L. Bean expressed concern that some customers may have thought we were suggesting that they would compromise their customers' trust by cheapening their products. Nothing could be further from the truth. L.L. Bean has offered quality products for years. And we have a great deal of respect for them.
>
> We therefore apologize to our friendly competitor in Maine for what was a regrettable error, and hope this corrects any confusion which might have resulted from our catalog advertising. No one respects the integrity of our honorable competitor more than we do at Lands' End.

After Smith apologized, Hartnett said that L.L. Bean was satisfied with his response and considered the matter settled. (In an interesting coincidence, it was about this time that L.L. Bean was well underway with its first-ever major redesign of the Maine Hunting Shoe. The following year, Mr. Bean's famous boot would receive a new heel protector and 50 percent stronger laces, and two years later, in 1999, the company would unveil a substantially improved version of its classic footwear, which would then be called the Bean Boot.)

On a more serious note, 1996 also saw the passing of Clifford Merrill "Mel" Collins at the age of eighty-seven. It had been Collins who'd taken over the job of clothing buyer following the death of Leon Gorman's father, John, in 1959, and who'd shown Leon the ropes upon his arrival in Freeport in 1960. "Mel had a Kardex binder with a card for each item in the catalog," Gorman recalled. "He recorded the beginning inventory for each season (spring or fall), added the receipts, and subtracted the ending inventory to calculate sales. Not hard to understand."[53] Between 1945 and 1949, and again from 1955 through 1974, Mel Collins photographed almost every item in L. L.'s original "cut-and- paste"-type catalogs, which showed "silhouetted" products with no backgrounds. The company's longtime use of Mel Collins's photographs in its famous catalog had given it "lots of credibility," said Leon Gorman

Less than two months after the passing of Mel Collins, L. L. Bean's longtime friend and hunting buddy George Soule died in Brunswick. Soule had tied fishing flies at Bean's store after graduating from Freeport High School, but eventually went on to create cork duck decoys using the insulation from an old refrigerator. Before his company started selling firearms, Gorman once described its position as being based on L. L.'s Maine Hunting Shoe, outdoor apparel, and items such as George Soule's legendary Coastal Decoys. What George Soule might be best known for, at least around Freeport, was the fact that he could scare up a grouse ("partridge") so it would fly in a direction where L. L. could actually shoot the thing. With the passing of George V. Soule at the age of eighty-four, the state lost one of its last links to Leon L. Bean and a simpler time when Maine's outdoorsmen were a breed apart.

In March 1997 L.L. Bean's employee bonuses returned following a one-year hiatus. While the company's domestic and overseas catalog sales for 1996 had remained stagnant at about $908 million, Bean's cost-cutting measures combined with its store sales of $108 million helped the company realize enough of a profit to pay out 9 percent bonuses as well as raises of 3 to 4 percent. (Overall, the cataloger's sales for 1996 had slumped by $40 million, from $1.08 billion to $1.04 billion.) In all, L.L. Bean handed out $15 million in bonuses, or more than $3,300 for each of the firm's 4,481 employees who'd put in more than 1,000 hours in the past year. The bonus paid in 1997 would foreshadow the company's lagging growth; for each of the next three Marches, there would be no bonus.

Toward the end of the year, *Forbes* magazine estimated Bean's net profit at $51 million, and an "operating profit" of $59 million. As usual, management at the privately owned firm held its cards close to its vest and neither confirmed nor denied the magazine's figures, acknowledging only revenues of "slightly more than $1 billion a year."[54] According to *Forbes*, the Freeport company ranked 181st among the nation's top 500 private companies, down 19 places from its previous ranking.

With the success of its recently introduced line of children's clothing, Bean soon decided it needed to capitalize on the line's profitability by giving it its own space. Or maybe it was thinking more about a space that would hold the youngsters' interest—one with activities such as a waterfall and trout pool, a climbing wall, and a mountain bike ride, while their parents occasionally convinced them to try something on. One story has it that the original idea for a kids' store had come from L. L.'s old friend Justin Williams (1912–2005), who lived just across Justin's Way on the other side of the retail store.

Whatever the reason, L.L. Bean solidified its commitment to its youngest customers when it opened the stand-alone L.L. Kids store. Built across Nathan Nye Street from the retail store, the two-story, 17,000-square-foot structure was designed to have the feel of a Maine camp, with cedar siding, gabled roof, and wraparound porch. The building would cost $3 million, but the company looked at its investment as money well spent on a profitable line. "For us it certainly represents one of the fastest-growing businesses that we have," said Michael Verville, Bean's director of retail sales.[55] The store's January groundbreaking marked the beginning of the second year of the company's three-year downtown building plan, so designed to make the project's costs easier to bear. (The three-year plan would actually cover parts of four years: parking in 1996, the L.L. Kids store in 1997, the Discovery Pond and expansion of the retail store in 1998, and the Discovery Park in 1999.)

While Bean's overall sales lagged, sales of its kids' apparel were climbing by an average of 15 percent a year, and had grown by an impressive 29 percent in the previous year alone. One thing the company had recently learned was that it had to take advantage of its strengths as quickly as it possibly could. In just its third year, L.L. Kids clothing was expected to do about $60 million, and the new store was intended to keep the division operating from a position of strength. That first year, the new store would have

700,000 visitors. (L.L. Kids would move into the main retail store in 2002, when it would be replaced in the smaller store by the Hunting and Fishing departments. Hunting and Fishing, in turn, would stay in the building until they moved into the flagship store's most recent addition and were replaced by the relocated Factory Outlet Store on Thanksgiving 2007. In 2009, the building would become Bean's Home store following the move of the Factory Outlet Store across Main Street to the new Freeport Village Station complex.)

On August 6, less than a week after the opening of L.L. Kids, L.L. Bean was already beginning its preparations for the upcoming holiday season, announcing the opening of a temporary call center in the central Maine city of Waterville. "It's a temporary remote call center," said Bean's public affairs director John Oliver. "We will be using it to facilitate our service during our peak coming into the holiday. . . . This is the first time we've done this. Lewiston and Portland have regular workforces."[56] The facility would be located in the vacant Rich's Department Store at the JFK Plaza on Kennedy Memorial Drive, and would employ as many as 700 people until Christmas. New workers there would start at about $8.50 an hour.

But temporary meant temporary, and L.L. Bean said it would stick with its originally planned December 21, 1997, closing date. The loss of 700 jobs caused by the folding of Bean's tent came on the heels of three other plant closings in the area and raised the local unemployment rate to 6.6 percent, which made the Waterville area eligible for federal assistance. On the other hand, the company had been pleased with the results of its first attempt to go to a new area and hire a temporary workforce. "It's been excellent, a fantastic experience,"[57] said Bean spokesperson Mary Rose MacKinnon. Bean's satisfaction with its Waterville venture would bode well for the area, and beginning in 1999, the call center would stay open year-round with a permanent staff of about 200.

With divisions like L.L. Kids doing well, Bean executives decided to head off on another tack to help shore up profits. Their latest idea was L.L. Bean Traveler, a 64-page catalog targeted toward people on the go that included "everything for travelers— from luggage to wrinkle-free clothing." The Freeport firm's latest offering put it in competition with a pair of California mail-order travel-gear companies: the Novato-based Travelsmith and Magellan's of Santa Barbara.

L.L. Bean was hoping in 1998 to avoid a repeat of its previous fiscal year when sales had started strong only to trail off during the crucial holiday season. As a short-term fix to its ongoing problem, the merchant hired 1,000 fewer seasonal workers than it had in past years. But Bean's management knew that to remain competitive in the increasingly crowded world of mail-order catalogs, they'd have to do more than cost-cutting. A lot more. One observer identified some of Bean's problems as follows: "The catalog has grown big and unwieldy, offering everything from clothes and camping gear to dog beds and sunglasses. The company's plain image doesn't attract new, younger customers. And the clothing often lacks a sense of flair." Another remarked that Bean's products had "gotten tired."

Yet again, L.L. Bean found itself in the all-too-familiar dilemma of needing to find a way to attract new customers without alienating its current ones. While Bean's core customers were an extremely loyal bunch, consumers in general were becoming increasingly fickle. The trick, of course, was to reach the fickle ones "without turning off the loyalists." Management responded by implementing the first phases of the long-term plan that had come out of the recent Strategic Review. Though Bean president Leon Gorman acknowledged his company's need to change with the times, he freely admitted to being less than comfortable with some aspects of the plan. He found it frustrating because Bean's had always sold "the steak without the sizzle. Now we've got to sell the sizzle along with the steak"[58]

Even the famous L.L. Bean catalog would be getting another makeover of sorts. Moving away from its familiar dense type and static poses, the catalog would soon feature "a lighter, more open style and more mood photos—from a shirt slung over an Adirondack chair to a landscape shot with a lone fly-fisherman standing in a valley stream." According to Leon Gorman, subtlety would be the key to these most recent changes. "The trick is that you still see it as the L.L. Bean catalog," he said. "We sort of don't want you to notice [the changes] too much."[59]

But the *Boston Globe's* Tony Chamberlain did notice, lamenting the day when Bean stopped using its employees as models and "replaced them with those big glossy shots of New York models, giving the catalog a distinctly Martha Stewart feel."[60]

The company also began sending out slimmer seasonal catalogs in an effort to avoid overwhelming the customers, and making it easier for them to find merchandise. "I don't know how many [colors of fleece] we have," said Catharine Hartnett, "but we have a lot. We're not sure we need to have that many. People get confused and close the catalog."[61] (Bean competitor Eddie Bauer also found itself jettisoning its recently added brighter color choices after customers avoided them in droves and Bauer's sales slumped more than 10 percent.)

There would also be more frequent catalog mailings targeting niche markets. One of the first of these new circulars came in July 1988 with the introduction of The Catalog for Active Women, which featured not only active wear, but also gear such as packs, sleeping bags, and even kayaks designed specifically for women. Later in the year, Bean came out with two new catalogs to supplement its traditional Christmas circular—one focusing on women's casual clothing, the other on men's. Next, in early 1999, L.L. Bean would launch its L.L. Home sub-brand, which consisted of three catalogs: Textiles, Furnishings, and Outdoor Living.

A little later in the year, "fashion" finally came to the house of L.L. Bean. "Women's fashion and L.L. Bean is almost an oxymoron to a lot of people," observed William Dean, publisher of a catalog industry newsletter. Dean's assessment notwithstanding, Bean was going to try to make a go of it, putting its first "affiliated brand," Freeport Studio, front and center as the first visible result of its recent Strategic Review. There would even be a Freeport Studio catalog, a "slick" affair that presented the product in such a manner that even the most devoted Bean fan would have a hard time discerning its origins. "We would not expect people to pick it up and say, 'Oh, it's from L.L. Bean,'" said company spokesperson

Catharine Hartnett. "We don't want to give the impression they'll get the same Bean apparel they've found in the past."[62]

By offering "more feminine" dresses, skirts, pants, and tops from new suppliers, the company hoped its new line would appeal to the busy woman who could wear it both at home and at the office. "The goal of all our clothes is to solve problems for today's busy women," said Fran Philip, a Bean VP and general manager of Freeport Studio. "Is it easy to take care of? Is it a wearable style? Is it flattering?"[63] And since women tend to buy business clothes on a fairly regular basis, the cataloger also hoped to create "dramatic profit opportunities" if it could pick up the slack during the slow season without hurting peak sales in the process.

The company tapped its extensive mailing list to send out nearly 25 million of its new catalogs—at a cost of 44 cents each—in the first year. "Relative to most catalog start-ups," said Philip, "that is a fairly aggressive number." (A new catalog would be sent to customers each quarter. These would be followed at one- and two-month intervals by "remails"—the same catalog with a different cover.) The first of the new line's catalogs mentioned its connection to L.L. Bean only in the fine print.

The goal of the Freeport Studio line was to generate "off peak" sales with a stylish line of women's clothing that would be easy to care for but wouldn't directly compete with the image Leon Gorman was still trying to maintain for the rest of his company. It was also expected to generate a gross margin of 55 percent.

Freeport Studio, said the company, offered "'high quality, well-designed sportswear (updated sportswear) for the active busy woman.' The line would include 'dresses, jumpers, skirts, slacks, jackets, and other related separates that are versatile, easy to wear, and easy to care for.'"[64] A separate call center, staffed by eighty specially trained "consultants," was set up for the line, and the first Freeport Studio catalog was mailed on January 15, 1999.

Once it began rolling off the presses, Bean's newest catalog revealed that the Freeport merchant had broken down its fashion line into four distinct categories: Working Assets, for the casual workplace; Comfort Zone, for casual or more formal settings;

Nature's Inspiration, a fresher take on the more traditional Bean look; and Basic Elements, wardrobe mainstays such as oversized white shirts and sweater sets. The company planned to ship out most of its Freeport Studio items in better-quality wrapping and already on a hanger. These customers would also receive a newsletter. Overall, the line was described as "fashionable but not frilly."

Because the January catalog had been mailed before a three-day holiday weekend, and its delivery was further slowed by bad weather, orders for the new line turned out to be about half of what the retailer had expected. In an effort to boost sales through brand recognition, the March edition of the catalog received a sticker on its cover (called a "Dot Whack" in the mail-order business) announcing that Freeport Studio was a "new L.L. Bean brand."

By November of 1999 the Sword of Damocles would be hanging over Fran Philip's head. After an up-and-down spring and summer, sales of Freeport Studio merchandise was 60 percent below expectations for the fall even though initial sales estimates had twice been reduced from their original $80 million to a final figure of $43 million. Projections for the new line had gone from a $5.7 million profit to a $2.2 million loss—and that was on top of $12.5 million of unsold inventory L.L. Bean was left sitting on.

Just a month earlier, Leon Gorman had said, "We never lost confidence in Fran. But when you miss forecasts by 70 percent, you've got some problems. Our bet was Fran would find the solutions so we'd break even by year two."[65] It couldn't have been easy to have such confidence in the line's eventual success given its dire circumstances.

By 2001 the company's leadership would decide that its Freeport Studio line of fashion just wasn't going to work out. The new line had underperformed in terms of growth and profitability right from the start, and when Freeport Studio showed no growth during 2000, the handwriting was on the wall. In a last-ditch attempt to bolster sagging sales, L.L. Bean had even moved some of the line's clothes, which had originally been catalog-only items, into some of its stores.

Ultimately, Bean's upscale line suffered from the same problem that did in the SBU concept; with its overhead, such as separate catalogs, call center, and marketing efforts, the company simply felt that the undertaking was no longer worthwhile. According to Bean spokesperson Rich Donaldson, the decision to pull the plug was made in early October 2001, but the company still planned to send out a spring catalog in January. L.L. Bean would continue to sell Freeport Studio items in its flagship store in Freeport and in the Portland and North Conway, New Hampshire, outlet stores, he said, until mid-2002.

"[W]e couldn't keep Freeport Studio separate from L.L. Bean if we wanted it to succeed, and that was a problem," Leon Gorman said. "Research revealed that customers thought it was inappropriate of Bean to be in dressy women's career apparel. It was confusing people about what we stood for."[66] In September 2000, a Harvard case study had chronicled the brand's start-up and first-year difficulties, and not even the benefit of a second-place tie for the line's circular (with the American Girl Holiday catalog) from *Catalog Age* would be enough to change the troubled line's fortunes.

Bill End's warning of nearly two decades earlier had proven to be prophetic: "If you want a guaranteed disaster, continue the shift towards women's apparel."[67] Freeport Studio certainly hadn't panned out the way the company had hoped, and L.L. Bean's women's fashion was once again an oxymoron. According to records in Augusta, L.L. Bean, Inc., officially canceled Freeport Studio on February 13, 2004.

One person for whom the survival of Freeport Studio wouldn't matter in the least was a young woman named Katherine Tyrol, who staged her own anti-clothing protest at the retail store in the wee hours of one August morning. L.L. Bean officials chalked up the incident as a crime of opportunity, owing to the fact that they're famous for always being open. "Some customers did happen to be in a position to catch an eyeful," said Bean's Catharine Hartnett. "She never told us what cause she was supporting."

"I was just kind of sick of the establishment and all that stuff," said the eighteen-year-old Tyrol after she'd emerged from Bean's lady's room and sprinted through the store wearing only a small backpack containing her clothes. "I think it's really oppressive that the government decides what part of me has to be covered," she protested. Tyrol was arrested shortly afterward when police stopped her and her friends in a car. Disappointed that people had missed her point by dismissing her as a streaker, Ms. Tyrol said that if she could to do it over again, she would "stay put and wait for police." She was charged with indecent exposure and ordered to appear in court before Labor Day—maybe so she could still wear white.[68]

Equally as ill-fated as Freeport Studio was L.L. Bean's strategic business unit structure. Intended to be more aggressive, more customer-focused, and quicker to respond to changes in the marketplace, SBUs were an attempt by Bean's executive committee to empower its managers to go after market share by becoming experts in their respective segments. The plan was implemented by dividing the company into seven SBUs: men's, women's, sporting goods, home, kids, travel, and Freeport Studio.

But the SBU structure would prove to be complicated and unwieldy, requiring even more changes to support it. It was, according to Leon Gorman, "supplemented by shared service units (SSUs), such as human resources, finance, and information services. We created seven product SBUs," he continued, "and six channel SBUs (in addition to catalog, e-commerce, and retail, we treated international, corporate sales, and factory stores as channels). We set them up in a matrix format, with each product area intersecting with each channel. An overall balanced scorecard of performance metrics for the company was developed and disaggregated to each SBU and SSU." There would also be "duplication of marketing and inventory management efforts; a lessening of expertise at the corporate level; and the need for many, many meetings."[69] The whole thing was overseen by Gorman and three senior VPs. In the end, the company's strategic business units concept would survive only about as long as Freeport Studio.

A major initiative to come from the Boston Consulting Group's Strategic Review was Bean's identification in early 1998 of three broad areas where the company could cut costs significantly. Chief among these was its cost of goods sold (COGS), or what L.L. Bean paid vendors for products. Within two years, the cataloger had gone from sixty knit vendors to six. Through longer commitments, better quality control, and improved communications with its remaining vendors, the company's attention to its "sourcing" enabled it to realize about $30 million in savings over the same time period—more than enough to justify the entire Strategic Review effort. The company's cost-cutting efforts were also aided by the recent economic slowdown in Asia, which forced Thailand, Indonesia, and the Philippines to devalue their currencies and made goods produced in those countries cheaper to buy.

Another ramification of the Strategic Review process, which one writer dubbed Bean's "introspective period," was the firm's acceptance of the fact that it needed to augment its outlets and flagship store with more retail locations. By 1995 even Leon Gorman had finally begun to lose confidence in his company's ability to grow by relying on its customers to turn to the catalog or website. In spite of all the new, fast, and easy ways to get the things they wanted, people still liked to go shopping in a store. "It was finally time," admitted Gorman, "to look hard at our retail options."[70] Interestingly, Bean's Internet sales would be double in 1998 what they'd been in '97, and triple during the holiday season.

"L.L. Regional" was launched in April 1998. "Retail might be a better way to strengthen our presence in the outdoor market," said Catharine Hartnett, acknowledging that most people want to try on a backpack or ride a mountain bike before buying one. Once the decision to build six to eight new retail stores by 2001 had been made and accepted, the firm's management needed to decide on the project's direction—whether to go with a few large regional stores, several smaller stores, or a mixture of both. In mid-1998, a large store in the Northeast (but outside of New England since the Freeport store was capable of drawing shoppers up from Boston) was the leading candidate for a planned 2000 opening.

Before the company began increasing the number of its retail stores, it first had to finish adding on to its flagship store. As had been the case with construction of the company's Desert Road facility, the latest addition to the store had been approved only after some lively discussion and over the protests of a few abutters who objected to the way their neighborhood had been rezoned. But the biggest roadblock to the expansion had been the cataloger's own finances when sluggish apparel sales in 1996 had forced it to institute a hiring freeze, reduce purchases from its vendors, and freeze all capital expenditures.

Once construction on the long-delayed expansion finally got underway in early 1998, it would end up being much smaller than the one originally proposed. It would also lack some key features of the original plans, which had called for the new section to be much larger than its eventual 25,000 square feet and to have a hiking hill (for trying out footwear) and a clock tower. The expansion was also supposed to have a rain room (for trying out rain gear) similar to the Gore-Tex–sponsored rain room at the new REI store in Seattle, and a loading dock along Morse Street would be converted to an indoor fly-casting pond. As it turned out, only the hiking hill would make the cut this time around.

Richard Balzer's exquisite, handmade $100,000 tower clock would make its way into the new addition, just not in a clock tower. Taking Balzer, his wife, son Tad, and "about eight assistants" two years to make, the clock resided temporarily in a glass case in the lobby of the existing store before being installed in an inside wall of the addition. The clock, called the Aaron L. Dennison Memorial Timepiece in honor of the Freeport native who is recognized as the father of American watchmaking, weighs 1,500 pounds, stands 6 feet tall, and has an 8-foot pendulum. It was originally designed for a tower above the store's entrance, "displaying the time across town with three 6-foot-wide faces." It also has a music box–style wheel, which plays nine selections depending on the locations of pins on its grid. Tad Balzer recalls that "L.L. Bean said, 'How much do you want for it?' and we were able to say, 'it's not for sale.'"

With the clock tower eliminated from the design, there was some discussion as to where the Balzers' clock, which they had given to the town, would end up. "The tower was ideal," affirmed the younger Balzer. "But if not the tower, it should stay in the main store of L.L. Bean in Freeport. . . . We'd like to see it stay with L.L. Bean, just because of the permanence of L.L. Bean,"[71] he said of the first mechanical tower clock built in the United States since 1963.

L.L. Bean finally opened the expansion of its Freeport store just prior to the start of the important holiday season.

One reason Bean's addition came about when it did was because of a tax increment financing package worked out between the cataloger and the town in 1996. In its original form, the TIF amended the 1988 TIF Bean had received for its Desert Road facility and was to last for twenty years. It also provided Bean with $3.4 million in property tax rebates and $2.4 million to pay for public improvements. Freeport would benefit by getting $3.8 million in new tax revenues and $5 million for a new 16,250-square-foot library at 203 North Main Street, behind the Baptist Church and the middle school.

The town would also save about $300,000 a year in the state's education funding formula and get to rent out the old library as retail space. Assistant librarian Vicki Lowe said moving the B. H. Bartol Library out of the crowded downtown's 1905-vintage Carnegie building would make it more accessible, especially for people driving to it. The new Freeport Community Library would be built on 3.5 acres purchased from James Gorman for $110,000, and would be more than twice as big as the old library.

While the TIF had been meant to keep L.L. Bean from moving some of its operations out of Freeport (nearby Yarmouth had recently lured away DeLorme Mapping with an attractive TIF package), not everyone in town had been in favor of giving the deal to the retail giant, especially in light of the fact that L.L. Bean had just cut 8.5 percent of its workforce (340 employees). "We seem to be trying to increase their overhead, and they seem to be trying to reduce it," said Freeport resident John Forest. "Maybe this is a time to let L.L. Bean be. Maybe they should do whatever they're going to do."[72] It was difficult for everyone to accept the fact that L.L. Bean was not invincible, that even the local catalog giant was susceptible to the market forces at work in the rest of the world, and that it was going to need a little help from time to time.

Others simply thought the whole thing was a bad deal for the town, saying that the cataloger was certainly big enough to "pay its fair share." Their comments were countered by those from the likes of Freeport landowner Kevin Kelly of Brunswick, who said, "We're only talking about new tax dollars. L.L. Bean or anyone is not going to receive a dime of existing taxes. This does help the average taxpayer."[73] Kelly's sentiments were echoed by Thomas McBrierty, state commissioner of economic and community development, who said that the proposed TIF package looked very balanced to him. "A large chunk of the money [would go] back into the infrastructure improvements in that area," said McBrierty. "I think that's great."[74] Bean VP Bill Shea pointed out that the expansion could create 150 to 200 new jobs in town. "When we first got into this whole idea, it was to benefit the town and L.L. Bean," he said. "We're not interested in pushing it if both sides don't see it as a benefit."[75]

At the urging of the town, L.L. Bean had gone ahead with construction of the much-needed 371-car parking lot in 1996, but not even that was accomplished until all aspects of the project had been extensively discussed. Primarily, citizens of Freeport had been concerned that the lot would be too close to the Morse Street School. "It's turning into a sea of asphalt," said Elizabeth Patten, a Morse teacher who had a seven-year-old son at the school. "What we're looking for is protection from traffic, and safety."[76] (The cataloger would later reclaim forty-six parking spaces for green space.)

The immediate solution to the problem was strategic landscaping consisting of fruit trees, trellises, fences, and blueberry bushes to provide a buffer between the two, for which the town allotted $20,000 and L.L. Bean contributed $5,000 to match a federal tree grant. The Friends of the Morse Street School, a group of teachers and parents eager to protect the school from sprawl, had wanted $40,000 for the project and were unhappy with the smaller sum, especially Bean's contribution. "We expect a bit more," Patten said. The company had not been interested in the school department's offer to sell them the fifty-year-old building.

The reality of the situation was that, since the land was now rezoned for commercial use, Bean's was not obligated to provide any additional landscaping for the school. "You'd like them to fund everything," said town council chairwoman Gloria Fogg DeGrandpre. "But in defense of Bean's, they have done a lot for the schools. They're a good business neighbor."77 Over the past decade, the company had given $250,000 to Freeport schools (not to mention the recent donation of $25,000 to the town's Hedgehog Mountain Project and an annual $8,000 contribution to Freeport Community Services). "We try to consider ourselves a citizen of Freeport," said Bean's Catharine Hartnett. "We have never been anything but. We don't benefit by not building good relationships," but she added that "we need to make business decisions so we can continue to grow at a healthy rate."78

One longtime Freeport resident who spoke up in defense of the retailer was Edgar Leighton, whose corner store across from L.L. Bean had been leased to Dansk after he'd been displaced by a fire. Leighton pointed out that without Bean, Freeport would most likely be a town of nothing more than empty shoe factories and vacant stores. L.L. Bean, Leighton noted, attracted retail, which provided a stable tax base. "For retail in Freeport to continue to be successful," he said, "you can't build a fence around it and say this is all there's going to be."79

Barbara Frissell, a retiree who'd lived in the neighborhood for twenty years, thought the parking lot was "beautiful," and agreed with Leighton's assessment of the situation. "The past is gone," she said, "and some people bitterly resent it. But without L.L. Bean, this town would be nothing."80

Shortly after Bean had originally proposed the 46,000-square-foot, $10 million expansion in early 1994, the town had enlarged the commercial zone to include the five acres behind the existing store. In recent years, the company had acquired four nearby properties in preparation for its upcoming expansion, specifically those at 8 and 9 Morse Street, 5 Nathan Nye Street, and 9 Cushing Avenue (which is now called Justin's Way). As had been the case with the previous expansion, the homeowners living along Morse Street protested that their property values would suffer if they weren't rezoned for commercial use, with two homeowners even suing to block the town council from acting on Bean's request. "An L-shaped row of houses with municipal property on one side and a major corporation on the other is not a neighborhood,"[81] said Philip Jones, one of the neighbors.

The homeowners dropped their suit three days later, after being told that officials would consider including their properties in the commercial zone. When that request was rejected three months later, the abutters were told that, since they were private homeowners, their request was not consistent with the town's comprehensive plan, which encourages the expansion of existing businesses and retention of local businesses. In other words, the rezoning request was turned down because it didn't include a plan for the land, the same reason it had been rejected in 1988. Quickly, the scope of the originally proposed expansion had grown to 64,345 square feet at a cost of $12 million but, by mid-October, the company's sagging profits had forced it to delay and then downsize the expansion even though it continued to get permits for the project.

Despite all the changes going on throughout L.L. Bean, the company and its president continued their support of worthy causes. To help people through the devastating January 1998 ice storm, L.L. Bean served free meals in its cafeteria, made showers available, and picked up half the cost of employee laundry expenses. The company also donated 600 parkas to electrical workers from away who'd come to help restore power. The following year, Leon and Lisa Gorman donated $1 million to The Nature Conservancy to help pay for the recent acquisition of a 40-mile stretch (about the size of Baxter State Park) of the upper St. John River. Because of that single contribution, the couple would be named as one of the fifty most important volunteers in The Nature Conservancy's fifty-year history.

With the company endeavoring to reinvent itself for the twenty-first century, it was also now time for L.L. Bean to reinvent its trademark boot—and to do it so that it still looked like it always had. Six and a half million pairs sold since 1912—does the Maine Hunting Shoe really need to change? And won't people be put off if Bean redesigns the thing? "That was one of the challenges," said Chris Brown, the company's product line manager for active footwear. "It is an icon, our premier product, but it really hadn't changed that much in decades."[82]

No one could have summed up the idea of redesigning the old standby better than veteran Bean beat reporter Edward Murphy at the *Portland Press Herald:*

> It's as though someone were to suggest that what Mount Katahdin really needs is some landscaping and a good hotel. And how about painting those drab white lighthouses a more fashionable teal?
>
> But redesign the Bean boot? Never!
>
> Until now, that is. . . .
>
> It's not often that people think of a boot as having "core values," but the Bean boot is more than just footwear. Along with lobsters and waves crashing against a rocky shore, the Bean boot is Maine.[83]

And the Bean Boot really wouldn't appear to change, at least to the untrained eye. "It may look the same on the outside," hinted the card that came with each pair of new boots, "but there's an inside story." In addition to the old version's shortcomings, "there are probably over a dozen products that are designed to look like the Bean Boot. You add them all up and, yes, it definitely chips away at the business," said Tom Armstrong, Bean's VP of outdoor apparel and footwear. "If we could just take a leap ahead of everyone with a new compound for our bottoms, it would be an exciting new offering," said Armstrong. "It's high-tech but low-tech," he pointed out. "It really looks the same, but the performance is improved. I think it's a metaphor for what we're trying to do at Bean: to keep the values and keep the customer service, but to improve the offering that we give to the customer."[84]

"It needed to look exactly the same," said A. J. Curran, Bean's active footwear developer. "We would have gotten a lot of letters if we had messed with the classic look. Finally the technology became available to make that happen."[85]

In its December issue, *Down East* magazine called the revamped footwear "A Better Bean Boot," reflecting the gumshoe's new official name. So why was the name changed? To deemphasize the boot's connection to hunting? A more likely scenario is that people had always referred to it as the Bean Boot and the nickname stuck. "In the sixties it was changed for a while," said Bean spokesperson Dave Teufel. "Then it went back to Hunting Shoe again. At one time L. L. himself changed it to Bean Boot."[86] As this is being written, it's still possible to get the boots with "Maine Hunting Shoe" on the heel label, but you'd probably have to ask for them specifically.

Down East also noted that while the boot still looks the same, "it no longer sucks socks." "Sock suck," a problem that had long plagued previous incarnations of the boot, had been caused by its too-large heel area, which conspired with gravity to cause the wearers' socks to slide down as their heels moved up and down in the boot. This problem was finally eradicated, after five years of research, by the new model's improved heel. "We reengineered the heel area," said Chris Brown, "narrowed it so it fit better. No more sock sucking."[87] Other improvements to Mr. Bean's classic boot included better waterproofing for the leather upper and more side support and breathability for the rubber bottom.

"Today, they're even better," said *Outside* magazine. "The 88-year-old Bean Boot was revamped for this winter to be tougher, warmer, and sturdier. Don't worry—they look *exactly* the same, with their chain-link tread, ribbed rubber bootie, and sumptuous leather cuffs. But the once-squishy sole is fortified with a steel shank, a sweat-wicking synthetic has replaced cotton in the lining, and the rubber is now injection-molded (in Maine) rather than vulcanized, making a lighter boot with surer traction."[88] The new boot's new sole is also lighter, warmer, and three times more abrasion resistant than before, and its new, softer leather upper is 100 percent waterproof.

About the only people who weren't happy with the new boot and its new Maine-made, injection-molded thermoplastic soles were the ones who worked at the LaCrosse Footwear Company of La Crosse, Wisconsin, to whom Bean's manufacturing "decision will result in a reduction of $1.5 million in sales to Bean . . . and will mean more layoffs in the second quarter."[89] But Tom Armstrong knew that the old hand-laid, vulcanized soles of the past wore out too fast and turned slippery. They just weren't going to cut it anymore.

The method of producing the new, improved sole for Bean's trademark footwear fell to L&A Molding of Lewiston, Maine, whose president, Oscar Cloutier, helped develop custom molds (at a cost of $100,000 for each shoe size) made by Apego Stampi in Italy. The injectable "rubber" was developed by the J. Von company of Leominster, Massachusetts, which "probably had 60 tests of the compound," before it finally "dialed in the right one." L&A Molding would manufacture up to 500 of the "thermo-plastic olefin" bottoms a day before Bean eventually moved its production to Arkansas.

"[Development of] the state-of-the-art injection-molded rubber bottom," notes the 2002 Bean company scrapbook, ". . . had not been market-driven, but part of Bean's Better Basics Process." Designing the "Y2K-compliant boot," said the L.L. Bean catalog, "took nine years, 35 prototypes, and 100 field tests" to keep it ahead of all the knockoffs out there. According to the Freeport merchant, its new old boot was 12 percent lighter, 14 percent more slip resistant, 35 percent warmer, and a staggering 250 percent more abrasion resistant.

But most people probably would have agreed that the greatest improvement of all to the new Bean Boot was the fact that it cost $6 less than its predecessor. The revamped Bean Boot and its nicer price were an immediate success: in the first six weeks they were available, sales were reportedly up by 39 percent for men and 49 percent for women.

The final chapter of the story of Bean's new boot would be played out in 2007, when the company returned the manufacturing process for the boot's rubber bottoms to Maine. The change in location wasn't just Bean's way of ensuring the quality of its rubber soles, it was also a matter of pride. "It means a lot to us" to make the boot in Maine, said Bean spokesperson Carolyn Beem. "It is a signature product for us so we have always been protective of the quality. It has also become a signature product for the state."[90] Bringing production back to Maine, which had lost 10,000 manufacturing jobs in the five years before the move, also proved to be "a public relations master stroke." Bean's was expecting to invest about $1 million in new machinery to facilitate the move. (The boots' laces and eyelets are supplied by companies in California and Rhode Island, respectively.)

At the same time the revised version of the boot he'd created was being introduced to the world, Leon L. Bean was also enjoying a shot of revived popularity. Besides making it into the *American National Biography*, L. L. Bean was also recognized in 1999 as one of the century's top entrepreneurs by the *Wall Street Journal*. In its November 29 edition, the paper hailed the Mainer, along with others such as Henry Ford, Bill Gates, and Sam Walton, as one of the "Ten Who Changed the World"—people who'd had the most influence on entrepreneurship during the past century. "The Bean name showed up on almost every product," said the piece, "and Mr. Bean's [catalog] prose was simple, down-home, and direct, the way his customers liked it. 'This is the shirt I personally use on all my hunting and fishing trips,' he'd write in his typical fashion.

"He offered advice too: 'A white handkerchief is dangerous for a hunter to use. They have been the cause of many shooting accidents. A red or blue handkerchief is much safer.'" (The reasoning behind L. L.'s advice, which was quoted from his 1942 book, *Hunting, Fishing, and Camping*, is that a white handkerchief can be mistaken for the white "flag" of a deer fleeing with its tail in the air.)

The Bean Boot wasn't the only thing getting a makeover in 1999. L.L. Bean also launched an entirely new website, "winning quick acceptance," said the company, "from customers and press alike." The following year, it would generate 15 percent ($164 million) of the cataloger's total sales. The *New York Times* called the company "an e-commerce star that is outperforming all but a few companies in its category on the Web. It has risen to that level by virtue of two core characteristics of the company: a stubborn adherence to customer service and a steadfast refusal to let excessive technological wizardry interfere with its shoppers' experience on the website."[91] For 2001, Bean planned to further broaden its Internet product line to appeal to younger customers. (The 16,000 products displayed in Bean's seventy different catalogs still accounted for 80 percent of the company's sales. During the year, L.L. Bean would mail more that 200 million catalogs to the 6 million active customers in its master file.)

The *Times* article gave another reason for the success of Bean's website: apparel. "[Bean's] Internet site has become the fourth most-visited apparel site on the web, according to Media Matrix, an Internet audience measurement firm, trailing behind only Old navy.com, Gap.com, and Victoriassecret.com." This was in spite of the fact that, up to that time, people had been wary of buying clothing online, a reluctance the company countered with its famous commitment to customer service. Bean's employees "love to serve customers in a way they'd like to be served," said Elizabeth Spaulding, the firm's VP for customer satisfaction.[92] This approach would be borne out in the coming years with L.L. Bean consistently excelling in one customer satisfaction survey after another. By 2006, Bean's online sales would exceed those of its catalogs.

About the only downside to Bean's increasing use of computers and the growth they'd brought to the company over the past fifteen years would be a few viruses and the looming of the new millennium along with its host of potential computer problems. In the months leading up to Y2K, the company reportedly spent as much as $10 million to ensure that its computers were ready for the date change.

Despite the growing popularity of online ordering, most of Bean's customers still preferred to place their orders by phone. This was good news for the employees of Bean's Waterville call center, many of whom were told in July that they'd be staying on after the holidays because the company had decided to keep the facility open year-round. (For two years it had operated on a seasonal basis.) "We are very proud to be able to be part of the Waterville community," said Elizabeth Spaulding. "We have been extremely impressed with the quality of the workforce that we have experienced during the last two peak seasons."[93] The call center, Bean's third year-round one in Maine, would employ about 200 people.

Unfortunately, not all customer attempts to call L.L. Bean were received in Waterville or any of Bean's call centers at all, for that matter. The problem started in August when one of the company's proofreaders, unaware of the new 877 prefix for toll-free numbers, "corrected" the number in the L.L. Kids catalog to "800," inadvertently making it the recently inactivated number for an unrelated kids business. Somehow the number ended up ringing in the home of a Virginia woman. "She was extremely gracious and good-natured and wonderfully helpful," said Bean spokesperson Mary Rose MacKinnon. "She even took orders for us, so no sales were lost." To compensate the woman for her help and patience, the company sent her "a very generous gift certificate"—and L.L. Bean immediately acquired the inactive toll-free number.

The company's efforts to drum up more business by way of its new advertising slogan, "Start Here, Go Anywhere" (created by the Mullen Agency), were bolstered by the mailing of 200 million catalogs during the year (but not through television advertising, as the recent glut of dot-com companies buying TV time had driven up the cost. "The cost of advertising essentially doubled," said Bean's Rich Donaldson, "and we decided not to throw our money away."[94]) While the firm's new slogan proved to be catchy and effective, it too would turn out to be problematic when Sullivan Creative, the ad agency of Massachusetts Bay Community College in Wellesley, unknowingly came up with the same slogan a year later. MBCC spokesperson Pam Eddinger asserted that Sullivan "had come up with the phrase independently," but acknowledged that the college was "aware of the conflict."

"We are of course interested in protecting our marks," said Bean's Rich Donaldson, but he conceded that "the Supreme Court has held that instruments of state governments, including community colleges, are immune from suit for federal trademark infringement, which limits our ability to do anything other than to appeal to such an institution's sense of fairness and good faith."[95]

Though Bean's sales remained flat (at $1.06 billion) and 1999 was the third straight fiscal year that the cataloger hadn't handed out a bonus to its employees, the outlook for L.L. Bean was good, with the changes it needed to make to return to profitability well underway. If all of the firm's recent trials hadn't been able to kill it (or even seriously injure it), they'd only make it stronger, and the still-changing company would finish the 1990s on a stable foundation and poised for growth.

Chapter 12

*Since its last big run at retail a few years earlier, L.L. Bean
had been hunkered down, learning how to do it right*

Between 1990 and 2000, L.L. Bean's annual sales had grown from $616.8 million to $1.169 billion. The problem was that most of that growth had come during the first half of the nineties, with the last half of the decade—which included the collapse of the company's Japanese business—being "a little better than flat," according to Leon Gorman.

March of 2000 saw the company's workers go without an annual bonus for the third straight year. The bonus, noted the company, is basically profit-sharing, and in 1999, much of the company's profits had gone toward new ventures such as more retail stores, a redesigned website, and specialized catalogs. The cataloger "had some modest growth in a competitive environment," said Rich Donaldson. "But we still fell short of any profit threshold in terms of paying out."[1]

Going without an annual bonus for four of the last five years got some of Bean's employees concerned enough to consider the possibility of unionizing. "[T]here's an interest at L.L. Bean to be . . . represented by the Teamsters," said Bill Turkewitz, a representative of Teamsters Local 340, who emphasized that it had been some of Bean's workers who'd contacted him, not vice versa. "I very seldom solicit," he said. "In fact I never solicit. As a rule, people come to me."[2] The initial two-hour informational meeting, held at the end of March in the union's South Portland hall, would attract about 200 people, and was closed to the press.

In Freeport, Bean's management was keeping an eye on the situation but didn't seem very concerned at that point. "From time to time over the years, unions have shown an interest in unionizing the company's workforce," said spokesperson Mary Rose MacKinnon. "Our employees have not elected to be represented by a union in the past, nor do we anticipate they will in the future. While we respect the right of our employees to unionize, we've found L.L. Bean managers and employees place a great value on the direct employee-employer relationship that we enjoy."[3] She also said that, even though the company hadn't paid a bonus for three years because of flat sales, pay raises exceeded the rate of inflation and Bean provided health insurance and other benefits. Company managers also met with employees to tell them why they didn't think a union was good for L.L. Bean.

(The union organizers would fold their tent in March 2001, a year after they'd started, when L.L. Bean gave its workers a 10 percent bonus—a total of $25 million to about 5,000 workers. Bean spokesperson Rich Donaldson said the bonus was based solely on profitability, and denied it had anything to do with some workers' recent movement to unionize, which had gradually been losing steam on its own. Bill Turkewitz said that many of the company's recent changes—such as the bonus, clarified policies, and regular hours for seasonal workers—had been the same ones sought by the union. "Bean is now doing the right thing by its employees," he said, but noted, "We're still keeping an eye on things."[4])

The unionizing effort was only a minor distraction to the company as it forged ahead with its growth plan: the opening in July of its second major American retail store, in McLean, Virginia, at Tysons Corner Center, the D.C. area's largest mall. Designed by Callison Architecture of Seattle, the three-level, 76,000-square-foot "core store" featured a decor that was decidedly Bean, including wood, stone, natural light, a trout pond, and a 16-foot waterfall. Forty Bean associates traveled down from Maine "to help start it up and inject some Bean character." The company's figures showed that about 1.5 million "L.L. Bean people" lived within a half-hour's drive of the new store. "The catalog takes customers to the store and the store takes customers to the catalog and online," said Candice Corlett of marketing firm WSL Strategic Retail. "Even if they don't buy anything in the store, it reinforces the brand identity."[5]

Of course people would buy things during the Tysons store's three-day grand opening, lots of things: $800,000 worth.

With the company's growth slowing in the catalog channel and growing in the e-commerce channel, "we needed to penetrate the retail channel where 90 percent of all sales occur," said senior VP Chris McCormick. "This was a competency we needed to develop quickly." L.L. Bean had opened its first American retail store outside Maine in its eighty-eight-year history on Friday, July 28 (although the number of the company's small Japanese stores was quickly approaching twenty). At the time, the company was planning to build another three to five stores in the Northeast relatively soon.

"A consensus emerged that we should go into retail whether I was sold on it entirely or not," Gorman would tell Forbes.com six years later. "I still like the traditional catalog business and direct marketing, but I couldn't avoid the fact that there's a big retail world out there."[6] But the company had, perhaps, planned a little too big. In April 2007 Ken Kacere, senior VP and general manager of L.L. Bean Retail, would tell *Retailing Today* that "based on our experience there, we know that [the Tysons Corner store is] larger than a L.L. Bean store needs to be."

In typical L.L. Bean fashion, the retailer contributed 5 percent ($40,000) of the store's opening weekend receipts to the National Park Foundation, the official nonprofit partner of the National Park Service, with the money earmarked for parks in the Virginia, Maryland, and D.C. area. "I know that L.L. Bean has a long history of helping people enjoy and respect the outdoors—from their environmentally sound business practices to their philanthropic presence," said NPF president Jim Maddy. "The National Park Foundation is especially pleased to number L.L. Bean among the friends we can count on to help people experience America's National Parks."[7]

Shoppers could also register to win a family vacation to Maine or a 2001 Subaru Outback "L.L. Bean Edition" loaded with camping gear. About the only downside to Bean's first full-line store outside of Maine was the fact that Virginia residents would now have to pay sales tax on the items they ordered from Freeport. The cataloger had notified about 140,000 of its "recent and repeat" customers in the state of the impending tax by sending them letters a month or so before the store opened.

The Subaru Outback H6-3.0 "L.L. Bean Edition" sports wagon shoppers in Virginia could try to win was the result of a recent collaboration between the Maine mail-order company and Subaru of America, which would assemble the vehicles at its Subaru-Isuzu plant near Lafayette, Indiana. Recommended to L.L. Bean by Leave No Trace, to which Bean had supplied equipment and Subaru had donated cars, the vehicle was the centerpiece of a strategic marketing partnership between the two companies.

In addition to a host of other amenities, the Bean Edition offered several exclusive touches including additional wood-grain trim, L.L. Bean embroidered floor mats and embossed two-tone leather-trimmed seats, an eleven-speaker McIntosh sound system, a Momo-designed mahogany steering wheel, and a one-year exclusive on Subaru's 6-cylinder, 212-hp engine. The vehicle was also covered by an L.L. Bean Carefree Performance Protection extended warranty.

Under the partnership agreement, Subaru and its dealers would have an L.L. Bean gear and clothing program and Subaru would become the "official" vehicle of L.L. Bean, Inc. "Both L.L. Bean and Subaru share a commitment to superior service, quality, and a dedication to the responsible enjoyment of the outdoors,"[8] said Leon Gorman during a tour of the Indiana assembly plant. The 2001 model-year vehicle was scheduled for release in late summer 2000 with an MSRP of $29,495 plus a $495 destination and delivery fee. Two weeks after taking delivery of the Bean Edition Outback, new owners would receive a specially designed Boat & Tote bag as a gift.

The new markets on which Bean's had its sights set weren't limited to those in the northeastern United States. In 2000 L.L. Bean had dissolved its nine-year Japanese partnership and established a wholly owned catalog, e-commerce, and retail business in Japan. The cataloger was also looking to the south for new growth; a nineteen-page Harvard Business School study (number IES088) looked at Bean's attempts to venture into the Latin American market. Late in the year, the Freeport firm would register a new division, L.L. Bean International, with Maine's secretary of state.

A couple of other Bean-related endeavors also taking place around that time were the partnership between Bean and W. L. Gore to provide the Weather Channel's on-location meteorologists with outerwear, and the publication of several new handbooks. The company's most recent how-to offerings included MacCauly Lord's *L.L. Bean's Fly Casting Handbook* (Lyons Press, 2000); *L.L. Bean's Canoeing Handbook* by Allan A. Swenson (Lyons Press, 2000); *The L.L. Bean Outdoor Photography Handbook* by Jim Rowinski and Kate Rowinski (Lyons Press, 1999); and *The L.L. Bean Hiking and Backpacking Handbook* (Lyons Press, 2000) by Keith McCafferty, who had also written *The L.L. Bean Family Camping Handbook* (Lyons Press, 1999).

There was another Bean-related book out that year that the company had nothing to do with: *The L&L Beancounter's Catalog: Survival Gear for Your Career* by Larry Bleidner and Peter Scott. (As a redheaded kid in the early sixties, Bleidner was the first person to say "betcha can't eat just one" to Bert Lahr in the famous Lay's potato chip commercial—Lahr had played the Cowardly Lion in *The Wizard of Oz*. Peter Scott had quit his job after winning $50,000 on *Jeopardy!* in 1998.)

Sort of an *Items from Our Catalog* for the business set, *L&L Beancounter's* featured helpful career tools ranging from the Golden Parachute Pack and the Aneurysm Detector/Calibrator to "big goofy slippers" for Ultra-Casual Friday. There were also more sinister-sounding items such as letter openers that made their users "someone to reckon with," shackles for temporary workers, cubicle periscopes, and the Human Resources Terminator Mask.

Published perhaps a little too close to home by Common Courage Press in Monroe, Maine, *L&L Beancounter's* joined a growing list of parodies of the famous cataloger, most of which the company simply ignored—with the notable exception of the drawn-out legal battle in which it had engaged with *High Society*'s publisher.

(In a very interesting coincidence, the day before *L&L Bean-counter's* was reviewed in the *Wall Street Journal*, the *Boston Globe* had run a piece called "Bean Counting." Published during the Teamsters union movement, the article included such enlightening tidbits as: "3—L.L. Bean's ranking among Maine's biggest employers. 3—Years employees say they've gone without a bonus. $1.03—Net sales, in billions, for the company in 1998. 14,820,143—Pairs of 6-inch-shaft Bean Boots you'd have to buy to run up a $1.03 billion bill," and so on.)

But it wasn't Bean's high finances that would give the company's management headaches; it was a much smaller figure that would take longer to wend its way through the legal system than had the cataloger's protracted fight with *High Society*. At issue was the sum of 55 cents which Rona F. Flippo of Cambridge, Massachusetts, felt she'd been overtaxed when she redeemed an L.L. Bean gift certificate. Specifically, when Ms. Flippo purchased a garment that cost $39.95, she used a $10 "Outdoor Advantage" coupon she'd earned by using her L.L. Bean/MBNA Visa card. When Bean's collected the sales tax for the full $39.95 instead of $29.95, Ms. Flippo felt she'd been overcharged 55 cents, since Maine's sales tax was 5.5 percent at the time. (Later versions of the story give the value of the coupon as $5 with a tax of 27 or 28 cents.) Lawyers got involved and the whole thing became much ado about little.

Bean's lawyer, David Bertoni, asserted that Flippo's attorneys were suing the wrong people, since L.L. Bean was simply collecting taxes for the state and was being held responsible for money it no longer has. Bean had even received, in writing, a ruling from Maine Revenue Services. "It's a common type of question," said Peter Beaulieu of Maine Revenue Services. "To us it's a clear-cut situation."

Portland newspaper columnist Bill Nemitz even weighed in on the matter, saying that Ms. Flippo's attorneys, who filed their court complaint as "R. F. Flippo, On Behalf of Herself and All Other Similarly Situated," clearly wanted "to sift through L.L. Bean receipts in search of a gold mine."

Flippo's lawyer, Daniel J. Mitchell, countered by saying that the case was "not about one woman claiming to be overcharged by 55 cents, but about potentially thousands of customers in this state who may have been overcharged sales taxes over the course of several years as the result of Bean's alleged misapplication of the state's sales tax law on certain types of purchases." The case would drag on for six more years before finally being resolved in Bean's favor.

In late May 2006, the Maine Supreme Judicial Court would overturn a lower court decision that found Flippo and others could be entitled to as much as $1 million in disputed sales tax. Because the retailer expects to collect the full value of the sale eventually, it is supposed to collect tax on the entire price. L.L. Bean had been right in collecting the sales tax for the entire price of the item, said the court, because it was going to eventually be reimbursed by MBNA for the full value of the discount coupon.

While its biggest employer was dealing with its sales tax issue, the town of Freeport was wrangling with its own unique problem. After many years of heated town meetings over what course Freeport should end up taking, it seemed clear that almost everyone involved had finally accepted the town's lot as a tourist destination when one of the community's most pressing issues was now that there were *too few* visitors. According to Bean VP Bill Shea, the number of visitors to L.L. Bean in 1999 had dropped by 8 percent— and this was on top of a 7 percent drop the previous year. It was an ironic twist for a town that, only a dozen or so years earlier, had been worried about becoming an overcrowded outlet-shopping Mecca. Now its business leaders were convinced that Freeport needed to become more—a destination complete with movies, music, theater, fine dining, and Maine-made crafts and art. "To be unique, we can't just be an outlet town," Shea told the town's business leaders. "It doesn't work anymore."[9]

Freeport needed to evolve into a location where people wanted to spend the evening or even stay overnight, instead of leaving once they were finished with their shopping. Besides the aforementioned amenities, another solution to the town's problem, said one expert, would be to build a train station down the hill from Bean's and (gasp!) a parking garage. It would be a nice parking garage, said the developer—it would look like an old four-story mill building and hold 800 cars. Fewer parking lots would mean room for maybe six more buildings, a kind of "inner village" between the train tracks and Main Street. It was the right idea, but the wrong time. (L.L. Bean had floated the idea of building a parking garage as far back as 1995, but had "determined it would not fit with the image Freeport wants to promote." Construction on Freeport's first parking garage, which would hold 550 cars, wouldn't begin until 2007.)

The notion of a parking garage wasn't the only major change the townspeople would have to ponder. Later in the year, Freeport voters would be asked to decide whether or not the town should lease out the old town hall, just a couple of blocks down Route 1 from Bean's store, for use as retail space. The proposal would lead to a spirited debate. "It's the only thing left of Freeport as it used to be," said lifelong resident Elizabeth Simpson. "I think it's an awful thing for them to be so hungry for money to want to rent it."(Three years earlier, voters had decided to lease the old Carnegie library near L.L. Bean to Abercrombie & Fitch for a reported $318,000 a year.)

Town councilman David Soley thought the building was "a ridiculous type of space for Town Hall to be in," adding that it could fetch more than twice the going rate for the best office space in Portland.

The building whose future the voters would soon be deciding had been designed by Maine architect John Calvin Stevens as the Grove Street School in 1894 for a fee of $100. In 1983, just as the outlet stores were discovering Freeport, the wood-shingled school was being closed and the building received an $800,000 renovation so it could be used as the town hall. The Freeport Historical Society mailed out fliers to registered voters urging them to reject the proposal to lease out the building. In the end, more than 80 percent of Freeport's registered voters would cast ballots, with 59 percent of them agreeing with the historical society. "The people have spoken," said Randall Thomas, executive director of the Freeport Historical Society. "It demonstrates the commitment of people who live in Freeport to the village center."[10] The town council said it would move forward with plans to add on to the building.

HOWEVER THE TOWN OF FREEPORT moved forward, it would have to do so without William E. Griffin, who'd died in January. "Wid" Griffin had started his career with L.L. Bean as an errand boy at the Hedgehog Mountain skeet range right after graduating from high school in 1935. He advanced with the company, working as a shipping clerk, fishing tackle buyer, and shipping room supervisor before retiring as vice president of distribution in 1979. His first big promotion, the one to fishing tackle buyer, wasn't really much of a promotion, at least at first, he once recalled, since L. L. liked to keep a pretty close eye on things at the time:

> I got involved in tackle buying about 1942, I guess. I was actually not the buyer at that time—L. L. was; he was everything then. I of course had done a lot of fishing; I'd fished with Mr. Bean, and knew something about the tackle and took care of it out back, as far as keeping the stock on the shelves and so forth. And so one time L. L.'s brother, O. R. [Otho Ralph], told him, "Why don't you let Wid take care of that for you?" And from that time on, I really began getting involved in the buying of the tackle. Actually L. L. supervised everything that I did! But I guess I actually became the buyer after World War II when I came home from the service, more or less took over the ordering and stocking and so forth.[11]

Griffin's promotion to the company's board of directors was a different matter. "I can remember now, L. L.—of course, he had a loud, booming voice, you know—and he came up through the office one day where I was working with all the others; and he sat on the edge of my desk, and he said—booming so loud that everyone in the whole factory knew—'Just keep this under your hat,' he said, 'but we're going to appoint you to the Board of Directors.'"[12] Except for L. L.'s accountant, Wid Griffin was the first person outside the family to be appointed to the board.

According to Griffin's own account, he and L. L. had met up once when he was out fishing as a boy. He was fourteen or fifteen at the time and had spent the day hiking and fishing along the Branch Brook, eventually making his way back to Goddard Pool at the bridge on the Poland Road.

> When I got there, L. L. and his brother Otho . . . were fishing and they were about ready to quit. And I was. I'd fished down from the other road! And so they were interested to see what I'd done, and they gave me a ride home. They were both real big men, you know, they were six-footers, 200 pounds, and they had a little Ford coupe. There really wasn't room enough for me in there, so I sat on L. L.'s lap! And they dropped me off where I used to live on the farm across the street.[13]

Wid Griffin was eighty-two when he died.

ALL THOSE BIG PARTIES that began on New Year's Eve 1999 notwithstanding, the New Millennium officially began on January 1, 2001—at least according to John Gould it did, anyway: "As we leap forthwith into the 21st century," he wrote in the *Christian Science Monitor*, "we find ourselves where everybody thought we were a year ago. Remember? Everyone thought 2000 was 2001, and you couldn't tell anybody anything. I knew the difference because I had Miss Fanny Dunham in the first grade, and she taught me to count, starting from one."[14] (Who can argue with logic like that?) In his column, "A Brief Personal History of the 20th Century," Gould recalled moving from Boston to Freeport as a boy, meeting Miss Dunham and one L. L. Bean, who, you'll recall, would later admonish him ". . . never to pay more than $3 for a pair of shoes, as the best shoes can be made to sell for that."[15]

Twenty years earlier, in a piece called "If the Shoe Fits," John Gould had written that it was in fact Raymond Stowell, one of L. L.'s "buyers" (". . . he was much more than that—his advice and assistance had much to do with the success of L. L. Bean, Inc.")

who'd told him, "Don't ever spend more than three dollars for a pair of shoes—the best shoes can be made for three dollars."[16] After sixty years of *Monitor* columns, his brushes with fame, and all the unique glimpses he'd given us of Freeport and Maine throughout his long career, it doesn't really matter if he occasionally mixed up a few of the details now and then. No one, with the possible exception of the lucky few who'd had the opportunity to work with him for an extended period of time, could have painted for us a clearer, more colorful portrait of Leon L. Bean. In 2002, Governor King would declare August 17 to be John Gould Day in Maine.

NOW THAT THE NEW CENTURY was finally upon us, Leon Gorman decided that it was a good time to step down from his day-to-day duties at the helm of L.L. Bean. "The way we're viewing this is as a change of leadership," said Rich Donaldson. "It's not an announcement of Leon's retirement. Therefore he'll continue to play an active role in the company."[17] Gorman planned to play that role by staying on as chairman of the board of directors (a position that had to be created for him) so he could focus on Bean's corporate governance and long-term strategy.

While the change in leadership may have come as a surprise to most people, company insiders had seen signs of its coming for quite some time. Following the departure of senior VP Bill End in 1990, Gorman had told the *Maine Times* that Bean "'never had a grooming operation going on. . . . Everyone was so young' a succession plan wasn't a priority. But now 'we're getting into succession planning.' Gorman noted that company by-laws require a search committee made up of board members to look outside and internally."[18] In 1998, he'd tipped his hand a bit when he told a reporter that there was no succession plan and wouldn't be until late 2000, when many of the company's new initiatives would be underway. But senior VP Bob Peixotto had picked up on some of the clues back in the mid-1990s, when he noticed that his boss—realizing that he was losing touch with the buying habits of the modern consumer—began to delegate responsibility for the company's future to the seven heads of Bean's strategic business units.

In other words, Leon Gorman didn't want to end up like L. L., whose business acumen, he believed, had begun to fade later in life. "One of the reasons I'm stepping aside is I didn't want to go twenty years beyond my capabilities," he said, obviously referring to his grandfather. "The Platform for Growth provided me the exit opportunity to step down from the day-to-day management of the business. I'd been with Bean nearly forty years and it was time to think about retirement. I had not reached the point, as L. L. did, of getting three meals a day and not wanting four, and I had no intention of hanging on that long."[19]

So, in 2000, the board of directors established a committee consisting of Leon Gorman and three others to find his successor (none of Gorman's children are involved in running the company). In November Chris McCormick learned that he was a leading candidate for the president's job, and the only one currently at Bean. In February he learned he'd been selected for the job, a decision that was ratified by Bean's ten-member board the following month. In May the rest of the family approved the change. "There was never any talk of selling the company," added Gorman. (In fact the board had unanimously adopted a resolution at the 1993 shareholders' meeting to retain family ownership of L.L. Bean, Inc.)

With sixty-six-year-old Leon A. Gorman now coaching from the sideline, his boots as president and CEO of L.L. Bean, Inc., would be filled by the forty-five-year-old McCormick, who'd been promoted at least every other year since joining the company, ascending to the position of chief operating officer just two months earlier. Chris McCormick had joined L.L. Bean from Garden Way (a Vermont-based mail-order garden supply company) in 1983 as assistant advertising manager, and had been instrumental in the development of both the firm's international business and its e-commerce venture.

With the recent implementation of the company's strategic initiatives showing strong results, Leon Gorman was certain that he'd handed over the reins to the right person. He had not only used the review process to position the company for growth, but also to assess his management team members as they engaged in various parts of the review. Gorman further tested McCormick by putting him in charge of a division he knew nothing about: women's clothing.

"Our new organization is in place with first-rate leadership," he said later, "and Chris has worked closely with me in setting our current course. Chris is a natural successor having both my confidence and the confidence of his colleagues."[20] McCormick's promotion to president and CEO had received final approval on May 18, 2001, effective immediately. The change in the company's leadership was announced in a headline of the *Bean Bulletin* three days later: "Leon Becomes Chairman of the Board; Chris McCormick Named L.L. Bean's President."

"I am honored to have been selected L.L. Bean President," said McCormick, the first non-family member to head the company. "Having worked with Leon for 18 years, I know the position I have to fill. I am fortunate in my new role that I will continue to have Leon's valued support, advice, and counsel. The organization is on firm footing and we have a very capable and highly committed workforce at all levels. L.L. Bean customers and the community will continue to see a company with a unique set of values committed to quality products, excellent customer service, our outdoor heritage, and respect for people."[21]

Shortly after succeeding Leon, McCormick sent him a note saying, "I won't let you down."

McCormick said he intended to stay the course set by Gorman, which meant sticking with e-commerce and introducing new retail stores around the Northeast. "It's a billion-plus dollar company, and, during peak, 10,000 or so employees are counting on me to make the right decision, and I'm energized by that,"[22] he said three days later, as he prepared to hike Katahdin with his brother and eighteen-year-old son. McCormick felt that, for now, his goal of increasing sales by 5 to 10 percent a year could be reached without the introduction of any new product lines.

The change in leadership was well received by Bean employees and the general public. Governor King proclaimed June 5 and 6 to be Leon Gorman Days in the State of Maine. On June 25, more than

700 people showed up at Bean's Fogg Farm facility for a potluck picnic to honor the man whose thirty-four years at the helm had taken the tired Freeport company with four seasonal catalogs, one rickety old store, and about $4 million in annual sales and turned it into an efficient retail powerhouse with fifty annual catalogs, multi-channel sales and distribution systems, and more than $1.1 billion in sales. In all, Leon Gorman had been with the company forty-one years, the first seven of which were spent trying to make L. L. and his Uncle Carl happy.

In 1999, the *Wall Street Journal* had carried a brief piece describing Gorman's office. Salient points of the article were phrases such as "Duck decoys. Fishing lures. A canoe paddle. No glitzy awards or photos with presidents. . . . Hand-painted mallards take flight over an antique partners' desk. . . . A cast iron doorjamb is shaped like a duck. . . . A shotgun on the wall belonged to his grandfather. . . . [R]ich colors and dark woods create a traditional feel. . . . A wastebasket is appliquéd with a pheasant. . . . A painted woods scene behind him served as a catalog cover some years back. . . . Reports and files spill out of a bookcase. . . . Reading material ranges from sports manuals to business tomes."[23] A small antique cannon Gorman kept near the door served as a memento of his Uncle Carl.

Of his office, Leon Gorman had explained, "Much of the decor reminds me of the wilderness experiences I enjoy. But the office design was more impromptu and spontaneous than anything else. There's no conscious theme."[24] After stepping aside, he'd do what he felt a true chairman of the board ought to do: spend a day or so a week at work reviewing overall strategies with McCormick, as well as advising him and acting as an intermediary between him and the board of directors. After Chris McCormick moved into the president's office, Gorman relocated to a small corner office for his part-time duties at the company.

Sadly, Leon Gorman's retirement had come right after the loss of his friend Lee Surace, a senior VP at Bean and the company's chief financial officer, whom Gorman had hired from Blue Cross and Blue Shield of Maine in 1970. Gorman remembers that Surace, with whom he'd discussed various succession candidates, was as big a part of the transition process as he had been in the growth of the company.

Leandro "Lee" Surace died of cancer on March 18, 2001, at the age of sixty-two. During his tenure with the company, Surace had served as chairman of the Advisory Council at the University of Southern Maine School of Business, from which he received the Alumni Association's 1998 Hilltop Award for outstanding service to the university. He was also instrumental in developing an internship program that places USM business students at L.L. Bean, and initiated a Maine Business for Scholars Award from L.L. Bean. Surace had earned an undergraduate business degree from USM in 1973 and an MBA in 1981. In 1991 he'd been chosen as one of Bean's Best. In his memory, Leon and Lisa Gorman, Jim and Maureen Gorman, and Tom Gorman donated $1 million to establish the university's first endowed chair, the L.L. Bean/Lee Surace Chair in Accounting at the USM School of Business. The company also changed the name of its Deering Building in Portland to the Surace Building.

"Lee was a mentoring kind of guy," said Leon Gorman. "He was considered an advisor and friend by virtually everyone who worked at Bean's including myself. He was a good listener and a good friend."[25]

While Chris McCormick's assessment of the company being on firm footing was correct and his goal of 5 to 10 percent annual sales increases was certainly achievable, men's clothing (up 53 percent), e-commerce (up 67 percent), and L.L. Kids (up 123 percent) all posted strong increases during the year, and Bean posted a sales increase of 4.5 percent over the previous year. (Catalog industry expert Bill Dean said the figures proved the company had needed its recent reorganization; "the question is, why didn't they do it 10 years ago?"[26]) And the bonus had returned, at least for a year.

But the company still found itself in a kind of "good news, bad news" situation. The bad news was that the firm had missed its 9 percent revenue-increase goal by a wide margin, Freeport Studio barely broke even, and the cataloger had expected e-commerce to increase by 90 percent (in November L.L. Bean had even published a "Webalog," a pocket-sized 28-page booklet designed to steer customers toward the Internet). The company had only managed to post strong profits, said Rich Donaldson, by cutting expenses and working its "cost-of-goods-sold" (COGS) initiative.

Also, a couple of the company's initiatives from its sweeping Strategic Review weren't panning out quite the way management had hoped. One early casualty was the strategic business unit concept, whose results simply did not justify the system's cost and complexity. For SBUs to even have a chance of working required changes in accountabilities, decision-making authority, systems support, and job descriptions. There were also meetings for policy making, feedback sessions, and "transfer of knowledge," not to mention the physical changes of offices and operating areas—all while still trying to operate a profitable business. In other words, the SBUs were simply more trouble than they were worth, and the company began recentralizing its organization in the fall of 2001. "It was like retrofitting your car's engine," said Gorman, "while doing 70 miles per hour on the Maine Turnpike."[27]

Also problematic for the company was another increase in its already significant mailing costs. In January, the U.S. Postal Service raised its rates an average of 6.9 percent, including those for bulk mail and periodicals. Bean spokesperson Rich Donaldson said that even though the cataloger's rate fell toward the lower end of the 5 to 12 percent increase, it still cost the company between 50 cents and $1.10 to produce, print, and mail a catalog, with about half of that cost being postage.

In February FedEx also increased its rates an average of 4 to 9 percent, which the cataloger managed to avoid through its annual contract with the shipper, although it still had to pay a 3 percent fuel surcharge. (In late 2000, L.L. Bean had begun using Airborne Express's airborne@home service for some of its package shipments. During its first year, Airborne shipped more than a million L.L. Bean packages, or about 8 percent of the firm's volume, to its Destination Delivery Units for home delivery by the Postal Service. "Airborne@home will help us improve our present backorder delivery program and provide tracking and tracing ability for these shipments,"[28] said Bob Olive, Bean's senior manager of logistics. Airborne@home replaced Bean's use of the U.S. Postal Service's Standard B Service—or parcel post—which the cataloger had been using since 1913.)

THE GOOD NEWS was that Bean's first foray into "brick-and-mortar" retailing was underway and progressing well. In addition to its already-operational Tysons Corner store, the company would open two more retail stores on the East Coast in 2001 and 2002. Bean's second retail store outside of Maine would be located thirty miles away from the first one, also in the suburbs of Washington, D.C., an area that turned out to be a strong one for the company. The 32,000-square-foot store, tucked in between Sears and Nordstrom at a mall in Columbia, Maryland, opened on Friday, May 4, 2001.

In 2002 L.L. Bean would open a small (40,000-square-foot), stand-alone "discovery" store at The Promenade at Sagemore in Marlton, New Jersey, eleven miles east of Philadelphia. (About "250,000 L.L. Bean customers live within a twenty-five-mile radius of Marlton," said the company.[29]) The firm's latest store, which it called its "store of the future" because of its single level and "race-track" aisles, would be its last for a while, as Bean management decided to take a "pause" on new retail sites. Senior VP Ken Kacere noted that any future stores would probably offer phone or computer ordering stations to supplement their in-store inventory.

The eighty-nine-year-old company's gradual opening of its new retail stores "gives us the opportunity to learn how to do it correctly," said Bean senior VP Brad Kauffman, "to make some mistakes without betting the farm. It's typical of Bean to walk before it runs."[30] Even walking had proved difficult at first. According to a later account of the company's first attempt at retail: "merchandise arrived without price tags or size stickers, the shops ran out of stock, and customers couldn't find products they saw in catalogs."[31] Customers had to lug kayaks through a mall. Bean president Chris McCormick admitted later that his company wasn't ready for retail at the time because it didn't know enough about it.

After completing the first phase, the company "stood back and tried to learn from that," said Ken Kacere. "We're a catalog company and we had one store for years. When we first ventured out from that, we were still a company focused on the direct-channel business."[32] One way Bean planned on learning from its recent retail expansion was by "tinkering" with the new stores, which Chris McCormick said may have been too large, and by setting up a prototype 15,000-square-foot store (not open to the public) in its offices at Northgate in Portland where it could experiment with different designs and layouts.

Leon Gorman had this to say about the pause: "It was clear the company needed to learn more about retail logistics and to develop the necessary retail systems prior to further expansion."[33] At the time, the company hoped to be opening stores as far west as Minnesota and then, maybe, Colorado by 2009, places where the firm's "colder-weather climate product line" would do well.

Back at the Freeport store, things were going full speed ahead. In late March visitors were treated to the sight of the mesmerizing ten-foot driftwood *Salmon 2001* sculpture that literally stopped people in their tracks. Originally slated to be displayed for a day or two to promote Bean's Fly Fishing & Spring Shooting Expo, the "gray, almost luminous sculpture with ghostly empty eye sockets" was still attracting a crowd a week later. "It's supposed to be a manifestation beyond reality," said Woolwich artist Mark Libby, who spent two years on the sculpture, "and I love to see grown men and kids standing there in their baseball caps, calling it 'awesome.'"[34]

Libby created his sculpture from more than one hundred pieces of driftwood and dead branches fastened together with resin and a nail gun. "In the end," he said, "it had its own evolution. It was a conversation between me and the piece of work. It had its own idea of what it wanted to be. It wasn't just up to me." As far as non-product displays go, Salmon 2001 had to be the most talked-about at Mr. Bean's establishment since Richard Balzer's exquisite clock. Maybe even since L. L. had put Herbert Talbot's twenty-six-pound turnip in the front window of his store in the Davis Block back in 1912.

Just down Main Street from Bean's retail store, another celebration of the company's values was on display for the summer at the Freeport Historical Society, which put on a major exhibit about the relationship of L. L.'s company with the community—and the rest of the world. Entitled "Merchant of the Maine Woods," the show featured paintings, L.L. Bean catalog covers, and articles of the Freeport firm's outdoor apparel.

Coincidentally, one of Mr. Bean's clothing design features had recently been the subject of a John Gould *Christian Science Monitor* article—about, of all things, buttons. A particular type of button, said Gould, that was invented by colonial settlers at Blastow Cove, near Deer Isle Township:

> The Colonial settlers of the region, roughly 400 years ago, considered themselves remote from button stores, so they developed the Blastow button. It's a bit of willow or alder sapling whittled with a groove around it to oblige a tying string. The wooden piece fitted through an opposite loop to make as good a button as anybody required those days.
>
> When Woolworth opened the five-and-ten, and a card of buttons was a dime, the Blastow model declined. It was brought back by L. L. Bean as a rustic touch on his parkas and snowmobile suits.
>
> You'll find Blastow buttons on stylish ladies' wear today at a great price, admired as chic, but nobody knows what to call the things.[35]

AFTER THE SEPTEMBER 11 terrorist attacks in 2001 everything changed; shopping was about the last thing on people's minds—but that didn't stop them from calling L.L. Bean. "These were not customers looking to place orders," said Chris McCormick, "but people who were just reaching out to a part of their world that felt comfortable to them. And by no means do I mean to trivialize such contacts . . . the fact that real customers called us looking for a break really speaks to the inimitable relationship that we enjoy with people all over the country. It also made us feel just that much better about doing as much as we did to help with relief efforts down there."[36] (L.L. Bean sent "500 blankets to the Federal Emergency Management Agency, 200 pairs of boots to the City of New York, as well as shirts for the teams of relief workers and booties for the rescue dogs,"[37] said Janet Wyper, the company's manager of community relations.)

In 2002, L.L. Bean, Inc., turned 90 on the 130th anniversary of its founder's birth. To mark this milestone for Mr. Bean's enterprise, John Gould took the occasion to put down some of his early memories of Freeport in his column, "The Home Forum," in the *Christian Science Monitor*, beginning with this paragraph:

> A good friend is having a big birthday, and I hereby join in the celebration. I was born in Boston and shortly persuaded my parents to move to Maine, where they fetched me up in the town of Freeport with the amazing success you now behold. A neighbor in Freeport was a gentleman about my father's age named Leon Leonwood Bean, who conducted a haberdashery in the village in partnership with his brother Guy.[38]

Unfortunately, L.L. Bean, Inc., started its ninetieth year with a 3 percent drop in sales (to $1.06 billion), a fact the company announced in early January—never a good sign as far as the prospect for an annual bonus was concerned, and when March rolled around, there wasn't one. (For the period from 1995–2002, during which the company handed out an annual bonus just three times, it averaged out to 3 percent per year. For 1987–94, the bonus had averaged 14.6 percent.) Since 1995 L.L. Bean's revenues had grown just 5 percent while those of rival Lands' End had grown by 46 percent. "Growth," said Bean president Chris McCormick, "is the number one issue facing our company."

Less than three weeks later, L.L. Bean laid off 175 employees, most of them salaried workers, first from the marketing department and then from merchandising. The cuts, said the company, were due to a recent reorganization that had left those departments overstaffed. One director position and two vice president slots were also eliminated. Bean spokesperson Rich Donaldson said that the layoffs were part of the firm's ongoing reorganization and were "not a knee-jerk reaction to a short-term softening of the business."[39] Prior to the layoffs, the company had had 900 salaried employees.

The news would get worse in October when L.L. Bean would lay off another thirteen people and offer early retirement to nearly 12 percent of its workforce. If not enough of Bean's fifty-five and older workers took the company's offer of a pension increased by 25 percent, said Rich Donaldson, then lagging sales could force another round of layoffs, which could come in January. "We're far enough behind," he said, "that it would have to be a holiday selling season like we've never seen before"[40] to make up the ground the company had lost. Bean's COO, Bob Peixotto, seemed equally pessimistic, indicating that layoffs would probably be necessary in the coming year, no matter how many of the 500 workers offered early retirement actually took it. About 200 would.

Sears, Roebuck and Co. decided to take another tack to deal with its sagging clothing sales; in a surprise mid-May move, it purchased Bean competitor Lands' End for $1.9 billion. "I think both of them will benefit," said analyst John Champion of Kurt Salmon Associates. "It gives Sears a strong brand in apparel, which has been a challenge for them, and it gives Lands' End a chance to get retail store presence."[41] According to the *Toronto Star*, "Lands' End is the largest specialty-apparel catalogue company and the biggest Internet seller of clothing in the United States, ahead of L.L. Bean in both categories."[42] Lands' End stock rose 20 percent on news of the buyout while Sears' stock rose slightly. (In November 2004, Sears, Roebuck and Co. would be bought by K Mart Holding Corp. for $12.3 billion, making the new company, Sears Holding Corp., the nation's third-largest retailer behind Wal-Mart and Home Depot.)

Back in Freeport, Chris McCormick squelched any rumors

about the Freeport cataloger by flatly stating that L.L. Bean still wasn't for sale and its family of owners had no interest in going public. "We answer to Main Street," he said, "not Wall Street."[43] The company was trying to get things back on track in its own fashion by printing 1,000 fewer catalog pages and reducing the number of circulars it issued by 13 percent.

But the biggest change the retailer would make regarding its catalogs would be one its customers wouldn't even notice when, in July 2002, it announced plans to go with a single catalog printer, Quebecor World, Inc. In October Bean and its new printer would sign a multi-year, $100 million contract for Quebecor to print the Freeport firm's 200 million annual catalogs at its plants in Evans, Georgia, and Franklin, Kentucky. The deal also called for Quebecor to make order forms and provide mailing lists to L.L. Bean. The Montreal-based company was the world's largest commercial printer, with 2001 revenues of $6.3 billion. The move represented a significant change for L.L. Bean, in that it gave one printer responsibility for its entire catalog production, said Quebecor's Tony Ross. "It is unusual for L.L. Bean to go with just one printer,"[44] noted *Catalog Age* senior editor Paul Miller.

Before the exclusive deal with Quebecor was struck, Bean's catalogs had been printed by both Quebecor and Quad/Graphics. The loss of Bean's business had been just one of the setbacks incurred by Quad/Graphics that year; during the summer company founder Henry V. Quadracci had drowned near his Pine Lake, Wisconsin, home and a ten-story portion of the printer's Lomira storage facility "collapsed and burned; catalog pages from L.L. Bean were among the ashes and stacks of partially burned paper."[45] The printer had also lost its contract to print *Sports Illustrated Women* when that franchise folded. In a statement, Bean cited Quebecor's "willingness to make significant capital investments" as a reason it had been selected for the contract.

By the end of the year, L.L. Bean would see somewhat stronger sales, thanks in part to recent changes in its pricing and shipping policies. Bean's Rich Donaldson characterized increased store sales as being in the "high single digits" over last year, while catalog and

Internet sales saw "an incredible surge during December."[46] The company also credited cold weather and a short holiday shopping season with motivating people to get out and shop.

In June the company had experimented with offering all sizes at the same price, instead of charging customers more for its "extended sizes." Donaldson said the new policy was "a marketing test, an experiment"[47] to see if the company could attract larger-sized shoppers without alienating regular-sized people. Which is kind of what happened; big people liked the idea of paying the same price as other people for their clothes, while regular people felt they should be charged less. Before long, L.L. Bean would revert back to its two-price policy.

Another temporary change would come in time for Christmas 2002 and, along with cold weather, would be responsible for much of the surge in Bean's sales both from the catalog and at llbean.com. From December 1 through the evening of the 21st, catalog and online Bean shoppers would receive free regular FedEx shipping on all purchases. (The cataloger would next offer free shipping during the 2005 holiday season.) In honor of its ninetieth birthday, the retailer was also offering double coupon dollars on purchases of $90 or more made with an L.L. Bean Visa card. Still, free shipping was only free to the customers, not the company, and sales for the year were still trailing those for 2001. In spite of the fact that cost-cutting measures and increased productivity would help the company meet its profit projections for the year, it would still have to lay off more workers in February.

Slow sales notwithstanding, the retailer managed to back worthy outdoors-related causes, which this year happened to take the form of a $1 million donation in support of Acadia National Park's Island Explorer shuttlebus service. The park's pollution problems "are of great concern" to the company said Bean president Chris McCormick. "L.L. Bean is making this contribution to help at a time when national parks throughout the country face increased use and underfunding," he said. "We want to help draw attention to the added burdens on park staff and park assets."[48] The white-blue-and-green buses cost $550,000 a year to operate.

The fleet, which had grown from six propane-powered buses to seventeen in its first three years of operation, carried 240,000 passengers in 2001, removing 80,000 vehicles from the roads of Bar Harbor and Mount Desert Island. Ridership on the Island Explorer had increased by 75 percent since the service began, sometimes reaching 5,000 passengers a day. Bean's contribution, administered by the nonprofit Friends of Acadia, would cover the shuttle's next four seasons and would allow it to add more buses and extend its service into the popular fall foliage season. "In the next two years, we're going to need at least eight more,"49 said FOA's Ken Olson. (In 2005 L.L. Bean would donate another $1.25 million for the Island Explorer and for educational and research programs at Acadia.)

Bean's connection to the area continued when, late in the year, Bar Harbor–based Jeff Dobbs Productions premiered its *Maine Biographies* series on Maine Public Broadcasting with the story of one Leon L. Bean. The *Bangor Daily News* said that Dobbs's hour-long film, narrated by then Bar Harbor resident Jack Perkins, "paints a well-rounded portrait of the man who created the merchandising giant," and "is lavishly illustrated with historical photos." (There are no known moving pictures of L. L. Bean.) "[T]he production does an admirable job of tracking how wise business decisions by the outdoorsman led to steady growth by his company, which later flourished as well under his grandson, Leon Gorman."50

One other interesting aspect of L.L. Bean's ninetieth anniversary was the company's new giant Bean Boot statue, which stands outside of the flagship store. Technically, the sixteen-week project was completed by Gelardi Design and Development of Biddeford and Kennebunkport, but the real credit for the creation goes to the firm's senior design engineer, twenty-three-year-old Deering High graduate Andrew Baker. "Andrew Baker was the brains, brawn and person who made the whole thing happen,"51 said owner Tony Gelardi. Baker created the statue by using a computer model of a Bean Boot, which he then enlarged to seventeen times the size of the real thing, making the finished statue sixteen feet long and fourteen feet tall. The 3,000-pound boot gets its shape from 2,000 pounds of Styrofoam in ninety-six two-inch slices.

In January 2003, L.L. Bean was the only Maine company to make the *Forbes* list of the 257 largest privately held companies in the United States. The fact that it came in at number 221 was small comfort to the 300 people who would lose their jobs the following month. This time, it was the hourly workers who were being let go. Among the reasons the retailer gave for having to trim its workforce were increasing health care costs, annual wage increases, and increased expenses such as advertising and free shipping. Bean's Internet sales had increased, allowing it to lay off workers who once processed orders or waited on customers.

Another reason cited by the company for layoffs was price deflation, a result of the sluggish economy. (A men's cotton sweater that Bean's had sold for $36 a year earlier, for example, was now fetching $20.50.) "There's clearly no reason to raise prices in a lot of sectors; clothing is one of them," said University of Southern Maine professor Charles Colgan. "That's why L.L. Bean is facing the problem it is."[52] He went on to explain that cheaper imports were allowing retailers to drop prices, plus consumers could now find the lowest price for an item online. Obviously, lower prices hurt profits, and the company was forced to become leaner. In just over a year, L.L. Bean had cut its regular workforce by 15 percent.

The good news was that even though Bean's sales fell from $1.14 billion to $1.07 billion, its drastic cost-cutting measures of the past year and the company's best-ever December meant that its profits increased by 20 percent, which translated to a 5 percent bonus for the firm's permanent employees—including most of those laid off the previous month and the 200 who had taken the retirement offer. It was only the second March bonus the cataloger had paid in the past in five years.

The news would continue to be good for the rest of the year. September's first half figures were up 2 percent, or good enough to get the employees a $100 (after taxes) bonus. These numbers reflected the company's 6 percent average price cut, which had come in July to help keep its prices competitive, along with more full-price sales and fewer returns. The trend continued through the third quarter and December sales, showing an 8 percent gain over the previous year. "We had a hugely successful holiday season," said Rich Donaldson. "I guess it would be an understatement to say it was a great surprise."[53] Even the weather seemed to be cooperating. With the help of an early-December snowstorm and cold weather, Bean's catalog and Web orders ended up running 20 percent ahead of projection.

In March 2003 the company had moved it's highly successful L.L. Kids division from its own building into the main store, so its Hunting and Fishing departments could take over the space. The previous September, Bean spokesperson Dave Teufel had remarked, "We want to get back to the cornerstone of our brand. Bringing back the feeling of the old L.L. Bean store would be a great way to celebrate that 90th anniversary"[54] (even though the switch couldn't take place until renovations to the Kids building were completed early the following year). The move would give Hunting and Fishing a much needed 2,000 additional square feet of space to display things like knives, compasses, and GPS units. Camping, and its related large items such as tents and sleeping bags, would stay in the main store.

The move, said Teufel, would put most of the company's clothing in one building. Some people speculated that the real reason Bean had made the change was because parents were less than thrilled with having to wrangle their kids across the parking lot and Discovery Park to another store, especially when it was cold or raining. (Hunting and Fishing would move back into the expanded flagship store with its former home becoming the L.L. Bean Factory Outlet Store in late 2007, and the space would become the cataloger's Home store in late 2009.)

In early May, L.L. Bean enhanced its Outdoor Discovery program with the purchase of thirty-three oceanfront acres on Freeport's Coskery Point. "It's a way to bring the Bean brand to life," said Rich Donaldson. "It's a brand differentiator."[55] Located about five miles from the store, on Flying Point Road, the former Flying Point Campground, for which Bean paid $2.6 million, gave the company about 1,200 feet of coastal frontage that it planned to use for its kayaking school, which was moving from nearby Wolf Neck.

While the company said it might move some of its other Outdoor Discovery programs to the site, it was initially undecided about future plans for its new property. "It was one of those opportunities that came up rather quickly," said Jim Gorman, Bean's real estate manager. "Thirty-three acres on the water doesn't come up on the market very often. When it did come, we felt the need to take advantage of it."[56]

THE SPECTER OF CASINOS coming to Maine would prompt L.L. Bean's leadership to become involved in a controversial political issue for the first time since Leon Gorman had come out in favor of keeping the Maine Yankee nuclear power plant open in 1980. When Governor John Baldacci promised to veto legislation allowing a casino, its supporters figured they'd have better luck letting the people of Maine decide the matter.

With a referendum question to legalize casino gambling in Maine now on the November ballot, the anti-casino movement got into full swing in April 2003 when the governor appeared as the featured speaker at a $250-a-plate fundraiser for Casinos No! at Freeport's Harraseeket Inn. Former governor Angus King, Bean president Chris McCormick, and chairman Leon Gorman were among of the event's prominent co-hosts.

Casinos No! was fighting efforts by the state's Passamaquoddy and Penobscot tribes to build a $650 million casino in the southern Maine town of Sanford, which had voted in favor of hosting such an establishment after Kittery, the group's first choice, changed its zoning laws to prevent it from coming to town. The tribes were receiving backing from the political action committee Think About It. According to the *Portland Press Herald*, Think About It, funded in part by Las Vegas casino developer Marnell Corrao Associates, had spent more than $420,000 on the issue as of January compared to less than $17,000 by the opposition during the same period. "We didn't want to wait [to raise money]," said Casinos No!'s Dennis Bailey. "It's going to be an expensive campaign."[57]

"They are joining with us because they are convinced a big

gambling casino will destroy Maine's way of life,"[58] said Casinos No! spokesperson James Bartlett, referring to the growing list of business leaders opposed to casinos. Soon after the Freeport fundraiser, Bean's Rich Donaldson announced that the company would be donating an unspecified sum to Casinos No! "Maine is truly one of the few states in the nation that enjoys a positive brand recognition," he said. "It's known for its rugged outdoors, natural beauty, low crime, family-friendly communities, corruption-free politics, and Yankee ingenuity. Casino gambling on the scale it's being proposed here really stands in stark contrast to those values."[59]

Bailey correctly felt that Bean's leadership in the casino fight would convince even more businesses to get on board. Shortly after Bean's credit card partner, MBNA, joined the anti-casino fight, casino supporters pointed out that there was something else to be considered—the unspoken concern that the casino industry would compete with L.L. Bean and other businesses for southern Maine's limited workforce and drive up wages. Maine AFL-CIO executive director Ed Gorham reasoned that "MBNA [and] L.L. Bean are both very large nonunion employers and they'd like to keep it that way."[60] In the end, Maine's voters chose to keep big casinos out of the state—until a new referendum in 2010, when the Beans and Gormans would donate 88 percent of the $328,000 raised by Casinos No!

While L.L. Bean's management knew exactly where it stood on the casino debate, and could see a definite timeline for the issue's resolution, the same couldn't be said for another matter the merchant would grapple with for the better part of a year. In early May, the news broke: L.L. Bean was thinking about buying Redmond, Washington-based rival Eddie Bauer from financially troubled Spiegel, Inc. Many retail analysts saw the purchase as a match made in retail heaven. Not only would it double Bean's $1.2 billion in revenues (Bauer had rung up sales of $1.4 billion in 2002), it would also speed the Freeport cataloger into hundreds of retail stores nationwide, not to mention landing the Freeport merchant Bauer's mailing list and distribution centers in Virginia and Ohio.

"There is a little bit of identity crisis at Eddie Bauer," said Wells Fargo Securities' analyst Jennifer Black, "and L.L. Bean is very good at figuring out who their target customer is." Besides, L.L. Bean—known for its "waterproof boots . . . and fishing equipment"—could only benefit from buying Eddie Bauer—famous for its "casual clothing and home decorations."[61] (The only time L.L. Bean had purchased another operating company was back in 1956, when L. L. bought the Small-Abbott Moccasin Company across the street.)

Spiegel, which filed for Chapter 11 bankruptcy in Manhattan on March 17, had acquired Bauer in 1988 and operated 586 Eddie Bauer stores throughout the country—although it said it planned to close 60 of them. Just as had been the case—to a point—with the original Abercrombie & Fitch company, frenetic growth, it seems, had been Bauer's main problem. With its "misguided retail strategy" alienating many of its core customers, sales at Bauer stores open more than a year had fallen 14 percent during the first three quarters of 2002, and the company was in the process of laying off 545 of its Seattle-area workers.

"Our interest is at a very preliminary stage," said Bean's Rich Donaldson, "simply because it still remains unclear how Eddie Bauer is to emerge from this process."[62] At this point, said Donaldson, the Maine company was only asking to be kept apprised of any developments from bankruptcy court. If Bean's were to buy Bauer, the price would probably be somewhere between $150 million and $200 million, and raising that much wouldn't be a problem for them, according to Bean president Chris McCormick. "There are banks that would love to lend us money."[63]

Speculation about the possible purchase was rekindled a couple of weeks later when Bean confirmed it was "hiring consultants to study Bauer's assets, and talking with investment bankers who could help structure a bid."[64] Still, the deal was far from done. McCormick said his company would be foolish to ignore the possibility of buying one of its bigger competitors, but cautioned that any decision was still months away. Spiegel spokesperson Debbie Koopman emphasized that the Chicago-based company was focused on reorganizing and was not in talks with anyone to sell its Eddie Bauer division.

As May became September, the matter of the possible purchase of Bauer was relegated to the back burner as L.L. Bean began to gear up for the holiday sales season. Spiegel wasn't due to present its reorganization plans to the court until mid-November but had put its Newport News catalog division on the auction block in the meantime. Chris McCormick said his company wasn't interested in Newport News ("reasoning that the line of bikinis and sarongs isn't a very close fit with Bean's parkas and hiking boots"[65]), but still had a keen interest in Eddie Bauer, even though doing the deal "could be a two-year process." No matter what the eventual outcome, McCormick looked at the matter as a win-win situation. "Spiegel knows that we're interested in Bauer and they've asked us to lay low for a while, so that's what we're doing. It's worth looking into still. If nothing else, getting market intelligence on a competitor is a positive thing."[66]

It's a good thing Bean's leader was content with gaining market intelligence on their competitor, because in the end that's about all he got. In November Spiegel had requested—and received— permission to delay the filing of its reorganization plan until February 10, 2004. It also got the go-ahead to open seventeen new Eddie Bauer stores, a move that both signaled its intention to hold on to its most profitable division and made it much more difficult—though still possible—for L.L. Bean to purchase Bauer. (Short-term plans called for the opening of just seven of the proposed stores with the rest to be put on hold.) A spokesperson for the Freeport company said it would "continue monitoring developments."

What developed was L.L. Bean's decision in early March to pass on the acquisition of the Eddie Bauer stores. In a memo to employees, Bean president Chris McCormick wrote that the financial condition of Bauer's parent, Spiegel, "is more complex and troublesome than we originally thought. We've decided that an acquisition of this size, and this one in particular, is not in L.L. Bean's best interests."[67] Not only did flagging sales at Bauer offer a limited opportunity for Bean, its licensing and merchandising agreements (such as the Eddie Bauer Ford Bronco, and a marketing deal with Target) further complicated matters. A spokesperson for Spiegel said that Bean's decision had not caused it to change any of its plans, since the company had never actually solicited buyers for the Eddie Bauer chain in the first place.

A month later, Spiegel, Inc., would announce that it had sold its Newport News catalog business to Pangea Holdings for $25 million, and that Bauer was, in fact, now up for sale. News of Bauer's availability elicited little response from Bean other than its reiteration that it still wasn't interested. And why should it be? The latest Harvard Business School case study (No. 504080, March 31, 2004) said that Bean's CEO saw his company in a good position to start to grow again. He was right. During its spring season, which ended on August 31, L.L. Bean's sales increased 13 percent, generating $930,000 in bonuses, or as much as $165 per longtime employee. "Bean is on a roll right now," said Rich Donaldson, "and this is a spring that can be described as a success, all across the board, all channels, all markets."[68] Store sales had increased by 16 percent.

Even without the acquisition of Bauer's assets, L.L. Bean's now-booming sales soon found the company in need of more call center capacity, a problem it had expected to remedy by building a new facility in Oakland, just outside of Waterville. But by early December, only six months after announcing its plan to build the facility in the FirstPark business park, Bean would pull the plug on the deal when it learned that it would be competing for area workers with another new call center owned by T-Mobile. Bean's Rich Donaldson said that T-Mobile's selection of Oakland was "good news for the area . . . but it does compromise our ability perhaps to meet our peak needs."[69]

Bean's announcement that it was scrapping its plan for an Oakland call center set off a flurry of activity throughout the state's cities and towns, each one hoping to make itself the most attractive to the Freeport retailer. Throughout the month of December, a bevy of Maine communities primped and preened and put together PowerPoint presentations in hopes of becoming the cataloger's latest interest. Sanford, Bangor, and Brewer entered the contest, as did Ellsworth (it did already have an L.L. Bean Factory Store, after all). Bangor's neighbor, Hampden, where Bean had intended to build a distribution center fifteen years earlier, soon threw itself into the mix of prospective sites as well. Even the Augusta-Waterville area still saw itself as being a viable candidate. University of Southern Maine professor Charles Colgan speculated that Bean would do best to look north of Augusta, where the labor market wasn't as tight as in Southern and Central Maine. Say, for example, Bangor.

As if to prove Professor Colgan correct, that's exactly where L.L. Bean decided to put its newest call center—in the former Irving Oil Company building near Bangor International Airport, to be exact. And to top it off, the 35,000-square foot building on Maine Avenue was already wired for telecommunications and had available property nearby for expansion. What tipped the scales in Bangor's favor, said Chris McCormick, was his company's review of the state's labor areas, which "led us to Bangor for its workforce capacity and ability to meet both our year-round and peak-season hiring needs."[70] The Bangor call center was expected to employ as many as 800 seasonal workers.

In the meantime, L.L. Bean prepared itself for the coming 2004 holiday season by opening a seasonal call center in the recently closed ICT call center on Route 26 in Oxford, just north of the Oxford Plains Speedway. Initially, the company said it couldn't commit to a long-term relationship with Oxford, but Bean spokesperson Carolyn Beem said that the cataloger "couldn't be more pleased with the response from the community"[71] and the number of qualified workers in the area, 300 of whom would earn about $9 an hour taking orders over the phone. (To help lure Bean's to Oxford, several local business leaders and other townspeople had donned their best Bean gear for a photograph, and hand-delivered a poster of the picture to the company's headquarters in Freeport.)

The same day it announced the Bangor site for its new call center, L.L. Bean also said that, even though an attempt to persuade the company to build a permanent call center in Oxford Hills had failed, the cataloger had signed a multi-year lease with owner John Schiavi to use the former ICT building as a seasonal call center. The company also decided to retain its seven-year-old call center in the former Rich's department store at the JFK Mall in Waterville. Initially the 225 year-round employees there had been scheduled to move to the new Oakland facility.

By 2005 L.L. Bean, Inc., was closing in on $1.5 billion in annual sales. The total for the 2005 fiscal year would run $1.47 billion, up 4 percent from the $1.41 billion the company had grossed in '04. In early March 2005 Bean's announced that its workers would receive bonuses of 12.5 percent for the previous fiscal year (when sales had increased by 9 percent), or about $3,300 for a typical sales representative. "Our 2004 sales results are no small accomplishment," said Leon Gorman, "and I'm pleased to announce that we are able to reward Bean people for achieving industry-leading sales results and solid profitability in a very challenging retail environment."[72]

Company president Chris McCormick also credited his hard-working employees, but in addition cited "the introduction of new colors, updated styles, improved pricing, and renewed strength in the company's hard-goods business"[73] as contributing factors in the firm's recent success.

The Freeport firm's sales would continue to hum along, if slightly less robustly, for the rest of the year. Prompted by concerns about rising oil prices because of Hurricane Katrina, the cataloger offered free holiday shipping from October 21 until noon on December 22. This incentive, offered for the first time in three years, would help L.L. Bean achieve a stunning 18 percent increase in sales over the previous December. For the entire fiscal year, Bean's e-commerce sales grew 28 percent, with Internet sales besting those placed over the phone or by mail. "You always think of L.L. Bean as the catalog company," said Chris McCormick, "but now we're the Web company."[74] With holiday sales rescuing the 2005 fiscal year, Bean's employees would see an 8 percent bonus the following March.

The residents of nearby Lewiston also reaped the fruits of L.L. Bean's recent success by means of the company's temporary

"Clearance Center" at the former Ames department store on East Avenue, which opened in early November and offered "factory seconds and discontinued merchandise" at savings starting at 30 percent. Despite the company's repeated assurances to the contrary, some local residents held out hope that the retailer would decide to make the Lewiston outlet permanent, but it wouldn't happen. In mid-January, Bean's Rich Donaldson said the store would be closing in five weeks, and that's exactly what happened. L.L. Bean packed up and left on February 12, just when it said it would.

Closer to home, things were jumping for other Freeport merchants—especially the ones closest to L.L. Bean's famous flagship store, a fact that hadn't gone unnoticed by the area's real estate agents. All anyone needed to do was look closely at the downtown's wildly varying lease rates, which is exactly what the *Maine Sunday Telegram* decided to do early in October. Not surprisingly, staff writer Tux Turkel found that spaces closest to Bean's store were by far the priciest. What was surprising was the fact that some of the lease rates on Freeport's Main Street were downright affordable. "The rents in Freeport are more locational than any market in Maine," said Portland real estate expert Tony McDonald. "And it's all driven by Bean."[75]

"Any building in the shadow of L.L. Bean does a lot of business," agreed Freeport developer George Denny. Digs close to the home of The Boot, such as those inhabited by Polo-Ralph Lauren, for example, were going in the $30- to $50-a-square-foot range, while storefronts a block or so away commanded $20 to $30 per foot. A couple of blocks north, on the other side of Main Street across from the post office, it was a different story; shops could be leased for less than $15 a foot, with one space listed at the bargain-basement rate of $2 a square foot (with the broker's listing sheet stressing that the price "is not a typo error"). Of course the reason for that area's fire-sale rates was its distance from L.L. Bean and the corresponding lack of foot traffic.

BUT MORE THAN JUST GROWTH came with the relentless passage

of time. It also meant the loss of more and more of the people who'd known L. L. Bean and helped him become the country's best-known outdoors merchant. In early July 2005, Freeport lost Sewall MacWilliams. He and George Soule used to tie flies for L. L. Bean in space they'd rented from him. Later the pair made those famous decoys from the mid-1940s to the early 1960s—4,500 a year, plus 1,000 decorative ones, at The Decoy Shop down on Staple Point Road. In 1963 MacWilliams went to work at the Freeport post office, where he'd work for twenty-six years—until he was seventy-seven. Sewall MacWilliams was ninety-three.

L. L. Bean's old friend John Gould, who'd given us so many fascinating glimpses of growing up in Freeport when the Maine merchant was in his prime, had died on the last day of August 2003 at the age of ninety-four. Upon his passing, the *Christian Science Monitor* ran an editorial about its longtime columnist, which concluded:

> Gould's essays were the literary equivalent of a roller coaster ride, complete with loop-de-loops. But the reader was always placed gently back on earth at the end, unruffled.
>
> Which brings us back to the secret of Gould's longevity. He was modest and generous. He never forgot that his readers were his guests. He greeted them, sat them down, made sure they were comfortable, and then he entertained, enlightened, and educated them. He respected his readers and sought to bless them. He once confided to us that he and his "first" wife, Dorothy, were spending $100 a month in postage to write back to readers who'd managed to discover their address.
>
> In short, John loved his readers. And, not surprisingly, his readers returned the favor.[76]

The previous August, L.L. Bean had named its book department in honor of John Gould, who had been nominated for the Pulitzer Prize in 2001 and would be nominated again in 2003.

In September 2005, L. L.'s friend Justin Williams passed away at the age of ninety-three. While he had worn many hats at L.L.

Bean, Justin Williams was best known for his skill as a hand sewer of shoes, including a pair for aviator Charles Lindbergh. His obituary noted that "for a time, the introduction that new hires at L.L. Bean went through included meeting Justin Williams." He could see the store from his home across Justin's Way, which had been named in his honor.

Another notable loss for the extended L.L. Bean family was the passing in late April of William A. Riviere, Sr., Maine Guide and author of *The L.L. Bean Guide to the Outdoors*, as well as several other books about camping, canoeing, and hunting. He wrote his first book in 1955, *Squire Rangeley Slept Here, or, Why I Came to Rangeley on Vacation in 1939 and Haven't Gone Home Yet!* He dedicated it to his wife, Eleanor, "who put in the commas and cut out the swear words."[77] Riviere also wrote a camping column for the *Boston Globe* for sixteen years during the 1970s and 1980s. He was eighty-eight.

IN 2006 L.L. BEAN RESUMED its retail expansion efforts, plans for some of which were very far-reaching. "We are actively searching out locations for retail developments in Asia and Latin America," said Zane Shatzer, head of Bean's international new-market division. "But we are also looking to boost our presence in Canada with an in-country catalog, website, and ultimately a retail presence."[78] Though the firm had distributed its famous catalog in Canada for decades, the company had realized a 30 percent increase in sales there over the past three years, making our neighbor to the north Bean's second-largest foreign market after Japan.

Though no timeline had been set for the merchant to open stores in Canada, Bean's Rich Donaldson noted that the company "had long been a resource to Canadian outdoor enthusiasts. The products we provide and the outdoor activities we encourage match up well with the interests of Canadians, and the fact that we are headquartered in a border state with two Canadian provinces [Quebec and New Brunswick] also helps to reinforce a sort of natural affinity between Canada and L.L. Bean."[79]

While the company's plans for its farther-flung stores were still in the incubation stage, the cataloger was busily opening new retail stores in New England and Pennsylvania. Short-term plans called for two Massachusetts stores: Mansfield (fall 2007) and Dedham (spring 2008). After opening as many as four more stores on the East Coast in 2008, Bean planned to open eight more in 2009 and probably another eight in 2010, according to Ken Kacere, Bean's senior VP of retail stores. "We're ready to go," he said. Adding stores means "anyplace you are, you're with Bean. Our goal is to allow a customer in that market area (where stores are located) to shop anytime, anyplace they choose with us."[80] Siting the stores in less developed areas, noted Kacere, was necessary so Bean could conduct its Outdoor Discovery classes, where people can learn how to use their new equipment.

Back in July of 2005, the Freeport firm had converted its 15,000-square-foot Factory Store at the Power House Mall in West Lebanon, New Hampshire, into a retail store and would continue that momentum into 2006. But Bean's real return to the expansion of its retail side would come in Burlington, Massachusetts, which got a 30,000-square-foot store at its Wayside Commons shopping center. A ribbon-cutting ceremony on September 15 was accompanied by music, refreshments, clinics and activities, and a gift-card giveaway. L.L. Bean also made a $30,000 donation to the Massachusetts Audubon Society. "In the spirit of our Flagship Store in Freeport," proclaimed the grand-opening handbill, "our new Burlington store will remain open 24 hours a day, throughout the celebration weekend!"[81]

Since its last big run at retail a few years earlier, L.L. Bean had been hunkered down, learning how to do it right. The firm started by hiring mangers with retail experience. Next the company got some pointers from fellow cataloger Williams-Sonoma, Inc., which had expanded into the bricks-and-mortar side of sales twenty years earlier. It was very important to Bean that things at the Burlington store went well. "This is huge," said Kacere. "The future depends on what happens in Burlington."[82] He needn't have worried; things went very well with more than 25,000 people showing up for the store's grand-opening weekend.

Five weeks after opening its Burlington store, Bean replayed its grand-opening routine at a store of the same size at The Promenade Shops at Saucon Valley between Bethlehem and Allentown, Pennsylvania. A bit closer to home, a summer, 2007 opening was planned for L.L. Bean's seventh retail store outside of Maine, another 30,000-square-foot affair at the Evergreen Walk shopping center in South Windsor, Connecticut. (Locating new stores farther south than Virginia, said Rich Donaldson, would further stress Bean's already-strained distribution system.)

With all of these new L.L. Bean stores cropping up within just a few hours' drive of Freeport, some people worried about the negative impact they'd have on Bean's flagship store. Kacere wasn't too concerned about that since the company had already made contingency plans to prevent such an occurrence. While the new stores, he said, would be "the everyday L.L. Bean shopping place," the Maine store would be more of a destination, an image the company planned to promote by holding special events and by keeping it "dynamic" through frequent changes. Exploring the historic Freeport store, he said, "is a special shopping event and we want to continue to make it that."[83]

One such special event was the May 2006 opening of the L.L. Bean Bike & Boat Store, located at 57 Main Street on the corner of Morse Street, where the Freeport merchant had opened its fourth Freeport "campus" store in the 16,000-square-foot space formerly occupied by Levi Strauss & Co. The four-day celebration (May 26–29) included clinics, demonstrations, and live entertainment. (In October the company would open its fourth Maine outlet store, a 13,000-square-foot shop up in Bangor at the Parkade Mall, just across Stillwater Avenue from the Bangor Mall.)

But Bean's wasn't the only outdoor retailer who was opening lots of new stores. Nebraska-based outdoor cataloger Cabela's had learned long ago that it needed to open stores to help fuel its growth. Started by Dick and Mary Cabela, Cabela's got its start in 1961 when the couple began selling fishing flies from their kitchen table in Chappell, Nebraska. By 1965 Cabela's had incorporated, and by 1991, it had opened two retail stores. In 2004, the company went public (NYSE: CAB) with an estimated $1.56 billion in sales, an increase of 50 percent since 2001. (L.L. Bean reported annual net sales of $1.4 billion for 2004.) Cabela's opened twelve stores between 1998 and 2005, and planned to have a total of at least twenty-five open by the end of 2007. Now it was scouting prospective sites in the Northeast, including one in Maine.

The site Cabela's would settle on for its first store in L.L. Bean territory was just off U.S. Route 1 and Interstate 95 in Scarborough, where the outdoors company's proposed 130,000-square-foot store would be the anchor for a $75-million project to include office buildings, restaurants, a bank, and a 200-room hotel. The store, which is about twenty-five miles from Freeport, opened in 2008.

But the matter of Cabela's locating in Maine was far from a done deal at the time. Just six weeks after it had more or less settled on the Scarborough location, Cabela's balked at Maine's sales tax and said it might just abandon its plan to locate here. For a while, Cabela's tried to convince Maine Revenue Services that its retail business was a separate entity from its mail-order and Internet business and, since the two were not related, the company shouldn't be obliged to collect the state's sales tax on catalog orders shipped to Maine.

Mainers weren't persuaded by Cabela's argument. An editorial in the Lewiston *Sun Journal* opposed special treatment for the interloper from Nebraska, calling Cabela's demand "high-handed and unacceptable." It continued with "companies with a physical presence in the state are required to collect and pay sales taxes on all their sales. We don't see how the state of Maine could possibly exempt Cabela's from paying the sales tax without exempting L.L. Bean. And if we exempt those two, wouldn't we have to exempt Sears, Wal-Mart, and a thousand other Maine retailers?"[84]

Of course L.L. Bean opposed an exemption for Cabela's, saying it would give them an unfair advantage. "It's not about competition," said Bean's Rich Donaldson. "Bring the competition on. It's all about playing by the same rules."[85]

While Ted O'Meara, spokesperson for New England Expedition, LLC, which put together the proposal, said that Cabela's had only been "seeking guidance from the state on a sales tax issue and had made no request to either bend or break the law,"[86] a business associate had a different take on the matter.

"It's a dealbreaker for Cabela's,"[87] said NEE's Gene Beaudoin.

But in the end it wasn't. Less than two months after the whole thing started, it was resolved with a creative compromise: if the company moved part of its catalog or Internet business to Maine (which had a lot of available telemarketing space at the time), Cabela's could collect Maine sales tax on catalog and Internet orders without setting a precedent for other states in which it had only retail stores.

Cabela's wasn't the first mail-order company to get caught up in the out-of-state sales-tax snafu—in fact L.L. Bean had found itself dealing with the matter more than once. In 1997, it had refuted a published report that said the company intended to collect sales tax on orders shipped to other states which had such a tax but where the cataloger had no physical presence. (At the time Bean had outlet stores in New Hampshire, Delaware, and Oregon—none of which had a sales tax.) And, back in 1986, Bean's had won a decision in which a Pennsylvania court ruled that the company didn't have to collect sales taxes on goods it sent to the commonwealth, saying that forcing the cataloger to collect the tax would amount to an illegal restraint of interstate commerce. (When L.L. Bean, Inc., opened a retail store in Pennsylvania in 2006, it was required to start collecting sales taxes on mail-order items it shipped there from Maine.)

The growth of Cabela's into Maine is about the only thing Leon Gorman doesn't address in his book about four decades with the company, *L.L. Bean: The Making of an American Icon* (Harvard Business School Press, 2006). "I'd always had the idea of writing about my experiences at L.L. Bean," he said. "I felt we had an interesting history that would be of value to others. When the Harvard Business School approached me in the late 1990s about writing my story, I was ready to go."[88] The idea for the book came not from Gorman but from the HBS Press in 1999. At the time, the publisher was looking for a business book that might cross over to mainstream readers—such as the many loyal customers of L.L. Bean.

Gorman's story of his time with the company his grandfather started chronicles both the bad times and the good—from the death of L. L. in 1967 and Gorman's struggle to grow the business while maintaining its identity and values to the boom days of the Preppy fad and the company's first heady years in the Japanese market. He also pulls no punches in describing the often tense relationship between himself and heir apparent Bill End. The book is an engrossing tale told with surprising frankness, especially considering how concerned Leon Gorman had been about details of his company coming out in M. R. Montgomery's 1984 book, *In Search of L. L. Bean.*

Released on October 3, 2006, *L.L. Bean: The Making of an American Icon*, had a first printing of 100,000 copies and featured a watercolor of a pair of Bean Boots by Charles Reid on the dust jacket. It came out just in time for Christmas sales—in fact it even made it into the holiday catalog (on page 4), which had been sent out in early September. Here's how the book was described in the catalog:

> Written by Leon Gorman, L.L. Bean Chairman and grandson of company founder Leon Leonwood Bean, this is a fascinating, true-to-life account of our nearly century old company. The story candidly reveals Gorman's struggles to balance change with tradition and how to shape a career—and a business—around bedrock values. Spanning four decades, it tells the funny, poignant and often engrossing details of managing the L.L. Bean legacy during the best and worst of times. Hardcover; 336 pages. USA.[89]

If L. L. were around to read the catalog copy for his grandson's book, he'd probably have said there were too many adjectives. The cover price of the book, which ended up being 304 pages including the index (plus 16 pages of photographs), was $26.95, but Bean's was selling it for $16.98 plus shipping.

BUSINESS WAS GOOD for L.L. Bean, Inc., in 2006, up 4 to 6 percent to $1.54 billion, or good enough for the company's nearly 5,000 regular employees to be awarded a 7.5 percent annual bonus. In February, before the company's sales figures had been made public and before his book was published—Leon Gorman and his wife Lisa donated $1 million to the University of Southern Maine to endow the Gorman Scholars Fund. "This is a magnificent gift," said USM president Richard Pattenaude, "one that strongly supports our goal of ensuring academic success for greater numbers of full-time undergraduate and graduate students."[90] The program provided $5,000 scholarships for seven in-state undergraduates and $3,000 scholarships for three graduate students; each could be renewed up to three times.

Bean's workers were also making out pretty well compared to others working similar jobs. In fact, one study showed that Bean's workers made out very well compared to those at other retailers: Among Maine's fifty biggest companies, L.L. Bean (with 6,500 workers) came in second behind Hannaford Supermarkets (7,500) for number of employees, and was nearly tied with Wal-Mart. Of Bean's workers, only 5.6 percent were receiving welfare of any kind compared to 8.8 percent of Hannaford's and 15.4 percent of Wal-Mart's. The study notes that it did not "differentiate between full and part-time work," and that employees "could have received one source of welfare or several."[91] The company even received an award from AARP for the fact that 36 percent of its workforce was over fifty—a sign of the job security enjoyed by the company's workers rather than the signaling of a return to Bean's aging workforce of the 1960s, most of whom couldn't afford to retire.

The previous September—when the Cabela's sales tax flap had put its planned 130,000-square-foot Scarborough store in jeopardy—L.L. Bean was announcing the details of a major expansion of its Freeport facilities. "When you look at everything in aggregate," said Rich Donaldson, "it's safe to say this is the biggest project Bean has undertaken."[92]

Bean's original expansion plans called for the leasing of its 3.6 acres across Main Street to Berenson Associates of Boston for the construction of a $45 million parking garage complex on land then occupied by the L.L. Bean Factory Store. The company also planned to build a new Factory Outlet Store adjacent to the Flagship Store and put an addition on its Desert Road Order Fulfillment Center, from which it shipped more than 16 million packages annually.

The 529-car parking garage would have 118,500 square feet of retail space attached to it, creating what Bean president Chris McCormick called "a major transformation" to downtown Freeport. "These changes will significantly enhance the overall experience for L.L. Bean customers and represent tens of millions of dollars of new commercial investment in our hometown of Freeport."[93] The other part of the plan, collectively called Freeport Village Center at the time (and now called Freeport Village Station), would have Bean's Factory Outlet Store moving to a new 14,000-square-foot building behind the main store—consolidating Bean's campus of stores on the west side of Main Street. The plan also called for adding 9,500 square feet to Bean's Hunting and Fishing store.

"We're very excited about the project and we see it as further implementation of Vision 2010,"[94] said Stephanie Slocum, executive director of the Freeport Economic Development Corporation, referring to the town's strategic plan for its village core. One of the primary principles of the town's 2010 economic development plan was to discourage "parking sprawl" by building garages.

The Desert Road facility was scheduled to have 330,000 square feet added on at a cost of $35 million to help the company keep pace with its growing catalog and Internet sales and its aggressive expansion into the retail store arena. One of the lessons the Maine firm had learned from its first foray into retail expansion was that it needed to keep its retail inventory and distribution system separate from its catalog/Internet operation.

But in February 2007, only months after first announcing its grand expansion plans, L.L. Bean gave them the boot. Part of them, anyway. While the addition to its Desert Road facility and the parking garage complex were still on track, Bean had greatly revised the plan for its own campus to one that was more cost effective and would improve traffic flow near the store, according to Rich Donaldson. For starters, the Bean Factory Outlet Store would now be moving into the 17,000-square-foot building occupied by Hunting and Fishing (formerly the L.L. Kid' store) on Nathan Nye Street in late 2007. Between the razing of Bean's old Factory Store and its relocation to the Hunting and Fishing building, it would be temporarily located at the old Eastland Shoe factory, just south of town on Route 1. (After forty-six years of operation, Eastland's Freeport factory fell victim to cheaper imports and ceased most of its operations there in September 2001. Most recently, the space had housed a Dexter Shoe outlet store.)

Where would Hunting and Fishing go? How about into a 33,000-square-foot addition onto the flagship store. (Perhaps not coincidentally, such an addition to L.L. Bean's existing 119,000-foot flagship store would increase its size to 152,000 square feet—more than 20,000 square feet larger than the one Cabela's was proposing for its Scarborough site.) About the only snag in the plan, said Donaldson, was the fact that the addition would encroach on Bean's small Discovery Pond, which would have to be filled in and recreated nearby at some point in the future.

While Cabela's grand new store was being built all at once, the sort-of-fits-together design of Bean's rambling store was the product of an evolutionary process which had taken place over several decades, and in spite of all its modern trappings, it still has its own type of rustic charm, part of which is its many-tiered layout. Immediately after going in the Main Street entrance, shoppers in 2007 were confronted with a number of choices as to which way to proceed. To the right were fifteen steps descending into the L.L. Kids department. Just beyond those stairs, six steps took shoppers up to men's outerwear, while bearing left through the lobby took them to camping (no steps up or down). Straight ahead from the front door, loomed a staircase (twenty-eight steps) up to the ladies' department, at the far end of which lay the shoe department. Climbing six steps up from ladies' took the intrepid shopper to the L.L. Home department. (The store also has three elevators.) During summer 2007, the 33,000-square-foot Hunting and Fishing addition was going up at the rear of the store adjacent to the shoe department.

Another slight snag in Bean's store expansion plan was the

matter of what to do with the historically significant Condon Barn located on Justin's Way behind the store. (A 1909 property map of Freeport village shows only a hose house and structures belonging to W. W. Fish and E. A. Buck along that part of what was then Cushing Avenue. Possibly, the hose house was later converted into a small barn.) The problem was solved when the cataloger sold the 100-year-old "barn/stable" to the Freeport Flag Ladies, Elaine Greene, JoAnn Miller, and Carmen Footer, for a dollar, and donated $5,000 to help with the cost of moving the 1,000-square-foot barn to Miller's Spring Street lot.

The trio of women had been displaying their patriotism in a number of ways since the September 11 terrorist attacks (freeport flagladies.com), and Greene and Miller have waved American flags on Main Street every Tuesday morning since the attacks. As a tribute to the barn's donor, "We're calling her Lady Liberty Barn," said Greene. The Ladies said they planned to use the barn to store items for yard sales, and proceeds would go to supporting our troops in Iraq and Afghanistan.

Another real estate transaction the company made in 2007 was the purchase of the small building in front of the store, then housing a Ben & Jerry's ice cream shop, on June 1. L.L. Bean paid $1.5 million for the building and 0.10-acre lot, more than three times its assessed value of $497,100. Though the company reportedly wanted to move the ice cream shop and turn the tiny parcel into green space, it would take its time doing so; Ben & Jerry's scoopers would still be serving ice cream at the same location three years later.

Completed well before the holiday shopping season began, Bean's magnificent lodge-like Hunting and Fishing store celebrated its grand opening on the first weekend of November. Besides stocking all the no-nonsense gear any interested outdoorsman could ever want, the roomy timber-frame structure also includes a Techno-Hunt virtual archery range, a bridge between the two sides of its upper level, and a large stone fireplace on the landing of the stairway leading up there. For those wishing to pursue their quarry outside, both resident and non-resident hunting and fishing licenses are available at the store's downstairs cash register through its Internet connection with MOSES, Maine Online Sportsman's Electronic Service.

The first-floor hallway connecting the addition to the rest of the store is where you can find the impressive 24-foot, 3,500-gallon riverbed aquarium stocked full of trout, salmon, and, for a while, painted turtles. It's complete with a viewing bubble in the bottom of one end so kids (and a few adults) can immerse themselves in the scene without getting wet. "This is the best-of-the-best and, perhaps, overwhelming. It's a funky store," said Mac McKeever, the firm's senior public relations representative. "This is just like a giant toy box for hunters and anglers, with enough features and attractions to make it a great shopping experience."[95]

According to the "L.L. Bean & Green Design" brochure available near the entrance, the company's latest addition was constructed using "Green Design" standards in compliance with the "Leadership in Energy and Environmental Design (LEED) Green Building Rating System." For example, the project used building materials manufactured within 500 miles of the store (in order to support the regional economy and reduce the environmental impact of transportation), and recycled 95 percent of the construction debris. "Most of the wood materials used to build the porch, interior wood ceilings, and many fixtures," says the pamphlet, "were salvaged from L.L. Bean's former Outlet Store." (By late 2010 all of L.L. Bean's Freeport facilities—Desert Road, the company headquarters, and the retail campus—would convert their heating systems from oil and propane to cleaner, cheaper natural gas.)

Three weeks after the Hunting and Fishing store's grand opening, the company's outlet store reopened in the renovated (recycled?) Hunting and Fishing location across Bean's village green, remaining open twenty-four hours a day through January 1.

Before the concrete in the foundation of the store's latest addition had even had time to completely cure, word got out that the retailer had an even bigger project in the works. In early June 2007, the *Portland Press Herald* came into possession of a confidential document asking hotel companies to spell out their qualifications for undertaking the development of a theme park–style adventure center just outside of town.

Once the cat was out of the bag, Bean agreed to discuss the project, which it described to the paper as being "on a fast track." Formal proposals from finalists would be due in a month and the whole operation, including theme park and hotel should be up and running in three years. "It's an aggressive timetable," said Carolyn Beem, "but if we're going to do it, let's do it. It's where we want to position ourselves."⁹⁶ The center could offer such activities as hiking, biking, golf, and cross-country skiing.

Capitalizing on the growing trend of experiential tourism, said Brad Kauffman, Bean's VP for strategic planning, "is consistent with what we think people want in terms of travel and vacation." A company document said, "The overreaching goal," of the project, which would be located on some of the company's 700 acres on Desert Road, "is to expand our relationship with our customers, enhance the customer experience (with [Bean]), and draw more customers to L.L. Bean's flagship store in Freeport, Maine, for a fuller experience of the brand."⁹⁷ The buildings would be financed and owned by the developer; Bean would offer a long-term lease on the land and planned to achieve "a reasonable financial return." (At the time, L.L. Bean was probably already Maine's top tourist destination—even ahead of the state's only national park—at least according to one newspaper: "No. 1: L.L. Bean is believed to be Maine's top tourist attraction. No. 2: Acadia National Park is the next most popular tourist attraction."⁹⁸)

While the company continued the process of building enough retail space so its stores could catch up to the catalog's sales, the Internet already had. In fiscal year 2006, L.L. Bean's website produced more revenue than either its stores or its catalogs. The website recorded 73 million visits for the period, a 13 percent increase over the previous year, and gathered the names of a record 1.7 million new customers. This rapid growth of the new medium came as no surprise to Leon Gorman.

Because of warm weather and no offer of free shipping for the holiday season, the firm's overall sales grew by only 4.6 percent, which was still enough to push its annual sales over the $1.5 billion mark for the first time. Even though they'd come in "a little shy of expectations," according to president Chris McCormick, Bean's sales still earned his 4,900 regular employees a 7.5 percent annual bonus (which cost the ninety-five-year-old company $25.5 million.)

But just because the company had gone high tech didn't mean that the old paper catalogs weren't still an essential cog in its well-oiled machine. In March 2007, the cataloger announced it had signed a multi-year, multi-million-dollar deal that renewed its association with Quad/Graphics, making that company Bean's exclusive printer. As part of the deal, the printer would establish a new prepress facility in Freeport, in or near Bean's headquarters, and manage prepress production at its service center in Braintree, Massachusetts. "We were impressed with their innovation, technology, and quality," said Steve Fuller, Bean's senior VP of corporate marketing. The contract was set to start in 2008.

Quad/Graphics had printed Bean's catalogs from the time the merchant parted ways with R. R. Donnelley, but had lost the contract to Quebecor in late 2002. "We are delighted to re-establish our print partnership with one of the nation's most remarkable catalogers,"[99] said Quad/Graphics president Joel Quadracci. The thirty-six-year-old company is the largest privately held printer of catalogs and magazines in the world.

L.L. Bean was very particular about the paper used in those catalogs—not just its quality, but also the impact its manufacture had on the environment. In May the cataloger announced that it wouldn't renew its contract with paper maker Verso's mills in Jay and Bucksport, Maine, because they couldn't meet Bean's new standards. "We made the change," said Bean's Carolyn Beem "because we are looking to increase the amount of recycled content in our paper, and we're also seeking to increase the certified fiber within the paper."[100] Beem said the paper would come from another supplier after the end of the year.

Verso spokesperson Bill Cohen said certification meant that the paper company followed sustainable forestry practices in planting, cutting, and logging. Maine is a leader in sustainable forestry practices, he noted, but was falling behind in the certification process because of the increasing number of small landowners involved in the logging process. Maine's paper industry, said Cohen, was getting help from state administrators in its effort to catch up in certification practices.

The bulk of the catalog paper Verso had made for Bean during their twenty-three-year relationship was produced in its Bucksport mill, which in 1993 (when it was owned by Champion International), had completed several capital improvements, and was looking at expanding into the production of recycled paper. At the time it was producing as much as 1,349 tons of paper a day, much of it coated paper that was used in publications such as *Time*, *Sports Illustrated*, *People*, and the catalogs of L.L. Bean and J. C. Penney. Beem said it was possible that Verso could do business with Bean in the future once it can meet the company's requirements.

Besides paper catalogs, L.L. Bean's other staple was, of course, its classic boot. While the company had long ago outgrown the capacity of Maine's Dingley Press to produce its catalogs, that didn't mean there was any good reason why the firm's famous boot couldn't be made entirely in the state (it had long been called the Maine Hunting Shoe, after all). In May 2007 Bean set about doing just that by leasing 50,000 square feet of the former Dion Distributors building at 75 Westminster Street in Lewiston from local developer George Schott.

A million dollars' worth of mold-making equipment was expected to arrive from Italy in June, with production due to start in September. "It's a significant investment for us and we're quite proud of where we'll be," said Carolyn Beem. "There's a great deal of excitement. This is an item that started the company, basically. For it to come from Brunswick and Lewiston is really a great [source of] pride for us."[101] The boot's leather uppers would still be made in Brunswick, where the uppers and bottoms would continue to be joined together.

It's appropriate that Bean chose to locate its sole-making facility in Lewiston, since the Lewiston-Auburn area is well known for its heritage of manufacturing high-quality footwear (it's said that in 1917, an Auburn factory had produced 75 percent of the world's supply of white canvas shoes). But this time the manufacturer of rubber bottoms for the twenty-four styles of Bean's boot wasn't going to be L&A Molding, as it had been around the time the boot received its invisible makeover in 1999, but L.L. Bean itself. Chamber of Commerce president Chip Morrison welcomed the news of Bean's bringing more jobs to Lewiston, where it already maintained a busy a call center. "Who doesn't have a pair of Bean Boots?" he asked. The sole-making operation was expected to create eight to twelve new jobs.

Almost as if it had been timed to coincide with the announcement that the company's boot-making process would return to Maine, L.L. Bean, Inc., scheduled its gala ninety-fifth anniversary celebration to begin on the Fourth of July. A full-page schedule in the *Maine Sunday Telegram* promised lots of activities during the five-day event, including a 10K race, fun run, and fireworks on the 4th, a kids' treasure hunt on the 5th, nature photography on the 6th, and the Weather Channel weather wall on the 7th. There were also a half dozen other daily activities and live concerts (including one by Grammy winner Paula Cole) each of the first four evenings. Another cause for celebration on the Fourth was Bean's donation, just before noon, of a park just off Bow Street to the town of Freeport.

A day later, on July 5, Leon Gorman signed copies of his memoir, *L.L. Bean: The Making of an American Icon*, in the Discovery Lobby of the retail store, while Maine humorist Tim Sample signed copies of his latest CDs upstairs in the L.L. Home department. "I told Leon," Sample remarked, "he had me here for the eightieth anniversary, the ninetieth anniversary, and now the ninety-fifth. He'd better have me back here for the hundredth."[102]

And there was one more thing for the cataloger to celebrate in its ninety-fifth year. Remember those Coty fashion awards of the mid-1970s and early '80s, and how Bean gear had become de rigueur among the Preppies? Twenty-five years later, in 2007, it was once again hip to wear Bean—or at least the Freeport cataloger's venerable boot. L.L. Bean's functional footwear had caught the attention of a new generation of the trendy and the fashion-conscious, this time at the *Washington Post*. Now Bean's "Rubber Mocs" (about $60) found themselves sharing the spotlight with such must-have fashion accessories as the $2,660 Louis Vuitton bag and Preppy-era Paul Frank calculator wristwatch ($75 at Urban Outfitters).

L.L. Bean cast its retail net further with the openings, in quick succession, of three new stores in Connecticut and New York, the first being a 25,000-square-foot store anchoring the Promenade Shops at Evergreen Walk, the newest section of the South Windsor, Connecticut, shopping center. The Hartford-area store was followed quickly by two more in New York: a 30,000-square-foot one at Colonie Center in Albany, which opened a month later, and a 15,000-square-foot outlet store at Towne Center in Fayetteville (near Syracuse), which had its grand opening in late September.

But news coverage of events concerning the company wasn't all positive. In September the Freeport firm was the target of a spoof posted on the website of the fake news publication *The Onion*, which claimed that L.L. Bean was the target of an ongoing boycott by African Americans. Posted on the Onion News Network on September 24, the two-minute video included:

> . . . a studio interview with L.L. Bean President Thomas McCormick [the real Bean president is Chris McCormick], who expresses mystification at the boycott.
>
> He pleads with leaders of the black community to step forward and explain why they won't buy the company's merchandise.
>
> McCormick says Bean researched its records and found it has sold fewer than 30 items to African-Americans since the company was established 80 years ago in "Greenwood, Maine" [which is actually where L. L. Bean had been born in 1872].[103]

Bean spokesperson Laurie Brooks said, "It's nothing new to us to be parodied. We've got an entire wall in our corporate offices covered with cartoons about L.L. Bean. We've been parodied countless times."[104] Afterward, the Freeport merchant declined to discuss the matter further, saying it didn't want to give more publicity to the story. The strategy worked, and the whole thing soon blew over.

With the latest swipe at its integrity growing smaller in its rearview mirror, L.L. Bean drove on toward the 2007 holiday season, its hopes for good sales bolstered by the offer of free holiday shipping on most items (from September 28 through December 21), an early December snowstorm, a ten-dollar gift card with every fifty-dollar purchase, aggressive online marketing, and unseasonably cold temperatures.

Another factor working in the company's favor in 2007 was its best-in-the-nation customer service, for which Bean had received an award in January from the third annual National Retail Federation Foundation and American Express Customer Service survey. Bean's best-in-the-nation status must have come as a surprise to some people who'd expected the award to go to, perhaps, a state famous for its southern hospitality, not one "that has fostered a whole genre of comedy based on little more than smart-alecky answers delivered deadpan to tourists seeking directions."[105]

"[W]hat does this award say," wondered a *Portland Press Herald* writer, "about Maine, a place populated by people who pride themselves on crustiness? People who had to invent the term 'from away' to describe everyone else in the world but them? People who deny native-Mainer status to children born here if their parents were not, noting that 'A cat can have her kittens in the oven, but that don't make 'em biscuits'?"[106] What *does* this award say? Believe none of what you hear? The survey, conducted by BIGresearch, asked nearly 9,000 people, "Which retailer delivers the best customer service?"[107] To come up with "a fair comparison, regardless of a retailer's size or geographic coverage, the consumer survey responses were compared to each retailer's 2006 revenues to develop the overall rankings."[108] L.L. Bean had moved up from third place in the previous survey.

Sales figures released by the company in early March 2008 showed that Bean had hit the nail on the head with its 2007 holiday sales strategy. While many retailers had experienced tough sledding in a challenging retail environment, L.L. Bean, Inc., had seen its sales increase by $80 million (5.5 percent) over the previous year to $1.62 billion, with catalog and Internet sales accounting for 75 percent of the take. "It was a solid team effort," said Bean president and CEO Chris McCormick, "deserving of recognition for our employees for their outstanding performance in a year that we faced stiff headwinds as a result of a weakening economy."[109]

Very strong spring and holiday sales more than made up for a "soft" fall season, while redemption of the ten-dollar gift cards helped the firm achieve good January sales. Bean's 5,000 permanent employees were compensated accordingly when the company paid out 5 percent bonuses totaling about $18.5 million.

For the first half of 2008, things continued to go fairly smoothly for the retail giant. It easily weathered the mid-May grand opening of the new 125,000-square-foot Cabela's store 25 miles down Route 1 in Scarborough by putting on Discovery and Family Fun weekends during the month in addition to holding a Memorial Day sale. Other attractions on the company's growing Freeport campus included a pair of new food and drink vendors: Linda Bean's Perfect Maine lobster rolls, which operated out of a walk-up window on the side of the Bike & Boat store, and the Portland-based Coffee by Design counter, which opened on the second floor of the retail store near the hallway leading to the new Hunting and Fishing store. (In 2010 Coffee by Design was relocated downstairs to the front of the store along Main Street.)

Besides the coffee shop, store patrons could also stop by Bean's own 1912 Café on the first floor. According to an in-store flyer, the new eatery, which opens daily at 11:00 A.M., features "all natural" ingredients, and specializes "in wholesome food and environmentally sound practices." Menu items included: salads, creative soups, artisan sandwiches, whole wheat personal pizzas, and organic drinks. The 1912 Café replaced the Dew Drop Inn snack bar, which had previously been located upstairs in Bean's homewares department.

As part of its plan to grow from twenty-three stores to thirty-two by 2012, the company forged ahead with the September openings of its first retail store in the Midwest, near Chicago, and its first store in China. The 30,000-square-foot Chicago-area store was located at the Arboretum, an open-air shopping center in the northwestern suburb of South Barrington. "L.L. Bean has many catalog and Web customers in the Chicago area, which is one of our largest markets," said Ken Kacere, Bean's senior VP of retail. "Our new stores will showcase a unique product selection for our active outdoor customers."[110] The new store, which employs about 125 people, was joined by another Chicago-area Bean store located in the Old Orchard Shopping Center in Skokie in November, when the Maine company also opened a store in the Pittsburgh, Pennsylvania, area.

Half a world away, Bean's first Chinese store was located at the Solana Mall in Beijing. The 3,000 square-foot store, which opened on September 27, was a joint venture between Bean's and the Youngone Corporation of Korea, and was the first of five planned for China. The product mix at the store consists of outdoor apparel, footwear, luggage, and hiking and camping equipment. (By 2011 L.L. Bean would have sixty-two stores in China.)

Bean's luck had even held during the previous month, when as much as five inches of rain in a twelve-hour period overwhelmed a six-foot metal culvert and washed out the roadbed of Desert Road, resulting in its closure for about a month. Fortunately for the cataloger, the storm of August 7 and 8 had washed out the road beyond Bean's cavernous Order Fulfillment Center, leaving the facility to deal only with some minor flooding on its floors. All of the OFC's merchandise, which is kept on racks, remained high and dry. Not so lucky was the Desert of Maine at the end of the road, which could be accessed by the sightseers and campers that it depended on for business only via a circuitous detour.

But by October 2008 the handwriting was starting to appear on the wall. The weakening economy, to which Chris McCormick had previously alluded, and a strong dollar made purchases for foreign customers more expensive. Earlier in the year, L.L. Bean had seen double-digit growth in its international sales, but began to experience "a slight slowdown" in those same sales beginning in early fall. "We're watching it closely," said Bean's Carolyn Beem of the fluctuating exchange rate. "We're not sure what will happen."[111]

Not wanting to be slow to react to the worsening economy and its growing Web sales, L.L. Bean had already taken the preemptive measure in June of deciding not to reopen its seasonal call center in Oxford for the upcoming holiday season. This decision left about 250 local people without the six to eight weeks of extra income they'd come to count on over the past four years. "It was a business decision we had to make," said Beem at the time. "It was a tough decision."[112]

By mid-October, L.L. Bean announced that it would be hiring 23 percent fewer seasonal employees to staff its stores, distribution facilities, and remaining call centers. The company's pessimism would turn out to be well founded; just before Christmas, it said it expected to miss its holiday sales goal by at least 10 percent, meaning the Freeport firm would probably end up experiencing only its third decline in annual revenues since 1960. "It appears that the Grinch has stolen a substantial piece of Christmas,"[113] read an e-mail from Bean president Chris McCormick, who said the company would try to cut costs through voluntary retirements and by opening just two of its originally planned eight new stores in 2009. "Even with those options on the table," he wrote, "it is now unlikely that we will be able to avoid some level of involuntary position elimination both to support our multi-channel transformation and to resize ourselves for a smaller revenue base."[114]

While the slumping economy was certainly the main culprit behind Bean's sagging sales, the fact that the cataloger didn't offer free shipping to most of its customers probably didn't help its situation any. Here's what happened. When the company parted ways with its Visa-card partner, Bank of America, at the end of June, holders of the L.L. Bean card had to reapply for a new one with Barclay's, which had recently opened a customer service center in Wilton, Maine. To sweeten the deal, the company offered free shipping only to those who applied for or had the new L.L. Bean Visa— but not to the rest of its holiday customers, who received a $10 gift card for every $50 purchase they made.

"The economy is in a very bad way and every sector, every segment, every distribution channel, every everything is taking a hit," said Donna Hoffman, a marketing professor at the University of California, Riverside, who is co-director for the school's Sloan Center for Internet Retailing. "I think the most significant tactic retailers have in their arsenal is free shipping. Offer free shipping and it really stimulates sales."[115]

And this year not even Mother Nature was giving L.L. Bean a break: high winds in late November toppled the company's giant outdoor Christmas tree, which had been trucked in and set up just four days earlier. No one was hurt when the tree came crashing down at around 4:30 in the afternoon, and the very next day—the day before Thanksgiving—a crew righted the tree and shored it up with more support at the base and extra guy wires.

In early March 2009, everyone's fears about the past year's sales were confirmed when the retailer revealed that its annual revenues had dropped for only the third time in nearly fifty years, shrinking 7.8 percent to $1.5 billion. Cost-cutting measures, said Bean president Chris McCormick, would include the laying off of as many as 200 workers, but not until April, after some others had taken advantage of the company's early retirement offer. In the end, about 150 people would be let go.

"We expect a further reduction in sales in 2009," McCormick told employees, "and we will be forced to resize and restructure the business to match the projected decline in sales and work volumes. The 2009 budget, the most difficult in my career, strikes the appropriate balance of cost cutting while continuing to invest in our future."[116] About the only good news for the merchant's 5,000 permanent employees was the small $330 "recognition gift" each of them received.

In late 2009, the company announced that it would be closing two of its Maine facilities during the coming year. First to go would be Bean's Waterville call center, which had operated full-time since 1999. Spokesperson Carolyn Beem said that once the facility closed in April 2010, its 200 full-time employees would be offered positions at the company's other call centers in Bangor, Portland, and Lewiston, and that as many as 100 workers might take part in a test program that would have them working from home.

Others, it should be noted, would very likely be able to secure positions in nearby Oakland, at the T-Mobile call center, which, just two weeks earlier, had announced it would be adding about one hundred workers to its current staff of 725. The ironic twist here is that it was T-Mobile's 2004 announcement of its plan to build a call center at Oakland's FirstPark that had forced L.L. Bean to scrap its plan to build there and locate its new call center in Bangor instead. During the holiday season, Bean's Waterville call center had employed as many as 500 people.

Shortly after announcing its plan to close the call center, the cataloger said it planned to close its Factory Outlet Store in downtown Portland in September 2010. Located at 542 Congress Street, the Portland store had opened in 1996 and employed fourteen people. One reason L.L. Bean gave for closing the Portland store was that it wanted to concentrate its "selling efforts" at its recently opened Factory Outlet Store in the new Freeport Village Station outlet mall located almost directly across the street from Bean's main campus.

With more than 20,000 square feet of shopping space, Bean's new Freeport Factory Store was one of the outdoor mall's main attractions, along with the cavernous Nike outlet. Joining Bean and Nike among the first stores to open in May 2009 was the Izod outlet, setting a trend that would see the new mall's storefronts fill up fairly quickly. "Janet Grady, spokesperson for Freeport Village Station's developer, Berenson Associates, Inc., a Boston firm that owns and manages retail developments in Massachusetts, Texas, and the Caribbean, said the complex should be 90 percent leased by the start of summer. 'I would say, given the economy, it has been amazing,' Grady said."[117]

Built on 3.6 acres owned by L.L. Bean, the new 120,000-square-foot mall suddenly accounted for nearly 20 percent of downtown Freeport's 530,610 square feet of retail space, all of which boasted a vacancy rate of just 9 percent. The shops in the $40-million development were constructed on top of and around a free 550-space parking garage. Part of the structure's south side was built around the town's historic Mallet Building, which briefly opened as a café. Other companies opening outlets during the mall's first year included Bass Shoes, Brooks Brothers, Calvin Klein, Coach, the maine dog [*sic*], Oakley, Van Heusen, and Famous Footwear.

Shortly after the outlet mall's grand opening, L.L. Bean unveiled another, altogether different attraction at its flagship store, this one showing nature at its full intensity. The best description of the new exhibit comes from its own sign:

> In May of 2006 Adella Johnson found the remains of two Bull Moose on her property in New Sweden. The Bull Moose had died after their antlers had become locked in battle during the previous fall's rut. Adella then donated the antlers to the Maine Department of Inland Fisheries and Wildlife to be used for educational purposes.
>
> The Department contacted L.L. Bean with the idea of partnering to bring these moose back to life by recreating their battle and sharing interpretive and educational information about these moose with the general public.
>
> L.L. Bean and the Department then engaged [Mark Dufresne at] Nature's Reflections Taxidermy of Gray, Maine, to develop this display. As far as we know, this is one of only two such displays in North America [the other is in New Hampshire].
>
> The antlers have never ever been separated since they first became locked in the fall of 2005.

The $55,000 exhibit, called *The Final Charge,* was set up for easy removal so it can travel to sportsmen's shows and other events. Two months before its official dedication, one of the diorama's first stops had been the July 24 grand opening of Bean's latest retail store, in Dedham, Massachusetts.

Just after Labor Day, as its employees began the lengthy process of decorating L.L. Bean stores for the holiday season, the company unveiled its new Home store, located in the building across Discovery Park from the flagship store—the one that had formerly been home to Bean's Kids, Hunting and Fishing, and Factory Outlet stores.

> "Our new Home Store space will allow our customers a much more interesting shopping experience and different ways to view our new product selection," said Ken Kacere, L.L. Bean's senior VP and general manager of retail. "The store will bring our catalog offerings to life, and customers will also discover one-of-a-kind handmade items, a selection of vintage pieces, as well as their favorite L.L. Bean home classics in great new colors."[118]

The new store, which is open twenty-four hours a day, was built in the style of an old-fashioned country store, featuring tin ceilings and fixtures made from local recycled materials. There, shoppers can find furnishings for bed, bath, and the outdoors, as well as hand-made items, specialty food products, and products for the kitchen. The space vacated by the Home department in the flagship store would soon be taken over by a revamped Kids department.

Another perk aimed at enticing holiday shoppers in 2009 was the return of L.L. Bean's improved gift card offer. The "improved" part came by virtue of the fact that shoppers now had to spend just $25 on purchases to earn the $10 gift card, instead of the $50 required the previous year. After the holiday shopping season, Bean continued the gift card promotion, but bumped the purchase requirement back up to $50.

"'We had the best real estate in the catalog for years,' said Morrill Worcester, owner and chief executive officer of the Worcester Wreath Co. 'I feel bad about what happened. We were with them for a long time.'"[119] What had happened to Worcester was that, after twenty-six years as Bean's sole supplier of Christmas wreaths, trees, and other evergreen products, his company would no longer be doing business with Maine's catalog giant. Making matters worse for Worcester was the fact that Bean's wreath business had gone not only to local Washington County competitor Whitney Wreath, but also to an out-of-state vendor, Teufel Holly Farms of Portland, Oregon.

The switch to other vendors had been made "primarily for financial reasons," said Bean spokesperson Carolyn Beem, who noted that the quality of Worcester's products had never been an issue. David Whitney said he expected his company to provide L.L. Bean with about 70 percent of its wreath products. The products originating in the Pacific Northwest would be made up of mostly noble fir, with the ones assembled in Maine consisting primarily of Maine and Canadian balsam fir.

THE GOVERNMENT'S EARLY NOVEMBER assertion that the recession recently gripping the country was coming to an end had given Maine's retailers hope for a better 2010. But for many, that sense of optimism was tempered by the fact that recent history showed stores selling discounted and used items were faring better than their full-price counterparts. Stores such as Wal-Mart, K Mart, and Marden's (the state's own chain of surplus and salvage stores), could expect to do better in the short term than full-price retailers like J. C. Penney and L.L. Bean.

This divide between discounters and regular retailers became evident for the Freeport company with the early March announcement of its sales figures for the previous fiscal year. When they were made public, the numbers revealed that L.L. Bean, Inc., had suffered its second consecutive decline in revenue, this time by 6.6 percent, to about $1.4 billion. Thanks to outerwear sales generated by heavy East Coast snowstorms early in the year, those figures were actually better than the company had projected, allowing it to give its full-time employees a 3 percent annual bonus.

"While we face many challenges ahead as the economy continues its slow recovery," Bean president and CEO Chris McCormick told workers in a memo, "we are optimistic about the future."[120]

Another blow to the company and the community had come on February 10 with the passing of Leon Gorman's seventy-nine-year-old brother John T. "Tom" Gorman, Jr. His obituary in Lewiston's

Sun Journal included the following information about the eldest Gorman brother and lifelong Yarmouth resident:

> He attended Yarmouth schools and was active in the Boy Scouts, the national defense effort, and qualified for his pilot's license at the age of 17. He graduated from Cheverus High School in 1949. The yearbook noted, "Tom is a swell fellow who never says much but is always willing to help. One of the 'brains' of the senior class." He received his bachelor's degree from Fairfield University in 1954.
>
> He was a member of the L.L. Bean family and spent his working years with the company. He had many friends and was a longtime member of the Yarmouth Lions Club, the Men's Club, and Sacred Heart Church. He traveled extensively and enjoyed coaching youth baseball, motorcycling, snowmobiling, and flying his Piper airplane.
>
> During his later years, he established a philanthropic foundation and was very active in aiding underprivileged residents of the state of Maine. Beneficiaries included those with mental health problems, cancer, and those in need of food [or with] aging issues. Thousands of very poor Maine people have benefited and will continue to benefit from his generosity.
>
> He is survived by his two brothers and their wives, James W. Gorman and wife, Maureen, and Leon A. Gorman and wife, Lisa; and numerous nephews and nieces.

One recent beneficiary of Gorman's JTG Foundation had been the Lewiston Junior High School, which had received a three-year, $500,000 grant to establish a pilot program geared toward improving its health and fitness facilities.

L.L. Bean's commitment to "adapting to the way its customers now shop through the design and features of its website"[121] helped it win a prestigious customer service award for the second time in two years. This time the merchant nabbed the top spot in *Bloomberg BusinessWeek*'s fourth annual ranking of the magazine's "Customer Service Champs." Kudos for the company came at the expense of such well-respected firms as USAA (insurance and financial services) and Apple, Inc. Also helping to put L.L. Bean ahead of the others were its return policies, including the company's switch to a Barclay's bank, which agreed to absorb half the cost of free return shipping to holders of the L.L. Bean credit card.

Toward the end of February 2010, L.L. Bean president Chris McCormick took out full-page ads in local daily newspapers to express his gratitude for the achievement:

Thank You
We're #1
Because of you!
Dear L.L. Bean Employees,
Last week, L.L. Bean was named #1 Customer Service Champ in *Bloomberg BusinessWeek*'s annual Ranking. Bloomberg *BusinessWeek* surveys consumers about customer satisfaction in many industries, including insurance, hotels, airlines, consumer products and retail. We couldn't be more proud that we came out on top. And, for the third consecutive year, Bean was named Top Retailer in Customer Service by the National Retail Foundation.

Our business was founded on superior customer service nearly 100 years ago. It was perfected under the leadership of L.L. Bean's longtime President Leon Gorman and remains the cornerstone of our business.

We would like to take this opportunity to thank our customers and employees for your part in making us #1. We couldn't have done it without you.
Sincerely,
[signed]
Chris McCormick
President and CEO
L.L. Bean

Even though Bean's online sales had exceeded catalog orders for the entire fiscal year for the first time ever in 2009, the firm's paper catalog was still seen as a valuable tool in its marketing campaign. In addition to generating plenty of sales on its own, the catalog still got a lot of the credit for sending legions of Bean's loyal customers scurrying to the company's website. "A lot of people like the catalog to browse and place orders online when they're ready," said spokesperson Carolyn Beem, "and some people like to do shopping online without the catalog."[122]

That the catalog still remained well worth its weight in standard, presorted postage in the era of e-commerce was not lost on L.L. Bean, whose printer, Wisconsin-based Quad/Graphics, signed a contract in February 2010 to become the company's exclusive provider of studio photography—meaning it had suddenly outgrown its space at the firm's Freeport headquarters. Bean's solution to this problem was to approve construction of a 16,000–square-foot digital photography studio 20 miles away in Westbrook. The new studio, which would be managed by Quad/Graphics Photography Services in conjunction with L.L. Bean's Photography Operations and Creative Department, consists of seven shooting bays, four with full daylight photography capability; a set-building shop; a prop room; production offices; dressing rooms; hair and makeup areas; and a merchandise handling area.

Now the new exclusive provider of studio photography would have a brand-new, state-of-the-art facility, to be called Studio 1912, in which to perform its increasing responsibilities—"photography for L.L. Bean's catalogs including the Men's, Women's, Kids, Fly-Fishing, Hunting, Traveler, and Home titles as well as its websites and e-commerce business."[123] Mark Kozlowski, Quad/Graphics' director of photography, said, "With this contract expansion Quad/Graphics will provide the best talent and technology, and together with L.L. Bean's creative direction we will create a best-in-class photography studio which will be a model for the catalog industry."[124]

Just as it had done with its catalog and website, the company decided to go with a mixture of the new and the old in the design of its latest clothing line. "Our almost 100-year history continues," announced the headline on the website for Bean's new Signature collection (llbeansignature.com), "with an updated fit and contemporary style—inspired by our archives." But since the company's new Signature line would be geared toward the younger market, that meant there would be more tweeting coming from Freeport than just that from the area's robins, cardinals, and black-capped chickadees. A January tweet from LLBean_PR alerted loyal customers to the new line's imminent launch, announcing: "L.L. Bean Signature website prelaunch starts today! Sign up for email, catalog & early items :)"[125]

Five days before its official mid-March debut, the line's designer, Alex Carleton, was on hand at Lewiston's Willy Beans Bistro & Café to get feedback on his nearly 200 designs from young men and women from nearby Bates College. This was the first of six college "trunk shows" scheduled for the collection before it went on sale online, by catalog, and at an L.L. Bean store in the Washington, D.C., area. "It's very J. Crew, Ralph Lauren," said Anne Cravero, a Bates freshman from New Hampshire. "Depending on how it's priced, I would choose L.L. Bean."[126] Items in the new line included skirts, tops, and dresses for women; shirts, sweatshirts, and polos for men; and footwear, pants, coats, bags, and accessories for both sexes. Prices ranged from $20 to $200. (Maybe it was just a coincidence, but two months later, New Albany, Ohio-based Abercrombie & Fitch would bring back its racy, ten-dollar A&F Quarterly catalog after a seven-year hiatus.)

Late in 2010 the *Wall Street Journal* caught up with the cyclical trend of rugged outdoor wear once again becoming de rigueur with the fashionable set, noting that "besides the reemergence of L.L. Bean and Pendleton, other vintage brands such as Stetson, Woolrich, Levi's, and Britain's J. Barbour & Sons are having second comings, either independently or collaborating with high-end runway designers" such as Gucci and Barney's, which, said the piece, "are taking cues from yellow-paged copies of *Field & Stream* and L.L. Bean catalogs."[127]

The same Internet technology that was helping L.L. Bean generate sales succeeded in turning a typical mid-March Saturday at the retailer's flagship store into a mob scene when a "flash mob," which had been organized on Facebook and Craigslist, suddenly descended on the place at around 1:30 P.M. Animated by the tunes from a member's boombox, the group's thirty-eight members (in Freeport, thirty-eight people qualify as a "mob") boogied out the door, down the steps past Ben & Jerry's, and took a left on Main Street, adding participants to their conga line as they went.

"People have enough stress in their lives," said the event's organizer, Nick Salve, of Southern Maine Flash Mobs. "If they show up somewhere and something ridiculous is happening, if it's able to make them laugh, that's what we're really doing it for."[128] The group then danced its way to Friendly's restaurant, from which it was turned away, before continuing north to McDonald's, where the group quickly dispersed.

Though an uneventful summer had given way to a fall shopping season fraught with retailer concern about soft holiday sales, consumer confidence rebounded enough to give sellers cause to be optimistic. L.L. Bean pulled out all the stops to attract customers. Free holiday shipping was back, as was giving shoppers a $10 L.L. Bean gift card with each purchase of $50 or more. The incentives worked. By early December, Bean's Carolyn Beem noted that seasonal sales were good, but that it was too early to tell if they were great. "Bean Boots are selling incredibly well," she said. "We're making those as fast as we can and selling everything we make. So there are a lot of bright spots. We are meeting or beating our expectations for the season."[129] Other big sellers included snowshoes, skis, children's items, and outerwear.

By the middle of the month there was more encouraging news from Freeport: the company was shipping out 145,000 packages a day; Internet sales shows strong, double-digit growth over the previous year; and overall sales were ahead of the 2.3 percent increase that the company had forecasted. (A cold and snowy January across much of the country would help the company continue its sales momentum well past the Christmas shopping season.)

All those indications of a good Christmas season proved to have been accurate when L.L. Bean released its final sales figures the following March. After two years of declining sales, the company realized a 5.7 percent increase in sales—to $1.44 billion—thanks to a cold, snowy winter in the eastern United States, which helped to increase the catalogers' online sales by 29 percent and sent the sales of its classic Bean boot up by a whopping 57 percent. Pent-up demand for men's clothing and outdoor sporting equipment also led to big gains in both of these categories.

Of his company's two previous slow years, Bean president and CEO Chris McCormick lamented, "The last time our sales fell off that much was after World War II. So we've never experienced this sort of decline for economic reasons, at least not in recent history."[130] But the bottom line for fiscal year 2010 had improved enough for each of its 5,000 permanent employees to receive a 5 percent bonus check for about $3,800 (the firm's total bonus outlay would come to $19 million). Chairman Leon Gorman called the extra employee cash a "well-deserved bonus."

In 2012 L.L. Bean, Inc., will celebrate its 100th birthday. Probably nowhere else but Maine would the combination of a state's rugged terrain and one man's wet, tired feet come together and lead to the invention of a boot that would begin a small empire.

For several decades, Leon Leonwood Bean had focused all his efforts on growing his company to a size that felt comfortable to him. Ironically, it nearly died from L. L.'s lack of interest as he aged during the fifties and sixties, only to be saved by his grandson. It was Leon Gorman who modernized the company and put it in the position to grow to the size it is today.

As we begin to emerge from a difficult recession, all signs point to continued growth for L.L. Bean. Sales are rebounding, the company's theme-park destination is taking shape, and even passenger train service will soon be returning to Freeport. Something else returning is Bean's famous year-round, no-strings-attached, free standard shipping to the U.S. and Canada. The family-owned business that transformed the once-sleepy coastal town of Freeport into Maine's shopping capital looks to be on solid footing to serve outdoorsmen and active people around the world for the next hundred years.

Acknowledgments

OBVIOUSLY A BOOK THE SIZE AND NATURE of this one is never the work of just one person. Dozens of people have given me plenty of help and advice over the past few years, and I thank everyone whose contributions, large and small, have led to the ultimate success of this huge undertaking.

As usual there are too many people for me to thank by name, but the ones who generously gave more time and assistance to me than I would have felt comfortable asking for deserve to be recognized by name. Kathy Christy talked with me about her father—and L. L. Bean's friend—John Gould. Lynette Thompson of the Dingley Press provided me with her history of the company. Vicki Lowe of the Freport Community Library let me pore over her carefully collected L.L. Bean archive and provided me with the names and addresses of numerous contacts. Earle G. Shettleworth, Jr., told me the wonderful story of how Mr. Bean' sign ended up on the roof of his father's building across the street. Fred Goldrup remembered how his grandparents had sewn the first pairs of L. L.'s Maine Hunting Shoes—he also searched in vain for old photos of Freeport. And Michael Perry recounted how he had been instrumental in starting what is now L.L. Bean's Outdoor Discovery Progam—and lent a huge file of documents to a person he'd just met.

I would also like to thank the Freeport Historical Society—especially Ned Allen—who provided many of the historical photographs in this book and never got tired of my asking to look through the collection "just one more time." Thanks also to the Bethel Historical Society, the Maine Historical Society, and the Peary–MacMillan Arctic Museum at Bowdoin College, for their help with images and information.

A special thanks goes to M. R. Montgomery, who answered my request to quote from his book *In Search of L. L. Bean* with, "You can quote as much as you want, as long as you want, as often as you want."

The biggest thanks of all go to the two women who helped me keep going on this effort. The first is Jennifer Bunting of Tilbury House, Publishers, whose patience, expertise, and support made this book possible. The other is Sue Potvin, without whom nothing would be possible, and to whom I owe so much in so very many ways.

Jim Witherell
Lewiston, Maine

Notes

Chapter 1

1. Descended from the MacBean clan of the Scottish highlands, Bean's coat of arms consisted of a wildcat above a shield containing a lion, a hand, a dagger, and a ship. Between the bottom of the shield and the name Bean is a banner bearing the motto "Touch not the cat bot a glove." In his autobiography, L. L. explains the escutcheon's symbolism: "The lion represents the red lion of the Royal Arms of Scotland. The hand with open palm signifies hospitality and loyalty to allies. The galley stands for the ship which early ancestors of the clan crossed from the north of Ireland to the islands on the coast of Scotland. They were later known as the Lords of Lorne. The dagger is the symbol of the Clan Chattan, the great clan consisting of 16 smaller ones of which Clan MacBean was one. The motto means: 'Beware how you molest us!' The word 'bot' means 'without.'" Leon Leonwood Bean, *My Story: The Autobiography of a Down-East Merchant* (Freeport, Maine: L.L. Bean, Inc., 1960), p. 37.
2. Josiah H. Drummond, *Joshua Bean of Exeter, Brentwood, and Gilmanton, N. H., and Some of His Descendents* (Portland: Smith & Sale Printers, 1903), p. 1.
3. Leon Leonwood Bean, *My Story: The Autobiography of a Down-East Merchant* (Freeport, Maine: L.L. Bean, Inc., 1960).
4. William B. Lapham, *History of Bethel, Formerly Sudbury Canada, Oxford County, Maine, 1768–1890, With a Brief Sketch of Hanover and Family Statistics* (Augusta: Press of the Maine Farmer, 1891), p. 15. Reprinted with a new historical essay by Stanley Russell Howe (Somersworth, NH: New England History Press, 1981), p. 421.
5. Ibid., p. 84.
6. Ibid., p. 421.
7. Ibid., p. 478.
8. Ibid.
9. Ibid., pp. 65–66.
10. The key to the mystery of George W. Bean's actual age at the time of his death comes from a Bean family history that's posted on (of all places) the website of Clemson University's Math Department. What happened was, somewhere along the way, a branch had fallen off the Bean family tree. The site accurately lists George W. Bean as having

been born on October 14, 1802, to Timothy and Hannah Bean, but this George W. Bean was, in fact, the younger brother (by six years) of Kimball Bean. Having the same name as his uncle, the other George W. Bean was born to Kimball and Lavinia Bean in November 1818. The problem is compounded by the fact that one history of Bethel lists both George W. Beans as having married Mary Ann Estes. L. L. Bean clears the whole thing up in his autobiography when he writes that his father was the son of George W. Bean born November 28, 1818. And on the previous page he notes that his grandfather was taken prisoner in the Civil War, died on June 26, 1864, and is buried in Andersonville, Georgia. (Civil War records at the Maine State Archives say that Private George W. Bean of Livermore was forty-four when he joined Company C of the 8th Maine Infantry on Sepember 7, 1861, and that he died as a prisonor of war on *August 24,* 1864.

11. Lapham, p. 483.
12. M. R. Montgomery, *In Search of L. L. Bean* (Boston: Little, Brown & Company, 1984), p. 10.
13. John Gould, "What This Country Needed Was a Good Hunting Boot," *Christian Science Monitor*, 2 Aug. 2002, p. 22.
14. Gordon Weil, *Sears, Roebuck, USA: The Great American Catalog Store and How It Grew* (New York: Stein & Day, 1977), no pg. cited.
15. Mina Titus Sawyer, "Small Town Maine Store is World Famous," *Lewiston Journal*, 21 May 1966, p.1A.
16. Tom Mahoney, *The Great Merchants: The Stories of Twenty Famous Retail Operations and the People Who Made Them Great,* (New York: Harper Bros., 1955), p. 295.
17. Arthur Bartlett, "The Discovery of L. L. Bean," *Saturday Evening Post,* 14 Dec. 1946.
18. "'L. L.'s Oxford County Boyhood," *L.L. Bean, Inc., Outdoor Sporting Specialties: A Company Scrapbook*, p. 1.
19. Florence G. Thurston and Harmon S. Gross, *Three Centuries of Freeport* (Freeport, Maine, 1940), p. 146.
20. Tess Nacelewicz, "Freeport and a Founding Family," *Portland Press Herald*, 22 Aug. 2007, p. B1.
21. Henry Milliken, "E. B. Mallet Was Freeport's Benefactor," *Lewiston Journal*, 5 June 1971, magazine section, p.1.
22. Thurston and Cross, p. 198.
23. Ibid., p. 197.
24. Ibid., p. 153.
25. Milliken.

Chapter 2

1. Thurston and Cross, p. 150.
2. "Ethel Williams," *L.L. Bean, Inc., Outdoor Sporting Specialties: A Company Scrapbook*, p. 13.
3. *State of Maine Guide's School Curriculum* (Augusta: Department of Inland Fisheries and Wildlife, 1996), p. 1.
4. Thurston and Cross, p. 192.
5. *Freeport on Casco Bay*, (Freeport: Freeport Chamber of Commerce, c. 1931), p. 3.
6. "Reported Burglars Started Big Fire," *Portland Evening Express and Daily Advertiser*, 28 Dec., 1909, p. 1.
7. Thurston and Cross, p. 151.

Chapter 3

1. *Freeport on Casco Bay*, p. 3.
2. John Gould, "A Brief Personal History of the 20th Century," *Christian Science Monitor*, 5 Jan. 2001, p. 23.
3. "L.L. Bean Dusts Off Old Covers," photocopy, no source cited, 1972.
4. John Gould, "Freeport Before Bean," *Christian Science Monitor*, 12 Oct. 1990, p. 17.
5. John Gould, "What This Country Needed Was a Good Hunting Boot," *Christian Science Monitor,* 2 Aug. 2002, p. 22.

Chapter 4

1. Thurston and Cross, p. 155.
2. Gould, "Freeport Before Bean," p. 17.
3. "Mail Order Catalog Wins First Prize," *Brunswick Record*, 31 Mar. 1927, no pg. cited.
4. John Gould, *And One to Grow On: Recollections of a Maine Boyhood* (New York: William Morrow & Company, 1949), p. 118.
5. John Gould, *Maine's Golden Road: A Memoir* (New York: W. W. Norton, 1995), p. 16.

Chapter 5

1. Thurston and Cross, p. 147.
2. Leon Leonwood Bean, *Hunting, Fishing, and Camping* (Freeport: L.L. Bean, Inc., 1942), pp. 92–93.
3. Percival Baxter quote on a bronze plaque mounted on a boulder by Katahdin Stream in Baxter State Park, Maine.
4. Franklin Gould, "My Brush With History: L. L. and the President's Missus," *American Heritage*, Apr. 1998, p. 43.

5. Ibid., p. 42.

6. John Gould, "What This Country Needed Was a Good Hunting Boot," *Christian Science Monitor*, 2 Aug. 2002, p. 22.

7. L. L. Bean, *My Story*, p. 10.

8. *Freeport on Casco Bay*, p. 4.

9. "L. L. Bean's Business Has Had a Phenomenal Growth," *Brunswick Record*, 23 Aug. 1934.

10. Montgomery, p. 33.

11. Carlene Griffin, *Spillin' the Beans* (Brunswick: 1992), p. 37. Her book was self-published.

12. Duncan Barnes, "A Pied Piper from Down East," *Sports Illustrated*, 8 Jan. 1968, p. 36.

13. Ibid., p. 37.

14. John Gould, "Mr. Bean's Venture Turns Out Just Ducky," *Christian Science Monitor*, 28 Dec., 2001.

15. Griffin, p. 114.

16. "Freeport Makes Enviable Record for Employment," *Portland Evening Express*, 1 July 1939, no pg. cited.

17. L.L. Bean, Inc., *Outdoor Sporting Specialties: A Company Scrapbook* (1987), p. 85.

Chapter 6

1. John Gould, introduction to *My Story* by L. L. Bean.

2. John Gould, "On the Bobcat Trail, a Plug for Socks," *New York Times Book Review*, 9 June 1957, p. 6.

3. L.L. Bean, Inc., *Outdoor Sporting Specialties: A Company Scrapbook*, p. 114.

4. Bean, *My Story*, p. 77

5. L.L. Bean, Inc., *Outdoor Sporting Specialties: A Company Scrapbook*, p. 114.

6. Griffin, p. 67.

7. L. L. Bean, *Hunting, Fishing, and Camping*, p. 50.

8. Leon Gorman, *L.L. Bean: The Making of an American Icon* (Boston: Harvard Business School Press, 2006), p. 12.

9. John Skow, "Using the Old Bean," *Sports Illustrated*, 2 Dec. 1985, p. 94.

10. John Gould, introduction to *My Story* by L. L. Bean.

11. Gould, "On the Bobcat Trail."

12. Bean, *My Story*, p. 114.

13. Thomas Ehrich, "Homey Hustlers," *The Wall Street Journal*, 5 Dec. 1973, p. 1.

14. Gorman, *L.L. Bean: The Making of an American Icon*, p. 10.

15. Bartlett, p. 97.

16. "Mel Collins," L.L. Bean, Inc., *Outdoor Sporting Specialties: A Company Scrapbook*, p. 117.

17. "Wid Griffin," *L.L. Bean, Inc., Outdoor Sporting Specialties: A Company Scrapbook*, p. 79.
18. Harold Boyle, "Many Hoped to Buy Bean," *Maine Sunday Telegram*, 15 Nov. 1981, p. 27A.
19. Montgomery, p. 133.
20. Gorman, *L.L. Bean: The Making of an American Icon*, p. 16
21. Mahoney, *The Great Merchants*, p. 298.

Chapter 7
1. Mary Richardson, interview of Carlene Griffin for WCVB TV Channel 5, Boston, circa 2002.
2. "The Ten Most Influential People in Maine," *Maine Times*, 6 Mar. 1981, p. 14.
3. Gorman, *L.L. Bean: The Making of an American Icon*, p. 53.
4. Ehrich, p. 1.
5. Montgomery, p. 148.
6. Leon Gorman, *L.L. Bean, Inc.: Outdoor Specialties by Mail from Maine* (Princeton, NJ: Princeton University Press, 1981), p. 13.

Chapter 8
1. Montgomery, p. 145.
2. Don Hansen, "Soap and Shoes Start Maine's Largest Mail Order Business—L.L. Bean of Freeport," *Brunswick Record*, 13 Aug. 1959, no pg. cited.
3. Gorman, *L.L. Bean: The Making of an American Icon*, p. 3.
4. Leigh Montville, *Ted Williams: The Biography of an American Hero* (New York: Doubleday, 2004), pp. 239–40.
5. "What No One Else Has as Good as," *Time*, 7 Dec., 1962, p. 9.
6. Gorman, *L.L. Bean: The Making of an American Icon*, p. 42.
7. Bill Nemitz, "He Draws the Line at Town Hall," *Portland Press Herald*, 27 Oct. 2000, p. 1B.
8. Montgomery, p. 164.
9. "L. L. Bean Has 93rd Birthday," *Brunswick Record*, 21 Oct. 1965.
10. Ibid.
11. Montgomery, p. 149.
12. Ibid., p.163.
13. Gorman, *L.L. Bean, Inc.: Outdoor Specialties by Mail from Maine*, p. 13.
14. "Tom Sidar," *L.L. Bean, Inc., Outdoor Sporting Specialties: A Company Scrapbook*, p. 207.
15. Montgomery, p. 177.
16. Edward D. Murphy, "The Man Who Believed in Bean's," *Portland Press*

Herald, 27 May 2001, p. 1A.

17. Nathaniel Benchley, "A Long Day's Shopping at L. L. Bean's," *Holiday*, Dec. 1968, p. 68.

18. Ehrich, p. 1.

Chapter 9

1. "The Space Age," *You Name It!* (later called *The Bean Scene*), Mar. 1971, p. 9.

2. Lew Dietz, "Bean, Maine, USA," *Down East*, Mar. 1970, p. 38.

3. "The Space Age," *You Name It*, Mar. 1971, p. 9.

4. Montgomery, p. 171.

5. Joan Cook, "Shopping by Mail Is a Thriving Business," *New York Times*, 4 Jan. 1971, p. 47.

6. Leon Gorman, letter to employees, *You Name It*, Mar. 1971, p. 1.

7. "Ethel Williams," *L.L. Bean, Inc., Outdoor Sporting Specialties: A Company Scrapbook*, p. 66.

8. "L.L. Bean Dusts Off Old Covers," photocopy, no source cited, 1972.

9. Rita Reif, "A Rustic Store That Became Awfully Chic," *New York Times*, 25 Nov. 1972, p. 18.

10. Montgomery, p. 177.

11. Thomas A. Eifler, "24-Hour Turnaround on a Million Packages a Year," reprinted from *Traffic Management*, July 1972, no pg. cited.

12. Ibid.

13. Griffin, p. 105.

14. Ehrich, p.1.

15. Michael Kernan, "L.L. Bean's Booming Despite Old-Time Atmosphere," *Washington Post*, reprinted in the *Portland Press Herald*, 28 Aug. 1975, p. 20.

16. John Lovell, "The Only Game in Town," *Maine Sunday Telegram*, 21 Apr. 1974, p. 1D.

17. Montgomery, pp. 182-83.

18. Donald A. Bluhm, "All Outdoors: L.L. Bean Busy for 75 Years," *Milwaukee Journal*, 6 Jan. 1988, p. 5E.

19. Montgomery, p. 182.

20. "Original L.L. Bean Store Succumbs to the Wrecker," *Brunswick Times Record*, 17 Feb. 1977.

21. James P. Brown, "Freeport, Inc.?" *Down East*, Sept. 1983.

22. Jim Dudas, "L.L. Bean is Stylish to Boot," *Cleveland Press*, 13 Oct. 1976, no pg. cited.

23. Cassie Mackin, *Today* interview of Leon Gorman, typed transcript on file at the Freeport Community Library, 15 Sept. 1976, pp. 1–2.

24. Gorman, *L.L. Bean: The Making of an American Icon*, p. 143.

25. Gorman, *L.L. Bean, Inc.: Outdoor Specialties by Mail from Maine*, pp. 18–19.

26. Montgomery, p. 222.

27. "Original L.L. Bean Store Succumbs to the Wrecker," *Brunswick Times Record*, 17 Feb. 1977.

28. Paul Downing, "Dan Rather: Not Impressed by Carter," *Portland Press Herald*, 21 Feb. 1977, no pg. cited.

29. Frank Sleeper, "L.L. Bean Fights Dickey-Lincoln," *Portland Press Herald*, 30 Sept. 1977, no pg. cited.

30. Jeff Wheelwright, "The Furbish Lousewort Is No Joke," *The New Republic*, 14 May 1877, p. 10.

31. Phyllis Austin, "L.L. Bean's Was in Trouble and Then They Started to Grow and Grow and Grow," *Maine Times*, 13 May 1977, p. 11.

32. Christopher Pope, "L.L. Bean Readies for Busy Season, Hires Hundreds," *Portland Press Herald*, 4 Sept. 1979, no pg. cited.

33. Horace Gower, "Data Processing at L.L. Bean," *The Bean Bulletin*, 27 Aug. and 3 Sept. 1982.

34. "Townscape Goal: Revitalize Downtown Freeport," *The Bean Scene*, Fall 1979, p. 7.

35. "Facilities Growth Continues," *The Bean Scene*, Fall 1979, p. 14.

36. "The Seventies," *L.L. Bean, Inc., Outdoor Sporting Specialties: A Company Scrapbook*, p. 107.

Chapter 10

1. "L.L. Bean Denies Jack Anderson Report," letter to the editor from Leon Gorman, *Portland Evening Express*, 6 Oct. 1980, p.10.

2. "NRC Sets the Record Straight," letter to the editor from Robert H. Gardiner, Jr., *Portland Evening Express*, 6 Oct. 1980, p.10.

3. Phyllis Austin, "The Beans of Freeport, Maine," *Maine Times*, 7 July 1989, p.15.

4. Paul Farhi, "Shop-by-Mail Industry Is Facing a Shakeout," *Washington Post*, 4 Nov. 1988, p. F1.

5. Susan Trausch, "The Case of the Costly Studies," *Boston Globe*, 7 July 1981, p. 1.

6. Austin, "The Beans of Freeport, Maine," p. 8.

7. "Bean's Hears from Customers," *Portland Evening Express*, 15 Oct. 1981, p. 9.

8. Bob Cummings, "Riviere & Bean: A Good Team that Could Be Better," *Maine Sunday Telegram*, 25 Oct. 1981, no pg. cited.

9. "The L.L. Bean Guide to the Outdoors," *The Bean Scene*, Feb. 1982, p.1.

10. Horace Kephart, *Camping and Woodcraft* (Knoxville: The University of Tennessee Press, 1988); introduction by Jim Casada, pp. xxvi–xxvii.
11. "A Message from Leon," *The Bean Scene*, Feb. 1982, p. 2.
12. M. R. Montgomery, "The Marketing Magic of L.L. Bean," *Boston Globe*, 27 Dec. 1981, p. 1.
13. Ibid.
14. Ibid.
15. Ibid.
16. Montgomery, *In Search of L. L. Bean*, p. 6
17. Bill Caldwell, "Maine Business 'Climates' Suit Bean Boss Just Fine," *Maine Sunday Telegram*, 1 May 1983, p. 114.
18. Gorman, *L.L. Bean: The Making of an American Icon*, p. 106.
19. James P. Brown, "Freeport, Inc.?" *Down East*, Sept. 1983, no pg. cited.
20. Eugene Carlson, "L.L. Bean's Success Attracts Other Stores to Maine Town," *Wall Street Journal*, 28 Nov. 1982, p. 37.
21. Gould, "Freeport Before Bean," p. 17.
22. Tux Turkel, "Freeport Shuffle," *Maine Sunday Telegram*, 2 Oct. 2005, p. F2.
23. Susan Levine, "Bean Sprouts: A Tiny Maine Town Gets a New Shot of Vitality," *Chicago Tribune*, 5 Aug. 1987, p. 25.
24. Turkel, p. F2.
25. "Taking a Potshot at L.L. Bean," *Newsweek*, 6 Dec. 1982, p. 155.
26. "The Maine Sporting Camp Guide," promotional brochure for the Maine Sporting Camp Association, Raven Maps and Images, 1990.
27. Tim Allen, "End Gives His View of Downtown Topics," *Portland Evening Express*, 13 July 1983, p. 1.
28. Dudley Clendinen, "L. L. Bean's Hometown Is Wary of McDonald's," *New York Times*, 3 Oct. 1983, p. I16.
29. Brown, *Down East*, no pg. cited.
30. Leon Gorman, "L.L. Bean in the Eighties," address at the University of Vermont, May 1986.
31. Ibid.
32. "L.L. Bean: Preppiness Has Bean and Gone," *The Economist*, 22 Oct. 1983, p.78.
33. Noah Deakin-Davis, "Calling L.L. Bean," *Down East*, Dec. 1985, p. 62.
34. Montgomery, p. 234.
35. Gorman, *L.L. Bean: The Making of an American Icon*, p. 146.
36. Tara Weiss, "Unfashionably Chic," www.Forbes.com, 19 Oct. 2006.
37. Tim Allen, "Bean's Buys Freeport Golf Course," *Portland Evening Express*, 15 Feb. 1983, p. 13.
38. "Bean's 'Good Neighbor' Status Has Critics," *Portland Evening Express*, 13 Jul. 1983, p. 12.

39. "MMC Wing to Honor Bean," *Portland Evening Express*, 22 Sept. 1983.

40. Loraine de Jong, "Bean's Parade Float," *Portland Evening Express*, 11 June 1983, p. 1.

41. "More Up Ladder at Bean's," *Portland Evening Express*, 2 Apr. 1983, p. 3.

42. Deakin-Davis, p. 62.

43. "I'm From Maine and Don't You Forget It," *Boston Globe*, 7 Aug. 1984, p. 1.

44. "VA Couple to Tie the Knot at L.L. Bean," *Washington Post*, 8 Aug. 1991, p. V4.

45. Laurie A. Kiernan, "The Town That Bean's Built," *Washington Post* (*American Journal* section), circa 1985, no pg. cited.

46. Roger Brown, "Freeport to Share L.L. Bean With City," *Portland Evening Express*, 17 Jan. 1984, p. 1.

47. Bob Cummings, "L.L. Bean—The Unauthorized Version," *Maine Sunday Telegram*, 13 Jan. 1985, p. 18A.

48. Christopher Lehmann-Haupt, "Books of the Times," *New York Times*, 16 Nov. 1984, p. C 29.

49. Gorman, "L.L. Bean in the Eighties," address at the University of Vermont, May 1986.

50. Skow, p. 95.

51. "L.L. Bean Selling Shotguns," *Maine Times*, 13 Sept. 1985, p. 6.

52. Ibid.

53. Eric Moody, "L.L. Bean, Inc., Beyond the Maine Hunting Shoe," *Southern Maine Business Digest*, Aug. 1991, p. 6.

54. Ray Routhier, "Backstage at L.L. Bean," *Portland Press Herald*, 12 Nov. 2006, p. E8.

55. Eric Blom, "Courting L.L. Bean," *Maine Sunday Telegram*, 1 May 1994, p. 7F

56. Ibid.

57. Skow, p. 95.

58. "Drunken Teens Pelt Singer's Bus," *Chicago Tribune* (UPI), 26 June 1985, p. 16.

59. Ken O'Quinn, "Woman's Career a Pillar of Maine Retail Institution," *Portland Press Herald*, 2 Jan. 1998, p. 1B.

60. In its day, spruce gum was very popular, as described in this piece from a Lewiston newspaper: "Alec Murray of Gardiner and Vital Bolduc of this place left here last week for the Penobscot River region on a gumming expedition which will occupy them until the first of November. Both are gummers and Mr. Bolduc has been at the business for a portion of each year since 1892. His plan is to put in about two

months in the woods in the fall and about the same time in the winter after a good depth of snow has fallen. With one partner, he has averaged to harvest and market about 300 pounds of gum, one especially fortunate season yielding twice that amount. In the early years, 75 cents was the usual market price, but this has continually advanced until this byproduct of the Maine spruce sells readily at $1.50 per pound. The whole forest area has been gummed over but yet Mr. Bolduc is able, with his long experience, to find a reasonably good harvest each year." "Looking Back; 100 Years Ago, 1907," *Sun Journal*, 22 Sept. 2007, p. C18.

61. Craig Wilson, "L.L. Bean's Believers," *USA Today*, 8 June 1987, p. 1D.

62. Stephen Fenichell, "Bean Sprouts: Taking a Great American Catalog Overseas," *Sky*, May 1996, reprinted in *L.L. Bean, Inc., Outdoor Sporting Specialties: A Company Scrapbook*, p. 210.

63. Jim Wright, "L.L. People: Bean's Own Secret," *Dallas Morning News*, 27 Dec. 1985.

64. Steven E. Prokesch, "Bean Meshes Man, Machine," *New York Times*, 23 Dec. 1985, Section IV, p. 1.

65. "L.L. Bean Grows and Grows," (Brunswick) *Times Record*, 11 Feb. 1986.

66. Cindy Skrzycki, "Rustic Pitch, Unique Service Pays Off for L.L. Bean," *San Francisco Chronicle*, 3 Apr. 1985, p. AA2.

67. Gorman, *L.L. Bean: The Making of an American Icon*, p. 193.

68. Ibid., p. 199.

69. Austin, "The Beans of Freeport, Maine," p. 8.

70. "The Company Turns 75," *L.L. Bean, Inc., Outdoor Sporting Specialties: A Company Scrapbook*, p. 164.

71. Dieter Bradbury, "New Bean's Builds on Old Bean Values," *Portland Press Herald*, 4 Sept. 1987, p. A1.

72. "Putting a Label On It," *The Bean Scene*, April 1987, p. 8.

73. "Maine News and Issues," *Maine Times*, 25 Sept. 1987, p. 12.

74. "Court Rejects L.L. Bean Suit Against Parody of Its Catalog," *Boston Globe*, 12 Feb. 1987, p. 98.

75. "L.L. Bean vs. the Preppified Pooch," *Newsweek*, 16 Mar. 1987, p. 53.

76. "L.L. Bean Plans Branch," *Boston Globe*, 27 Feb. 1987, p. 7.

77. Ted Cohen, "North Conway Allows L.L. Bean Store," *Portland Press Herald*, 17 Oct. 1987, p. 23.

78. Paul Farhi, "Shop-by-Mail Industry Is Facing a Shakeout," *Washington Post*, 4 Nov. 1988, p. F1.

79. Karen Houppert, "L.L. Bean Spells Out Plans," *Portland Evening Express*, 1 April 1988.

80. Founded in 1955 by Jonas Klein (1922–2007), Eastland Shoe eventually grew to include 800 workers in all its divisions: Westland Shoe (Bidde-

ford), Northland Shoe (Fryeburg), and Eastland's Lisbon division. It was said that Klein knew the names and life stories of every one of his Eastland employees. By 2001 the company realized that the only way it could remain competitive was to import more of its shoes, and it closed its Freeport factory, putting 150 people out of work. About 50 employees were retained to run Eastland's offices, warehouse, and distribution operations.

81. Lyn Riddle, "For Some in Maine Town, a Boom Was No Boon," *New York Times*, 30 Oct. 1988, p. 54.
82. Nancy Perry, "All-New Bean Is the Same Fierce Competitor," *Portland Press Herald*, 28 May 1992, p. 10A.
83. Ken O'Quinn, "L.L. Bean Heir Takes on Brennan," *Brunswick Times Record* (AP), 11 Feb. 1988, no pg. cited.
84. Joseph Pereira, "L.L. Bean Scales Back Expansion Goals to Ensure Pride in Its Service Is Valid," *Wall Street Journal*, 31 July 1989, p. 1.
85. Moody, p.5.
86. Pereira.
87. "Catalog Industry Honors Bean," *Bean Bulletin*, 12 May 1989, no pg. cited.
88. "Bean's 'Hunt Couture' Styles Still the Clothes That Make the Man," *The Denver Post*, 22 Sept. 1989, no pg. cited.
89. John W. Porter, "L.L. Bean Will Close Plant, Cut Work Force," *Portland Press Herald*, 20 Oct. 1990, no pg. cited
90. Andy Rooney, "A Closet Full of Nothing/Remnants Past," *San Francisco Chronicle*, 13 Aug. 1989, p. Z6.
91. Abby Zimet, "Soviets Study Capitalism at L.L. Bean," *Maine Sunday Telegram*, 29 Oct. 1989, p. 1A.
92. Augie Favazza, "'You'll Need a Map' to Get Around in L.L. Bean Addition," *Portland Evening Express*, 27 May 1989, p. 11.
93. Patricia Gallagher, "Lands' End Sees Drop in Earnings," *USA Today*, 12 Dec. 1989, p. 1B.
94. Austin, "The Beans of Freeport, Maine," p.8.
95. Ibid., p. 11.

Chapter 11
1. Gorman, *L.L. Bean: The Making of an American Icon*, pp. 259–60.
2. L.L. Bean, Inc., *Outdoor Sporting Specialties: A Company Scrapbook* (2nd ed.), p. 190.
3. William C. Hidlay, "In Freeport, Shoppers Pay the Price for Paradise Retailing," *Los Angeles Times*, 9 Dec. 1990, p. 4.
4. John W. Porter, "Bean's Free Shipping Days Over," *Portland Press Her-*

ald, 26 Feb. 1991, p. 1B.

5. M. R. Montgomery, "L.L. Bean Gives the Boot to Free Shipping," *Boston Globe*, 7 Mar. 1991, no pg. cited.

6. "North by East," *Down East*, May 1991, p. 25.

7. Tim Warren, "A Stodgy Publication Enters the '90s and Loses Its Essential Nature," *The Baltimore Sun*, 4 Oct. 1992, p. 5C.

8. Jeff Smith, "Worker Bonuses Balloon After Big Year at L.L. Bean," *Portland Press Herald*, 20 Feb. 1993, p. 1A.

9. Catharine Hartnett, Amy Binder, and Joseph K. Fisher, *Business Wire*, New York, 3 March 1992, p. 1.

10. Colin Nickerson, "For L.L. Bean, Japan 'Easy Street,'" *Boston Globe*, 9 Mar. 1992, p. 20.

11. Catharine Hartnett, "L.L. Bean Announces First Japan Store Opening," *Business Wire*, New York, 6 Nov. 1992, p. 1.

12. Colin Nickerson, "Far East Goes Down East," *Boston Globe*, 28 Feb. 1993, p. 1.

13. Nickerson, "For L.L. Bean, Japan 'Easy Street.'"

14. Phyllis Austin, "Bean Ad Has Company Upset," *Maine Times*, 8 May 1992, p.13.

15. Royal Ford, "Maine Race Forecast: Congress by Fire," *Boston Globe*, 25 June 1992, p. 26.

16. Jeff Smith, "Bean Customers Confused About Candidate," *Portland Press Herald*, 12 Sept. 1992, p. 1A.

17. Steve Campbell, "Control Defined Bean's Lost Bid," *Maine Sunday Telegram*, 8 Nov. 1992, p. 14A.

18. Robert Lovinger, "L.L. Bean Goes All Out on 80th," (New Bedford, Massachusetts) *Standard Times*, 20 Sept. 1992, business section, no pg. cited.

19. Shelby Gilje, "Caller ID Is Coming and in Some Ways Is Already Here," *Seattle Times*, 27 Dec. 1992, p. D15.

20. Lisa Duchene, "L.L. Bean Takes Plunge into Children's Clothing," (Brunswick) *Times Record*, circa 1993.

21. Rob Gavin, "L.L. Bean, Developer Huddle on Major Expansion Plans," *Portland Press Herald*, 9 July 1992, p. 9A.

22. Rob Gavin, "L.L. Bean Seeks to Calm Abutters," *Portland Press Herald*, 26 Aug. 1992, p. 1B.

23. Thomas Petzinger, Jr., "The Front Lines," *Wall Street Journal*, 16 Apr. 1999, p. B1.

24. Senator Smith (1897–1995) was elected to the House of Representatives in 1940 following the death of her husband, Clyde, and in 1948, became the first Republican woman elected to the U.S. Senate and the first

woman to serve in both houses of Congress. Two years later, Senator Smith opposed the Red-baiting beliefs and practices of Senator Joseph McCarthy (R-Wisc.) when she delivered her famous "Declaration of Conscience" speech.

25. "Manufacturing Wins Margaret Chase Smith State Quality Award," *Bean Bulletin*, 8 Oct. 1993.
26. Ellen Neuborne, "Catalog Crunch: How L.L. Bean Keeps 10 Million Items Moving," *USA Today*, 17 Dec. 1993, p. 1A.
27. "Deep Freeze Heats Up Sales at L.L. Bean," *Bangor Daily News* (AP), 3 Feb. 1994, no pg. cited.
28. Eric Blom, "L.L. Bean Tops List of Clothing Catalogs for Overall Satisfaction," *Portland Press Herald*, 29 Sept. 1994, p. 12B.
29. "L.L. Bean Unveils Gift-Registry Service," *Houston Chronicle*, 3 May 1994, p. 2.
30. $100,000 Worth of L.L. Bean Clothing Stolen," *Bangor Daily News* (AP), 25 Oct. 1994.
31. Edward D. Murphy, "Maine Firms Wary of Orders via E-Mail," *Portland Press Herald*, 20 Oct. 1995, p. 1B.
32. Kim Strosnider, "L.L. Bean to Offer Ordering by Internet," *Portland Press Herald*, 2 May 1996, p. 1A.
33. "L.L. Bean Worldwide Web Site Launch," *L.L. Bean, Inc., Outdoor Sporting Specialties: A Company Scrapbook*, 2nd ed., p. 214.
34. David Sharp, "Lagging Sales Baffle L.L. Bean," (Peoria, Illinois) *Journal Star*, 20 Dec. 1995, p. A 2.
35. Eric Blom, "L.L. Bean to Delay Freeport Expansion," *Portland Press Herald*, 19 Oct. 1995, p. 1A.
36. Eric Blom, "If Shoe Doesn't Fit Bean Profile, Keep Walking," *Portland Press Herald*, 23 June 1995, p. 1A.
37. Kim Strosnider, "State Rushes to Fulfill State Tourism Promotion," *Portland Press Herald*, 22 Jun. 1995, p. 1A.
38. William Safire, "Grammar Is Sold Short in Catalogs," *Pittsburgh Post-Gazette*, 26 Nov. 1995, p. B8.
39. Blom, "L.L. Bean to Delay Freeport Expansion."
40. John W. Porter, "'Perfect Companies' Undergoing Change," *Portland Press Herald*, 20 Jan. 1996, p. 6A.
41. Kim Strosnider and John W. Porter, "L.L. Bean Responds to Poor Retail Year with Planned Cuts," *Portland Press Herald*, 20 Jan. 1996, p. 1A.
42. William C. Symond, "Paddling Harder at L.L. Bean," *Business Week*, 7 Dec. 1998, p. 72.
43. Booklet in L.L. Bean's Corporate Information Kit, c. 2002.
44. Kim Strosnider, "New Distribution Center Will Speed Shipments,

Bean Says," *Portland Press Herald*, 27 June 1996, p. 8B.

45. Kim Strosnider, "L.L. Bean to Open on West Coast," *Portland Press Herald*, 16 Apr. 1996, p. 1C.

46. Kim Strosnider, "L.L. Bean to Issue Its Own Visa Card," *Portland Press Herald*, 7 May 1996, p. 1C.

47. "North by East," *Down East*, Nov. 1996, p.44.

48. Victoria Brett, "L.L. Bean Adds an Inch to the Waist," *Portland Press Herald* (AP), 15 Aug. 1996, no pg. cited.

49. Ibid.

50. "North by East."

51. Mark Shanahan, Ted Cohen, and Lindsay Tice, "Reporters' Notebook," *Portland Press Herald*, 8 Jan. 2000, p. 1B.

52. Kim Strosnider, "Lands' End Apologizes for Remark About Boots," *Portland Press Herald*, 26 Jan. 1996, p. 1C.

53. Gorman, *L.L. Bean: The Making of an American Icon*, p. 27.

54. Edward D. Murphy, "Forbes Ranks Bean in Its Top 500, But Not with Bean Help," *Portland Press Herald*, 9 Dec. 1997, p. 2C.

55. David Hench, "L.L. Kids Building Beginning to Sprout," *Portland Press Herald*, 24 Feb. 1997, p. 1B.

56. "L.L. Bean to Open Waterville Call Center," *Portland Press Herald*, 6 Aug. 1997, p. 3B.

57. "L.L. Bean to Close Call Center," *Portland Press Herald*, 19 Dec. 1997, p. 5B.

58. David Sharp, "L.L. Bean Takes Steps to Protect Itself in Stormy Catalog Market," *Los Angeles Times*, 16 Dec. 1998, p. 7.

59. "L.L. Bean Makes Marketing Changes," *Bangor Daily News* (AP), 29 June 1998, p. 1.

60. Tony Chamberlain, "Bean Gives the Boot to Its Hunting Heritage," *Boston Globe*, 29 Oct. 1999, p. E15.

61. Greg Gatlin, "L.L. Bean Changes in Store, in Fashion," *Boston Herald*, 8 Sept. 1998, p. 33.

62. Ibid.

63. Edward D. Murphy, "Can't Be Bean, Can It?" *Maine Sunday Telegram*, 20 Dec. 1998, p. 1F.

64. Rajiv Lal, and James Webber, "Freeport Studio" (Harvard Business School Case Study 9-501-021, Boston, 2000), p. 5.

65. Ibid, p. 1.

66. Gorman, *L.L. Bean: The Making of an American Icon*, p. 261.

67. M. R. Montgomery, "The Marketing Magic of L.L. Bean," *Boston Globe*, 27 Dec. 1981, p. 1.

68. Shortly after he'd started with his grandfather's company, Leon Gor-

man had kept a little black book in which he made notes on how he'd improve the business, if he had the chance. One of his notes to himself read, "Stock a line of merchandise to the extent that if a person walked in without a stitch on he could be completely outfitted for a trip anywhere." Gorman, *L.L. Bean, the Making of an American Icon*, p. 46.

69. Gorman, *L.L. Bean, the Making of an American Icon*, p. 255.

70. Ibid., p. 251.

71. Will Bartlett, "L.L. Bean Scales Down Main Store Expansion," *Portland Press Herald*, 6 Mar. 1998, p.1A.

72. Scott Thomsen, "L.L. Bean Awarded Big Break in Taxes," *Portland Press Herald*, 21 Feb. 1996, p. 1A.

73. Scott Thomsen, "Freeport Residents Split Over Tax Break for Bean Expansion," *Portland Press Herald*, 7 Feb. 1996, p. 1A.

74. Scott Thomsen, "Town Council to Meet on L.L. Bean Tax Plan," *Portland Press Herald*, 15 Jan. 1996, p. 1B.

75. David Hench, "State to Review L.L. Bean Tax Plan," *Portland Press Herald*, 12 Jan. 1996, p. 12B.

76. Scott Thomsen and Edward D. Murphy, "School Gets Money to Screen Bean Lot," *Portland Press Herald*, 3 Apr. 1996, p. 1B.

77. Ibid.

78. Scott Thomsen, "Realities of the '90s Strain Bean–Freeport Relationship," *Portland Press Herald*, 24 Feb. 1996, p. 1A.

79. David Hench, "Planners OK Bean Zoning Change," *Portland Press Herald*, 30 Mar. 1995, p. 1B.

80. Peter Pochna, "Bean's New Parking Lot Panned, Praised," *Portland Press Herald*, 30 July 1996, p. 1A.

81. "Neighbors Sue Over L.L. Bean Expansion Plan," *Bangor Daily News* (AP), 13 Apr. 1995, p. 1.

82. "A Better Bean Boot," *Down East*, Dec. 1999, p. 8.

83. Edward D. Murphy, "The Sole of Maine," *Portland Press Herald*, 5 Sept. 1999, p. 1A.

84. Ibid.

85. Candus Thomson, "Old Bean Look, New Boot Fit," (Bergen City, New Jersey) *The Record* (reprinted from *The Baltimore Sun*), 4 Oct. 1999, p. L9.

86. Chamberlain, p. E15.

87. "A Better Bean Boot."

88. Christopher Borrelli, "Classics: The Bean Boot," *Outside*, Feb. 2000.

89. Doris Hajewski, "Boot Maker Expects Sales to Slip," *Milwaukee Journal Sentinel*, 28 Mar. 1998, p. 1.

90. "L.L. Bean Wants Sole Control in Maine," *Sun Journal* (AP), 9 Feb. 2007 p. B8.

91. Bob Tedeschi, "L.L. Bean Beats the Current by Staying Mainstream," *The New York Times*, 20 Sept. 2000, p. H7.

92. Ibid.

93. "Waterville Chosen for New L.L. Bean Catalog Call Center," *Bangor Daily News* (AP), 17 July 1999, p. 1.

94. Chris Reidy, "L.L. Bean in It for 12-Month Haul," *Boston Globe*, 8 Dec. 2000, p. D3.

95. Alex Beam, "Rudy's Back in the Barn," *Boston Globe*, 7 Dec. 2000, p. B13.

Chapter 12

1. Joshua L. Weinstein, "Bean Says No Bonuses for Workers," *Portland Press Herald*," 14 Mar 2000, p. 1C.

2. Joshua L. Weinstein, "L.L. Bean Workers Consider a Union," *Portland Press Herald*, 29 Feb. 2000, p. 1C.

3. Ibid.

4. "Changes Lead Teamsters to Abandon Effort to Unionize at Bean," *Portland Press Herald* (AP), 17 Mar. 2001, p. 6D.

5. Paul Tolme, "L.L. Bean No Longer Just a Maine Attraction," *Seattle Times*, 25 July 2000, p. E1.

6. Tara Weiss, "Unfashionably Chic," www.Forbes.com, 19 Oct. 2006.

7. "L.L. Bean Announces Gift to National Park Foundation," New York: *PR Newswire*, 27 July 2000, p. 1.

8. "L.L. Bean President Leon Gorman and Subaru Executives Showcase New 2001 MY Subaru Outback H6-3.0 L.L. Bean Edition," *PR Newswire*, 19 Sept. 2000, p. 1.

9. Tom Bell, "Freeport Leaders Say Shopping Isn't Enough," *Portland Press Herald*, 28 June 2000, p. 1A.

10. Lindsay Tice, "Freeport Voters Say No to Turning Town Hall into Store," *Portland Press Herald*, 9 Nov. 2000, p. 1B.

11. "A Visit With Wid," *The Bean Scene*, Fall 1979, p. 2.

12. Ibid.

13. Ibid.

14. John Gould, "A Brief Personal History of the 20th Century," *Christian Science Monitor*, 5 Jan. 2001, p. 23.

15. Ibid.

16. John Gould, "If the Shoe Fits," *Christian Science Monitor*, 21 Aug. 1981, p. 20.

17. David Sharp, "L.L. Bean Executive Leaves Post," *Bangor Daily News* (AP), 22 May 2001, p. 5.

18. Phyllis Austin, "At L.L. Bean, It Isn't the End for End," *Maine Times*, 14 Sept. 1990, p. 3.

19. Edward D. Murphy, "The Man Who Believed in Bean's," *Portland Press Herald*, 27 May 2001, p. 1A.

20. Edward D. Murphy, "Bean Icon Stepping Down," *Portland Press Herald*, 22 May 2001, p. 1A.

21. "L.L. Bean Announces Leadership Change," *PR Newswire*, 21 May 2001, p. 1.

22. Meredith Goad, "L.L. Bean's New Leader 'Energized' by Job," *Portland Press Herald*, 24 May 2001, p. 1A.

23. Nancy D. Holt, "Workspaces: A Look at Where People Work," *Wall Street Journal*, 8 Sept. 1999, p. B10.

24. Ibid.

25. "Lee Surace," *L.L. Bean, Inc., Outdoor Sporting Specialties: A Company Scrapbook*, 2nd ed., p. 209.

26. Edward D. Murphy and Allan Drury, "L.L. Bean to Pay Bonus to Workers," *Portland Press Herald*, 10 Mar. 2001, p. 1A.

27. Gorman, *L.L. Bean: The Making of an American Icon*, pp. 264–65.

28. "Airborne Express Welcomes New Customer L.L. Bean," *PR Newswire*, 21 Aug. 2000, p. 1.

29. Sheri Day, "L.L. Bean Tries to Escape the Mail-Order Wilderness," *New York Times*, 27 Aug. 2002, p. C1.

30. Gus G. Sentementes, "L.L. Bean Gets Ready for Columbia Opening," *The Baltimore Sun*, 29 Apr. 2001, p. 1D.

31. Jenn Abelson, "6 Years Later, L.L. Bean Gets Back in Gear for Expansion," *Boston Globe*, 1 Sept. 2006, p. A1.

32. Edward D. Murphy, "Bean Rolls Out Retail Strategy for Northeast," *Portland Press Herald*, 20 June 2006, p. C1.

33. Gorman, *L.L. Bean: The Making of an American Icon*, p. 278.

34. Lloyd Ferriss, "Salmon Sculpted from Driftwood Hooks Customers at L.L. Bean," *Portland Press Herald*, 2 Apr. 2001, p. 1A.

35. John Gould, "Button, Button. . . ." *Christian Science Monitor*, 9 June 2000, p. 23.

36. Alison Bulman, "Chris McCormick: The UN-Bean," *Portland Monthly*, Nov. 2001.

37. "Businesses Step Forward," *Portland Press Herald*, 20 Sept. 2001, p. 2A.

38. John Gould, "What This Country Needed Was a Good Hunting Boot," *Christian Science Monitor*, 2 Aug. 2002, p. 22.

39. Edward D. Murphy, "L.L. Bean Retooling, to Cut Jobs," *Portland Press Herald*, 5 May 2002, p. 1A.

40. Edward D. Murphy, "L.L. Bean Paring Work Force by Offering Early Retirement," *Portland Press Herald*, 25 Oct. 2002, p. 1A.

41. Dave Carpenter, "Sears Buys Lands' End for $1.9 Billion US," *Toronto*

Star, 14 May 2002, p. D2.

42. Ibid.

43. Clarke Canfield, "New L.L. Bean Head Orders Change," *Houston Chronicle*, 14 July 2002, p. 2.

44. Rick Barrett, "L.L. Bean Discontinues Account with Quad/Graphics," *Milwaukee Journal Sentinel*, 1 Nov. 2002, p. 1 D.

45. Ibid.

46. "L.L. Bean Reports 'Strong Finish' to Holiday Season," *Portland Press Herald*, 4 Jan. 2003, p. 7D.

47. Marc Fisher, "Trying to Lure a Larger Market" (Bergen County, New Jersey) *Record* (Washington Post News Service), 1 June 2002, p. F8.

48. Meredith Goad, "Bean Gives $1 Million for Shuttle at Acadia," *Portland Press Herald*, 19 June 2002, p. 1B.

49. Ibid.

50. Dale McGarrigle, "Film Details L. L. Bean the Man, the Empire," *Bangor Daily News*, 4 Dec. 2002, p. 1.

51. Katie Gallagher, "Give 'em the Boot," *Portland Press Herald*, 12 Dec. 2002, p. 1E.

52. Matt Wickenheiser, "Deep Discounts Mean Retail Stores Feel Pain," *Portland Press Herald*, 5 Feb. 2003, p. 10A.

53. Edward D. Murphy, "Maine Stores Report Strong Holiday Sales," *Portland Press Herald*, 30 Dec. 2003, p. 1A.

54. "L.L. Bean Switching Hunting, Kids' Areas," *Portland Press Herald*, 7 Sept. 2002, p. 7D.

55. Matt Wickenheiser, "Bean Buying Coastal Land for Outdoor School," *Portland Press Herald*, 6 May 2003, p. 1A.

56. Ibid.

57. Grace Murphy, "Casino Foes Ready to Raise Money," *Portland Press Herald*, 22 Mar 2003, p. 2B.

58. Ibid.

59. Kelly Bouchard, "L.L. Bean Joins Fight Against Casinos," *Portland Press Herald*, 19 Apr. 2003, p. 1A.

60. Grace Murphy, "Credit Card Giant MBNA Embraces Anti-Casino Stand," *Portland Press Herald*, 12 July 2003, p. 1A.

61. John Cook and Christine Frey, "L.L. Bean May Court Bauer," *Seattle Post-Intelligencer*, 3 May 2003, p. C1.

62. Ibid.

63. Edward D. Murphy, "This Is an Opportunity That L.L. Bean Has to Consider," *Portland Press Herald*, 21 May 2003, p. 1A.

64. Ibid.

65. Edward D. Murphy, "Optimism, Opportunity on the Rise at L.L.

Bean," *Portland Press Herald*, 16 Sept. 2003, p. 1C.

66. Ibid.

67. Edward D. Murphy, "L.L. Bean No Longer Interested in Bauer," *Portland Press Herald*, 6 Mar. 2004, p. 1A.

68. Edward D. Murphy, "Spring Sales: 'Bean Is on a Roll,'" *Portland Press Herald*, 21 Sept. 2004, p. C1.

69. Edward D. Murphy, "Bean Scraps Plan for Oakland Call Center," *Portland Press Herald*, 3 Dec. 2004, p. C1.

70. "Outfitter to Open Call Center in Bangor," (Lewiston) *Sun Journal* (AP), 25 Mar. 2005, no pg. cited.

71. Gail Geraghty, "Bean Jingles Oxford Economy," *Sun Journal*, 30 Nov. 2004, no pg. cited.

72. "L.L. Bean, Inc., Reports 2004 Net Sales Results," *Business Wire*, New York, 5 Mar. 2005, p. 1.

73. Ibid.

74. Edward D. Murphy, "L.L. Bean Pays Bonus: 8 Percent," *Portland Press Herald*, 11 Mar. 2006, p. D7.

75. Tux Turkel, "Freeport Shuffle," *Maine Sunday Telegram*, 2 Oct. 2005, p. 1F.

76. "Good as Gould," *Christian Science Monitor*, 5 Sept. 2003, p. 10.

77. Avi Steinberg, "William A. Riviere, Sr.," *Boston Globe*, 5 May 2005, p. C15.

78. Hollie Shaw, "L.L. Bean Looking to Open Canadian Stores," (Don Mills, Ontario) *National Post*, 26 Jan. 2007, p. F1.

79. Ibid.

80. Murphy, "Bean Rolls Out Retail Strategy for Northeast," *Portland Press Herald*, 20 June 2006, p. C1.

81. Handbill distributed at the information desk in L.L. Bean's Freeport store.

82. Abelson.

83. Murphy, "Bean Rolls Out Retail Strategy for Northeast."

84. Editorial, *Sun Journal*, 29 Aug. 2006.

85. "Cabela's Balks at Maine Sales Tax," *Sun Journal* (AP), 29 Aug. 2006, no pg. cited.

86. "Chamber Mediates Tax Spat of Outfitters," *Sun Journal* (AP), 7 Sept. 2006, p. B7.

87. "Cabela's Balks at Maine Sales Tax."

88. Ray Routhier, "Backstage at Bean," *Portland Press Herald*, 12 Nov. 2006, p. E8.

89. Christmas 2006 catalog, L.L. Bean, Inc., Freeport, ME, p. 4.

90. "Bean Chairman, Wife Give $1 Million for USM Scholarships," *Sun*

Journal (AP), 14 Feb. 2006, no pg. cited.

91. "Maine's Top 50 Employers and Welfare [table]," *Sun Journal*, 14 Nov. 2005, no pg. cited.

92. Donna Goodison, "L.L. Bean Planning Stores in MA," *Boston Herald*, 22 Feb. 2006, p. 28.

93. Clarke Canfield, "Bean Plans Its 'Biggest Project,'" *Portland Press Herald* (AP), 22 Feb. 2006, p. C6.

94. Tess Nacelewicz, "New Stores, Parking Proposed in Freeport," *Portland Press Herald*, 30 Aug. 2006, p. B1.

95. Terry Karkos, "New L.L. Bean Hunting, Fishing Store Opens Its Doors to Oohs and Aahs," (Lewiston) *Sunday*, 4 Nov. 2007, p. C1.

96. Tux Turkel, "Bean Sees Theme Park on Horizon," *Portland Press Herald*, 5 June 2007, p. A1.

97. Ibid.

98. "By the Numbers: Tourism in Maine," *Sun Journal*, 7 Dec. 2007, p. B1.

99. "Quad/Graphics to Become Exclusive Printer for L.L. Bean Catalogs," *PR Newswire*, 26 Mar. 2007, no pg. cited.

100. Donna Perry, "L.L. Bean Cancels Longtime Verso Job," *Sun Journal*, 16 May 2007, p. A1.

101. Kathryn Skelton and Carol Coultas, "Sole Supplier," *Sun Journal*, 24 May 2007, p. A1.

102. Brief conversation with author at L.L. Bean retail store, Freeport, ME, 5 July 2007.

103. Dieter Bradbury, "Any Truth to New L.L. Bean Spoof?" (Waterville, Maine) *Morning Sentinel*, 28 Sept. 2007, p. 2A.

104. Ibid.

105. "L.L. Bean's Service Tops Nation's Friendlier Regions," *Portland Press Herald*, 18 Jan. 2008, p. A6.

106. Ibid.

107. "L.L. Bean Wins Service Plaudits," *Sun Journal*, 29 Jan. 2008, p. B 6.

108. Ibid.

109. "L.L. Bean: Holiday Sales Boosted 2007," *Sun Journal* (AP), 3 Mar. 2008, p. B8.

110. Andrew Schroedter, "L.L. Bean to Open Store in Suburbs," (Chicago) *Crain's*, 25 Feb. 2008.

111. Noel K. Gallagher, "A Borderline Dollar; Its Recent Surge in Value Might Take a Toll on Maine by Slowing Exports to Canada and Making It Costlier for Foreign Tourists," *Portland Press Herald*, 24 Oct., 2008, p. A1.

112. Leslie H. Dixon, "Sluggish Economy, Web Sales Disconnect Oxford Call Center," *Sun Journal*, 26 June 2008, p. A1.

113. David Sharp, "L.L. Bean Seasonal Sales Off 10 Percent," *Sun Journal* (AP), 24 Dec. 2008, p. A1.

114. Ibid.

115. "Web Deals Create Late Shoppers' Paradise," *Sun Journal*, 19 Dec. 2008, p. B7.

116. "L.L. Bean Sales Fall; Layoffs to Come," *Sun Journal* (AP), 10 Mar. 2009, p. B4.

117. Beth Quimby, "Recession Can't Stop Growth in Freeport," *Portland Press Herald*, 1 Apr. 2010, p. A1.

118. "L.L.Bean to Open a Home Store," http//www.hometextilestoday.com/CA6695409.html, 9 Sept. 2009.

119. Dennis Hoey, "L.L.Bean Looks Beyond Maine for Wreaths for First Time in Years," *Sun Journal* (*Portland Press Herald*), 19 Nov. 2009, p. A3.

120. David Sharp, "L.L. Bean Sales Fall in 2009," *Sun Journal* (AP), 13 Mar. 2010, p. B8.

121. "L.L.Bean Tops Bloomberg BusinessWeek's Fourth Annual Ranking of 'Customer Service Champs,'" *Business Wire*, New York, 18 Feb. 2010.

122. Justin Ellis, "L.L.Bean Shoppers Move to the Web," *Sun Journal* (*Portland Press Herald*), 6 Mar. 2010, p. A5.

123. "Quad/Graphics, L.L.Bean Expand Partnership," *PR Newswire*, 10 Feb. 2010

124. Ibid.

125. Bag Lady and Good-Buy Girl, "Bliss Thru Shopping," *Sun Journal* 22 Jan. 2010, p. B2.

126. Kathryn Skelton, "L.L.: Cool for School, Again," *Sun Journal*, 11 Mar. 2010, p. A1.

127. Steve Garbarino, "Off Duty—Style and Fashion: Is L.L. Bean Driving the Runway?!" *Wall Street Journal*, 25 Sept. 2010, p. D1.

128. Molly F. McGill, "Only for a Moment," *Sun Journal*, 14 Mar. 2010, p. C1.

129. Lindsay Tice, "Holiday Sales Looking Strong," (Lewiston) *Sun Journal,* 8 Dec. 2010, p. 1.

130. David Sharp, "L.L. Bean Reverses Two Years of Sales Declines in 2010," (Lewiston) *Sun Journal* (AP), 15 March 2011, p. B4.

Index

Photograph by Sue Potvin

JIM WITHERELL is a master Maine Guide and the creator of hiking maps for Acadia National Park and Baxter State Park. Also an avid cyclist, he is the author of *Bicycle History* (McGann) and working on a book about the Tour de France. He lives in Lewiston, Maine.